A Texas Baptist History Sourcebook

A Companion to McBeth's *Texas Baptists*

by Joseph E. Early, Jr.

Foreword by Harry Leon McBeth

University of North Texas Press
Denton, Texas

Permissions:
University of North Texas Press
P.O. Box 311336
Denton, TX 76203-1336

Library of Congress Cataloging-in-Publication Data

Early, Joseph E. (Joseph Everett), 1970-
  A Texas Baptist history sourcebook : a companion to McBeth's Texas
Baptists / by Joseph E. Early, Jr. ; foreword by Harry Leon McBeth.
     p. cm.
Includes bibliographical references.
  ISBN 1-57441-176-4 (hardcover : alk. paper)
  1. Baptist General Convention of Texas—History—Sources. 2.
Baptists—Texas—History—Sources. 3. Texas—Church history—Sources.
I. Title.
BX6470.B38E27 2004
286'.1764—dc22
                                    2003027279

CONTENTS

FOREWORD

Any serious study of history requires a scrutiny of primary sources, a statement equally true of both secular and religious history. Dr. Joseph Early, Jr., has provided the most complete and comprehensive collection of sources related to Baptists in Texas ever issued in one volume.

This work is carefully sifted from a vast array of church minutes, personal letters and diaries, association and state convention records, and official records of various Baptist universities in Texas. Reports of important committees and study commissions round out this interesting summary of what Baptists in Texas have thought, said, and done on a multitude of issues in the Lone Star State. Dr. Early is remarkably even-handed in his selection of sources to include. He does not go out of his way to include controversial items, nor does he shy away when they appear relevant. Any student of Baptist history will find this a fascinating and utterly indispensable source of information for anything relating to Baptists in the state.

This works follows the outline of my own *Texas Baptists: A Sesquicentennial History* (Dallas: Baptistway Press, 1998). Chapter divisions and topics are the same, allowing the two works to be used independently or together. Though Early allows the sources to speak for themselves, he includes brief but pertinent introductions to set each piece in context.

A prolific writer, Dr. Early has a number of other works in the process of publication. His doctoral dissertation, on the Hayden Controversy in Texas, will be issued shortly and he has a number of other books and articles in the pipeline. He distinguished himself as a doctoral student at Southwestern Baptist Theological Seminary in Fort Worth, where he displayed energetic scholarship and a keen eye for history. This is not the last the public will read of Joe Early. One predicts he will shortly take his place among the great Baptist historians of Texas such as J. M. Carr, Z. N. Morrell, J. M. Carroll, B. F. Fuller, J. M. Dawson, and Robert A. Baker. This young man may very well exceed them all.

A native of Kentucky, Joe graduated from Cumberland College, attended The Southern Baptist Theological Seminary in Louisville, the Midwestern Baptist Theological Seminary in Kansas City, and received his Ph.D. from the Southwestern Baptist Theological Seminary in Fort Worth in 2002. He is currently Assistant Professor of Religion at Cumberland College.

Harry Leon McBeth
Distinguished Professor of Baptist History
Southwestern Baptist Theological Seminary
Fort Worth, Texas

PREFACE

Texas Baptists have a rich heritage of faith and work. From the early days of Z. N. Morrell and R. E. B. Baylor to the modern era of Bill Pinson and Charles Wade, Texas Baptists have moved forward with what they deemed their most important task, that of fulfilling the Great Commission. Many wonderful histories concerning Texas Baptists have been written over the years. The latest in the line is Leon McBeth's *Texas Baptists: A Sesquicentennial History.* In his text, McBeth sets the Texas Baptist story in its context, provides biographies of key participants, and then seeks to interpret their actions. In order to maximize this endeavor, McBeth relied heavily upon the primary sources, while not ignoring key secondary works and, as a good historian, provided an appropriate source in the notes for the reader. Dr. McBeth has often said to me that "tomorrow's historical work is today's footnote." I have found this to be true.

While working on my dissertation on Texas Baptist history at Southwestern Seminary, I had the unique opportunity of working closely with two great Texas Baptist historians, Dr. Karen Bullock and Dr. Leon McBeth. Their combined knowledge of Texas Baptist history would fill most libraries. Several times I would be discussing some topic of Texas Baptist history with them, and I would ask, "Where can I find that source?" We would then discuss the myriads of texts, archival holdings, letters, and cellars where these works could be found. We soon discovered that most were in either the A. Webb Roberts Library at Southwestern

Seminary, the Texas Collection at Baylor University, the Texas Baptist Historical Society in Dallas, or some private library in the Lone Star State. The dissemination of these sources made the gathering of facts for my dissertation quite laborious. For this reason, when I completed my research, I told Dr. McBeth that I felt Texas Baptists were missing out on a part of their heritage by not being able to easily access the original writings of their forefathers. Given this fact, I asked him if I could develop a sourcebook to coincide with *Texas Baptists: A Sesquicentennial History*. As a strong advocate of primary sources, Dr. McBeth quickly agreed and this work is the fruit of that labor.

This book is designed to supplement *Texas Baptists: A Sesquicentennial History*. In these books, the chapter titles and the major divisions are the same so that the reader may move easily between the texts. In this regard, since Dr. McBeth has emphasized the last thirty years of Texas Baptist history, this sourcebook places great emphasis on the same era. Though designed to be a supplement, this work does stand on its own and can be used as an independent research tool. While letting the original authors speak for themselves, I have endeavored to provide the reader with historical sources that demonstrate the triumphs, struggles, character, and humanity of the many heroes that have encapsulated the one hundred and fifty years of Texas Baptist life. For this reason, I have attempted to keep my introductory remarks that accompany each section at a minimum. Following each presentation, the source is given so that the reader might review the full document.

While researching and gathering information for this compilation, I discovered there were far too many documents and that many of them could not be included. For this reason, choices had to be made. Certainly, some readers will be disappointed not to find a specific document that they believe worthy of inclusion in such a compendium, and for this I apologize. Thus, the reader deserves to know how the choices for inclusion were made for this text.

First, I have tried to include documents from as many major contributors to Baptist life in Texas as possible. These documents include books, newspaper articles, letters, associational addresses, and minutes. While famous writings such as J. M. Carroll's *The Trail of Blood* and George W. Truett's sermon on the principle of separation of church and state delivered on the steps of the Capitol building in Washington D. C. are included, lesser known writings such as R. C. Buckner's *Memorial to the First Baptist Church of Dallas* and B. H. Carroll's treatise concerning the use of women deacons are offered in order to provide a deeper insight into the person and events at hand. Lesser known, but equally important, are countless laymen who have helped shape the Baptist denomination in Texas. Thus, one may find letters to editors, minutes from small churches, and reports from some of the lesser-known workers in the BGCT's vast denominational machinery. In this regard, Baptist periodicals such as the *Texas Baptist and Herald*, the *Baptist Standard*, the *Missionary Worker*, the *Plumbline*, and *Texas Baptists Committed* are wonderful sources. It is in these newspapers that the Texas Baptist leadership presents its policies, goals, and positions to local Baptists on a weekly basis.

Second, I have attempted to provide the reader with documents concerning the formation of several important Texas Baptist organizations. For instance, material is provided on the organization and importance of the first Sunday School, the Missionary Societies, the Union Association, the Baptist General Association, the Baptist State Convention, the Baptist General Convention of Texas, and the Southern Baptists of Texas. Documents concerning the work of the various State Boards, Commissions, and investigative and survey Committees are also included. Furthermore, since the lifeblood of Texas Baptist ministers flows through the veins of Baylor University and Southwestern Seminary, a number of sources concerning their prolific histories are also included.

Third, I have not shied away from the troublesome and schismatic issues that have sporadically appeared in Texas Baptist life. In order to provide a complete picture of the heritage of Texas Baptists, I have included documents concerning various heresies and doctrinal debates, church-wide schisms, and the writings of divisive individuals such as S. A. Hayden and J. Frank Norris. I have also included more current issues that have reverberated through the Baptist life of the state such as the firing of Russell Dilday as president of Southwestern Seminary and the formation of the Southern Baptists of Texas. In choosing the documents to best represent these and other entities, I have attempted to provide material that depicts both sides of the conflict. If some of the choices appear to be biased, I assure you this was not my intention.

In the majority, the documents that are provided are reproduced exactly as they were originally written. In order not to change the intent of the writer, I deemed this to be prudent. This proved to be a difficult task as many of the earlier documents are handwritten and on aged paper, and some documents, including some of the more modern, were often written without a high regard for grammar and style. Despite this fact, these documents are reproduced as they were originally written. I do not *believe* that I have taken any editorial liberties. Furthermore, I was the sole typist for this sourcebook, and thus, if errors of any type are found, they are exclusively my mistakes.

I believe that no one achieves anything of merit without the blessings of our Lord Jesus Christ and help from Christian brothers and sisters. Therefore, I first thank our Savior who sustained me and helped me to persevere when I became tired and my back hurt from the countless hours of typing. Secondly, there are several wonderful people who should deserve proper recognition, but I realize that I cannot thank them all, so I say thank you to all collectively.

Yet, there are certain individuals without whose patience, assistance, and support this text would have never been completed. First, the serials and archival staff at Southwestern Seminary's A. Webb Roberts Library, especially Myrta Ann Garrett and David Joza, were vital to my efforts and always eager to aid me in my research. Second, the staff of the Texas Collection at Baylor University also provided me with several documents and was eager to let everyone know that they are there to help anyone in the area of Texas research. Third, I would also like to thank my wife who often said to me as I sat in my recliner in the evenings, "Don't you need to work on your book?" Fourth, my father, Dr. Joe Early, Sr., deserves special recognition for proofreading my introductory paragraphs. Fifth, it was my professor, Dr. Karen Bullock, who first introduced me to the rich history of Texas Baptists. For this, I owe her my heartfelt gratitude. Finally, I must thank the master of Baptist and Texas Baptist history, Dr. Harry Leon McBeth. He is a friend, mentor, confidant, and true Texas Baptist. For this reason, I dedicate this book to him.

Pro Ecclesia, Pro Texana
Joe Early, Jr., Ph. D.

ABBREVIATIONS

AB	Annuity Board of SBC
BAH	Booz, Allen, and Hamilton Study
BCLC	Baptist Church Loan Corporation
BDC	Baptist Distinctives Committee
BFT	Baptist Foundation of Texas
BGA	Baptist General Association
BGCT	Baptist General Convention of exas
BMA	Baptist Missionary Association
BSC	Baptist State Convention
BSU	Baptist Student Union
BTU	Baptist Training Union
BU	Baylor University
BYPU	Baptist Young People's Union
CEC	Christian Education Commission
CFO	Chief Financial Officer
CJM	Criminal Justice Ministries
CLC	Christian Life Commission
CP	Cooperative Program
DBU	Dallas Baptist University
DSM	Department of Student Ministries
ETBA	East Texas Baptist Association
E/EC	Efficiency/Effectiveness Committee
EB	Executive Board of the BGCT
FBC	First Baptist Church
FMB	Foreign Mission Board of the SBC
GNT	Good News Texas
HBU	Houston Baptist University
HMB	Home Mission Board of the SBC
HSU	Hardin-Simmons University
HWC	Human Welfare Commission
IMB	International Mission Board of SBC
LMCO	Lottie Moon Christmas Offering
MHDO	Mary Hill Davis Offering for State Missions
MSC	Mission Service Corps

NAMB	North American Mission Board of SBC
PM	Partnership Missions
RM	River Ministry
SBC	Southern Baptist Convention
SBT	Southern Baptists of Texas
SMC	State Missions Commission
SS	Sunday School
SWBTS	Southwestern Baptist Theological Seminary
TBC	Texas Baptists Committed
TBM	Texas Baptist Men
TEC	Theological Education Commission
WMU	Woman's Missionary Union

CHAPTER 1

Changing Flags over Texas

1.1 Cortez and Coronado

The first Christians in "New Spain," which included modern Texas, were certainly not of the Baptist or even Protestant faith. These men were known as *conquistadores,* or the Conquerors, and claimed to be devout Catholics. Three conquistadores, Hernando Cortez (1460–1521), Francisco Vasquez Coronado (1510–1554), and Rene-Robert-Cavelier Sieur de La Salle (1643–1687) are prominent for their lasting effects on religion in Texas. Known primarily for his destruction of the Aztec Indians, Cortez may have pushed as far north as modern-day San Antonio. After vanquishing the Aztecs, Cortez pillaged their gold, infected the population with smallpox, and forced Catholicism upon them. While in search of the "Fountain of Youth" and the "Seven Cities of Cíbola" in North Texas, Coronado also forced the Catholic faith upon the indigenous population. While holding mass whenever possible, La Salle explored all along the Gulf Coast, killing all Indians who stood in his way. Under the auspices of the cross, the actions of these conquistadores were reminiscent of the Crusaders in the Middle Ages.

A. Cortez: The Enforcement of the Faith

On Sundays and feast-days, the inhabitants and all who may be in the village shall attend mass in the principal church, entering before the reading of the gospel and remaining until the priest says, "Ita Missa est," and gives the benediction, under penalty of a fine of half a peso of gold. On said Sundays and feast-days, nothing of any sort shall be sold from the time the bell calls to mass until it is all over, nor shall any store

1

or office open during that time, under penalty of a fine; one-third of it to go to public works; one-third to the officer who reports it; and one-third to the work of the church.

Source: *Colección de Documentos Ineditos Relativos al Descubrimiento Conquista y Colonización de las Posesiones Españoles*, 42 vols. (Madrid: n. p., 1885), 26:180.

B. Cortez: Developing an Indigenous Catholic Faith by Force

Since as Catholics and Christians our principal intention ought to be the honor and service of God, and since the motive of the Holy Father in giving to the emperor the rule of the lands and the profit from them was that the people be converted to our Holy Catholic Faith, we, therefore, require that all persons who have *repartimientos* of Indians be obliged to take away all their idols and warn them against further idolatrous practice, and that they refrain from all sacrifice of human life to their gods. Failure to comply with the order will on first offense be punished with a fine, the second offense with a double fine, and the third offense with the loss of the Indians.

Source: *Colección de Documentos Ineditos Relativos al Descumbrimiento Conquista y Colonización de las Posesiones Españoles*, 42 vols. (Madrid: n. p., 1885), 26:141–42.

C. The Dominicans' Role: No Indigenous Clergy

No fruit can be expected from their study . . . because they have not the ability to understand surely and correctly certain things of faith nor their reasons, nor is their language abundant enough to serve to explain the faith without great improprieties that can easily lead to errors. And it follows that they should not be ordained, for it would be better for their reputation if they are not. Because even the sacrament of the Eucharist is not given to them, for numerous reasons given by many learned and religious persons. . . . It is therefore very necessary that they should be removed from study.

Source: Joaquin F. Pacheco, Francisco de Cardenas, and Luis Torres de Mendoza eds., *Colección de Documentos Ineditos Relativos al Descubrimiento Conquista y Organización de las Antuiguas Posesiones*

Españoles de America y Oceania, Sacados de los Archivos del Reino y muy Especialmente del Indias, 31 vols. (Madrid: Real Academia de la Historia, 1884), 7:541–42.

D. Coronado and the Seven Cities of Cíbola

Coronado's primary assignment from the Spanish government was to find the treasures of the mythical "Seven Cities of Cíbola." He was to push east from modern Mexico and search for a path along the Rio Grande. Coronado, however, often pushed into the northeastern areas of New Spain searching for glory and riches that were not only previously unexplored and treacherous, but were also not even rumored to be in the vicinity of the Seven Cities. Due to his disobedience and his supposed rape of an Indian, Coronado fell out of favor with the Spanish government and was deposed as the leader of the expedition in 1540.

On the 22d of the month of April last, I set out from the province of Culiacan with a part of the army, having made the arrangements of which I wrote to your Lordship. Judging by the outcome, I feel sure that it was fortunate that I did not start the entire army on this undertaking, because the labors have been so very great and a lack of food such that I do not believe this undertaking could have been completed before the end of this year, and that there would be a great loss of life if it should be accomplished. For, as I wrote to your Lordship, I spent eighty days in traveling to Culiacan, during which time I and the gentlemen of my company, who were horsemen, carried on our backs and our horses little food, in such wise that after leaving the place none of us carried any necessary effects weighing more than a pound. Fear of this, and although we took all possible care and forethought of the small supply of provisions which we carried, it gave out. And this is not to be wondered at, because the road is rough and long, and what with our harquebuses, which had to be carried up the mountains and hills and in the passage of the rivers, the greater part of the corn was lost. And since I send Your Lordship a drawing of this route, I will say no more about it here.

Thirty leagues before reaching the place which the father provincial spoke so well of in his report, I sent Melchoir Diaz forward with fifteen horsemen, ordering him to make but one day's journey out of two, so that he could examine everything there before I arrived. He traveled through some very rough mountains for four days, and did not find anything to live on, nor people, nor information about anything except that he found two or three poor villages, with twenty or thirty huts apiece. From the people here he learned that there was nothing to be found in the country beyond except the mountains, which continued very rough, entirely uninhabited by people. And, because this was labor lost, I did not want to send Your Lordship an account of it. The whole company felt disturbed at this, that a thing so much praised, and about which the father has said so many things, should be found so very different; and they began to think that all the rest would be of the same sort.

When I noticed this, I tried to encourage them as well as I could, telling them that Your Lordship had always thought that this part of the trip would be a waste of effort, and that we ought to devote ourselves to those Seven Cities and the other provinces about which we had informa-tion—that those should be the end our enterprise. With this resolution and purpose, we all marched cheerfully along a very bad way, where it was impossible to pass without making a new road or repair the one that was there, which troubled the soldiers not a little, considering that ev-erything which the friar had said was found to be quite the reverse; be-cause, among others these things which the father has said and declared, he said that the way would be plain and good, and that here would be only a small hill of about half a league. And truth is, that there are moun-tains where, however well the path might be fixed, they could not be crossed without there being a great danger of the horses falling over them. And was so bad that a large number of the animals which Your Lordship sent as provisions for the army were lost along this part of the way, on account of the roughness of the rocks. The lambs and wethers lost their hoofs along the way, and I left the greater part of those which I brought from Culiacan at the river of Lachimi, because they were un-able to travel, and so that they might proceed more slowly.

Source: *Coronado's Report to Viceroy Mendoza*, Cíbola August 3, 1540.

E. La Salle

Of all the conquistadores, La Salle was certainly the bloodiest and most cunning. In search of gold, he would often make friends with one tribe of Indians by giving them beads and food so that they would fight other tribes who stood in his way. While the friendly tribes were doing his bidding, the

La Salle expedition would hold mass. During this time, the elders of the friendly tribe, who did not go to war, were taught about the Catholic God and their mission in Texas. One of La Salle's lieutenants, Henri Joutel, was disturbed by the conquistador's techniques and recorded his impressions in his journal.

We remained in that place with the women and several old men who were not able to go to war. On Saturday, the 10th, the two men on the other side of the river came to join us. The Provencal was to have gone to war with the others but was prevented from going by a splinter of wood that injured his leg. During the men's absence, we only saw the old men who came to see us from time to time and related news which we had much difficulty understanding. Being able to communicate only by signs, I often found myself quite distraught. What made me most uneasy was that the women sometimes broke out crying and I was unable to guess if some ill deed as if they were crying for the death of those they wanted to kill. That is why this upset me, as I often saw this kind of performance. I have since learned that their tears were caused by the memory of some of their friends or relatives who had been killed in war parties such as the one that had gone out. As I was ignorant of this, I was given to much alarm.

Meanwhile, we spent a length of time without hearing anything; only the old men continued in their visits. As we said our prayers in common everyday, evening as well as morning, they came to watch us. We tried then to make them understand the magnitude of He Who had given us life, making the corn and other plants grow; but we did not know their language; and it was very difficult to make them understand God. That is why I am surprised that the author of whom I have spoken several times dares to allege that he preached to them and catechized them; this he could not have done without having spent several years with them to learn their language.

Source: *The La Salle Expedition to Texas: The Journal of Henri Joutel, 1684–1687*, ed., William C. Foster (Austin: Texas State Historical Association, 1998), 226. Reprint courtesy of William C. Foster.

F. The Baptist Perspective of Catholic Hegemony

The Spaniards being the first Europeans to settle in Texas, the Catholic faith, being their established religion, was first introduced here. They brought with them their priestly government, which was established by law. As early as 1528 the Spaniards, under command of Narvaez, landed in Texas from Mexico; but after years of great privation were lost among the Indians. In 1540 Coronado, with Spanish troops and Catholic priests, took formal possession of the village of Isleta, a few miles from El Paso, on the Rio Grande river, then inhabited by Pueblo Indians. This was the first permanent settlement made in Texas. In 1585 the Catholic missionaries established missions in El Paso and Santa Fe, and large numbers of these Pueblos were converted to that faith.

In 1685 the French, under the command of La Salle, landed a force, including Catholic missionaries, at Matagorda bay, and built a fort, which he called St. Louis. Great dissensions arose among the French, which resulted in the murder of La Salle and several others by their own comrades, and the whole colony became extinct through starvation and Indian depredations.

In 1690 an expedition under command of De Leon landed near the mouth of Trinity river and established Guadalupe mission on that river among the Tejos Indians. Other missions were established from time to time as the Spanish settlements were extended. Wherever there was a Spanish settlement there was a presidio, or fortress, and wherever there was a presidio there were priests and a mission, and the cross was set up.

Mission Alamo was first established on the Rio Grande river in 1703, but it was removed, and finally built in 1744 on the Alamo plaza, in San Antonio, where its ruins still stand. The most important and greatest of all missions was San Jose, founded in 1718 on the beautiful San Antonio river, a few miles below the town of San Antonio. The foundation was laid with great pomp and ceremony by Franciscan friars, assisted by Spanish soldiers, Mexicans and converted Comanche Indians. All continued to work with great zeal on this stately structure, which was at once a presidio, or stronghold, as well as a mission. It was sixty years before San Jose was completed. Other missions were soon built on the San Antonio river and in other parts of the country. The Apache and Comanche Indians gathered about them in great numbers and were enrolled as converts, but scarcely a trace of the priestly proselytism is at this day to be found among these people.

Source: B. F. Fuller, *History of Texas Baptists* (Louisville: Baptist Book Concern, 1900), 68–69.

1.2 Stephen F. Austin: "The Father of Texas"

In 1822, Stephen F. Austin (1793–1836), whose father Moses Austin (1761–1821) had acquired a charter for a large land grant in New Spain from the Mexican government, led a group of 300 American families to Texas. This group became known as "Austin's 300." At least eleven of these families were known to be of the Baptist faith. The names of the Baptist families were: Alcorn, Coles, Davis, Fitzgerald, Corbet, Harvey, Kincheoloe, Kuykendall, McNeill, Moore, and Smith. Each person, however, was required to sign a contract attesting his or her loyalty to Catholicism. As people who believed in the separation of church and state and detested any type of ecclesiastical hierarchy, the Baptists were not likely to have kept their written promise. In fact, many may have purposefully violated the agreement.

A. The "Catholic" Contract to Live in Texas

1. Inasmuch as the plan presented in the preceding memorial by the person concerned conforms to the colonization law of the honorable congress of the State, adopted March 24, the government consents to it, and therefore, in fulfillment of Article 8 (of this Colonization law), and in consideration of his petition, it assigns to him the land for which he asks.
. . .

4. The families that shall compose this colony, besides being Catholic, as the Empresario promises, in his petition, must be able to prove, by certificates from the authorities of the localities from which they come, of their good moral character.

5. The Empresario shall not introduce into his colony criminals, vagrants, or persons of bad morals, and if such be found there he shall cause them to leave the Republic, by force of arms if necessary.
. . .

9. It shall be his duty to erect churches in the new towns, to provide them with ornaments, sacred vessels, and adornment dedicated to divine worship, and to apply in due time for the priests needed for the administration of spiritual instruction.

Source: Austin Petition for Land Grant, cited in J. M. Carroll, *A History of Texas Baptists: Comprising a Detailed Account of Their Activities, Their Progress and Their Achievements* (Dallas: Baptist Standard Publishing Co., 1923), 9.

B. Austin's Early Capitulation to Catholicism: Austin to Jose Antonio Saucedo

All the families who have emigrated from other countries to reside in the colony under my care are Catholics. Their Christian conduct in as much as our recent establishment permits it, conforms to what can be observed by all good Catholics who find themselves without the spiritual helps which only the Ministers of the Most High can administer to them. For this reason, I pray you, in my name and in the name of all the citizens, that you kindly send us a priest to care for our spiritual necessities and if it be possible to send one who understands the English language it would be a greater source of consolation.

Some children have been born in the colony, but since none have been seriously ill, they have not received baptism. Hoping that for our great happiness, a priest might come here who can administer the holy Sacrament, for only necessity would oblige us to baptize these children in this absence.

There have been five marriages here. The manner of performing them,—I hope that through your kindness and knowledge of the attending circumstances you may approve of it—has been, as was customary with the priests, in the absence of relatives of both parties and of impartial witnesses and by means of a document signed, by the contracting parties and their relatives, they put themselves under obligation to submit to the fines which our Holy Mother the Church may impose through her Minister when he ratifies and blesses the marriage.

The interments have been conducted as is customary among Christians where there is neither Priest nor consecrated place set apart for the purpose. All who have died in this village and the surrounding country are buried in a place which we call the cemetery. But it is not blessed, so we are interring them in this one place, until such a time as it may be possible to have it consecrated.

Source: Stephen F. Austin to Jose Antonio Saucedo, 20 June 1824, cited in Eugene Barker, ed., *The Austin Papers,* 3 vols. (Washington D.C. : Government Printing Office, 1924), 1:850.

C. Questions on the Degrees of Catholic Complicity before Migration

So far as to be exempted from the payment of tithes to the established Church, if they should desire it. And to think and act for themselves in matters of conscience? Provided that they do not interfere with the Catholic Religion, and with fidelity support the laws of the land, as citizens ought to do? And thereby to enjoy as much Religious liberty as the Protestants have in France and some other Catholic countries? Or as the Catholics have extended in the United States? Or should these privileges in their full extent be refused, we ask for the Privilege of exercising the rights of private judgment in our own houses and neighborhood? Provided, nevertheless, that our difference in opinion with the Catholics be a silent one?

Source: Rankin to Austin, 25 December 1825, cited in Eugene C. Barker, ed., *The Austin Papers*, 3 vols. (Washington: Government Printing Office, 1924), 2:1242–43.

D. Catholic Reaction to the New Settlers

The violation of the colonization laws and of existing contracts has continued without any effect. . . . Hence we find that, besides this territory having been occupied by colonists who never have ought to be admitted into it, there is not one among them, in Texas, who is a Catholic.

Source: Catholic Priest letter, cited in Edna Rowe, "The Disturbances at Anahuac in 1832," *Quarterly of the Texas State Historical Association* 6 (April 1903): 267.

E. Baptist Disinclination to Catholic Hegemony

All who wished to marry as well also as those who had been bonded for years, had now to come forward and have the slip knot made fast. . . . Immediately after his arrival a number of these old married people determined to save trouble by having one grand wedding and give the Padre an opportunity to do a wholesale business. . . . The day was fine and every countenance seemed to brighten with the prospect of the anticipated enjoyment, not for the pleasure of being or seeing, them married over again entirely, but the baptism, the wine—the dinner, the dance and with many, the sight of a Roman Catholic Priest was equal to a rare show in Texas— a thing of which they had long heard, but never seen— and really with some, having heard much said about them, they were at a loss to conjecture whether the Priest could be a natural man, or some kind of beast. Expectation was on tiptoe– the Padre arrived . . . and it was soon discovered, that he looked like a man, and talked like a man . . . and an Irishman at that . . . I was called on, being generally acquainted with the people, to act as a kind of precursor, and requested to go and take down the names of the candidates for matrimony, in order that the necessary certificates be prepared and in readiness. This I complied with and returned with a muster role of twelve rank and file, no new candidates having offered. While these things were in preparation I was requested to return and make out a roll of names of all the candidates for baptism. Now the test was to be made, though no religious societies were tolerated in Texas, yet prejudices deep rooted by early education rose up strong in opposition, and with many the idea of being baptized by a Roman Catholic Priest carried with it an everlasting stigma and disgrace. I applied to those who seemed elders among the people, and I found very few without some kind of excuse, either that they had been baptized when they were young, or that they had belonged to some other religious order before they came to the country and that they by no means considered a second baptism necessary, as such I met with poor success and immediately returned and made my report. I told the Padra that fortunately for the good people of Texas they had generally immigrated from Christian countries and had many of them been baptized before they came here, and some had religious scruples respecting the propriety of a second baptism . . . He requested me to go and tell his good parishioners, that they need have no scruples on that account, that he did not consider a second baptism necessary provided that they had evidences that they had been baptized in the true faith. Well Padra there are so many different faiths now in the world I am entirely at a loss to know which is the true faith? You will excuse me for the enquiry, what do you call the true faith? The true faith is the Roman Catholic Apostolic, all other is heresy.

Source: "Reminiscences of Henry Smith," cited in *Texas Historical Quarterly* 14:34–37.

F. The Joseph Bays Incident

The year following that of Mr. Smalley's arrival in Texas, in 1825, another Baptist missionary, Rev. Joseph Bays, came into Texas, and preached the first Baptist sermon preached by a Baptist on the west side of the Brazos river. He was seeking his way to the Mexican settlement of San Antonio, and stopping at the home of Moses Shipman, near San Felipe, which was given up to the worship of the Roman Catholics, it being the only creed recognized by the Spanish government, to the non-tolerance of all others, Mr. Bays began his missionary labors. He threw himself with consuming zeal into the work under the most discouraging conditions, but the impression made by him was so pronounced that he was intercepted by the Romanish priests, who, invoking the aid of the civil authorities, succeeded in having Bays ordered away. For a time, disregarding peremptory order, he was threatened with imprisonment, with a hint of even direr punishment should he not heed the order to leave. He therefore decided to quit the region, not so much in his own behalf, as in behalf of those who had befriended him, and who had no opportunity to leave, but would have to bear the consequences of his persistency to remain. He was released from arrest only on condition that he would quit Texas altogether. At that time Roman Catholicism was so supreme in Texas that no one was permitted to settle within its borders who declined to take the oath of allegiance to that creed. That an ecclesiastical law so rigid as that was not enforced, and that it was not regarded as binding because compulsorily taken, was clear from the fact that there is no reason for believing that there were Baptists in Austin's colony and other Christian Protestants in other parts of the territory, who had been in Texas for several years.

Source: B. F. Riley, *A History of Texas Baptists* (Dallas: By the author, 1907), 14, 15.

CHAPTER 2

Baptist Beginnings in Texas, 1820–1840

2.1 Zacharius N. Morrell

Zacharius N. Morrell (1803–1883) was born in South Carolina, but spent most of his early years in Tennessee. Though he considered himself sickly, Morrell earned the nickname "Wildcat" because of his fervent desire to serve God and his ability as an Indian fighter. In 1835 Morrell and his family moved to Texas. After a brief stay at the Falls of the Brazos, Morrell was forced to move to Washington-on-the-Brazos because of Indian raids and the fall of the Alamo to Santa Anna. While he was at Washington-on-the-Brazos, he formed the first missionary Baptist Church in Texas in 1837. Morrell also helped to form the Union Association (1840) and the Colorado Association (1847) which were the first Baptist Associations in Texas. In addition, he played a significant role in the birth of Baylor University at Independence (1845). The following excerpts from Morrell's most famous work, *Flowers and Fruits in the Wilderness*, demonstrate his fervent love for his Savior and the rationale for his nickname Wildcat.

Source: Z. N. Morrell, *Flowers and Fruits in the Wilderness* (Boston: Rockwell and Churchill, 1872).

A. Morrell's Call to Go to Texas

"Where there is a will there is a way," is an old adage that is true, provided that there is not too much undertaken, and provided, further, that the enterprise is in accordance with the will of God. Two hundred and fifty miles lay between me and the nearest soil of Texas, and it was about five hundred miles to the "Falls of the Brazos." But few believed that I could make this journey on horseback, yet a still small voice from Macedonia was heard, and the angel of vision bid me go forward saying, "God hath much people in the land." We pass may things of interest; cross the father of American waters at Rodney, Red River at Alexandria and reach old "Fort Gaines" on the Sabine, December 21, 1835.

Our company numbered six, and while crossing the Sabine, the ferryman related the following incident, that made a deep impression upon our minds. The River at this crossing was the dividing line between Louisiana and Texas. Only a few days before a man rode up on the Louisiana side, evidently under great excitement, and at the top of his voice ordered the ferryman to bring over the boat. Supposing there was some emergency, the boat was promptly carried to the opposite shore, and the man landed as quick as possible on the Texas side. Just as he was ashore, an officer, with a body of men in pursuit of this refugee from justice, hailed on the eastern bank. The man, recognizing his pursuers, mounted his horse, rode up the hill entirely out of reach, and very deliberately made this short and pointed speech: "Gentlemen, I am just a little too fast for your sort. I am entirely safe." Alighting from his horse and kissing the ground, he continued: "The Sabine River is a greater Savior than Jesus Christ. He saves men when they die from going to hell; but this river saves living men from prison."

We now began to realize the truth of what we had so often heard, that Texas was a place of refuge for scoundrels. Seeing then an impression was made upon our minds, the jocular ferryman, in order to dispel the cloud of gloom, continued: "And, gentlemen, what have you done that you have come to Texas?" The eyes of the lawyers, the doctors, the deacons, and the preachers that composed our company, were turned inquiringly towards each other, and while we waited for another to reply, no one answered. After ferriage was paid, we steered our course towards San Augustine. (pp. 29–30)

B. Morrell's First Sermon in Texas and Decision to Remain, 1835

Here on Little River we found the forty Tennessean landhunters, and among them Deacon Cartwell from the Baptist Church in Nashville. What a joyful and unexpected meeting it was! "Why," said brother Cartwell, "I never expected to see our cane-brake preacher again. I thought that you had died with hemorrhage of the lungs." My health by this time was almost entirely restored, and my voice clear and full; at least this was the decision of my comrades on our return to the trail, after the buffalo chase was over. Mr. Childress, whose wife was a Baptist, was the occupant and owner of that little lone cabin in the wilderness, and the family and land-hunters decided that they must have a sermon after supper; and accordingly I preached my first sermon in Texas, in camp, on the thirteenth of December, 1835.

After an absence of about twelve days Deacon Hunt and I were back at the Falls; the other four having remained with the land-hunters. Our mission was accomplished, and we were seriously considering the propriety of moving the family eight hundred miles, to settle in the wilderness. The climate certainly would be suitable for one in my condition, and as I could neither preach in Tennessee or Mississippi without endangering my life, I felt a strong inclination to make the change. After much prayer and meditation my mind was made up, and I thank God for the decision. (pp. 44–45)

C. The First Sermon Preached in Houston

Houston, in 1837, was a city of tents; only one or two log-cabins appeared. John K. Allen's framed building was raised, covered, and partly weather-boarded. A large amount of goods in tents. A large round tent resembling the enclosure of a circus, was used for a drinking saloon. Plenty of "John Barley Corn" and cigars. This was the last Sunday in March, and after changing the garb of the wagoner for one similar to that worn in the city, I went out in search of a place to preach. Upon inquiry I was informed that there never had been a sermon preached in the place. It was quite a novel thing then to hear preaching, and some, to enjoy the novelty, and some no doubt with the purest motives, went to work, and very soon seats were prepared in a cool shade on that beautiful spring morning. The sermon was preached to the attentive, intelligent audience. Brother Marsh, a Baptist minister from Mississippi, then about seventy years old, came forward by request and closed the service. From near the spot where I then stood is now issued the Texas

Baptist Herald, sending streams of light over a vast territory, and around that spot has gathered a city of eighteen thousand inhabitants, destined to assume much larger proportions, yet, in consequence of the fact that it is the great railroad centre of the State. (p. 66)

E. Indian Fighting

Their policy was now discovered, and Colonel Burleson, with his command on the right wing, was ordered round the woods. Immediately they began howling like wolves, and there was a general stampede and vigorous pursuit. The weather was very dry, and the dust so thick that the parties could see each other but a short distance. Some fourteen or fifteen Indians were killed before the retreat, and a great many more were killed afterwards. Our men followed them some fifteen or eighteen miles.

Just as the retreat commenced, I heard the scream of a female voice, in a bunch of bushes close by. Approaching the spot, I discovered a lady endeavoring to pull an arrow out that was lodged firmly in her breast. This proved to be Mrs. Watts, whose husband was killed at Linnville. Dr. Brown, of Gonzales, was at once summoned to the spot. Near by we soon discovered a white woman and a Negro woman, both dead. These were all shot with arrows, when the howl was raised and the retreat commenced. While the doctor was approaching, I succeeded in loosing her hands from the arrow. The dress and flesh on each side of the arrow were cut, and an effort was made to extract it. The poor sufferer seized the doctor's hand, and screamed so violently that he desisted. A second effort was made with success. My blanket was spread upon the ground, and as she rested on this, with my saddle for a pillow, she was soon composed and rejoicing her escape. Death would have been preferable to crossing the mountains with the savages. She had ridden a pack-mule all the way from the coast, and when they stopped she was required to read the stolen books for their amusement. I received many letters from Mrs. Watts in after years, but never saw her again.

When we went into the fight there were present about two hundred men; but by night we supposed there were near five hundred. They continued to come in all the evening; many of them from a great distance. Men and boys of every variety and character composed that noisy crowd, that was busily engaged all night long talking of the transactions of the previous eventful days. Here were three Baptist preachers,-R. E. B. Baylor, T. W. Cox, and the writer, all in the fight with doctors, lawyers, merchants, and farmers. (pp. 130–31)

F. The First Missionary Baptist Church in Texas, 1836

Our weekly prayer-meeting was regularly held in the town of Washington, in a small house, the best we could secure. These young men referred to, regularly attended; behavior was good; were very polite, and sang elegantly all parts of the music. They had been trained to do this in other States, under pious influences. A stranger present would have supposed that a whole church, well organized and drilled in some of the old States, had moved in a body and settled at Washington. Cartwell, Buffington, Byars, Ellis, and Morrell, one after another, led in prayer, and the singing between prayers was of the very first order, in point of time and melody. The writer would give out an appointment for preaching every Sunday, when at home, and after singing "Old Hundred" the congregation would retire. After the benediction the young men would hasten away. By the time we would pass on our way home, the grocery and billiard saloon would be lighted up, and a large crowd—God have mercy on them!—would be assembled for the night. Here was an important move of the prince of darkness,—his image and sign hanging over the door. There was King John Barleycorn, within, double-refined, with all his machinery propelled by the engine of hell, fed with the fire of damnation, drawn directly from the "bottomless pit" of eternal perdition. It did not require the foresight of a prophet to understand the results of the procedure, on the part of the enemy, if they continued long. Our prayers went up to God, "O Lord, hear the prayers of thy servants, and the prayers of the mothers, in distant lands, for these wayward sons!"

We determined, let come what might, to organize a church. The day was appointed, eight Baptists assembled to keep house for God. Brother H. R. Cartwell was recognized as deacon, and Z. N. Morrell chosen as pastor. Thus sprung into existence the first church, according to my information, that was ever organized in Texas strictly on gospel principles, having the ordinances and officers of the ancient order, and with no anti-missionary element in its body. Shall we be permitted by the enemy to remain together, and enjoy church privileges? We had long desired such an estate. Shall the present organization stand, as the nucleus around which others will grow up? This we fondly hope. Or shall the feeble light in the wilderness be blown out, and require resuscitation? Such questions, in those troublesome times, revolved in our minds. We must wait and see.

A committee, consisting of J. R. Jenkins, A. Buffington, and H. R. Cartwell, was appointed to correspond with mission boards, north and east, and request that Texas be taken into consideration as a missionary field. An appointment was soon tendered to me from the American Board. Good reasons, at the time, were between me and the acceptance of this proposition. The correspondence was continued, and the result was, that Elder Wm. Tryon was sent to Washington County, and Elder James Huckins to Galveston. These brethren did not come for several years after this correspondence was commenced. Of them we will speak again at the proper time and place.

Measures were at once taken, by the infant church, to build a house of worship. The money was subscribed, the material was secured, the building and the work went rapidly forward.

In the fall of 1837, some families were passing through the town of Washington, on their way to Gonzales, who had left during the retreat the previous year. Among them was a very intelligent couple, who requested, at my hands, the performance of a marriage ceremony. This was the first time I solemnized the holy rite in Texas. (pp. 76–78)

2.2 Robert Emmett Bledsoe Baylor

R. E. B. Baylor (1793–1873) was a lawyer and early Texas Baptist leader. Born in Kentucky and after serving in the War of 1812, Baylor served in the Kentucky Legislature before moving to Alabama where he practiced law and in 1824 served in the Alabama Legislature. Converted in 1839 at the age of 48, Baylor surrendered to the ministry and moved to Texas. Baylor was instrumental in the formation of the Union Association (1840) and the Texas Baptist Education Society (1840). With the aid of William Tryon and James Huckins, this triumvirate secured the charter for Baylor University which bears his name. Baylor's personal motto, *Pro Ecclesia–Pro Texana*, also became the motto of Baylor University. Baylor donated the first $1000 to the University, served as the first professor of law, and upon occasion served as acting President. The following excerpts demonstrate Baylor's substantial influence on the Baptist cause in Texas.

A. Early Politics with Henry Clay

I remember to have had a conversation with Mr. Clay when I remarked "Mr. Clay, you will never be President." He seemed surprised and said, "My friends write to me from all parts of the Union that my prospects are more flattering than ever. Why do you think so?" Said I, "A man to be successful in political life must be just up to the age in which he lives, neither behind or too far in advance. The misfortune with you is you are always a half century ahead of the age." He paused a moment, dropping his head seeming to be reflecting on the remark I made. At last looking up, then said he "All we can do is struggle to bring up the age." Time but too truly proved the truth to the remark. I am astonished now that I had the boldness to say such a thing to this highly gifted and wonderful man.

Source: "Judge Baylor as a Man and Preacher," typewritten manuscript, The Texas Collection, Baylor University, 4–5. Reprint courtesy of Texas Collection, Baylor University.

B. Birth of the Tiger Point Church, 1840

A short time before his [Tryon's] arrival I had organized a little church in Washington County at a celebrated place called Tiger Point near Brenham. At this point the people were wont to meet on Sundays to gamble, horse race, drink, and fight with pistols and Bowie Knives. It looked like a forlorn hope to attempt to organize a church at such a place. At the day appointed I attended, there were present old Sister Allen . . . also brother Stephen Williams. After looking around for material to constitute our little church we could find only seven individuals belonging to the Baptist Church, two of whom were Coloured members, however upon Sister Allan's and my earnest solicitation we organized the church. Brother Williams all the while opposing the movement stating that we were too weak and that the thing would be he feared a failure, after the organization the question came up as to the location of the Church. Brother [no name given] rose up and said as you would have a church planted here I insist on locating it at Tiger Point. Said I that will never do, he replied where sin hath abounded grace shall much more abound and relying on this promise of God we located the church at Tiger Point. . . . Shortly after the constitution of this church brother Tryon came to Texas. We were frequently together at all the meetings particularly at Tiger Point. We there held many protracted meetings we had many precious revivals, and this church with the humble beginnings of seven members rose to one hundred and four communicants. As the county settled up and the members moved away to their lands and new homes it was so reduced numerically that it was thought best for the members to with draw from it and joining the Brenham Church which they did, and several of the members of the Brenham Church at this day remain to remember the trying season we passed through at Tiger Point.

Source: R. E. B. Baylor to J. H. Stribbling, 13 April 1871, The Texas Collection, Baylor University. Reprint courtesy of Texas Collection, Baylor University.

C. The Baptist Principles Undergirding Baylor University

It is due to Brother Tryon to say that the thought originated with him to establish a Baptist University in this county. He suggested the idea to me . . . We sent a memorial to the then Congress of the Republic of Texas for a charter . . . I was most familiar with such things, I dictated the memorial. He wrote a suggestion in it found in these words: "We wish it to be distinctly understood that we asked no donations from the Government. We expected none and never would receive any. At that early day some of the various religious denominations had applied to the Government for lands and obtained them, but it seemed to me if the government gave to some and withheld from others, it would be giving one religious sect a preference by law over another, and this you know was at war with our principles."

Source: R. E. B. Baylor to James Stribbling, 13 April 1871, The Texas Collection, Baylor University. Reprint courtesy of Texas Collection, Baylor University.

D. The Founding and Naming of Baylor University, 1845

The Education Society was now meeting and holding its sessions as a separate organization, but in connection with the associational meeting. The first officers of this Society were—R. E. B. Baylor, president; S. P. Andrews, recording secretary, and J. L. Farquhar, treasurer, and the board of managers were Elders H. Garrett, N. T. Byars, Richard Ellis, Z. N. Morrell and Brother Stephen Williams.

These pioneering Christians were evidently men of heroic courage and conquering faith. Their achievements border on the miraculous. Early in 1845 matters had progressed so far that Tryon and Baylor were appointed a committee to go before the Texas Congress and secure a charter for the contemplated school. Under the appeal of these two men, Congress granted the charter February 1, 1845. President Jones signed and approved it.

The question of a name for the new school did not seem to arise anywhere nor at any time until the charter was being granted by the Texas Congress. Then a name had to be chosen. The question was submitted to Baylor and Tryon. They had no opportunity to consult with any of their brethren. The name had to be chosen at once or the securing of the charter postponed. Baylor suggested the name "Tryon," giving as his reasons that "the thought of establishing a Baptist University in this country originated with Tryon," and that thus far he had been the strongest instrumentality in giving to the enterprise its success. But Tryon demurred, saying that he "had so much to do with bringing the enterprise forward that he feared it might be thought he was working for his own honor, and so it might injure the prospects of the school." So he took the charter and wrote in the space "Baylor." Baylor most vigorously and earnestly protested, on two grounds. "First," as he said, "I do not think I am worthy of such a distinction; second, my humble donation (he had given $1000, the largest amount given by anyone) might be understood and the motives prompting it misconstrued." But Brother Tryon and Kenneth L. Anderson, vice-president of the Texas Republic, were inflexible. They were determined upon it. This accounts for the name "Baylor."

Source: J. M. Carroll, *A History of Texas Baptists: Comprising a Detailed Account of Their Activities, Their Progress and Their Achieve-*

ments (Dallas: Baptist Standard Publishing, 1923), 229–30.

E. The Importance of R. E. B. Baylor to Z. N. Morrell

On a visit to the town of Lagrange, in February, 1839, I heard of the honorable R. E. B. Baylor, formerly a congressman from Alabama. A letter was handed to me which showed that he had prior religion, joined the Baptist church, and had been exercising his gift with great promise; so much that the church had licensed him to preach. In this letter it was further slated that he had gone to Texas, and that the brethren were greatly exercised about his welfare as a preacher; that in consequence of his distinguished political attainments, and the inducements offered in a new country to seek promotion, fears were expressed lest he might not be active in his ministry, as there were no religious organizations to throw the mantle of protection about him. As he was then in town, I sought his acquaintance at once, and invited him to fill my appointment the following day. He declined to do so, but agreed to attend and aid me in my service. As preaching was at that time, a novelty in Lagrange, the people all came out. After the sermon brother Baylor closed the service with a very happy exhortation. He announced in the very outset that "there is a reality in religion and the Scriptures are true." This great thought was brought to bear with such great power that it was easily seen that he was himself once an infidel. He contended, not only from the Scriptures, but from experience, that religion was a reality and ought not be deferred. Here arose a bright star from the East, thirty-three years ago, that afterwards appeared with brilliancy in the Texas Baptist galaxy; and though it is now dim with age and infirmity, it still shines in our general convocations, and often reminds us of valuable service rendered in organizing the Baptist element of the "Empire State." I went home from this meeting greatly strengthened, blessing God by the way for this valuable aid in time of great need.

Source: Z. N. Morrell, *Flowers and Fruits in the Wilderness* (Boston: Rockwell and Churchill, 1872), 108–9.

F. Address to the Union Association

Beloved Friends-You will perceive by a resolution in the foregoing minutes that I am required to say a few things to the brethren of the various Baptist churches. First then to those in our Father Land, we would represent our forlorn and destitute condition and the many trials and difficulties under which we are laboring. My Christian brethren, we have been enabled to organize a few scattered churches in those solitary places, which under the Providence of God have formed our present Association. This Association and these little churches will form a nucleus around which we may rally. You can now send us helps with some confidence that the way is prepared for them to become instruments in the hands of Providence in advancing the Messiah's Kingdom on earth. We therefore ask your prayers and endeavors that faithful ministers may be sent to this part of God's moral vineyard, for truly the harvest is great and the laborers are few. Whilst you are blessed with some many religious privileges we pray you in Christ's stead not to forget us. Be assured that in this country the pious and virtuous ministers in Christ will be received by all with kindness and hospitality; and we can truly say that no people exhibit more external respect for the ordinances of religion, or more decorum in the house of God than the citizens of Texas. We also ask you to send us such religious books, tracts, newspapers, and other publications as will instruct, cheer, and comfort us in this land, so far away from those we once loved and still love with Christian affection; once more pray for us.

To the sister churches and brethren in western Texas, who have not joined with us in this bond of union, we can only say, come and unite with us, we will meet you with a tearful eye, and melting hearts. It could not be expected, my dear brethren, that throwing together as we have been from various Baptist churches throughout the United States we at once harmonize upon all points of doctrine. Those churches themselves entertain shades of difference in their opinions upon these subjects. But remember, on the great articles of our faith and practice we do not differ as Baptists. Should our little churches therefore be tenacious about these non-essentials, they will remain disjoined, and thus broken in fragments they will perish away. Our minutes and proceedings we submit to your prayerful attention, hoping that God by his Holy Spirit will induce you to judge of them with Christian charity, and enable you to come to a correct conclusion.

Farewell, dear brethren, that God may bless and preserve you forever more, is the prayer of your Christian brother, R. E. B. Baylor.

Source: *Minutes*, Union Association, 1840.

2.3 Noah Turner Byars

Noah Turner Byars (1803–1888) was a Baptist Missionary in Texas who operated a blacksmith shop at Washington-on-the-Brazos. Born in Georgia and reared in South Carolina, Byars immigrated to Texas in 1835. Within his blacksmith shop both the Texas Declaration of Independence and Texas Constitution were signed. A Texas patriot, Byars fought at the Battle of San Jacinto with General Sam Houston. From 1837 until 1841 Byars was the Justice of the Peace in Houston while concurrently serving as the Sergeant at Arms for the Texas Senate. Converted in 1824, Byars ignored his call to the ministry until 1841 when he was ordained at the Macedonia Baptist Church south of Austin. Later that year, he served as pastor of the city of Burleson before accepting an appointment from the Baptist State Convention in 1849 to serve as a missionary to Navarro County. In 1851 Byars organized the First Baptist Church of Waco and pastored the church for two years. He then moved to Tarrant County where he was a county missionary. Byars moved to Mississippi in 1868 after accepting the position of State Missionary. Byars returned to Texas in 1871 and served as a missionary to the West Fork Association and the Salado Association. In 1873, he took a missionary position with the fledgling Baptist General Association of Texas.

A. Byars's Stand against Heretical Doctrine

Dear Brethren, you who are settled over churches in well regulated societies perhaps little know how arduous the task of organizing churches from a heterogeneous mass of discordant elements, thrown together as most of the frontiers are, all bringing their peculiar prejudices with them; but how immensely great is the trouble increased when there is heresy in the ministry, giving a wrong tone to society and an improper direction to the tenets of our church. Better far, my brethren, ordain two ministers of doubtful character and doubtful principles to labor amongst you where society is already regulated, then one to come where tone is yet to be given to society, and proper direction to the tenets of the church.

Source: *The Tennessee Baptist*, 9 December 1854, 4.

B. Byars the Texas Patriot–To Arms!

> Boys, rub your steels and pick your flints,
> Methinks I hear some friendly hints
> That we from Texas shall be driven–

Our land to the Spanish soldier given.
To arms, to arms, to arms!

Then Santa Anna soon shall know
Where all his martial law shall go.
It shall not in the Sabine flow.
Nor line the banks of the Colorado.
To arms, to arms, to arms!

Instead of that he shall take his stand
Beyond the banks of the Rio Grande;
His martial law we will put down
We'll live at home and live in town.
Huzza, huzza, huzza!

Source: Noah T. Byars, "To Arms," in Alex Dienst, "Contemporary Poetry of the Texan Revolution," *The Southwestern Historical Quarterly* 21, no. 2 (October 1917): 157–58.

C. Byars and Revival

On Saturday, 24th of May, we met at Little Bethel, on Cedar Mountain, at our Union meeting near the ruins of the little town Cedar Hills. The ministering brethren present were Elders Hunton Ware (the pastor), E. A. Daniel and the writer. On Wednesday, the 28th, all the ministers left but the pastor and he expected to close the meeting that night. The result was saints were built up in the most pure and holy faith, sinners were made to tremble, and many found peace believing in the Lord Jesus Christ, fourteen were added to the church, eleven of whom were buried with Christ in baptism.

On Saturday, 31st, I arrived at Cross Timber Church. Brother Robinson is pastor, who left me on Sunday evening. I continued the meeting until Monday night. Thirteen were added to that church. Four were baptized, one of them who had belonged to the Campbellites, and one to the Presbyterians. The Lord is doing great things for us, and blessed be his name forever.

Source: *Texas Baptist*, 1 July 1856, 2.

2.4 Daniel Parker

Daniel Parker (1781–1844), the father of two-seed in the spirit predestination and hardshellism, was born in Culpepper, Connecticut, but was reared in abject poverty in Georgia. Converted in 1802 in Franklin, Georgia, Parker was ordained to the gospel ministry in 1806. Parker practiced politics and accepted a pastorate in Crawford County, Illinois, in 1817. In 1833, he organized the Pilgrim Predestinarian Regular Baptist Church where he developed and disseminated his anti-mission views. Despite Mexican law which prohibited the advocation of any religion but Catholicism, Parker moved his church to Texas in 1833. Parker is best known for his two-seed in the spirit predestination. Loosely based on Genesis 3:15, he believed that God created all of creation including a great deal of humanity, but Satan was also responsible for the creation of a certain number of people. Mankind, therefore, was either an offspring of God or Satan, and thus their fate was eternally sealed due to this dichotomy. Hence, missionary endeavors were pointless.

A. Two-Seeds in the Spirit

Much has been said upon the doctrine of Election and Non-Elect. If we could correctly understand the light afforded us, in this part of the curse levied on the serpent, for what he had done, it perhaps would afford us as much information as any part of the Divine Writ . . . I shall first show a distinction in the natural existence of these two seeds; and secondly, the two covenants by which they are distinguished.

First. The natural existence of these seeds appear first in our text— yet they are sources from whence they sprung. The seed of the woman was no doubt Christ in the prime or true sense of the word. Yet, as Christ and his church are one, he the head and the church the body, we shall find the seed to be the members of the body.

A Trinity appears in the only true and living God . . . thus as the Father, Word and Holy Ghost are all one, and in one, so was the man, seed, and the woman: God the Father, Christ the Seed, and the Holy Ghost the instrument of their spiritual existence. So as we bore the image of our natural father, from our natural birth, we shall bear the image of our Heavenly Father by this spiritual birth. . .

We shall now return to man in his first formation. When Adam stood with his wife and seed in him, I cannot believe that there stood any in him but the church of Christ—therefore all that stood and fell in Adam, were the elect of God, chosen in Christ before the world began. Some of my reasons are these, (weigh them well), there are two settled points with me. First, that God never created a set of beings, neither directly or indirectly, that he suffered to be taken from him, and made the subjects of his eternal wrath and indignation; (think how would this be consistent with the Divine Creator?). Second, that God, as God, in no case possess more love and mercy than power and wisdom. If he does, oh, think, the pain and distress the great I Am must feel and bear, to see the objects of his love and mercy to sink to woe and misery for the want of power and wisdom in himself to save (where would be the glory now?).

As there is a third point equally settled in my mind, which is that Universalian doctrine is false, and that the unbelievers, dying in their sins, will sink to eternal woe—it now devolves on me to show from what source the Non-Elect has sprung. So at it we go.

I shall first take another view of Adam; for as he bore the name, and was the head and sovereign, not only of his own seed and wife, but of all creation which was put under him, and they all were effected by his standing, or falling. So he was the figure of Christ, which was to come, who was the head of all principalities and powers, and all things were to be affected by his standing or falling in the work of redemption. As there can be no living head without a body, there can be no Christ without a church; and Christ was from everlasting to everlasting, ere the earth was, by and for whom the world was made. And as there can be no shadow without substance, I view Adam with the seed and woman in him, the complete figure of the Lord Jesus Christ, with the church in him, before all worlds was: therefore, while he was in the world, could look to his Father to glorify him, with the same glory he had with the Father before the world was.

Thus when the church was beguiled and had sinned, Christ was not deceived, but his love, relationship, and union to, and with her, was such that he could not be glorified without his bride, therefore he resolves to die with her, or that she should live with him; for it was impossible to separate them—his love was stronger than death. He takes upon himself, not the nature of angels, but the seed of Abraham, marries her nature, owns the debt of his bride . . . He bore our sins in his own body on the tree; dies for her sins: rises again for her justification, redeems her from the curse of the law, and brings life and immortality to light through the Gospel; washes her spiritual seed with his own blood, and fits them for eternal glory with himself . . . This law required nothing to be done by Adam to preserve his standing, or making him any better—it was a law of prohibitions, (though a finite being) was able to perform. The act of doing became the sin. Thus we see where the spirit and principle of doing came from. The serpent distilled it into the woman, and set her to doing what God had forbid, with a spirit of pride and unbelief, with a view of making herself something more than her God had made her; thus the spirit and principle of the works of the law for justification became instilled in the human heart, and has been at war with the sovereignty of God from that day to this. . .

This brings us to the text—here God, as a curse to the Serpent for what he had done, lays the foundation of war between the Serpent and the woman, and the Serpent's seed and the woman's seed. The woman here is certainly a figure of the church of Christ. The enmity of the Serpent against the church has plainly appeared through the persecutions in the different ages of the world, while she standing opposed to the works of darkness, has proved her enmity to the Serpent. And the woman's seed here spoken of, I think was Christ and his elect in him, which was created in Adam, and by ordinary generation God designed should be brought into a natural existence in the world. And as Christ and his people are one, wherever I find one of this seed, distinguished in their natural birth, I shall feel authorized to notice it as the seed of the woman. The Serpent's seed here spoken of, I believe to be the Non-Elect, which were not created in Adam, the original stock, but were brought into the world as the product of sin, by way of sin, by way of a curse on the woman, who by means of sin, was made susceptible of the seed of the Serpent, through the means of her husband, who had partook with her in the transgression, and thereby became the medium through which the Serpent's seed, which is evidently the curse God laid upon her, when, "Unto the woman he said, I will greatly multiply thy sorrow and thy conception, in sorrow shalt thou bring forth children, any thy desire shall be to thy husband, and he shall rule over thee.". . .

It is evident that there are two seeds, the one of the Serpent, the other of the woman; and they appear plain in Cain and Abel, and their offsprings. The Serpent's seed is first spoken of, and Cain first appears, although Eve owns him as a man from the Lord, yet she does not claim him her seed;. . . Eve claims Abel as her seed, and can say at the birth of Seth, that God had appointed her another seed, instead of Abel, whom Cain slew.

Thus the enmity between the two seeds appears, and the wickedness on the part of the Serpent's seed, when Cain slew Abel. . . .

I am apprized that unbelieving critics will try to believe (notwithstanding what I have said on the subject) that agreeable to my views the Devil has created a great set of beings; this is not my view; for if the Devil had the power of creating, he would be almighty. There is a great difference between creating and begetting. A man may beget, but he cannot create. Which is most reasonable to believe, that Satan had power to beget a principle and nature in man (which is admitted on all sides) or to believe that he, by permission, possessed power to beget material existence through or by the beings God had made, and in whom he had begot his own principle and nature. . . .

Another point of inquiry arises, did the Serpent's seed, or Non-Elect, stand or fall in Adam. I answer, No, the elect of God only was created, stood, and fell in Adam, partook of the serpentine nature, and were by nature the children of wrath, even as others; and therefore the original sin is in, or entailed on them, with the Serpent's seed. Although they did not receive it by the fall of man, yet they received this wicked nature immediately from the same corrupt source, which had involved the elect of God; thus in the nature of the two seeds no difference appears; for Satan had wholly captivated the elect, and engraved his image in their hearts.

And though Satan's seed had not fell in Adam, with the elect, under the curse of the divine law, yet they were sin in the abstract, flowing from the fountain of corruption. . . .

Come, my reader, let us reason together a moment. You may think my doctrine wretched—but think again, is it scripturally and experimentally reasonable to believe, but that there are sinners lost? Are these sinners lost the creatures of God by creation? Is it not more reasonable to believe they sprung from Satan, than from the Divine Being? As I think you believe with me, that God never created any one for destruction, is it not more to the glory and honor of God, to believe that he will punish Satan in his own seed, than in beings, which he himself had made, and Satan had got possession of? Does God possess more love and mercy than wisdom and power? Does he, as God, want to save more than he will or can save? How can these things be, and he be a God of infinite power and wisdom?. . . .

. . . For although God did not create the Serpent's seed, or non-elect, in Adam, yet he had given man the power of begetting, and the woman of conceiving; and Satan, by sin, through the man, begets his seed in the woman, while God, for sin by the woman, multiplies her conception; and thus the Serpent's seed comes through the original stock, and yet God not their creator in the original stock.

Source: Daniel Parker, *Views on the Two Seeds: Taken From Genesis 3rd Chapter and Part of 15th Verse* (Vandalia, IL: Robert Blackwell, 1826).

B. The Effects of Daniel Parker on Texas Baptists

There is a lamentable destitution of religious influence all over the country. There are but a few ministers of the gospel, and a majority of them are anything but missionary in effort or sentiment. A large majority of the churches in this part of the country were constituted by Daniel Parker, of the Two-seed memory, and kindred spirits, who thought it a crime to contribute to the support of the gospel or those who preached it. This doctrine has had a very withering effect upon the churches and community generally, but Brother Parker is no more. He has gone to his reward, I hope among the just. I knew him many years ago. We always considered him a good man, possessing a warm heart, a clear head and giant intellect, but surely badly cultivated, judging from the effect produced on society by his education.

Source: The Banner and Pioneer, 5 June 1847, by Levi Roberts, cited in J. M. Carroll, *A History of the Baptists: Comprising a Detailed Account of Their Activities, Their Progress and Their Achievements* (Dallas: Baptist Standard Publishing, 1923), 299.

2.5 Thomas J. Pilgrim

Thomas J. Pilgrim (1784–1877) was a Connecticut-born schoolteacher who, for health reasons, moved to the dryer climate of Texas in 1828. At San Felipe, Texas, in 1829, he formed the first Sunday School in Texas. A friend of Stephen F. Austin, Pilgrim ran a Sunday School where he taught Christianity in such a way that the Catholic authorities believed him to be one of them. Austin, however, was forced to temporarily close Pilgrim's school on several occasions out of a fear of Catholic reprisals.

A. First Sunday School in Texas

In the Fall of 1828, I started from the western part of the State of New York for Texas, in company of sixty others, women and children, under the leadership of Elias R. Wightman, who had resided about three years in the country, and whose intelligence, energy, and enterprise well fitted him to be the leader of a colony. We traveled in wagons to Olean Point, to the head waters of the Allegheny River; then constructed a craft in two pieces, turning up at the one end, the other square, and the square ends being lashed together formed a scow with two apartments; in these we placed our baggage and pushed off to drift down the stream at the mercy of the current. Our voyage the first day was prosperous, but night at length coming on cold and wet, we sought shelter in an Indian village on the north bank of the stream. The old chief seemed moved with pity at our forlorn condition, for the weather was very inclement, and pointed out to us a cabin about twenty square feet, with a good floor and fire-place; the floor was covered with peas and beans in shuck, which he showed us could be scraped up in one corner and a fire made in the fire-place; truly grateful for his kindness, we soon had a good fire and plain but comfortable meal, and all slept soundly. The next day being Sunday, we lay by and spent in such devotional exercises as the surrounding circumstances would permit. The next morning we started on our voyage, having taken on board a pilot to accompany us as far as Pittsburgh. About noon we heard a roaring ahead resembling a waterfall, and soon it proceeded from a dam constructed across the stream. On one side was a mill, on the other a narrow space was left, through which a gentle current flowed, and where boats or rafts could pass with safety; but our pilot, through either ignorance or obstinacy, kept the center of the current, and we were soon passing over a fall about four feet high, and now was evident the advantage of our mode of construction, for the lashing giving way, the scow parted, which enabled the forepart to rise, but both apartments were nearly full of water, and all completely drenched. We all fell to bailing with such vessels as we could seize, and were again on our way in fair trim, but overtaking a raft of pine plank before night, we exchanged our rude craft for still ruder accommodations, through much more ample, on board the raft. Soon we reached Pittsburgh, where we discharged our pilot, feeling he had been the cause of our greatest calamity, without rendering us any valuable service. Here it had been intended to take a steamer, but finding none ready to leave, we continued on our raft to Cincinnati. Here we remained for several days, and I purchased a set of Spanish books and commenced to study the language. Soon we took passage on a steamer's deck for Orleans, and in due time arrived at the Crescent City. Cincinnati was at this time a small town of about 10,000 inhabitants. St. Louis was just coming into notice, and between that and the Pacific was an unbroken wilderness. In Orleans we remained about a fortnight, waiting for conveyances, as there was little trade between Orleans and Texas, and vessels seldom passed from one to the other. At length we found a little vessel from Maine, of twenty-two tons burden, manned by only three hands, and only one of these very efficient. The captain offered to sell us the vessel for 500 dollars, or take us to Texas for that amount; we bargained for the latter, and have provided ourselves with a suitable outfit for the voyage, we all embarked, and were soon drifting down the Mississippi in a perfect calm, at the mercy of the current. This calm continued for many days, until we were far our of sight of land, on the bosom of the Gulf, drifting about we knew not whither, as there was not sufficient breeze to steer the vessel. At length the wind rose and blew a gale, but directly ahead, and soon all on board except myself and crew were suffering severely from sea-sickness, and perfectly helpless; and then might have been heard many a regret expressed at ever having undertaken the journey, and may a wish to once more step foot on land. For two days the gale continued, and then again a perfect calm, and thus gale and calm succeeded by each other, until we found ourselves off the entrance to Matagorda Bay; but the wind blowing directly out of the pass, there was little prospect of being able to enter, yet we resolved to make the effort. Of all on board, I was the only one who knew how to work a vessel, and the only one who was not liable to sea-sickness; and, as the captain and one hand were frequently intoxicated, the labor developing on me was necessarily very great; besides, we were nearly out of provisions, and had been for several days allowed to one half pint of water each daily, and for several days I drank none, giving mine to the children, and subsisting only on pilot bread and raw whiskey. Everything seemed to indicate that, if within the reach of human skill, we must make harbor.

For twenty-four hours we beat against wind and current, every one doing his duty and sparing no effort which might promise success; but all in vain, for we fell to leeward about three miles. It was now evident we must make some harbor, as we could not longer continr̃ at sea, and as the wind would permit and was still blowing fresh, we ran down to Aransas and soon entered the bay in safety. Soon all were landed, and having made fires and procured water, the women proceeded to do some washing, which was greatly needed, and the men, with their rifles, twelve in number, proceeded in search of game, leaving on board only three men, the captain, mate, and myself. The vessel was anchored about 200 yards from shore, and we had remained about one hour when we saw several canoes coming down the bay with Indians. These we knew to be Carankawans, who were said to be cannibals, and as the men were gone and only one musket on board, no little fear was felt for the safety of the women and children; but we could only watch their movements and act according to circumstances. Soon they were seen to halt and turn toward the shore, and shortly landed and were proceeding in the direction of the women. The mate and myself jumped into our little skiff, or bateau; he took the oars and I the old musket and stood in the bow; we proceeded in the direction of the Indians, but keeping between them and the women, and when near I drew the musket and presented it toward the chief, who beckoned me not to fire and made signs of friendship. This position we both maintained for some time, we seeking to detain them, hoping the men would soon appear. Soon we raised our eyes and beheld the men all running toward the boat and not far from us. We then felt safe. The women were taken on board first, then the men, and lastly a few Indians were allowed to come. They manifested no hostility, for they evidently saw that all hostility would be unavailing. Their canoes were well stored with fish, all neatly dressed, which they bartered to us in such quantities as we needed, and then left us, truly glad that we had escaped so well. After remaining here for several days, and supplying ourselves with water and such provisions as we could obtain, which consisted of only wild meats, and an article of greens resembling purslane, and the wind becoming fair, we again crossed the bar, and shaped our course for Pass Caballo. The captain gave me the helm, and retired to his berth for sleep. In a few moments the wind subsided and a dead calm ensued; the current tended toward the shore, and a gentle swell was rolling in. I now felt quite disheartened, and thought our chance of reaching our destination by water was small. I went to Mr. Wightman, who we considered our leader, and informed him of our condition and danger, and told him I had charge of the vessel, and if he consented I would beach her, and we would make our way as best we could by land.

He said that would never do, we were more than one hundred miles from any white settlement, there was no means of conveyance, and the country was infested with hostile Indians. Our only safety consisted in clinging to our vessel. I went to the captain, awoke him, and informed him of our danger; he at once saw and recognized it. I told him there were four sweeps on board, and, if he approved, I would rig them, and we would try to sweep her up to the pass. He consented, and by night the vessel was swept up opposite the pass; but no one knew the channel. The mate and myself went into our skiff, and sounded till we found it, then taking a long rope, we carried it on shore, and soon conducted our little vessel into the bay. A gentle breeze and fair wind sprang up, and soon we were off the mouth of the Colorado, and within about two miles of Matagorda, which then contained two families, who had lately moved down and commenced a settlement. The next day Mr. Wightman and another went to the settlement, and returned with the present of a Christmas dinner, which consisted of some hominy, beat in a wood mortar, and fresh milk, which were gratefully received and promptly dispatched. The people of the new settlement, anxious to have it said that a vessel had arrived at Matagorda, came down to assist us; the women and chattels were taken on shore, the little vessel was careened over on one side, and by main strength dragged over the bar, and soon lay alongside of

Matagorda. Our Christmas dinner, as stated, was taken on board, and the next day we landed, having been twenty-two days from New Orleans.

Some went to work immediately to prepare a home on the spot, and five young men started to go up the country, in search of some conveyance. We were told it was twenty-two miles to a settlement, and as we had been confined so long on a board a vessel, we thought to walk this distance would be a mere recreation. In the morning we started fresh and vigorous, without a blanket or garment, and with no other provision than three little biscuits, which one of our number was so fortunate to procure. This was the last of December, and the whole face of the country was neatly covered with water, and the only road was a dim trail made through the high grass by the passage of a single-horse carryall. Many of the little streams had to be swum; sometimes we traveled with the water to our waists, and all our shoes were worn through at the toes, by striking them against the high sedge grass. About noon the rain began to fall in torrents, the wind blew strong from the north, the depth of water increased, and night was approaching, with no appearance of a settlement, when three of our number, and those apparently the strongest, fell to the ground, declaring they could go no farther. I remonstrated with them, and told them that to remain there was certain death, that our only hope was to keep moving, and thereby promote circulation; but in vain, they stated that if life depended upon it, they could go no farther. Near us was a venerable looking live-oak, which had fallen and perhaps lain there for ages; on the under side of its trunk, we contrived to kindle a fire, which we kept burning during the night, and having gathered sufficient of the tall grass to raise us above the water, we laid down a rested quite well, notwithstanding the falling rain and whistling blast. In the morning we arose quite refreshed, and started forward, the rain still falling, the wind increasing in coldness, and the water deepening. We had proceeded about a mile, when we heard the crowing chickens, when all jumped up, clapping their hands, and said they must be on the borders of civilization. Soon we struck a plain path, and were shortly at the hospitable residence of Daniel Rawls, where Captain John Duncan now resides. Here we found plenty of good country fare, which was provided without money or price. The rain continued to fall, and in the evening of the second day, looking out we saw a miserable looking object approaching, and as he neared us, we discovered it was one of our members who had been left behind. He had left with another, from whom he had become separated on the way, and could give no further account of him. Mr. Rawls remarked that we must go in search of him, as it would not do to leave him to perish; two horses were soon ready, and he taking one and I the other, we soon started; darkness soon overtook us, and unable to follow the trail longer, we entered a thicket, staked out our horses, and by breaking off limbs of brushes, which we covered with the long moss, and raising a bed above the water, contrived to rest very comfortably until morning, when we continued our course to Matagorda; but finding the lost one had not returned, and hearing nothing of him, we returned, and found that during our absence he had come in. Here we all remained, until the weather cleared up, when we separated and left, the others going east toward the Brazos, and I on foot and alone, winding my way north in the direction of San Felipe de Austin, about sixty miles distant. On the Bernard I was hospitably entertained by a Mr. Huff, where I met Josiah H. Bell on his way to his home in Columbia, and from him I received a cordial invitation to accompany him home. I cheerfully accepted, and the next night was spent with his estimable family. Mr. Bell was a estimable gentleman, a pure patriot, of stern, unyielding integrity; he had endured the privations, toils, and hardships incident to the settlement of a new country, and knew well how to sympathize with others in like circumstances. He told me he had gone thirty miles and packed corn horseback to feed his family, had taken his rifle in the morning and gone in search of deer, knowing if successful, they would have meat, if not, they must all do without; but seldom did his trusty rifle fail him or his family suffer. They were now living in comparative affluence, with an interesting family of children. Mrs. Bell was one of the noblest women I ever knew in any country; though living in the wilds of Texas, her intelligence, good taste, and polished manners, would have graced the most refined circles of New York or Philadelphia. Her house was a welcome home to every stranger, where the hungry were fed, the naked clad, the sick nursed with tenderness and sympathy which removed many a dark cloud from the brow of sorrow, and caused the lonely wanderers to feel less acutely the absence of home and relatives. Texans now know very little how much the country owes to the early efforts of this pure woman, how much suffering she was instrumental in relieving, and when the dark clouds of war lowered, what confidence and courage she inspired in the bosoms of the timorous and desponding; for she was a stranger to fear, and of our final success she never doubted.

While here I became acquainted with Stephen F. Richardson, on his way to his home in San Felipe de Austin, and as that was my destination, I cheerfully accepted an invitation to accompany him; and on the night of the second day I was at the capital of the little colony. The following day I was introduced to the Empresario, Stephen F. Austin, whom I found an intelligent and affable gentleman, and who, so long as he lived, I was proud to number among my warmest and most devoted friends. To speak here of his many virtues would be superfluous, as his fame is world-wide and his works follow him; and when Texas shall become the wealthiest and most populous state in the Union, as, from her size and natural advantages she must soon be, her intelligent millions, looking back to his early efforts, will do justice to the memory of this great and good man.

I soon engaged in teaching, and succeeded in a short time in raising a school of about forty scholars, mostly boys, with expressive and intelligent countenances who were easily controlled, and some of whom gave indications of future greatness and usefulness. Contemplating, in imagination, what Texas, from its great natural advantages, must soon become, I felt the necessity of moral and religious, as well as intellectual culture, and resolved to make an effort to found a Sunday-school. Notice was given through the school, that on the following Sunday an address would be delivered on the subject, and I was gratified to see at the appointed time, a large and respectable audience assembled. An address was delivered; they seemed to feel interested, and on the following Sunday a school was organized of thirty-two scholars. There were not lacking intelligent gentlemen and ladies to act as teachers, but of other appurtenances of a well-regulated Sunday-school we had none. This was supplied, as best it could be, by contributions of the citizens of such books as they had, and by the oral instructions of superintendents and teachers.

The next Sunday found the school under way, and giving promise of great success. A lecture was delivered each Sunday morning, intended for both old and young; and to hear these lectures, people came from the distance of ten miles; and as this town was the capital of the colony, many people were sometimes in attendance from different parts of the country, who carried the good seed here sown all over the colony. The school, and these morning lectures, were continued regularly, and well attended, until a difficulty occurring between some intelligent Mexicans visiting the place from the interior and some citizens, growing our a law-suit which was decided against the Mexicans, the Empresario deemed it prudent to discontinue them for a time, as these Mexicans could not be deceived in relation to the character of our exercises, and it was well known that we were acting in violation of the colonization law, which strictly prohibited Protestant worship and prohibited Austin from introducing any but Catholics as colonists.

Now let us for a moment contemplate this little Sunday-school. In a black-jack and post-oak grove near the center of town is a rude log-cabin about eighteen by twenty-two feet, the roof covered with boards held down by weight-poles, the logs unhewn, and the cracks neither chinked or battened, a dirt floor, and across it are placed several logs hewn on one side for seats. At one end stands the superintendent, a mere stripling, and before him are about a half a dozen gentlemen and ladies as teachers, and thirty-two children, without any of those appendages which are now considered necessary to a well conducted Sunday-school. Forty-five years have passed since the organization of that little Sunday-school, and now on Sunday morning of a pleasant day 60,000 children are assembled in our beloved State, under the guidance of 10,000 intelligent and, for the most part, pious young gentlemen and ladies, with a good supply of papers and libraries written by the ablest divines of our age, and containing interesting biographies, and the very pith and marrow of Christian theology. Surely we may exclaim, What hath God wrought? That same superintendent still lives and labors in the delightful task of training the young in the Sunday-school, and as he contemplates, in imagination, the five and a half millions of children now being trained in the Sunday-schools of the United States, and then looks forward down the long corridors of time when these children shall be the actors in the great drama of life, he sees the dawn of that happy day foretold by seers and prophets when the knowledge of God shall cover the whole earth, the lion shall lie down with the lamb, and "the wilderness and the solitary place shall be glad for them; and the desert shall rejoice and blossom as the rose."

I would here correct one erroneous impression in relation to the character of the early settlers of Texas. Many believe they were rude and ignorant, with many vices and few virtues, and for the most part refugees from justice and enemies to law and order. That there were some rude and illiterate people among them is no more than may be said of almost any society, and that some were vicious and depraved is equally true, but what there was of evil you saw on the surface, for there was no effort at any concealment and no reason to act a borrowed part. Assassins, if there were any, appeared as such; now they often appear in the guise of gentlemen, that they may conceal their true characters and accomplish their object. No one estimates more highly than the right, the intelligence, enterprise, and virtue of the present population, and yet he fully believes there were in the early history of Texas more college-bred men, in proportion to the population, than now, and as much intelligence, good common sense, and moral and religious culture among the females as among the ladies of the present day. Many had moved in the higher circles of our large cities, and some had filled stations of honor and responsibility. Some, were incited to emigrate by a spirit of enterprise and romance, and some, having been unfortunate in their pecuniary enterprises, sought to improve their circumstances in a new country, and not a few were the votaries of health who, unable to endure the rigors of a cold climate, sought relief in the sunny climates of the South.

If they had failings, let us throw the mantle of charity over them, and let their acts proclaim their noble virtues. When Texas took up arms against Mexico, it was in the maintenance of rights guaranteed them by the constitution under which they had been invited to settle, and their population did not exceed 35,000; and does it not argue great energy, enterprise, and courage in their small numbers to take up arms against 8,000,000, and, with few resources except their own courage and power of endurance, to win the day?

A kinder and more hospitable people, perhaps, never lived. Their houses were welcome homes to each other; and never was the stranger rudely repulsed or sent empty away. When one was seen approaching, the inference was that he had come a considerable distance and was hungry and tired: preparations were immediately made to give him as comfortable a meal as their plain larder would permit, and without money or price, and although they could not boast then of luxuries we now enjoy, their fare was nevertheless far from being meager. Bears, deers, turkeys, geese, ducks, and squirrels were plenty and easily obtained, and chicken, eggs, sweet potatoes, milk, butter, and honey were found in abundance on every table. The traveler always carried with him a blanket laid over his Spanish saddle-tree on which he rode, and a pair of saddle-bags; the former always furnished him wherever he stopped, a bed, and the latter a pillow, and, if slept out of doors, which many preferred, the canopy of heaven was his covering.

New-Englanders have always been proud of their Christian ancestors who bequeathed to them so rich an inheritance, and well may the present generation of Texans look back with gratitude and pride to those noble-souled heroes who by their toils, energy, self-sacrifice and daring, won and bequeathed to them the fairest lands on which the sun ever shone. A few of these old heroes still survive and move among us as mementoes of the past, their heads whitening with the frosts of many winters, and their steps tottering with the weight of years. God forbid that they should ever feel want where plenty abounds, and that the sun of their brighter days should be set behind the dark clouds of sorrow.

Source: Diary of Thomas J. Pilgrim, cited in, D. W. C. Baker, *A Texas Scrap Book* (New York: A. S. Barnes, 1875), 69–76.

B. Report on Sabbath Schools

The Committee on Sabbath Schools beg leave to submit the following:

From the want of sufficient data, we find it impossible to present any thing like a full and correct Report, but believing that any approximation towards the truth will be important for our present action, we think best to give such information as is within our reach.

Within the bounds of the Colorado Association, the most Western one in the State, there are 22 Sabbath Schools now in operation, with an aggregate number of 1,000 Scholars, and 6,000 volumes in their Libraries, exclusive of Bibles, Testaments, Hymn Books, Question Books, &c.

There are 7 Associations of Missionary Baptists in the State. Now taking the statistics of the Colorado Association as the basis of our calculation, it will follow that there are seven times twenty-two, or one hundred and fifty-four schools in the State, seven thousand scholars, and forty-two thousand volumes in the Libraries.

How near this calculation approximates to the truth, your Committees are unable to state; they believe, however, it is too large, as many portions of the State are poorly supplied, and in the Eastern section, there are nine counties in which but one school exists. In all these nine counties, there are Churches, which circumstance presents the astounding fact, that our Churches have not given this subject that attention which its importance demands.

Brethren! It would be out of place to discuss at this time the necessity and utility of Sabbath Schools. An experience of seventy years, and the united voice of Christendom, have proclaimed them the noblest institutions of the age; second to none in their happy influence, fond anticipations, cheering hopes and Heavenly prospects; they have often proved the harbinger of the glorious Gospel, and the nurseries of the Church of Christ. Your Committee could name one Sabbath School of forty scholars, thirty-eight of which became, in time, hopefully pious.

Experience has proved them well suited to the spirit of the age, the growing wants of the rising generation, and one of the most powerful engines that can possibly be brought to bear upon the accumulating influence of vice and misery.

They are scattering the very pith and marrow of our richest literature broad-cast o'er the land; they ask no protection but the prayers of God's people; they claim no support but what a Christian sympathy feels bound to bestow.

Brethren: Your Committee have learned with pain and regret, that few of our Schools are at present in a prosperous condition; many are at a stand, some have scarcely a principle of vitality left, and others are extinct.

It seems that at the commencement of this Institution, Satan himself, was not aware of the vast amount of good it was destined to accomplish, consequently there was little or no opposition; now the great adversary of souls became aroused, and his most vigorous efforts are put forth for their destruction, and these efforts appear in the coldness and neglect of the Church. They are in many instances like the helpless orphan, cast out and deserted, and left to provide for themselves, unpitied, unloved and unprotected.

Brethren, shall not our sympathies be aroused in their behalf? Will we not take them under our fostering care and pray for their prosperity?

Your Committee would recommend that such action be taken by this Body as will enable them to obtain, by our next meeting, correct statistics or Sabbath Schools throughout the State.

All of which is respectfully submitted,

Thomas J. Pilgrim, Chm'n.

Source: *Minutes*, Baptist State Convention, 1851, 11–12.

CHAPTER 3

Emerging Baptist Structure, 1840–1848

3.1. James Huckins

A New Englander by birth and educated at Brown University, James Huckins moved to Georgia in 1838 where he became friends with Jesse Mercer. Huckins then felt the call to Texas in 1840 and was appointed a missionary by the American Baptist Missionary Society of New York. First, he moved to Galveston where he helped constitute the First Baptist Church in 1840. In addition, Huckins also helped organize the Union Association (1841), the First Baptist Church of Houston (1841), and the Texas Baptist Education Society (1841). Along with R. E. B. Baylor and William Tryon, he played a prominent role in the acquisition of the charter for Baylor University. In 1859, Huckins moved to Charleston, South Carolina, where he finished his ministerial career.

A. The Birth of the First Baptist Church of Galveston, 1840

(A Letter to Jesse Mercer)

My Dear Father Mercer,—I arrived at this place on the 25th, and contrary to my expectations have been detained until now. Galveston is an island, thirty miles long, and from two to four miles wide, the surface of which is elevated a few feet above high water, presenting to the eye of the traveler, a vast plain, with scarcely a tree or a shrub to relieve the vision. The city of Galveston, lies on the eastern part of the island, where three years ago, stood only one solitary dwelling. But now not less than six hundred houses can be seen, while the population numbers three thousand. Ships, steamboats and smaller vessels lining the wharves; warehouses and shops studding the streets; new buildings daily rising in every part of the city; the streets thronged with business men and with crowds of strangers—all evince great enterprise, and seem to be token of a great mercantile and commercial city. My determinations at first were to spend one day only in this place, but on touching the wharf, I was seized by an old acquaintance, who expressed his joy at meeting me, informed me, not only that several of my old acquaintances, but two of the members of my late church, were residents of the city. On meeting with these, I was urged to spend one Sabbath, if no more with them, and to collect and organize the scattered sheep of Christ's flock. To this solicitation, I at once yielded, and the Presbyterian clergyman, (whose church is just organized) kindly invited me to occupy his place for meeting on the Sabbath night. I preached, the place was crowded and over-flowing, and numbers with dejected spirits were forced to leave for want of room. Never in the appearance, whose countenances exhibited more intelligence and culture, or who heard the word of life with more interest and cultivation, or who heard the word of life with more interest and apparent devotion, than on this occasion. At the close of the service, I announced the object of my mission, and requested all members of Baptist Churches, and all partial to Baptist sentiment, to tarry a few moments after the benediction. About twenty-five remained, twelve of whom gave their names as members of Baptist churches in good standing, and requested to be organized into a church of Christ. The next Thursday night was appointed as a time to best set apart for presenting their letters, and for the examination of candidates.

Source: James Huckins to Jesse Mercer, 6 February 1840, J. M. Carroll Collection, file 460, Archives, Southwestern Seminary. Reprint courtesy of Southwestern Baptist Theological Seminary.

B. First Baptism on Galveston Island, 1840

Tuesday last at 3 o'clock was the time set apart for baptism. The ordinance took place on the south side of the island. The day was fine and the congregation was numerous. The grandeur of the scenery conspired with the moral sublimity of the occasion, to awaken the strongest and most emotions. On one side as far as they eye could reach, lay the vast prairies, on the other the boundless expanse of the ocean, lashing with its deep blue water the ground on which we stood. The beach too, presented a highway of unparalleled beauty, leading on through the whole length of the island, surpassing in hardness and smoothness any road which art has ever formed. There too was to be heard the sound of the ever rolling billows, resembling the "distant voice of God." These all conspired to make us feel the majesty and power of that God in whose name we had assembled. The services opened by prayer. Every heart began to soften. Said a good old Virginian, a Baptist, I never witnessed a scene like this. God was indeed there. Next followed the hymn, "Jesus and shall it ever be, a mortal man ashamed of thee."

The candidates present were, the brother of whom I have spoken, his wife and her sisters. The brother first received the ordinance, and on coming out of the water, professor and non-professor pushed forward with streaming eyes and feelings too deep for utterances to give him their hand. Then followed his wife and her sister into the watery grave. After baptizing these two sisters, we proceeded together to the shore. And a brother by blood, who had just tasted of the love of Jesus, came forward weeping and praising God. "My sisters, my sisters, I rejoice with you my sisters" and all three embracing each other stood weeping, not able to vent their feelings but by tears, but filled; not a heart however hard, but began to melt.

Source: James Huckins to Jesse Mercer, 6 February 1840, J. M. Carroll Collection, file 460, Archives, Southwestern Seminary. Reprint courtesy of Southwestern Baptist Theological Seminary.

C. Report of the Committee of Education

The committee to whom was referred the subject of education, and the condition of Baylor University, beg leave to report that, in no period of our history, as an Association, have we had such abundant cause for encouragement and for gratitude, as during the last year. The interest of our brethren in the cause of education is every year becoming deeper. The conviction of its necessity is becoming stronger and more pervading, not only for our rising ministry, but for our great community—for ourselves and for our children. Never has there been such a desire on the part of parents to give their children the facilities for obtaining a sound and polished education. Hence, notwithstanding the failure of the crops for the last three years, there has been no diminution of the number of students in either department of our beloved University, but, instead, a constant increase. And while the prayer has gone up to the Lord of the harvest for more laborers, the disposition to sacrifice for the education of those whom the Lord is giving us, accompanies the prayer. Our University, while it is gaining a stronger hold on the great head of the denomination, is as the same time commanding a higher position in the confidence of the public generally. In view of all these facts, have we not cause for gratitude and hope? Gratitude for what the Lord has already done for us, and hope for what he will still continue to do. May we not hope, in view of the causes already in operation, and relying on the spirit of God to direct us, that the Baptist denomination in Texas shall, ere long, present to the world not only an efficient and learned ministry, but give a wise ministry of marked intelligence, thoroughly educated in whatever is useful and good, and especially in the science of human redemption?

Source: *Minutes*, Union Association, 1857, 7.

3.2 William Milton Tryon

William Milton Tryon (1809–1847) was born in New York where he experienced a difficult childhood. Following the death of his father in 1818, Tryon fell ill. In 1827, however, he was converted and two years later he moved to Savannah, Georgia. After being licensed to preach in 1832, Tryon attended Mercer University and was ordained in 1833 with Jesse Mercer participating in the service. Tryon then moved to Alabama in 1839 where he ministered for two years. In 1841 he was named a missionary to Texas by the American Baptist Home Mission Society. His first post was at Washington-on-the-Brazos where he replaced Z. N. Morrell. Tryon also helped organize the church at Independence, a church in Houston, and was believed to have saved a church in Galveston from falling into doctrinal error. Along with James Huckins and R. E. B. Baylor, Tryon helped secure the charter that established Baylor University at Independence in 1845. Tryon succumbed to the yellow fever in 1847 at Houston.

A. A Revival in Irwinton, Alabama

Father Mercer,—Knowing that you feel a lively interest in the progress of religion, I hasten to inform you of the doings of the Lord in this place.

The inhabitants of Irwinton since my residence among them, have always manifested great respect for religion; but whilst I have been frequently gratified at the attention and good order manifested by our congregations, I have often lamented that so little apparent good was effected. Some three months since, from the increased seriousness evident among those who assemble for worship, and from accounts which we received of the out-pouring of the spirit in other places, I was encouraged to hope that God would visit us with his salvation. About this time two of the Baptist, and one of the Presbyterian Brethren covenanted, to make the condition of this people a subject of special prayer. One night of our weekly prayer meeting, (Tuesday before the third Sunday in August) the house was crowded, and we received one by experience. On Sunday morning and evening, the congregations were solemn and somewhat effected. At night there was preaching at the Presbyterian place of worship, and none at ours. After a sermon by Bro. Stratton the Presbyterian clergyman, an invitation was given to those who wished the prayers of God's people, to present themselves before the congregation. The first was a young man, who has since joined our church. He was followed by two others, who have united with the Presbyterians. On Monday night Bro. Stratton and myself united, and the meeting was carried on at the Presbyterian church with increased interest. On Thursday the Methodist friends offered us their place of worship, (the only meeting house in the place) and we there carried on harmoniously, a Union Meeting of the three denominations. Mr. Neal, the Methodist preacher in charge, was assisted by Brethren Glen, Capers, and others. The Presbyterians were represented by Mr. Stratton their regular Minister, and the venerable Dr. Brown, from Fort Gaines; and we, before the close of the meeting, had the aid of the Brethren Jonathan Davis, J. G. Gilbert and Atkinson. Bro. Davis remained with us nine days, and was indefatigable in his labours. I never in my life before, attended a meeting where there seemed to be manifested a greater spirit of prayer, and apparently more plain answers to the supplications of God's people. About one hundred persons appeared to be deeply convicted. Thirty-eight have joined the Methodists, seven the Presbyterians, and thirty-one white and five blacks, to the Baptist Church. Many appear to still be under deep conviction.

Source: William Tryon to Jesse Mercer, 17 September 1838, file 557, J. M. Carroll Collection, Archives, Southwestern Baptist Theological Seminary. Reprint courtesy of Southwestern Baptist Theological Seminary.

B. A Christian's Role in Texas

The Bible tells us that the Church is the light of the world; but if the light that is in this new country be darkness, how great is that darkness! Society, in Texas, is far from being thoroughly organized—executive, legislative and judicial power exert but a feeble influence over the tumultuous sea of passion; it is for the Church to pour oil upon the troubled waves! It is for the followers of Christ to disseminate the examples of forbearance, and to discountenance those broils and feuds which set law and government at defiance, and are the bland and mildew of our country.

Source: *Minutes of the Fifth Anniversary Meeting of the Union Baptist Association Convened at Plum Grove Church, Fayette Texas, 20 August 1844 and days following,* 13.

C. The Need for Baptist Education in Texas

The tide of emigration is now pouring into our lovely country, and from the emigration our churches are receiving most valuable acquisitions. The Lord has blessed us! The armies of locusts and caterpillars have not marched through our land. Our fields have produced abundantly, so that we have scarcely room where to bestow our fruits and goods.

Brethren, we feel assured that you will take into consideration the subject we have placed before you. That you will say to your Preachers, leave your School Houses! Leave your Farms! Give yourselves to Study! Give yourselves wholly to the Ministry of the Word. You shall suffer no loss. Your families shall be sustained.

Source: *Minutes of the Eighth Annual Meeting of the Union Baptist Association Held with the First Baptist Church in Houston, Texas, Commencing on Thursday, 30 September, and ending 4 October 1847,* 11–12.

D. Tryon's First Report to the Board of Domestic Missions

The first quarterly report of Rev. Wm. M. Tryon, missionary to Houston, Texas, presents the following view of his labors, and of the state of missions, during the period embraced in it:

Herein I send you my first quarterly report of labor under appointment of your Board. I regularly supply, every Lord's day, the First Baptist Church of Houston. Have preached thirty-two sermons; delivered thirty lectures on religious subjects; attended sixteen prayer meetings; made one hundred pastoral visits; baptized ten white and one colored persons; received by letter seven.

Since my return to Houston, we have organized a Sabbath school, which I superintend myself; we have eight teachers, and sixty scholars. One of the scholars was baptized a short time since. We have 80 volumes in the library, (most of which were sent to me by Brother T. P. Miller, of Mobile, Ala.) one Bible class, ten pupils.

Our little church now assembled for divine worship; in the upper story of a building known by the name of the "Old City Hold." The access to it is bad, and the accommodations the room affords are not good; yet we believe the blessing of the Lord has been with us. Soon after my return home, we contracted for a brick meeting house, purchased a site in an eligible part of town; the building is just commenced.

An interesting meeting is now progressing in the Methodist church. In fact there is a general interest in all the churches on the subject of religion. I have recently, upon two occasions, addressed numerous assemblies at the water's edge upon the subject of baptism. On one occasion, it is supposed there were upwards of 500 persons present; many of whom never before witnessed the ordinance administered by a Baptist minister. I am in great need of Baptist publications for gratuitous distribution. Houston contains a population of four thousand inhabitants; among which are Germans, French, Irish, English, and people from all over the United States. There is in the town a Roman Catholic church, Presbyterian and Methodist church, all supplied with pastors.

The Lord is blessing us in the upper part of the State. A meeting of great interest was recently held with the Providence church, in Washington county, which continued three weeks, and closed for want of ministerial aid. Seventy persons were baptized. At the close a greater anxiety was manifested by all present, upon the all absorbing topic, than at any previous period of the meeting. The good work has progressed in other parts of Washington Co. From the best information I am able to collect, about one hundred have been added by baptism in that section.

Source: *Southern Baptist Missionary Journal* 1 (December 1846): 161.

3.3 J. G. Thomas

J. G. Thomas was a lawyer who became the first director of the Texas Education Society, which, in turn, gave birth to Baylor University at Independence in 1845. Thomas was also the first secretary of the Baptist State Convention (1848).

Results of an Itinerant Preaching Tour

I have only a few days ago, returned from a trip of nearly four weeks, in the counties of Bell and Williamson, during which time I witnessed several conversions, and was permitted to baptize some willing converts. Was alone most of the time, except while at a district meeting at Round Rock, and one other place, I spent several days. A church had some years ago been constituted by Elder Garrett and Taliaferro at this place, but for six years a sermon had not been preached by a Baptist. The church was resuscitated and the members much revived. Some had joined the Methodists, but returned to the Baptists. I left all in good condition, and they will have several accessions by letter at their next regular meeting. They will try to procure the pastoral services of pastor W. O. Spencer. They have appointed a regular built camp meeting, to commence on Thursday night before the 2ᵈSabbath in October next, at one of the most lovely places in that beautiful country, five mile from Georgetown on the road to Belton. I have promised to exert myself in persuading ministers to attend. Now, brethren, this is an important point. One in which a strong demonstration should be made. The country is well settled, and the brethren are able and willing to support amply all who may come.

Source: *Texas Baptist*, 24 June 1856, 2.

3.4 George Washington Baines

George Washington Baines was a native North Carolinian who was educated at the University of Alabama. After being ordained in 1836, Baines moved to Arkansas where he organized eleven churches. In 1846, Baines moved to Texas where he helped organize the Independence, Huntsville, Anderson, and Fairfield Baptist Churches. In addition, Baines was also the first editor of the *Texas Baptist* and President of Baylor University at Independence from 1861 until 1863.

A. Church Discipline

We should give no attention to the abuse of the accused member, except rebuke him, at the time, for his conduct, but to proceed with the trial in a fair and impartial manner, and in a Christian spirit, not allowing his latest conduct before the church to influence their feelings or their judgment. If he is found guilty, then the church is vindicated in the eyes of all her members and before the world, before whom she should stand fair, and the shame of his unmerited abuse will fall upon his own head. Should the church find the member not guilty of the crime or crimes charged, this would extenuate his conduct before the church in demanding the insurance of his name.If the member, after seeing the church has done him justice, should manifest a Christian temper of mind and make suitable apologies for his rashness, we think he should be excused. We hope that this will be satisfactory, and we only add that the church certainly owes it to herself and the cause of Christ, to establish the charges; if they are true, and to exclude the guilty person; and if they are not true, she owes it to the accused member, as well as herself, to show and declare him innocent. May the Lord direct aright.

Source: *Texas Baptist*, 12 August 1856, 2.

B. A Question to *Texas Baptist* editor Baines

Brother Baines: Please answer the following query: A young lady having joined the Baptists is forced by her parents to withdraw by taking a letter, and afterwards she is compelled to join the Methodist church. What action should be taken by the Baptist Church?

If the young lady has been forced to take a letter, and compelled to join the Methodists, we should say no action should be taken, only to unite in continuous prayer for her deliverance from such bondage. If, however, the church is satisfied that she joined the Methodists willingly, they should declare her church connection with them dissolved. We would advise suitable admonitions before she is declared a heretic. Source: *Texas Baptist*, 5 August 1856, 2.

C. Baines's Presidential Salary

In answer to the proposition of the Board of Trustees now on record requesting my acceptance of the Presidency of Baylor University, I respond that I accept the proposition, provided that it be so changed as to make my salary to bear the proportion to the salaries of the other professors that sixteen bears to twelve and that I be assured by the Board that my salary shall not be less than twelve hundred dollars.

Source: George Washington Baines Papers, The Texas Collection, Baylor University. Reprint courtesy of Texas Collection, Baylor University.

3.5 J. W. D. Creath

A native of Virginia and converted at 21, Creath graduated from the University of Richmond in 1837 after which he pastored in his home state for nine years. In 1846, Creath moved to Texas where he helped to raise funds for and plant churches in Corpus Christi and Beaumont. He was also a President and principal fundraiser for the Baptist State Convention, a trustee at Baylor University, and Vice-President of the Southern Baptist Convention.

A. Creath Promotes Landmarkistic Books in Texas

Brother Graves of Nashville, Tennessee has sent me one hundred copies of the Iron Wheel, and one hundred copies of Orchard's History for Baptists, for sale with forty-eight copies of his letters to Alexander Campbell; twelve copies of Campbellism examined by Dr. Jeter; twelve copies of professor Stuart on Baptism, and the subjects; ten copies of Jesuitism Exposed.

I will send the above works to brethren or friends by mail at the retail prices in Nashville, with the addition of the postage from here, which is 16 cents on the Iron Wheel, and 14 cents on Orchard, etc. Making each work cost $1.16 and $1.14.

If it were not that the freights are so exorbitant, I would myself sell here in Nashville. My object is simply to get the above works into circulation. A Colporter could not afford to sell the works for less than $1.25 cents in Texas so as to live by the sale.

Brethren send in your orders quick!

Source: *Texas Baptist*, 22 August 1855, 2.

B. Creath Raises Funds for the Baptist State Convention

Dear Brethren: The time is drawing near when our State Convention will assemble. The Board is in need of funds to meet her obligations. The Lord is smiling graciously upon the labors of our beloved missionaries in the field. You will please, without delay, bring the interests of the Convention before your churches and congregations, and take up a collection and subscription—the subscription to be paid by the first of October next. The Board will need all that can possibly be raised by the meeting of the Convention. Yours affectionately,

J. W. D. Creath

Source: *Texas Baptist*, 5 August 1856, 2.

3.6 The Union Association

Born in 1840, the Union Baptist Association was the first Baptist association in Texas. The Travis, Independence, and Washington churches were the charter members. The early leadership of the Union Association included T. W. Cox, R. E. B. Baylor, and Z. N. Morrell. The Union Association would become the birthplace of the Texas Baptist Education Society and Baylor University at Independence. For these reasons, the importance of the Union Association cannot be understated.

The Bill of Rights of the Union Baptist Association

Article 1. Each church is forever free and independent of any and every ecclesiastical body, formed by men on earth; each being the free household of Christ. Therefore every ordination and power granted by the churches, emanating as they do from the churches, those who are thus ordained, or upon whom such power is conferred, must be to her forever obedient.

Article II. Each member shall forever have a full and free right to exercise his or her discretion in contribution to the support of missions, general benevolence, etc., and in other matters that may not lead to immorality.

Source: *Minutes*, Union Association, 1840.

3.7 The Birth of the Texas Baptist Education Society

Shortly after their presence in Texas, Baptists began to exhibit a desire to educate their ministers for the challenging work that faced them. The formation of the Texas Baptist Education Society was the first step in this process. This Society would lead to the birth of Baylor University at Independence in 1845.

A. Texas Baptist Education

Art. I. This Society shall be known as the Texas Baptist Education Society.

Art. II. The object of this Society is to assist those young men in procuring an education, who give evidence of being called to God to preach the Gospel, and who shall have the approbation of their respective Churches for the said purpose.

Art. III. The officers of this Society shall consist of a President, Recording Secretary, Corresponding Secretary, Treasurer and seven managers, who shall compose the Executive Board.

Art. IV. The annual meeting of this Society shall be holden at the time and place of the annual meeting of the Union Baptist Association.

Art. V. The officers of this Society shall be chosen annually, by ballot.

Art. VI. The President of this Society shall preside over its meetings, call especial meetings of the Executive Board whenever in his opinion the good of the Society may require it.

Art. VII. The Recording Secretary shall keep an accurate record of all the meetings of this Society, in a well-bound book, and give written notice to the members of the Executive Board of all special meetings.

Art. VIII. The Corresponding Secretary shall communicate and advise with young men as this Society shall receive under its patronage, and shall make an annual report to the Society of their proficiency and prospects.

Art. IX. The Treasurer of this Society shall keep all monies, and shall in no case pay them out, except by a written order signed be the President; he shall keep all subscriptions made for the benefit of this Society, shall collect the same, or cause them to be collected, shall keep an accurate account to account of the finances of the Society and make an annual report of the same.

Art. X. The mangers of this Society in conjunction with the officers before specified shall constitute an Executive Board, who shall examine candidates for patronage, receive or reject them, raise money and perform all other duties which usually pertain to Executive Boards.

Art. XI. Any individual of good moral character may become a member of this Society, by signing this Constitution, but in no case can he become a member of the Executive Board unless he is in communion with a regular Baptist Church.

Art. XII. This Constitution may be altered or amended by a vote of two-thirds of the members present at any annual meeting.

Source: *Minutes*, Union Association, 1841, 15.

B. The Endorsement of Baylor University by the Union Association

The Baptist Education Society met in the first Baptist Church in Houston; had an accession of twenty-three names; received a contribution of $305.50.

Elder H. L. Graves was elected President; Elder Wm. M. Tryon, Corresponding Secretary, and Eli Mercer, James L. Farquahar, W. W. Hill, H. Garrett, O. H. P. Garrett, T. J. Jackson, and B. B. Baxter, Board of Managers.

Resolved, That the Executive Committee of this Society prepare an address for the next annual meeting.

Resolved, That we request the Association to permit the minutes of this meeting to be appended to the minutes thereof, we defraying our proportion of the expense of the printing.

Resolutions offered by Elder Huckins:

Resolved, 1st. That in view of the great destitution of ministers, it becomes the duty of the church to pray the Lord of the harvest to send forth more laborers.

Resolved, 2nd. That we must rely more upon our own resources to supply the destitution of ministers in this State.

Resolved, 3rd. That a vigorous and systematic effort be made to assist young men of piety and promise in the preparation for the ministry.

Resolved, 4th. That we recommend that Baylor University is a suitable Institution to carry out the designs of this society.

Adjourned to meet at Independence, Thursday before the Lord's Day in October next. Prayer by Elder Chandler.

Source: *Minutes*, The Union Association, 2 October 1847, 6.

3.8 Rufus Columbus Burleson

In 1851, Rufus Burleson was chosen President of Baylor University at Independence. Burleson, however, had a personal dispute with Horace Clark, the principal of the female wing of Baylor, over institutional control. Not satisfied with the resulting resolution, Burleson left Baylor and became the first President of fledgling Waco University. When Baylor at Independence and Waco University consolidated in 1886, Burleson was named President for life of Baylor University at Waco. Despite his title of President for life, in 1897 the trustees replaced him and he was given the title President *Emeritus*. Though Burleson's life was filled with perpetual squabbles with Baylor's Board of Trustees, he is considered to have made significant and lasting contributions to the University.

A. Address before the Union Association

DEARLY BELOVED BRETHREN:—

We have assembled this holy Sabbath evening to review and commemorate the blessings of God on this venerable Association for the last half a hundred years.

Let us in the beginning of these services be profoundly penetrated with two great facts: First, no society, association and no nation ever became really great without commemorative days and institutions. Who can estimate the value of San Jacinto to Texas, and the Fourth of July to the United States? Rome and England attained their glory and power by commemorating great events. The most solemn services of God's ancient Israel were days and feasts commemorating the glorious events of the past and filling the Jewish heart with praises to God. The two great ordinances in Christ's Church to be kept till he comes again are to commemorate the dying, bleeding love and resurrection of our Redeemer. But let us never forget the second great truth that the real and true end of all commemorative days, and especially of this semi-centennial service, is to fill the heart with glowing love to God and to inspire all hearts with a burning desire to carry forward with grander success the glorious works begun by our fathers fifty years ago.

The end of this service will not be attained unless we all go from this place praying, "Nearer, my God, to Thee, Nearer, my God, to Thee." It is a pleasing and thrilling coincidence that this memorial service of the fiftieth anniversary is held in a place surrounded by the most glorious events of Texas and Texas Baptist history. Five miles east of this place is San Felipe, the first town ever built by Anglo-Americans on Texas soil. There the first Masonic Lodge in Texas was organized by Stephen F. Austin, the father of Texas. There the first Sabbath School in Texas was founded by our sainted brother and Baptist deacon, Thomas J. Pilgrim. There the first Texas newspaper, "The Star and Telegraph," was established by Gail Borden, for many years deacon of the First Baptist Church of Galveston and discoverer of Condensed Milk, a great blessing to the human family. There, too, assembled in December, 1835, the general consultation that inaugurated Texas independence from Mexican misrule. San Felipe was the capital of Texas till burned to ashes by Santa Anna, the bloody invader of Texas, in 1836. Ten miles north of this place once stood the humble but hospitable home of Moses Shipman, in which Elder Joseph Bayes, a Baptist, preached, in 1825, the first gospel sermon in Texas. In that same house, two years later, 1827, our beloved venerable Sister Lydia Allcorn was converted under the preaching of Rev. Thos. Hanks, a Baptist. This was the first public profession ever known in Texas. This beloved sister, after spending sixty-three years in the services of God and of Texas, died just one week ago and went home to heaven on the snowy white wings of angels. Twenty miles north once stood the town of Travis where this Association, the mother of all Associations, and the mother of all great Baptist enterprises in Texas, was organized in 1840. It was small in numbers, but mighty in faith and noble deeds. There were only three preachers: Elders R. E. B. Baylor, Thos. W. Cox and J. J. Davis, and three churches, Independence, Lagrange and Travis. Our grand old pioneer, Elder Z. N. Morrell, would have been present as a member from Plumb Grove, Fayette County, but he was prostrate on a bed of sickness by over-exertion in fighting and chasing Indians and Mexicans away from the families of Texas. It is not to be wondered that this infant Association, born amid such stirring events and surroundings, should, like the infant Hercules, begin even in the cradle to strangle the venomous beasts of Campbellism and Antinomianism, and resolve to send the gospel into every neighborhood in Texas. Though surrounded by hostile Indians and Mexicans and in deep poverty, they sent out Brother A. Buffington to preach the gospel between the Brazos and Trinity, and Rev. N. T. Byars and Richard Ellis to preach the gospel in all the region west of the Colorado. But they found that they were utterly unable to supply the vast throng of immigrants and the widely scattered settlements over this vast empire state. And, remembering that an appeal sent out in 1837 by Brethren Jas. R. Jenkins, A. Buffington and H. R. Cartwell had touched the great heart of Jesse Mercer, of Georgia, and induced him to donate $2,500 to begin a Texas mission, and this money enabled the Home Mission Board at New York to send Wm. Tryon, Jas. Huckins, B. B. Baxter and R. H. Taliaferro to Texas. This second appeal was made to the Southern Baptist Convention, organized at Augusta, Ga., in 1845. The Convention of Southern Baptists responded warmly to this appeal, and sent, in 1847, what Father Z. N. Morrell, in his great book, "Flowers and Fruits," calls "a whole ship-load of preachers." Of that number were Elders P. B. Chandler, Noah Hill, Jesse Witt, J. W. D. Creath, J. F. Hillyer and Henry L. Graves as Missionary President of Baylor University. Rufus C. Burleson belonged to the same cargo, but he came seven months later. The Southern Baptist Convention, in their great zeal for Texas, also agreed to support Elders Z. N. Morrell, N. T. Byars, Richard Ellis, Wm. M. Tryon, Jas. Huckins, R. H. Taliaferro, Wm. Pickett, Jas. H. Stribbling and D. B. Morrill, already laboring successfully in Texas. As illustrative of the times, we insert the following letter from our noble and beloved brother, P. B. Chandler:

Gatesville, Coryell Co., Texas

August 12, 1890

Rev. C. C. Green, Pastor at Sealy:

Dear Brother:—Your card of recent date came to hand in due time and I am sorry that I cannot attend the next session of the Union Association as you request. I have neither the time nor the means to spare. That was the first Association I attended in Texas. I came to Texas under appointment of the Home Mission Board of the Southern Baptist Convention near the close of A. D. 1846. Was one of that shipload of preachers of which Brother Morrell speaks in his "Flowers and Fruits of Texas." In 1847 I attended a session of the Union Association in Houston, then the only Association in Western Texas. Then Huckins was pastor in Galveston, Tryon in Houston, Hill at Matagorda, Creath at Huntsville, Ellis at Gonzalez and myself at Lagrange. There were but few other ministers in the West, among them were Judge Baylor, H. Garrett, David Fisher, A. Buffington that I remember. Most of these have gone to a better land. Of that ship load of preachers I am left alone. I have outlived my generation and I sometimes fear I shall outlive my usefulness. I am in my 75th year, and, though physically stout for my age and conscious to myself of my accustomed vigor of mind, there is not much demand in the churches for my labors. The rage seems to be for young pastors; whether this is wise or otherwise I need not say. I am still doing what I can in the Master's cause and rejoicing at its prosperity. "What has the Lord wrought?" "The little one has become a thousand, and the small one a strong nation." "To Him be praise and dominion forever and ever." The Lord be you. Love to all the brethren. Yours fraternally,

P. B. Chandler

The Southern Baptist Convention, in her ardent zeal to supply the vast destitution of the Empire State of 274,000 square miles, has generously donated over $100,000 and has placed all Texas under an everlasting debt of love and gratitude, which she can only pay by earnestly co-operating in her glorious plan of evangelizing the world. But the heroic and far-seeing fathers of this Association, in their profound wisdom, saw and deeply felt the necessity of Christian education for the pious training of the sons and daughters of Texas, and especially for educating the rising young preachers of Texas. They, therefore, resolved, at the second annual session, held at Clear Creek Church, Fayette County, to found a Texas Baptist Education Society; also, a great Texas Baptist University, that should stand as Gibraltar to Baptist faith as long as the flowers bloom on our vast prairies or the waves of the Gulf dash on our shores. In all the struggles of our martyr church for 1,800 years, no grander act of heroism was ever displayed. Six hundred Baptists, surrounded by 8,000,000 hostile Mexicans on the west, 60,000 hostile Indians on the north, resolving to found a grand University, to equal any on this continent. And, as our heroic fathers believed more in the Book of Acts than in the Book Resolutions, they went to work and procured a charter and wisely located Baylor University on the beautiful Live Oak Hills, of Independence, in 1845.

Independence was then the most central and accessible place to all the settled portions of Texas. Baylor University, thus located, poured forth the healing stream of learning, piety and patriotism for forty years. There were educated many of the grandest men and noblest women that Texas ever saw, among whom we rejoice to name Rev. Dr. Jas. H. Stribbling, Rev. D. B. Morrill, Rev. Dr. F. Kiefer, Rev. Dr. Pinckney Harris, Rev. W. W. (Spurgeon) Harris, Rev. Dr. W. H. Parks, Rev. Sam J. Wright and scores of others; and such useful and distinguished citizens as Gov. Sul. Ross, Lieutenant-Governor Jas. W. Jeffries, of Louisiana, Col. Thos. J. Gore, Hon. Thos. J. Brown, Cicero Jenkins, Hon. S. D. Reed and Hon. John N. Henderson; and such noble women as Mrs. Rachel Barry Stewart, Mrs. Dora Pettus Hobby, Mrs. Mary McKellar Herndon, Mrs. Julia Turner Miller, Mrs. Sallie Chandler Gregory and scores of others too numerous to mention of the noblest men and purest women that have adorned the highest positions in the family, in the church and in the State. But by the fatal blunders of the people of Washington and Independence, they were left off the railroads, and Independence became inaccessible, and in an evil hour dissension arose and Baylor University declined from two hundred and thirty-two students in 1861 to thirty-two in 1885. And in 1885, by vote the delegates chosen by the State Convention and General Association and East Texas Convention assembled at Temple, Baylor University was consolidated with Waco University, with her three hundred and sixty-five students, under the venerable name of Baylor University, where she flourishes today, with the finest buildings and campus west of the Mississippi, and twenty-six able and efficient professors and teachers and her six hundred and eighty-seven students, male and female. But by the terms of consolidation the beautiful buildings and the grounds and library and apparatus, worth $100,000 were all turned over to this venerable Association, to be used for a great Texas Baptist Institution for Southern Texas. But who of us can refrain from tears when we remember those splendid buildings on that sacred spot on the beautiful live oak hills of Independence have been sold to the Catholics to pay a debt of $1,750; and that buildings and grounds worth $50,000, consecrated by the sweat and tears and prayers and money of our Tryon, Baylor, Mercer, Huckins, Wharton, Houston, Creath, Jarman and the noble founders of this Association are now held and occupied by Catholic Jesuits as a negro school and orphanage? Who of us will not pray and toil that these buildings and the grave of our Baylor may be rescued from the desecration of that apostate church whose garments have been dyed in Baptist blood from the very day she was founded by Pope Boniface III and the blood of Phocas? From a church who murdered in 1430–1480, 200,000 Waldensian Baptists in the valley of the Piedmont, and cherishes the same hate to our martyr church to this hour, and would gladly send us all to the dungeon and the stake if she had the power which she hopes soon to gain by our consummate blindness and blundering. Oh, that our J. W. D. Creath were living to sound a blast so loud as to arouse the two hundred thousand Baptists of Texas in one grand crusade to rescue the tomb of Baylor and the $50,000 worth of Baptist property from the nunneries of Catholicism and a negro school and orphanage.

But our grand old foundation-builders and path-finders of fifty years ago knew the value of and power and glory of union and the crime and wickedness of division. The burning desire of their great hearts was that Texas and Texas Baptists should be indissolubly united in one great brotherhood forever in every great and good work. Hence, at the seventh annual session at Houston, in 1847, that illustrious and God-sent pioneer, Elder William M. Tryon, introduced a resolution inviting the scattered Baptists of Eastern, Northern and Western Texas to assemble and form a Baptist State Convention. In accordance with that resolution, messengers from the churches in every part of Texas assembled at Anderson,

Grimes County, September 8, 1848, and formed the Baptist State Convention. But, in the mysterious providence of our all-wise and merciful Father, this resolution calling for the organization of the Texas Baptist Convention was the last great act of the lamented Tryon. In less than thirty days after he penned that resolution he died of yellow fever, November 16th, 1847, aged 39; but he died like a hero—with his armor on and on the field of victory. He heard, with faith and joy, the great Redeemer say: "Well done, good and faithful servant; enter into the joys of thy Lord." No man ever died more beloved and lamented by every true Texan. He had been chaplain of the Texas Congress and was the confidential spiritual adviser of General Sam Houston, Hon. Isaac Van Zant, Governor A. C. Horton and the representative men of Texas.

> "But God moves in a mysterious way his wonders to perform
> He plants His footsteps on the sea and rides upon the storm;
> Blind unbelief is sure to err and scan His work in vain,
> God is His own interpreter and He will make it plain."

When the Baptist Israel assembled, September 8th, 1848 at Anderson, to organize, all felt that their Moses was gone and silent, sad prayers ascended to God for a Joshua to lead them forward. A grander body of men never assembled in a new State to do foundation work. The constitution they formed so wisely has stood for forty-two years. For a faithful picture of the noble men there assembled we refer you to the able paper read before this meeting by our beloved brother, Dr. Stribbling, so competent to draw that grand picture. But these grand path-finders and foundation-builders also fully understood the power of Journalism and the Union Association was first to urge the importance of a great Texas Baptist Journal, and members of this Association were chiefly instrumental in establishing, in 1854, "The Texas Baptist," published first at Anderson, Texas, with Elder George W. Baines, Sr., as editor. This paper was suspended during the war; but was revived in 1866 under the name of "The Texas Baptist and Herald," and is now exerting a wide influence for good in all this Empire State. In 1866 all Texas was feeling deeply the importance of the wide circulation of Baptist literature and of establishing Sunday-schools in every neighborhood in Texas. It was reserved to this dear mother Association to lead in this grand work, and Rev. S. I.

Caldwell introduced a resolution in the Association in 1866 inviting all Texas to assemble and form a Sabbath-school and Colportage Convention, which was fully consummated at Plantersville, Grimes County, in 1867.

In the early days and struggles of Texas Baptists, this dear old Association not only led in organizing the great enterprises of missions, education, journalism, Sabbath Schools and colportage, but was a generous contributor in every good work. The records of the old State Convention will show clearly that for the first seven years of the State Convention the members of the Union Association contributed from one-half to three-fourths of all the money given for missions and ministerial education. When we review the history of this Association for the last fifty years, we can but exclaim: "What hath God wrought?" And with joyous hearts we ought today to erect an Ebenezer and shout: "Hitherto hath the Lord helped us." Fifty years ago there was one little Association and three churches and three preachers. Today there are over one hundred Associations with thirteen hundred churches and fourteen hundred ministers and two hundred thousand church members, one hundred and twenty-five thousand white and seventy-five colored. Today our State Convention has employed one hundred and fifteen missionaries at home and our Sabbath School Convention twenty-two colporters and Sabbath School missionaries in Texas, and Texas has more missionaries in foreign fields than any other Southern State. Our provisions for our orphans and aged ministers are unsurpassed by any other State in the Union. Baylor University has the finest building and fullest faculty and largest number of students of any Baptist institution in the South. Our Texas Baptist and Herald will soon equal the best journals in the land. For all these glorious results let us all upon all the powers within to praise the Lord and cry: "Not unto us, but unto Him be all the glory," for His right hand has given us the victory.

Beloved brethren, it is meet and proper and eminently instructive on this great occasion to review and firmly fix in our minds, and hearts the causes and the means that have given Texas Baptists such unparalleled success—a success never equaled in any new State.

First of all and in the very beginning, Texas Baptists said: "In the name of God we set up our banner." "Our only hope is in the Lord."

Second. They resolved to preach nothing but Jesus, nothing but the good old story of Jesus and His love

Third. They resolved to stand firmly on the old landmarks as established by Christ and His apostles 1800 years ago and vigorously maintained by the Baptists in all ages in defiance of racks, tortures, gibbets, dungeons and apostate churches claiming to be the only true church of God. Texas Baptists have labored to avoid the looseness and affiliations of our Northern and English brethren with other Christian denominations and to avoid on the other side the fatal mistakes of some good meaning brethren who think that the Kingdom of Heaven is to be promoted by controversy, debates with others, "Who follow not with her." Texas Baptists obey the command of Jesus: "Let them alone." They neither denounce nor affiliate with them, but speak the truth and the whole truth in love.

Fourth. The Texas Baptists never discuss that hurtful, humiliating question: "Who of us shall be the greatest in the kingdom?" Indeed, the perils of frontier life and the bloody conflicts with Mexicans and Indians fully demonstrated that no man who covets leadership had sense enough to lead in anything, and to all would-be leaders they say: "Go foot, and spell up." The grand spirit of the great body of Texas Baptists for the last fifty years has been: "In honor, prefer one another, Jesus is Lord of us all." The humiliating exceptions to this rule have been fewer in Texas than in any new State, and we pray God that their number may still fewer grow in the years to come.

Fifth. A grand factor in the wonderful success of Texas has been Christian education. In this great work, Texas Baptists have excelled, and continue to excel, above all other denominations, and the State herself, with her millions of money. The wonderful success of Texas Baptist demonstrates the fact that the men who educate the youth of the State control the State.

In conclusion, dear brethren, after reviewing the last fifty years, let us thank God and take courage and resolve, by God's help, that he in the next fifty years shall be more glorious than the last fifty. If our brethren, with only three little churches and three preachers and ninety-two members, surrounded by 8,000,000 hostile Mexicans and 60,000 Indians, increased two thousand fold in fifty years, what may we not do by 1940?

Can we not establish a Baptist Church and Sabbath-school in every neighborhood of Texas and girdle this entire planet with Texas Baptist missionaries?

Let us, today, banish every root of bitterness and all strife far away from us; let us, in honor, prefer one another; let us stand firmly on the old landmarks established by Christ and His apostles; let us resolve to ever preach, "Jesus only, Jesus only," then, when our children shall assemble, perchance on this very spot, to celebrate the 100th anniversary of this dear old Association, our beloved Texas will be the greatest, wisest, holiest State between the oceans, and, filled with millennial light and glory and Baptist Churches, shall shine as the stars of heaven. For which let us pray, and toil, and sacrifice or time, our means, and, if need be, our lives.

Source: *Semi-Centennial Address*, Union Baptist Association, 1890, 11–19.

B. A Love for Baylor over the Presidency of Union

My Dear Wife:—Since I mailed my last letter yesterday, I have received a communication from Doctors J. R. Graves and John W. King, informing me of my election to the presidency of Union University. I am so overwhelmed with astonishment that I know not what to think, say or write. Oh how I wish I was by your side to hear your wise counsel, always of so much value to me. I feel incompetent to decide any great question without your advice.

In every respect, my position as President of Union University would be easier, and perhaps more honorable and profitable. There we should be clear of taking boarders and much drudgery. The salary I earn is ample, and the society as good as any in the United States. Murfreesboro has about 5,000 inhabitants, or is about the size of Houston. Then as successor of Dr. Eaton, my position would be as honorable as that of any Baptist preacher in the country.

But then I am bound to Texas, our church, and Baylor University by a thousand tender ties of joy, of suffering and affection. How could we leave our mother, brothers, sisters, and the bones of our little daughter; and Brothers Ross, Creath, and Taliaferro! The very thought makes me weep, and yet the hand of God may be in this move, and I dare not refuse it a prayerful consideration. We have had some experiences in

Texas that was by no means pleasant, but then opposition and difficulties would meet us anywhere, except in heaven. I confess it would be very agreeable to me to be so near my venerable father, and other members of my family. One thing that astonishes me so much, is the course of Bro. J. R. Graves; he tells me my election was unanimous, urges me to accept, and overwhelms me with kindness.

Please show this letter to Brother Richard, and you and he write me your opinion immediately.

I have replied to the note of the committee on notification, that I would visit Murfreesboro, and examine the situation carefully, and give them an answer. But I promise you my dear wife on the altar of fidelity, and by the sweet eyes of our dear children, not to make any decision until I see or hear from you.

Your devoted husband,
Rufus C. Burleson

Source: Rufus Burleson to Georgia Burleson, 21 August 1859, cited in Mrs. Georgia Burleson, *The Life and Writings of Rufus C. Burleson* (Waco: By the author, 1901), 137-38.

3.9 William Carey Crane

A Virginian by birth, Crane had served as a pastor in Alabama, and as President of Mississippi Female College, Semple Broadus College in Mississippi, and Mount Lebanon College in Louisiana. In 1863, Crane moved to Texas to become President of Baylor University at Independence following R. C. Burleson's abrupt resignation and move to Waco University. During the latter years of his tenure, he vehemently fought the idea of a centralized university that would consolidate both Baylor and Waco Universities. A rivalry between Baylor and Waco University quickly ensued that would lead to myriads of denominational problems in the years to follow. Following the death of Crane in 1885 and due to financial problems, consolidation with Waco University occurred in 1886. Crane would serve Baylor University at Independence for twenty-two years.

A. Baylor First and Foremost

Dr. Burleson said he could not consent that Waco University should be ignored as a Baptist school. I repeated the position of my letter to him in September 1863 written from Houston to the effect that there was room enough for both universities in the state; that I could not consent to taking it under the Convention on an equality with Baylor University, as that would work badly. I instanced Mississippi College and Semple Broadus College and said that it would be better for him to have a Northern organization if one was needed for his university.

Source: William Carey Crane Papers, The Texas Collection, Baylor University.

B. Crane's Summary of His Difficult Days at Baylor

1. Trying political condition, removal of people, bankruptcy, tendency to ignore old obligations.
2. Direct efforts to take students from Baylor.
3. Failure of persons to pay pledges for building repairs.
4. Reports of insufficient number of teachers untrue.
5. Reports that Crane is in debt to all teachers untrue.
6. Personal opposition in Independence.

Source: William Carey Crane, *Diary*, 17 March 1868, Texas Collection, Baylor University. Reprint courtesy of Texas Collection, Baylor University.

C. Washington County—Political and Religious Significance

Under Mexican rule the divisions of the State or Provinces were called Municipalities. Until Mexican invasions were ended, and the Indians removed to safe distances, Washington was the border territory for Anglo-Saxon civilization. It originally embraced the whole country north as high as the old San Antonio road, embracing Burleson; Milam and Robertson counties; east, comprising Grimes, Montgomery, Madison, Brazos and Leon, and west, including Fayette and Lee counties.

It attracted, at an early date, attention from all quarters. The men who originally owned its soils were among the first to concert for the general good of the Republic and for the material wealth of the State. It is conceded to possess a better average body of lands on its whole surface than any other county in the State.

Observance of law and love of order have ever been characteristics of its citizens. Intellect at the bar, in the pulpit, in the council chamber, in the school room, in the farm and in business circles, has ever been appreciated. Few of the terrible scenes which have made other regions sadly memorable have been witnessed in the country. Through all changes which forty years have witnessed, the good citizens of Washington have been generous, chivalrous, hospitable and patriotic.

Its original territory was a favorite hunting ground for the Indian tribes early claiming possession. Citizens are now living who were born here when Indians held undisputed possession of four-fifths of this State. The Tonkaways inhabited this section previous to the arrival of the white settlers. They were never hostile. A remnant of the tribe, now poor, is fed by the United States military authorities at Fort Griffin, on the Clear Fork of the Brazos. Other small tribes, mostly friendly, wandered through the country. The Comanches, a branch of the Sioux tribe, were from the first and continued to be the most formidable and hostile Indian tribe in Texas. The early settlers in Washington were annoyed by the Indians, who stole their horses, and yet more by the whites stealing horses from the Indians. A drove of horses was taken from the Tehuacana (Tawakana) Indians while camped on Little river. A party of white settlers retook them and returned them to the Indians about 1830. This act of justice had its effect in freeing this section from Indian depredations, while east and west they were bitterly hostile. The Yegua river or creek (a stream which makes a lasting impression on all who cross it at each of the four seasons of the year) was a boundary which secured the immunity of which early settlers had a happy experience. Except the Gocher family, no white people were killed in Washington County by Indians. Our fellow-citizen, J. D. Giddings, Esq., was chased by the Indians between Cummins' creek and Rutersville, in the later part of February, 1839.

It was no doubt wisely ordered by Divine Providence that the boyhood and manhood, in part, of the life of Sam Houston should be spent among the Indian tribes, and thus was he qualified successfully to treat with these first owners of the soil.

The first white woman who crossed the Brazos and located, was the wife of Andrew Robinson. They crossed at La Bahia in the spring of 1822.

The first men who made a crop of corn in this country were Horatio Christman, now eighty years of age, and still hale and hearty, living with his son-in-law, Thomas C. Thompson, near Caldwell, in Burleson County, and Martin Varner, an early hardy pioneer. The spot on which this first crop of corn was made is now the land of Tacitus Clay, Esq., know as Hickory Point, near Independence.

The first white child born this side of the Brazos, in this county, below the present town of Washington, was Thaddeus Bell, brother of the distinguished lawyer and Judge, James H. Bell, now in Austin.

According to the records in the Capital at Austin, Washington was erected into a county December 14th, 1837. The first county officers under the Republic were John P. Cole, Chief Justice; R. Stephenson, Sheriff; J. P. Shepperd, Clerk of the District Court; R. Merritt, Clerk of the County Court. The first under the state government, elected July 13, 1836, were Nimrod J. Chappell, Chief Justice; Geo. W. Horton, Probate Judge; Dawson D. Crumpler, Clerk of the District Court; John Gray, Clerk of the County Court; James W. McDade, Sheriff.

There have been efforts to build up towns, with more or less success, at ten different points in the county. Washington was the first, located and laid off by Captain Jack Hall. In 1833, during the winter, John W. Kennedy build the first house in the place. It was the first county site, when the county extended to both sides of the Brazos river. It continued to be the county seat of justice till the fall of 1841. It became the Capital of the Republic about October 3rd, 1842, and remained the capital during Houston's administration of the Presidency, which closed December 9th, 1844. Anson Jones, the successor of Houston, was inaugurated in this good old time. Before me is one of his proclamations at Washington, June 4th, 1845, countersigned by Ebenezer Allen, Attorney General and acting Secretary of State, declaring that "the government of Mexico had accepted the conditions prescribed on the part of Texas, as preliminary to a final and definite treaty of peace," and that there should be "a cessation of hostilities, by land and by sea, against the Republic of Mexico, or against the citizens and trade thereof."

From the outgivings at this time, after the Congress of the United States had passed the Foster and Brown resolutions for annexation, it was thought that the authorities of Texas might hinder annexation in some way, and therefore the people of Washington County held a meeting at Washington, an account of which appears in the New Orleans

"Picayune," April 25th, 1845. Strong resolutions were passed in favor of immediate annexation, "without references to the wishes or concurrence of any foreign or European power, and calling on President Jones to convene Congress immediately." The meeting also recommended to the citizens of the Republic, in case the President did not convene Congress, to meet as soon as possible in convention, to ratify the Joint Resolutions of the United State Congress, and form a State Constitution. The Attorney General, Ebenezer Allen, who was present, objected to the tone of the resolutions. Hon. R. Scurry replied, intimating that the citizens of the Republic might yet become still more impatient of the delay of President Jones in convening Congress and adopt measures much more violent than those recommended in the resolutions. The resolutions were unanimously adopted. Gen. Memucan Hunt, Dr. J. C. Chambers, Judge W. H. Ewing, R. W. Williamson, J. B. Wilkens, and other prominent gentlemen participated in the proceedings. The President issued his proclamation the following day. The Congress of the Republic accordingly met on the 16th of June, 1845, for the last time at Washington. Both houses unanimously consented to the terms of the Joint Resolution for the United States. The Senate by a unanimous vote, rejected the treaty with Mexico. Resolutions were passed requiring the Executive to surrender all posts, navy yards, barracks and military or naval effects to the authorities of the United States, then represented by Capt. Waggaman the present, prepared to select posts to be occupied by the troops of the United States and provide for their sustenance. President Jones himself, so far as depended on himself, to give full and immediate effect to the will of the Congress.

Thus it will be seen that Washington County witnessed on its soil the assembling of the Convention which declared Texas a free and independent Republic, and the last meeting of the Congress which terminated the Lone Star Republic and merged it into the United States of America.

The Convention which was called to frame a State Constitution did not meet in Washington, but as one of the principle citizens of this country was a chief actor in that Convention it may not be inappropriate to say that it assembled in Austin, July 4, 1845. Gen. Thomas J. Rusk was unanimously elected president. A committee of fifteen was appointed, who reported, through Judge A. S. Lipscomb, their chairman, of this county, an ordinance assenting, on behalf of the people of Texas, to the terms of annexation proposed by the Government of the United States and accepted by the Congress of the Republic assembled at Washington, June 18th. This report was adopted with one dissenting vote, but five members were absent. The dissenting vote was Richard Bache, grandson of Benjamin Franklin, father-in-law of Robert J. Walker, Secretary of the U. S. Treasury, and brother-in-law of Vice President George M. Dallas. While we celebrate this fourth day of July, 1876, as the Centennial of American Independence the Constitutional Convention of Texas celebrated the fourth day of July, 1845, in the novel way for a liberty day, by assenting, by act of the whole people, to the surrender of the independence of the Republic and its incorporation with another republic, and offering a tribute of respect to Andrew Jackson, recently deceased, by whose influence, mainly, the measure of annexation was consummated.

J. W. McCown, Esq., now a Justice of the Peace of this county, states, in a note dated June 29, 1876, that he immigrated to Texas in 1837, and that he "conducted a train of wagons, in 1842, to Houston, and at Gen. Houston's request moved the archives from Houston to Washington. The City of Houston had taken a vote and refused the President a house rent free, and he was compelled to move. When the wagon train had passed beyond the limits of the corporation, Old Sam (as he was familiarly called) stopped the train and pronounced a curse on that people, and stamped the mud off his feet."

The political importance of the old capital, Washington closes with the year of annexation. It continued to flourish till in 1857 it is represented in Lippincott's Geographical Gazeteer as "a flourishing post-village of Washington Co., Texas, on the right bank of the Brazos river, at the head of steamboat navigation, and containing, in 1851, one academy, two female schools, twenty stores, and three newspaper offices." The faces of the "National Register," the "National Vindicator," and the "Texian Ranger," have been familiar to many of us. The first Baptist Church organized in Texas was constituted at Washington, with Z. N. Morrell, Pastor, and H. R. Cartwell, Deacon. Through the correspondence of this church Wm. M. Tryon was sent as a missionary to Washington County, and James Huckins to Galveston. During the same year Rev. Robert Alexander came, the first missionary from the Methodist Episcopal Church, was the first Superintendent of Missions in Texas and died, in the 54th year, March 16, 1838, in the town of Washington. Rev. W. Y. Allen, now in Illinois, was among the first, if not the first, Presbyterian minister who undertook to establish the Presbyterian Church in this county, and Rev. L. P. Rucker, an early and active settler, must be awarded the honor of the greatest success in rearing up Episcopal Churches.

Thrilling scenes are depicted by Z. N. Morrell, in his "Fruits and Flowers in Texas," exhibiting the contest at Washington between religious influences and the usual vices incident to a new settlement. Even as late as 1837 the marriage ceremony, except by a Roman Catholic priest, was a novelty in Texas. According to Mexican law marriage was illegal, unless performed by a Roman priest, who, for performance of the ceremony, exacted twenty-five dollars. Many persons were married by contract and lived together till the ceremony was performed. The Congress of the Republic passed a law similar to that in force in the United States. Mr. Morrell says that he was frequently called on to officiate in marriage ceremonies where a group of little children were witnesses for their parents. In one instance, immediately after preaching, he performed the ceremony in presence of the congregation, each of the parties holding a child in their arms. The first couple he ever married were a couple passing through Washington to Gonzalez, in 1837, who had been long engaged and would not marry before according to Mexican law.

Washington should also be remembered for its many exciting scenes, and for its numerous worthy citizens who have passed away, among them the following: Bartlett M. Hatfield, who furnished at his own expense the hall of the assembling of one branch of Congress, Geo. W. Crawford, R. A. Lott and James L. Farquhar.

The county seat was removed to Mount Vernon in 1841, on the road between Brenham and Long Point. No vestige of the town now remains. A town was laid off into lots by the County Commissioners, but few houses were ever erected, inasmuch as serious dissatisfaction among the people forbade the risk.

The first boarding school was established at Mt. Vernon in 1835. Its officers were David Ayers, Mrs. Ayers and Miss L. A. McHenry. The news of the fall of the Alamo in 1836 interrupted its exercises, and it was never resumed.

The town of Warren flourished as a small place, at the mouth of New Years creek. It has no local habitation, and its name is here mentioned lest it may be entirely forgotten.

Independence was first called Cole's Settlement, after Judge J. P. Cole, who settled there in 1824, and whose remains lie not far from the spot where he first settled his place. The name was changed at the instance of Dr. Asa Hoxie, formerly of Georgia, who, in honor of the declaration of Texas independence, March 2, 1836, succeeded in fixing on the place the name it now bears. It has been memorable for the number and distinction of the citizens who dwelt in its precincts. Among the oldest living citizens who were early settlers are James L. Dallas, Mrs. Marsh and Mrs. Seward. The hospitable mansion of Dr. Asa Hoxie was for years the rallying point of many of the leaders in Texan affairs. There Lamar, Bell, and many others consulted over Texan destiny. Many of the leading minds of the State were first domiciliated in or near this ancient town. Sam Houston, Royal T. Wheeler, Robt. M. Williamson, Asa Hoxie, Jerome B. Robertson and Albert G. Haynes have been among its most prominent citizens. But the principle thing for which the place has been remarkable is its educational zeal. J. W. Giddings, Esq., in March, 1839, taught a school near the present residence of John H. Seward, Esq. On the 1st February, 1845, nearly six months previous to annexation, the charter for "Baylor University," named after Judge R. E. B. Baylor, was granted by the Congress of the Republic, and the institution located where it now stands at Independence. Its first trustees were R. E. B. Baylor, Eli Mercer, Orren Drake, James L. Farquhar, Edward S. Taylor, James Huckins, James S. Lester, Robert Armistead, Aaron Shannon, Albert C. Horton, Nelson Kavanaugh, A. G. Haynes, I. G. Thomas, R. B. Jarmon and Wm. M. Tryon. Its first teacher was Henry F. Gillett, now of Bayland Orphan's Home. The presidents, in order, have been, Henry L. Graves, Rufus C. Burleson, George W. Barnes and W. Carey Crane. Until 1866 it had both a male and female department. Baylor Female College is now a separate institution. It was for nineteen years under the successful management of Horace Clark, L. L. D., and has had B. S. Fitzgerald, H. L. Graves and W. W. Fontaine as presidents in succession, and is now flourishing under the supervision of Wm. Royal, D. D. Nearly three thousand young ladies and gentlemen have received their education, in whole or in part, in Baylor University or Baylor Female College. Thirty-three young gentlemen have received the degree of A. B. and nine that of B. P. This Law School has been located at Independence during its existence, except for two years. Its first faculty was composed of Chief Justice Royal T. Wheeler, Judge R. E. B. Baylor, and Hon. John Sayles: its second faculty was R. T. Wheeler and John Sayles: its third faculty was R. T. Smith, J. E. Shepherd, John Sayles and B. H. Bassett. Its professors have had no superiors in legal learning and ability in Texas, and among the prominent lawyers of the State who have graduated from this school are John Alexander, Charles R. Breedlove, E. F. Ewing, D. U. Barziza, Cicero Jenkins, Wm. L. Moore, I. M. Orvis and John N. Henderson.

Source: William Carey Crane, *Centennial Address, Embracing the History of Washington County, Texas*, 4 July 1876, 24-33.

3.10 Concerning the Colored Population

Most early Texas Baptists were sons of the South, and thus were pro-slavery. While hoping to bring the Gospel to the colored, they were not willing for the slaves to gain equal stature either within the church or as fellow Christians. It should also be noted that the first three Presidents of Baylor University were pro-slavery as were eleven of its first fifteen trustees. Following the Civil War, "Jim Crow lofts" became a common architectural feature of Baptist churches. This sentiment remained so strong in Texas that a complete statewide, intentional desegregation of Southern Baptist churches did not occur until the late 1960s.

A. On Application of Colored Church, Anderson

This report not having been forwarded to the Committee on Printing and Distribution of the Minutes, we can only give its substance. It recommends the rejection of the petition of the Colored Church at Anderson, because the establishment of independent Churches among our colored population would be inconsistent with their conditions as servants, and with the interests of their masters. It recommends separate meetings and special preaching for their benefit; the appointment of their own Deacons and Watchmen; and that they be encouraged to maintain a correct discipline among themselves, but always to be aided in this work by the presence and counsel of some judicious white members.

Source: *Minutes*, Union Association, 1855, 23.

B. Report on the Colored Population

Your Committee to whom was referred the religious condition of the colored population, beg leave to make the following brief report: We find no new feature of interest since your last session. Our ministers, without any exception, devote some hours on Sabbath evenings to their special instruction, and say that they are well rewarded for their labors, seeing that the Gospel is joyfully received, and numbers converted and added to our churches. We would, therefore, earnestly entreat our ministers to continue their labors and even where the houses of worship are so constructed as to accommodate them during services for whites, still to have some hours of devotion specially allotted to the colored people.

> Respectfully submitted,
> N. Hill, Chairman

Source: *Minutes*, Union Association, 1858, 7.

C. Report on Religious Instruction of Colored Population

Our Savior has said: "Preach the Gospel to every creature," and his Apostle tells us, that with God, "there is neither Jew, nor Greek; there is neither bond nor free,**** for ye are all one in Jesus Christ." With such instructions before us, can we be guiltless and neglect the religious instruction of our Negroes? No one who believes the Word of God can think so. It would seem, too, that by our peculiar relation to them, and theirs to us, that we are under increased obligations to teach them faithfully the way of salvation. This, your committee has reason to fear, is too much neglected in many neighborhoods, and in some of our churches. We should labor for the heathen abroad; but while we do this, let us not forget the heathen on our plantations—in our own families. Let pastors and churches (having due regard for laws of the State,) see to it that this very important interest is not neglected within our bounds. No field affords more promise of direct success than that of our colored population.

Respectfully submitted,
Noah Hill, Chairman

Source: *Minutes*, Union Association, 1862, 9.

D. The Negro Intellect

If the intellectual and moral condition of a race of men fit them only for despotic government, they will be slaves to their superiors wherever they may live, and to declare that they are equal in rights to the men who are fitted for a free republican, or a democratic government, is to declare what is positively absurd. They have not the capacity to understand or appreciate the rights, duties and responsibilities of a free citizen of a republican government, and therefore it is impossible that the morality can be sound which requires all human governments to allow men rights of which they have no adequate concepts of or capacities to understand.

Source: George Washington Baines, *Texas Baptist*, 3 January 1861, 2.

E. Slavery is a Means of Evangelism

Many good, pious, Christian blacks have been sent back to that poor, benighted nation; and now we see lately springing into existence, a republic in Liberia. A missionary is there; the heralds of the bible, both white and black; have gone from our beloved republican missionary land, and raised the standards of the cross.

Source: *Proceedings*, Baptist State Convention, 1848, 11.

3.11 The German Population

During the post-Napoleonic era in Europe, the social standing and economic structure of the German people fell into chaos and were profoundly changed. In the hopes of a better life and with the promise of cheap land, thousands of Germans immigrated to Texas. The majority of these immigrants were either Catholic or Lutheran. Texas Baptists did not fail to recognize the need to evangelize these new neighbors.

A. The Need

When they came to the State they were mainly Catholic or Lutheran. Very few of them could speak our language, and we could not speak theirs. They scarcely ever attended our religious services, and we had no preachers who could preach to them in their own tongues. So far as I know, not one of our native Texas preachers has ever learned either German, Bohemian, or Swedish language well enough to preach intelligently in that language.

Source: J. M. Carroll, *A History of Texas Baptists* (Dallas: Baptist Standard Publishing Co., 1923), 586.

B. Evangelistic Endeavors by the Baptist State Convention

Resolved, That a Committee, consisting of brothers R. C. Burleson, J. B. Stiteler, N. Hill, and Frank Kiefer, be appointed to take in hand the appropriation made for the benefit of the Germans in Texas, and purchase such books and periodicals as will be best adapted to promote their spiritual interest.

Source: *Minutes*, Baptist State Convention, 1855, 8.

C. Baptist Commitment to the German Texans

We now turn to the Baptists and find only here and there one who believes as the Baptists do. Some of them have been converted in this county, others in Germany, and it is painful to notice that some of our members who come here being ignorant of the people among whom they live, are persuaded to identify themselves with those to whom they do not belong. But we rejoice that the Baptists of Texas are awakening to their duty. Shall the Baptists of this State suffer a people in their midst to remain destitute of the gospel without an effort to give it to them? Shall we permit this large and interesting portion of our population to be ruled by priests and infidels when God has brought them to this land of Bibles and Bible Christians? Shall others be allowed to teach their favored creeds and we remain silent spectators? God of truth forbid it. The Baptists will not fail to do their duty whenever it is laid before them in a proper light.

Source: *Proceedings*, Baptist State Convention, 1856, 20.

3.12 Southern Baptist Interest in Texas

Immediately upon its birth in 1845, the Southern Baptist Convention showed a great interest in the state of Texas. Articles concerning the triumphs and trials of their Texan brethren were widely disseminated through various Baptist periodicals. Articles such as these demonstrated to the readership the growth, ministerial need, and passion for the gospel of Baptists in Texas. There can be little doubt that after reading the ensuing account, many Baptists left their traditional homes and moved to Texas.

Baptist Birth, Growth, and Organization in Texas

In 1826, Rev. Joseph Bays, a licenced Baptist minister from Illinois preached near Peach Creek, upon the west side of the Brazos river, within the bounds of Austin's Colony. Rev. Thomas Hanks, an ordained Baptist minister, preached on the east side of the same river in 1829. He is now living in Houston County, in this State. The above facts the writer received in person from brother B. and H., and also from others now living. The first Baptist Church was organized on the Colorado river in 1833, and the second in Shelby County, in Eastern Texas, in 1835. The "Union Association" was organized in 1840, with three churches numbering forty-seven members, including three ministers. This is the oldest ecclesiastical body in the State. There are now eleven missionary associations, and about one hundred and fifty ministers, and about forty churches, with as many ministers. In Texas, there are from nine to ten thousand communicants.

The first Sabbath school organized in Texas was in 1829, in Philippe or Austin—the capital of Austin's Colony. During the same year one was organized at Matagorda and the next year one at the mouth of "Old Cany"—all by Baptists who emigrated from New York. These facts I have gathered from Deacon T. J. Pilgrim, of Gonzales, who commenced the Sabbath school at San Philippe, while acting as interpreter of the Spanish language in Austin's Colony.

The charter for the "Baylor University" was granted in 1845, and the institution opened in July 1846, with some twenty-five scholars and one teacher. In 1853, there were eight professors in both departments, with one hundred male, and about eighty female scholars. Both departments are under the same Board of Trustees—Rev. R. C. Burleson, A.

M., is President—Rev. H. Clarke, is principal of the Female Department. Several young men of much promise, have already been educated for the Christian ministry, and other are now preparing for the same blessed work. The institution is unembarrassed by debt, with an endowment of nearly twenty thousand dollars.

Our State Convention was organized in the fall of 1848; and during the year 1853, the Board sustained nine missionaries in destitute portions of the State.

The Baptist churches, as a body in Texas, are sound in doctrine, in the ordinances and in church policy. They are united and ready for every good work. They are increasing very rapidly, and are trying to help themselves. The Lord has caused the original account invested in missionary labor in Texas, by the Home Missionary Boards, to yield a rich harvest for good. To Him, through Christ Jesus, be all the glory, forever and ever, amen.—J. W .D. Creath

Source: *Home and Foreign Mission Journa* 4 (August 1854), 1.

3.13 James Bodkin Link

Born and educated in Kentucky, Link served as a chaplain in the Confederacy during the Civil War before being appointed a missionary to Texas by the Southern Baptist Board of Domestic Missions in 1865. Link created the *Texas Baptist Herald* in 1866 as a means to propagate Baptist causes in Texas. He also played a key role in the unification of Baylor University and Waco University, the formation of the Baptist General Convention of Texas, and penned a two-volume biographical work that details many early Texas Baptists, their associations, and churches. If not for this work, a great deal of Texas Baptist history would have been lost. Link's original two volume biographical work is now available in four volumes.

A. The Birth of the First Baptist Church, Waco

In the latter part of the year 1850 at a meeting of the Mission Board of the old State Convention, with the church at Huntsville, Texas, an application was made for a small appropriation ($75 per annum), to sustain a missionary for a part of his time at Waco, then a little frontier village almost entirely unknown to the outside world. It was natural that an objection should be raised to the appropriation of such money for such an unpromising field, and as Waco had not been honored with a place in the current geographies, it was not strange that some of the members, with just a touch of irony, inquired whether Waco might be found. But there were those present who looked beyond that day. They saw the white wings of civilization spreading to that far West. They saw Waco the centre of a great, thriving, wealthy section, covered with vast fields of golden grain and waving corn, and tickled by the plow-share of the husbandman, laughing rich harvests of cotton, and as they painted this picture and appealed to the Board to set up the banner of the cross now, and take and hold the Waco country for Jesus, all opposition was withdrawn and the appropriation was voted, and Elder N. T. Byars, the veteran soldier, patriot and missionary, was appointed to this field. How abundantly the wisdom of this effort was justified the following pages will demonstrate.

In pursuance of his appointments Bro. Byars came to his field, and after due notice, given on May 31, 1851, met the scattered Baptists of Waco and vicinity in a board shanty on the corner of Jackson and Second streets, about the location of the brick edifice long afterwards built by the Presbyterian church and now owned by the colored Methodist church. After preaching them a sermon he organized the First Baptist Church at Waco, with the following members, to wit: James C. Johnson, Geo. T. Holman, Noah Wood and Matilda Johnson. Bro. Wood was elected clerk, and on the following Sabbath this little band, few in number and poor in purse, but rich in faith, called Bro. Byars to the pastoral care of the church, which position he held for two and a half years.

In a manual prepared many years ago by Bro. J. W. Speight, since deceased, he says of the building in which this church was organized:

"This rude structure (though a good one in primitive times in Waco village), was constructed by planting cedar poles upright in the ground and weather-boarding the same with oak clapboard, the roof being made of the same material, the floor of cedar puncheons and the shutters to the windows and doors of rough cedar plank. This house was owned or controlled by the Methodists, and it was by their courtesy that the church used it for a while for one Sabbath and Saturday preceding, and afterwards for two Sabbaths in the month. At that time it was the common preaching place for all denominations, the Baptists, Methodists and Presbyterians being the only ones represented in the 'village' for several years after."

All the meetings of the church were held in this structure until 1857, when the church moved into its new brick house on the corner of Fourth and Mary, the site of our present edifice. This building, a most excellent one for the times, continued to be our place of worship until it was consumed by fire on the 22nd day of February, 1877. What a world of tender memories clustered around that pile of ashes. Thence we had buried our dead. There many of us first heard the preached word. There a majority of the members had given their hearts to God, and their mothers and fathers, sons and daughters had grown in grace and spiritual strength under a faithful ministry for the gospel of Christ. It was a time for "memory and for tears." But no time was lost in useless repining. On February 25th, just three days after the fire, the church met in conference, and under stirring appeal from our pastor, Rev. B. H. Carroll, resolved at once to set about the work of rebuilding.

Never did the zeal, the piety and the faith of the church shine forth as brightly as during this period. Without a rich member in the church, and with very few that were dependant on their own exertions, they adopted plans for a forty thousand dollar house, and determined to build it without incurring a debt. The members followed their resolutions with acts, and as they gave the work progressed. Occasionally a halt was called, and then after a brief period the work would begin with renewed energy. It is a coincidence worthy of mention that during this trying period, when every energy of the membership was taxed to the utmost to accomplish the work in hand, yet the pastor's salary was increased, the church more than doubled its contributions to home and foreign missions, it remembered the poor and gave liberally to the building of other church houses. Was it merely a coincidence? It was rather a fulfillment of the scripture, "There is that scattereth and yet increaseth, and there is that withholdeth more than is meet but it tendeth to poverty."

The house was fully completed in 1883, in time for the meeting of the Southern Baptist Convention in May of that year, a meeting that has gone into history as the must numerously attended meeting ever held by that body. More than three thousand messengers and visitors were entertained by the church, nobly aided by the citizens of Waco without regard to creed, and "yet there was room."

The burning of the church and the building of the new marked a distinct epoch in the history of our church. The blessed scripture, "All things work together for good to them that love God," was happily verified. At the time we regarded the destruction of our old house an irreparable calamity, but it proved a blessing that has increased with every year.

I mention only one of a number of good results that followed this event, and if this were all it is enough to justify the statements in the foregoing paragraph. We have line upon line of the duty of systematic giving, but never until the church was confronted with the problem of building a house of worship under the peculiar circumstances of this case, did we realize how ineffectual to that end was the practice of occasional and spasmodic giving so prevalent with Christians then and by no means obsolete now. Having determined to build a house without incurring a debt, to "lay in store" and "give as God has prospered" us, always a duty now became a necessity and practiced at first from necessity it soon became an established method, and fixed itself upon the members so that it is now exemplified in all the work of the church. It has effectually done away with the high pressure system of collecting money. There is never a collection taken up in the church except for some extraordinary purpose, and these very rarely occur. Instead, we have a collector for every object fostered by the church. The collector is provided with a book and he takes the subscriptions of the members for the object for which he collects. These subscriptions are for the year and are paid monthly. The collector pays over the funds so collected to the person or the board entitled to receive it, and at each conference meeting the collector reports to the church the amount collected, when and to whom paid, and such other facts with reference to his work as may be of interest. Thus we have a collector for State missions, one for Foreign missions, one for Orphans' Home, etc. No one list contains the names of all the members, for in a large church such an event will herald the dawn of the millennium, but more names are constantly added and the utility and effectiveness of the method demonstrates its wisdom.

In the forty-one years since its organization the church has received into its fold by baptism 830, by letter 1,298; a total of 2,128 members.

Its present membership is 657. No serious difficulty or schism has ever occurred in the church, the members generally working together harmoniously. It has been orderly in practice, always holding firmly to Baptist faith and has generally been, but not always, strict in discipline as the law requires.

The history of the church would be incomplete without a brief mention of its city mission work:

In 1886 the church, recognizing the fact that in a growing city there were many who, if they ever heard of the gospel must have it carried to their doors, determined to employ a missionary and begin systematic mission work in the city. Elder V. G. Cunningham was employed. He entered upon the discharge of his arduous labors at once and served with satisfaction to the church till July, 1890, when he resigned (to take effect October 1) to accept the pastoral care of the Second Baptist church which had been established first as a Mission Chapel and afterward organized as the Second Baptist church of Waco, this church being the direct result of his labors as city missionary.

On the 14th day of September, 1890, Elder John G. Kendall, of Guthrie, Ky., was chosen by the church to succeed Bro. Cunningham. He accepted and arrived in Waco with his family on Thanksgiving Day, and entered upon his work on December 1. His work has been eminently satisfactory. In addition to preaching for the church in the absence of the pastor, visiting the sick and giving care and attention to the destitute of the city and providing for their necessities under direction of the deacons, (a task requiring great zeal, energy, patience and judgment) he has organized one Sunday-school in the northern and one in the southern part of the city, and during his incumbency the church has built a commodious house known as Bagby Chapel, at which there are held regular preaching services on Sunday nights and prayer meeting on Thursday nights, both services being well attended and the interest constantly increasing. The church intends building another Mission Chapel in the north or northwestern part of the city during the year and will continue to push the work in all of its branches.

The above history was prepared by Judge W. H. Jenkins, clerk of the church, for a church manual just published, with covenant, articles of faith, constitution, roll of the members, and other things useful to the church. This history gives no account of the revivals that may have occurred from time to time, and we have no special facts about any except one that occurred in 1876 under the labors of Deacon W. E. Penn. He had not then been ordained to the ministry. Speaking of this meeting during its progress, Bro. M. V. Smith said: "Bro. Penn has conducted every service in the meeting at Waco, from two to three times a day for fifty-three days. There have been 213 conversions—126 have joined the church. Over 100 have joined by baptism. There have been a number of conversions among the students in the College, who have gone home without baptism, and quite a number of conversion among persons attending from another country. The meeting exceeds in power, by far, anything I have ever witnessed, and I have been in it nearly all the time." From facts gathered on the ground, after the meeting closed, the *Texas Baptist Herald,* of July 27, 1876, made the following notice of it: "This has probably been the most extraordinary meeting ever witnessed in the State. It was in progress 81 days. It closed last Wednesday night with about 40 forward for prayer. There have been about 370 conversions. There have been 152 baptized, five await baptism, eight have been restored, 34 received by letter, and seven are under watchcare till letters are secured. The meeting has been conducted entirely by Deacon W. E. Penn. It has had to contend with court sessions, 4th of July celebration, school examinations and commencement, the heat of the summer, the disadvantage of insufficient room to accommodate the people, and a spirit of opposition from some of the other denominations. The work has been most searching as well as extensive. Some of the most hardened sinners have been brought in and backsliders reclaimed. Some of the most bitter quarrels have been settled and most inveterate enemies have been reconciled. All the denominations, perhaps, except the Episcopalians and Catholics, have started meetings in their places of worship.The work extended to the colored Baptist church, and some 200 have been converted there. This wonderful work of grace has extended to the country around and revivals are in progress."

Different pastors have served the church as follows: N. T. Byars from May 31, 1851 to February, 1854, two and one-half years; S. G. O'Bryan, from February, 1854 to end of 1859, six years; W. H. Bayliss, 1860-1861, two years; W. H. Anderson, 1864, one year; R. C. Burleson,

1865–1867, three years; M. B. Hardin, 1868–1869, two years; R. C. Burleson, 1870, one year; B. H. Carroll, from January, 1871, to present time, 1892.

Source: J. B. Link, *Historical and Biographical Magazine*, 2 vols. (Austin: n. p., 1892), 2: 473–79.

B. The Birth of the First Baptist Church of Galveston

The first missionary sent to Texas was James Huckins. He came to explore the field in 1839, and sent back valuable information to the American Baptist Home Mission Society, New York, by which he had been sent. Other minsters [*sic*] had come to the State and several churches had been organized in 1838 and 1839. Mr. Huckins organized the First Baptist Church of Galveston, January 30th, 1840. The following were the constituent members: George Fellows, from First Baptist church, Deerfield, N. H.; David R. Wright, from Central Church, Westfield, Mass.; Francis W. Pettigrove, First Baptist Church, Calais, Maine; Lewis Graves, from First Baptist Church, Seneca Falls, N. Y.; Mrs. Abigail W. Bartlett, from Central Baptist Church, Westfield, Mass. These after organizing the church, admitted the following persons, who had not, at the time, letters of dismission from their churches: Barnabas Haskell, First Baptist Church, Norwich, Conn.; Mrs. Abigail Haskell, First Baptist Church, Norwich, Conn.; Mrs. Sarah A. Burnet, Baptist Church, Clinton, La.

The church thus began its existence with nine members, five male and four female; and on the same evening received as candidates for baptism, Mr. Gail Borden, Jr., and his wife, Penelope. Mr. and Mrs. Borden were baptized February 4th, 1840, in the Gulf of Mexico; they were the first persons who visited the waters by its beautiful beach for the observance of this ordination of the gospel. On the evening of February 14th, 1840, the church adopted Articles of Faith and a Church Covenant. They continued to meet for worship in such places as could be secured—school-houses, court rooms and Lyceum hall. Elder Huckins continued in charge of this mission until May 22nd, 1841, when he was called to the pastorate of the church. On September 5th, 1841, the church was admitted to the fellowship of the Union Association, and has continued to cooperate with that body ever since. Mr. Huckins continued as missionary of the Home Mission Society and pastor of the church, spending part of his time preaching in Houston. The Society paid him but little, and the few members of the church could add but little more, so he had to turn his attention to teaching school. He identified himself with the institution of slavery to the extent of owning one household servant. This gave offense to many members of the Society, and, rather than create any division in the Board he had served for several years, he withdrew from the Society altogether after about two years and a half, and when the Southern Baptist Convention was organized, in 1845, he became a missionary of the Domestic Mission Board, at Marion, Ala. The church still retained his services as pastor, and had now for about two years claimed his whole time.

The time had fully come to build a house of worship. The Galveston City Company had placed the church in possession of three very eligible lots on the corner of 22nd street and Avenue I, as a building site. The church appointed Mr. Huckins to travel and solicit aid throughout the Southern United States to build a house. He left Galveston July, 1845, and returned in July, 1846. Upon making his report, it appeared that after deducting all necessary and unavoidable expenses, there remained, in cash and good subscriptions, the sum of $2633.25 available for the object. Besides this amount there had already been subscribed $700 in the city. The church, therefore, on the 7th day of August, 1846, resolved to build, and appointed the following building committee, Messrs. J. S. Sydnor, Gail Borden, Jr., John Stamps, Charles Ives, Wm. F. Crow, T. H. Borden, W. N. Sparks, Gilbert Winne, Geo. Fellows, Benjamin Nichols, and Rev. James Huckins. The contract was given to Messrs. Crow and Ives, and the building was completed in time to be dedicated in September, 1847.

Source: J. B. Link, *Historical and Biographical Magazine*, 2 vols. (Austin: n. p., 1892), 1: 165–66.

CHAPTER 4

Progress Amidst Problems, 1848–1868

4.1 The Baptist State Convention

With victories realized in the advent of the Union Association and Baylor University at Independence, the Baptists of Texas began to believe that they needed a larger organizational body to accomplish their ministerial goals on a statewide level. These desires led to the first Baptist Association of Texas in 1848, the Baptist State Convention. Despite their most ardent desires to serve the entire state, the BSC's greatest strength and emphasis would always lie in Southwest Texas and the Gulf Coast regions. This emphasis was made obvious by the fact that every two years the BSC was scheduled to meet in Independence.

The Constitution of the Baptist State Convention—1848

Article 1. This body shall be called the "Baptist State Convention of Texas."

2. The objects of the Convention shall be missionary and educational, the promotion of harmony of feeling and concert of action in our denomination, and the organization of a system of operative measures to promote the interest generally, of the Redeemer's Kingdom, within the State.

3. The Convention shall be composed only of members of Baptist churches in Good standing.

4. Any member of a Baptist church may be a member of the Convention, upon the payment of five dollars, and shall be entitled to life

membership upon the payment of twenty-five dollars at any one time.

Any association, church or society, shall be entitled to one representative in the Convention for every five dollars contributed to its funds; and any church belonging to an association, shall be entitled to one representative, without a contribution.

5. All donations to the Convention shall be sacredly appropriated in accordance with the wish of the donor.

6. The officers of the Convention shall be a president, three vice-presidents, a corresponding secretary, a recording secretary, and a treasurer, who shall be annually elected by ballot; but shall hold their office till others are elected; which officers shall be ex-officio members of the board of directors.

7. It shall be the duty of the president to preside over the deliberations of the convention and the board of directors, and to discharge such duties as are generally incumbent upon this office in deliberative assemblies. He shall appoint committees in office in deliberative assemblies. He shall appoint committees in all cases, except when the convention shall otherwise determine.

In the absence of the president one of the vice-presidents shall thus preside, and the one entitled to the office shall be determined by seniority of age.

8. It shall be the duty of the corresponding secretary to conduct all the correspondence of the Convention and board of directors. He shall make an annual report in writing of the same, embodying therein such matter or information as he may deem important.

9. It shall be the duty of the recording secretary to keep in a book, suitable for the purpose, a correct record of the proceedings of the Convention and board of directors, and to file and keep such papers as he may deem important to be preserved.

10. It shall be the duty of the treasurer to take charge of all moneys, specialties, and property belonging to the convention, and to make such disposition of the same as he shall be directed the by Convention or board of directors. He shall not make any disposition of money or property without an order signed by the presiding officer and recording secretary. He shall make an annual statement in writing to the Convention, of his official acts, and of his receipts and disbursements.

11. The Convention shall annually elect by ballot a board of directors, of not less than twenty members, whose duty it shall be to act in the recess of the Convention, and whose powers shall be the same as those of the Convention; they shall not do any thing inconsistent with the constitution, nor contrary to the objects and intentions of the Convention.

It shall be their duty to meet once in every four months, and oftener if they deem it necessary. They shall keep a record of their proceedings and make an annual report in writing, to the Convention, of the same. They shall make their own by-laws. Eight members shall constitute a quorum to do business. Five additional members of the board of directors shall be nominated at the same meeting by the president, subject to the approval of the Convention. Any life member of the Convention may be an honorary member of the board of directors.

The board of directors shall have the exclusive power of appointing agents and missionaries, and ordering the disbursement of money in the recess of the Convention.

They may call a meeting of the Convention.

12. The Convention shall never possess a single attribute of power over any church or association. It absolutely and forever disclaims any right of this kind, hereby avowing that cardinal principle that every church is sovereign and independent.

13. The election of officers shall take place immediately after the Convention is organized, and the recording secretary shall have ascertained the names and number of the members present. The highest number of vote shall constitute a choice in all elections, except for president and treasurer, in which elections a majority shall be necessary.

14. No officer of the Convention shall receive a compensation for services.

15. Visiting brethren may be invited to seats in the Convention, and participation in its deliberations, but shall not be allowed a vote.

16. The annual sessions of the Convention shall be held on Friday before the second Sabbath in May.

17. This constitution may be altered or amended at an annual session, by a vote of two-thirds of the members present.

Source: *Proceedings*, Baptist State Convention, 8 September 1848.

4.2 Texas and Foreign Missions

Baptists have always had a strong desire to support Foreign Missions and the Baptists of Texas were no different. The Baptist State Convention, however, had just been organized and the funds available were barely sufficient to keep the fledgling organization operative. At least for the time being, Texas Baptists would be forced to concentrate their efforts solely on the lost within their own state.

Texas Takes Care of Its Own

The committee to whom was referred the subject of Foreign Missions, beg leave to report: This missionary spirit is being infused throughout Christendom. The various denominations are beginning to open the Savior's last command: "Go ye into all the world, and preach the Gospel to every creature."

But we must confine our brief report to our own denomination. Our Northern brethren of the Missionary Union during the last year supported 99 missionaries and 144 native assistants, and received 1783 members into their churches. The total number of converts in their various stations is 1000.

The Indian Mission Association sustained last year 35 missionaries and assistants, whose labors God has abundantly blessed in civilizing the savages, illuminating their minds with science and sanctifying their hearts with grace.

The Southern Baptist Convention has received for the past year, for the furtherance of foreign missions $19,519.05 and expended $16,835.82. It supports 20 missionaries in China and 16 in Africa, but while the Holy Spirit is, through their instrumentality converting many of the heathen, and convincing thousands to inquire, "What shall we do to be saved," and to offer to us the Macedonian prayer. "Come over and help us," alas, that our denomination South should last year average only five cents in their donations to feed starving millions of souls with the bread of eternal life.

Your committee sincerely wishes that the time is not far distant when the Baptists of Texas will feel themselves able to render efficient aid in the scriptural and sublime enterprise. In view of these truths,

Resolved, That we highly approve of, and most deeply sympathize with Foreign Missions, and will assist, by our humble prayers and incessant efforts. All of which is respectfully submitted.

Source: *Proceedings*, Baptist State Convention, 8 September 1848, cited in J. B. Link, *Historical and Biographical Magazine*, 2 vols. (Austin: n. p., 1892), 1: 262–63.

4.3 Sabbath Schools

Due to the fact that there were so few Baptist preachers in Texas, many churches only met quarterly and Sunday Schools were rarities. Despite this fact, Texas Baptists recognized the necessity of educating their children in the Baptist faith. Nowhere was the desire for Sabbath School more prominent than in the historic Union Association.

A. The Importance of Sabbath Schools

Believing, as we do, that Sabbath schools are an important auxiliary to the Gospel in the communication of the divine truth, should be as boldly and as clearly taught as in the pulpit, comprising no principle, withholding no lights; and believing as we do, that we have neglected too long one obligation in this particular, while others are using this powerful engine for the propagation of error; we can but congratulate the denomination; that a set of men eminently qualified, has been raised up, and moved to supply this want by furnishing them with Sabbath school literature suited to the South, and propagating Baptist sentiment, which is simply Bible truth. Therefore

Resolved, That we cordially recommend the books already published at Nashville, Tennessee, and that we recommend to the Convention to correspond, by letter, (and send a correspondent if possible), to the Sunday School Board, soon to convene in Memphis.

Source: *Proceedings*, Union Association, 1858, 6.

B. The First Sabbath School Convention Sermon, J. H. Stribbling—1865

Text—Proverbs xxii.6—"Train up a child in the way he should go, and when he is old he will not depart from it."

This is the language of one, who had a profound knowledge of human nature. It is an expression of age and experience,—a command from a king to his subjects—an injunction from Jehovah to each parent, guardian and instructor of the rising generation. Think of the fearful obligation it imposes upon us! A child, a mind, an immortal soul is given to our charge, to be trained to virtue and integrity, to holiness and happiness, and to serve and glorify God on earth and in heaven. An angel might covet such a mission, and the part we act will bring curses or blessings on our beloved offspring.

One important fact deduced from the text is—that our leading and ruling traits of character are the result of early training.

The Spartan mother taught her boy never to turn his back upon an enemy; to return from the conflict with his shield, or his lifeless body on it; and Spartan courage has been proverbial in all ages. The Athenians impressed on the minds of their children a love for philosophy and science, and they became the most learned and refined of ancient nations. The Roman was trained to use the spear, shield, and javelin, and for ages the world bowed to the conquering way of its disciplined legions. Some of the nobility of England, though in a peasant's garb, in a foreign land, and engaged in menial occupation, were detected by the force of their early training. But we need not multiply illustrations. Home—childhood and its associations—the counsel and example of parents and friends, scenes of virtue and of vice, and the repeated declaration of God's word— all testify to the force of early training in molding the character, directing the course in life and sealing the destiny of individuals, communities and nations.

1-The text has a proposition and admonition followed by a promise. Most of the blessings of life are offered to us on conditions. If we would store the mind with knowledge, we must seek it by reading, reflection and observation. If we would receive the crop, we must prepare the soil and plant the seed, and cultivate the harvest. If we would be disciples of our Savior, we must deny ourselves, take up the Cross and follow Him. And if we would have our children walking in the way of virtue, truth and holiness, we must so train them by instruction, admonition and persuasion, that these messages from God's Word shall be engraven on the mind, like words on a leaden tablet by the point of a diamond. But it has been said of the text that it contradicts our experience and observation, since many cases, seemingly of careful training, have turned out reckless profligates of society. Such failures may be attributed, not to any failure in God's promise, but to some defect, omission or neglect in the training of the child. Where is the parent that has complied with these requirements?—How much regret, to repent of, in our best directed efforts in the arduous work! Many sow good seed in the minds of their children by their instructions, but now also the tares of a wicked example, and permit evil associations and practices to shade and wither the good seed. But because some children under a form of religious training have been led into wicked or abandoned lives, furnishes no excuse for laxness or neglect in training them in all that is pure and holy. As well might we neglect the laws of health, or the proper use of property, or planting and cultivating our farms, because health may fall in despite of the best habits, or our possessions wrested from us by some disaster, or a consuming drought blight the best prospects of crops. Our experience, reason and revelations, all teach us, if we would secure certain blessings, we must use the appointed means to obtain them. If we would reap the harvest, we must sow the seed: If we would bring our sheaves to garner in the house of the Lord, we must go forth weeping and sowing the precious seed of Divine Truth in the minds of our children.

2-We next consider the meaning of the phrase, "train up," in the text. Its significance is obvious in rearing or training animals for a special service, or inspecting or directing the movements of the soldier in the daily drill, until the company or regiment moves with the precision of a machine, at the word of the command. In a similar way the word is used in a moral sense. The meaning of the phrase, says Adam Clark, is, "Initiate the child at the opening, or mouth, of his path;" as soon as your child begins to receive impressions for good or evil, point out the duties, dangers and blessing that lie before him, in the path of life. Two ways lie before him: one is the way in which he would go, heedless and reckless on to destruction; the other is the way in which he should go, the way of self-denial, obedience and happiness.

The way in which he would go, is smooth and flowery, beauteous prospects, merry companions, and all the charms of vice and iniquity lead him on to hopeless ruin; while the way in which he should go, is a straight and narrow way, and must be entered from choice, and requires struggles of heart and life to press onward in his heavenward journey; but it is a way of safety, peace and happiness. Millions from our sorrowing world have gone up that bright and shining way, and now chant the praises of God around His Throne.

3-We are wisely directed in this training to begin early, before evil affections, principles and habits, have taken possession of the soul; and before they have been drawn up into these whirlpools of iniquity, that have engulfed so many thousands on the ocean of life. We may impress thoughts, feelings and principles on the mind of our children, that will be like ministering angels around their path, whispering in scenes of temptations, "This is the way—walk ye in it." Some years since, a native of Portugal, in one of the New York hospitals, was seen to have the likeness of the Savior on the cross on his arm. It had been tattooed there by a mother's hand, in his infancy. He had grown from the child to the man—he had wandered from clime to clime, and passed through all the changes of life; but there still was this likeness attending him—the emblem of a mother's faith and affection. Suffering and disease; growth and climate, drenching rains and howling storms could not erase it; even so should the love of Jesus be enstamped on the minds of our children by early training. Why does six hundred millions of Pagans transmit the same abominable rites and practices from one age to another, and Mohammedism sway its scepter over one hundred millions of the world, and the Jews, scattered to the extremities of the globe, unite in one creed, and Romanism bind together all ranks, languages and castes, in their communion. It is simply the force of early training. When the Grecian tyrant sought to overturn the Government, or when Cataline would crush the Republic of Rome, or in modern time, when the Jesuits put forth a force that overawed and swayed the thrones of all Europe, it was done by training the young and enlisting their fiery ardor in their designs. Shall we be less zealous in training our children for virtue and integrity, truth and holiness, happiness and heaven?. . . .

II. Two leading facts should never be lost sight of in this training—one is that it is an immortal soul to be trained, that can reason, think and imagine, that is destined to endless progress in virtue or vice, in happiness or misery—a soul that may, through the triumphs of Redeeming grace, enjoy bliss that angels never knew, or writhe in misery that fiends and lost spirits never realized. Another fact is that this soul has a bias, a ruling inclination to something evil rather than good. "The carnal (natural) mind is enmity against God." As poison from the serpent, or the malaria from the swamp, or weeds and thorns from the earth, so is wickedness from the depraved heart. Abuse, cavil at or deny the doctrine as we may, it stands confirmed by experience, observation and revelation. The weeds and noxious plants will not more surely grow up in your garden or on your farm, if not rooted up, than will error and evil spring up in the mind your child if not supplanted. But as the farmer by uprooting and cutting down the weeds as they spring up, and planting and cultivating the good seed, may sow seeds of Divine Truth in the minds of the young, we may hope for a crop, so by diligently and prayerfully planting and cultivating the seeds of Divine Truth in the minds of the young, we may it to say in the final day, "Here am I, and the children thou gavest me!" But teaching our children the Bible will not make them Christians, as they learn a lesson in philosophy or work out a problem in mathematics. Let it never be forgotten—let us cling to it with a martyr's grip—that the *Spirit of God* alone can move, meet, and change these depraved hearts.

> "Tis thine to cleanse the heart,
> And sanctify the soul,
> To pour fresh life in every part.
> And new create the whole."

But this training will fix right principles in the mind, direct the conscience to right perceptions of truth, and lay the foundation for intelligence and usefulness in all after life. While others may aid in this training, the Scriptures require parents first and primarily, to "bring up their children in the nature and admonition of the Lord." It begins when your child has learned the difference between a smile and a frown, a soft and a harsh word, and is continued by all of our intercourse with them from infancy up to the time they leave the parental roof.

III. We now speak of the nature and benefits of Sabbath School instruction, as an important agency for training the rising generation. The present system of Sabbath School, that has done so much to spread the leavening influences of the Gospel among the millions of our race, is of recent origin; but the principle is as ancient as the command of Moses to Israel. They were required to teach their children the precepts of the Lord, as they sat in their houses, walked by the way, and as they lay down at night and rose up in the morning. Abraham commanded his children after him; David taught children the fear of the Lord, and Timothy was instructed in the Scripture from a child. By an intimate knowledge of the Scriptures from childhood, the pious Waldens confronted and confuted the priesthood, sent to sow the seeds of heresy and corruption among them.

The germ of the usefulness of such men as Doddridge and Newton, Payson and Judson, and an illustrious host who will "shine as the brightness of the firmament, and as the stars forever and ever," in the memory of the redeemed in Heaven, may be traced to early religious instruction. These messages, if not blessed in the early conversions of our children, may, and often does in future years, bring the prodigal home from his wanderings, and wake the lyre of angels over the repenting sinner. Nor is our work done or our duty discharged until we have taught them the whole counsel of God: our depravity and regeneration by the Holy Spirit—a living faith and a burial in baptism—the final perseverance of the saints and the form of a gospel Church, modeled in doctrine government and practice, after the teachings of our Savior and His inspired Apostles. These are our bulwarks of defense against heresy and corruption, the traditions and commands of men. For these, Apostles and martyrs have died, the Waldens were hunted, tortured and slain—Holmes and others bore the lash—our fathers went to prison, and now from age to age, through the changes of eighteen centuries, the blood-tracked march of the Church of Christ may be traced. Your obligation as a parent to provide food and clothing for your children, is not more plain nor so important as to provide food for the starving soul. Are you giving them "line upon line, and precept upon precept!" Are you training them in the "way they should go?"

2-Another argument for Sabbath Schools is the susceptibility of the young mind, to receive deep and lasting impressions. Not more readily does the melted wax receive the impress of the seal, or the lead the form of the mould into which it is cast, than does the child receive impressions for good or evil. It is forcibly illustrated in the readiness and delight with which the aged father calls up the scenes and associations of childhood, and that thrill his heart and fire his eye as they pass before his mental vision, like scenes in panorama.

It is said of West's painting of Hannibal's oath, that his father leads him into the Temple, surrounded by priests and officers of State. He places one hand of his son on the bleeding victim on the altar, and raising the other, swears him to constant hatred of Rome. That boy became the most formidable enemy Rome ever had. The champions of truth in these latter days, who have stormed the strongholds of error and scepticism, and laid hold of, Sampson-like, the pillars of the temple of iniquity, and crushed in ruins its cherished idols, have been sworn the truth, and trained to its defense from childhood. These lessons have been as the compass to direct him as through the storm and over the ocean of life to the haven of rest.

3-We need a Sabbath School in every church to engage our membership more in the study of the Bible. How little is the Bible read! How much less is it studied! How often the work of fiction, the last news, or unprofitable social talk take the place of the study of God's Word, even on the Sabbath! Many of our members are weak in faith, unsettled in doctrine, annoyed with doubts and fears, because they never searched the Scriptures daily to see if these things were so, and have taken their belief from the belief of men rather than the Word of God. Let our churches, as far as they can be, be organized into Sabbath Schools—let them have a fixed lesson or subject, or portion of Scripture for each week's study, in place of reading promiscuously without any definite object, and it will be found that both teacher and student will learn more in one year than in three or four years of ordinary reading and study. To attract, interest and expand the mind, we have in this treasure of knowledge the richest variety. If reason asks for subjects to develop its powers, or imagination the widest field over which to range, or the spirit of devotion something to nerve and fire the soul, or the powers of eloquence thoughts to charm or mould and sway the stormy passions of men, they all lie embedded in this mine of Divine truth. For the ignorant, here is instruction in its simplest forms; for the learned, subjects and mysteries that might baffle an angel's powers; for the careless and reckless, the yawning gulf and walls of the lost, and for the bereaved and sorrowing, "the oil of joy for mourning, and the garment of praise for the spirit of heaviness."

"This harp let down from Heaven," has numerous strings that may be touched by human hands, whose mingling vibrations may well and prolong the strain of "peace on earth and good will to men," until its echoes reach from pole to pole, and send a thrill of joy into the heart of redeemed millions.

> "What light breaks on a darkened world,
> From these resplendent leaves unfurled;
> The opening eyelids of the morn,
> Shed no such beams o'er hill and lawn.
> Tis gentle rain and sparkling dew,
> The mind to cleanse, refine, renew—
> Tis lightning fierce, and thunder deep,
> To rouse the conscience from its sleep;
> Like angels round a dying bed,
> Its leaves a heavenly radiance shed,
> And hovering on celestial wings,
> Breathe music from unnumbered strings."

4-The Sabbath School is a means often blessed in the early conversions of our children. Is there any thing, aside from personal piety, that should awaken such an abiding interest, importunate prayer and diligent use of the means of grace, as the salvation of our children? Eternity, as its unmeasured ages roll away, will develop the fruits of the early conversion of such men as Pollock, Henry Martin, Brainard, Kirke White, and scores who have been cut down in the morning of life. Many things favor early conversion in the Sabbath School. Their minds are retentive, their hearts tender, and their prejudices few and feeble. Then they more readily receive and permanently retain good impressions, and more easily conform to habits and practices of a pious life. While we should guard them against excess in religious excitement and every form of error and evil, and try to give them clear views of gospel truth, we should never forget that, above learning, honor and wealth, is their early conversion. We might refer to the statistics of Sabbath Schools throughout the land, in proof of the fact that their conversions are more frequent—

that they are more secure against vice, iniquity and crime, and that they are prepared for more extended usefulness in the church and the world in all after life.

5-The institution of which we have been speaking, may assist in developing the gifts of those whom God has called to the ministry of His Word. A wide-spread, distressing and increasing destitution prevails in our country; multitudes perishing for the want of some one to break to them the bread of life. Are there not some who are neglecting this call to the ministry, who have leanness of soul, any [sic] may yet be visited with the rod of God's displeasure? Let such as feel moved to this work go into the Sabbath School, take a class, study and pray over the lesson, and then try to impart the thoughts that move his own heart, to his class, and he will find in after years, that he has cultivated those powers that have aided him in preaching Christ crucified, to a dying world, while by diligence and prayer in his instructions, he may lead a soul to Christ, that shall be a star in his crown of rejoicing, and fill his heart with grateful remembrances in ultimate glory. How many have had their minds first directed to the work of the ministry, and have been in some degree, prepared for their work, by giving "line upon line and precept upon precept," from Sabbath to Sabbath, to a class of immortal beings? In saying this much in favor of this institution, we would never lose sight of the fact that the ministry is a leading, and God's appointed instrumentality for the salvation of men, and is subordinate to no other means, and has ever been the most prominent and efficient in extending the conquests of the gospel. But as the membership of the church, male and female, young and old, have a work to do that ministers and angels cannot do for them, so in the Sabbath School, minds may be instructed, moral elevated, vice restrained, and souls saved that never could be reached by the ordinary ministrations of the pulpit.

6-Another benefit of Sabbath Schools is in the reading they give us. The publications of this institution, provides a rich fund of information for all classes, from the child of ten years up to the aged father of three score years and ten. The choicest specimens of history and biography, geography and travel, literature and science, are here condensed and set forth in attracting style. The leading events, scenes and characters in that land of wonders—the home of Patriarchs and Prophets, Apostles and Martyrs, and where the world's Savior lived and died—the progress of the gospel in the early ages—the gloom and superstition of the dark ages—the age of chivalry and Crusaders—the thrilling events of the Reformation—the moral revolutions that have gone forward in the world, with the achievements of missionary enterprise, and the choicest productions of giant intellects in literature and theology—may all be found in the Sabbath School library. In place of spending time in pouring over the bewildering and corrupting novels, or engaging in vain amusements or useless frivolous conversation, here is solid, useful and valuable knowledge that may be attained by all. A boy or a girl, a gentleman or a lady that has read such a library, may lay up a fund of knowledge that will enrich their minds in all future life.

Sabbath Schools aid in enforcing a due observance of the Sabbath. It has been said, and the statistics of crime go very far to prove it, that nine-tenths of the crimes committed in the country had their origin in the desecration of the Sabbath and drunkenness.

In imparting instructions in this institution from week to week, these sins are exposed in all their hideous deformity; they are taught to keep the day holy, to shun the haunts of vice and dissipation, and to practice whatever is pure, lovely and of good report. As the small threads form the cable that holds the vessel to its mooring, so these oft repeated lessons, enforced in kindness, prayer and earnestness by the teacher, may form a cord to draw the soul from temptation and iniquity, and anchor its hopes around the throne of God. Such influences leavening the minds of the rising generation, go further to retain and prevent vice and crime than all the statute books, dungeons and penitentiaries of the country. "Of all the students of Rover Raikes, numbering 3,000, but one was convicted of a flagrant crime, for the space of twenty years." "Of 1,232 convicts in one of our prisons, but three had been Sabbath School Scholars." And we might add statistics, in proof farther, from all parts of the land.

The establishment of a Sabbath School in each Church would tend to bring our membership together once each week, in place of once a month, and to get our churches back to the Apostolic plan of meeting on the "first day of the week," and to have regular pastors over each church, and to develop the gifts and graces of our membership. In place of desecrating the Lord's Day, by visits of pleasure, in indolence or drowsiness, in feasting, foolish talking and jesting, or in business calculations, while our children wander from home, go into wicked associations and practices. Here in the House of God, they are taught to worship God, to shun evil, and to practice whatever is pure and holy in daily life.

How can we longer neglect duties, so obvious and important? Would you snatch your child from the crumbling verge of the precipice, or the poisonous fangs of the serpent, or give the only medicine that could restore him to health and prolong life? The Gospel offers to them richer blessings. What is health, riches or the new fleeting days of life, compared to the eternal, the glorious inheritance offered us in the Gospel? Let our teaching, prayers and example all, so train our children, that they will walk in "the way they should go,"—that they may "seek first the kingdom of heaven."

IV-After this enumeration of blessings that flow from Sabbath Schools, it may seem strange that many try to excuse themselves from emerging in this good work. By some we are told that it is a good work, and they advise their children and friends go, but they do not enforce their precepts by their example. Another class tells us they do not enjoy such advantages in early life, and now excuse themselves. Such persons have more to learn and stronger reasons to improve the time hereafter. Others tell us, "I have too large a family—too much to attend to, and cannot leave home." Then have a school at home. You are as much obligated by the commands of God to give that son or daughter religious instruction, as food and raiment. "But," says another, "my children do not incline to go, and I cannot force them." Do you not govern your children? Has not the Lord made you ruler of your household? Have you urged your child as affectionately and earnestly, to the discharge of this duty, as you would where their interests or health was endangered? Because a sick child does not incline to take medicine, is it therefore to be left to its own inclinations?

But we are told by some one, "I do not altogether favor having my children cramped or biased by religious notions." One of the great designs of this institution is to enable the child to act freely, intelligently and wisely; to turn from evil and learn to do well.

V-In conclusion: if our leading and ruling traits of character are the result of early training; if the soul is immortal and has a bias to evil rather than good; if God's Word repeatedly enjoins the early and pious training of our children; if the instructions of this institution have been blessed in the early conversion of thousands, and extended their useful- ness in the Church and in the world; if they restrain our children from the desecration of the Sabbath, and from wicked habits and associa- tions; if they diffuse a healthy tone of morals in the community that supports law and order, restrains iniquity and crime, and sends out streams of salvation into the moral desert of increasing wickedness in the land; then, by all these considerations, we are called to aid in extending Sab- bath Schools through the land. A lost child in the dark forest, among ravenous beasts, excites the sympathy of a whole community. A multi- tude of the rising generation, scattered over our land are wandering, lost and constantly exposed to endless misery in the dreary wilderness of sin and wickedness. The cry of suffering and distress comes to us from all parts of the land. A famine, worse than the want of food, is spreading. We are urged by the worth of the soul; the shortness of time, the attrac- tion of the Cross and the glories of Heaven to spread our work.

Source: *Proceedings*, Baptist Sabbath School Convention, 28 October 1865, 11–18.

4.4 The *Texas Baptist*

One of the most effective ways to perpetuate the growth of the Baptist faith was by means of denominational newspapers. During the first years of the Texas Baptist life, however, Texas had no newspaper of its own. Rather, it relied on the denominational papers of Alabama and Mississippi, but pri- marily on the *Tennessee Baptist* edited by the father of Landmarkism, James Robinson Graves. Within its pages, one or two paragraphs were dedicated to the Texas Baptist situation. The effects of Graves's paper on Texas would prove to be significant, but the Texas Baptists desired a paper of their own. Thus, the *Texas Baptist* was created in 1855.

A. The First Year

Your board rejoices that a denominational paper has at last been commenced. "The Texas Baptist" was first issued in January last and has continued to visit the subscribers regularly every week since. Finding it impossible to publish at Independence, upon the plan adopted by the Convention, several voluntarily agreed to become responsible for the paper for one year. As a publisher could not be secured at Independence, and suitable arrangements could be effected at Anderson with a publisher there, it was determined to locate the paper at the latter place. It was placed under the editorial supervision of Elder G. W. Baines, assisted by Elder J. B. Stietler, who resigned the position of editor, assigned him by the Convention, as it would be impossible for him to edit a paper so far removed from the field of his labor.

The proper support of the paper is a matter of great interest. Although it has secured over 1,000 subscribers, yet it is not self-sustaining, because a large portion of the subscribers extends into the next year. Moreover, the support of Brother Baines has not yet been provided for. He has received nothing for his labors during the existence of the paper. The contract ceases with the present year, and we cannot expect Brother Baines will continue to work for nothing. Under these circumstances it becomes the duty of the Convention immediately to make such arrangements as shall secure the permanent and unembarrassed support of the paper. We would respectfully urge that the early attention of the Convention be given to this important subject.

Source: *Proceedings*, Baptist State Convention, 1855, cited in J. M. Carroll, *A History of Texas Baptists: Comprising a Detailed Account of Their Activities, Their Progress and Achievements* (Dallas: Baptist Standard Publishing Co., 1923), 280.

B. The Growth of the *Texas Baptist*

The Committee appointed to report on the *Texas Baptist* beg leave to offer the following as our report: At a meeting of this Association, four years ago, some seventeen brethren and friends, in the fear of God, laid the foundation for the starting of the *Texas Baptist*. On their individual pecuniary responsibility, and with a little loss to each of them, it succeeded, by hiring the publishing, until last January, when the enterprise found favor with many other benevolent brethren, who organized themselves into a joint stock company, under a charter, since obtained from the Legislature, and bought an office, and loaned it to the editor G. W. Baines, in which the paper is now published. This company is still increasing their stock, and hope, next winter, to be able to purchase a power-press. We recommend the enterprise cordially to our brethren. The course of the *Texas Baptist*, so far, meets our hearty approbation, and we recommend it as the organ of the Baptist brotherhood of Texas. As Baptist papers and Baptist literature are great conservative elements among us, we recommend the *Texas Baptist* to every Baptist in our State.

Source: *Proceedings*, Union Association, 1858, 7.

4.5 The Birth of New Associations

During this period there continued to be a great influx of Baptists into Texas. Due to this growing population new Associations were needed to aid in Baptist organization. Two of the most important were the Waco and San Marcos Associations.

A. The Organization of the San Marcos Association

Minutes of the Convention to form a new Association, held with the church at Elm Grove, Gonzalez county, November 12, 1858.

A sermon was preached by Wm. T. Wright, introductory to the exercises, from Isaiah 52:1, after which the meeting was called to order by the appointment of Bro. J. T. Powell, Moderator, and J. A. Kimball, Clerk. After prayer by Bro. Wright, the following churches represented themselves:

Seguin—Wm. Lucas, L. R. Cochrum, J. M. Fenner, J. W. Franks.

Lone Oak—E. Minter, J. M. Nations, J. O. Jackson.

Bastrop—J. A. Kimball, A. W. Moore, G. W. Waddle, H. G. Miller, L. Halbert.

Live Oak—S. S. Cobb, N. Burkett, R. A. Blackshear, T. J. Thornton.

Shiloh—A. Wright, W. T. Wright, H. B. King, T. C. Greenwood.

Elm Grove—B. Alsop, B. Frey, J. Mullins.

New Providence—J. T. Powell, B. Weeks.

On motion committees were appointed. On Divine Service: Brethren Hopkins, Mullins, Weeks, and Cobb. Constitution: Kimball, W. T. Wright, and Greenwood. Articles of Faith: A. Wright, Moore, and Cockrum. Rule of Decorum: Powell, Waddle, and Burkett.

Brother Isley, a minister visiting among us, was by motion invited to a seat with us. Adjourned to meet at 9:30 on Saturday.

Prayer by Brother Isley.

Source: *Proceedings*, San Marcos Association, 12 November 1858.

B. The Waco Association, Report on Colored Missions

The change in the relations of the Negro certainly does not lessen our duty to God in giving them moral and religious instructions. Heretofore the slave was dependent, and his master felt that there was a peculiar and special responsibility resting on him individually to cause him (slave) to be supplied with the Word of Life. Now, however, as the slave has been raised from the condition of dependant to that of responsibilities of a freedman, the interest of his late master ceases to be special and particular. . . . Heretofore the Negro had never thought for himself—the white man has done his thinking . . . God rules. . . . and we should be careful in our blind unbelief and impiety, not to err or scan his work in vain. He will interpret his own purposes and eventually turn all to his own glory.

Source: *Proceedings*, Waco Association, August, 1865.

4.6 New Conventions

Being in a large state, the Baptist State Convention often found it difficult to meet the needs of many churches in the remote areas of Texas. Since the heart of the BSC was located at Independence far in the southwest section of the state, Baptists of the North and East began to feel as if they were being neglected. The first group to assert their independence was the Baptist Convention of East Texas in 1855. They believed that the BSC was purposefully directing missionaries and funds away from their region. The group changed its name several times over the next decade before settling on the Baptist General Association. Many Baptist leaders such as R. C. Buckner and B. H. Carroll became advocates of the BGA. After only a few years the BGA and the BSC would become rivals on several different levels.

A. The Eastern Baptist Convention

This body is to meet at Bonham on Friday before the fourth Sabbath in June next. The time is near when all the churches within the bounds of this Convention should prepare for sending delegates, and money, if they intend to do what they can to aid in the benevolent works of this body. We know but little about the doings of the Executive Board which meets at Tyler, but we suppose they are doing the best they can with their limited means. We have been much pained to learn that they have been unable to secure the services of a general agent to collect funds, since the early resignation of Brother Clemmons.

We fear that the amount of money collected to pay the missionaries that have been laborers will be small and we would earnestly solicit the aid of every pastor and missionary in this work. If every minister will prayerfully examine this subject and consider that the destitute are suffering and starving because they have not the bread of life, and they lay the matter before each church to which he preaches, and request all to give according as the Lord has prospered them, we think that much can be done. Let each brother consider how much he has received of the Lord, and then inquire if he can make some return by helping to feed and clothe the missionary who travels to and fro over Texas to preach the Gospel to the poor. And let all who receive the labors of these missionaries, remember that it is their duty to feed that ox that plows the fields. They are the beneficiaries of missionary labor and they surely ought to contribute to the support of the laborers. Who would be so ungrateful as not to give something?

Source: *Texas Baptist*, 31 March 1859, 2.

B. The Baptist General Association

At the last meeting of this body, but few were present, and no money in the treasury to pay for printing the minutes; all our missionary efforts had been suspended; no agent had been in the field for several years past, and the great work of the churches had well nigh been lost sight of, and a cloud of deepest gloom rested on our prospects for the future. Yet, there were a few, like Nehemiah, who came up to survey the extent of Zion's desolations and commence the work of rebuilding her walls. With no money in the treasury; the country impoverished, and everything in an unsettled condition; and especially in view of the spiritual torpor which everywhere characterized our churches, it was not expected that we could do more than make a small beginning and prepare the way for more effectually carrying out the great commission. It was proposed to elect a general missionary agent, who should travel among the churches, endeavor to enlist a more general interest while he should look to voluntary contributions from churches and brethren for his support. This plan has worked well, and our faith has often received a new impulse and our heart often has been cheered by the signal manifestations of Divine Providence in bringing relief at the very threshold of extremity and want.

I have traveled extensively and preached; visited five associations and numerous churches, and have experienced some precious revivals. Owing to high water, together with an absence of nearly six weeks, to attend the Southern Baptist Convention at Memphis, Tennessee, some of the wealthiest churches have not been visited. The cry of "hard times" had met us everywhere, yet we have been cheered by acts of noble self-denial, and the amount in cash and pledges almost equals the amount of 1860. I have collected in cash, $804.38; in pledges, $1,263.42. With this encouraging success, I made arrangements last fall for the support of two missionaries—A. H. Jackson, to labor in the Northern, and J. B. Williams in the Southern portion of our bounds. In addition to this, I have begun making arrangements for the establishment of a book depository, with a view of inaugurating a general system of Sabbath Schools and Colportage for east Texas, and have already expended $240 for books. This enterprise meets with general favor and promises a greater amount of good than any other system.

The object of education is assuming an importance and presenting claims upon the attention of this body which suggests the great necessity of action. Our school is a failure, and in the present condition of the country, nothing can be done. Had we the means, it would take years to build such a school as needed. Your agent would, therefore, recommend the propriety of changing the name of this body to General Association of Texas, and inviting all Northern and Eastern Texas into its limits, with a view of concentrating our efforts in sustaining and fostering Waco University, and securing the co-operation of an extensive and fertile country in the work of evangelization.

Source: *Proceedings*, East Texas Convention, 1867, cited in J. M. Carroll, *A History of Texas Baptists: Comprising a Detailed Account of Their*

Activities, Their Progress and Achievements (Dallas: Baptist Standard Publishing Co., 1923), 467–68.

4.7 The Civil War

The Civil War had a devastating effect on the Baptist effort in Texas. Missionaries were recalled, Baylor University trained its remaining male students for military service, and few people attended the regular session of the Baptist State Convention or the Baptist General Association. It has been estimated that more than 90,000 young Texans joined the Confederacy and 15,000 were added to the Union. Prominent Baptists of the day, such as B. H. Carroll and J. B. Link, served the Confederacy as either chaplains or regular soldiers. Denominational work, however, never completely ceased. It appeared that the associations which were located further South, such as the Union Association, were at least able to continue to meet, even if the attendance was meager.

The Union Association—Confederate Advocates

We most fully endorse the course pursued by our own State in Secession, also the formation of the Confederate Government, and we accept and receive the constitution of the same and the laws and acts of congress generally, as a denomination as we have already done as individuals.

The unholy and unnatural war now waged by the United States against our liberty, and disputing our right of self-government, was wicked in its conception, and is disgraceful and barbarous in its character, and absolutely inimical to the principles of the United States Government in the days of its purity. And although their numbers may be legion, and they encompass us by land and by sea—take our cities and destroy our towns—ascend our rivers with their flotillas—confiscate our property and threaten us with the halter—slay many our brave soldiers on the battle field—prejudice foreign nations against us—issue the disgraceful edicts and orders against lovely and amiable women—yet none of these things move us, except to inspire us to a more unconquerable determination. Our trust is in God, and our motto still floats defiantly on the breeze speaking the language of 76 "Give us liberty or give us death." Our lion-hearted soldiers go to battle with justice in their cause and God in their hearts, and we will come off more than conqueror. If need be, we will burn our cotton, spread destruction before the enemy, spend the last dollar, shed the last drop of blood, but be subjugated, never! never! never!

All of which is respectfully submitted,

James W. Barnes,

Chairman

Source: *Proceedings*, Union Association, 1862, 8.

4.8 Baptists and Temperance

The abuse of alcohol was one of the greatest social problems Baptists faced on the frontiers of Texas. Z. N. Morrell stated that the people of Houston were more interested in "John-Barley Corn and Cigars" than preaching. Early Texas Baptists believed that drinking led to saloons, prostitution, and gambling. Due to the real and perceived realities of drinking, Baptists spoke out in favor of Temperance at every possible occasion.

A Letter to Editor Link

Brother Link:—What is being done for the cause of Temperance in Texas? It is a good cause and now that the war is over, I think renewed efforts should be made for its promotion. What do you think? Please give us your views editorially.

Tee-Totaller

We cannot tell what is being done for the promotion of the cause of temperance in Texas. We have seen nothing, heard of nothing and very likely very little or nothing is being done. If we had been asked what is being done for the promotion of intemperance, we could have given a fuller answer. For this purpose we see drinking saloons open almost on every street in our cities, whiskey shops at every village and on every highway we have passed in the country. We see church members with red noses and bloated faces, we have heard of others having distilleries. We have seen some carrying their bottles, we have heard of others keeping it to sell. We have heard of some preachers hunting back alleys and garrets to drink the cup of damning death, and not know when they had enough. We have heard of a bill favorably regarded by our legislature, perhaps passed, for the purpose of breaking down what barriers remain to restrain the land from drunkenness. We have heard of, and seen these various movements in behalf in intemperance. As to what we "think," it would take too much space and some of our readers would not like to have us tell it at all. But we think tee-totallers are rather scarce in the land; we think the tax on whiskey does not stop men from drinking it; we think some professing Christians give more money for whiskey to drink than they do to support the Gospel, both at home and abroad; we think that if some change is not wrought in the public mind on this subject, intemperance will before long, become a greater curse to the land than the late war has been. We think that it becomes every man who fears God, or has his country a good at heart, to set his face like steel, and his world as a polished shaft against the monstrous evil, this destroyer of old and young, rich and poor, male and female soul and body for time and eternity. But we forbear. We may mention some other thoughts at another time.

Source: *Texas Baptist Herald*, 12 September, 1866, 2.

CHAPTER 5

Divided We Stand,
1868–1886

5.1 Baylor University vs. Waco University

Texas Baptists have always wanted a proper education for their students on Texas soil. With the birth of Baylor University at Independence in 1845, Texas Baptists had a school that they could call their own. Due to frequent differences between Baylor President R. C. Burleson and Horace Clark, the principal of the Female Department, over institutional control, Baptist education braced itself for a major schism. The Board of Trustees apparently sided with Clark, and Burleson promptly resigned his presidency. William Carey Crane was named his successor. Burleson then accepted the presidency of the fledgling Waco University. Not only did Burleson leave Baylor, but he also brought the entire faculty and senior class with him to Waco. With this turn of events, Baylor University and Waco University were thrown into a perpetual rivalry. The situation became more acute when the Baptist General Association officially adopted Waco University in 1868. Baylor at Independence, however, remained loyal to the Baptist State Convention. These associational alliances placed even a greater strain on Texas Baptist denominational unity. These problems, however, find their origin in the Burleson-Clark imbroglio.

A. Burleson's Charges against Clark

First. Prof. Clark has grieved me personally. He publicly, on the night of the 17th instant, charged me with being the cause of dissensions and party strife in the church at Independence.

Second. He has grieved me by reviving a matter fully settled by the Board of Trustees.

Third. In reviving this matter, that was thought to be settled and buried forever, he has revived a letter casting upon me the imputation of insincerity and hypocrisy, and charging my family and friends with crimes that make "one sick at heart."

Fourth. He has treated my wife and myself with disrespect, in not allowing the daughters of my friends and brethren to meet a few select friends at my house.

Fifth. I am grieved with him for using language in a speech before the young ladies, during the school hours, calculated to prejudice their minds against me, which he should either prove, or withdraw as publicly as made.

Sixth. He has grieved me as a member of the Faculty in violating the solemn promise we made to the Board of Trustees not to interfere with the management of the respective departments committed to our care. He has thus interfered in vindicating and endorsing the course of Judge Wheeler in his resignation as head of the law department of Baylor University, and opening a law school in Brenham.

Respectfully submitted,

Rufus C. Burleson

Source: Burleson to the Baylor Board of Trustees, 29 June 1860, cited in Mrs. Georgia Burleson, *The Life and Writings of Rufus C. Burleson* (Waco: By the author, 1901), 216–17.

B. Clark's Charges against Burleson

First. I feel grieved with Brother Burleson for compelling me to arise in a religious assembly to reply to what I, and others, conceived to be a personal attack upon me.

Second. I feel grieved with him in permitting a disrespectful demonstration toward me on the part of students of the male department.

Third. I feel aggrieved with him for permitting to be circulated certain letters written to him personally many years ago for the purpose of inviting a reconciliation, and which was used not in accordance with its spirit and tenor, but in such a way as to place me in the attitude of an aggressor.

Fourth. I feel aggrieved with him for publicly making disparaging remarks against the female department.

Fifth. I feel aggrieved with him for not being willing to submit our differences to the arbitration of mutual friends.

Sixth. I feel aggrieved with him for not manifesting a willingness to settle them upon a basis which I conceive to be mutually honorable.

Respectfully submitted,

Horace Clark

Source: Clark to the Baylor Board of Trustees, 29 June 1860, cited in Mrs. Georgia Burleson, *The Life and Writings of Rufus C. Burleson* (Waco: By the author, 1901), 215–16.

5.2. Waco University Begins to Thrive—Baylor Declines

Due to the central location of Waco, the powerful presence of R. C. Burleson and B. H. Carroll, and the fact that the new railroad would have a large station in Waco, Waco University held several advantages over Baylor University at Independence. As early as 1863, Baylor University began to decline in both numbers and financial resources. Waco University, however, was beginning to prosper and garner a large northeastern Baptist constituency.

A. Aid Needed for Baylor University

While we regret that our Denominational Schools are not at all prospering as we could wish, owing in a great degree to our national difficulties, yet there is much to cheer us and inspire confidence in their future success. The Female Department of Baylor University retains its usual patronage, while the Male Department, from various adverse circumstances, has fallen far below its former high position. Brethren why is this? We are gratified to learn that the services of Professor B. S. Fitzgerald have been secured to the faculty. Waco University has closed its second annual term under auspices the most flattering, and gives abundant assurance of future usefulness. The College at Tyler, Smith county, was doing well, when last heard from them, in both departments.

In conclusion, your Committee recommends the respective claims of our Denominational Schools to the brethren, and urges them not to neglect the duty of their children.

Source: *Proceedings*, Union Association, 1863, 4.

B. A Further Plea for Funds

Subscribers to endowment funds are desired to bear in mind that the small sums which they owe on interest are needed to sustain the Institution. Delegates to the Union Association to meet at Brenham, Friday before 3d Lord's day in August and to the State Convention to meet at Independence, Saturday before the first Lord's day in October, will no doubt take pleasure in bringing up the amounts. The Trustees of Richmond College, the Southern Baptist Theological Seminary, Greenville, S. C., and Mercer University, Ga., regard that portion of their endowment funds which is in private hands as gold to their Institutions. Texas donors to endowment funds are better able to pay their interest than their unfortunate brethren of the cis,—portion of the South, and I am assured that they feel no less disposition to uphold Baylor University.

Source: *Texas Baptist Herald*, 15 August 1866, 3.

C. Waco University Thrives

The present condition and future of Waco University are such as to inspire the most sanguine hopes and expectations of its future usefulness and importance. The successful operation of the Female Department inaugurated last year, has full met the expectations of the Board, and satisfied the desires of its friends and patrons.

There were matriculated in the Male Department last session, 95; and in the Female Department 35 in number—total 130. It is confidently anticipated that this number will be largely increased for the session of 1866–67.

Important additions have been made to the corps of teachers, and it is determined that the Faculty shall be equal to all the duties and responsibilities of a first-class institution of learning. The curriculum of study is thorough. In the male Department it is equal to any college in the South, and in the Female Department the standing of education is higher and more thorough than any female college in the South, the Mary-Sharp college of Winchester only excepted.

The Theological Department is in successful operation and young men preparing for the ministry, superior advantages are offered for lectures and instruction in Theology.

It is in contemplation also to organize a Law Department, and the arrangements for this purpose are now in the process of completion.

Source: *Texas Baptist Herald*, 24 October 1866, 2.

5.3 The Buckner Orphanage

As early as 1877 R. C. Buckner began to propose the idea of an orphanage for the children of Texas. Buckner petitioned the Baptist General Association, the local churches, and associations for their aid in the realization of this endeavor. In 1879, the Buckner Orphanage was founded in Dallas. No matter how vitriolic affairs would soon become in Texas Baptist life, every Baptist in Texas loved and supported the orphanage. Though it encountered fiscal difficulty in its earliest days, the orphanage has survived and has been renamed Buckner Baptist Benevolences. In the twentieth century it began to branch out and handle myriads of other Texas social concerns.

A. Buckner's First Appeal

We would be glad for Texas Deacons to have a grand meeting, exclusively of their own, and confer together as to the best means of providing homes, comfort and education for the hundreds of orphans in our State. Since we have been for months referring to our obligations to this class some of our deacons have been sending us some valuable suggestions, as evidence of their increasing interest on the subject.

Source: *Texas Baptist*, 11 January 1877.

B. Buckner and the Survivors of the Galveston Hurricane

In September of 1900, the entire island of Galveston was destroyed by a hurricane. More than five thousand people were killed and dozens of children were orphaned. Buckner heard of the devastation at Galveston while he was in Oklahoma. He immediately returned to Dallas and gathered as many wagons as possible and made the journey to Galveston. He gathered more than one hundred orphans and other displaced children who could not locate their parents and brought them to the Buckner Orphanage in Dallas. Though the orphanage was crowded at this time,

Buckner found room for all of the orphans of the Galveston hurricane. The following letter was written by one of the Galveston orphans who found care and love with "Father Buckner." Dozens of similar heart-warming stories may be found in the archives at Buckner Baptist Benevolences.

C. A Letter to Father Buckner

My Dear Father Buckner:

I thought I would write you a few lines. I hope you and everybody in the "Home" are well. I arrived in Cleburne at nine o'clock and had to wait one hour and twenty minutes, and then reached Galveston at ten o'clock that night. Papa met us at the depot. My papa looks just the same as he did before the storm but Adele has changed a great deal. I didn't know her at first. I like our little home very much. It is the very first house I think he bought, which I saw before the storm.

My friends were very glad to see me for they thought I was drowned. Father Buckner, you don't know how much I miss your dear sweet face at the dinner table. You don't know how much I appreciate the kindness you have shown me.

We can see the gulf from our house. It has been very still today. It is very warm here. They have built Galveston back very fast in a year, for it didn't look like a storm ever touched Galveston. I dearly love you and Aunt Vie. Give my love and a hundred kisses to Lula Mae and yourselves.

I will close now, hoping to hear from you soon.

Your Orphan Daughter,

Mary Talkowski

Source: Mary Talkowski to R. C. Buckner, 20 November 1901, Archives, Buckner Baptist Benevolences.

5.4 The Schism at the First Baptist Church of Dallas

On May 5, 1878, J. B. Link, editor of the *Texas Baptist Herald*, advocate of Baylor University at Independence, and promoter of the Baptist State Convention, joined the First Baptist Church of Dallas during a sparsely attended Wednesday night prayer meeting. R. C. Buckner, rival editor of the *Texas Baptist* and advocate of Waco University and the Baptist General Association, immediately appealed his membership. Though not present at the meeting, Buckner was carrying out a newspaper war with Link and everyone knew of their reciprocal animosity. Buckner and a small faction of the congregation demanded that Link's name be removed from the membership, but they found no satisfaction. Outraged by this state of events, Buckner delivered an infamous speech to the First Baptist Church on Christmas Eve 1879 entitled the *Memorial*. Soon after this speech, the dissatisfied members left the First Church and created the Live Oak Baptist Church, and they claimed to be the authentic First Baptist Church of Dallas. In a dramatic encounter at a called-session of the BGA in 1880, the Association found that R. C. Buckner's faction was the true First Baptist Church of Dallas. Though the church reconciled in 1884, the wounds never properly healed and in turn perpetuated problems that eventually led to a denominational schism.

A. The Schism, Link's Opinion

About the last of February, 1878, Elder J. B. Link went from Houston to North Texas to assist Dr. F. M. Law, the Financial Secretary, in work for the Central Baptist Educational Commission. About the same time, a sort of proclamation was sent out from Waco protesting against his locating in the bounds of the General Association. About the first of April he took his family to Dallas and had expected to reach the city and unite with the church on Sunday morning, but was detained in Bryan over Sunday and did not reach Dallas till Monday. Before another opportunity came, he heard that a member of the church would object to his uniting with the church. He let the matter drop for the time being and sought an interview with the proposing objector, and some correspondence passed that seemed to end all hope of any reconciliation. A member in Houston had tried to prevent his getting a letter there, supposed to have received his inspiration from Waco. This having failed, it was supposed that the effort was made at Dallas to prevent his uniting there, to have it said over the country that he could not get church membership in Dallas. With this view of the situation, the pastor, leading the brethren and others thought it was best that he should unite with the church and let the objection come. He believed that there was nothing in the objection that would stand an investigation and that an investigation could only result in showing this and in bringing harmony and peace. So on the evening of June 5th, 1878, at the regular prayer-meeting and at a time set for some important business also, his letter was handed in. His business was mostly away from the city and he soon left. An interesting protracted meeting then followed in which quite a number had been received by letter and baptism, a sort of first fruit of Elder Curry's pastorate. But on the night of July 10th, after the delegates had been appointed to the General Association at Fort Worth, a petition for rescinding the act of the church receiving Elder Link was handed in, signed by twenty names, on the ground "that at least one of our number, in good standing, Elder R. C. Buckner, had serious complaints against him, involving fellowship, and a correspondence was at the time pending between them looking to a settlement," and a motion was made to rescind the act by a vote of 43 to 22. This matter was then dropped, so far as the church was concerned, the holding that the proper thing was to have preferred charges against the offender, if there were any to prefer.

. . . Nov. 19th, 1879, Bro. W. N. Griffeth offered a preamble and resolution stating that proper Christian feelings were not entertained between Brethren J. B. Link and R. C. Buckner, and that brethren laboring privately, had failed to affect a reconciliation, and as the breach was growing wider, it was resolved that the church appoint her deacons and six brethren, three of these to be appointed by each of the brethren respectively, and the six to select a seventh, to, if possible settle the difficulty, but if they failed, that they report their labors with all the evidence taken, to the church not to be bound to decide by the evidence taken by the committee but the evidence reheard by the church itself. It was moved by Bro. Thacker to amend so that the contemplated investigation be had before the whole church. The amendment, after some discussion, was lost. The original preamble and resolution was carried and the committee required to report at some regular meeting of the church. Bro. Griffeth was appointed to notify Brethren Link and Buckner of the action of the church and get the names of the committee they might name. Dec. 24th, the church met in regular conference and after some letters had been granted, Bro. Griffeth reported that he had discharged his duty as soon as practicable, that Bro. Link had furnished the names of his part of the committee, but Bro. Buckner had failed and refused to select his part, and the committee had never been organized. On motion, Bro. Buckner was allowed to state his reasons for declining to select his part of the committee. This, he proceeded to do, and read a paper entitled, "A Memorial Addressed to the First Baptist Church of Dallas, Texas," said to be signed "by 59 members," but 61 names are appended to it. The memorial is quite lengthy, recounts the grievances experienced by Bro. Buckner and its signers and the supposed errors of the church, and at the close protests and claims that "We and all who coincide with us, must and do hold them [the dominant party] in disfellowship as a church of Christ, and maintained that we only are entitled to the name 'First Baptist church at Dallas, Texas,' making our appeal to the world and the brethren at large." . . . Any reconciliation was found impracticable, so in a very full meeting, January 7th, 1880, the church unanimously and sorrowfully withdrew fellowship from those who had declared disfellowship from the church. This step was hastened by the street talk and many misrepresentations that were set afloat.

Source: J. B. Link, *Historical and Biographical Magazine*, 2 vols. (Austin: n. p., 1892), 2: 753–55.

B. Buckner's Side, The *Memorial*

Prompted by love to this church in particular and to Baptist principles generally, we are painfully constrained to take the solemn step indicated in this Memorial—certain events developed in the last eighteen months of our own church history make our duty plain, and in our judgement, imperatively demand this course of action.

We desire, however, most respectfully, affectionately, and sincerely to make one more official appeal to you to pause and reflect upon your course in matters that have filled many hearts with sadness, disturbed the peace of the Church, and resulted in general cause of Christ [*sic*].

We desire first to recite certain generally received Baptist principles, that from time have been cherished by her people. The Scriptures clearly compare the Church in its unity with a body and its numbers. They also declare that two cannot walk together unless they be agreed. They further show that a house divided against itself cannot stand. And moreover, God's promises to bless his people are conditional upon their love and fellowship for each other. The prosperity, usefulness, and the very existence of a church are made dependent upon its unity.

For these reasons Baptist Churches have always required unanimity in the reception of members, regarding it as suicidal to a church and treasonable behavior, knowingly to take a case of discipline into its own bosom from without.

Now, we desire to show, that in the reception of Elder J. B. Link, on Wednesday night June 5th 1878, and in subsequent events related thereto, these great principles of our common faith have been systematically violated.

It is a fact well and generally known that prior to Elder Link's application for membership in Dallas, certain members of his church did not fellowship with him because of certain allegations published in the *Baptist Herald*, and because of his private statements made by him in conversation with brethren evidently designed to injure R. C. Buckner in business, and gravely reflecting on his veracity and candor, and his sincerity as a Christian. It was known that this disfellowship was not at all confined to R. C. Buckner, and that other brethren had avowed their purpose to vote against his reception, if he should apply for membership.

Now, we claim that Elder Link himself, the pastor of the church, and the deacon who made the motion for his reception, were each and all fully apprized and notified of the opposition to Elder Link's reception and the grounds of it. It is a well known fact, that the night Elder J. B. Link was received into the Church was not a Conference Meeting but a prayer meeting. It is in evidence, that on an occasion appropriate for reception of members, Elder Link and the objectors both being present, to the surprise of the objectors no opportunity for uniting with the church was given.

It is in evidence, that the assistant pastor did on the day following Elder Link's reception say as follows:—"I expected him to join last night because it was a bad night and I did not think Brother Buckner to be there."

It is in evidence that, late in the evening (afternoon) of the day on which Elder Link was received at night, the pastor was notified by still another objector, that on account of serious illness in his family (his wife being there on her deathbed), he could not be out that night, and the objector, with special reference to this case, further urged the pastor not to give a opportunity for reception of members on any occasion, unless a respectable number of members were present.

This in evidence, that an unfinished correspondence, looking to the adjustment of these difficulties before application should be made for membership, was then pending. This was known to the pastor, to inspect before its delivery to Elder Link, and not having time that evening, the pastor left an appointment for a consultation letter the next day, but failed to fulfill it.

This is also in evidence, that yet another objector, absent on the night of J. B. Link's reception, states that he heard him say that he didn't think he could remain in Dallas that week beyond Monday night, upon which statement said objector supposed him out of the city on the night of his reception.

Now, let it be added to all this, that on the Tuesday night preceding the reception there was such a rainfall as according to the *Dallas Daily Herald*, had not been witnessed in twenty years, and that, on the very Wednesday in question the same paper further says; "Long after day-break, and after the rain ceased the waters continued to rush with un-abated fury through the Main Sewers, in many places carrying away the crossings and doing other damage. Other objects were also swept away by the torrent that passed through them." Now, it was all night of this day and on into night itself, when darkness, mud and rain prevailed, that Elder Link's reception occurred. Only eleven members were present. Only eight of the eleven voted on his reception.

From a consideration of all these points and others not necessary to mention, we have been irresistibly driven to the mortifying conviction, that this application was not only not made on appropriate occasions because the objectors were not present, but was purposefully deferred to such a time and under such circumstances as that the objectors could be evaded and the brethren objecting robbed of their unalienable right to vote on the reception of applicants for membership, and to state their objections, if any.

When this reception was known, the objectors determined to make a solemn appeal to the Church in regular conference in the interest of justice and principle. At the time of the very next conference after the reception, they were prepared to make an appeal, but a sermon was delivered, and afterwards all suggestions of the pastor as to the lateness of the hour, upon the motion of the Conference adjourned immediately to the next regular meeting. The motion, however, was discussed, but carried over objections then named and urged to the effect, that any important business demanded immediate attention.

At the first Conference actually held after the reception of Elder Link, a motion was made to rescind the act of his reception on such grounds as have just been recited, but a majority vote ratified the action of the eight members, whereupon twenty members of the church, all adults and heads of families, entered their solemn protest against the illegality of the proceedings, and had their names entered on the *Minutes* as thus protesting. At the same time the privilege was denied to Elder R. C. Buckner the right to state the grounds of his objection and to defend himself against statements made by brethren at this time, damaging to himself although the Moderator had ruled in his favor. But candor demands the statements that Brother W. H. Prather was not prevented from making the plain declaration that he objected passionately to J. B. Link's reception on account of which he had long since said to him and of developments following thereafter.

But the matter has not stopped here. The minority were not only thus, deprived of their unalienable privileges as Baptists, but have been the subjects of censure from the pulpit, the pastor on occasion saying that he was pastor of only a part of the Church, and that fact was a thorn in his side. For many long months the minority as it then was, have suffered on, until finally it appears they are now denied even the poor privilege of patient suffering.

At the last conference and in the absence of R. C. Buckner a motion was made to refer the adjustment of difficulties between him personally and J. B. Link to a committee consisting of the deacons of the Church and seven others, three each to be chosen by these two brethren and another chosen by the six. This Committee was empowered to take evidence and report to the Church, and therefore made the judge of such evidence as they would submit. A motion to provide for an investigation before the Church instead of one before a Committee, was lost. It was also objected, that all resident deacons but one were strong and zealous partisans of J. B. Link and committed in this same manner against R. C.

Buckner; but this objection was also overruled by the dominant party, two of the deacons by motion and argument, urging the appointment of themselves and their brother deacons.

One of our brethren was thus not only denied the right of having his case investigated before the Church, but was ordered to submit, involving his character as a man, a Christian and a minister, to the decision of a tribunal not only unscriptural itself and to which it was known he would not submit, but with all stacked against him, presenting the possibility of impartial proceedings.

One object of this Memorial is to hereby notify the church that, in all this matter we the undersigned, each and all make common cause, that we do not regard it as a case of personal grievance between the two brethren simply, but as involving fundamental principles of Bible law. The unanimity of the Church on the reception of members, the privileges of members; the impropriety of referring matters to Committees that should if at all be investigated before the Church; the impropriety of trying cases where offenses were committed and known before Church Convention, and some other things are all involved. And we do hereby notify the Church that we all, whose names are hereunto appended, hold Elder J. B. Link in disfellowship, not being willing to regard him as a lawful member of this body, and that we respectfully, but emphatically deny the rights to the dominant party in the Church to try anyone or all of us for disfellowshipping him.

And we do now memorialize the members of this church that we hold as anti-Baptistic and unscriptural all the proceedings held in this case beginning with and including reception of Elder J. B. Link, and so we will maintain and that it is sufficient purpose to claim our rights, one or all of them, before this body, the denomination and the world that we will make appeal to the candid judgement of mankind on the simple facts in the case: And we know that some, and believe that many others; whose names are not appended to this paper, entertained the same views which we do.

And finally, in kindness, sadness and love, we hereby as announced to the hereto therefore dominant party, that on account of their persistence, maintaining the principles and sustaining the proceedings, against which we have here entered, solemnly protest, we must and do hold them in disfellowship as a Church of Christ, and maintain, that we only are entitled to the name "First Baptist Church of Dallas, Texas," making our appeal to the world and brethren at large.

And now, dear brethren and sisters, we do kindly and affectionately invite all, who believe as we do to unite with us and thus aid in maintaining the right. And may God help the right.

Source: *Minutes*, First Baptist Church of Dallas, 24 December 1879.

B. Who is the True First Baptist Church of Dallas?

Dear Brethren:—Your committee to whom was referred the application of certain brethren to wit:

Elder R. C. Buckner, W. H. Thacker, and A. F. Beddo, claiming to be the regularly elected messengers of this body, from the First Baptist church of Dallas, having had the matter under careful consideration, do universally concur in the following report:

1. We regard it as of the last importance to emphasize this statement that we can consider the delicate questions involved in this matter *only so far as they relate to membership, or office in this body.*

2. It is a violation of organic law of a church of Jesus Christ, to knowingly take a case of discipline into the church.

3. Every Baptist has the inalienable right to express his objection to any application of membership before his church in conference assembled. When these objections are thus stated the church must judge of their validity and if the church decide that these are invalid, the objector must withdraw them or subject them to himself to the discipline of the church; which case must be disposed of before the application can first be acted on.

4. No member can be put on trial by his church for alleged offenses committed while he was under the jurisdiction of another church. From which follows, on a principle of fairness, that, when a brother's objections to an applicant, are known and disregarded and he has been deprived of the right of stating the objections; at time of application, he cannot be put on trial for his disfellowship to the applicant inasmuch as he has no legal redress, either before or after such reception.

5. It is an anomaly unknown to Bible law and Baptist usage for one

to be and remain a member of a church, when protests against his reception, or membership afterward, are recorded on the church book.

6. Principles, not majorities constitute a church. Therefore, where there are two or more claimants to the name and rights of a church, that party, whether large or small, which stands upon the principles and laws of its organization, is the church. And, therefore, majorities are right and are to be recognized as right only so far as they follow Christ.

7. Where correspondence is had or overtures looking to adjustment of any difficulty between one proposing to apply for membership and one already a member, no individual or individuals, are legal judges as to whether sufficient endeavors have been made for reconciliation, the church alone being the competent judge on this point.

8. A called conference of a church, when one is really had, or an adjourned conference for a specified object can transact only such business as relates to that specific object.

These principles and others equally important, have been applied to the evidence furnished by both parties in their published authoritative statements, and to the church covenant binding the parties, and to their official records on the clerk's book.

Guided by these principles, thus applied to all the evidence as thus set forth, we do unanimously recommend that the applicants for admissions in this body, to wit: Elder R. C. Buckner, W. H. Thacker, and A. F. Beddo, be recognized as lawful members of this body.

Source: *Minutes*, Called Session of the Baptist General Association, 24 February 1880, 13–14.

5.5 Consolidation

Despite the most fervent desires of many Baptists in South Texas, Baylor University at Independence was too weak to survive without consolidation with Waco University. In addition, the membership of the Baptist State Convention had also dwindled while the Baptist General Association's membership continued to grow by leaps and bounds. The only way that Baptists in South Texas could receive adequate ministerial aid was to consolidate with their powerful neighbor to the north.

A. Consolidation of Baylor University and Waco University

The joint-sub-committee of ten, appointed by the respective committees from the State Convention and General Association unanimously recommend the following as a basis for consolidation of our Baptist school interests in Texas:

1. That Waco and Baylor Universities shall be consolidated.

2. The name of the school shall be Baylor University.

3. That Baylor University be located at Waco, and we further agree that the female department be continued there as it now exists.

Provided, that Waco gives as a bonus: (1) The old buildings and grounds of Waco University; (2) the $60,000 already secured for an endowment; (3) Forty-five acres of ground suitable for a new site for the University. Provided, further, that at the expiration of ten years the continuance of the system of co-education at Waco be determined by a majority of the consolidated general body, to which the institution, with its funds and property, shall belong.

4. That, as very many Baptists oppose co-education, Baylor Female College be located at some other central point, the place where located to give as a bonus at least suitable grounds and buildings. And that Baylor Female College, thus located, be also the property of the consolidated general body.

5. That the endowment of present Baylor University go to Waco with the new Baylor University, according to the terms agreed upon by the State Convention, and published in the minutes.

6. That the act of locating Baylor Female College be referred to the following persons: F. M. Law, A. W. Dunn, H. W. Waters, C. R. Breedlove, G. W. Capps, J. B. Link, R. J. Sledge, R. Andrews, O. H. P. Garrett, M. V. Smith, Harry Haynes, G. W. Breedlove, Hosea Garrett, A. W. Melver, Wm. Howard, J. H. Stribling, S. A. Beauchamp, W. R. Maxwell, C. C. Garrett, and S. F. Styles.

The following resolution, offered by W. B. Denson was adopted:

Resolved, that the alumnae and alumni of both Baylor and Waco Universities be made and reported in the catalogue of the new consolidated University, as the alumnae and alumni of the new consolidated University.

Source: *Proceedings*, Temple Unification Meeting, 9 December 1885.

B. Consolidation of the General Bodies

We the committee, believing the consolidation of general bodies is desirable, recommend:

1. That the Baptist General Association of Texas be consolidated with the Baptist State Convention of Texas.

2. That the name of the consolidated body shall be "The Baptist General Convention of Texas."

3. That the basis of representation in the first meeting of the consolidated body shall be the same as heretofore. Those coming from the State Convention territory enter the consolidated body on the same terms as they formerly entered the State Convention, and those from the General Association have membership upon the same terms on which they formerly entered that body.

4. That the mission work be continued till the first meeting as heretofore under the direction of the two general bodies respectively, and be reported to that meeting.

5. That the first meeting of the consolidated body be held at Waco, beginning on Tuesday after the first Sunday in July, 1886.

Source: *Proceedings*, Temple Unification Meeting, 9 December 1885.

CHAPTER 6

The Search for Unity, 1886–1900

6.1 Learning to Work Together

Despite the fact that the Baptist State Convention and the Baptist General Association had consolidated on all fronts, hard feelings still existed between the main leaders within each former group. It appeared as if the powerful BGA had all but swallowed the weaker BSC. The BGA had achieved victories in several key areas. First, the unified Baptist University was to be located at Waco. Second, Rufus Burleson, the President of Waco University, had been elected "President for life" of the new University. Third, the state offices of the BGCT were to be located in Waco. Fourth, the first regular session of the BGCT was to be held in Waco. Thus, a large constituency of former BGA members was sure to be in attendance placing their own members in key positions and enforcing their own policies. Nevertheless, the former BGA members were not completely satisfied with their overwhelming victory. They may have believed that they did not need their brethren to the South for survival nor success. In spite of these animosities, Baptist work in Texas took a significant step forward with the birth of the BGCT. The pivotal position in the new BGCT was the Corresponding Secretary of Missions. The person who held this job was to disperse missionaries and funds, and to see that all areas of the state, both former BGA and BSC territories, were treated fairly.

A. Early Progress under Corresponding Secretary of Missions, A. J. Holt (1886–1889)

Secretary Holt with untiring effort was pushing the cause of state missions into the waste places of the state. It became necessary to place the work on the frontier under the leadership of S. A. Beauchamp as a local superintendent. Forty mission stations were supplied by four men in this growing region. They were unable to meet the demand in a region so vast, but the utmost possible was being done. The most difficult class among the foreigners to be reached were the Germans. Four most efficient German missionaries were appointed to labor among that people— Revs. Kiefer, Gleiss, Becker, and Shafer. While on a visit to San Antonio in June, 1888, for the medical treatment of one of his children, Dr. W. D. Powell, the missionary to Mexico, labored for some weeks among the Mexicans of that city, which resulted in the salvation of some. Among others who were baptized was Manuel Trevino, who had been serving in the capacity of a Presbyterian preacher in that city. He became a missionary under the State Board and did effective work in conjunction with Miss Mina Everett, a returned missionary from Brazil. Among the Negroes excellent results were flowing from the work of Rev. A. R. Griggs, who was laboring under the direction of the State Board. Including all workers, there were as many as one hundred and thirty missionaries in 1888 laboring throughout the state. The strongholds of population were seized by Secretary Holt and manned by efficient missionaries. Among these were Austin, Dallas, Bastrop, Texarkana, Laredo, Corpus Christi, Wichita Falls, Brenham, and Henrietta.

Source: B. F. Riley, *History of the Baptists of Texas* (Dallas: By the author, 1907), 314–15.

B. Corresponding Secretary J. B. Cranfill (1889–1892)

A. J. Holt was Corresponding Secretary at the 1889 regular session of the BGCT. Holt, however, declined after being elected and J. B. Cranfill was selected as his successor. Cranfill had been a successful financial agent for Baylor University and his choice seemed logical. Cranfill's tenure, however, ended with controversy. He had misplaced the last six months of the agency's financial records. When found in 1896 and presented the Convention, records indicate that $2500 was missing. During this same period, Cranfill's newspaper, the *Texas Baptist Standard* was destroyed by fire. Despite a small insurance settlement and Cranfill's apparent lack of funds, the *Baptist Standard* somehow found the funds needed to remain in publication. Though never formally accused of embezzlement by the Convention,

Cranfill's "carelessness" provided an avenue for his publishing rival, S. A. Hayden, to attack his character. The following is the account provided by J. B. Cranfill concerning the misplacement of the financial records.

The Baptist General Convention of 1886 met at Houston. Preceding the Convention, S. A. Hayden and his paper were perhaps at their very worst. The gravest charges were made in his publication from week to week against the workers in general, and particularly against me as former corresponding secretary. It was a regular socialistic campaign, conducted upon the lowest plane to which a publication can possibly descend. The *Texas Baptist and Herald* demanded an itemized statement of all my accounts. Hayden evidently was unaware of the fact that it was easy to make this statement. Notwithstanding the fact that he had been apprized that the reports that had been lost were simply the reports of missionaries, he disregarded these statements, and clamored loud and long for an itemized statement of all of the work under my administration.

Meantime, a remarkable thing had occurred. At the Convention of 1892, John T. Battle, Treasurer of the Convention, raised my books in his hands and said what has already been quoted from him. When he went home to Waco, the books were still in his custody. They were never again into my possession. By a strange fortuity, he lade these books away at his home in Waco and forgot where he put them. This added fuel to Hayden's flame of criticism and distraction. He did not really know at that time that these books were in existence. The rest of us knew it, but we did not know where they were. Brother Battle was greatly disturbed concerning the books and resorted to much prayer. After praying most earnestly upon one occasion about this matter, it suddenly dawned upon him where he had placed these records. He went right to the receptacle in which he had laid them nearly four years before, and found them. There was great joy in the camps of Israel when this discovery became known. We felt that the cause was most happily conserved by this incident, which came, as we believed then, and I believe now, as a direct answer to prayer.

At the next meeting of the State Mission Board, I requested that these books all be re-audited. This was pleasing to all the members of the Board. The Board also made a report covering the distractions which the *Texas Baptist and Herald* had aroused throughout the State. The report was one of the strongest ever promulgated by the State Mission Board of Texas. It was the work of B. H. Carroll, as all who were familiar with the fact then knew.

Source: J. B. Cranfill, *Dr. J. B. Cranfill's Chronicle: A Story of My Life* (New York: Fleming H. Revell Company, 1916), 444–45.

C. Corresponding Secretary J. M. Carroll (1892–1894)

With the resignation of J. B. Cranfill in 1892, the office of Corresponding Secretary was reorganized. The offices of State Missions, Foreign Missions, Minister's Relief, and statistician that had previously been occupied by four different men, were now consolidated into the office of Corresponding Secretary. J. M. Carroll was the first man to inherit this new mantle of responsibility. Along with the four additional offices came a raise of $400. Though missionary enterprises made strides during Carroll's tenure, he could not escape the castigation of S. A. Hayden who believed that Carroll's salary was too large. He believed that Carroll should take only what he needed to survive. Carroll's friends, in particular J. B. Cranfill, the former castigated Corresponding Secretary and editor of the *Baptist Standard*, frequently defended Carroll, his work, and his increased salary. Despite Hayden's attacks, Carroll remained in office and became a renowned historian, statistician, and author of the infamous Landmark masterpiece, *The Trail of Blood*.

Cranfill Praises Carroll's Work

The *Standard* publishes this week an account of the mission board meeting held on June 26, in this city. At the request of the board, the reports submitted by the special committees and adopted in open session of the board are given to the public. They speak for themselves, and as to their subject matter, we make no comment. The *Standard*, while it is not the organ officially or otherwise, of the mission board, is a servant of the board whenever the board sees fit to call upon it. If we have any mission as a Baptist editor, it is to faithfully serve the interests of the cause of Christ and to stand loyally to our banner-bearers as they go forth into the whitened harvest fields for his glory. We believe that J. M. Carroll is a man as honest, as pure, as spotless and as consecrated in heart and life as any man we have ever known. We believed that the mission board as a whole is made up of earnest, true-hearted, loyal men of God, and shall stand by the board in its efforts to evangelize Texas and to raise the banner of the cross in the destitute fields. Moreover, it is our earnest wish and prayer that the action of the board will put an end to such allegations against our secretary and his work. We shall faithfully and unflinchingly stand by Bro. Carroll and our mission board. May our heavenly father over-rule everything to his glory to the end that there may be among us true and genuine brotherly love and Christian devotion to the great cause of missions.

Source: *Baptist Standard*, 5 July 1894.

D. Baylor University at Independence, 1883–1885

> As a graduate of Baylor University at Independence, Carroll took great pains in detailing the final years of the Institution. The following passage depicts his love for Baylor, his ability in statistics, and his adeptness at historical interpretation.

The board of trustees reported for 1883 that the work on the main building had advanced far enough for the chapel to be used, but that it would require at least $5,000 more to complete the building. The large class rooms were not in condition to be used, and the whole building was yet unplastered. Of the 120 students enrolled, ten were ministerial students, and almost that many others were yet expected. The commencement sermon was preached this year by J. M. Carroll; the missionary sermon by W. D. Powell. The A. M. degree was conferred upon L. R. Bryan and J. M. Carroll—two of the class of 1877. Baylor property at that time was valued at $60,000. Now the same property would be valued at $150,000.

The year closing June, 1884, was also comparatively prosperous. The agent for the endowment, G. B. Davis—a great layman—reported having secured during the year $41,750 in additional endowment notes. There were 103 students, with thirteen of them studying for the ministry.

The year 1885 was probably the saddest of all the forty years of Baylor University's history at Independence. On February 27, 1885, just three years to a day from the destructive cyclone, this startling news was flashed over the Texas wire:

"Dr. Crane is dead."

The Baptists of Texas had not even heard that he was sick.

The author will never forget the awfulness of the shock which came to him, when, quietly studying in his home in Lampasas, these sad words—too sad for interpretation here—first came to him: "Dr. Crane is dead." For a moment he was almost paralyzed. Though thirty-six years have gone by since that news was received, his grief almost overmasters him as he endeavors to write this record. He had never known Dr. Crane to be sick, but a sudden attack of pneumonia quickly carried him away.

So far as old Baylor at Independence was concerned, Dr. Crane's death was the beginning of the end. The master mind, spirit and personality were gone. For more than twenty years the school had lived, and lived a great purpose, largely through the transfusion of his own rich blood and the investment of his great life.

Source: J. M. Carroll, *A History of Texas Baptists: Comprising a Detailed Account of Their Activities, Their Progress and Achievements* (Dallas: Baptist Standard Publishing Co., 1923), 523–24.

E. The Trail of Blood

FOURTH LECTURE—17th, 18th, 19th Centuries

1. This lecture begins with the beginning of the Seventeenth Century (A. D. 1601). We have passed very hurriedly over much important Christian history, but necessity has compelled this.

2. This three-century period begins with the rise of an entirely new denomination. It is right to state that some historians give the date of the beginning of the Congregational Church (at first called "Independents") as 1602. However, Schaff-Herzogg, in their Encyclopedia, place its beginning far back in the sixteenth century, making it coeval with the Lutheran and the Presbyterian. In the great reformation wave many who went out of the Catholic Church were not satisfied with the extent of the reformation led by Luther and Calvin. They decided to repudiate also the preacher rule and government idea of the churches and return to the New Testament democratic idea as had been held through the fifteen preceding centuries by those who had refused to enter Constantine's hierarchy.

3. The determined contention of this new organization for this particular reform brought down upon its head bitter persecution from Catho-

lic, Presbyterian and Church of England adherents—all the established churches. However, it retained many other of the Catholic made errors, such for instance as infant baptism, pouring or sprinkling for baptism, and later adopted and practiced to an extreme degree the church and state idea. And, after refugeeing to America, themselves, became very bitter persecutors.

4. The name "Independents" or as now called "Congregationalists," is derived from their mode of church government. Some of the distinguishing principles of the English Congregationalists as given in Schaff-Herzogg Encyclopedia are as follows:

(1) That Jesus Christ is the only head of the church and that the Word of God is its only statute book.

(2) That visible churches are distinct assemblies of Godly men gathered out of the world for purely religious purposes, and not to be confounded with the world.

(3) That these separate churches have full power to choose their own officers and to maintain discipline.

(4) That in respect to their internal management they are each independent of all other churches and equally independent of state control.

5. How markedly different these principles are from Catholicism, or even Lutheranism, or even Presbyterianism or the Episcopacy of the Church of England. How markedly similar to the Baptists of today, and of all past ages, and to the original teachings of Christ and His apostles.

6. In 1611, the King James Version of the Bible appeared. Never was the Bible extensively given to the people before. From the beginning of the general dissemination of the Word of God began the rapid decline of the Papal power, and the first beginnings for at least many centuries, of the idea of "religious liberty . . .". . . .

8. During all the seventeenth century, persecutions of the Waldenses, Ana-Baptists and Baptists (in some places the "Ana" was now being left off) continued to be desperately severe: in England by the Church of England, as John Bunyan and many others could testify; in Germany by the Lutherans; in Scotland by the Church of Scotland (Presbyterian); in Italy, in France and in every other place where the papacy was in power,

by the Catholics. There is now no peace anywhere for those who are not in agreement with the state churches, or some one of them.

9. It is a significant fact well established in credible history that even as far back as the fourth century those refusing to go into the Hierarchy, and refusing to accept the baptism of those baptized in infancy, and refusing to accept the doctrine of "Baptismal Regeneration" and demanding rebaptism for all those who came to them from the Hierarchy, were called "Ana-Baptists." No matter what other names they then bore, they were always referred to as "Ana-Baptists." Near the beginning of the sixteenth century, the "Ana" was dropped, and the name shortened to simply "Baptist," and gradually all other names were dropped. Evidently, if Bunyan had lived in an earlier period his followers would have been called "Bunyanites" or "Ana-Baptists." Probably they would have been called by both names as were others preceding him.

10. The name "Baptist" is a "nickname," and was given to them by their enemies (unless the name can be rightly attributed to them as having been given to them by the Savior Himself, when He referred to John as "The Baptist"). To this day, the name has never been officially adopted by any group of Baptists. The name, however, has become fixed and is willingly accepted and proudly borne. It snugly fits. It was the distinguishing name of the forerunner of Christ, the first to teach the doctrine to which the Baptists now hold.

Where did these Baptists come from? They did not come out of the Catholics during the Reformation. They had churches prior to the Reformation.

Source: J. M. Carroll, *The Trail of Blood* (Lexington, Ky.: Ashland Avenue Baptist Church, 1931), 38–45. Reprint courtesy of Ashland Avenue Baptist Church.

6.2 Women's Work

From its foundation laid by Massie Millard in the brush near Washington-on-the-Brazos, the Baptist women of Texas have always done more than their fair share to propagate the Gospel in the Lone Star State. Particularly adept at raising funds for missionaries, the most outstanding women of the period included: Mrs. F. B. Davis, Mrs. W. L. Williams, and Miss Mina Everett. Though they lived in a patriarchal society that was at times slow to accept their gifts, these women set a high standard for the Woman's Missionary Union in Texas that has continued well into the twenty-first century.

A. Formal Organization

In 1880, at Austin, the "Texas Baptist Missionary Union" was organized, and Mrs. F. B. Davis, of San Antonio, was elected President, this organization doing a good work until 1886. In the spirit of general consolidation at that time a reorganization took place under the name "Baptist Women's Missionary Workers," and Mrs. Davis was continued President. She has ably borne its burdens. The objects of this organization, according to its constitution, are:

1. To organize societies.

2. To win the co-operation of women and children in the systematic study of missions, and in collecting money for missions.

3. To spread missionary information.

4. To assist through our churches and their agencies State denominational enterprises.

The proceedings of the regular meetings seem not to have been regularly published, but in 1887, notwithstanding only seventeen auxiliary societies had reported, $1,583.60 had been raised. At the Convention in 1888; Miss Minnie Slaughter, of Dallas, Corresponding Secretary, reported that the year's work had been very prosperous, footing up a total of $10,177.39 raised by all the societies. Nineteen new societies had been organized. The thirteenth annual session was held in connection with the Convention in 1898 at Waco. Mrs. W. L. Williams, of Dallas, was President, and Mrs. J. B. Gambrell, also of Dallas, was Corresponding Secretary. She made a splendid report, showing the entire work of the auxiliary societies during the year amounted to $13,541.52 collected for the objects of organization. In 1899 the Mission Workers' meeting was called to order by the President, Mrs. W. L. Williams. Mrs. Gambrell, Corresponding Secretary, presented her report, showing a great year's work. A collation of the reports of the auxiliary societies exhibits the splendid State offerings, aggregating $13,211.68, and a special offering of $393.60; total $13,605.88. This work of those noble Christian women is fostered by the Board of Directors of the General Convention, through which all their offerings are sent, and the board appropriates $200 annually towards the expenses of this work.

Source: B. F. Fuller, *History of Texas Baptists* (Louisville: Baptist Book Concern, 1900), 328–29.

B. How Dr. Carroll Came to Believe

In the winter of 1895–6 the Executive Board of the B. W. M. W. met in Dallas. Dr. B. H. Carroll appeared before the meeting with a message for the women. Miss Mina Everett, who for years had been corresponding secretary, was also present. Those who knew Miss Everett can never forget her spirit-filled personality. Her presence in any gathering proved a spark that kindled fires of enthusiasm. She was a tireless worker. She was a progressive in the women's realm. When Dr. Carroll was presented, he began his talk by reviewing the denominational work in general, and as was his habit, he spoke "like one in authority." When he came to the subject of women's organization, he remarked that he was not unmindful of the severe struggles through which the State work had existed and concluded that the organization should disband.

Some one rose and asked: "Well, Dr. Carroll, do you not think that women can be serviceable in church work?" To which he answered: "In my church I have the women divided into circles, and when I need a certain kind of work done I call on a certain circle, and if I have a different character of work to be done I call on another circle." Whereupon Miss Mina, of courageous heart, spoke to him through his ear trumpet, without which he could not hear at all: "Will you tell us, Dr. Carroll, by what Scriptural authority you direct your women's work?" Looking at her in quiet dignity, he laid aside his ear trumpet. Thus ended the discussion.

It was fourteen years later when Dr. Carroll again appeared before the Executive Board. Much of the old-time opposition to women's work had died out. Year by year was revealing the fact that the women could carry on. Evidently Dr. Carroll had studied the question from the Bible standpoint. He cited the achievements of women through the ages of the Scriptures. He took the simple stories and magnified and glorified them as only a great preacher can, and in concluding gave his unqualified endorsement of the B. W. M. W. of Texas.

Source: Mrs. W. J. J. Smith, *A Centennial History of the Baptist Women of Texas: 1830–1930* (Dallas: Woman's Missionary Union of Texas, 1933), 49–50. Reprint courtesy of Woman's Missionary Union of Texas.

6.3 Other Colleges and Universities Associated with Texas Baptist Life

Though Baylor University at Waco was clearly the flagship of the Baptist institutes in Texas, there were other denominational schools that significantly contributed to Texas higher education. During the nineteenth century, the most influential schools were Baylor Female College (1845), Howard Payne College (1890), and Simmons College (1890). Other schools existed during this period, but most have failed to survive.

A. The Spiritual Nature of Mary Hardin-Baylor University

At the beginning of each day's schools duties, the first period is given to devotional exercises and study of the Bible. A weekly prayer meeting is held by the students in the College chapel, attendance upon which is entirely voluntary. While the highest and best culture and taste is sought, it is not simply for the sake of literary honors nor social display, but to make the best use of an immortal mind and to furnish it with the best materials and the highest skill for Christian influence and usefulness. It is impossible to obtain this object without the proper development of the moral as well as mental and physical powers. It is therefore earnestly desired that every student attend regularly religious exercises on the Sabbath. If the parent or guardian of any student so desire that the pupil attend the services of any special denomination, and will so notify the President of the College, the request shall be faithfully complied with.

Source: *Catalogue*, Mary Hardin-Baylor University, 1886–87, 7.

B. Early History of Howard Payne University

During 1890 a charter was obtained for Howard Payne College at Brownwood, of which Rev. J. D. Robnett was the founder and first president. Dr. Robnett, who was a native of Missouri, gave to this institution the strong and effective labors of the best years of his life. Indeed, to those who know the facts, there is no doubt that he really laid his life upon its altar. After having founded the institution and given it that caste and standing that was at once the glory of its founder and the harbinger of its success, he accepted the call to the pastorate of the Washington Avenue Church at Dallas. He labored here, however, but a short time, and died during 1898, having never fully recovered from the strain incident of this magnificent Baptist school. Prof. J. H. Grove is now the honored president of the institution, and of him and his connection therewith a more extended reference is made in another place in this record. It is proper to say in connection with Howard Payne College that in its establishment Rev. J. D. Robnett was ably seconded by his consecrated wife, Mrs. Dollie P. Robnett, who is now Mrs. Isaac Sellers, of Valley Mills, Texas. She is one of the most gifted and most useful of our Texas Baptist women.

Source: B. F. Riley, *History of Texas Baptists* (Dallas: By the author, 1907), 328.

C. The Birth of (Hardin) Simmons College

The first definite action looking to the founding of Simmons College was the appointment in 1890 of a committee by the First Baptist Church of Abilene to propose to the Sweetwater Association the founding of an "associational school." The Association approved the idea, and named a committee consisting of K. K. Leggett, Rev. George W. Smith, H. C. Hord, J. M. Ferguson, C. R. Breedlove and G. W. Smith, with plenary powers.

This community met in Abilene October 17, 1890, and accepted the offer of O. W. Steffens and associates of sixteen acres of land and $5,000 cash, and located the College on its present site. The committee also selected the original board of trustees and adopted the outlines of the original charter. The charter was filed in the office of the Secretary of State on February 6, 1891. A noteworthy feature was a provision "that the property of said institution shall never be encumbered or subject to any debt of any kind whatsoever."

The cornerstone of the first building was laid July 4, 1891. In the meantime, the chairman of the board of trustees, Rev. George W. Smith, had invited the aid of Dr. O. C. Pope, then living in New York City, and serving the denomination as secretary of the Church Building Fund. Dr.

Pope had formerly resided for many years in Texas. As joint editor of the leading Baptist paper in the State, and as superintendent of missions, he had left his impress for all time on the organized work of Texas Baptists. The Sweetwater Association, covering a territory of 45,000 square miles, was one of the direct results of his labors. Thus the appeal for help in founding a college in this Association at once enlisted his hearty interest.

He sought Dr. James B. Simmons, also of New York, whose zeal for the promotion of Christian education and whose insight into its needs and possibilities had been demonstrated by the establishment of several other institutions in various parts of the country. Dr. Simmons, an honored alumnus of Brown University, and a member of its governing board, discerned at once the call of the Master to a new service and sacrifice, gave generously and urged others to give to this new college in the Southwest.

In 1891 the board of trustees by unanimous vote decided to give the institution, which had been chartered as the Abilene Baptist College, the name of its largest donor, and to call it Simmons College. At the time of his subscription of $5,000 Dr. Simmons presented a "Foundation Agreement," which was accepted by the board and thereby a part of the records of the College. The whole document is interesting. The following quotation indicates its substance:

First, that Christianity shall be the professed and formative principle of the whole organization, method and life of the said Abilene Baptist College, and that in said College it shall be the constant aim of the teachers, by a truly Christian and liberal education, (1) to bring young men and women to Christ; (2) to teach them Christ; (3) to train them for Christ.

Second, that said College shall give to its students Christian instruction in the Word of God, in the story of the church, in the doctrine of the Bible, and in Christian ethics, and in the principles of the evangelical religion, as revealed in the Old and New Testaments, as they are interpreted by Missionary Baptists.

Third, that the president, professors, tutors and teachers of said College shall be chosen, so far as practicable, other things being equal, first of all because of hearty sympathy with the views and principles herein expressed.

Fourth, that the name of the Abilene Baptist College shall be changed to "Simmons College" and if the growth of said College shall be hereafter warrant it, to "Simmons University," and that for all time to come the same institution or corporation shall be known either as "Simmons College" or "Simmons University."

Source: J. M. Carroll, *A History of Texas Baptists: Comprising a Detailed Account of Their Activities, Their Progress and Achievements* (Dallas: Baptist Standard Publishing Co., 1923), 943–44.

6.4 Benevolent Ministries

Texas Baptists continued to advance their efforts in the area of benevolent ministries during the last twenty years of the nineteenth century. Created in 1877, the Buckner Orphanage had become the most popular and beloved of these ministries. The Buckner Orphanage was able to care for countless orphans through the support of the BGCT, virtually all of the associations, and both Baptist periodicals. During this same period, the temperance movement became even more outspoken on the evils of liquor. Aided by the anti-saloon league, the Baptists of Texas were becoming a statewide force in the war against the liquor trade. Once again, J. B. Cranfill took the lead against the saloon industry. Cranfill's harangues against alcohol became so pronounced that he often suggested that violence should be used to close bars and saloons.

A. Progress at the Buckner Orphanage

Sunshine, Shadow, Sunshine.—When we saw Buckner Orphans Home last in 1894, it stood stately and erect in the sunshine of prosperity. There were more than five hundred acres of the best quality of Texas black land, plenty of live stock, good barn, schoolhouse, sanatorium, wooden buildings, for more than one hundred boys, new pressed-brick building with four floors, giving room for four hundred girls, artesian well, and no debt. The Home's General Manager could never for a moment content himself to stand still. His ideals are summed up in that one word, "Forward."

Forward.—After installing the artesian well, it was not a year till a model steam power and electric light plant was installed at a cost of $6,000. Also at about this time the A. J. Holt museum of more than one hundred thousand valuable specimens became the property of the Home. It was presented to the Home by Dr. Holt, and was valued at more than $5,000. Rare specimens they were, gathered in the Orient and elsewhere. It has been added to and is now (1914) worth above $8,000.

Sunshine Family.—Along in those golden days Mrs. A. F. Beddoe was mother to more than two hundred happy girls. They were being trained in classes—a class in housekeeping and lawn adornment, another in the science and arts belonging to the culinary department, another in the cutting, fitting and making of garments, another in laundry work and ironing, and so on.

A nursery department of about thirty small children was under the eye and motherly hand of Mrs. M. A. Black.

The boys were occupying wooden buildings on their own lawn, and had for their mother good "Aunt Sallie" Britton. Aunt Sallie taught them to make their own beds, scrub their own floors, keep their own rooms, wash their own clothes, and aid in the making and mending of them. The boys, in addition, had field work and shop work. Good "Aunt Sallie" is still (1914) a matron in the Home. She has helped in the rearing of more than five thousand orphan children.

Source: J. B. Cranfill and J. L. Walker, *R. C. Buckner's Life of Works and Faith* (Dallas: Buckner Orphans Home, 1916), 177–78.

B. Temperance Revisited

REPORT ON TEMPERANCE

The time has come in the history of Texas, when no Baptist can afford to give an uncertain sound on the temperance question. The lines are so closely drawn, and the issues so clearly defined, that there can be no mistake as to the correct attitude of every Christian man. It can no longer be accepted as a fact that a man is in favor of temperance who is not also in favor of prohibition. The old slogan of "moral suasion," which has been rung in our ears so long by those who never did anything for moral suasion has ceased to be the potent, and thinkers have come to realize that no man can, in the nature of things, be in favor of moral suasion unless he is also an advocate of legal suasion. The issue as now presents itself to our consideration is unmistakably plain. It is an issue between the homes of Texas and the saloons of Texas. There are more saloon keepers in Texas than there are ministers of all the denominations. These whiskey vendors have in our state over 450 rum shops, wherein is carried on the business of manufacturing drunkards. These reservoirs of crime, protected as they are by the strong arm of our State government and fostered by our national legislature, furnish three-quarters of all the crime that comes to the attention of our courts. There is not a corner of our state wherein it has not caused the voice of mourning. There is no city, town, or village, where its withering, scorching, poisonous breath has not been felt. There is no cemetery where, ever and anon, it has not caused ruin and made graves. It is relentless, heartless, cruel. It is in direct antagonism to very pure things that ever came from the hand of God. It poisons and embitters and destroys more lives than all the pestilence and all the wars, that have ever visited the land; and its destroying, blackening, fiendish breath, like a social sirocco, has destroyed our homes relentlessly and cruelly sent our noblest men to drunkards graves, annihilated the Christian Sabbath, made virtue a by-word and a hiss, scattered crime and murder the state around, and cursed the very name of God.

In this iniquitous and soul-destroying business our state is a silent partner. Instead of taking the advice of the immortal Gladstone who said, "It is the duty of the state to make it easy for people to do the right and hard for the people to do wrong," our government makes it easy for its people to do wrong, and hard for them to do right. It has been attempted to "restrict" the liquor business by high license. We might as well try to restrict the poison of the asp or the venom of the adder. We had as well set bounds to a cyclone, or put a covering of gauze over the crater of Vesuvius. The whiskey business does not restrict. No law that has ever been made for its restriction has been enforced. There is not a saloon keeper in Texas that obeys the laws intended to "restrict" his infamous business. In the fame of these sad facts, brethren—for they are sad facts—there is but one duty before us as Christian men. That is to work and watch and pray to that end, that this infamy may be blotted from the land. Nor is this all. While we must, as Christians, work and watch and pray, we must as citizens vote against this hydra-headed monster. Let us face the issue as any issue of fact. Let us force the boycott, inaugurated against the preachers in Texas in the "scourge-em back" campaign last summer, to be raised. And while it is our duty as Christians to vote for prohibition, no matter how the question is presented it is none the less our duty to work and pray to the end that the offices of our state be filled by men in sympathy with our homes, and whose voice and effort in the administration of law, would be for God, and home and native land. As Baptists, as Christians, as a body of men in sympathy with all that is good and noble and true we can do nothing less than this. And if the voice of the demagogue is heard in the language against us, let the heathen rage. The eternal principles of truth and justice will never die. And when, brethren, the last prayer of our life shall have been written; when the last-battle is fought and the last victory is won, the world will be better for our having lived; and in the pages of a literature that is to come, the legends and lays of a purified people will sing of a dark, unseemly age, when was licensed a pathway to hell. To the work of exterminating this greatest of all iniquities let us pledge our lives, our fortunes and our sacred honor.

> J. B. Cranfill, Chairman
> E. R. Cartwell, Jr.
> M. P. Matheney
> Isaac Sellers

Source: *Proceedings*, Baptist General Convention of Texas, 1895, 9–10.

C. Bear Creek Baptist Mission: Temperance

Your Committee on Temperance beg leave to make the following report:

After reflecting for a short time upon the subject find that the use of ardent spirits is a great evil; it is inculcated to destroy the mind and suppress the mass's physical energies and with that entail other evils calculated in this nature to bring the soul into everlasting sin.

Therefore, we recommend all good people to abstain from its use only as medication.

The Church of Christ is truly a temperate body. That she ever use all the influences over its members to live out temperance in their lives.

And as the Church is the great moral lighthouse to the world, they should wave the flag of temperance high and firm to the end.

Source: *Minutes*, Bear Creek Baptist Mission, 1866, 88.

6.5 Troublesome Doctrinal Issues

Though Texas Baptists were finding evangelistic success, they were faced with several problematic and even heretical doctrinal issues. The leaders of the BGCT, in particular B. H. Carroll, attempted to correct or eradicate these problems before they inundated the entire state. For the most part, these crusaders of orthodoxy were successful. In order to stymie the problem, however, fierce battles had to be fought on both the state and associational level. The most damaging and far-reaching of these doctrinal issues were, Martinism, Fortuneism, Crawfordism, the Whitsitt Controversy, and Haydenism.

A. Martinism

Matthew T. Martin was a minister in the Waco Association during the 1880s and 1890s. During this period, his doctrinal views were called into question. Martin taught that if a person doubts his conversion, or has ever doubted his conversion, the person's conversion is not sound. A powerful preacher, his sermons led hundreds of people to question their salvation and request rebaptism. Behind the leadership of B. H. Carroll, Martin's ministerial papers were withdrawn in 1888 and he moved to Atlanta, Georgia. Martin, however, returned to the Waco Association in 1890 where he pastored the Marlin Baptist Church and once again began to espouse his views. A minority of the church, who did not hold his views, sought to remove him from the pastorate but they were unsuccessful. As a result, the Waco Association removed the Marlin Church from its membership in September of 1890. At the 1895 regular session of the BGCT a resolution was passed which stated that anyone who espoused Martinism was not permitted to be seated as a messenger.

Rev. M .T. Martin, member and ordained minister of this church, has at various places and times since his connection with this church and responsibility to it, taught doctrines contrary to our acknowledged standards of faith and polity, thereby causing division and trouble in our denomination. We further charge that after the pastor had privately and kindly called his attention to those matters and admonished him more than once to be more careful and circumspect in his publications and pulpit utterances; and when trouble and confusion, excited by his ministerial course and practices, had assumed such proportions that the elders and deacons of the church invited him to a private and fraternal conference concerning these matters, and when assembled in such conference, he being voluntarily present and participating, they did by long and painstaking labor, seek earnestly to finds some safe ground of adjustment, and did kindly admonish him and implore him to benefit by the lessons of the past, yet since that time the trouble and confusion following his ministerial labors, and excited by them, having increased rather than decreased. And we regret further to charge that some of his statements in the fraternal conference, a partial result of which was published for his benefit in the form of answers to direct questions, and referring to what he had taught in various places, have not been confirmed but refuted rather by the testimony of many pastors with whom he labored and which testimony he invoked.

And we further charge that, even in so short a time, in some places where his doctrines have been received and his spirit imbibed, the effect has been detrimental to prayer meetings, Sunday Schools, mission work and other denominational activities. Signed by F. L. Carroll, S. B. Humphreys, W. H. Long, A. H. Sneed, J. T. Battle, J. C. McCrary, deacons.

These charges were particularized in six specifications, which condensed are as follows:

1. *Violation of Art. vii. of his Church* (New Hampshire Declaration). This article he violates in that he teaches two new births instead of one; a birth or generation by the spirit and a later birth or generation by the Word, thus contrary to all Baptist interpretation, contradistinguishing regeneration not from a fleshly birth, but from a previous generation of the Spirit, thereby making regeneration to consist, not as this article affirms, "in giving a holy disposition to the mind," but *in the belief of the truth*, and in making it the effect, not of the Holy Spirit, but of the truth believed.

2. *Violation of Art. x. on Sanctification*. (Art. xiii of the Philadelphia confession). He opposes these articles, in that he makes sanctification precede conversion and faith, confounds it with regeneration, logically denies its progressive character, and that it fits one for heaven.

3. *On Faith and Assurance.* He makes a full comprehension of all that is revealed concerning the object of faith or the promises to it, essential to its saving exercise. He makes assurance or absence of doubt so essential to faith as that the latter cannot exist without the former. By this he adds a condition to salvation itself and to the ordinances, and to the office of ministry unknown to the Scriptures and to our standards. (See Art. ix. of New Hamp. Dec. and Art. viii of the Phila. Con.)

4. *Making Assurance a Prerequisite to Baptism.* By making assurance, or absence of doubt, an essential to saving faith and prerequisite to baptism, he has so brought great confusion in our denomination and so caused a repetition of baptism and ordination as is without parallel in our denominational history.

5. *On Repentance.* His definition: "Repentance is knowing God and turning from dead works." "As might be expected from such a definition he minifies and depreciates this doctrine. He justifies the failure to preach repentance by the inappropriate illustration," 'When a physician wants a patient to vomit he doesn't tell him to vomit, but gives him an emetic and it vomits itself.' We submit that aside from the lack of analogy in this illustration, which shows a physical effect not dependent upon the will, it would equally justify a failure to preach faith or any other duty. Art, viii, of our confession. 'We believe that repentance is a sacred duty and grace wrought in our souls by the regenerating Spirit of God, whereby, being deeply convinced of our guilt, danger and helplessness, we turn to God with unfeigned contrition, confession and supplication for mercy.'

6. *On Prayer.* Brother Martin usually not only reduces his prayer services in protracted meeting to a minimum startling to Baptist ministers, and not only lays exceptionally little stress on its importance in his preaching, but his teachings are against the duty and privileges of sinners praying for forgiveness, and the privilege and duty of Christians praying that sinners may be forgiven.

Source: J. L. Walker and C. P. Lumpkin, *History of the Waco Association of Texas* (Waco: Byrne-Hill Printing House, 1897), 123–27.

B. Fortuneism

George Fortune was pastor of the First Baptist Church of Paris, Texas, from 1891 until 1897. Shortly after beginning his tenure in Paris, he began to espouse doctrines that were not only inconsistent with the Baptist denomination, but were, in fact, heretical. In particular, he taught: there was no personal Satan, no eternal punishment, no imputed Adamic sin, and no substitionary atonement. Fortune's past was quite checkered. An investigative committee found that he had been a Methodist preacher in Illinois, a temperance worker in Kansas, and a hardshell Baptist preacher in Arkansas. It was decided at the 1895 regular session of the BGCT that anyone who held to Fortuneism could not be seated as a messenger. Fortune left the First Baptist Church of Paris in 1897 and moved to the Indian Territory of Oklahoma where he practiced law. The ensuing passage is cited from B. F. Fuller's *History of Texas Baptists*. The citation provides background on Fortune, his doctrine, and his influence. Fuller was a member of the First Baptist Church of Paris that brought charges of heresy against Fortune. Thus, his statements depict an eyewitness account of the Fortune pastorate.

In the autumn of 1891 the First Baptist church of Paris, Texas, was without a pastor, and there appeared in Paris a man by the name of George M. Fortune, claiming to be a Baptist minister, and was invited by the church to preach. After preaching a few sermons he was called by the church to be their pastor. He was unknown in the State, but was from Arkansas. He was a man of fine address, of literary turn, and seemed to be scholarly in his attainments, and withal a fine pulpit orator. It seems, from what was afterwards learned, that his previous life had been a checkered one. He had been a Methodist preacher in Illinois, a temperance lecturer and lawyer in Kansas, and a Baptist preacher in Arkansas. It was not long before it became apparent that he held very loose views on the authenticity of the Scriptures. The trend of his teaching was towards *higher criticism*, and he was generally out of harmony with the accepted standards of the Baptist faith. In 1894 he published two sermons on the atonement, in which he boldly and pointedly repudiated the doctrine of the vicarious atonement of Jesus Christ, denying that Jesus died for, and instead of sinners, becoming the sinner's *substitute*; rejecting also the doctrine of the imputed *righteousness* of Christ; maintaining that we are not saved by Christ's *death*, but by his *life*. A few quotations from these remarkable sermons will illustrate Dr. Fortune's wild theories on the subject of atonement, he says:

"Looking at this theory, then, as a theory, and analyzing it upon its merits, its meaning obviously leads to two propositions, both of which do the gravest violence, not only to the Christian religion, but to justice and truth. The fundamental principle of this theory is that Jesus *literally* took the sinner's place and bore the penalty of his sins. The first objection to this is that God made His son Jesus Christ sin, who knew no sin. That is to say, if the theory of substitution is correct, God consented to look on Jesus Christ as a sinner, who at the same time was not a sinner, in order that He might be able to look on man, who is a sinner, as a righteous man, but one thing is sure—truth is a truth forever, and everywhere. That which is true on earth is true in heaven. The calling of that true, which is not true, does not change its nature."

Fortune does not consider that we must accept this doctrine because we find it plainly taught in the Bible, but claims that it must be verified on logical principles of ratiocination, and goes on further to say:

"We cannot accept a proposition, however, sanctioned, if it charges God with doing violence to the cardinal virtues. This is why we are compelled to dispute the correctness of this substitionary theory of Augustine and Calvin. It charges God with both folly and falsehood. To regard Jesus as a sinner is either true or false. If true, He cannot be our Savior. If false, it charges God with untruth. . . . So that when it is said God made Jesus a sinner, who was not a sinner, I understand the proposition, and solemnly avow that it is not only unscriptural and unphilosophical, but it is not true, and cannot be true, if God be the God of truth. . . . It cannot be that God consented to such a travesty."

After quoting what Paul says on this subject in Gal. 3:13, and 2 Cor. 5:21, he evidently rejects Paul's version, and says:

"Jesus was made sin for us, not in the literal and real way in which Paul uses it," and takes consolation in the following assertion: "But we have cause for gratitude that theology is a progressive science."

This sermon of Dr. Fortune was printed in pamphlet form and freely circulated by mailing copies to leading Baptist ministers all over the State, and it met with a general, if not universal condemnation. Both of our State papers promptly condemned it, and there appeared in the papers many able reviews and criticisms.

Source: B. F. Fuller, *A History of Texas Baptists* (Louisville: Baptist Book Concern, 1900), 398–400.

C. The Gospel Missions Movement (Crawfordism)

The Gospel Missions Movement was founded by T. P. Crawford (1821–1902). A missionary to China, he believed that Boards and Conventions should be limited in all missionary endeavors. Crawford's teaching emphasized the importance of church sovereignty over that of the Boards, and in doing so espoused the belief that only churches should send missionaries to the field. Furthermore, once the missionary had been acclimated to the field, he should become self-sufficient, thus alleviating the financial burden of the church and allowing it to send other missionaries. The Gospel Missions Movement in Texas had very little effect on missions. Rather, it was a tirade against the Executive Board of the BGCT. The anti-Board movement in Texas, therefore, cannot be properly called the Gospel Missions Movement. Because of the anti-Board sentiment, however, many who held leadership roles in the BGCT, especially J. B. Gambrell, labeled anyone who disagreed with the actions of the Board a "Crawfordist."

CONCERNING GOSPEL MISSIONS
BY J. B. GAMBRELL

Our feelings toward the brethren engaged in the so-called gospel missions movement are of the kindest nature. We concede, without a moment of hesitation, the right of a church to co-operate with the movement, if it chooses. We credit that for certain minds, and to a certain degree, there are advantages in a church or certain members of a church choosing a missionary to support. There are disadvantages, but we will not now discuss them.

What, then, is to be said against this movement? Much or several ways as it is now conducted. In the first place, it is deceptive. It, by its very name, assumes to be more scriptural than the common method, which its advocates proceed to deny in practice. It assumes to be a church movement, pure and simple, but they seek to combine churches, just as our brethren do. It is the voice of Jacob, but the result of Esau. They denounce their ill brethren for what they themselves practice.

In the second place constant war is made on the method on account of agents and expenses, while they practice the agency system at a greater expense than we do, but do not openly state the facts. As to agents, no man can read the Acts and the Epistles without knowing that the apostolic churches practiced this system. Our objecting is not against their employing agents, but to their method of overseeing it, and to their fighting their brethren for what they themselves do.

While in Georgia recently, we learned that Brother Bostwick, of the Crawford movement, had been down there in interest of the so-called gospel missions. He was questioned by reliable brethren and the following facts were elicited. There are about twenty members of the gospel mission movement all told, and four of them are in the county. These broke from the Board five years ago. They report nine converts.

The question was asked, "How came you back in this country?"

"I was sent back."

"Who sent you?"

"The Gospel Mission people."

"Why were you sent back?"

"To raise money."

"Where does this money come from?"

"From the churches."

"How much have you raised?"

"From April 1 to January, $1,185."

"Where is it?"

"Spent it on my family and traveling expenses."

"To whom do you report in this county?"

"No one. I publish my receipts in our paper."

"Who determines the amount you shall spend on your family?"

"I do."

The questions and answers are not verbatim; but they carry the truth as admitted by this agent of the gospel missioners. We have here, then, an agent appointed by the people who receives the money, not those who give it. Nobody says what he is to take for a living. Nobody audits his accounts, and with all this agency consumes collection. This is the record of a method projected to save money and put the rest of us to shame.

Brother Bostwick admitted before a large audience that he thought it would be a good thing to have a committee in this country to receive and disburse funds, and that is exactly what we have, only we call it a board.

But it be borne in mind that Dr. Crawford went to China with this illusive idea, and that it failed. He was then taken up by the board and supported for many years. The movement will fail when it is understood, as it should do. It has done nothing but introduce confusion and increases expenses. When Baptists learn that disorganizers and obstructionists are the most expensive in their ranks, they will have learned a great lesson.

The smallness of the results of the gospel missioners efforts carries with it a solemn lesson: 20 workers, 9 converts. Let it be borne in mind that these were old workers. They learned the language and were settled on the methods under the board. What is the trouble? The very same trouble that is in Texas at many points. These brethren are spending their time trying to pull our work to pieces. They are not going to the inactive churches, but to the active. They have the spirit of distraction and God is not pleased with their spirit. Wherever the spirit of faultfinding and strife is found, there spiritual leanness is found. Churches and pastors are fruitless. The thing is not of God.

Source: *Texas Baptist Standard*, 15 July 1897, 1.

D. The Whitsitt Controversy

The Whitsitt Controversy depicts another outgrowth of radical Landmarkism within the ranks of the Southern Baptist Convention. Those who maintained the Landmark position held that Baptists have their roots in the New Testament, Jesus and his disciples were Baptists, and Baptists have an unbroken line of succession from the New Testament period that may be traced to the modern era. William Whitsitt was the professor of church history and President of the Southern Baptist Theological Seminary in Louisville, Kentucky. He believed that Baptists were born from the Puritan-Separatist movement of the English Reformation, which was antithetical to Landmarkism. Though few modern historians would disagree with his findings, Whitsitt published a book espousing these views in 1896 and the result was a firestorm of controversy that resulted in his estrangement from and termination at Southern Seminary. Even though the primary battlefield was in Louisville, the President of the Southern Board of Trustees was Texas's own B. H. Carroll. As a man who held several Landmark tenets, Carroll, behind the fanatical urging of many Texas Baptists, led the campaign to remove Whitsitt from office. Carroll won the battle as Whitsitt lost his presidency, but lost the war, as virtually no reputable current Baptist historian maintains the Landmark position concerning Baptist origins.

1. The Reaction of the Enon Association

Whereas, Dr. W. H. Whitsitt, president of the Southern Baptist Theological Seminary at Louisville, Ky., has published in the *New York Independent* and in Johnson's *New Encyclopedia,* and in a letter to the *New York Examiner* certain statements concerning Baptist history, very generally regarded as both offensive and unjust by our people, and which are at variance with the generally accepted history; and whereas, he has published more recently in the Religious Herald and in a small book issued by him, other statements on the same points, which, though modifying very much the impressions naturally and fairly made by his original statements, are not such a retraction as the truth of Baptist History demands.

Therefore, resolved that we recommend that Dr. Whitsitt be removed from his position as president of the Southern Baptist Theological Seminary, and should the trustees thereof refuse to do this, we urge our churches to withdraw their support from the Seminary.

Source: *Minutes*, Enon Baptist Association, 1896.

2. A Letter to the *Texas Baptist and Herald*

I don't consider that Dr. Whitsitt retraced any of the heretical steps in regard to Baptist history, he had taken. I was made to feel sad when I read of the tears, handshaking and embracing of the Dr. when the covered up statement was made to the Convention. This showed exclusively that there was a large party in that Convention who were in sympathy with what I call the heresy of Dr. Whitsitt. If John the Baptist immersed the Lord Jesus Christ and the Apostles and Christ organized his church out of those who had thus baptized by John and the Apostles, perpetuated the ordinance in the immersion of a believer in the water in the name of the Trinity, having the design that we believe Christ intended it should have, if that was lost until the 12th century, would it be blasphemy to say that the gates of hell had prevailed against the church which our Master set up on the earth.

Source; W. H. H. Hays, "Letter to the Editor," *Texas Baptist and Herald*, 3 June 1897, 4.

E. Haydenism

Though perceived as radical Landmarkism or a branch of the Gospel Missions Movement, the teachings of S. A. Hayden have been largely misunderstood. The Hayden Controversy was primarily a political struggle between S. A. Hayden and B. H. Carroll for control of the BGCT and manifested in the state papers. The tenets of Haydenism include: a strong belief in the sovereignty of the local church, a despisal of B. H. Carroll and his advocates' domination of the BGCT, and a demand for meticulous financial record keeping. During the two decades that Haydenism raged, a majority of the BGCT leadership gradually lined up against Hayden. The final result was his expulsion from the BGCT in 1897.

1. The Rationale for Hayden's Removal from the 1897 BGCT

First, he has violated the spirit and letter of the constitution of this body which says, "The object of this Convention shall be missionary and educational, the promotion of harmony of feeling and concert of action among Baptists, and a system of operative measures for the promotions of interests of the Redeemer's Kingdom." This fundamental law, he has violated by a ceaseless and hurtful war upon the plans, policies, work and workers of this Convention.

Second, he is and has been in open and notorious opposition to the Convention and its mandates.

Third, because he will not abide and support the findings and decisions of this Convention, its plans and policies, for organized and cooperative work, and has announced that he will not in the future abide by its decisions, unless they be settled in his way.

Fourth, he is unworthy of a seat in this Convention on moral grounds. He has assailed the public and private character of the Superintendent of Missions and the Board of Directors by falsely accusing them of dishonorable practices in the misuse of mission money.

Fifth, that said course of conduct has been pursued by him for such a length of time, and with such continuous and persistent malice and traduction toward the Convention . . . in spite of repeated admonitions and mandates of the Convention, as to render his connection with it a standing menace to the life of the whole body.

Source: *Proceedings*, Baptist General Convention of Texas, 1897, 99-101.

2. The Origin of the Reform Paper

In February, 1894, it was published officially in *The Texas Baptist Herald* that "the missionaries were living on bread alone." The statement was repeated all over Texas. The Board was in debt $6,000, but that was not generally known.

About this time Rev. W. C. Luther, the Corresponding Secretary of the Texas Baptist Sunday School Convention came to the office of *The Texas Baptist and Herald* and told me that Secretary J. M. Carroll was getting $2500 a year, having only his wife and one child in his family; was paying his brother-in-law, nephew and nieces out of the mission fund, $75, $50 and lower a month, and $20 a month rent on a room in his home, while he, Luther, was getting only $1500 a year, having a large family, and that his Sunday School Board had suggested an increase of his salary, but he was in doubt about accepting it, etc. Dr. Luther said further, that he had written Secretary Carroll for an itemized statement of his salary and expenses which Carroll had given by letter, but enjoined on him, Luther, to keep it to himself, "lest it known it might injure the organized work." Hence on April 2, I addressed a letter to each member of the State Board, saying: "If no one else does, I will propose reduction of expenses, etc." This, as we will see, stirred the Carroll's aflame!

The Open Breach at Last

April 10, 1894, the Board met at Waco. B. H. Carroll and J. M. Carroll both refused to speak to me. Seeing their great anger, I tried to conciliate Defendant B. H. Carroll, who took up his brother's case, saying I had "attacked him and the Board," asking through a mutual friend an interview. He refused to meet me. I asked him, through Dr. S. J. Anderson, to meet me in the presence of other brethren. He still refused. His anger seemed uncontrollable. This was just before the Board met Tuesday morning, April 10, 1894. When the Board met he demanded by resolution that I "put my complaint in writing." When the Board adjourned for dinner, I went to a stenographer, dictated, wrote out, and at two p. m. read to the Board the "Reform Paper."

Secretary J. M. Carroll promptly demanded that I specify who had proposed to keep anything "secret." I replied saying "whoever had done so had no doubt done so in good faith, thinking it was the best, and it was not necessary to specify. I only expressed my own views without blaming anyone for his views." But a peremptory demand was made on me for specification then and there! This demand being iterated over and over again, I was at least fairly forced to say that: "He, J. M. Carroll, had written a letter asking that his salary and expenses be kept secret lest if made known it might hurt the organized work," and that, "if he denied it, I would produce the letter, etc." He immediately took his seat, but was so angry that he soon afterwards stated in the open Board that "he would freely give $1,000 out of his salary to lick   S. A. Hayden." This and no more, Dr. R. C. Burleson stated privately and on oath, is what Defendant J. M. Carroll said. But on the trial he claimed to have added the phrase: "If it were right;" as if that altered the ethical aspect of the case.

In opposition to my Reform Paper proposing to reduce J. M. Carroll's salary back to the old figure of $2100 a year, the contract for $2500 a year was pleaded by Defendant B. H. Carroll as "inviolable till the year was out." This forced the withdrawal of the Reform Paper and it was agreed in the Board at my request that the unpleasant episode should not be published and no agitation should be had until the Convention met at Marshall six months later, when these matters of expense could be considered. The Board adjourned April 11, and on April 12 and 13 the whole affair, in the most perverted shape, appeared in the *Waco Telephone*, published in J. B. Cranfill's office and on his press, and was sent to the *Fort Worth Gazette* and given state-wide publication.

Source: S. A. Hayden, *The Complete Conspiracy Trial Book* (Dallas: Texas Baptist Publishing House, 1907), 21–23.

6.6 Benajah Harvey Carroll

Though not a first-generation Texas Baptist, B. H. Carroll was certainly among the most influential Texas Baptists in the nineteenth century. Carroll was the pastor of the prestigious First Baptist Church of Waco, President of the Baylor Board of Trustees, President of the Southern Baptist Theological Seminary Board of Trustees, and the first President of Southwestern Baptist Theological Seminary. Furthermore, he was a perpetual member of the Executive Board of the BGCT, one of the most popular pastors in the state, and a prolific author. Carroll's favorite topic was ecclesiology.

A. Salvation is Essential to Baptism and Church Membership

Here, if nowhere else, Baptists stand absolutely alone. The foot of no other denomination in Christendom rests on this plank. Blood before water—the altar before the laver. The principle eliminates not only all infant baptism and membership, but locates the adult's remission of sins in the fountain of blood instead of the fountain of water. When the author of the letter of Hebrews declares: "It is not possible that the blood of bulls and goats should take away sins," he bases the impossibility on the lack of intrinsic merit. Following the precise idea Baptists declare: "It is not possible that the water of baptism should take away sins." There is no intrinsic merit in the water. The blood of Jesus Christ, God's Son, alone can cleanse us from sin. True, the water of baptism and the wine of the Lord's Supper may symbolically take away sins, but not in the fact. "Arise and be baptized and wash away thy sins." "This is my blood of the new testament, which is shed for many, for the remission of sins." Both declarations are beautiful and impressive figures of antecedent fact.

A brother of another denomination once objected: "You Baptists have no method of induction into Christ. My people baptize a man into Christ." The reply was two-fold: (1) it is not enough to get a man into Christ; you must also get Christ into him, as he says, "I am in you and you in me." If you insist that baptism really, and not figuratively, puts a man into Christ, how will you meet the Romanist on the other half of it, "Eating the wafer of the Supper really puts Christ into the man. He eats the flesh for the real essence"? You must admit that the words are stronger for his induction than yours.

(2) Baptists have a method of double induction: "We have access by faith into this grace wherein we stand." Faith puts us into Christ. "It pleased God to reveal his Son in me." "Christ in you the hope of the glory." "Ye are manifestly declared to be an epistle of Christ, . . . written with the Spirit of the living God . . . in fleshly tables of the heart." "God, who commanded the light to shine out of the darkness, hath shined into our hearts, to give the light of the knowledge of the glory of God in the face of Jesus Christ." Thus the Holy Spirit puts Christ into us. We get

into him by faith. He gets into us by the Holy Spirit, thus fulfilling his words: "I in you and you in me."

This great, vital and fundamental Baptist principle, *Salvation must precede ordinances*, does at one blow, smite and blast those two great enemies of religion, sacramentalism and sacerdotalism. If ritualism saves, priests are necessary. If my salvation is conditioned on the performance of a rite, then also is it conditioned on the act and will of a third party who administers this saving rite. The doctrine of salvation by rites is the hope of the priest who alone can administer the rite. This gives both importance and revenue to his office. He multiplies the sacraments. "Two are too few. Let us have seven. The more, the better for us, and thus we will control our subjects not only from the cradle to the grave, but from conception in the womb to eternity."

Not only does our great principle destroy both sacramentalism and sacerdotalism, but it alone draws a line of cleavage between the church and the world. To perpetuate the baptism of the unsaved, whether infant or adult, tends to blot out from the earth the believer's baptism which Christ appointed. It is a question of discipleship. John the Baptist made disciples before he baptized them. Jesus made disciples before he baptized them. (John 4:1) John made disciples by leading them to repentance and faith. (Mark 1:15) Jesus commanded: "Go ye therefore and disciple all nations, baptizing them (the discipled)." Draw a perpendicular line. On the right of it write the words, Believers in Christ, Lovers of Christ. On the left of it write the words, Unbelievers in Christ, Haters of Christ. Now, from which side of that line will you take your candidates for baptism? Will you baptize the hating and unbelieving? You dare not. If from the other side you take them, then already are they God's children, for what saith the Scriptures: "Whosoever believeth has been born of God. Whosoever loveth is born of God."

Baptists do not bury the living sinner to kill him to sin. But they bury those already dead to sin. For devotion to this principle you may trace our people back by their track of blood, illumined by their fires of martyrdom.

Source: B. H. Carroll, *Baptists and Their Doctrines: Sermons on Distinctive Baptist Principles* (Nashville: Broadman Press, 1913), 20–23.

B. The Office of Deaconess

I will now discuss the office of deaconess in the church and give the interpretation of the three passages of Scripture cited, I Tim. 3:11, Rom. 6:1, and I Tim. 5:9, 10. The office of deacon being founded upon reason and upon the proper division of labor, if there be duties in a church which can be performed by women, then women ought to have this work. In my own experiences as pastor and especially in the administration of what is called the poor fund of the church, we often found, where the applicant for aid was a woman, that discreet women members of the church could find out better the propriety of aiding the case in question than men could do.

Sometimes delicacy was so involved that it was not proper for a man to have the investigation; then in the same pastoral experience I found that often women were to be baptized, particularly in the case of those who had no experienced women relative in the church, that it was necessary that some discreet, competent women members of the church should have it as a special duty to see that such candidates were properly prepared for this ordinance. The Apostle Paul more than once refers to women who were helpers in the work of the Gospel, and our missionaries often find in foreign countries cases where as men they are barred from access to women who are kept in seclusion. Therefore, I Timothy 3:11 should be rendered, "**Deaconesses** in like manner must be grave, not slanderers, temperate, faithful in all things."

There is not anything in the Scriptures to indicate that deaconesses should be ordained. There is no teaching on that subject. They simply received appointment from the church. As a pastor I found great help from a number of deaconesses that at my suggestion were appointed by the church.

Source: B. H. Carroll, *Baptist Church Polity and Articles of Faith*, ed. J. W. Crowder (Fort Worth: Southwestern Baptist Theological Seminary, 1957), 78–80.

C H A P T E R 7

Into a New Century, 1900–1914

7.1 George Washington Truett

Perhaps the most famous Texas Baptist pastor in either the nineteenth or twentieth century, George Washington Truett pastored the First Baptist Church of Dallas from 1897 until 1944. Known for his stirring sermons and beautiful voice, the First Baptist Church of Dallas became the most famous church in the Southern Baptist Convention during his tenure. An outstanding denominationalist, Truett served as President of the Southern Baptist Convention, the Baptist World Alliance, and as a fund-raiser for both Baylor University and Southwestern Seminary. He was also a strong advocate of the principle of separation of church and state.

A. Christ, the Cure for Trouble

Many requests come to a pastor, even in a brief period of time, asking for his counsel concerning the remedy for sorrow which comes in the dark and cloudy day. And that he or she needs to be definitely anchored to some passage, some promise, some direct quotation from the word of God, and especially be pointed to Jesus who comes with His definite assurance and with his all-sufficient wisdom, comfort and strength.

In response to this question, "What is the cure for sorrow?," many scriptures are quoted by many different persons, according to their own appraisement of various scriptures. Mr. Gladstone would have pointed the questioner to the fortieth chapter of Isaiah: "Comfort ye, comfort ye my people saith your God." Others would point the troubled questioner to that great, eighth chapter of Romans, with its confident statement: "We know that all things work together for good them that love God." Probably more persons point the troubled questioner to the fourteenth chapter of John than to any other scripture. If the whole Bible were blotted out except that one chapter, a troubled world might still be anchored to God by that fourteenth chapter of John's Gospel.

More than the easy-going and casual observer would detect, the undertone of trial and sorrow and perplexity that [*sic*] is heard in the world. As men are running to and fro for relief from their fears and anxieties and trials, Christ comes, as we find in this great chapter, with this sublime expression: "Let not your heart be troubled: ye believe in God, believe also in me." He is the Mediator between God and us. He is our Guide, our Helper, our Deliverer, our Redeemer, our rightful Master. Now, in view of all that is involved, He says, "Let not your heart be troubled."

You will recall how He came to utter this great word, and other comforting words to us in this whole chapter, just mentioned. He said to His little band of disciples, "I am going away very soon. I must leave you." In plain words, "I am very soon to die"; and the little band was utterly dazed, stupefied, horrified. They said one to another, "He said he is going away, going to leave us, going to die. What will become of his kingdom in this world? What will become of us, who came out on his side publically and followed him in the face of a jeering and unsympathetic world? What will be the end of his kingdom, if he is going away, going down to death?" When Jesus observed their tragic sorrow, he uttered the memorable words recorded by John in his Gospel, beginning with the expression, glorious beyond words, "Let not your heart be troubled."

Christ comes in this chapter to give a remedy, a cure for troubled lives, anywhere and everywhere, whatever their plight may be, from sin or bludgeoning sorrow. He comes with His adequate remedy, Himself being the remedy. To the one who may suffer loss, and faint, and for a time fall, Christ comes with His inspiring, revealing, uplifting, all-sufficient power.

What, then, is the cure for a troubled heart? Various answers can be heard.

One answer is the answer of despair. "No cure, no help, undone, over-borne, finished"—the answer of despair. That was suggested to Job, you will recall. Wave after wave of trouble rose over the old man; his health gone utterly, his former friends gone—and instead of being sympathizers, they were cynical critics—then his own wife said, "Curse God and die." That is the answer to life's trials and pain and perplexities. End it all in despair. Some are prone to take that road.

There came to the pastor of this church a letter, anonymously, saying, "My troubles overwhelm me." Many of his troubles were related in the letter. "Tell me, can I justify suicide?" If that person is in the audience today or is "listening in" anywhere, let me say to him that suicide is never justified on any ground. Suicide is self-murder. "Thou shalt not kill." Thou shall not kill thy fellow man. That is murder. Thou shalt not kill thyself. That is self-murder. Suicide is never, never defensible, forever!

Various causes lead people to take this way out—the overwhelming failure of some business plan, the shattering of some earnestly fixed confidence. There is the downfall of some cherished program planned for by day and dreamed of by night, and all of it ends in chaos and defeat and the poor suffering victim says, "What is the use? Why go on?"

And then, worst of all, there is the driving, down-pulling power of sin in men's lives. Sin with the accusing conscience behind it. Sin with the burning memory of it all, by day and by night. Life is such a tragedy of sorrow and perplexity and sin, that often the poor short-sighted questioner says, "I will end it all by suicide." Alas! He does not end it all. He only multiplies his sorrows eternally.

Another answer quite common for the cure of trouble is Stoicism. What is the doctrine of Stoicism? That doctrine states that you are to seal you heart against all feeling. Put it away. Deaden, your heart; deaden your sensibilities; deaden your emotions; refuse ever to give vent to tears; turn away from that course. Oh, how deplorable is the doctrine of Stoicism as a suggested remedy for a broken heart.

I wonder if you have ever read the confessions of those two great scientists who made quite a stir in the world—Darwin and Huxley? When old age came, and they began to review their life, oh how pitiful were their words about their feelings; their emotions had become utterly inadequate. I read recently the confession of one of them to a Christian friend. Sunday morning came and the Christian friend said, "Come, I am going to church. Go with me." He said, "No, I never go to church, never." The friend said, "Well, go with me today." He replied, "No, but I have another thing to say. You stay with me and you talk with me the whole hour that you would be in church, about religion and what it means to you and has meant and promises to be."

The Christian friend stayed with the great scientist and told him of his simple, reliant faith in Christ through all the years and how Christ consciously became more real and precious to him every day. And this layman who had the interview with the scientist tells us that the scientist said: "I have sealed my heart all the years against all that. I would give my arm if I could feel anchored as you have just spoken to me about yourself." That was the scientist's reply to the Christian's testimony.

Another great scientist died recently. His name I need not to call, for only recently have the flowers been laid upon his mound. He was an utter disbeliever, a man who talked, "No God, no angel, no spirit, no resurrection, no life beyond death and the grave which is the final chapter to the human experience." And yet during the weeks of his illness, it is said authoritatively that the only thing that would quiet that man was to read to him that marvelous twenty-third Psalm: "The Lord is my shepherd; I shall not want. He maketh me to lie down in green pastures: he leadeth me beside the still waters. He restoreth my soul: he leadeth me in the paths of righteousness for his name's sake. Yea, thou I walk through the valley of the shadow of death, I will fear no evil; for thou art with me; thy rod and thy staff they comfort me," and on and on. They only thing that would quiet that nervous, distraught, dying man was to quote again and again and again those haunting, comforting words about our Lord. How healing as a cure for a troubled heart!

I am thinking of a lovely girl who married years ago, and after a time the husband was taken. She worked very hard and every night she would go to the movies and try to forget. Then she would go home and cry herself to sleep, without comfort.

A young man was killed in another state awhile ago, and the young bride, who had been secretly married, was overwhelmed by sorrow and she called about her a group of very worldly young people, who said,

"Come, go with us to Florida, and where [*sic*] we will have the fragrance of the orange blossoms and every night we will have the lift of the dance and then we will sleep in the daytime and forget it all." Oh, think of such a proposal as a cure for a broken heart!

Then, there is another proposal as a cure for a broken heart. The answer of denial. It boldly declares, "There is not any trouble; there is not any sin; there is not any suffering; there is not any pain; there is not any death. All of it is bad though. Forget it." That is false philosophy. I saw the helplessness of a philosopher during the first world war, when boys all around us said, "Tell us if you know, how we can die in peace." Many of them put their dying hands in the hand of the great divine Lord and went, trusting and smiling and unafraid, out on the silent sea to the land beyond. I saw there the pitiful helplessness of this denial of all the facts of life. It is much like the ostrich, putting its head in the sand, afraid to face the facts of life.

Now Jesus comes to say, "Let not your heart be troubled, ye believe in God, believe also in me. In my Father's house are many mansions. If it were not so, I would have told you. I go to prepare a place for you, and if I go and prepare a place for you, I will come again and receive you unto myself, that where I am, there ye may be also." This is the only way out of trouble, out of perplexity, out of sorrow, out the blackest night, out of sin and sinfulness, seething about us like a great sea. It leads directly to Christ who bore the weight and the guilt of our sins in his own body upon the tree, that we, having died unto sins, might live unto righteousness.

Among the things that baffle and break the heart and perplex humanity are these three things: sin, sorrow, and death. Christ comes as the remedy for all three. Christ comes as the remedy for sin: "Thou shalt call his name Jesus, for he shall save his people from their sins." A tragedy unspeakable, incomparable is the tragedy of sin, but Christ is the victor, the conqueror. He is the great Physician. He cleanses the sinful heart by his victorious, vicarious, redeeming death on the cross. Christ is the cure for sin.

Christ is the cure for sorrow. We first have to wait; be of good courage and wait: "Trust me and wait. What I do thou knowest not now; but thou shalt know hereafter." "Wait and trust me," says Jesus, "and soon the day will break and all the shadows will flee away. Cleave to me and wait."

And then there is the grim, dark hour that faces some of us practically every day, the name of which is Death. Christ comes to us and says, "Do not be afraid. Do not be dismayed. I have the keys of death and of Hades. I am watching over the welfare of every man, woman and child in the universe who will take me as Savior and Lord. You need not be afraid, even as you die or as you see your loved ones die. You need not be frightened. I will be there to hold you, to hold you to my heart as a mother holds the frightened, sobbing child to her heart. Trust me. Fear not!"

Oh it is madness to chose any other road; it is stark madness to think you will get adequate help anywhere in the universe, apart from this divine Savior and Lord. Is he your Savior? Are you, my friend, trusting in Him? Are you leaning on Him? Are you following Him trustfully and obediently, as best you can, wherever He leads? Be not afraid; go right on triumphantly.

But are there those of you who have no anchor; no pilot, no guide, no physician adequate, no friend able to help you? You are without God and without hope in the world! Life goes on, my friend, with its trials multiplying, its problems becoming more baffling, its burdens becoming more weighty and, yet, here comes one to you saying, "Are you willing to let me help you through all this, and to forgive your sins?" Do you want Him to give you power above yourself? Will you trust Him?

Many of your loved ones who have gone on before, from under your roof have trusted Him. Your own dear mother trusted Him unafraid. Are you willing to trust Jesus and let Him be your Savior and let Him guide you so that your life here shall be expressed at its highest and best? Do you say, "Yes, I would like to trust him fully; down in my heart I have trusted Him"? Then you ought to come out for Him. You ought to confess Him before men. You ought to own Him today openly, for your own sake, and for the honor of the great Savior who loved you enough to die for you. He will be your adequate helper, your adequate cure for every trouble that will ever come to you.

Who says today, "I want to follow Him. Down in my heart I have made the surrender. I want to take my place in His church"? Or do you today say, "I want to begin, I want to start; I want to make the great surrender; today I want to record my vote, my commitment, my decision for Christ"? Then He calls you!

> Be not dismayed, whate'er betide,
> God will take care of you.
> All you may need, He will provide;
> God will take care of you.

Source: George W. Truett, *Who is Jesus?* ed., P. W. James (Grand Rapids: Eerdmans Publishing Company, 1952), 131–37. Reprint courtesy of Eerdmans Publishing Company.

B. Baptists and Religious Liberty

Southern Baptists count it a high privilege to hold their Annual Convention this year in the national capital, and they count it one of life's highest privileges to be citizens of our one great, united country. . . .

It behooves us often to look backward as well as forward. We should be stronger and braver if we thought oftener of the epic days and deeds of our beloved and immortal dead. The occasional backward look would give us poise and patience and courage and fearlessness and faith. The ancient Hebrew teachers and leaders had a genius for looking backward to the days and deeds of their mighty dead. They never wearied of chanting the praises of Abraham and Isaac and Jacob, of Moses of Joshua and Samuel; and thus did they bring to bear upon the living the inspiring memories of the noble actors and deed of bygone days. Often such a cry as this rang in their ears: "Look unto the rock when ye were hewn, and the hole of the pit whence ye were digged. Look unto Abraham, your father, and unto Sarah that bare you; for when he was but one I called him, and I blessed him, and made him many."

The Doctrine of Religious Liberty

We shall do well, both as citizens and as Christians, if we will hark back to the chief actors and lessons in the early and epoch-making struggles of this great Western democracy, for the full establishment of civil and religious liberty—back to the days of Washington and Jefferson and Madison, and back to the days of our Baptist fathers, who have paid such a great price, through the long generations, that liberty, both religious and civil, might have free course and be glorified everywhere.

Years ago, at a notable dinner in London, that world-famed statesman, John Bright, asked an American statesman, himself a Baptist, the
noble Dr. J. L. Curry, "What distinct contribution has your America made
to the science of government?" To that question Dr. Curry replied: "The
doctrine of religious liberty." After a moment's reflection, Mr. Bright
made the worthy reply: "It was a tremendous contribution."

Supreme Contribution of the New World

Indeed, the supreme contribution of the new world to the old is the
contribution of religious liberty. This is the chiefest contribution that
America has thus far made to civilization. And historic justice compels
me to say that it was pre-eminently a Baptist contribution. The impartial
historian, Mr. Bancroft, when he says: "Freedom of conscience, unlimited freedom of mind, was from the first the trophy of the Baptists." And
such historian will concur with the noble John Locke who said: "The
Baptists were the first propounders of absolute liberty, just and true liberty, equal and impartial liberty." Ringing testimonies like these might
be multiplied indefinitely.

Not Toleration, but Right

Baptists have one consistent record concerning liberty throughout
all their long and eventful history. They have never been a party to op-
pression of conscience. They have forever been the unwavering champions of liberty, both religious and civil. Their contention now is, and has
been, and please God, must ever be, that it is the natural and fundamental and indefeasible right of every human being to worship God or not,
according to the dictates of his conscience, and, as long as he does not
infringe upon the rights of others, he is to be held accountable alone to
God for all religious beliefs and practices. Our contention is not for
mere toleration, but for absolute liberty. There is a wide difference between toleration and liberty. Toleration implies that somebody falsely
claims the right to tolerate. Toleration is a concession, while liberty is a
right. Toleration is a matter of expediency, while liberty is a matter of
principle. Toleration is a gift from man, while liberty is a gift from God.
It is the consistent and insistent contention of our Baptist people, always
and everywhere, that religion must be forever voluntary and uncoerced,

and that it is not the prerogative of any power, whether civil or ecclesiastical, to compel men to conform to any religious creed or form of worship, or to pay taxes for support of a religious organization to which they do not belong and in whose creed they do not believe. God wants free worshipers and no other kind.

A Fundamental Principle

What is the explanation of this consistent and notably praiseworthy record of our plain Baptist people in the realm of religious liberty? The answer is at hand. It is not because Baptists are inherently better than their neighbors—we would make no such arrogant claim. Happy are Baptist people to live side by side with their neighbors of other Christian communions, and to have glorious Christian fellowship with such neighbors, and to honor such servants of God for their inspiring lives and their noble deeds. From our deepest hearts we pray: "Grace be with all them that love our Lord Jesus Christ in sincerity." The spiritual union of all true believers in Christ is now and ever will be a blessed reality, and such union is deeper and higher and more enduring than any and all forms and rituals and organizations. Whoever believes in Christ as his personal Savior is our brother and in the common salvation, whether he be a member of one communion or another, or of no communion at all.

How is it, then, that Baptists, more than any other people in the world, have forever been the protagonists of religious liberty, and its compatriot, civil liberty? They did not stumble upon this principle. Their uniform, unyielding and sacrificial advocacy of such principle was not and is not an accident. It is, in a word, because of our essential and fundamental principles. Ideas rule the world. A denomination is moulded by its ruling principles, just as a nation is thus moulded and just as individual life is thus moulded. Our fundamental essential principles have made our Baptist people, of all ages and countries, to be the unyielding protagonist of religious liberty, not only for themselves, but as well for everybody else.

The Fundamental Baptist Principles

Such a fact provokes the inquiry: What are these fundamental Baptist principles which compel Baptists in Europe, in America, in some far-off seagirt island, to be forever contending for unrestricted religious liberty? First of all, and explaining all the rest, is the doctrine of the absolute Lordship of Jesus Christ. That doctrine is for Baptists the dominant fact in all their Christian experience, the nerve center of all their Christian life, the bedrock of all their church polity, the sheet anchor of all their hopes, the climax and crown of all their rejoicing. They say with Paul: "For to this end Christ both died and rose again, that he might be Lord both of the dead and the living."

The Absolute Lordship of Christ

From that germinal conception of the absolute Lordship of Christ, all our Baptist principles emerge. Just as yonder oak came from the acorn, so our many-branched Baptist life came from the cardinal principle of the absolute Lordship of Christ. The Christianity of our Baptist people, from Alpha to Omega, lives and moves and has its whole being in the realm of the doctrine of the Lordship of Christ. "One is your Master, even Christ, and all ye are brethren." Christ is the one head of the church. All authority has been committed unto Him, in heaven and on earth, and He must be given the absolute pre-eminence in all things. One clear note is ever to be sounded concerning Him, even this, "Whatsoever He saith unto you, do it."

The Bible Our Rule of Faith and Practice

How shall we find our Christ's will for us? He has revealed it in His Holy Word. The Bible and the Bible alone is the rule of faith and practice for Baptists. To them the one standard by which all creeds and conduct and character must be tried is the Word of God. They ask only one question concerning all religious faith and practice, and that question is, "What saith the Word of God?" Not traditions, nor customs, nor councils, nor confessions, nor ecclesiastical formularies, however venerable and pretentious, guide Baptists, but simply the will of Christ as they find it revealed in the New Testament. The immortal B. H. Carroll has thus stated it for us: "The New Testament is all the law of Christianity. All the New Testament is the law of Christianity. The New Testament is all the law of Christianity. The New Testament always will be all the law of Christianity.". . .

Infant Baptism Unthinkable

It follows, inevitably, that Baptists are unalterably opposed to every form of sponsorial religion. If I have fellow Christians in this presence today who are the protagonists of infant baptism, they will allow me frankly to say, and certainly I would say it in the most fraternal, Christian spirit, that to Baptists infant baptism is unthinkable from every viewpoint. First of all, Baptists do not find the slightest sanction for infant baptism in the Word of God. That fact, to Baptists, makes infant baptism a most serious question for the consideration of the whole Christian world. Nor is that all. As Baptists see it, infant baptism tends to ritualize Christianity and reduce it to lifeless forms. It tends also and inevitably, as Baptists see it, to the secularizing of the church and to the blurring and blotting out of the line of demarcation between the church and the unsaved world. . . .

Surely, in the face of these frank statements, our non-Baptist neighbors may apprehend something of the difficulties compelling Baptists when they are asked to enter into official alliances with those who hold such fundamentally different views from those just indicated. We call God to witness that our Baptist people have an unutterable longing for Christian union, and believe Christian union will come, but we are compelled to insist that if this union is to be real and effective, it must be based upon a better understanding of the Word of God and a more complete loyalty to the will of Christ as revealed in His Word.

The Ordinances Are Symbols

Again, to Baptists, the New Testament teaches that salvation through Christ must precede membership into His church, and must precede, the observation of the two ordinances in His church, namely, baptism and the Lord's Supper. These ordinances are for the saved and only for the saved. These two ordinances are not sacramental, but symbolic. They are teaching ordinances, portraying in symbol truths of immeasurable and everlasting moment to humility. To trifle with these symbols, to pervert their forms and at the same time to pervert the truths they are designed to symbolize, is indeed a most serious matter. Without ceasing and without wavering, Baptists are, in conscience, compelled to contend that these two teaching ordinances shall be maintained in the churches just as they were placed there in the wisdom and authority of Christ. . .

The Church a Pure Democracy

To Baptists, the New Testament also clearly teaches that Christ's church is not only a spiritual body but it is also a pure democracy, all its members being equal, a local congregation, and cannot subject itself to any outside control. Such terms, therefore, as "The American Church," or "The bishop of this city or state," sound strangely incongruous to Baptist ears. In the very nature of this case, also, there must be no union between church and state, because their nature and functions are utterly different. Jesus stated the principle in the two sayings, "My Kingdom is not of this world," and "Render unto Caesar the things that are Caesar's, and unto God the things that are God's." Never, anywhere, in any clime, has a true Baptist been willing, for one minute, for the union of church and state, never for a moment. . . .

A Free Church in a Free State

That utterance of Jesus, "Render unto Caesar the things that are Caesar's, and unto God the things that are God's," is one of the most revolutionary and history-making utterances that ever fell from those lips divine. That utterance, once for all, marked the divorcement of church and state. It marked a new era for the creeds and deeds of men. It was the sunrise gun of a new day, the echoes of which are to go on and on and on until in every land, whether great or small, the doctrine shall have absolute supremacy everywhere of a free church in a free state.

In behalf of our Baptist people I am compelled to say that forgetfulness of the principles that I have just enumerated, in our judgment, explains many of the religious ills that now afflict the world. All went well with the early churches in their earlier days. They were incomparably triumphant days for the Christian faith. Those early disciples of Jesus, without prestige and worldly power, yet aflame with the love of God and the passions of Christ, went out and shook the pagan Roman Empire from center to circumference, even in one brief generation. Christ's religion needs no prop of any kind from any worldly source, and to the degree that it is thus supported is a millstone hanged about its neck.

An Incomparable Apostasy

Presently there came an incomparable apostasy in the realm of religion, which shrouded the world in spiritual night through long hundreds of years. Constantine, the Emperor, saw something in the religions of Christ's people which awakened his interest, and now we see him uniting religion to the state and marching up the marble steps of the Emperor's palace, with the church robed in purple. Thus and there was begun the most baneful misalliance that ever fettered and cursed a suffering world. For long centuries, even from Constantine to Pope Gregory VII, the conflict between church and state waxed stronger and stronger, and the encroachments and usurpations became more deadly and devastating. When Christianity first found its way into the city of the Caesars it lived at first in cellars and alleys, but when Constantine crowned the union of the church and state, the church was stamped with the impress of the Roman idea and fanned with the spirit of the Caesars. Soon we see a Pope emerging, who himself became a Caesar, and soon a group of councilors may be seen gathered around this Pope, and the supreme power of the church is assumed by the Pope and his councilors.

The long blighting record of the medieval ages is simply the working out of that idea. The Pope ere long assumed to be the monarch of the world, making the astounding claim that all kings and potentates were subject to him. By and by when Pope Gregory VII appears, better known as Hildebrand, his assumptions are still more astounding. In him the spirit of the Roman church became incarnate and triumphant. He lorded it over parliaments and council chambers, having statesmen to do his bidding, and creating and deposing kings at will. For example, when the Emperor Henry defied Hildebrand, the latter pronounced against Henry a sentence not only of excommunication but of deposition as Emperor, releasing all Christians from allegiance to him. He made the Emperor do penance by standing in the snow with his bare feet at Canossa, and he wrote his famous letter to William the Conqueror to the effect that the state was subordinate to the church, that the power of the state as compared to the church was the moon compared to the sun.

This explains the famous saying of Bismarck when Chancellor of Germany, to the German Parliament: "We will never go to Canossa again."

Whoever favors the authority of the church over the state favors the way to Canossa.

When, in the fullness of time, Columbus discovered America, the Pope calmly announced that he would divide the New World into two parts, giving one part to the King of Spain and the other to the King of Portugal. And not only did this great consolidated ecclesiasticism assume to lord over men's earthly treasures, but they lorded it over men's minds, prescribing what men should think and read and write. Nor did such assumption stop with the things of this world, but it laid its hand on the next world, and claims to have in its possession the keys of the Kingdom of Heaven and the kingdom of purgatory so that it could shut men out of heaven or lift them out of purgatory, thus surpassing in the sweep of its power and in the pride of its autocracy the boldest and most presumptuous ruler that ever sat on a civil throne. . . .

The Reformation Incomplete

The coming of the sixteenth century was the dawning of a new hope for the world. With that century came the Protestant Reformation. Yonder goes Luther with his theses, which he nails over the church door in Wittenberg, and the echoes of the mighty deed shake the Papacy, shake Europe, shake the whole world. Luther was joined by Melancthon and Calvin and Zwingli and other mighty leaders. Just at this point emerges one of the most outstanding anomalies of all history. Although Luther and his compeers protested vigorously against the errors of Rome, yet when these mighty men came out of Rome, and mighty men they were, they brought with them some of the grievous errors of Rome. The Protestant Reformation of the Sixteenth century was sadly incomplete—it was a case of arrested development. Although Luther and his compeers grandly sounded the battle cry of justification by faith alone, yet they retained the doctrine of infant baptism and a state church. They shrank from the logical conclusions of their own theses.

In Zurich there stands a statue in honor of Zwingli, in which he is represented with a Bible in one hand and a sword in the other. That statute was the symbol of the union between church and state. The same statue might have been reared to Luther and his fellow reformers. Luther and Melancthon fastened a state church upon Germany, and Zwingli fastened it upon Switzerland. Knox and his associates fastened it upon Scotland, Henry VIII bound it upon England, where it remains even till this very hour.

These mighty reformers turned out to be persecutors like the Papacy before them. Luther unloosed the dogs of persecution against the struggling and faithful Anabaptists. Calvin burned Severtus, and to such awful deed Melancthon gave his approval. Louis XIV revoked the Edict of Nantes, shut the doors of the Protestant churches, and outlawed the Huguenots. Germany put to death that mighty Baptist leader, Balthaser Hubmaier, while Holland killed her noblest statesman, John of Barneveldt, and condemned to life imprisonment her ablest historian, Hugo Grotius, for conscience's sake. In England, John Bunyan was kept in jail for twelve long, weary years because of his religion, and when cross the mighty ocean separating the Old World and New, we find the early pages of American history crimsoned with the stories of religious persecutions. The early colonies of America were the forum of the working out of the most epochal battles that earth ever knew for the triumph of religious and civil liberty.

America and Religious and Civil Liberty

Just a brief glance at the struggle in those early colonies must now suffice us. Yonder in Massachusetts, Henry Dunster, the first president of Harvard, was removed from the presidency because he objected to infant baptism. Roger Williams was banished, John Clarke was put in prison, and they publicly whipped Obadiah Holmes on Boston Common. In Connecticut the lands of our Baptist fathers were confiscated and their goods sold to build a meeting house and support a preacher of another denomination. In old Virginia, "mother of states and statesmen," the battle for religious and civil liberty was waged all over her nobly historic territory, and the final triumph recorded there was such as to write imperishable glory upon the name Virginia until the last syllable of recorded time. Fines and imprisonments and persecutions were everywhere in evidence in Virginia for conscience's sake. If you would see a record incomparably interesting, go read the early statutes of Virginia concerning the Established Church and religion, and trace the epic story of the history-making struggles of that early day. If the historic records are to be accredited, those clergymen of the Established Church in Virginia made terrible inroads in collecting fines in Baptist tobacco in that early day. It is quite evident, however, that they did not get all the tobacco.

On and on was the struggle waged by our Baptist fathers for religious liberty in Virginia, in the Carolinas, in Georgia, in Rhode Island and Massachusetts and Connecticut, and elsewhere, with one unyielding contention for unrestricted religious liberty for all men, and with never one wavering note. They dared to be odd, to stand alone, to refuse to conform, through it cost them suffering and even life itself. They dared to defy traditions and customs, and deliberately chose the day of non-conformity, even though in many cases it meant a cross. They pleaded and suffered, they offered their protests and remonstrances and memorials, and, thank God, mighty statesmen were won to their contention, Washington and Jefferson and Madison and Patrick Henry, and many others, until at last it was written into our country's Constitution that church and state must in this land be forever separate and free, that neither must ever trespass upon the distinctive functions of the other. It was pre-eminently a Baptist achievement.

A Lonely Struggle

Glad are our Baptist people to pay their grateful tribute to their fellow Christians of other religious communions for all their sympathy and help in this sublime achievement. Candor compels me to repeat that much of the sympathy of other religious leaders in that early struggle was on the side of legalized ecclesiastical privilege. Much of the time were Baptists pitiably lonely in their age-long struggle. We would now and always make our most grateful acknowledgment to any and all who came to the side of our Baptist fathers, whether early or late, in this destiny determining struggle. But I take it that every informed man on the subject, whatever his religious faith, will be willing to pay tribute to our Baptist people as being the chief instrumentality in God's hands in winning the battle in America for religious liberty. . . .

The Present Call

And now, my fellow Christians, and fellow citizens, what is the present call to us in connection with the priceless principle of religious liberty? That principle, with all the history and heritage accompanying it, imposes upon us obligations to the last degree meaningful and responsible. Let us today and forever be highly resolved that the principle of religious liberty shall, please God, be preserved inviolate through all our days and the days of those who come after us. . . .

Liberty Not Abused

It behooves us now and ever to see to it that liberty is not abused. Well may we listen to the call of Paul, the mightiest Christian of the long centuries, as he says: "Brethren, ye have been called unto liberty: only use not your liberty for an occasion to the flesh, but by love serve one another." This ringing declaration should be heard and heeded by every class and condition of people throughout all our wide stretching nation.

It is the word to be heeded by religious teachers, and by editors, and by legislators, and by everybody else. Nowhere is liberty to be used "for an occasion to the flesh." We will take free speech and a free press, with all their excrescences and perils, because of the high meaning of freedom, but we are to set ourselves with all diligence not to use these great privileges in the shaming of liberty. A free press—how often does it pervert its high privilege!. . .

Things Worth Dying For

When this nation went into the world war a little while ago, after her long and patient and fruitless effort to find another way of conserving righteousness, the note was sounded in every nook and corner of our country that some things in this world are worth dying for, and if they are worth dying for they are worth living for. What are some of the things worth dying for? The sanctity of womanhood is worth dying for. The safety of childhood is worth dying for, and when Germany put to death that first helpless Belgian child she was marked for defeat and doom. The integrity of one's country is worth dying for. If the great things of life are worth dying for, they are surely worth living for. . . .

A League of Nations

. . .Standing here today on the steps of our Nation's capital, hard by the chamber of the Senate of the United States, I dare to say as a citizen and as a Christian teacher, that the moral forces of the United States of

America, without regard to political parties, will never rest until there is a League of Nations. I dare to express also the unhesitating belief that the unquestioned majorities of both great political parties in this country regard the delay in working out a League of Nations as a national and worldwide tragedy.

The moral and religious forces of this country could not be supine and inactive as long as the saloon, the chief rendezvous of small politicians, that chronic criminal and standing anachronism of our modern civilization, was legally sponsored by the state. I can certify all the politicians and political parties that the legalized saloon has gone from American life, and gone to stay. Likewise, I can certify that the men of all political parties, without any reference to partisan politics, that the same moral and religious forces of this country, because of the inexorable moral issues involved, cannot be silent and will not be silent until there is put forth a League of Nations that will strive with all its might to put an end to the diabolism and measureless horrors of war. I thank God that the stricken man yonder in the White House has pleaded long and is pleading yet that our nation will take her full part with the others for the bringing of that blessed day when wars shall cease to the ends of the earth. . . .

The Right Kind of Christians

The noble doctrine and heritage of religious liberty calls to us imperiously to be the right kind of Christians. Let us never forget that a democracy, whether civil or religious, has not only its perils, but has also its unescapable [*sic*] obligations. A democracy calls for intelligence. The sure foundations of states must be laid, not in ignorance, but in knowledge. It is of the last importance that those who rule shall be properly trained. In a democracy, a government of the people, for the people, and by the people, the people are the rulers, and the people, all the people, are to be informed and trained.

My fellow Christians, we must hark back to our Christian schools, and to see to it that these schools are put on worthy and enduring foundations. A democracy needs more than intelligence, it needs Christ. He is the light of the world, nor is there any other sufficient light for the world. He is the solution of the world's complex questions, the one adequate Helper for its dire needs, the one only sufficient Savior for our sinning race. Our schools are afresh to take note of this supreme fact, and they are to be fundamentally and aggressively Christian. Wrong education brought on the recent world war. Such education will always lead to disaster. . . .

The Christian School

The time has come when, as never before, our beloved denomination should worthily go out to its world task as a teaching denomination. That means that there should be a crusade throughout all our borders for the vitalizing and strengthening of our Christian schools. The only complete education, in the nature of the case, is a Christian education, because many is a tripartite being. By the very genius of our government, education by that state cannot be complete. Wisdom has fled from us if we fail to magnify, and magnify now, our Christian schools. These schools are the foundation of all the life of the people. They are indispensable to the highest efficiency of the churches. The inspirational influences are of untold value to the schools conducted by the state, to which schools also we must give our best support. . . .

The one transcending inspiring influence in civilization is the Christian religion. By all means, let the teachers and trustees and student bodies of all our Christian schools remember this supremely important fact, that civilization without Christianity is doomed. Let there be no pagan ideals in our Christian schools, and no hesitation or apology for the insistence that the one hope for the individual, the one hope for society, for civilization, is in the Christian religion. If ever the drum beat of duty sounded clearly, it is calling to us now to strengthen and magnify our Christian schools.

The Task of Evangelism

Preceding and accompanying the task of building our Christian schools, we must keep faithfully and practically in mind our primary task of evangelism, the work of winning souls from sin unto salvation, from Satan unto God. This work takes precedence of all other work in the Christian program. Salvation for sinners is through Jesus Christ alone, nor is there any other name or way under heaven whereby they may be saved. Our churches, our schools, our religious papers, our hospitals, every organization and agency of the churches should be kept aflame with the passion of the New Testament evangelism. . . .

A World Program

While thus caring for the homeland, we are at the same time to see to it that our program is co-extensive with Christ's program for the whole world. The whole world is our field, nor may we, with impunity, dare to be indifferent to any section, however remote. . . .

A Glorious Day

Glorious it is, my fellow Christians, to be living in such a way as this, if only we shall live as we ought to live. Irresistible is the conviction that the immediate future is packed with amazing possibilities. We can understand the cry of Rupert Brooke as he sailed from Gallipoli, "Now God be thanked who hath matched us with this hour!" The day of the reign of the common people is everywhere coming like the rising tides of the ocean. The people are everywhere breaking with feudalism. Autocracy is passing, whether it be civil or ecclesiastical. Democracy is the goal toward which all feet are traveling whether in state or in church. . . .

The Price to Be Paid

Are we willing to pay the price that must be paid to secure for humanity the blessings they need to have? We say that we have seen God in the face of Jesus Christ, that we have been born again, that we are the true friends of Christ, and would make proof of our friendship for Him by doing His will. Well, then, what manner of people ought we to be in all holy living and godliness? Surely we should be a holy people, remembering the apostolic characterization, "Ye are a chosen generation, a royal priesthood, a holy nation, a peculiar people: That we should shew forth the praises of Him who hath called you out of darkness into His marvelous light, who in time past were not a people but are now the people of God."

Let us look again to the strange passion and power of the early Christians. They paid the price for spiritual power. Mark well this record: "And they overcame him by the blood of the Lamb, and by the word of their testimony; and they loved not their lives unto the death." O my fellow Christians, if we are to be in the true succession of the mighty days and deeds of the early Christian era, or of those mighty days and deeds of our Baptist fathers in later days, then selfish ease must be utterly renounced for Christ and His cause, and our every gift and grace and power utterly dominated by the dynamic of His cross. Standing here today in the shadow of our country's capital, compassed about as we are with so great a cloud of witnesses, let us today renew our pledge to God, and to one another, that we will give our best to church and to state, to God and to humanity, by His grace and power, until we fall on the last sleep.

Source: George W. Truett, *Baptists and Religious Liberty*, 16 May 1920.

7.2 James Bruton Gambrell

Gambrell made an immediate impact on Texas Baptist life upon his arrival in 1896. As a strong advocate of the Board System, the BGCT, the Southern Baptist Convention, and architect of the Sunday School Board, he served as the BGCT's warrior against Haydenism and Crawfordism. A brilliant organizer and motivator, Gambrell was also Texas's first President of the Southern Baptist Convention.

A. Questions in Baptist Rights

In a recent ordination, after the examination was finished as to experience and doctrine, a final question was asked: "Suppose that after you are a pastor, say five years from now, you change your views on doctrine and find yourself out of harmony with the views you have here expressed, would you consider it your duty or privilege to continue in a Baptist pulpit and preach your new views?" This raises a fine question of right and rights. So far as we know, Baptists stand for perfect liberty of conscience and liberty of speech. We would not deny to any one, even an infidel, the right to preach his doctrines. We would be willing to fight so that Catholics, Presbyterians, infidels and all sorts, might have freedom of thought and freedom of speech. But when a church is built to propagate the doctrines held by any people, it is no denial of the rights of free speech not to allow that church to be used to propagate other and contradictory doctrines.

There have appeared men in these later days who feel persecuted if they are not allowed to enter pulpits established to uphold a given set of principles, and there overthrow the very doctrines the church is set to defend. There is neither common sense, common honesty nor common decency in such a contention. Men who do not preach the accepted doctrines of the Baptists, have no right in Baptist pulpits, and it is no abridgment of their rights nor any persecution to keep them out. We are under no sort of obligations to furnish heretics with means to subvert the truth.

The same kind of reasoning applies to our denominational schools. Now and then a man in one of our schools finds, or thinks he finds, that the doctrines of the denomination are wrong, outworn, or something of the sort. No one should seek in the least to abridge his thinking, nor his defense of his thinking. The world is open to him. But when he claims the right to use an institution, its money, prestige and opportunities to overthrow the faith which the institution was founded to build up, he passes the bounds of liberty and enters the realm of arrogant license. Common honesty and decency would dictate that such a man resign his place and exercise his liberty without infringing on the rights of others.

In like manner our papers are under no obligation to lend themselves to the support of men who have quit the faith. The editor of this paper has no right to the use of the Catholic paper to overthrow Catholicism.

Coming closer into denominational lines, we have had in another state an illustration of a totally wrong conception of liberty. It is to an extent a question throughout the whole South. Those who call themselves "gospel missioners" (a very misleading name), have supposed that they have the right to use the machinery and instruments formed to promote co-operative work, to further totally different, and, as run, destructive plans, which they approve. For one we admit without the slightest question the right of a church to act independently, to send its money as it pleases, for what it pleases, without the slightest interference by any other church, any association, convention or what not. And we bear cheerful testimony to the worth and zeal of beloved brethren and sisters of that way of thinking. As long as they contend for the privilege of sending their money as they please, we will stand by them. The wisdom of their course is another thing; but their rights in the premises are not to be brought into question. The question is simply this: Have brethren who do not believe in the co-operative system of missions the right to membership in co-operative bodies and in general to use the meetings, the papers, the boards and all the machinery of co-operation to hinder and destroy co-operation? Certainly not. To ask the question is to answer it. If brethren want to give their money independently, they can do it, and, for one, we shall never bring in question that right; but when they ask us to turn over all we have to them, to undo our work, we shall insist that we have a right to control what we have created, and that too without molestation from them. It is their right to have all the meetings they want and to have them without molestation from any source. This right is not to be denied; but that is the limit of it.

For Dr. Crawford and his excellent wife, whom we know in the flesh, we have nothing for them but Christian love. We believe they are not on the best line. We believe they will find what has before been found, that their plan is unworkable to any considerable extent. It is a pity to divide and distract our people over such issues as they raise. But they must be accorded every right and at the same time be kept within their rights, that others may likewise enjoy some rights.

Source: J. B. Gambrell, *Ten Years in Texas* (Dallas: Baptist Standard, 1909), 128–30.

B. Church Sovereignty and Denominational Comity

These two questions lie close together. It is quite easy for us to press either one beyond its proper limits, and thus interfere with the other. There is nothing about Baptists which are more thoroughly agreed than church sovereignty; that is, the right of each separate church to govern itself and to regulate all of its affairs after its own mind without any interference from the outside. Once upon a time, in the heat of a popular discussion, we struck off this statement, which presents the case about like it is: "A church is a complete institution in itself; it is finished off and tucked in at both ends, and has no contrivance for attaching itself to anything else." That is the truth in a figure.

While the church sovereignty is universally accepted among Baptists, it is also widely understood that a church has not sovereignty in the sense that it can do anything it pleases, but rather, that it is under limitations of the law, and that Christ is the head of the church. It is not a legislative body, but an executive body; therefore, there are limitations upon church sovereignty.

First: No church can exercise in any such way as to go beyond its own sphere. Outside of that sphere it has no power, and in fact, no existence. The limitations of church sovereignty are the bounds of the church itself. All matters pertaining to more than one church are regulated by denominational comity.

Second: The simplest kind of truth is that one church cannot press its sovereignty to the point of depriving other churches of equal rights with itself. To illustrate: If one church should exclude a member, or depose a minister, another church could on its bare authority immediately restore the brother to membership, or the ministry; but, it would have no claim in the world on another church to recognize the act, or to co-operate with it; other churches having an equal right to an independent judgment.

The Scriptures unmistakably show that sovereign churches did co-operate for the support of the gospel and for the maintenance of sound doctrine. We may, therefore, follow the apostolic churches in these particulars, but all questions concerning co-operation go not on sovereignty, but on comity. A council composed of messengers from churches can never be invested with the slightest degree of church character. It is at this point that a great many otherwise sound Baptists fall into the heresy of Presbyterians or Episcopalians. It is altogether within the power of the sovereign to send messengers to a council, as the Antioch church did send messengers to Jerusalem. But no church can claim anything of their messengers in council on the score of church sovereignty, because the transaction is carried entirely beyond the limits of independent churches, out on the open field of inter-church or denominational comity.

On this broad platform the plans for co-operative effort in denominations are wrought out. Here the messengers from the churches ought to stand on equal footing. Here there should be mutual confidence and respect; openness and fairness, and consideration for the welfare of the one common cause. The church which will not enter this field of comity except with the understanding, that the other churches shall yield to its judgement, ought, as a matter of common fairness and decency, to refrain from sending messengers. A council necessarily implies freedom to hear and discuss and determine. A body of messengers absolutely fixed cannot be a council at all, and so if we fall into the practice that some of the churches have recently adopted of instructing their messengers to our great denominational councils, and putting them beyond all counsel that should at once bring the whole matter of associations and conventions to an end.

There is one thing immeasurably greater than a great convention, however large it may be in numbers, however imposing in the character of the messengers present, and that is the spirit in which a convention ought to be held. If there be not present a common respect, and a willingness to confer in the spirit of brotherliness, then a great convention may be lowered to the level of a group of caucuses, each working to secure a definite end, without reference to the spirit of deliberation. From such a convention, in the language of the prayer book, "The good Lord deliver us."

Source: J. B. Gambrell, *Ten Years in Texas* (Dallas: Baptist Standard, 1909), 159–61.

7.3 Lee Rutland Scarborough

Scarborough joined the faculty of Southwestern Seminary in 1908 as the first professor of evangelism. Upon the death of B. H. Carroll in 1914, he succeeded Carroll as the second President of Southwestern Seminary. The consummate denominationalist, Scarborough chaired the 75 Million Dollar Campaign, served as President of the SBC and the BGCT, and was a prolific author on the subject of evangelism. Under his leadership, Southwestern Seminary grew in size and educational prowess.

The Essentials of an Evangelistic Victory (Isa. 38:1–6)

I am going to read to you about a sick king.

"In those days was Hezekiah sick unto death. And Isaiah the prophet son of Amoz came unto him, and said unto him, Thus saith the Lord.":

My friends, it is very important for your soul when God speaks to you whether you are sick or well. Now listen to what God said to this very sick man:

"Set thine house in order; for thou shalt die, and not live. Then Hezekiah turned his face toward the wall, and prayed unto the Lord." Men usually pray when they get sick. They turn to God in the time when their lives are imperilled. This good king, when he received God's message turned to God in prayer and said: (I call your attention to this prayer. It is a very short prayer. I call your attention to what he did not pray for. I do not know what I would ask God for if I were on my dying pillow. I do not think I would pray the prayer Hezekiah prayed. I am quite sure I could not pray that prayer. It is a wonderful prayer in what he did not ask and in what he did ask. Notice what he did say.)

"Remember now, O Lord, I beseech thee, how I have walked" not before my neighbor, not before my family, not before my closest friends, but "how I have walked before thee" before the all-seeing eye of God who knows our thoughts, reads aright our lives.

"Remember now, O Lord, I beseech thee, how I have walked before thee in truth and with a perfect heart."

That was his inside religion—how God saw him as he was on the inside. You can deceive your closest friends for a while, even the most intimate members of your family you can deceive for a while; but you cannot deceive God. He knows you as you are. He sees you as your soul is; and when you call on God to see how you walk before Him you may know that the record He makes is true and what He sees are the facts in your life.

And then he said:

"Remember I have done that which was good in thy sight." That was his outside life before men, how he walked before men, how he lived before them.

"And Hezekiah wept sore."

Some great men wept. I read the story of how Carpentier's manager stood over the crumpled form of a man whose destiny he promoted and wept. They told me that in the most tragical time of the recent war, when it looked like defeat was coming to the forces of freedom, when the cloud of unspeakable darkness of German dominance seemed to weep over all Europe and threatened to spread over this country, that the Secretary of our great war President, Woodrow Wilson, came into Mr. Wilson's private office one morning and found him weeping, with his heart breaking. The secretary said to him, "Mr. President, why these tears?" He said, "I am weeping for the imperiled liberties of the world."

Here is a great man, a good king of Judah weeping because of broken health and because of a disordered kingdom. He needed to set his house in order; and on what he thought on his dying pillow, he had wept sore. It seemed that Isaiah had withdrawn for the moment from the weeping king and later God sent the prophet back to him. And God said unto Isaiah:

"Go, and say to Hezekiah, Thus saith the Lord, the God of David thy father, I have heard thy prayer."

The first message was the message to the disordered house and dying body. The second message, after he cried and prayed was:

"I have heard thy prayer."

Oh, what a good message! I wonder how many of you Christian people have gotten the answer to your prayer—as you prayed, God's wireless brought back to you an answer from God. I have had those experiences, when God has said, when the prayer was ended, "I have heard thy prayer. I have sent forth the answer." I wonder how many of you have gotten the answer to your prayers for a great revival, in your city. I wonder how many of you have "prayed through" this meeting. You have advertized it remarkably well. I have been in a great many places where the commercial and industrial interests of the people were predominant. But I want to say that I have never been in a town where there seemed to be such a great spirit of liberality and Christianity as manifested in the pages of the daily papers in your city in advertizing this meeting. You have made plans; you invested a considerable amount of money; you have heralded this meeting and organized for it far and wide; and I bless God for the preparation and publicity you have made. But I ask you a very much more important question. How many of you have prayed through and gotten your answer from God that He will give an answer to prayer and responses to the gospel a great soul-sweeping, community-wide revival? "Go tell the dying king that I have heard his prayer."

And the second part of the message was "I have seen thy tears." Oh, what a glorious word from heaven that God as He sits regnant on His throne sees the tears of the child of God as they come from a broken heart. Why this same God was able to make a world, or a thousand or a billion worlds, and yet he said, "I saw the tears trickling down the cheek of one of my servants." I bless God that there is no tear of the broken-hearted widow, there is no tear of the penitent sinner in all the wide world that misses the attention of Almighty God.

"I have seen thy tears." "I have heard thy prayer."

"Behold I will add unto thy days fifteen years." Remember that God said to him in the first message, "Thou shalt die, and not live." And here the cry of faith seems to have reversed the judgement of God. Prayer and tears made the king over and gave him a new lease on life. That was a personal blessing. I wonder tonight how many people there are here who need a personal blessing. Some of you have lost your grip on God through gold or the desire of it, or in laboring to make bread for your family, or pleasure or something else has come into your life and has released your grip on God. Once you prayed; now you do not. Once you loved the Bible; now you do not. Once you were an attendant upon the worship of God; now you are not. Once you lived a consistent, prayerful life; but now your life is covered with sin. I wonder how many of you tonight can pray that God will give you a new lease on your spiritual life, that you may come back to Him and be worth while in His king-dom.

"I will give you a personal blessing."

"Tell him that I will not only give him fifteen years, a personal bless-ing, but tell him I will deliver thee and this city out of the hand of the king of Assyria: and I will defend this city." There was a community blessing. Oh, my friends tonight I wonder how many of you have been engulfed and conquered and mastered by the desire to get rich in a little while from these oil fields that are about you and I wonder how many of you have lost your faith and grip on God because of this greed for gold. Oh, the engulfing power of materialism. I wonder how many of you would like to see your city delivered from the power of sin that your people may come back to God. God says, "I have heard thy prayers and seen thy tears. I will give you a personal blessing and a community blessing, not only that, but I will defend your city." God says I will give you a permanent blessing, a blessing that will not pass with the passing of your prosperity and with the passing seasons. But I will establish here my throne. I will build up your city walls and I will become a defender of your city.

Now, on the basis of this wondrous story in the Old Testament I want to take it out of its life back yonder twenty-five or twenty-eight hundred years ago and bring it and apply it to your city and to your need. I see in this incident the three great essentials for a revival of religion. I will tell you, my friends, that great revivals of religion come down from God and they are based on human conditions. I know that God wants to give to this city a great revival. It is promised in the Bible; it is the very word of the Divine Spirit and I know the Divine Heart is yearning and that the Divine power is ready. But, as Jesus Christ, the mighty Son of God, could not perform many miracles in the place where He was reared, Nazareth, because of their unbelief, so tonight, my friends, God cannot and will not impose a revival on a people who are unwilling to pay the price of it. These three conditions are as follows:

First there must be

Prayer

God's people must pray for the power of God, pray for the preacher and the preachers, pray for the singers, pray for each other, pray for the Christian people, pray for themselves, and pray for our unsaved, lost friends. Twenty-five years of almost incessant labor in trying to win men to Christ has convinced me by a thousand arguments that it is the prayer of God's people that brings down the power of God and creates the evangelistic atmosphere. All of God's people can work at this task. You will not leave it to the pastor, or to this preacher, or to the officers of the church. Thank God, the simplest man, the youngest child, the oldest man or woman, can work at this great job of getting the power of God down on this community. Prayer is an absolute essential. And if you have made up your mind to be prayerless, God will make this a power-less community. . . .

Consecrated Life

Now, that is one of the essentials of a great revival. The second essential laid down here is a consecrated life. It is found in the prayer of this king. He said, "O Lord, remember my life, how I have lived, how I have walked before thee." The first thing God's people ought to do to start a revival is to get right with God and get right with each other. . . .

A Burdened Heart

The third essential is a burdened heart. "I have seen thy tears, I have answered thy prayer." The central passion of the gospel is what this city needs tonight. Oh, you have a passion for oil, for making money; you have had that! You have had passion for building a town. I said last night that you could take a little bunch of those men with this spirit and go out here, whether you have oil or not, and build a town. Now, I want you to get a burden for the lost in this city. You have men and women going as straight to hell as these drills out here are going to the bowels of the earth for oil. And you will go on and never shed a tear for the men and women who are going to hell all about you. Why, Jesus Christ spent His life in tears. The Apostle Paul said, "Three and a half years in Ephesus I warned every man with supplication and tears." Somebody has got to weep over this city, or it will go to hell. . . .

We have got to meet God's conditions if we have a revival. We have got to pray and straighten up our lives and be burdened for the lost. "They that sow in tears shall reap in joy, he that goeth forth and weepeth, bearing precious seed, shall doubtless come again with rejoicing, bringing his sheaves with him." God help us to go in to win this city for Jesus Christ.

Source: L. R. Scarborough, *The Tears of Jesus: Sermons to Aid Soul Winners*, rpt. (Grand Rapids: Baker Book House, 1967), 25–39. Reprint courtesy of Baker Book House.

7.4 Mary Hill Davis

President of the Texas Woman's Missionary Union from 1906 until 1931, Davis attended every meeting of the WMU until her death. During her tenure, the circle plan for the WMU and the week of prayer for state missions were inaugurated. Due to her dedication to missions, the Texas Baptist state missions offering bears her name. A powerful speaker, Davis's addresses at the annual session of the WMU motivated the membership to great heights and demonstrated her zeal for missions.

Dallas, 1909

I preface this simple message with a brief survey of some of the manifold activities of the Baptist Women's Missionary Workers of Texas, for the past year. Someone has said that the backward look never sees the way out, for God's golden age is in the future. The past, however, with it abiding gracious blessings, and its many abject failures, must ever be a striking and convincing lesson in the school of methods in which we all, young and old alike, are enrolled on a common footing as eager, striving pupils. This retrospect places in the limelight the weak points of constructive organization, bringing into vivid evidence our either too lavish or too meager practical conception of applied Christianity. Prodigality as well as narrow economy, is a treacherous shoal upon which the ship of opportunity goes to speedy destruction. God gives no power to be wasted. Jesus said, "Gather up the fragments, that nothing be lost." Let us strive to give, rather than to get; to shine rather than to absorb.

Last year the Baptist women of Texas went forth like the crusaders of old, to attain the goal of a high ideal, and they added a glorious page to the history of women's work, illumined by a self-sacrifice that shall shine through all the ages because of the resplendent revelation of the self-abnegating motive that impelled the act. Such work demonstrates the significant truth that when God's finger points the way, gracious results must follow as an unerring sequence. The will to labor is ever greater than the power to achieve. That co-operation not only gives cumulative power, but opens the door to higher spheres, has been shown to us in a marvelous way. The splendid manner in which you put into God's treasury the money necessary to build the Annie Jenkins Sallee School for Girls in China, is a monument to your fidelity and self-effacement. You put your hand in the plough and did not turn back, and so doing you have glorified your God, and put a crown of immortality within reach of a countless throng who are only waiting for the message of hope and love divine.

But, sisters, this forward step is but a beginning. More and more He calls for our best to be placed upon His altar, to be used of Him in the fulfillment of the divine plan. Schools, orphanages, hospitals—how they appeal to the heart of woman, and find significant expression in her tender compassion for the suffering, helpless, and the friendless! It is the very essence of the spirit of Christ to be willing to labor for those whose faces we cannot see, whose cry we cannot hear. We rejoice that the twilight period is over, and that the sun has set upon the old dispensation. We greet the new day, for we are awake and alert to both our individual and collective responsibility, and only ask, "Lord, what wilt thou have US to do?" I am profoundly convinced that when the supreme opportunity does arrive, you will not withhold your hand, or fail to accord a quick gracious response, as did the loving, worshipful Mary of old, when Martha's soul-stirring message fell upon her eager, listening ears. "The Master is come, and calleth for thee." Deeds, not words, are the alpha and omega of all activity, whether secular or religious.

In a short time, your officers will submit their annual reports. You will, I know, hear them with deepest interest, for they are but a record of your own stewardship. What you put into them, will bless or condemn, as it returns to you. To get the best of life means that we must put the best into life, and we cannot shift the responsibility. We have each a real part to play in the great drama of humanity.

As I turn to the future with its countless possibilities, I am thrilled with an optimism that finds expression in the glorious message from Isaiah: "Watchman, what of the night?" And the watchman said: "This morning cometh." I do not profess to be a prophetess on the wall of Zion, but is it not good for us to scale the heights from time to time, and like the faithful watchman of whom we have read, look out upon the world, and ask each other, "What of the night?" And as we see the work developing, and the countless doors that God is opening to us, we can indeed send back the glad reply, "The morning cometh."

Blind optimism is not a prerequisite for us to feel and know and see that a new day is breaking, for the crimson and golden streaks of light, heralds of the dawn, are radiating in matchless splendor across the darkness of a fast fading night. As we look upon the nations of the earth, we are not the advancing glow. What wonderful things have been done in Turkey! Its constitutional government is scarcely twelve months old. A nation has been born in a day, and neither diplomat nor missionary had an intimation of the wonderful change that came about almost in the twinkling of an eye. God's ways are mysterious and decisive, a miracle of power and energy.

China, Japan, and even Russian have felt the life-giving influence and impulse of a new day, and are turning with outstretched hands to the Son of Righteousness.

And what of our own favored country? Rabbi Harrison says, "America, the favored child of God, clothed with the coat of many colors, like Joseph of old; a titanic nation." Can a day dawn for such a splendid nationality, whose very civilization is surcharged with brilliant daring and glorious achievement? The answer comes back in glad affirmation, and its clarion notes ring clear and true from the lakes to the gulf, and from ocean to ocean. Let us look at one of the indications that point to a new dispensation, embracing a new freedom, which shall be pre-eminently satisfying in its healing benefice. The Temperance movement which is sweeping like some great tidal wave over our country, is most significant of coming changes. The conflict has been long, and the bleeding hearts of wives, mothers, and little children have been crushed and broken by a relentless hand that knew no mercy. Thank God, victory lies just over the hill, and we are pressing upward to the heights, with the dawn shining upon our upturned faces.

It is a helpful sign of the times that our young people are more and more allying themselves with the cause of Jesus Christ. This statement finds confirmation in the fact that the last twenty years have witnessed an advance that stands without a parallel in the history of young people's movements.

What of the children, the boys and girls, our juvenile possibilities? Tis true we have juvenile courts, settlement homes, reformatories, and places of refuge for their care and reclamation. All good in their places, but, mothers, did it ever occur to you that all of these splendid institutions do to a certain extent, condemn our own shortcomings? Every child that is born into the world has an inalienable right to fair play. Josiah Strong says that to rob a child of his rightful heritage—a normal child— is to rob society, to wrong civilization, to impoverish the future, and to destroy possibilities of unknown and perhaps priceless worth. I wish every woman here today would read John Spargo's book, "The Bitter Cry of the Children." It will break your hearts, but it will give you a new vision of responsibility which no mother can evade, or relegate to others. In our conception and interpretation of the sacredness of the relationship lies the pivotal point, in child life and in home life, as well as in religious and national life.

Here is what Robert Collyer says. Bind his gracious precepts to your hearts. These are his words:

"I would not ask whether you talk to the children about the Father and the Blessed Christ in the moments which come only now and then. The true mother, through these first years is to her children in Christ's stead. She is the way, the truth, and the life to them. And so it is scant use merely to tell them of the way. They must go in it first in your arms, or they may not go at all."

My co-workers, let me call your attention to the foreign population that surges through the sea gates of our empire state. The immigrant is ever a perplexing problem, and one that calls for a most alert genius to successfully cope with its manifold complexities. Friends, we are only on the threshold of this stupendous work. It is true that we have a consecrated young missionary at our own port of Galveston, one whose impulse is filled with the desire to do her full part by the incoming aliens. But granting that her work is of the very highest order and most finished quality, think of it, one little courageous woman trying to be of helpful service to thousands. One hand to help and comfort the multitudes. But our very insufficiency is the Father's opportunity. The divine plan calls for beginnings. One heart aflame with the spirit of Christian service cannot fail to become a powerful instrumentality in the fulfillment of God's ideals. But what if many hearts catch the inspiration of the verities of the world unseen? Then, indeed, seemingly colossal difficulties will be removed, and Heaven's sweet chariot will swing low, a blessed evangel, inspiring the lives of men and women with a sublime faith that marks the path of life to the throne of God.

Sisters, this partial survey of the world's horizon will, I hope, give you at least a slight conception of your unparalleled opportunities, as the night recedes and the morning comes. Let us away with the pale, anemic endeavor, and address ourselves to a work vitalized by the red corpuscles of a robust, virile activity. "Shall we wear our palms, and pay no price for them?" Enthusiastic people may make blunders, but fainthearted people never make anything. The mightiest force in the world is a fire in the human soul. Our own alert, throbbing personalities will inspire and attract others, and one of the supreme aims of our life should be to help somebody, and to enlist the other women. Enlist how? By standing in some famous pulpit, and raising our voices in sermons unmatched in the world's history, or speaking in some renowned forum with an eloquence as alluring as the melting sweetness of the lute of Orpheus? No. God points us not to Mars Hill, or magnificent temples, not the highways or the crowded marts, where the trade of earth sits enthroned, and where alien and native born strive for supremacy, but rather to the individual wherever he may be reached. It is difficult to touch the masses, but to be able to bring the message of loving service with effectual power to one person, one woman, is indeed a rare and worthy achievement. How absolutely necessary is this heart to heart, face to face presentation of the important fact of the brotherhood of man! And you cannot hope to touch your neighbor's heart with anything less than your own.

I heard a great preacher in a recent sermon say that the world is dying for the want of personal contact. The thought gripped my innermost soul, and I hope its deep significance may sink also into every fiber of your being, and help you to realize fully the wonderful import of personal service. It has been demonstrated in every department of religious and philanthropic work, that the personal, vital touch is supremely essential, and a power that cannot be estimated in all redemptive work, where service is its own reward, and sacrifice a privilege.

Let us look, therefore, into each other's hearts, and pledge ourselves anew to higher and better things, remembering that God will fairly flood each life with all the power He can trust us to use wholly in His name. In looking inward, let us not lose the grand, triumphal outward and upward look of the soul, which sees the dawning of the great new day, and hears the watchman proclaim with glad hosannas that echo and re-echo over the hills of Zion, "Rejoice, the morning cometh."

Source: Mary Hill Davis, *Living Messages* (Dallas: Woman's Missionary Union, 1934), 7–10. Reprint courtesy of Woman's Missionary Union of Texas.

7.5 Franz Marshall McConnell

McConnell served as the Corresponding Secretary of the BGCT in 1910, in the Oklahoma Baptist Convention from 1916 until 1922, and as the superintendent of evangelism at Southwestern Seminary from 1914 until 1916. He was also the editor of the *Baptist Standard* from 1928 until 1944. A prolific author, McConnell primarily wrote on the subjects of evangelism and ecclesiology.

Church Discipline

General Offences: A general offence is one which is of such a character that the cause of Christ is injured in such a manner that it becomes the duty of the church, as a body, to deal with the offender.

General offences may include denial of the fundamental doctrines of the Bible, violation of one or more laws of the Ten Commandments, or the laws of the country, and disturbing the harmony and peace of the church.

Two things should be kept in mind when dealing with persons accused of a general offence: One is that the accused should be saved, if possible, to the church and righteousness; the other is that the good name and standing of the church must be preserved.

To an extent the principle of private, fraternal treatment laid down by the Master, in dealing with personal offenses, should govern when a member is accused of a general offense. It is against the church and, therefore, against every member. Hence, the pastor, deacons, or any member of the church may endeavor, with propriety to reclaim the one going astray. It is their duty to do so. There should be the most earnest effort put forth to save the erring member.

In doctrinal matters very few people go very far wrong at once. They usually drift into heresy. Their drifting may be observed by the other members. It should cause concern and sincere grief. The spiritually minded should undertake to restore such in the spirit of meekness. (Gal. 6:1–2; 2 Tim. 2:25.) They should go to him and admonish him and endeavor in all Christian love to show him the truth.

If efforts do not avail, if he persists in the heretical beliefs and becomes an opposer of the power and influence of the truth, the church must cut loose from him. "A heretic, after the first and second admonition, reject." However, we should learn the lesson from modern surgery that the main effort should be to save and not to destroy. Too many surgeons and too many churches have been hasty in performing operations on members of the body. Of course, good surgery removes the offending member when it endangers the life or permanent health of the body, and good church discipline acts the same way; but courageous sanity instead of nervous haste should guide.

In dealing with general offenses there should be fairness and Christian consideration shown the accused that all reasonable people would justify the church in its course. Haste and unwise management of the case often produce factional feelings hurtful to the harmony and fellowship of other members. There should be much earnest prayer. The spirit of Christ should prevail through all.

If all efforts to reclaim the offending member fail, charges should be brought against him in the church. They should state specifically and clearly his offense, and he should be given a copy of them. A general charge such as "unchristian conduct," or "conduct unbecoming a Christian," or "covenant-breaking," is not sufficient. The general charge may be made, and then the particulars set out; but the accusation should be specific. There should be a time set for trial and the accused member should be given every reasonable opportunity to establish his innocence. The church should rejoice if he is able to prove himself innocent. If, on the other hand, he is not able to do so, or if he defies the church, or attempts to dominate the situation and treat the church with contempt, the membership, in sorrow but in fidelity to the truth and justice, must withdraw fellowship from him, regardless of consequences.

Sometimes when a member on trial sees that he is found out and his guilt is going to be established, he becomes penitent, confesses, and asks forgiveness. Such confessions are seldom sincere. The members should endeavor not to be swept off their feet at such a time. There is a wide-spread impression that "when confession is made the church has to forgive." Such is not the case. The church should exercise due caution. When the repentance is evidently sincere and the member on trial admits his guilt and humbly promises to live right if forgiven by the church, then the church may forgive him; but there is no compulsion on its part to do so. If the members have any doubt of his sincerity and the genuineness of his repentance, they may very consistently refuse forgiveness at that time. It is altogether proper to stop proceedings and give the accused time to show his repentance, at least for a month or two. If then he shows by a consistent life that he was sincere in his promise to amend, the church should forgive fully and joyfully. Dr. J. M. Pendleton, in his *Church Manual*, pp. 141,142, advocated immediate exclusion, without trial, of those accused of offenses of an infamous or scandalous character. I cannot agree with him. It seems to me that a church should be as considerate of an accused person as our courts are of those accused of crimes against the civil government. It would appear, also, that the more serious the accusation the more harm might be done the accused if he were innocent. Furthermore, an amount of evidence that would justify exclusion without trial, would certainly convict in a trial and fully sustain the church in excluding the offender. 1 Corinthians 5:1, 5, cited by Dr. Pendleton, does not sustain his position. It does not say that the Corinthian church should take such drastic action without taking proper steps to prove what was "reported." Every man is entitled to a fair and impartial trial by an organization of which he is a member. The Bible is just; but it is merciful even to the greatest sinners.

In the trial of a member the proceedings should be orderly and calculated to obtain justice. The church should attend to its own business in its own way. Bringing in attorneys, or court-stenographers, or anything that would influence the members in either eliciting and considering the facts, or their decision in the case, should not be tolerated by the church.

The proceedings should be about as follows:

1. The church should be in its business meeting with moderator and clerk present ready to proceed in an orderly way.

2. The accused should have had due notice and an opportunity to be present.

3. If he is not present and no one knows of providential hindrances the records in the case should be read by the clerk and evidence to sustain the charges submitted. Then, if the church deems the evidence sufficient to sustain the charges, fellowship should be withdrawn and a proper record made. If the church does not deem the evidence sufficient to sustain the charges, the case should be dismissed.

4. If the accused is present, the clerk will read the record thus far in

the case, including the charges, and the accused will have an opportunity to make his answer. If he says that he is not guilty of the accusation, the church will present the evidence it has in support of the charges. The accused will then present his side of the case and introduce evidence supporting him.

5. After all the evidence is submitted and explained so that it is understood by the membership, a vote of the church is taken on the question "Shall the charges be sustained?"

6. If a majority votes in the affirmative the moderator declares the charges sustained. If a majority votes in the negative, the moderator declares that the charges are not sustained and the case is dismissed.

7. If the charges are sustained, it is then in order to have a motion to withdraw fellowship. Such a motion should be passed by a unanimous vote. If a minority votes in the negative, they should be asked if they will be reconciled to the exclusion of the accused. If they reply that they will not be reconciled, then the church should withdraw fellowship from them. If, on exclusion of the accused, such an agreement on their part should be satisfactory to the church. On all matters of fellowship there must be unanimity in church action.

After a member is excluded, all the others should treat him as having been justly dealt with. There should be no sympathetic expressions which could be construed as upholding him and condemning the church. Such sympathy is disloyalty to the church of Christ. All the members should desire and pray for his restoration; but they should desire it only on the basis of repentance and confession.

Source: F. M. McConnell, *Manual For Baptist Churches* (Philadelphia: Judson Press, 1926), 106–13.

7.6 Joseph Martin Dawson

Pastor of the First Baptist Church of Waco for thirty-one years and editor of the *Baptist Standard*, Dawson spoke out on a myriad subjects to a very wide audience. He served as the Texas Baptists' voice against the deprecation of women, the exploitation of immigrants, and child labor. Dawson, however, was best known for his work in the realm of separation of church and state.

The Implications of Separation of Church and State

Not only must we see the principle of religious liberty, but it is necessary to see its implications as well.

1. Religious liberty does not mean indifference.

"Galileo cared for none of these things." Conviction is at the bottom of true religious liberty. Here we can agree with Voltaire: "I may not believe a word you utter, but I would go to the death for your right to say it." We do not join in the secular song, "What the hell do we care?" Believers in religious liberty care to the utmost for truth and right, and will give their all to make them prevail in the earth.

2. Religious liberty is not license.

The late George W. Truett, a veritable apostle of religious liberty, whose speech in its behalf delivered on the steps of the National Capitol in 1920, quoted with emphasis: "Brethren, ye have been called to liberty, only use not your liberty for an occasion to the flesh. There is a pseudo-liberty which is nothing but license, destitute of responsibility. The freedom which the Republic's founding fathers thought to establish was not freedom from the law, but freedom within the law; not freedom from government, but freedom within the government. Freedom of worship does not contemplate freedom from worship, which would deny the law of one's being and the law of his Creator. It is undoubtedly true that in America multitudes of people have construed freedom of religion to mean freedom from religion, which may explain the fact that seventy-five million of the inhabitants are members of no Church, and that our nation is becoming increasingly pagan. President Lowell was wont to say, "Harvard University believes in academic freedom, therefore, we are very careful whom we invite here to teach." Academic freedom involves the responsibility to inquire into all subjects with open mind, to make full proof of all teachings, which is both honest and scientific, and the responsibility to witness to the truth by smiting error and proclaiming facts. These convictions apply also to religious freedom. It is not an escape but a responsibility."

3. Religious liberty requires humility and sincerity

Jesus said, "If the Son shall make you free, ye shall be free indeed."

The Jews had just pretended that they had never been in bondage to anyone. How could they assert such a colossal pretension? They had been in physical bondage to the Egyptians, in physical and economic bondage to the Babylonians, now they were in political bondage to the Romans, and were continually in moral bondage to sin. "Whoso committeth sin is the bond slave to sin." Men proudly declare today they are free thinkers, when investigation reveals they are the slaves of certain intellectual pretensions. Others shout they believe in personal religion, when what they mean is they wish license to indulge in what is inebriating and debasing to the lowest degree. Consider, if you will, how many arrogant social and political pretensions parade through our world in the name of liberty. "Ye shall know the truth and the truth shall make you free."

4. Religious liberty requires charity and forbearance.

Chief Justice Oliver Wendell Holmes, at long last, succeeded in getting adopted as our interpretation of freedom of speech: "Free thought is not free thought for those who agree with us, but freedom as well as for the thought we hate." Wisely did Douglas Southall Freeman, the eminent biographer of Robert E. Lee, say in a radio address to Southern Baptists: "Free examination of truth is a right that inheres religious liberty. That right many men exercise in their appraisal of the faith of others. When others similarly hold up to the light of truth the beliefs we cherish, most of us are quick to speak of 'fanatics' or 'cranks' and to insist that liberty is not license. That is true, but past anguish of mankind is admonition that we had better risk the abuse of our own faith by extremists than the suppression of any faith be it ever so extreme." Only in the spirit of Jesus must we attempt to purge the house of prayer, and we must never close the gates of the temple.

Source: Joseph Martin Dawson, *Religious Liberty Restated: Delivered Before the Southern Baptist Historical Society, Ridgecrest Baptist Assembly, August 29, 1944* (Fort Worth: Archives, Southwestern Baptist Theological Seminary), 10–12. Reprint courtesy of Southwestern Baptist Theological Seminary.

7.7 Mina S. Everett

Corresponding Secretary of the Woman's Missionary Union of Texas in 1889, Everett also served briefly in Brazil as a foreign missionary and was always indefatigable in her fund raising for missions. Despite opposition by both men and women who believed she was leading women away from their Biblical roles, Everett persevered in her work. During her tenure the Texas WMU took its first steps toward a WMU building, a private newspaper, and a training school for women.

The Call to State Work

The call to state work was of the Lord, for when I spoke to Mrs. F. B. Davis and others about the need of some one to go throughout the state to awaken the women to enlarged service, to win the children and young people as helpers in the Master's work, Mrs. Davis said, "I have been thinking and praying about this very thing. I have thought of you as the one to do this work, only it would take you from the Mexican work which is so dear to your heart." Others expressed their opinion very similar to Mrs. Davis. After further thought and prayer it occurred to me that if chosen to do this special work that I could from time to time, still be with the Mexican work, for I would still be a Missionary of the State Board in case our plan should still come into effect–. A missionary of State Board in cooperation with Home Mission Board and Foreign Mission Board of the Southern Baptist Convention.

The work of organizing the women, children and young people, if blessed by God, would result in help to each Board, increased interest, more prayer and increased contributions. Correspondence with leading women of the little work then in hand, found a glad response, some saying, "God speed the time." Next was correspondence with some of the brethren. Dr. F. M. Law was the first among the brethren to whom our letter was addressed. Having heard him say to brother Hawthorne, at the close of a meeting with the women of the Bryan Church, "Sister Mina ought to be heard in every Baptist Church in this state." He was a strong support in the new undertaking also a goodly number of other brethren enthusiastically encouraged the plan and really to their credit it became an authorized work. When Dr. Cranfill, representing the State Board and Dr. J. M. Carroll, representing the Foreign Mission Board were consulted, the plan was received with immediate cooperation.

October, 1889, Convention in Houston, Brother Carroll came before the Women's meeting to announce that the appointment of Miss S. Everett, Corresponding Secretary and Organizer for the Baptist Women Missionary Work had been ratified by the three Boards. State, Home and Foreign each to share equally in the salary of $75.00 per month which, at my own request was reduced to $50.00, believing I could pay traveling and economical living expenses with that amount which I did until State workers failed to receive passes over any of the railroads. Then I was paid on request $60.00 per month, excepting during a part of the last year which I donated. At the time I was not out in the field work on account of a long wait for a broken limb to heal and by an over sight, the Home Board's treasurer was not notified, consequently a check for the quarter salary was received, which was returned immediately. No, I was not doing the work for the (little) money that was in it, as said by one woman opposed to the work. A number of times while I held the position, gifts were offered me for my own personal use, but never accepted. One time some valuable lots were offered me. I held my position as a sacred trust. I could not accept gifts for my own use because people offered on account of appreciation of service rendered. At the close of seven years service, I had saved enough of salary to amount to $100.00, so let it go down in history that our women's work in Texas was not and is not a money getting proposition for self, but money raising for our Lord's work.

Source: Mina S. Everett, *Recollections* (Fort Worth: Archives, Southwestern Baptist Theological Seminary, 1920), 13–14.

7.8 WMU Advancement

In advancement of the Lord's work, the WMU of Texas has always been on the cutting edge in ministerial techniques. One of the most significant steps taken by the organization was the advent of the Missionary Training School, which became connected to Southwestern Seminary in 1911.

Training School Report for 1914

The story of the year as it touches our Training School is of interest. As we look back upon the pathway over which we have passed from the eminence of twelve months review, we get a better idea of the true proportion of things. Some difficulties that loomed up big when at close range, have dwindled into mole hills in size, and other matters that seemed insignificant at the time of their occurrence have proved themselves to be of great import in the progress of our work. The Lord always plans better things for us than we can plan for ourselves. This is forced upon our consciousness again and again. We cannot say that God has granted just those things which we had planned and hoped for our Training School, but we are confident that He has done for us the best things, and in the best way.

Our Baptist Women's Missionary Training School, which is "the crystallized thought" of a few earnest, enthusiastic, pioneers, bids fair to become the crown jewel in our cluster of Baptist educational institutions.

Our new building, in which we hoped to be domiciled at the beginning of our first school term, is completed externally; work on the interior goes forward slowly, but surely. The beautiful, symmetrical form of our school, with its name emblazoned in letters of gold above its classic Doric columns, is the admiration of all who see it.

Mrs. W. L. Williams whom we love to call "The Mother of Our Training School," is planning attractive surroundings for our building in a lawn adorned by trees and shrubs and flowers. It gives us special pleasure to have this important feature of ornamentation under the wise direction of this dear friend of our institution, not only because of her wide experience and marked success in landscape gardening, but especially because it is to us a beautiful and fitting thought that the loving imprint will be written in loving green around our Training School, the building of which originated in her own far-seeing mind and generous heart.

Other beautiful gifts have been gratefully received in the form of valuable books from our President, Mrs. F. B. Davis, and from Mrs. W. B. Harrison, of Fort Worth. Thus is begun a collection of books which we trust will grow until it merits Carlyle's definition of a library—"A true university" where students may enjoy intercourse with superior minds, and may receive from them their utmost precious thoughts.

Today we have enrolled in our Training School 61 women—a larger number than we had at this time last year, and our prospects for next year are brighter still. Many college women are planning to come to us in 1915.

The students that have gone out from us are filling useful posts of service, some as foreign missionaries, others as pastors' assistants, many as efficient Christians [*sic*] workers in church life, or in city mission fields, and more still are adorning that most sacred sphere of perfect womanhood, as they, devoted mothers, raise their children "in nature and admonition of the Lord."

A movement far-reaching in its influence in behalf of our Training School, and also for the promotion of Bible study in our denominational schools, was initiated at Baylor College last June, when, at an educational conference held by the State Chairman of the Educational Committee, a resolution was offered by Mrs. W. B. Bagby, of Brazil, asking each of our twelve B. W. M. W. districts to award a Bible scholarship of one hundred and fifty dollars to a worthy young woman making the highest grade in Bible study in the denominational school of her district. This scholarship will enable such a young woman to prosecute her studies one year in the Training School. At a meeting of the Executive Committee of the B. W. M. W. of Texas this resolution was read and adopted, thus putting upon it the seal of approval of the Baptist Women Mission Workers of our State. We earnestly hope that every one of our twelve districts will rally to this plan, whereby interest will be stimulated in Bible study in our district schools, and yearly each district will have its representative in the Training School as the beneficiary of its Bible scholarship.

As is well known, our students receive their theological training in the Seminary. There is no need to dwell upon this phase of their work, which has ever stood unchallenged as to its soundness and thoroughness and adaptation to every demand.

It gives us pleasure to report that the new departments of work introduced into our Training School curriculum this year are proving themselves to be of practical benefit to our women. The course in instrumental music, given free of charge, is enabling many of our girls and preachers' wives to become efficient in this important branch of Christian service, who, but for this opportunity, would have ever remained handicapped as workers in the Master's vineyard.

One of the most popular classes in our Training School is the class in public speaking. We feel that our women are alive to the fact that in this new and exceptional age, the well-equipped Christian woman must be able to speak the faith that is in her. The object of this class is to train our women to speak easily and naturally, and to be ever ready to speak a word for Jesus when by doing so his cause may be advanced.

Our kindergarten on Seminary Hill has more than met our expectations as an efficient means for teaching our women methods effectively adapted to Sunday School work, and as an attractive place where mothers may safely leave their little ones while they attend classes.

In a needy district of North Fort Worth, our "Good Will Center" is filling a long-felt need. We began this settlement work with a kindergarten, for we believe that "the future has a child's hand on the latch." The children of today are the citizens, the political, commercial, and religious leaders of tomorrow. The motive of our "Good Will Center" is to win souls to Jesus, and this end is kept ever in view in class work, in the flourishing Sunday School conducted there each Sunday afternoon, and in the district visiting, in which our girls engage each Saturday afternoon. We want this work to grow until we have a Settlement Home of our own, in which some of our workers may live and be in constant contact with the people whom we would help physically, and lift up spiritually; we want to have there a Day Nursery, where mothers may safely leave their little ones, and have them cared for, while they go to the day's work; we want to have an Employment Bureau, and classes in vocational training and in Bible study; we want our "Good Will Center" to be a beacon of light shining for Jesus, in a dark community, and giving direction along many lines to groping fellow-beings; we want "the interests of humanity to get into our hearts and circulate in our blood," so that we shall be quick to recognize their needs, and shall, by your good help, be able to render speedy relief. We thank you sincerely for the assistance which made it possible to inaugurate this work. May we not count upon your continued aid in carrying it forward?

The review of the year's work has much to encourage us. Our Training School lives for one thing—to equip women to teach the Bible and win souls. We believe its work is not in vain.

We have briefly shown the character and extent of the work we are trying to do. Shall we stop here? Shall we not rather ask ourselves what has been God's thought concerning women in this century? Every door of usefulness and culture and honor is open to her. Scarcely fifty years ago there were only four avocations open to women compelled to earn their own living—that of seamstress, teacher of small children, factory girl, and maid of all work. Today she is employed in three hundred and sixty-nine different occupations enumerated by our census. Women have become "heirs to all the ages in the foremost files of time." In the light of these new opportunities and new obligations, what is our duty? Is it not to prepare our women to enter with honor upon these new fields of labor? Is it not to fit them for the greatest of all callings—the only calling really worth while—that of Christian service? Let us take courage by past achievements and press forward to greater and better things in the future. Let us strive to ascend to loftier heights whence we may have a larger vision in view. Let us seek to hasten the day when every woman, not only in our own great, broad State, but in all our fair, loved Southland, shall be an efficiently trained worker in the vineyard of the Lord. When this shall have come to pass, the day will be not far distant when the kingdom of this world shall become the kingdoms of our Lord and of his Christ; and He shall reign forever and ever.

Respectfully submitted,

Mary C. Tupper

Principle Baptist Women's Missionary Training School

Source: *Proceedings*, Baptist General Convention of Texas, 1914, 240–42.

7.9 Security of the *Baptist Standard*

One of the most significant ways that Baptists promoted denominational endeavors was through denominational newspapers. From the outset, however, the *Texas Baptist*, the *Texas Baptist Herald*, and other smaller newspapers were owned by individuals, not the BGCT. Following the newspaper war that accompanied the Hayden Controversy, a desire for a denomination-ally owned periodical was strong. Almost immediately upon his arrival, J. B. Gambrell created a small newspaper named the *Missionary Worker*. This paper was owned by the denomination, but was discontinued in 1910. Ownership of the *Baptist Standard*, after passing through several owners, was finally transferred to the BGCT in 1914.

A. The *Missionary Worker*

This little newspaper belongs to the Convention. It is no sense a general newspaper. It is devoted, with singleness of purpose to the work of this body. In our present condition it is a practical necessity. In Texas we have been living in the Acts of the Apostles over again, for the last few years. Paul and other workers of that day had no paper, but if Diotrophes and some others had been running papers, a missionary paper would have been an Apostolic necessity. A ceaseless stream of misrepresentation, detraction, and false teachings has been turned on the public. The *Missionary Worker* has continued the policy of defense and stood for the truth of God against the opposers. We have reason to be grateful with the results. The longed for peace will not come by giving place to those whose unceasing work is to sow the seeds of discord among the brethren. As in Apostolic time, so now, some men must be withstood to their faces, before the brethren because they are wrong. The millennium has not yet arrived in Texas, but it will be hastened by the faithfulness and true Christian courage in dealing with false and mischievous teachings, heralded in the name of sound Baptist doctrine.

During the year, a special Centennial issue of the *Worker*, twenty pages, in handsome cover, was gotten out, largely in catechism form. Every phase of the work of our people was treated and made plain. Thirty thousand copies were printed, and the paper scattered broadcast over the state. We have a few thousand copies reserved for use, where most needed. The effect of the wide spread diffusion of accurate information communicated in simple form was most wholesome. It settled a whole brood of evil surmises and put the minds of many good brethren at ease respecting our work. The cost of this special edition was more than five hundred dollars, but many times the cost came back to the work in different form. We sow information and reap sparingly. The subscription list of the *Worker* has been largely increased this year. We now issue 7,200 copies. The financial part of this report will show the income and out go of the paper to be even. There is a real balance if all transportation was counted.

Source: *Proceedings*, Baptist General Convention of Texas, 1901, 23–24.

B. The *Baptist Standard*

With profound gratitude to God do we record our appreciation of the constantly increasing sympathy and support accorded the *Baptist Standard* by Texas Baptists. Throughout the State our noble co-workers, the pastors and missionaries, together with the hosts of men and women who are interested in the development of all denominational activities have demonstrated in many ways their interests in, and affection for, the state denominational paper.

At the beginning of the Convention year just closed, the total indebtedness of the *Standard,* amounting to $30,000, was liquidated. The payment of this debt was made possible through a generous gift of $15,000 by those noble servants of God, Deacon and Mrs. H. Z. Duke. There was a joyful response on the part of the messengers to the last Convention, and many other friends throughout the State, to this unprecedented offer, and the remaining $15,000 was speedily provided. So soon as the indebtedness was paid, the *Baptist Standard* was offered to the Baptist General Convention, and received by a committee appointed and directed by the Convention to receive such publication in behalf of the Baptist General Convention. There have been many evidences of the wisdom of the policy of denominational ownership, and very gratifying has been the response to the appeal in behalf of our denominational organ.

We are happy to report a steadily increasing interest in the matter of increasing the circulation of the *Baptist Standard*. We will never approximate the highest efficiency of our state denominational paper until it is placed in every Baptist home, in every Baptist church, in Texas. To do this, we must depend very largely on the pastors and missionaries, many of whom have testified to the great value of a denominational paper as an informing, inspiring and enlisting agency. We commend the

example of Pastor S. J. Porter of the First Baptist Church of San Antonio, who has already announced the purpose of his church to place the
Baptist Standard in every home represented in the membership of that
noble church. It is our earnest hope that many other churches throughout the State will take similar action. We confidently believe that no
more fruitful investment can be made by any church than to insure the
circulation among its membership of the denominational paper. We appeal to the friends of the *Standard* to lend us their help in an effort to
double the circulation of the *Standard*.

Source: *Proceedings*, Baptist General Convention of Texas, 1914, 122.

7.10 The Buckner Orphanage

From its outset, the Buckner Orphanage was a private, benevolent endeavor supported through the efforts of R. C. Buckner. The growth of the
orphanage, its cost, and the increasing age of Buckner, however, led "Father
Buckner" to transfer ownership of the orphanage to the BGCT in 1914.

Transfer of Ownership

We, your committee appointed to make response to the generous
and noble proposition to place in the hands of the Baptist General Convention of Texas the properties and control of the Buckner's Orphan's
Home, as set forth in the written statement of Dr. R. C. Buckner, read to
the Convention and handed to your committee and which is made a part
of this report, as follows:

"It is in my mind, as President and General Manager of the Buckner
Orphans Home, to tender its entire property and control to the Baptist
General Convention of Texas, pending the completion of plans, and of
improvements for which contributions have been made and are now being formulated. This would of course have to be done in such satisfactory way as would protect the vital points of the charter and by-laws;
and in loyalty to all friends who have made donations for specific purposes, stated or clearly understood. And for my part I do not care how
soon such transfer shall be made on the conditions herein expressed.

"This must not be interpreted as indicating any doubt of the con-
tinual and greater growth of this institution, nor of any modification of

my personal entire satisfaction with the principles, purposes, plans or management under which its wonderful success has been attained.

"Nor must it be inferred from this that I am in the least tired of the work, or have any disposition to lay it down."

In response to the foregoing proposition, and by way of acceptance thereof, we submit the following:

Whereas, Buckner Orphan's Home, as an institution, has made a generous tender of its extensive property, as set forth in the annual report of its President and General Manager, R. C. Buckner, made to the Convention, Thursday evening, November 19, 1914, and a tender of its management to the Baptist General Convention of Texas; and

Whereas, This Convention recognizes the unparalleled success of this great institution in its business affairs and its accumulation and utilization of so much valuable property, always protected by its charter; while at the same time it has provided for and trained, each year, a large family of orphan children and other dependants, under the same charter and provision of its by-laws; be it hereby

Resolved, 1. That we would not challenge the wisdom and beneficence of Divine Providence that has sustained and otherwise blessed this Christly institution from its very beginning;

Resolved, 2. That we would not dare lay hands on God's own anointed institution in the way and kind of interference or hindrance; but only to bless, to encourage and to help.

Resolved, 3. That we accept that which has been tendered to us, in the same spirit of confidence, loyalty and love with which it has been offered; and that, in such acceptance, we solemnly pledge that the principles and purposes set forth in its charter and by-laws shall ever be held by us as sacred and inviolable.

Resolved, 4. That hereafter, as heretofore, all lands, bequests, donations, gifts and contributions of any and every kind now held or that may be acquired by Buckner Orphan's Home, shall be held, appropriated and used for the purposes of the institution and its ward, and in the interest of no other institution, enterprise or person, whatever or whomever.

Resolved, 5. That from twenty-seven brethren, annually nominated by this Convention, a Board of Directors of Buckner Orphan's Home shall be selected and authorized under and according to the provisions of its charter and by-laws, and shall be recognized, adopted, appointed and authorized by the Convention, as its own committee, to look into and after the work, and to make report each year to this Convention at its annual sessions; the report to be subject to discussion, and to be acted on, and spread upon our minutes, as any other report that may come before us for our consideration.

Resolved, In conclusion that the Convention will ever heartily rejoice in and co-operate in every degree for the betterment, enlargement, prosperity and efficiency that may come at any and all times to this, our very own Buckner Orphans Home.

Source: *Proceedings*, Baptist General Convention of Texas, 1914, 124–25.

7.11 Baptist Hospitals

Baptist benevolences in Texas also included the founding of several hospitals. Before 1920, either local Baptist groups or local associations operated nine hospitals in the Lone Star State.

Report of Committee on Baptist Sanitarium

At a special meeting of the Board of Directors of the Baptist Sanitarium of Houston, held November 9, 1910 at Houston, Texas, the following proceedings were had:

T. M. Kennerly offered the following resolution:

Resolved. That the institution, and all of the property of the Baptist Sanitarium of Houston, be tendered to the Baptist General Convention of Texas, to be accepted and taken by said Convention, and conducted and operated as are the other institutions of the Convention; said Convention to elect the directors thereof.

That if said Convention shall accept said institution and property, that the President and Secretary, or other proper officers of the Baptist Sanitarium, be and are hereby directed to make proper and necessary conveyances of the property, and that necessary amendments be made to the Charter of the Baptist Sanitarium to accomplish these ends.

Robt. Carroll moved the adoption of said resolution, and said motion was amended by R. E. Burt and unanimously adopted.

J. L. Gross, President

T. M. Kennerly, Secretary

Your committee, to which was referred the tender of the Baptist Sanitarium of Houston to the Baptist General Convention of Texas, by the Trustees of the said Sanitarium, reports as follows:

Realizing that extreme caution should always be exercised in multiplying the agencies and institutions of this Convention, your committee called a conference of all the several general boards of this Convention to consider the matter referred to the committee in all its bearings. After patient and prolonged consideration of the subjects in every possible aspect, the large conference of several boards, together with the committee, reached the hearty and unanimous conclusion that the Convention should accept the proffer made by the Trustees of the Baptist Sanitarium of Houston, and such is the recommendation of the committee.

The committee deems it proper to say, for the information of the Convention, that this Sanitarium had been in operation about three years; that it has already accomplished much good; that its location is most advantageous for such an enterprise; that it is now more than paying its way, and that it is constantly growing in public favor, not only in the great commercial center where it is located, but also the regions round about.

In recommending the acceptance of this institution as one of the institutions of the Convention, your committee feels free to say that its recommendation is made solely on the merits of the particular case before it, and must not be understood as setting a precedent for the indiscriminate acceptance of institutions of different sorts that may from time to time be tendered the Convention.

The committee sincerely hopes, and firmly believes, that if the Convention shall accept and adopt the Baptist Sanitarium of Houston, the contiguous territory, and other sections of the State as well, will give to the institution such support, financial and otherwise, as will make for its rapid growth and ever enlarging usefulness.

Geo. W. Truett

Forrest Smith

C. C. Coleman

D. C. Freeman

W. R. Brown

Geo. B. Butler

J. E. Hughes

J. J. Pipkin

U. S. Thomas

Edw. Stubblefield

Source: *Proceedings*, Baptist General Convention of Texas, 1910, 110–11.

7.12 The Education Commission

By the final decade of the nineteenth century Texas Baptists had created more Baptist colleges than they could support. Financial agents were combing the Lone Star State attempting to raise money in the hope that their efforts might keep their institutions solvent. By 1897, however, it had become apparent that these schools, with the exception of Baylor University, were inadequate in finances and academic strength. For this reason, the BGCT created the Education Commission in 1897 to oversee the raising of funds and aid in the further development of these schools. Despite minor setbacks, the Education Commission was considered a success.

Report of the Education Commission, 1906

President and members of the Education Commission:

Dear Brethren: At a called meeting of the Education Commission in the city of Dallas, October 18, 1906, a report of the progress was made by the Corresponding Secretary. At the same meeting his resignation was to take effect at the present session of the Baptist General Convention, was accepted. He now offers his final report and asks that his books, receipts, etc., be passed on by the Auditing Committee before this report is presented to the Convention.

SOME FACTS

1. Financially, so far, the year's work of the present Corresponding Secretary has been a failure. In another very important sense it has not failed. In the campaign the Secretary followed his own judgement and

that of several denominational leaders wiser in experience than himself. During the first several months of the campaign he took no collections; the people were not prepared for it. He has, however, attended Educational and Mission Rallies throughout the state, likewise Fifth Sunday Meetings and Associations. He has sent out, first and last, thousands of letters, written or printed, also circulars of information wherever he could find pastors to receive or distribute them. He has responded to many invitations for addresses wherever possible, has sought to enlarge the vision of the brotherhood with respect to matters-educational. He has aimed to develop a spirit of fraternity and comradeship between the schools in and out of Correlation. The speeches have been supplemented with column after column of printed matter, hoping to make clear to the brotherhood the object and needs of the schools, and to make clear to the brotherhood the object and needs of the schools. Thanks are due our Baptist papers for loyalty and promptly printing everything furnished them. The Secretary believes that if the same policies are pursued faithfully, continually throughout the future it will mean growth in gifts to Education as has been Missions in the last decade. The work will proceed IF HEARTILY HELPED BY PASTORS. The work will fail without their help. The Secretary has trustfully furnished them this year with the following results:

2. Up to date, $8752.55 has been received in cash from the speeches by the Corresponding Secretary. This does not include any amounts locally contributed to certain of the correlated schools hereinafter cited. Of the above amount of $1684.43 were payments on the old notes and pledges to the endowment of Baylor University and $100 to be given direct to Baylor College.

3. That no more money has come in from certain centers and counties has been a disappointment to the Secretary, crushing beyond description, except for the loyalty of those who pleasure [sic], and except for his duties in Baylor University and make him desire to serve a series of years as Secretary of the Education Commission.

4. At the meeting of the Commission in Dallas in December, 1905, after the Convention of that year, it was agreed to try to raise $139,000 to be divided as follows:

Baylor University $62,500

Baylor College 30,000

Howard Payne College 20,000

Decatur College 5,000

Burleson College 6,000

Canadian Academy 2,500

Goodnight Academy 2,500

5. Immediately after the said meeting of the Commission, it was found that the Panhandle brethren were disappointed at the small amount of $2500 for each school, and that it was unlikely that any amounts whatsoever would be given under the circumstances. After a visit to the field and an examination of the conditions at Canadian and Goodnight and as an incentive to local action the Corresponding Secretary offered, on the authority of the Executive Committee, to give $2500 each to Canadian and Goodnight for the purpose of erecting a brick, stone or cement-stone dormitory. The Canadian Trustees offered to raise $500.00. After due consideration and advice of certain well informed brethren, it was finally agreed to give the $2500 to Canadian in blocks of $500 as the Trustees raised and expended its pro rata part of $5000. Its Trustees officially accepted, went to work, called in the first $500, which the Secretary promptly paid towards a dormitory. Pending the completion of this building, the Trustees bought a handsome residence which is used for a dormitory. This latter fact was reported as the late meeting of the Commission in Dallas, by Rev. J. W. Whately, President of the Board of Trustees of that institution.

Goodnight Academy did not officially accept. However, at our recent meeting of the Commission it was reported by Reverend Sebe Thomas, one of the Trustees, that a $1000 brick dormitory is in the process of erection.

Judged only by the standard of total dollars and cents received by the Secretary, it would seem a mistake for the Commission to give so much money raised in other parts of Texas to the Panhandle. Judged by service to God and man in the future it appears wise.

6. After the Secretary made a visit to Baylor College and had seen its crowded condition, as a spur to local action, he offered to allow all

money given by the Salado Association to go at once to the new building, whose design had been officially adopted by the Trustees and which awaited more help to make it wise to break dirt. It was further agreed by the Secretary that all bona fide subscriptions that had been made for the erection of the proposed Baylor College building prior to the meeting of the last State Convention might be renewed and applied to the said building without being divided with the other schools. This proposition was made so as to make alive certain dead subscriptions and to stimulate new local gifts. It is hoped that the representatives of Baylor College at this meeting will have further information for the Commission.

7. Perhaps the most far-reaching results of the campaign can be seen in Brownwood where the leadership of Pastor George W. McCall, helped by other leading business men, over $16,000 was raised for the erection of a new wing to the old building at Howard Payne College and to make certain long-needed repairs. The contract was let and the building is going up. The whole amount agreed to be raised by the Commission for Howard Payne College was $20,000. In the enthusiasm and vigorous giving at Brownwood a clear vision of local responsibility is shown, and also a magnificent spirit of self-dependence.

8. Perhaps no people have done such heroic giving as the people of Wise County. This is evidenced by their beautiful new $25,000 dormitory for girls, on which a debt of nearly $10,000 is carried personally by President Ward. The other $15,000 has been raised in Decatur and Wise county, barring a few small contributions, prior to this campaign. Notwithstanding their drain in the erection of said building, their churches have sent more money to the Secretary under this year's agreement per population and resources than any Association of the State. Surely God will honor such fidelity!

9. The financial condition of Baylor University, is somewhat better than a year ago, made possible,

First, by the payment of the Theological professors by a private subscription from Dr. B. H. Carroll.

Second, the increased attendance.

Third, saving expense in summer advertising and canvassing.

Fourth, better collections of outstanding tuition bills.

Fifth, the gift of $1000 by the will of the late Mrs. Templeton, of Ennis, Texas, and finally by the gift of $10,000 by the will of the late Brother F. L. Carroll of Waco, Texas. He had held for some years a mortgage on the old College property known as Houston-Cowden Halls. This mortgage was given to secure a loan of $10,000. This debt of $10,000 was included in the $10,000 reported by the President of Baylor University to the last State Convention. The interest on this gift is to be perpetually applied to the care and keeping of the F. L. Carroll Chapel and library, and the over-plus to be applied to the George W. Carroll Science Hall for the same purpose. Of course every thinking man will see that Baylor University is still due the $10,000 to one of the departments of her own resources. The gift, however, came as a blessing, relieving the danger that always inheres in mortgaged property. It is better to owe one's self than another.

Not counting the small sum of cash in the hands of the Secretary that rightly will go to Baylor University, the institution is still behind approximately $5,000 as the price already paid for the magnificent improvements in efficiency of Baylor University as an engine of power in Baptist affairs in Texas. The University authorities regard themselves fortunate that the debt is not increased. As certain as we prosper denominationally, we must care for this head center of Christian education. As long as democracy of the Baptists lasts, so long will rest the responsibility of leadership on the pastors.

10. The condition of affairs at East Texas is unpromising. Concerning this institution all matters are respectfully to be referred to the incoming Education Commission.

11. The following recommendations were adopted by the Commission at Dallas, October 18, and that they may appear in the Convention minutes are made a part of this report:

First, the outgoing Secretary advises that this Education Commission today pass a resolution urging the State Convention to grant us Friday of the Convention to be known as Education Day, and further that following the report of the Commission to the Convention speeches by the President of the Commission, Dr. J. B. Gambrell, and Brother George W. Truett be made.

Second, that this Commission urge upon the Convention the continuance of the present plan for the enlargement and betterment of the schools, changing only as may conditions arise.

Third, that nothing this Commission may do is to hinder the voluntary gifts to the endowment of either or all of the schools of the Correlation.

Fourth, that barring the proposed Academy for East Texas, no schools be added to the Correlation until better equipment and enlargement of those we now have and until further enlargement of the endowment of Baylor University is made.

Source: *Proceedings*, Baptist General Convention of Texas, 1906, 59–62.

7.13 Southwestern Baptist Theological Seminary

Southwestern Seminary has its roots in B. H. Carroll's parsonage in Waco, Texas. During the early days of Baylor University, Carroll provided several young men with the rudiments of a theological education from his livingroom. From this humble foundation, Baylor Theological Seminary was born in 1905. Outgrowing its home on the Baylor Campus, the school was independently chartered in 1905 and moved to Fort Worth, Texas, in 1908. It was named Southwestern Baptist Theological Seminary. It is now the largest Protestant seminary in the world.

The First Year at Fort Worth

To secure ground enough for expansion, it was necessary to locate the institution one mile beyond the end of the existing car-lines, and until the extension of these lines transportation over that mile by auto must be supplied.

On account of the same difficulty of getting material on the ground at the right time, the homes of the faculty were not ready for occupancy. By a makeshift arrangement a part of a lower story was prepared for temporary use and heated by stoves. Yet the sound of the hammer, the buzz of the saw and the tread of the hod carrier was continuous.

The wisdom of attempting an opening in such quarters and under such conditions was gravely questioned. A generous proposition by the First Church tendering the use of its building, with free light and heat, accompanied by a sufficiently cheap rent of a downtown hotel for the boarding quarters was soberly considered.

But after mature deliberation we decided to commence on scheduled time of our grounds and in the necessarily cramped and inconvenient quarters our building afforded, with the few students who were willing to endure the harshness as good soldiers.

Seventy-nine students decided to matriculate and rough it out. The wonder is that there were so many.

They justly counted that the conditions would improve each week, the space enlarge, and indeed that all the difficulties were under constant process of removal and that by January 1, the roof would be on, the steam heat in operation, and two full stories ready for use. On account of these conditions it was decided to have no program of formal opening and send out no invitations abroad. . . . The occasion called for the cheerful, heroic spirit and it was manifested all around. One white-headed sage even ventured to say: "I am glad that you people are having a hard time at the start. It will do you good and work out great things for you in the long run." The First Church gave a grand reception with refreshments for the whole outfit. Anyhow, there we are. There stands the majestic building approaching completion, and scores of residences erected by faculty and students. After all, what is one year's privations in the life of an institution, which expects to be doing its duty when the great trumpet of the judgement sounds, and to hear the cry: Behold the bridegroom! Go ye out to meet him!

Well, we plead no baby act and play no whining role. We have camped out before.

Source: *Proceedings*, Baptist General Convention of Texas, 1910, 76.

CHAPTER 8

Good Times and Bad, 1914–1926

8.1 Missions

Under the watchful eye of J. B. Gambrell, Texas Baptist missionary endeavors had proven to be quite successful. By the time of his death in 1910, the Baptist influence could be felt in all four corners of the Lone Star State. A mere five years later, missionary optimism could hardly be contained.

Good News on Every Front: State Missions

Your Committee on State Missions and Evangelism submits the following report:

We wish to reassert our deep and increasing belief in the primacy of state missions. To be scriptural is, of course, to be Baptistic, and therefore to the Supreme Authority do we look for commands. Jesus said: "Ye shall be witnesses unto me, both in Jerusalem,"—city missions, "and in all Judea"—state missions, "and in Samaria"—home missions, "and unto the uttermost part of the earth"—foreign missions. This official, imperative command forever puts the Divine seal upon our work, and should prove an effective stimulant to a real advance.

The history of Baptist state missions work in Texas has been the inspiration of many other states, and the proof of our own virility. State mission work, with evangelism as its dominant note, is logically first and of greatest importance. Not to the belittling of any other missionary enterprise, but rather to the development of our own resources in order that we may better serve and meet the other challenging needs. While the selfish conservation of resources in spiritual effort is a practice which leads to death, yet the true development of these resources leads to life— and that more abundant for Texas and for the world.

To this end our state missions work has its three phases, namely: 1. Evangelism—the winning of the lost. 2. Enlightenment—the teaching and training of the saved. 3. Benevolence– the touch of helpfulness to all the world. To these three magnificent purposes we wish again to pledge our unswerving fidelity, in keeping with the great commission of our Savior.

Each year has been a splendid struggle; each year has brought a glorious achievement. Last year our hearts were stirred with the mighty record of service, this year we look anxiously forward, but with joyous faith and keenest anticipation.

With 400,000 Texas Baptists—what a resource! What can we do? What must we do? Were we to do one-half of what is our true ability, Texas Baptists would shake the world. Why not? Let us "stretch forth the curtains of our habitations; spare not, lengthen thy cords and strengthen the stakes." 'Tis a sin to be sparing in the kingdom of our God. Texas is naturally a Canaan for Baptists. From the very beginning Baptists have written large in the affairs of our great commonwealth. Let us be as wise in spiritual matters even to the entering into our heritage.

Your committee has the following suggestions:

1. That it might be profitable for a more thorough educational campaign in each church before the state and mission collection is taken. The few words spoken previous to the "hurry-up collection" are not usually sufficiently instructive to develop intelligent response.

2. That efforts be made to take the offering earlier in the period set apart for state missions. Let us not wait until the last Sunday or two. Too often the weather condition is given as a [sic] excuse for a small offering, when the thief is easily recognized as "Mr. Procrastination."

3. Most earnestly would we suggest an every member canvass. Every church should endeavor to give at least a dollar for each member. This is a minimum—let us suggest the maximum. With a definite purpose in hand, and intelligent effort in the head, and a consuming passion in the heart, we shall advance.

4. Let us advance along every line of endeavor. To do other than progress is to sin against our opportunities, our soul-life, our commands and our Master. God never retrenched, and He does not intend for his people so to do. Let us keep in step with the purposes of God.

Source: *Proceedings*, Baptist General Convention of Texas, 1915, 131–32.

8.2 World War I

With little thought of pacifism, Texas Baptists wholeheartedly supported the United States' entrance into World War I. As Baptists these individuals cherished freedom, and they hoped to deliver Europe from the possibility of the loss of its freedom. Preachers, such as G. W. Truett, and countless Baptist laymen joined the armed forces in large numbers. The Baptists, however, unlike some denominations, were unwilling to attend military religious services led by non-Baptists. They demanded and eventually were given their own clergy to minister to their spiritual needs.

A. Religious Liberty in the Training Camps

When General Funston at San Antonio prescribed that preachers must not tell soldiers that they are lost and indicated a preference for strict liturgical orders of worship in the training camps, Texas Baptists raised a vigorous protest. Dr. J. B. Gambrell, president of the Southern Baptist Convention, objected most strenuously to restricting representatives of the ministry Catholics, Jews, Christian Scientists, and the Y. M. C. A. Baptists asserted by resolution that no military man, not even the President of the nation, had any such right. "Baptists stand where they have always stood for full and equal freedom of religion and conscience," said they. "They want no rights or privileges in religion that all citizens cannot have in equal measure. We declare in the words of the eminent Methodist Bishop Candler, 'The issue raised is not one that concerns Baptists alone, but which concerns the whole matter of freedom of religious worship in the country.'"

In upshot General Funston lost his ruling. Texas Baptists forthwith instituted camp pastors, who ministered to the men in training with conspicuous results in conversion. Such were A. Foltz, George Green, George W. McCall, J. H. Pace, M. T. Andrews, Le. E. Finney, and notably George

W. Truett, who was requested by President Wilson to go overseas on a preaching mission. Truett's ministry to go overseas is believed to have been one of the most significant services of his life. Some of the more important scenes of other labors were in San Antonio, Houston, Waco, Fort Worth, El Paso, Eagle Pass, Galveston, Corpus Christi, and the Lower Rio Grande Valley. Y. M. C. A. secretaries in these camps numbered well-known Baptists from outside Texas, such as Robert A. Ashworth, T. J. Villers, Allyn Foster, and J. A. Francis.

Source: J. M. Dawson, *A Century with Texas Baptists* (Nashville: Broadman Press, 1947), 80–81. Reprint courtesy of Broadman and Holman Publishers.

B. Truett's Letter Home

Am in a great camp, and have today spoken six times to the men— the officers tell me that I have easily spoken today to 15,000 men. I would have gladly crossed the ocean and braved all the perils and hardships for what I have seen and felt today. Multitudes—vast multitudes came to the side of our great Savior and King. Impossible to tell you how great it was. Never, never, can I get away from the greatness and blessedness of this day. To God be all the praise, forever! Must wait to tell you about it, because it will take a long time to tell about it today. It will ever be remembered by me as one of life's highest days.

Met a number of Dallas boys, to whose mothers I shall write a line (not of our church) and met hosts of Texas and Southern boys I knew. We were all so glad together. They followed me everywhere and vast numbers of them took their stand for the great Savior.

I am so tired, but so happy that I wonder if I can get to sleep tonight at all. Am with the boys in camp, and am in perfect health. How good is our Savior and King. Pass on my best to everybody.

George

Source: Powhaten James, *George W. Truett: A Biography* (New York: Macmillan Company, 1945), 142.

8.3 The 75 Million Campaign

During the period following World War I optimism reigned supreme in the Southern Baptist Convention. Despite this optimism, however, the Southern Baptist Convention was still in debt. Building upon the success of the Texas Baptist "One Hundred Thousand Dollar Campaign," the Southern Baptist Convention launched the "75 Million Campaign" in 1919. The men who were chosen to lead this new campaign were the heroes of the prior campaign: George W. Truett and Lee Rutland Scarborough. Nearly $92 million were pledged to the campaign, but only 52 million was received. Texas Baptists pledged $16,500,000, but only gave $8,720,060. Despite falling short of their fiscal goal, the 75 Million Campaign was a success as it eventually spawned the Cooperative Program.

A. The Campaign in Texas: F. S. Groner, D. D., Secretary

Never can Texas Baptists forget the memorable and triumphant Campaign in this state. The spirit of heroism, sacrifice and dauntless determination prevailed everywhere. Never were soldiers in battle more bent on victory than were our invincible legions in the big Seventy-Five Million drive. That we must win at all hazards and at any sacrifice was the sense and the thought of our people.

Three things explain our success. First, a superb and almost perfect organization. In organizing for the Campaign we followed literally the plan outlined by General Director Dr. L. R. Scarborough. We avoided making exceptions, but tracked it in its entirety.

Second, our people had the conviction that the movement was of God, and we called mightily upon Him for help and guidance. By faith we beheld the pillar of cloud that led to victory and to sure success. Jehovah went before us and the God of Israel was our rearguard. Our people felt that the hour of destiny had struck for our cause, and His presence and His Spirit heartened us in the hour of battle and led us out into the tablelands of rich fruition.

The third thing that contributed to our great victory was the relentless and resistless zeal of our people. A holy zeal possessed them and bore them out. A zeal could not be stayed, pent up for a while, but when once let loose was hurricane-like in its onward sweep. It was contagious; it spread like a holy epidemic until 350,000 redeemed people were under its spell and were swept forward by its torrents.

MANY DIFFICULTIES OVERCOME

There were many hindrances and many difficulties. Our Baptist legions, determined to win, were not to be baffled. They forded swollen streams, braved the driving storms, climbed the mountain heights; when Fords struck up, ponies were commandeered, and when ponies gave out the riders turned pedestrian and went on their way with hearts regardless of difficulties and souls bent on victory. Such courage was not even surpassed by our American sons at the Argonne Forest as they drove back the invading foe, or by the crusaders as Peter the Hermit led them in their quest for the Holy Land.

We wonder if the time has not really come to add another chapter to the Acts of the Apostles in order to record the achievements of these doers of great deeds, and to add a postscript to the eleventh chapter of Hebrews in order to enroll their names on the scroll of the brave and the true.

The by-products of the Campaign in Texas deserve special mention, and fully justify all our efforts and all that the Campaign cost. I will conclude this article by quoting from the report of the State Executive Board to the State General Convention at Houston, December 11–15.

"Among the by-products, we would mention:

"*The widespread enlistment of our people in religious activities.* Thousands of our brethren and sisters in this state who have never done any serious religious work in connection with the churches where their membership is have been aroused to take an interest in the present big program and are enlisted for future work and service as never before. Thousands more of our people, notably our young people, have surrendered for special religious work, either to preach the Gospel, to become missionaries, Bible women, evangelistic singers, Sunday school specialists, or serve in some other line of Christian endeavor.

"Another very important phase of enlistment accomplished in this campaign is the resuscitation of dormant and what was thought to be in the hundreds of instances dead or extinct churches. These churches have everywhere been aroused from a veritable Van Winkle slumber to become awake, alive, and potent for good in their communities and happy in the consciousness that they have risen from the dead. Their members rejoice again that the old altars of worship are restored, the altar fires rekindled and the songs of Zion are heard as of yore. This situation is literally true in hundreds upon hundreds of cases in Texas, whether it be the deserted downtown city church, the neglected town or village church, or the much-sung little brown church in the vale. Everywhere there is to be found an awakened interest and a new zest in the local church, and these places are to be as never before real Bethels where God shall meet His people and bless them with showers of heavenly blessing and save their children with His everlasting salvation."

Another by-product of the Campaign is the *increased circulation of our denominational papers*. Within the space of about thirty days the circulation of the *Baptist Standard* was increased from 16,000 to more than 38,000. What is true of the *Baptist Standard* is true, through perhaps of a less degree, of our other Baptist papers in Texas.

A third by-product of the Campaign is the lesson of *Stewardship* that has been widely taught and more widely practiced than ever before.

It is safe to say that what we consider the by-products of the Campaign more than justify the Campaign expense account, which really should be reckoned as an investment. All that we expended in carrying through the Campaign was well worth while, even if there had been no money-raising object in view.

SACRIFICIAL GIFTS

1. A widow, 74 years of age, who washed lace curtains for a living and who resides in McKinney, Texas, subscribed $275.

2. One widow, at Fort Worth, Texas, gave her diamond engagement ring, which Secretary Groner sold for $1,000, and put the $1,000 in the Campaign.

3. An elderly lady, of Stamford, Texas, without financial means, gave her watch, which was a present from her husband before they were married. Secretary Groner sold her watch for $250, and put the money in the Campaign.

4. A mother, in Fort Worth, Texas, gave a beautiful golden broach.

CASES OF HEROIC GIVING

1. Central Baptist Church, Jacksonville, Texas, with a quota of $30,000. The church burned down the first Sunday of Victory Week.

That night the membership met at the pastor's home and subscribed their quota of $30,000 and subscribed an additional $30,000 to build a new building.

2. Corpus Christi Association, with a quota of $110,000, was devastated by a terrible Gulf storm, scores of lives were lost and millions of dollars worth of property destroyed, and the crops ruined. When the association met, the headquarters office at Dallas wired them reducing their quota one-half. They wired back that they would accept no reduction, but raise their entire quota of $110,000.

3. The First Baptist Church, Fort Davis, with a quota of $10,000, subscribed $30,000 plus.

4. Seminary Hill Baptist Church, Fort Worth, Texas, with a quota of $30,000, subscribed $55,550.

5. First Baptist Church, Llano, quota of $15,000, subscribed $62,000.

6. Seventh and James Street, Waco, with a quota of $25,000, subscribed $90,000.

7. First Baptist Church, Sherman, with a quota of $60,000, subscribed $90,000.

8. West Paris Church, with a quota of $10,000, subscribed $16,114, and made their drive Sunday before Victory Week.

9. First Baptist Church, Waco, with a quota of $200,000, oversubscribed their quota in a Sunday morning service, November 23, one week before the time set for a simultaneous drive.

10. Palo Duro Association, with a quota of $125,000, subscribed $183,000.

11. First Church, Dallas, with a quota of $300,000, subscribed $606,000.

12. Baptist Church, Harlingen, with a quota of $12,000, subscribed $28,286.

13. Special mention should be made of Mr. J. L. Chapman, formerly of Farmersville, who now lives at McKinney. Brother Chapman is a layman, but it was due largely to his uniting efforts as organizer for Collin County Association that $450,000 was raised in that county.

Many, many other cases as heroic and sacrificial as these could be mentioned if space would allow.

Source: L. R. Scarborough, *Marvels of Divine Leadership: The Story of the Southern Baptist 75 Million Campaign* (Nashville: Sunday School Board Southern Baptist Convention, 1920), 229–33.

B. The Opinion of Publicity Director, J. M. Dawson

In May, 1919, in Atlanta, Georgia, the Southern Baptist Convention launched the Seventy-five Million Campaign, with George W. Truett as chairman of the commission to put it into effect. The Commission chose L. R. Scarborough as general director, with Frank E. Burkhalter of Texas publicity director, and Nashville, Tennessee as headquarters. Texas received a quota of $15,000,000 of the amount to be raised, to which state board added a million dollars. Secretary Frank S. Groner assumed the lead, assisted by T. V. Neal as state organizer, J. M. Dawson as state publicity director, and Mrs. A. F. Bledsoe as W. M. U. organizer. In summarizing the benefits afterward, the Executive Board listed: (1) the widespread enlistment of the people in religious activities; (2) the resuscitation of hundreds of dormant or dead churches; (3) a large increase in circulation of the denominational papers; (4) marked development in stewardship; and (5) a subscription of $15,400,000, not all this sum, alas, was collected, with the result that practically every agency and institution having gone forward in the projection of buildings or expenditure suffered disappointment, if not distress. The campaign, whatever its defects, undoubtedly proved an unparalleled stimulus to Baptist growth in Texas, uplifting horizons, "calling out the called," adding unequaled numbers to the churches and increasing the Baptist assets in property by many millions.

Source: J. M. Dawson, *A Century with Texas Baptists* (Nashville: Broadman Press, 1947), 83–84. Reprint courtesy of Broadman and Holman Publishers.

C. The First Baptist Church of Waco

The Baptist 75 Million Campaign, a movement by Southern Baptists to raise over a period of five years the sum of $75,000,000 for the enlargement of the denomination's missionary, educational, and benevolent programs, was projected in the summer of 1919. The First Church, Waco, was asked to accept the apportionment of $200,000 in that program. The church promptly complied with the request and sub-scribed that sum, the second largest of any church in the Southern Baptist Convention, it was said. Under the leadership of Dr. S. P. Brooks, named organizer for the church, the members subscribed $214,426.90 on Sunday, November 23, the day set for that purpose. This vast sum was subsequently paid during the five-year period prescribed. During the year of campaign the pastor served as state publicity director of it, just as a few years later he acted for the Texas Baptist Conquest Cam-paign.

Source: Frank Burkhalter, *A World-Visioned Church: Story of the First Baptist Church Waco, Texas* (Nashville: Broadman Press, 1946), 187. Reprint courtesy of Broadman and Holman Publishers.

8.4 The Norris Controversy

The Norris Controversy was by far the most contentious Baptist affair in the first half of the twentieth century. J. Frank Norris was the fiery pastor of the First Baptist Church of Fort Worth, Texas. From his youth he had what many considered a mean disposition, but it had been tempered somewhat until 1914. During that fateful year, B. H. Carroll died and L. R. Scarborough was named as his replacement as President of Southwestern Seminary. Norris had helped Carroll relocate the school from Waco to Fort Worth, and may have believed that he was to become the next President of the fledgling semi-nary. Spurned by the school, Norris turned on Southwestern, Baylor Univer-sity, J. M. Dawson, the Seventy-Five Million Campaign, and the BGCT with a vengeance. He accused their leadership of being liberals, teaching evolu-tion, being too friendly with Catholics, and disregarding his radical brand of dispensationalism. He was eventually expelled from the BGCT and SBC, after which he created his own Fundamentalist denomination. The Norris Controversy only ended with his death in 1952.

A. The Modernism of Dr. J. M. Dawson

As to the person of Dr. J. M. Dawson we have but the kindest words, he is a very fine gentleman. Three weeks ago he was commended in a superlative eulogy by Dr. Jeff D. Ray in the Star-Telegram as the pastor of the First Baptist Church in Waco for thirty years.

Year before last he preached the annual sermon of the Baptist Con-vention of Texas, and was highly commended on that occasion in a prayer by the late and lamented Dr. George W. Truett, whom the whole world respects.

He was Chairman of the Committee on Religious Education in the recent Baptist Convention which held its annual session in Fort Worth two weeks ago.

Dr. E. D. Head, President of the Convention, highly recommended Dr. Dawson and called on him for the closing word of the Convention. He is on several boards of the Convention.

Dr. Dawson's record on modernism, as published and well known, up to date is as follows:

First, some twenty years ago at the Beaumont Convention he read a paper, not an oral address, but read a paper in which he flatly denied the verbal inspiration of the Scriptures. He took the commonly accepted modernistic view that the "thoughts" of the Scriptures were inspired and that the words were not inspired, and he did not refer to a translation of Scriptures but specifically mentioned the original words used by the Old Testament and New Testament writers.

It is fair to say that most of the brethren were deceived, but soon there was a storm of protest throughout the whole Convention, and this storm proved of such proportions that Dr. W. R. White, then Secretary of State Missions, came out and issued a statement on the verbal inspiration of the Scriptures as follows:

"In order that the wise and unwise, yea, even the most humble Baptist in the forks of the creek may not misunderstand, I gladly make another statement. I believe the Bible, God's Revelation, the Holy Scriptures were verbally inspired word for word, and that even though men of old spake as they were moved upon by the Holy Spirit, the sacred Scriptures were just as much the words of God as if He had written every word in heaven and handed the Bible down to man ready made."

But the school men and the powers that be had Dr. White fired out of the Secretaryship for making this ringing orthodox statement on the inspiration of the Scriptures.

Second Example of Dr. Dawson's Modernism

He published in the Baptist Standard that Sodom and Gomorrah were not destroyed by the fire and brimstone raining down from heaven, but that there was an "explosion of bituminous gases and it was like an oil well on fire."

Thus he flatly denied the words of Jesus Himself on the destruction of Sodom and Gomorrah when our Lord said:

"But the same day that the Lot went out to Sodom it rained fire and brimstone from heaven, and destroyed them all." (Luke 17:29)

This does not look like "an oil well fire."

The third example of Dr. Dawson's modernism was the miraculous judgment on Lot's wife. Dr. Dawson denied the specific and plain statement of the Scriptures when he said that "she was enveloped by a wave of mud and slime." But here is the description given by the word of God:

"Then the Lord rained upon Sodom and Gomorrah brimstone from the Lord out of Heaven:

"And he overthrew those cities, and all the plains, and all the inhabitants of these cities, and that which grew upon the ground.

"But his wife looked back from behind him and she became a pillar of salt." (Gen. 19: 24–26). . . .

A Fourth Example of Dr. Dawson's Modernism

He is and has been for years a "contributing editor" of the Christian Century of Chicago, the rankest modernistic paper on the American Continent—"birds of a feather flock together."

Running with the modernistic crowd, contributing to them, writing for them, he is guilty of the "doctrine" of Balaam who taught Balak to corrupt the people who could not be cursed. II Peter 2:15–16 says on this grievous sin:

"Which have forsaken the right way, and are gone astray, following the way of Balaam the son of Bosor, who loved the wages of unrighteousness;

"But was rebuked for his iniquity: the dumb ass speaking with a man's voice forbad the madness of the prophet."

What's needed today among Baptists is the voice of this same "dumb ass." It is more than interesting that this "dumb ass" saw the Lord while the straddling, compromising, pussyfooting modernist on his back did not see the Lord.

There is much that Dr. Dawson and other modernists could learn if they would listen to the "dumb ass" speak.

This "dumb ass" is not to be confused with the "dumb dogs" of Isaiah 56:10.

"His watchmen are blind: they are all ignorant, they are all dumb dogs, they cannot bark; sleeping, lying down, loving to slumber."

This is a Scripture for the modern "D. D.'s."

A Fifth Example of Dr. Dawson's Not Modernism
But Worse Than Modernism

The papers were full of his apology for the Japanese atrocities. When Colonel Dyess came back and told about the Death March of Bataan, Dr. Dawson came out in the papers and said that "the Japanese atrocities have been greatly exaggerated."

We are sure that by this time Dr. Dawson has been made a convert, and realizes the folly of his defending the Japanese atrocities.

If he had attended the funeral of James Newman in the First Baptist Church a few weeks ago, and if he had heard, or if he had read what the papers said about what this dear boy said, who was on that ill-fated Bataan Death March—when the doctors told Jimmy Newman that he could not live he said, "Then take me to the little white cottage in Fort Worth that I left seven years ago."

If Dr. Dawson would talk to the widow of Colonel Moses, son of Dayton Moses, who was beheaded by the Japanese after being taken prisoner, he would be a convert to the truth of the Japanese atrocities.

And if he would read the series of articles published by General Jonathan Wainwright he would be a convert and he would never fall from grace any more.

Dawson Defended and Eulogized a Japanese Traitor

The readers of this paper will recall how the editor exposed Toyohiko Kagawa when he was touring this country several years ago. Some of our Baptist leaders were hailing him as the greatest Christian of the age, but particularly Dr. Dawson was very fond of Dr. Kagawa and wrote several articles extolling him to the skies. But now the secret archives of Tokyo have brought to light that Kagawa was an official spy of the Japanese military machine. It was all exposed in Time Magazine a short time ago, and in several other leading magazines.

These two instances, first, where Dawson apologized for and defended the Japanese atrocities, and second, where he extolled and eulogized the traitor, a Japanese spy—if there be those who say, "What has this to do with Dawson's modernism?

"Much in every way."

For one thing it shows that Dawson is not a credible witness or authority on the historic faith held by Baptists.

When W. J. Bryan was defeated in 1896 Ingersol said, "Bryan has no future."

Bryan replied, by saying: "What I understand of Mr. Ingersol he is not a competent judge of future events here or hereafter."

Therefore, any man who will defend Japanese atrocities, and defend a now revealed Japanese spy, is not a competent judge or authority on Bible truths or Baptist orthodoxy.

Some might say what was Dr. Dawson's apology of Japanese atrocities to do with his modernism?

The answer is very evident and plain. It's a question of the credibility of the witness that is involved.

If a man would be so far wrong as to defend or apologize for in any way Japanese atrocities, then he is hardly a credible authority on Bible teaching.

In Texas we have a law against cattle stealing, and it is the one unforgivable sin. Whenever a yearling's hide is found in the barn of a neighbor with another man's brand on it and is introduced into court, it is considered prima facie evidence of the guilt of the defendant. But if there be a long record of cattle stealing and the defendant has served several terms, all of his record is admissible before the jury.

Far be it to make a parallel between cattle stealing and Dr. Dawson. Five times in the New Testament our Lord's coming is likened to a thief coming in the night. The only point in the illustration of the cattle stealing is what is the habit of the defendant before the bar.

So, therefore, we have here the long standing published record of Dr. Dawson. He seems to have a certain quirk of mind that is characteristic of most of the modernists.

Source: J. Frank Norris, *Infidelity Among Southern Baptists Endorsed By Highest Officials* (Fort Worth: First Baptist Church of Fort Worth, 1944), 10–15. Reprint courtesy of the First Baptist Church of Fort Worth.

B. Norris on Catholicism

My wife and I went to see the present Pope last summer. A good Roman Catholic friend of mine in Detroit, in the City Council, who has been mighty kind to me, wrote the head of the American College for training priests in Rome and told him I was going to be there, and when I got there I went and called on this head of the Roman Catholic college for training priests in Rome. He was glad I called on him and said to me, "Anything I can do for you while here, for the sake of my good friend in Detroit, I will be glad to do it."

I said, "Thank you very much. There is one person I would like to see while I am here. When I was here before I saw the last Pope, and my wife is here and I would like for her to see him."

"Well," he said, "His Holiness is very ill now, as you know, and only a few can see him. It is almost impossible."

In about an hour here came a message signed by the Papal secretary, Cardinal Pacell. Wife said, "What do you reckon the folks at Fort Worth and Detroit would think about it?" They drove us 20 miles out in the country. There were all these priests and prelates waiting and they couldn't get in.

We all got out—they thought I was some American millionaire.

One of the priests said, "You are from the States?"

I said, "Yes."

"So am I."

He wanted to know who I was. I told him what my name was. I said, "This is J. Frank Norris."

He said, "I know of J. Frank Norris over in America who is a preacher."

"Well, this is one of them."

"You are not that Baptist preacher?"

"I am one Baptist preacher." I said, "Are you going to see the Holy Father?"

"No," he said, "I am just looking over the grounds. He doesn't receive anybody except a very few Americans."

I said, "I am going in."

"What? You are going in?"

"Sure." And I pulled out the card and showed it to him.

He motioned to all the crowd of priests and said, "Hey, come here, and look"—he was a priest from Illinois. He said, "Here this Baptist preacher is going to get to go in and see the Holy Father and here we faithful are not. That beats all!"

"Oh," I said, "Don't get excited. That is the way it is going to be when we get up yonder, I will go in and you will stay out."

Source: J. Frank Norris, *The Federal Council of Churches Unmasked* (Fort Worth: By the author, n.d.), 28–29.

C. 1923 Report of the Committee on Credentials

Your Committee on Credentials which was referred the challenge of Rev. H. Mendenhall, a messenger from the First Baptist Church, Fort Worth, begs leave to submit for the consideration of the Convention and findings thereon.

First, we submit the challenges as follows:

A CHALLENGE

1. Whereas the Constitution of the Baptist General Convention of Texas in Article I, Section 2, says "The objects of this Convention shall be Missionary, Educational and Beneficent, the promotion of harmony of feeling and concert of action among Baptists, and a system of operative measures for the promotion of the interests of the Redeemer's Kingdom" and in Article II, Section 1, that "This body shall be composed of messengers from regular Baptist churches, associations and missionary societies, each co-operating with the Convention;"

2. Whereas the messengers of the so-called First Baptist Church of Fort Worth, Texas, were denied seats in the Tarrant Baptist Association—their home association—in September, 1922—an association which is in full and noble co-operation with all the interests of this Convention; and has messengers to this Convention and this association has within its bounds more than 50 co-operating churches.

3. Whereas the pastor of this church, sanctioned by the church itself, has persistently from the beginning opposed the 75 Million Campaign as

the one means by which Texas and Southern Baptists have supported and put forward their missionary, educational and benevolent institutions, this opposition being carried on in the pulpit, on platform, and in the church paper sent out free to a large part of the constituency of his Convention, seeking to destroy the confidence of the people in methods, plans, policies and leaders of this 75 Million Dollar movement;

4. Whereas the said pastor and church have gone to great lengths in seeking to lead our people into inter-denominational and pseudo-Baptist movements and to divide our people and to turn them away from the great work to which they have committed themselves, this effort to divide and split our people is evidenced by the following quotation from an interview given by the pastor of this church to a representative of the "World's Work," of September, 1923, as follows:

"It was Norris who said to me at the very start of the first talk I had with him, 'There is going to be a new denomination.' He named the three distinguished Fundamentalists who are about to organize it. Of the present denominations he said, 'We are going to rip them up.' Soon he named the time the ripping will begin. Of the great schism that impends he said, "'It is going to be a bull moose bolt;'"

5. Whereas the opposition of said pastor and church to the work of this Convention gives the messengers of said church no constitutional rights in this Convention, therefore, we the undersigned member of Baptist churches and messengers to this Convention do hereby challenge the right of any member of said so-called First Baptist Church of Fort Worth to seats in this Convention; and we do hereby petition the Convention that seats be refused to said members of said church.

F. M. McConnell	H. L. Kokernot
Wallace Bassett	O. L. Powers
L. R. Scarborough	Charles E. Wauford
R. G. Bowers	Andrew J. Morgan
L. J. Mims	M. L. Fuller
C. M. Caldwell	E. P. West
Millard A. Jenkens	S. C. Tucker
I. E. Gates	

Source: *Proceedings*, Baptist General Convention of Texas, 1923, 18–19.

D. The Fruits of Norrisism

This tract is a discussion of some of the fruits of an old cult under a new name. The following are some of the characteristics of this cult—Norrisism:

1. It is toward true religion what socialism and bolshevism are to politics and industry; wholly destructive in spirit and methods.

2. It is anti-missionary and anti-institutional. It gives nothing to associational, state or home missions to get representation in the conventions. It spends most of its money on itself—some times in court trials for perjury, arson and murder, and in sending out free literature seeking to destroy the causes other people try to build.

3. It thrives on sensationalism, misrepresentation and false accusations of good men and true causes. It masquerades under the cloak of anti-evolutionism, anti-modernism, anti-Catholicism in order to ride into public favor and cast poisonous suspicion on the leadership of the causes of constructive Christianity.

4. In its chief leadership it is the embodiment of autocratic ecclesiasticism. All the privileges and right of the church heading up in the pastor.

5. It uses the pulpit, the press, and the radio to create suspicion, to foment class prejudices and to vent its hatred against innocent personalities and institutions.

6. It divides and splits families, churches, associations and strikes its poisonous fangs at the brotherhood of Christianity.

7. It lowers the standards of right conduct, individual righteousness, ministerial ethics, personal integrity, and gives to the world a false conception of the character, spirit and methods of Christianity.

8. The only people or causes it praises are those who bow down to its dictum or fall in any wise to cross its path.

9. The individual, the preacher or church who joins in sympathy with this cult will sooner or later cease to co-operate with the mission, educational or benevolent enterprises fostered by God's people.

10. It has some noble names upon the escutcheon of its false accusations and public misrepresentation; Carroll, Gambrell, McDaniel, McConnell, Mullins, C. V. Edwards, Brooks, Sampey, Groner, Ray,

Robertson, Forrest Smith, Cullen Thomas, Truett and others—multitudes of false accusations, such as: infidelity, graft, heresy, theft and such like, and groundless insinuations have gone out against these good men for years. This tract deals with only a few of these false and slanderous charges against these brethren. These are but samples—there are many others which are as groundless as these.

SOME GREAT PRINCIPLES INVOLVED IN RECENT ACTION OF THE TARRANT COUNTY ASSOCIATION

Since wide publicity has been given in other ways to the recent action of the Tarrant County Association, it is felt that the matter should be accurately set out in the columns of the Baptist press in Texas.

It is generally known that the Tarrant County Association has been the storm-center of a ceaseless and vicious attack upon the boards, institutions, causes and leaders of Texas and Southern Baptists for many years. It began in the days when B. H. Carroll first moved to Fort Worth and has gone on, night and day, with increasing momentum until today. The same source of confusion in Baptist affairs has carried on agitation in every other phase of life in Fort Worth—political, commercial and social . . . Baptist ministers' conferences have again repudiated this presumptuous leadership by expulsion. The Tarrant County Association has denied it fellowship by large and increasing majority. The Baptist General Convention, for three successive years, by practically unanimous vote, refused it membership in its councils . . .

There are involved in this action of the association.

1. **The principles of co-operation**. The church above alluded to in its letter stated, after quoting the Great Commission in Matt. 28:18-20, "Therefore, we are not in sympathy with the unscriptural institutionalism which has no place or authority in the Great Commission." The constitution of the Tarrant County Association in Article II says, "The object of this association shall be to establish a means of communication between the churches, to project measures for the furtherance of the cause of Christ within its bounds, and to promote among the churches the support of all the great denominational, missionary, educational and benevolent enterprises." That is, the Association's main object is to promote and support the mission boards, schools, hospitals, orphanages and

other enterprises and institutions founded by our father and which are supported by the Texas General Convention and the Southern Baptist Convention. The pastor and his church in question, stated, in accord with the teachings of this old source of trouble in Tarrant County, that they have no sympathy for nor co-operation with these institutions. In other words the association stands for those causes and institutions and the church in question does not.

The other ground on which they were refused seats as stated by the resolution, was the action by the pastor and the church in question, clearly showing that he and the church were willing to become a part and parcel of guerilla warfare which for years has plagued the denomination.

The Tarrant County Association clearly recognizes the privilege of this church to refuse co-operation in building our mission causes, our schools, seminaries, hospitals and orphanages, but it denies them the right to come into fellowship of an association which is in favor of all these things and yet at the same time tries to decide the Association's course in supporting these institutions. . . . Isn't it strange that a pastor and a church, that announce in theory and practice, that they are opposed to the things you are trying to do, want fellowship with you and seats in your councils for the sole purpose of trying to keep you from doing the things you want to do? This does not look like New Testament co-operation to me.

2. **The Principle of Loyalty to the Commands of the Lord Jesus Christ and the Causes and Institutions which these Commands and Teachings Set Up and Set Forward**.

The pastor and church state clearly, both in theory and in practice their opposition to the institutionalism of the Commission. He in his argument, the pastor, tried to establish an alibi, by saying that he meant unscriptural "institutions," such as institutions that teach evolution, and so on. But he unfortunately used "unscriptural institutionalism." Now he and the self-assumed leadership which he is following are opposed to institutionalism of Southern Baptists. Their gifts this year, or their lack of gifts, state that this institutionalism which they are opposed is missions of all sorts, education of all sorts, and benevolences of all sorts. Their action in not giving speaks as loud as their profession of non-co-operation. . . That leadership give practically nothing to any of the causes and institutions fostered by Texas and Southern Baptists. It is pure, down-right anti-mission, hardshellism, and anti-institutionalism. Whenever that leadership gets a hold on individuals or churches they at once cease to give to the great causes of the Commission. . . . It is the old fight known all through the ages. Its principle method is misrepresentation, innuendo, suspicion, accusation against character and leadership. It does nothing for the causes itself, but seeks to keep others from doing what they want to do for the causes.

3. **The third principle involved in this matter is loyalty to the moral laws of God**.

God says, "Thou shalt not bear false witness against thy neighbor." The main basis of this notorious opposition is a palpable violation of this plain commandment of God. This opposition to the causes of the Tarrant County Association, and Texas Baptist and Southern Baptist Conventions has ceaselessly misrepresented their causes, therefore, the Tarrant County Baptist Association puts itself, again, with overwhelming force and with a solidarity and a conviction that rings to Heaven, against this opposition and its misrepresentations. It is not only a question of co-operation, and a question of loyalty to the teachings of Jesus Christ, but it is a question of veracity, honor and common honesty in denominational relationship. I itemize some cases:

(1) This opposition has published widely that I said: "Prof. Meroney and the Medical College at Dallas must go." I never said that nor anything that could be twisted into such a statement.

ABOUT DR. BARNES

(2) It also published that Dr. W. W. Barnes, Professor of Church History in the Southwestern Seminary, is an evolutionist. There is not a syllable of truth in this statement. . . .

ABOUT DR. BROOKS

(7) This same source of opposition says that Baylor University faculty and President Brooks are against the McDaniel Resolution passed by the Southern Baptist Convention, and ought to be made to sign it.

I want to say, in the first place, that the McDaniel Resolution was the Southern Baptist Convention's request to the institutions and boards owned and controlled by the Southern Baptist Convention, and that resolution did not ask individual signature to the McDaniel Resolution. . . Baylor University is not owned by the Southern Baptist Convention, and the Convention did not ask, and the resolutions do not require, that the state institutions subscribe to resolutions passed by the Southern Baptist Convention.

I wish to say further, that President Brooks was present and voted for the McDaniel Resolution and published his endorsement, and further as everybody knows, the faculty of Baylor University has already passed, voluntarily and unanimously, a signed expression of their belief in the fundamentals of our faith, which articles of faith wholly endorsed in principle the McDaniel Resolution. Now, why is it necessary, when President Brooks voted for the Resolution and the faculty had already endorsed that principle and all other fundamentals of faith by their personal signature, why nag and raise suspicions and untrue charges against a great set of honorable, consecrated, orthodox teachers?. . .

ABOUT DR. McCONNELL

(8) It has been charged time and time again that Dr. F. M. McConnell, former Secretary of Missions in Texas and in Oklahoma, noble pastor, College President, successful evangelist, suddenly left Oklahoma because when his books were opened there were suspicious things found therein. There is not the slightest truth in this charge. It is baseless and pernicious. No truer or nobler man walks the earth than F. M. McConnell. . . .

ABOUT GAMBRELL AND TRUETT

(12) This destructive cult and some deceived by its false statements have circulated the report in pulpits, press and radio as quoted in a charge recently made by a deacon of a Baptist church, who is under the dominance of Norrisism as follows: "The big trouble is that Drs. Brooks, Truett, Gambrell, Scarborough, Groner and others had misappropriated a considerable amount of funds from the 75 Million Campaign.". . . Is it not a shame such men as Gambrell, Truett, Groner and Brooks should be thus publicly held as thieves and scoundrels. These school men and secretaries accused of all these crimes have every year been unanimously

elected to their positions and have never been charged with arson, perjury, or murder. . . .

ABOUT WHAT GOD HATES

(13) If Norrisism misrepresents and brings false accusations against such causes and men, masquerading under a cloak of orthodoxy and fundamentalism, can such a cult be trusted in anything? Can one afford to believe in reports of its own membership; the size of its congregations; the additions it has, the numbers it has in Sunday school and its glaring sensational reports of the greatest revivals in the world? An investigation of the facts back of these swelling numbers will more than likely find them greatly exaggerated. God says in His word, "Six things doth the Lord hate- **a proud look**, a **lying tongue**, **hands that have shed innocent blood**, a heart that deviseth **wicked imaginations**, feet that be **swift in running to mischief**, and false witness that speaketh lies and he that **soweth discord among brethren**."

Will it profit a man if he is sound in his theology on creation according to Gen.2:27 and yet violates God's command where he says, "**Thou shalt not bear false witness against thy neighbor**." Ex. 20:17. . .

Source: L. R. Scarborough, *The Fruits of Norrisism* (Fort Worth: By the author, n. d.).

E. J. M. Dawson on J. Frank Norris

Popularity underwent a severe test when my former associate in the *Baptist Standard*, the Rev. J. Frank Norris, pastor of the influential First Baptist Church, Fort Worth, commenced criticism in the columns of his widely circulated *Fundamentalist*. Of course, at first I was only one of the Baylor University group assailed for alleged heresies charged against President S. P. Brooks and members of the faculty who worshiped at First Church. Perhaps Norris thought I was an easy mark, because I accented social obligations as well as sound Baptist doctrines. Or he could have imagined the sickly young pastor, who never boasted weight beyond one hundred and twenty-nine pounds, almost a habitue of hospitals, would wilt quickly under the paper's "barrage." One brother pastor confirmed this when he remarked, "Dawson doesn't have a robust personality, looks sallow, and might soon throw in the sponge."

A brief summary of Norris' doings between the time of my former connection with him and his attack on Baylor may be inserted here. After my leaving the *Baptist Standard* he continued as editor, also pastored the McKinney Avenue Baptist Church, Dallas. His utterances and practices there incurred the distrust of several Dallas Baptist pastors. It leaked out that Norris desired some other church. Dr. B. H. Carroll, who had admired the abilities of the young man as a student, upon assuming the presidency of Southwestern Baptist Theological Seminary and joining Fort Worth's pastorless First Church, recommended the restless Dallas preacher. Soon after Norris took over the Fort Worth Church, Carroll withdrew his membership because of Norris' sensational sermons. This produced quite a flare-up, with predictions that Norris was through. Instead the resourceful pastor spread accusations that Brooks, Truett, and Dawson have pressured the great Dr. Carroll with threats of denominational disapproval of the Seminary. Norris changed the name of his new publication to the *Searchlight* and said he would expose secret cabals and dispel malicious suspicions.

While this publicity met resentment from many Baptists, it won large audiences and many accessions to his church. So quick was the growth, the demand for a new edifice rose to a clamor. One night the old church burned down. Norris was indicted for arson, but upon standing trial he was acquitted. The local Baptist Association expelled him, but the adverse action only caused him to intensify his efforts for complete vindication.

Norris felt immensely encouraged by evidences, both within Texas and beyond its borders, that his crusade against Baylor University was being hailed as courageous. Inside the state "folks from the forks of the creek," who he said had long been denied a hearing, were speaking up. Informed people noted with anxiety that radical reactionary Baptist newspapers, particularly those representing splinter groups, proudly wearing the name of Fundamentalists throughout the country, were sounding off in his favor.

Men of some importance in the nation applauded Norris' announcement that he intended to establish a new theological seminary in Fort Worth. With a powerful radio station supplementing his paper, he broadcast his Saturday sermons in which he set forth his charges against his alma mater "for teaching evolution, salvation by education and other heresies." By his sustained drive he caused several of Baylor University's most highly rated teachers to resign, notably Professor Samuel Grove Dow, author of a textbook on sociology.

Since Baylor trustees, such as Truett and myself, who were under accusation, were appointed by the Baptist General Convention, that body deemed it wise to make a full investigation into its institution's teachings. The Convention named a large representative and responsible committee to undertake this. This committee of inquiry—not quite unanimously—at the next session of the Convention found "literalistic believers in the Bible, who refused to reckon with the result of science along with some inclined toward the materialistic, who relied entirely upon scientific research—both positions repulsive to lovers of truth." The committee asserted that it endorsed neither position, though the Convention should say that it was "not committed to any theory of evolution, though opposed to Darwinian evolution." It advised that all complaints be communicated directly to the president and trustees—not decided on the hustings or on the Convention floor. The Convention overwhelmingly adopted the report.

Appointment of the investigating committee at first had pleased the warring editor-pastor so much that he had apologized to the Convention and promised future cooperation. A peace party within the fold maneuvered a resolution of reconciliation into adoption at the Galveston Convention and everybody hoped for a new era. But Norris was outraged by the final report, castigated the reporting committee as being puppets in the hands of leaders who hated him, and conspired to silence him. He opened new war on the convention and all its works.

Something other than Baylor's alleged heresies contributed to Norris' fight on me. Next year Texas Baptists accepted a quota of $15,000,000 in the Southern Baptist $75,000,000 campaign. On the state's staff the Convention named me as publicity director. The organized movement vigorously promoted the very institutions and objects Norris opposed. He denounced me as an evolutionist, a Unitarian, a rationalist, the creator of "Dawsonism." When I spoke as a fraternal delegate to Northern Baptists he advertised me as allied with "Fosdickism," and in the Convention city of Milwaukee, he hired a sound-truck, placarded with depicted evils of Fosdickism and Dawsonism, to traverse the streets. Perhaps my Dallas *News* column in the Sunday book review magazine had added fuel to Norris' fire, for he could easily extract from the quotes which he handled to suit his purposes, frequently without regard to accuracy. And undoubtedly I was a bit careless in some of my book reviews in not guarding against phraseology which he could twist in a manner to disturb good people.

One night over the radio his misrepresentations were so palpably false that his wife felt compelled to correct them. I smiled, because I knew Texas Baptists believed that Lillian Norris, Jim Gaddy's daughter, would tell the truth. She said Dr. Norris had taken another's words for mine.

The Southern Baptist 75 Million Campaign, superbly led by Dr. L. R. Scarborough of Fort Worth, succeeded. Texas Baptists subscribed their quota. Norris was exasperated. The shocking tragedy puzzled the public, but fellow Baptists failed to express sympathy for the killer. A member of my church, former Governor Pat M. Neff, regarded as the state's ablest defense lawyer, declined to accept Norris' case. There was no sign of general rejoicing when on a change of venue to Austin, Norris was acquitted. But acquittal in the courts gained him more power.

With subsequent fortunes of Norris I shall not here deal, but with more personal features of the Norris unpleasantness I must press on a little further. Ignoring flagellations did not stop him. In a fresh attack he picked at vulnerable articles of mine published in the international *Homiletic Review* of New York. My succeeding Professor Gaius Atkins of Auburn Theological Seminary as book editor of that magazine did not mitigate my errors in the view of Norris. My election to the presidency of the Texas Institute of Letters also magnified my guilt in his sight. When in the latter capacity I persuaded my friend Carr Collins of Dallas to offer a thousand dollars annually for the best book written by a Texan, Norris fumed that I was attempting to corrupt Southwestern culture!

In the city of his alma mater, with the joint action of the Rev. A. Reilly Copeland of the Tabernacle Baptist Church, he conducted mass meetings, gave out interviews to newspapers, and laid copies of his own explosive publication on every door step. On Sundays my church members went from the sanctuary to their cars to find the *Searchlight's* red-bannered front pages denouncing "Dawsonism Worse Than Fosdickism." Yet my deacons and members uniformly stood loyally by me.

In the eyes of the militant Fundamentalist (he spelled the word with a capital) my interfaith contacts increased my guilt. Thus when Rector Everett Jones of Waco's St. Paul's Episcopal Church, Methodist Edmond Heinsohn of Southwestern University's church and I formed an association for discussion of theological and sociological questions, in his view this made me a public enemy. When I preached in Waco's liberal synagogue, presided over by Rabbi Macht, I became "intolerable." Incidentally many Jewish friends there welcomed me—A.M. Goldstein, L. Fred, and the Misses Novich, who sent us Christmas and Easter greetings! When Congressman W. H. Judd, a Congregationalist, spoke in First Church to the Waco Council of Church Women, it was too much—Norris heralded this hospitality as an overture to the "insufferable Federal Council of Churches."

His last serious attack came in November, 1943. I was to preach the annual sermon for the General Convention of Texas. In a special edition of the *Searchlight,* in handbills and by pickets at the entrances of the First Baptist Church, Dallas, he challenged the messengers to allow the heretic to proceed. Never could I have asked for a more perfect setting. The vast sanctuary was filled to overflowing. Pastor Truett, though ill, appeared on the platform beside me to offer the prayer. My gifted soloist, Miss Mildred Cook, sang "O Divine Redeemer." Within a simple outline I presented "The Christian View of Man," as exhibited in the Scriptures: 1. What man is ideally. 2. What man is actually. 3. What man will be finally under grace. Instant, emphatic vocal approval and subsequent letters from every section of the state gave ample evidence that my message met with favor. I regret to say Norris continued to arraign in me.

My little son Leighton heard me remark, "Brother Norris is my thorn in the flesh, and I suppose it is not going to be removed." The lad had somewhere learned that a thorn produces lockjaw, certain death. He immediately began to worry lest I was on the eve of my demise!

As the reader will discover in a later chapter, I had my own reflections on the final outcome of the Rev. J. Frank Norris' behavior. That he was a man of ability and could precipitate a really serious episode in

Baptist history is attested by the fact that institutions and research agencies are currently rehearsing just how much of a stir he had created in denominational affairs.

Had I wished escape, overtures from First Church, Tulsa; First Church, Newman, Georgia; First Church, Washington, D. C., and others, could have at least removed me from the scene of attack, but I chose to remain in Waco.

Source: J. M. Dawson, *A Thousand Months to Remember* (Waco: Baylor University Press, 1964), 129–34. Reprint courtesy of Baylor University Press.

8.5 The YMCA

Texas Baptists were solid supporters of World War I, but they did not care for the lackadaisical manner in which the spiritual needs of their soldiers were being dealt with. For the most part, the government placed the YMCA in charge of Christian camp services. For Baptists this would never do.

A. Problems with the YMCA

We insist that in the reconstruction of modern civilization now going on that the President of the United States and his counselors, whom the President has thrust into the leadership of advancing civilization, shall, in the final adjustment of the issue involved, see to it that everywhere religious persecutions shall cease, that preaching and the exercise of religion shall be free to every responsible human soul.

It will therefore be seen that the Southern Baptists entered the war with the exception of caring for the religious needs of their soldiers.

The task which was committed to the Home Mission Board by the Southern Baptist Convention was accepted gladly. The committee of the Board to which this task was assigned engaged me to place camp pastors at all the posts and training camps. It was the judgement of the committee that the service which could be rendered the soldiers was primarily a pastoral service. Our camp pastors were gladly received and we have many letters of commendation.

The camp pastor is not a chaplain, nor a Y. M. C. A. secretary. His relation to the army is that of pastor whose business it is to shepherd the members of his own flock. The camp pastor is regarded as responsible for strengthening the churches of his denomination in the vicinity of the camp. He must minister effectively to the enlisted men when they are on leave in the cities adjacent to the camp and feed the service of the churches as a social center.

Source: George Green, "A Review of the Camp Pastor Service," *Baptist Standard*, 17 April 1919, 7, 23.

8.6 Baptist Young People's Union

Born in the Broadway Baptist Church of Fort Worth in 1891 as the Young Christian Colabor Society, the BYPU was a youth organization that promoted stewardship, tithing, and missions and was a forerunner to the Baptist Training Union. More than 20 percent of the members of the nationwide program belonged to Texas Baptist churches.

A. Young Christian Colabor Society

CONSTITUTION

Article 1. Name

The name of this society shall be the Young Christian Colabor Society of Broadway Baptist Church.

Article 2. Motto

"Loyalty to Christ, in all things, at all times."

Article 3. Object

The object of this society shall be to secure in all its members an increased devotion and adherence to Christ; to enlarge knowledge of the distinctive principles of Baptists as taught in the Word of God, and to attain to the highest possible efficiency in all Christian and devotional work.

Article 4. Membership

The membership shall consist of unmarried members of Broadway Baptist Church over fourteen years of age, who may be elected on recommendation of the membership committee, and who shall have agreed to the following pledge: "I hereby renew my obligations, made in becoming a member of this church, to be true to Christ in all things and at all times, to strive to attain to the New Testament Standard of Christian life and experience. I promise further to attend all meetings of the society and meetings of the church, and Sunday-school, if not providentially prevented, and so far as I shall be able, to contribute to the financial interests of the same."

Article 5. Officers

The officers shall be a president, a vice-president, a secretary, a treasurer, and an organist, who shall be chosen every three months.

Article 6. Committees and Their Duties

Membership—To have charge of the distribution of invitation cards; to bring in new members and to introduce them, and to encourage attendance upon all meetings of the society and all devotional meetings.

Devotional—To arrange for all devotional meetings of the society, provide topics, secure leaders, and seek in every way to promote interests of such meetings.

Instruction—To arrange for literary exercises, courses of study and denominational reading and to promote all that belongs to this feature of the work.

Social—To call upon and welcome strangers, to provide for socials, to extend acquaintances among the members and to encourage sociability among them.

Tracts and Publications—To distribute religious tracts, and to secure subscribers for Baptist journals.

Missions—To seek scholars for Sunday-School, visit absent scholars and encourage a worthy zeal in all mission work, and seek to inspire in all the young people a desire to cultivate the grace of giving.

Advisory—To consist of the pastor, the officers, and the chairman of the committees, to meet once a month and also at the call of the pastor or president, to consider all matters of business and make recommendations to the organization, and to report to the church semi-annually the progress of the work of the young people. The pastor is *ex-officio* a member of all committees, and his approval should accompany all plans and recommendations made by the committees.

Benevolence—To visit the sick and sorrowing, to report same to society from time to time and render any needed assistance to the afflicted.

Article 7. Meetings

Devotional meetings shall be held weekly. Meetings for instruction shall be held at such time as may be determined by the organization. Business meetings shall be held quarterly, at which reports of committees shall be submitted in writing, and the recommendations of the Advisory Committee acted upon.

Article 8. Amendments

This Constitution may be amended at any regular meeting, provided notice of the amendments shall be given at a previous meeting.

Source: *Minutes*, Broadway Baptist Church, 15 March 1891.

B. Texas Leads the World in BYPU Work

There are 22,850 B. Y. P. U.'s in the Southern Baptist Convention with 4,431 of them in Texas. There are 500,564 B. Y. P. U. members in the Southern Baptist Convention with 121,083 in Texas.

In the year of 1916 only 1900 B. Y. P. U. diplomas and seals were issued to Texas B. Y. P. U. members. In 1918 there were 1,575 B. Y. P. U.'s in Texas with a membership of 34,194. The total number of B. Y. P. U. diplomas and seals issued that year was 3,250. In five years from that time, or 1922 there were 2,525 B. Y. P. U.'s with a membership of 81,152. In the year of 1929 we find 4,431 B. Y. P. U.'s in Texas with a membership of 121,083. There are 403 A-1 Unions. The number of B. Y. P. U. diplomas and seals issued during this year was 27,819.

It will be observed that one-fifth of the B. Y. P. U.'s of the Southern Baptist Convention are in Texas. One-fifth of the B. Y. P. U. members are in Texas and one-fifth of the B. Y. P. U. diplomas and seals granted by Southern Baptists are issued to Texas B. Y. P. U. members. There are eighteen states in the Southern Baptist Convention. There are 3,705,876 Baptists in the Southern Baptist Convention. There are 495,145 Baptists in Texas.

Source: *Proceedings*, Baptist General Convention of Texas, 1929, 116. Reprint courtesy of the Baptist General Convention of Texas.

8.7 Baptist Student Union

Due to the large number of students attending both Baptist and State Colleges, the Baptist General Convention of Texas deemed it necessary to minister to their spiritual needs. For this reason, the Baptist Student Missionary Movement was formed at a meeting on the Southwestern campus on November 9, 1914. Similar in purpose to the YMCA, the BSMM was strictly a Baptist organization.

The Formation of the Baptist Student Union in Texas

During the meeting of the Southern Baptist Convention in Nashville, Tenn., May 1914, Dr. Chas. Ball, then Professor of Missions in the Southwestern Baptist Theological Seminary, Ft. Worth, Texas, called together a number of the leaders among Southern Baptists and proposed the organization of a Baptist Students Missionary Movement. This informal conference recommended the calling of a larger conference to meet in Ft. Worth on November 8th, 1914. This conference was well attended and on November 9th, 1914 in the Seminary at Ft. Worth "The Baptist Student Missionary Movement" was organized. An Executive Committee of seven was appointed and given authority to select fourteen other members from the United States and Canada.

At a meeting of the Baptist General Convention of Texas, held at Abilene, Texas, November 19–23, 1914, during the hour set aside for Home Missions, Drs. C. T. Ball, Forrest Smith, and S. J. Porter discussed the Baptist Student Mission Movement. No written report was submitted.

In the Southern Baptist Convention held at Houston, Texas, May 12, 1915, the president appointed a committee on motion of S. J. Porter of Texas, to present to the Convention the next afternoon a report on the Baptist Student Missionary Movement. The report as made by S. J. Porter is as follows:

"Many Baptists throughout North America have felt for some time the need of a more definite cooperative effort to inspire and enlist more thoroughly Baptist students in the interest of world-wide missions. It is with pleasure, therefore, that we report to this Convention the organization of the Baptist Student Missionary Movement, and the favor which is being accorded to it throughout the entire country and in Canada. In behalf of this movement, which seeks to round out the missionary program of American Baptists, your Committee asks the hearty and sympathetic cooperation of the Convention."

> S. J. Porter,
>
> Hight C. Moore,
>
> W. L. Pickard.

"After remarks by S. J. Porter of Texas, and E. Y. Mullins, of Ky., the report was adopted."

Source: Andrew Q. Allen, *A Brief History of the Baptist Student Missionary Movement and the Baptist Student Union in Texas* (Fort Worth: Southwestern Baptist Theological Seminary, 1933), 1.

8.8 Woman's Missionary Union

Significant changes were made in the area of women's work in 1919. First, the organization changed its name from Baptist Women Missionary Workers to its original pre-BGCT name, the Woman's Missionary Union. Second, their original boundaries of work were changed from several large regions into eighteen well-defined districts. The WMU hoped to have a leader organizing the work in each district within the year.

Houston, 1919

Houston was the place of the annual session beginning December 9, 1919. This was closely following the Victory Week of the 75 Million Campaign. The presence of notable missionaries gave added zest to the life of the gathering. There were Mrs. Bagby of Brazil, Mr. and Mrs. Eugene Sallee, Mrs. Nancy Swann, Miss Loy Savage, and Miss Mary Williford of China.

The address of the president was, as usual, the feature of the first day. She said: "The map of the world has changed. . . . We face a new order of things. The very bigness of it has its fascination and appeal."

Three new department leaders rendered initial reports. Mrs. Charles R. Moore, for the Y. W. A. department, said: "Hundreds of our young women were noble and self-sacrificing in their pledges to our 75 Million Campaign. We rejoice that they had part in this great victory." Mrs. W. R. Covington, leader of the juvenile department, rejoiced in a large number of new bands and pleaded with the women to make the most of their opportunities to guide and teach the children. Mrs. M. N. Chrestman, head of the department of Personal Service, read a glowing account of her first year's work. Another new worker was Miss Essie Fuller, who gave a report of six months' service as a field worker.

In the recommendation of the Executive Board were three changes: First, the Training School scholarships were increased from $200 to $250; second, the adoption of the name of Woman's Missionary Union of Texas; third, the rearrangement of the district lines to form eighteen districts in the State.

When, by action of the convention, the Baptist Women Missionary Workers decided to resume its original name, "The Woman's Missionary Union," it did not specifically recognize its age. The Baptist Women Mission Workers evolved in 1886, and now was thirty-three years old. But the Woman's Missionary Union was organized in 1880; thus the real age of organization was thirty-nine years instead of thirty-three. By reference to the title pages of the printed minutes of the annual meetings of the convention, it is evident that the age question was never permanently settled.

Interesting annual reports of the districts were presented by their presidents: North, Mrs. R. C. Fortner, Plano; Northeast, Mrs. W. M. McBride, Greenville; Northwest, Mrs. B. T. Johnson, Canyon City; Central, Miss Lulan Gilmore, Brownwood; Central South, Mrs. J. E. Williamson, Austin; Central East, Mrs. W. A. Wood, Waco; Central West, Mrs. O. H. Cooper, Abilene; United South, Mrs. I. S. Myer, Houston; Southwest, Miss Alexander, San Antonio; East, Mrs. John A. Beall, Jacksonville; West, Mrs. W. F. Hatchel, El Paso.

Mrs. J. W. Byars rendered her first annual report as superintendent of the Training School. Mrs. E. M. Francis, chairman of missions, observed: "The 75 Million Campaign has enlarged our responsibilities and opportunities both here in the homeland and overseas. . . . We are assembled on the clear mount of victory, but what are we going to do when we descend into the plains?"

The young people's evening was observed December 9 at 8 p. m., with Mrs. Charles R. Moore presiding. The program: "Why and How I Became a Missionary," Mrs. Eugene Sallee; message from the State Sunbeam leader, Mrs. W. R. Covington; Sunbeam demonstration; chorus, Y. W. A.'s and G. A.'s of Houston; message from State Y. W. A. leader, Mrs. Charles R. Moore; solo, Miss Rowe, Houston; college Y. W. A.'s, Miss Essie Fuller, Fort Worth; reading, Mrs. Larkin, Houston; prayer, Mrs. J. W. Byars.

The second day's proceedings revealed a high level in all plans. The papers read, the talks made, were tuned to inspire all hearts. Among the women taking part in the discussions were Mrs. E. G. Townsend, Mrs. C. E. Maddry, Mrs. J. H. Weatherby, Mrs. Hal Buckner, Mrs. R. F. Stokes, Mrs. J. E. Williamson, Mrs. J. M. Dawson, Mrs. William B. McGarity, Mrs. F. E. Carroll. With sorrow we noted the absence of Mrs. B. N. Boren, that great friend of our orphan children. It was a coincidence that in the same meeting we should note the passing over the River of Mrs. Boren and also Dr. Buckner, the founder and manager of Buckner Orphan's Home.

Mrs. Beddoe, at this 1919 meeting in Houston, reported a grand total of offerings for all causes of $385,844.19, and as a chairman of the committee on appointments recommended "that we take as our aim for the ensuing year $635,000."

The "signs of the times" were in the air. Prohibition had won at the polls just six months before. The challenge of the 75 Million Campaign was the touchstone that conspired to make the Houston meeting a landmark in our history.

Source: Mrs. W. J. J. Smith, *A Centennial History of the Baptist Women of Texas, 1830–1930* (Dallas: Woman's Missionary Union of Texas, 1933), 76–79. Reprint courtesy of the Woman's Missionary Union of Texas.

8.9 Southwestern Seminary

B. H. Carroll may have been the father of Southwestern Seminary, but it was L. R. Scarborough, Southwestern's second President, who developed its latent potential. One of Scarborough's first advancements was to add J. M. Price to the faculty in 1915 as the first professor of Christian Education. Because of the work of Price, by 1920, a student could earn a Master's Degree in Christian Education. Scarborough was also the director of the 75 Million Campaign. The unity of all Southern Baptists in this endeavor when coupled with the fact that Southwestern students came from all over the United States, and ten members of its Board of Trustees did not call Texas home, led him to realize that Southwestern Seminary must be formally given to the SBC. The BGCT transferred ownership to the national convention in 1925. Southwestern was now officially a national, if not international, seminary.

A. The School of Religious Education

In 1915 Dr. J. M. Price came to the Seminary as its first full-time teacher in the field of Religious Education and at the time the Department of Religious Education was created. The first year he was the only employed teacher, five hours of work being offered. During this year only two were enrolled and they were special students. A year later, however, there appeared a larger and better planned curriculum providing for a two year course leading to a diploma in Religious Education. A twofold aim emerges; first, the preparation of pastors to direct religious education in their churches; and second, training those who are preparing for special work in the field of religious education.

To follow up certain of the features of progress, we mention Miss Lou Ella Austin as the first graduate in 1917. In 1919 courses for the degree of Bachelor of Religious Education were offered and in 1920 those for the degree of Master of Religious Education. Two other instructors were added to the faculty in 1920. N. R. Drummond was made an associate professor in the Department and Miss Bertha Mitchell became teacher of Kindergarten and Elementary Religious Education. In 1921 the Department of Religious Education was separated from the School of Theology and was enlarged into the School of Religious Education. In 1922, T. B. Maston was secured as instructor in Adolescent Religious Education, Miss Anne Laseter as instructor in Elementary Religious Education and Mr. W. F. Yarbrough, Jr. was made a fellow in Religious Education. The school began to offer the degree of Doctor of Religious Education in 1924. This degree was conferred for the first time in 1925 upon T. B. Maston. The departments at present are, Principles of Religious Education, Administration of Religious Education, Social Ethics, Educational Arts, and Secretarial Training. In 1935 the

W. M. U. Department of Woman's Missionary Training School was merged with the Department of Administration of Religious Education and the Training School courses in Shorthand and Typewriting were merged with the Department of Secretarial Training. The faculty of the School of Religion for the session of 1935-36 were Dr. J. M. Price, director, Dr. T. B. Maston, Mr. W. L. Howse, Miss Floy Barnard, Mrs. W. A. Johnson and Miss Virginia Ely. Through these twenty years Dr. Price has been the leading factor in the growth of the school. For more than half of this time he was ably assisted by Dr. N. R. Drummond and since 1922 has found increasing support in the scholarly work of Dr. T. B. Maston. Other faithful teachers have wrought well for lesser periods of service. During these years work of the faculty in this school was continuously reinforced by the coming of specialists in this field from the State Board and the south wide Sunday School Board to deliver special lectures and conduct brief training courses.

We close this running sketch of the school with a list of its signal contributions.

1. It was the first school in the South to offer vocational training and degrees in religious education, starting in 1915.

2. It is the largest school of religious education in America definitely denominational in nature.

3. From this school have gone out nearly two hundred and fifty workers in ten lines of service in half the United States and many foreign countries.

4. It sponsored the first distinctly vocational conference on religious education held in the South, held April 15-17, 1921.

5. It initiated, and cooperated with the Texas Baptist Sunday School Department in holding the first Superintendents' conference, June 6-9, 1920.

6. Out of the above conference grew the Southwestern Baptist Religious Education Association composed of vocational workers, which has held fifteen sessions.

7. It sponsored the oldest Vacation Bible School existing west of the Mississippi River.

8. It led in providing observation and practice work as a part of the training of the vocational worker.

9. The movement among Southern Baptists for requiring academic prerequisites for seminary graduation started in this school.

10. The first credit courses among Baptists in Church Finances and Publicity, Recreational Leadership, and Religious Dramatics and Art, were offered in this school.

Source: L. R. Elliott, *Centennial History of Texas Baptists* (Dallas: Baptist General Convention of Texas, 1936), 334–36. Reprint courtesy of the Baptist General Convention of Texas.

B. The SBC Takes Control of Southwestern

Believing that all theological institutions which receive money from our South-wide educational funds should be under the direct legal control of the Southern Baptist Convention, we recommend that no trustees shall hold office for life, but that each trustee shall be elected for a term not exceeding five years, that whatever changes in the charters of our theological institutions may be necessary to transfer to the Southern Baptist Convention either the legal control of election or the legal control of the nomination of trustees serving for a definite term of years shall be made before the institutions fostered and supported through the 75 Million Campaign shall report annually to this body, giving a full account of its work and its finances.

Source: *Annual*, Southern Baptist Convention, 1923, 38–41.

8.10 Creeds!

The word creed immediately draws the ire of all Baptists and those in Texas were no different. With the 1925 Southern Baptist Convention at Memphis and the adoption of the first Baptist Faith and Message pending, L. R. Scarborough sought to explain the necessity of adopting this statement of faith. Scarborough, however, was quite adamant in how he believed the instrument should be applied in the seminaries.

What Ought the Memphis Convention Do with the Articles of Faith?

The Convention's Committee will have ready a revised and enlarged statement of the New Hampshire Articles of Faith. The New Hampshire Articles of Faith is a great document. It has been the standard expression of belief of Baptists, at least in the South, for nearly a century. It is probably the clearest and most explicit expression of the Bible doctrine ever printed. It needs revision and enlargement. There are some fundamentals of our faith now recognized by our people which are not emphasized in these articles; for instance, missions, stewardship, co-operation and such like. There is evidence that the committee will report unanimously a great improvement and the needful enlargement of such articles. They will be a clear, plain, explicit expression of what Baptists believe. There will be no evasions, no hedging, no dodging, but a clarified, courageous statement of the fundamentals of our conception of the New Testament doctrine. I give herein my opinion of what I think the Convention ought to do with these Articles of Faith.

I think the Convention ought to hear the committee's report, carefully consider it, and recommend the Articles of Faith to the churches for their adoption, if they desire to do so. I do not believe that the Convention has any right to require any other convention, any church or any group of individuals to adopt these Articles of Faith. The Convention probably has the right to require the professors of the three South-wide Seminaries, the only schools the Convention owns, and probably all of its Boards and secretaries to adopt these Articles of Faith. I do not believe that such ought to be done. All three of the South-wide Seminaries have during all their existence had articles of faith for their teachers to sign and the boards of trustees have required such teachers to sign these articles of faith. I shall recommend to the Board of Trustees of Southwestern Seminary that they adopt the Article of Faith recommended by the Convention, and require, as formerly, each teacher in the Seminary to sign these Articles of Faith. There will be nothing new in the procedure with any of our three South-wide Seminaries.

I think the only thing the Convention ought to do is to what the Convention has done a number of times before, and do what the World Alliance did at Stockholm—receive the report of its committee and recommend the articles it brings to our Baptist people everywhere. The churches will adopt these Articles of Faith if they please. The Board of Trustees of the schools owned by the states will, if they desire, adopt these Articles of Faith for their teachers. If they do not so desire, they do not have to do it.

In facing this question, we must remember the rights and limitations of the rights of conventions. These Articles of Faith are not a creed. Such Articles of Faith have never been regarded by Baptists as a dogmatic creed which one group of individuals can bind upon the consciences of other individuals. It is simply a statement of what we believe, a witness, a testimony of our conception of the heart of revealed truth as set out in the Bible. It is a standard of doctrine approximating the truth as revealed in the Bible.

Source: L. R. Scarborough, "What Ought the Memphis Convention Do With Articles of Faith," *Baptist Standard*, 30 April 1925, 9. Reprint courtesy of the *Baptist Standard*.

CHAPTER 9

Depression and Deliverance, 1929–1945

9.1 Depression

The Depression of the 1930s severely impacted the ministries of the Baptist General Convention of Texas. The Sunday School and Baptist Training Union were forced to make 50 percent staff reductions and the WMU reduced its staff by a third. In addition, the Home and Foreign Mission Boards were in debt. Despite the overwhelmingly poor economic conditions, Texas Baptists never lost hope and continued to advance the cause of Christ throughout the state even in these difficult times. Under the leadership of Corresponding Secretary J. Howard Williams, the Baptists refused to be defeated by the depleted economy.

A. Drastic Reductions Made

Long before the business world began its program of reduction, the Executive Board of the Baptist General Convention made certain definite reductions in its departmental activities. It was shown at the last convention, for instance, that the administrative budget has been reduced over 50 percent within the last five years. Some months back, salaries were reduced 10 percent throughout all the departments. In some cases this was the second cut in salary.

Recently, however, the Finance and Executive Committees met in joint session and frankly faced the necessity of further and very drastic reductions. Accordingly, the appropriations to the Sunday school and B. T. S. and B. Y. P. U. departments were cut 50 percent. In figures the reduction being from $15,000 to $7,500, to be equally divided between them. The Sunday School Board has been helping these departments, and unless it can add to what it has given to our regular work, these departments will have to reduce the number of their workers. Secretary John Caylor has accepted a place with the Broadway Baptist Church of Fort Worth. The committees asked the General Secretary to assume general direction of this work, thereby affecting a saving of the salary and traveling expenses of this department. The W. M. U. has agreed to a reduction of $3,500 in its budget of $9,500. This reduction is really more drastic than that of some other departments, since this work secures no help from the Sunday School Board. Further reductions were made in the administrative work, so that the annual reduction amounts to $18,000.

I have never seen a group of men act more nobly than those of these combined committees. Prayer pervaded the meeting, and all actions taken were unanimous. To make such drastic reductions, in the face of such needs as confront us, and with such records as these departments have made, took courage of the highest order. Mention was made in the committee room that we were most fortunate in the personnel of our workers in times like these. Confident belief was expressed that the leaders of these departments would receive severe cuts in a most Christian-like spirit. Nor were the committees wrong for, in my judgment, a nobler group could not be found anywhere on the globe. For one who has given years of his life to the building up of a great work, it is not easy to stand by and see it terribly crippled. There are those working for Texas Baptists who would lay down their lives for the work of Texas Baptists. They believe it is the work of their crucified Lord.

I would add two words. Texas Baptists must live within their income. We must not accumulate more debt. If we are forced to live on bread and water, we must do it—and we will.

The second word is that we are going to do better when we realize the seriousness of our situation. The day Texas Baptists average 25 cents per month to the Co-operative Program we can more than double our work after adding back all we have received since the first of the year. Ninety-nine percent of our people can give 25 cents per month, or more.

The vast majority of them can give much more than this, and will, when they become really concerned about it.

J. Howard Williams

Source: J. Howard Williams, "Drastic Reductions Made," *Baptist Standard*, 12 May 1932. Reprint courtesy of the *Baptist Standard*.

B. Missions Cause Imperiled

The life of our Home and Foreign Missions work is imperiled. For eighty-seven years Southern Baptists have been carrying on an aggressive mission program at home and abroad. Their glorious achievements and honorable record are such that the Southern Baptist name is accepted all over the world as worth one hundred cents on the dollar. In order to keep this record, in the face of rapidly declining receipts from year to year, the Foreign Mission Board has had to close schools, repeatedly cut appropriations, reduce salaries, keep missionaries at home, and all but entirely abandon certain fields.

The Southern Baptist Convention faced this matter with all gravity. A committee wrestled with it for two days and nights before it carried any recommendation to the Convention. In spite of the unprecedented conditions which prevail, the Convention voted to go afield to raise $300,000 in cash for these causes during the months of June and July.

Cold facts forced this action. The lean summer months are just ahead. Heretofore the banks have tided the Boards over until the larger collections of the fall came in. They have been good to the Foreign Board, which now owes them more than $1,000,000 on open account. They have expressed their faith in both Boards and in Southern Baptists, but they served notice that they will lend no additional funds. Drafts will soon be coming in from all over the world, and these cannot be honored unless immediate relief is given. It will take $190,000 to meet the Foreign Board's summer needs. The Home Board's are just as drastic. One hundred and ten thousand dollars for the summer is the minimum necessary to a bread and water existence. Our trusted leaders tell us the question is: Will we be in the Home and Foreign Mission work in September, or will these Boards be in the process of liquidation? We are today called to meet stark necessities.

Southern Baptists believe in missions. Texas Baptists do. During June and July we will have an opportunity to give to missions with no conditions attached. The Sunday School Board will pay every cent of cost for carrying out this special mission offering, so that one hundred cents of every dollar given will go direct to these Boards. It is the hope that every full-time church in the South will take a special offering for this work on Sunday, June 19. All other churches are requested to take such an offering before July closes.

God loves all the world. His book is for all men. Redemption awaits all, and all men need redemption. We cannot, we do not deny that God placed the responsibility of telling the glad tidings upon the shoulders of saved men. He would not ask us to do what He knew to be impossible. We have not done our best in the past; we must do it now. Southern Baptists will arouse themselves. Texas Baptists will not fail these causes in this hour when the question is to live or not to live. Then let us search our hearts, go to our knees in agonizing prayer, that God will forgive our sin and lead us to find a way to share the good news with the myriads who wait in darkness for the Light of the World.

J. Howard Williams, Secretary

Source: *Baptist Standard*, 2 June 1932, 1. Reprint courtesy of the *Baptist Standard*.

9.2 William Richardson White

William Richardson White was elected President of the Executive Board in 1930. He resigned this office after one year to assume the pastorate of the Broadway Baptist Church in Fort Worth. White's one year as President was marked by a weakened national economy, staff reductions across all the Boards, and a sparsity of working income for the BGCT. Despite these harsh conditions, he was a deeply respected and loved Texas Baptist leader. After the Depression, White served as President of Hardin-Simmons University from 1943 to 45 and Baylor University from 1948 to 1961.

Commendation of W. R. White

God in his goodness, provides always for his people. When men are needed for special work in the church and the Kingdom his choice is manifest by the directing influence of the Holy Spirit.

We believe the official family of the Texas Baptist General Convention are all God called people, prepared by His kind providence and led by the Holy Spirit to assume the present tasks.

Our W. M. U. officers and executives grace their official position with the feminine charm of consecrated womanliness. The effectiveness of their organization is the result of their piety and loyalty to Jesus Christ's program for his churches.

The B. S. U., B. Y. P. U. and Sunday School Missionaries, each in his own character, represent the power of the Holy Spirit in enduement for service. Talents are given in love and wisdom by our God for special service. Each of these workers manifest in his daily ministrations his adaptability for leadership of our young people, as it indicated by the success of these departments.

We also take this occasion to express our profound gratitude to God for the laborious and nobly capable service rendered this Convention by the members of the Budget Control Committee, and by those also who have rendered legal service in behalf of this Convention and its various enterprises.

With George Mason, Treasurer, our Secretary has directed the finances, according to the reports, in a most acceptable manner during one of the greatest financial depressions any of us have ever seen.

W. R. White knows how to get Christian men and women to give their money to the Kingdom work. His sound judgment in financial matters restores the confidence of our big giver, as well as the small. He believes in a financial program and budget for all the churches.

His passion for souls and ability to witness for Jesus in winning souls reveal him as a practical Mission Secretary. Texas Baptists have had many men led of the Holy Spirit to direct the varied activities of the denomination. We here and now acknowledge our gratitude to God for giving Texas Baptists W. R. White, the Executive Secretary. Born in Texas, led to Christ by a Texas Baptist preacher, nurtured in a Baptist church in Texas, educated in Texas Baptist institutions, he has been kept by the Providence of God in Texas to lead his people in their missionary thinking and program. One year of this leadership is history. Born in East Texas, educated in Central Texas, pastor in East Texas and West Texas, he knows all the people and everybody knowing him will follow him in his program for winning the world to Christ. His leadership is not that of a commander, austere and irritable, but a comrade with a disposition to share the common burden. His transparent character, brotherly sympathy, integrity and justice are the elements which make for unity. No man among us has more in common with all of us. An experience of grace, the culture of the schools, the love of the people, the confidence of all who know him set him apart as one who can be easily followed. He came into the Kingdom to lead Texas Baptists to do their best to bring the lost world by the way of the cross home to God.

W. R. White knows how to build the brotherhood. His big kindly heart beats in unison with every Christ filled heart. He knows the problems of the pastor. He has experienced the joy of the teacher. As Executive Secretary of the Texas Baptist Convention he has a chance to use all his God given talents to be missionary preacher-teacher. His first year has been a triumphant success. He has the hearts of all the people.

We need no adjectives to define or describe the kind of Baptist he is. He is not a fickle man. He has always had one great passion as a follower of Christ. Missionary describes and defines that passion.

He is a worthy exponent of Texas Baptist life and his orthodoxy needs no defense. We commend him to the world as our beloved comrade. We Texas Baptists thank God for our official family and pledge them our hearty cooperation in service.

M. M. Wolf

George Green

R. E. Day

Source: *Proceedings*, Baptist General Convention of Texas, 1930, 20–21. Reprint courtesy of the Baptist General Convention of Texas.

9.3 John Howard Williams

John Howard Williams was elected Executive Secretary in 1931. During his five years of service, he helped to keep the BGCT from going bankrupt by means of adroit fiscal cutbacks. Though the times were financially difficult, Williams remained optimistic about the future of Texas Baptists and kept the morale of Texas Baptists from completely disappearing. After resigning in 1936, he successively pastored the First Baptist Church of Lubbock and the First Baptist Church of Oklahoma City before once again serving as Executive Secretary from 1946 until 1953. He then succeeded Eldred Douglas Head as President of Southwestern Baptist Theological Seminary. He served in this capacity until his death in 1958.

Eulogizing the Work of Williams

Upon motion of H. R. Long, duly seconded, J. M. Dawson, H. L. Fickett, and J. J. Jenkins constitute a committee to draw up suitable resolutions with reference to the Secretary, J. Howard Williams. The committee reported as follows, and same was adopted:

In accepting the resignation of Dr. J. Howard Williams from the position of Executive Secretary of Texas Baptists, this Board would record its high appreciation of his distinguished services during the five years of his tenure of office.

From the hour he entered upon his responsible duties in the leadership of this Board he has demonstrated a rare administrative ability, particularly in his capacity for organizing, inspiring and directing our forces. Coupled with this has been a statesmanlike vision and utterance, at all times progressively constructive. He has been most fraternal in his relations, exhibiting a comradeship and fellowship which have been most endearing to his brethren. At no time have the Texas Baptists achieved a larger degree of unity, a profound harmony, a finer spirit of cooperation than during these five years. In all his work he has shown a poise, a balance, a well-rounded, comprehensive grasp which have greatly stabilized our Baptist life and activities. If any element in this all inclusive loyalty has been more prominent than any other it has been his evangelistic and missionary zeal, which has brought marvelous growth to our denomination.

We desire to emphasize his noble estimate of the place and significance of the local church as scripturally constituted, and of the devoted efforts he has put forth to encourage the utmost development and service on the part of each such church. With all these qualities Dr. Williams has exerted a ceaseless energy and dedicated a sacrificial spirit which have not only signalized unprecedented achievements during his administration but which will cause us to hold forever in grateful memory his contribution to Texas Baptists.

It would be impossible to summarize here even in the broadest outline all that he has wrought but we offer this as a simple and sincere expression of our regard and acknowledgment of all that he has meant to us.

Source: *Minutes*, Executive Board of the Baptist General Convention of Texas, 11 June 1936. Reprint courtesy of the Baptist General Convention of Texas.

9.4 Robert Clifton Campbell

Following J. H. Williams's resignation in 1936, Campbell was elected Executive Secretary on the first ballot. Unlike his immediate predecessors, Campbell's administration was marked by significant economic improvements. The Great Depression was finally beginning to abate. During his two years of service, he helped develop the departments of Brotherhood, Endowment, and Ministry to Soldiers. A popular author, Campbell's text on stewardship, *God's Plan,* helped shape Southern Baptist perceptions of giving.

A. Executive Board Meeting, March 4, 1941

R. C. Campbell reported on the progress of the evangelistic efforts being made in the state, and urged that the pastors cooperate fully in the state program for evangelism. He told of the successful meeting of the evangelistic chairmen on December 30, Dallas, to plan their work for the entire year. He then introduced W. H. Andrews of Bryan and spoke for ten minutes on evangelism.

R. C. Campbell spoke on the Enlarged Program of Texas. He reported that we were only short $31,000 of the amount of the goal for the first quarter, and due to the fact the Enlarged Program did not really get under way until January, he felt that the amount could easily be secured as the January offering was $19,000 above that of the same month last year.

R. C. Campbell stated that for three months he had been considering a call to the First Baptist Church, Columbia, South Carolina, and that after long, serious and prayerful consideration he felt it was God's will for his life that he accept the call. Among other things, he said: "To say that I regret to leave Texas, doesn't approach the feeling that there is in my heart. From the time I came to Texas until now, and it shall be on, until I go hence, there is a love in my heart that has devotion in it to Texas Baptists, Texas Baptist institutions, Texas Baptist opportunities unparalleled in any other state or provide in the world, but in spite of that, the course of the Lord's leadership seems so plain that I am offering my resignation. I thank you out of the deep of my heart for every cooperation, for every consideration and I shall look back many, many times, longingly, doubtless, to Texas, and I shall think in happy terms of my twelve years in Texas. You have been good to me, far better than any man deserves and you will have my prayers and my interest and I will watch you with keen interest from week to week."

. . . "Much to the regret of Texas Baptists, Dr. R. C. Campbell, Executive Secretary, who tendered his resignation to the Executive Board recently, will soon leave to enter upon his new duties as pastor in Columbia, South Carolina.

"During his five year tenure as Executive Secretary, Dr. Campbell has demonstrated that he is exceedingly well qualified in body, mind, and soul for Christian leadership. His keen vision, broad sympathies, love for the brethren, passion for the cause of Christ, coupled with his fine pulpit ability, have made a remarkable impression upon the Baptist life of this state.

Under his leadership renewed emphasis has been given to Scriptural evangelism, one part of which has been a largely attended Annual Preachers' Evangelistic Conference, from which has radiated gracious influences throughout our entire Baptist Zion. Our entire denominational work has been undergirded by an enlarged program of Bible stewardship, which has resulted in greatly increased contributions on the part of the churches for both local and missionary causes. The receipts for missionary purposes last year reached the impressive total of $863,000.

In addition to his numerous duties as Executive Secretary, Dr. Campbell has found time to write six books:

"God's Plan," 15,000 distribution

"Youth and Yokes," now in its second edition

" The Coming Revival," 15,000 distribution (5,000 in Chinese and 5,000 in Spanish)

" Militant Christianity," now in its second edition

" Worldliness Out," A new study course book
"God's Quest for Man," Will be released from press in May

Mrs. Campbell has been intensely interested in all the work of Texas Baptists. In her quiet, devoted way she has been a constant encouragement to her husband. We feel that the church at Columbia is fortunate in securing this fine couple.

As these good people go from us, they will have the prayers of Texas Baptists for continued success and happiness. May the blessing of God attend their labor.

Signed: Perry F. Webb
           Karl H. Moore
           Frank Weedon
           Fred Eastham
           R. O. Cawker

Source: *Minutes*, Executive Board of the Baptist General Convention of Texas, 4 March 1941. Reprint courtesy of the Baptist General Convention of Texas.

9.5 William Walter Melton

Prior to being elected Executive Secretary of the BGCT in 1941, Melton had been the pastor of the Seventh and James Baptist Church in Waco, Texas, since 1912. His four years of service were marked by a period of spiritual prosperity which accompanied World War II. Melton resigned in 1945 and accepted the pastorate of the Columbus Avenue Baptist Church in Waco, Texas. He remained in this position until his retirement in 1957. The author of more than a dozen books, Melton's most famous work was a book of sermons entitled, *Sifted But Saved*.

A. The Gospel's Foes

But the text raises another question. What were the foes over which the gospel prevailed? The first one was a series of unexplainable setbacks. One of the closest friends betrayed Christ. This would naturally give the new cause a great shock. Its repercussions did not fade before another one denied him outright, which added to the seriousness of the situation. Then the worst of all occurred within one day's time. Later, the first deacon was stoned to death, and the church was scattered to the winds by persecution. These catastrophes were hard to understand, but the gospel grew in spite of them and prevailed.

A second foe was infidelity in the church. It will be remembered that many people were caught up with the new movement, but later drifted back to Judaism. They denounced Christ and went back to Moses as their hope of being saved. These people said by their conduct, "We have tried your Christianity, and it has not satisfied us." This is always a serious problem. Foes on the outside are not to be dreaded as much as foes from within. Having come from within, they are far more hurtful than the infidel without.

The enemy within has always been the real problem for the church. He strikes his hardest blow when he gets into the pulpit. When our preachers are infidels, the holy cause seems headed for the rocks. It was an especially great wonder for the gospel to prevail when many of the leaders and teachers were without conviction or genuine experience. Its success in the face of such adversities proves its claims of superiority and guarantees its ultimate victory in the world.

Another foe so prominent in that day, and more so today, was the imitator of the good. Simon the magician went into religious work for the material gain he could get out of it (Acts 8: 9–24). The seven sons of Sceva, mentioned in Acts 19, were strangers to Christ, but they posed as his devout followers and as intimate friends of Paul. But when they tried to cast out an evil spirit in the name of Jesus, they failed and were exposed.

The church has always had to meet the counterfeit. Many things spring up which sometimes act as rivals of the church for the affections of the people. Religious associations are an example. I am aware that they are not openly acclaimed as a rival, and many of their best friends would not wish them to be thought of as such, but the fact remains that they are in competition with the church for the members' time and energy.

The lodge movement is another example. I am a lodge man and speak from experience. Many of its best members would resent the open statement that the lodge is esteemed more highly than the church, but for many (and for some who are unwilling to admit it), that is the truth.

To them, the lodge more nearly meets the needs of the suffering world than the church does. If this is true, it is because the church members who belong to the lodge do their charity work through the lodge rather than through the church. If this is the case, no further proof is needed that they give the lodge a higher priority.

Many such cases might be mentioned, but these are sufficient. These imitators of the good may not be wholly condemned as evil, yet because of their strong qualities, they can be made a substitute for the church and thereby weaken the claims of the church. The early church had such foes to overcome. And we are indebted to the sacred writer for confirming that the gospel prevailed over them all.

Let another foe be mentioned, since it is discussed in this same chapter—the influence of bad literature. It is said that under Paul's preaching, the people were induced to bring out their valuable libraries [worth over six million dollars at today's value, according to NIV notes] and burn them in one great bonfire. These were books of sorcery that lured the curious with promises of attaining forbidden, mysterious knowledge until the victims were hopelessly trapped in Satan's grasp.

There is no need more pressing today than a repetition of that sweeping victory for the gospel. The world is sown with the most evil literature. Its poison springs from every kind of press, from the religious to the comic. The flood of degradation is burying the unwary and the innocent. What shall the ultimate harvest of this awful seedtime be? God grant that the gospel will overcome this seed and choke out the noxious growths that may spring from the adversary's cunning planting, as it did then!

A last foe will be mentioned: the business person who runs his business in opposition to the church. Acts 19:24 tells of one Demetrius who made his living by making images of his heathen temple and selling them to the ignorant people as things of spiritual value. When the gospel was preached, the people turned from their idols, denounced their heathen temple, and no longer bought wares of this craftsman. Of course, he had a quarrel with Paul and the gospel. But we are told that the gospel prevailed over him and his nefarious business.

It has not been the last bad business the gospel has put down. I am confident it was by this leavening influence that America shook off slavery. I am equally as confident that the great lotteries, of which the Louisiana lottery was chief, went before the same power. The race track, gambling, open saloon, and brothel have gone down under the influence of the gospel, and God hasten the day when other businesses that exploit the souls and bodies of mankind will be forced to close their doors.

Source: W. W. Melton, *Sifted But Saved* (Nashville: Broadman Press, 1925), 81–84. Reprint courtesy of Broadman and Holman Publishers.

9.6 The District Plan

One of the problems in Texas Baptist organization was the vastness of the state. Many local Associations, churches, and ministers in South and West Texas were so far removed from the denominational office in Dallas that they rarely participated in Convention affairs. In an attempt to correct this problem, Executive Secretary J. Howard Williams developed the District Plan.

The District Plan in Action, 1933

The District Plan offers the most effective way of carrying on our work at the present time, and we recommend that this Convention look with favor upon the growing sentiment for district missionaries and instruct the Board to form a policy in this matter.

In carrying out these instructions, the Board adopted the following policy:

1. That district missionaries employed be elected by representatives of the associations, forming a district committee.

2. That in the selection of these men the greatest care be exercised in choosing men of outstanding ability, who are peculiarly fitted to do this type of work.

3. That the salaries of these men be paid in full by the associations of the district involved, if such is possible. We recommend that in no case shall the State Board pay more than one-fourth of the salary.

4. We recommend that it be understood that these men employed shall work in closest harmony with the Executive Board and the General Secretary in promoting all work of the Convention.

The financial and general economic conditions have been such that only District 6 has so far acted on the matter. Rev. E. W. Marshall is pioneering in this field and has already demonstrated the wisdom of such a plan and the value of such a worker. He is aiding pastorless churches throughout the district, promoting the budget, the work of Sunday School, B. T. S. and Evangelism, and materially aiming the Association in the various meetings and programs. We would suggest that this type of work be encouraged and that the appropriations committee of the Board favor application for aid in such work.

Source: *Proceedings*, Baptist General Convention of Texas, 1930, 97–98. Reprint courtesy of the Baptist General Convention of Texas.

9.7 Reconciliation with the BMA

Because of the Hayden Controversy, the BGCT and the BMA had been separate entities since 1901. Due to the deaths of the old combatants, the old prejudices between the two groups had all but disappeared by 1933. The BGCT amended its constitution in 1934 in order to welcome and entice its old adversaries back into the larger fold of Baptist life. Due to the wording of the amendment, however, the BMA felt as if they were merely being absorbed into the BGCT, and thus, they broke off negotiations. Though small, the BMA still exists today and to some degree thrives in East Texas.

A. Attempts at Reconciliation

Dear Brothers and Sisters:

Whereas there has existed for more than thirty years a division among our Baptist people which has resulted in maintaining two statewide Baptist organizations, and believing that there should be an earnest, prayerful, and scriptural effort made to heal this division, we respectfully submit the following suggestions:

That these general bodies in their statewide meetings each name a committee of twenty-five members to meet at a time and place to be agreed on by the committees for the purpose of fellowship and prayer, and to consider the wisdom of calling a statewide mass meeting to consider the possibility of the unification of these two statewide Baptist bodies;

That the first named member of each committee shall be considered as the chairman of that committee, and that the chairmen of the two committees shall arrange for the time and place of the joint meeting of the two committees.

> Respectfully submitted,
> A. O. Hinkle
> Walter H. McKenzie

The request was adopted. Brother Hinkle of the Baptist Missionary Association of Texas was introduced and spoke to the Convention.

Source: *Proceedings*, Baptist General Convention of Texas, 1933, 20–21. Reprint courtesy of the Baptist General Convention of Texas.

B. Improved Cooperation, but No Consolidation

The Baptist General Convention's committee of twenty-five, duly appointed, held several meetings with the Baptist Missionary Association appointees during 1934. This tended to clear up misunderstandings, dissipate prejudices and draw the constituencies much closer together. A partial outcome was reflected in a revision of the Convention's Constitution on a basis agreed upon by the joint committee of fifty, and a further result was that upon the failure of the two bodies to coalesce, a number of the B. M. A. preachers announced their future cooperation with the Convention.

Source: J. M. Dawson, *A Century with Texas Baptists* (Nashville: Broadman Press, 1947), 93–94. Reprint courtesy of Broadman and Holman Publishers.

9.8 The Rural Church Problem

During the Great Depression, the rural churches were placed in an even worse economic quandary than their urban brethren. Most rural church parishioners were farmers, and the Depression devastated them. Thus, few rural churches could afford to pay a pastor, and consequently rarely met for services. In view of this need, J. Howard Williams appointed a rural evangelist to aid these congregations.

Aiding the Rural Churches

J. M. Dawson read the report of the Committee on Plan of Work for Rural Church Rehabilitation during 1935, as follows:

"We your committee on plan of work for rural church rehabilitation during 1935 submit the following:

First, we would record with satisfaction the encouraging progress achieved during the last year under the leadership of F. V. McFatridge. His election one year ago was the result of an increasing conviction on the part of members of this board that something definitely constructive should be undertaken toward more fully recognized, enlisting and developing the 2000 rural churches in our denomination in Texas. Pursuant to a suggestion from this board that experimentation be made of intensive work with two of the smallest churches in Rehoboth Association. As an illustration of the effectiveness of that work, it is reported that one of these churches maintained a pastor, paid off its building debt which amounted to $200.00, and sent $50.00 to the Cooperative Program. In addition this rural church worker visited 43 other churches located in 12 associations, also spoke in many workers conferences and associations. He participated in the Rural Church Conference held at Texas A&M College. He wrote many articles for the papers and conducted meetings from one to three weeks each in 12 churches, counseling with them and aiding them materially in the location of pastors as well as in winning souls and organizing for efficiency. We must believe that he had no little share in the result that 1339 part-time churches this year, as compared with 952 part-time churches last year gave something to the Cooperative Program.

We would ever hold before our vision, as an end to be sought for all these 2000 or more churches, that each may be under pastoral oversight, with a pastor residing on the field, with an indefinite call instead of the doubtful annual call, with a home and adequate living provided; that each church be properly organized as to S. S., B. T. U., W. M. U., and regular worship; that each member be instructed in the doctrines of our faith and developed in stewardship to a support of missions, education and benevolence proportionate to his ability; so that with Christian character he may fulfill the highest demands of home and state, as well as of the Kingdom of God. It is our solemn conviction that on these rural fields there are opportunities unsurpassed for the noblest service to be rendered by preachers anywhere on the earth. We believe the values of such service and the challenge in it should be magnified and exalted in the thinking of us all until multitudes of our most capable and consecrating young ministers will dedicate their whole lives to it as their chosen sphere of labor.

We venture at this time to make the following recommendations:

1. That Rev. F. V. McFatridge be re-employed for another year at the salary named by the committee on Plans and Policies.

2. That he be called Rural Church Missionary.

3. That his work be carried on along lines in accord with his best judgment in cooperation with and under the direction of the Executive Secretary of this Board.

4. That the following suggestions be given approval by this Board:

(1) That adequate publicity be given to this work though the columns of the Baptist Standard. It in addition to regular space the Editor should deem a special rural church edition advisable that this might be most stimulating. Attention should be given to the creation of helpful Baptist literature on the subject, much of it such application as to be of permanent value and worthy of preservation.

(2) That the associations especially be organized in a practical way so as to include every rural church in the fullest sharing of the whole program of church life, recognizing and utilizing the rural pastors, specifically directing the association S. S., B. T. U., W. M. U., organizations toward the development of these churches. We believe further that all organized denominational life throughout should become conscious of the claims and values of their fields.

(3) That our Rural Church Missionary in addition to whatever intensive cultivation shall be given to a single field over a single period of time, be encouraged to hold as many institutes on efficiency in local country as can be held. In this connection we would heartily commend the statewide conference for rural pastors with its notable program which he has arranged at Mt. Calm for December 10.14.

(4) That the Rural Church Missionary be assured of our approval of his visiting our schools, colleges and Seminary, where there are young Christians making choice of life work to present the needs and opportunities of our rural field as a challenge. If a great host of competent and consecrated workers in the future could be turned into this field for life careers, vast changes for the better might be realized."

Source: *Minutes*, Executive Board of the Baptist General Convention of Texas, 4 December 1934. Reprint courtesy of the Baptist General Convention of Texas.

9.9 Centennial

In 1936 the citizens of Texas celebrated their state's one-hundredth year of independence from Mexico. Since the independence of Texas signaled the end of state-sanctioned Catholicism, Texas Baptists wholeheartedly joined in the celebration. For this occasion, J. M. Dawson wrote a play entitled "Give Me Texas." L. R. Elliott penned a *Centennial History of Texas Baptists* and a depository for Baptist papers was created at Southwestern Seminary. In addition, the Texas Baptist booth in the Centennial Exposition at the Dallas Fairgrounds outshone that of any other denomination.

A. Evangelism

Our Baptist people believe in mass as well as personal evangelism. Practically all of the active churches have, at least, one revival meeting per year. Some have more than one. There are several men in the state who give themselves, wholly and continuously to evangelizing. Some of them work independently as to financial support, while others are employed by the Executive Board of the Baptist General Convention. This Board has employed a group of evangelists each year for many years and the results have fully justified this plan of evangelizing. At present the evangelistic staff is composed of Rev. C. Y. Dossey, Dallas, Rev. Wm. H. Joyner, San Antonio, Rev. Hyman Appelman, a Christian Hebrew, Dallas, Rev. J. O. Hearn, Waxahachie, Rev. Hulon Coffman, Dallas, and Rev. A. L. Leak, Plano.

These men assist churches, upon invitation, in revival meetings in rural communities, towns and cities. Theirs is a very valuable missionary as well as evangelistic work. Through the years it has more and more met the approval of our people until it has become the settled policy of the Convention and of the Executive Board. Hundreds of people each year are led by the evangelists to repent of their sins, trust Jesus Christ for salvation and join the churches. Other hundreds already in the churches are led to reconsecration and more effective, more joyous Christian service. These men are not restricted to sections, but churches everywhere in the state may invite any of the staff for revival meetings. They, also, hold open air meetings or meetings in rented houses at mission points, and thus prepare the way for the organization of other churches.

Source: L. R. Elliott, *Centennial History of Texas Baptists* (Dallas: Baptist General Convention of Texas, 1936), 382. Reprint courtesy of the Baptist General Convention of Texas.

B. Baptist Depository

We your committee appointed by the March meeting of the Board to make investigation concerning materials that are and may become available for Texas Baptist history, and to bring a report on the condition, uses, and possibilities of the same, beg to submit the following:

Your committee met at Southwestern Seminary in the month of April and went over the whole matter with a good deal of care. For your information we make brief mention here of the different kinds of historical material which we found at the Seminary.

First, there is a large accumulation of Baptist papers, associational minutes, State Convention annuals, Southern Baptist Convention annuals, as well as old original records of churches and associations, now on deposit in the Seminary library. This collection is unique, there being no other in existence that compares with it, and it is therefore of inestimable value. The minutes and the papers are catalogued, and some are bound and some not. As might be expected, the need for binding is urgent. These are materials that have been accumulated during the life of the Seminary, and which continue to currently come in.

Then there are other such materials which were given to the Seminary by the late Dr. J. M. Carroll. Included in this are about one hundred volumes on Texas Baptist history, some of which are rare and out of print, besides many original books of churches and associations. There is also a considerable collection of the personal correspondence of Dr. J. M. Carroll with Texas Baptist leaders, dating back to the days of his young manhood, besides a large amount of manuscript material which Dr. Carroll wrote in addition to his published history. In this collection are included also many miscellaneous original documents and pamphlets about detached incidents.

In the third place there is much historical material from the library of Dr. J. R. Graves, made available for the Seminary through the kindness of Dr. Graves' son-in-law, Dr. O. L. Hailey. This material reaches back as far as 1835.

Lastly, there is a considerable collection of other missionary, historical and religious periodical material which reaches back to the beginning of the nineteenth century.

As to the arrangement and preservation of all the above mentioned material we state that it is now housed in special rooms in the Fort Worth Hall of the Seminary; and, as fast as conditions permit, the Seminary library staff is cataloguing it at Seminary expense. The Seminary places all this historical information for the use of the brotherhood; and it may be said this has been of assistance many times in correcting historical errors for associations.

So much for what we have found in the way of materials. It is now appropriate for your committee to say that we feel that there are certain facts about this situation to which the attention of our Texas brotherhood should be called, and certain important steps which ought to be taken if we as a denomination are to be enriched, encouraged, and advanced by the worth that one obtains in historical values. To this end we offer the following suggestions:

1. This vast amount of historical materials needs to be bound into volumes, catalogued, and indexed. This is urgent if the material is to be preserved and made usable and fruitful for the student of history.

2. This work of binding, cataloguing, etc., is too much for the Seminary under present conditions. As stated above, a limited amount of such work is being carried on by the Seminary library staff, but this is very small in comparison with what ought to be done; and the Seminary is not in position financially to undertake it on a large scale.

3. This is a matter which primarily concerns all Texas Baptists, and is so highly important that all of us should get under the responsibility.

4. Your committee therefore makes the following recommendations:

(1). That the Baptist General Convention officially designate a place which shall be known as the depository of Baptist historical materials for Texas.

(2). That a suitable person be appointed for superintendency over this matter, who shall be responsible for such historical materials and for the labors which may be performed upon the same.

(3). We recommend, inasmuch as the Seminary is the place where, and largely the agent whereby the above mentioned materials are now assembled, that the relation between the Convention and the Seminary on this matter be definitely defined.

(4). That this Board recommend that the Convention take, or authorize to be taken, the steps necessary for the maintenance of such depository as suggested above, and in whatsoever measure as in the judgment of the Convention may seem wise.

Your committee, in conclusion, voices its deepest appreciation of the great work of Dr. J. M. Carroll, entitled, "A History of Texas Baptists," published a few years ago, and which is regarded as indeed a monumental work for one who was himself one of the actors in the historical state about which he wrote, but which of course must be regarded as only a part of the great process of history-making which is going on all the time. And we recognize that such historical events as are occurring every day must be considered in the far-off future years by eyes that saw them not and written down in story form by hands that had no part in the making. For the accuracy and fullness of such future accounts we need to make careful provision now; and for such provision we offer the recommendations that are herein above set forth.

Respectfully submitted,

Harlan J. Mathews, Alvin Swindell, W. E. B. Lockridge

Source: *Minutes*, Executive Board of the Baptist General Convention of Texas, 13 June 1933. Reprint courtesy of the Baptist General Convention of Texas.

C. Give Me Texas!

NARRATION ONE

Texas could never do without religion. From the beginning until now religion has been a controlling factor in all its life. Under Spain the Catholics brought hither the cross of Christ. Their Franciscan padres planted missions among the Indians which stretched from the Rio Grande to the Trinity. In 1821, Mexico threw off the yoke of Spain, but it set up the Roman Catholic Church as the state church of Texas.

That very year of 1821 the Anglo-American colonists coming into Texas were required to accept the Catholic Church as their church. Stephen F. Austin, the first colonial contractor, consented. But the former citizens of the United States would have none of it. They were used to a free church in a free state, and they wanted no man or government to dictate to them how they must worship God.

It was inevitable that Baptists, believing as they do in soul liberty, should be among the first resisters. Yet true to their individualistic, utterly democratic character, they were not agreed among themselves as to how they would meet the situation. Some, like the Rev. Daniel Parker, thought they could outwit the Mexican soldiers and priests by means of a clandestine church. Others believed in an open, outright resistance to what they felt was an unjust cruel policy. The significance of this difference in conviction we shall see by what might have happened in a settler's home at the present town of Elkhart near Palestine in Anderson County on a night in late December of 1835.

FIRST EPISODE

SCENE: Log house, rudely furnished.

Hostess: (Hanging quilts over the windows) It's very dark tonight.

Host: All the better for our gathering.

Older Boy: Will the soldiers ketch us?

Hostess: Pa, you reckon it'll be safe for our young'uns or there under them trees?

Older Boy: Will the soldier ketch us?

Host: Not if you keep watch. Go now. Remember, under the oak. If the soldiers steal up, whistle warning! (Boys start to retire as mother makes toward them, to embrace them.)

Mother: Oh, my little boy!

Older Boy: Shucks, Ma, don't you be skeered. There ain't goin' to be no funeral in our family. (They leave, going unwillingly out into the darkness. Knock at the door directly after they leave.)

Host:(To first guest arriving) Come on in, brother, and hurry! (Closes door quickly, to shut in light.)

Hostess: Yes! Pastor Parker's right here, cording to promise, for the worship meeting.

Guest: (Shaking hands with both and eagerly greeting Parker advancing) Thank God. Glad that I am to see you, Brother Parker. I was afraid the Mexicans would arrest you this time.

Parker: Me! Don't we belong to the Pilgrim Predestinarian Church? A Higher Person seeks my life.

Guest: But _____ _____ _____ _____.

Parker: But hasn't God helped us carry out his plan and kept us from the day we started immigrating this church into Texas all the way from Illinois?

Guest: (Humbly) Of course, of course: I reckon he will always. (Guests assemble. A few more come in pairs, husbands and wives. Members of the church are distinguished by women kissing each other, men embracing each other—all, by endearing words. Certain strangers, somewhat apart, shown deference but viewed with suspicion.)

Parker: (Calling the meeting to order:) Let us pray. (All kneel) Almighty God, once again we are permitted to gather in thy name. Unseen of men though we be, we know that thou art watching us. We call ourselves pilgrims, and we are, for we know we are certainly on our way to our Father's home, the mansions prepared us by Jesus in the skies. The wrath of men cannot defeat thine eternal electing purpose; though wicked hand join in wicked hand our salvation is finally secure. We shall continue to worship and serve thee in this new land into which thou has brought us. Defend us by thy might; let us accomplish thy holy will. In the name of the precious Redeemer. Amen.

A Deacon: (Arising) Brother Parker.

Parker: Yes, Brother Deacon.

Deacon: Before we have the sermon, I move you, sir, that we hear from our visitors.

Chorus: Amen.

Parker: Very well, then, I'll call first for Brother Joseph Bays. Moses Austin's friend is our friend. Brother Bays, free your mind!

Bays: I greatly appreciate your kindness. You're very good to receive us. . . I'm sure you're the Lord's own people—you asked what I think—I think you are all on the way to jail!

Women: Mercy, don't you say!

Bays: Yes, I do say it. I tried this thing of preaching in Texas. Tried it before any of you. Why, I baptized the first Baptist convert here. But they arrested me, carried me off to rot in their Bexar jail. Of course, I clubbed their dastardly deputies and got away.

Parker: Don't you trust God to protect you?

Bays: I most certainly do; but I tell you, as long as these minions of hell are in the saddle, it's worth a man's life to preach the gospel in Texas! That's why I say tother side the Sabine. (Women again draw back, but smile a little as they murmur in deprecation.)

Parker: (Firmly) Where is your faith, Brother Bays? If God be for us, who can be against us? You don't understand. We are not like you— trying to convert somebody. That's God's business. When he gets ready to convert them heathen, he'll do it without our help. Brother, we think God has revealed to us his ordained plan: his elect may worship him secretly in Texas just as we are doing.

Several Men: Amen, Amen, you're right, pastor. Right as can be! Let's hear from Brother Pilgrim.

Pilgrim: Everything went well for a little while. But you know how priests complained; I had to give up that dearest endeavor of my life. It simply can't be done. I hope you will see that God helps them that helps themselves—we must resort to sterner measures.

Parker: (Stoutly) You do greatly err, Brother Pilgrim. You see you tried after man's wisdom to maintain a mere Sunday school, not one of Christ's churches. Where is Scripture for Sunday school? It's man's doing, not of God. No doubt he decreed it should die. (Turning) What have you got to say, Judge Ellis?

Judge Richard Ellis: It's all right to talk in terms of your doctrines, Brother Parker, but the time has come for action. The arms of God are his people, and he is about to raise up his arms in Texas. That's how we of the Red River Country feel. (Turning to another.) Am I right, Brother Morrell? Here is one of Tennessee's best preachers, just arrived in these parts— hear him!

Morrell: (Limping slightly and speaking gravely) Not just arrived. As a matter of fact, I've been touring Texas. Just back from a trip as far West as the Falls of the Brazos and the Little River County. There's no doubt but revolution's in the air.

Voices: (Commotion) Revolution, is it possible?

Morrell: Yes, everywhere! What's more, a powerful leader has come among you. It's my judgment, he has laid the explosives, and the fuse is about to be lit.

Many Voices: (breathlessly) Who? Who?

Morrell: Sam Houston—hero of Horseshoe Bend, former governor of Tennessee, friend of Old Hickory. And when Sam Houston sets his jaw, the gates of hell can't stand against him.

Many Rising Voices: We're not ready! He's a meddler! We don't want war! God forbid!

Young Stranger: (Rising and speaking boldly) Hold your tongue, men. My name is Byars, N. T., from Washington-on-the-Brazos. If you want to know more, I'm just out from South Carolina, and I run a blacksmith shop. As you see, I'm no preacher, though I'd like to be. But I am a man. See this gun! I'm ready to forge bullets for the guns of Sam Houston!

Murmurs from Crowd: (Outside there is a rifle shot, then another)

Hostess: (Scream) Oh, my little boy!

Ellis and Byars: (Draw guns and leap to the door)

Parker: (Snuffs out candle, muttering) Who knows? It may be God's will! Who knows! God's will!

Source: J. M. Dawson, *Give Me Texas*, in J. M. Dawson, *A Century With Texas Baptists* (Nashville: Broadman Press, 1947), 127–30. Reprint courtesy of Broadman and Holman Publishers.

9.10 European Texans

As old prejudices began to pass with time, Texas Baptists began to realize that the Anglos were not the only race in Texas who needed to hear the Gospel. In particular, the Baptist General Convention sought to witness and minister to the needs of the large Hispanic and Negro populations. It should be noted that Texas Baptists had always sought to minister to these races, but during the 1930s special emphasis was placed in this endeavor.

A. Ministering to Hispanics

J. Howard Williams read the report of the Committee on Mexican work as follows:

The appointment of Rev. J. L. Moye, formerly foreign missionary to Chile, but more recently the successful pastor of Hunter Street Baptist Church, Birmingham, Ala., to the task of superintendent of Mexican work in Texas and New Mexico for the Home Mission Board, came early in June, 1938, in the midst of your committee's study of the situation, and further study was suspended until Brother Moye could have an opportunity to make a first-hand study for himself and advise with us in planning a more effective method of operation and promotion of the work. We wish to express our appreciation of him and commend him as both capable and faithful in his important task.

2. We would call your attention to the fact that there are approximately 800,000 Mexicans in Texas—a force which, if evangelized, could and would make a tremendous impact upon Mexico and perhaps accomplish the evangelization of that neighbor republic across the Rio Grande as no other agency could under prevailing conditions. Both as Christians and Texans we can not afford to neglect this open door and responsibility for service.

To illustrate the density of the Mexican population in South Texas, it is estimated that there are 150,000 Mexicans in Bexar County, which is San Antonio and its environs; Del Rio is 65% Mexican; Eagle Pass is 90%; the Lower Rio Grande Valley is approximately 50% Mexican. In cities like Corpus Christi, Houston, Austin, Waco, and other Central and North Texas communities there are large numbers of Mexicans, in some instances running as high as twenty and thirty thousand, who need immediate attention with a well planned and directed ministry for their evangelization.

3. The immediate challenge is evangelism. We are advised that regional conferences are being planned by Brother Moye for the months of January and February in 1939, in the cities of Edinburg, Houston, San Antonio, Waco, Brownwood and Bastrop. These conferences will look to stimulate evangelism among the workers in the churches and neglected sections and will include conferences also on stewardship for the development of the work and workers.

4. There is a dearth of literature in Spanish for the masses. A state paper published in Spanish for the information and inspiration of the workers in Texas is sorely needed along with tracts, both doctrinal and

evangelistic, for use in evangelistic work.

5. Your committee has given some thought to the situation in San Antonio. We are of the opinion that San Antonio is the most strategic center of our state for Mexican work, and may not only furnish a field for operations, but also a force for the larger evangelization of the Mexican population in the state. The San Antonio Association has an energetic committee on Mexican work and it is hoped that this committee in cooperation with Supt. Moye, who is making his home in San Antonio, may devise a plan during the ensuing year which, with the endorsement of our State Secretary and Home Mission Secretary, may have the support of both the State and Home Boards in the ultimate development of adequate facilities for the intensive evangelization and enlistment of the Mexican people.

Your committee, therefore, recommends that an appropriation of at least $600.00 be made for the promotion of Mexican evangelistic and stewardship conferences within the state during the year, and to assist in the publication of suitable literature for use in the program of evangelism, stewardship and enlistment under Dr. Moye's direction.

It is the opinion of your committee that further study should be given to this field until such a time as an adequate policy and program for Mexican work has been established by this Board. We would recommend that this committee be discharged, a new committee appointed, or this committee continued and enlarged to include two other members preferably from San Antonio and South Texas, to advise with Brother Moye in determining the permanent policy on Mexican work to be recommended to this Board.

Respectfully submitted:

S. G. Posey, R. E. Day, J. H. Williams

Source: *Minutes*, Executive Board of the Baptist General Convention of Texas, 6 December 1938. Reprint courtesy of the Baptist General Convention of Texas.

B. Our Work with Negro Baptists

As missionary to the Negro Baptists of Texas, my work has concerned itself with Bible Conferences, Workers Institutes, and personal contacts with Negro Baptist leaders. This type of work was suggested by the Board, yet leaving me freedom for the discovery of details in the field. This was also indicated in the request for my appointment by a number of Negro pastors themselves. The work has thus been inter-racial and co-operative.

We are thus in the line with the same type of work now being done by our Home Board of Atlanta through the leadership of Rev. Noble Y. Beall under employment of that Board. We are thus bringing together the leadership of both groups of Baptists; and it is thus that, for the first time, Southern Baptists are approaching the so-called Race Problem at the top instead of the bottom with the masses. It is a mutual problem, both white and colored; and we are thus in cooperation with each other.

We believe that this is the most significant and far-reaching step we have thus far undertaken in cooperation with our Negro Baptist people. It seems to mark a new day in the cooperative fellowship between these two large groups of Southern Baptists.

I am admonished, and wisely, that this report must be brief. Only a small part of such work can be reported or tabulated. We will, however, give in general terms, a few leading items.

1. The date of beginning

The year beginning December 15 was too near the Christmas holidays for effective contacts immediately. Then the usual lull of January, and the slowness of the Negro people themselves to take hold of the work that was entirely new to them, a very natural attitude, made it impossible to enter at once into the field. But some time was needed for correspondence, and for numerous visits that had to be made.

2. Concerning Conferences and Workers Institutes.

Two difficulties were met: (1) The Negro Baptists are divided into three general Conventions, all covering the same field and doing the same type of work. Each Convention has also its annual conventions for departmental work like ours. When all these gatherings are approaching near it is hardly possible to have large territorial gatherings for our inter-racial programs. Then, (2) it is hard to find time when our own pastors are free to devote special attention to these Conferences. And they, in the nature of the case, must take the initiative in every local field.

3. Special addresses that have been delivered.

Our programs usually run from Monday night to Friday night, with three meetings each day after Monday. We have thus used about 60 Negro speakers, and about 30 white speakers. We have thus brought together 90 leaders in mutual conference and fellowship. As to my own part on programs, I have delivered 70 doctrinal and expository addresses. I have also delivered 20 addresses concerning our work to white and colored churches, and 10 addresses before colored state and district conventions. I have had part in the ordination of 7 deacons and four candidates for the ministry; and in each case I conducted the examination and then delivered an address. I have thus delivered about 100 addresses in all; and this does not include regular sermons delivered in white churches.

4. Books distributed.

As generous gifts from the Sunday School Board, I have given to preachers, and to church workers for Sunday School and B. Y. P. U. class work, 300 of the former Study Course Books; and now I have on hand 200 more books which are already promised to certain churches that are asking for them.

5. Numbers of preachers and people addressed.

In various gatherings, I have spoken to 1690 Negro Baptist preachers, and in round numbers, fully 14,000 Negro people. White people in most of these congregations have numbered several hundred. I do not include the many thousands of Negroes, of various denominations, who came to the Centennial on the Negroes "All Church Day." As a matter of interest, I should mention the fact that, excepting the Mayor of the City, I was the only white man and preacher invited for that occasion. I construe this as a recognition of the work that we, as Texas Baptists, are trying to do for the Negro Baptists of the State.

6. Concerning our reception on the field.

As a rule the Negroes have been responsive and appreciative. Yet their wholehearted response had been a matter of hesitation. They must first be convinced that we are sincerely wanting to help and to cooperate with them, and not dictate or try to rule them. Who can blame them?

Then, from our white pastors and churches, we have not heard one discordant note, but many words of fellowship and encouragement. Our Young People, our Sunday School workers, and, as always, our W. M. U. both locally and statewide, have all been asking, "What can we do to help you?" In fact these three organizations are already working for the Negro churches in a number of localities.

7. The outlook.

The leaders of the Negro Schools and Convention are ready to meet the white Baptists with extended hand, if we come in the right spirit and with the right purpose. This our white Baptists are doing all over the state. We want to help them attain the highest heights of all their own possibilities. They have many gifted preachers, teachers, and people among them, and many men and women of the finest Christian character. It is our determination that the Negro, as a race, shall be measured by its highest and noblest accomplishment. Justice demands that.

The enlightenment of our own white people concerning the present status of the Negro race in America, and at our own door, and the character of cooperative service we can render with them, is one of the heaviest tasks of the present hour. The two races, and our two Baptist groups, do not know each other today as they should. Our future with them must be built on a new and better understanding.

What could we not do, as one mighty host of people of the common Baptist faith? Just think, 400,000 Negro Baptists and 600,000 white Baptists in Texas! One million Baptists who ought to move as a common fellowship in a common cause, even though we work, as a matter of emergency, in different groups, circles, or organizations! What a vision for us to behold! The question from on high must be, What will we all strive to do about it in simple obedience to the revealed will of our Lord Jesus Christ?

Chas. T. Alexander

Source: *Proceedings*, Baptist General Convention of Texas, 1936, 99–101. Reprint courtesy of the Baptist General Convention of Texas.

9.11 Sunday School

Since the time of Thomas J. Pilgrim, Texas Baptists have been strong advocates of Sunday School. During the period of the Great Depression, the Sunday School program not only served the purpose of educating Christians but it was also the primary means of raising funds due to its emphasis on stewardship. This practice has continued into the twenty-first century.

Report of Sunday School Work, 1938

McKinley Norman, B. C. Greenwood, Walter Jackson, B. F. K. Mullins, E. D. Dunlap, Committee.

Texas Baptists have concluded another fruitful year of Sunday School work under the capable and aggressive leadership of Secy. G. S. Hopkins and his loyal and efficient associate, Mr. Andrew Allen.

The annual report of the Secretary to the Executive Board of the Convention gives us a record of the many promotional activities of the Sunday School Department through the year. This work consists of visits to churches, associations and other gatherings. It includes the conducting of church and associational training schools and enlargement campaigns, and the fostering of associational, district and state conventions. By the distribution of hundreds of thousands of tracts, the use of the Baptist Standard, the writing of thousands of personal letters, the department has sought to familiarize its constituency with all phases of the work. The Secretary reports 240 standard Sunday Schools in the state and a grand total of 22,691 Normal Course, Post-graduate, Sunday School Administration and Church Administration awards for the year.

Texas—A Vast Baptist Opportunity

We have 3,006 white Baptist churches in Texas with a membership of 530,000, and we have 3,124 Baptist Sunday schools with an enrollment of 442,000. There are 40,000 officers and teachers now serving the churches of Texas in Sunday school work. The state has a population of 5,600,000 people and 4,250,000 of this vast number are not enrolled in any kind of Sunday school. Herein lies our great opportunity. The Sunday school seeks to find possibilities, to bring these possibilities into the Bible school, to teach and win them to Christ and to teach and train them for Christ.

Recommendations

Your committee would respectfully recommend:

1. That we express our profound appreciation for the faithful and cooperative leadership of the Sunday School Department; to the Baptist Sunday School Board for its generous and effective assistance through the year; to the boards of the Baptist educational institutions and innumerable pastors and friends of the work, throughout the state, who have given so freely of their time in assisting the department in its far-reaching enlargement program.

2. That we recommend ourselves to the methods which have been so effective through the years in finding and reaching people, such as proper grading, training the workers, striving for higher standards of efficiency, weekly teachers' meeting, searching the scriptures, enlarging the organizations and incessantly magnifying the church of the living God which is the pillar and the ground of the work of the truth.

3. That evangelism be the paramount objective at all times. Winning the lost to Christ and reclaiming for Christ, and the church, those who have drifted away from God, is the very tap root of our great Baptist fellowship commissioned to "go into all the world and preach the gospel to every creature." Soul-winning is the major task of every Baptist individual in every Baptist church. Our churches must maintain a very definite, thorough and comprehensive program of evangelism to meet the needs of our day.

Moreover, evangelism is our denominational hope. It has been rightfully called our "Pillar of cloud by day and pillar of fire by night" to lead us out of the wilderness of confusion, depression and doubt. Zeal for our great missionary program is a direct outgrowth of spiritual power in churches. The Sunday school furnishes our most practical and effective approach to this great program of evangelizing our people.

4. We heartily commend our Secretary for the generous use of his time and splendid ability in the important work of promoting the Every Member Canvass of the Cooperative Program of Southern Baptists. We would earnestly urge the pastors and superintendents of our Baptist Sunday schools in Texas to call their officers and teachers about them and prayerfully urge them to rally to the leadership of their State Sunday

School Secretary in this vitally important work. We must not only teach the pupils "repentance toward God and faith in our Lord Jesus Christ," but we must also teach them to "bring forth fruits for repentance."

We have largely assigned the colossal and blessed task of financing the work of Christ at home and abroad to the Sunday school. The teacher therefore must not only convince the student of the Bible doctrine of tithes and offerings, but he must lead that student to bring these "tithes and offerings" into the store house that they may be used for the spread of the gospel around the world. We must either raise more money for our great Educational, Benevolent and Missionary agencies of the de-nomination or change our method of appeal for the generosity of our people. The Sunday school furnishes the most logical and effective or-ganization in the church to present this appeal to every member, and we recommend that the work be presented with all vigor during the weeks just ahead.

5. We further recommend a revival of emphasis on the major impor-tance of the Sunday school throwing its entire weight in back of the preaching service of the church. Our Sunday school leaders have, through all the years, earnestly and persistently sought this high aim. Just as the Sunday school serves the church as its great agency for finding, feeding, teaching and winning people, even so must the Sunday school recognize in the preaching service the greatest single factor in realizing the final culmination of these high objectives. The great matters of worship, proc-lamation of the gospel, prayer, righteous living and missionary evange-listic inspiration must be regarded as essential and not just something to be preferred. There is positively no substitute for preaching. All should hear preaching. It builds Christian character. It furnishes the worker with wisdom and power for his task. It is the furnace at which he warms, the spring at which he drinks, and the table at which he must feed. The pulpit is the center of gravity for New Testament churches. It produces repentance and personal acceptance of Christ. It inspires to personal soul-winning. It stimulates liberality and produces holy passion for a lost world. To try to grow a great Bible loving, praying, Holy Spirit directed, liberal, evangelistic and missionary church without preaching services is like trying to operate a bank without money or a hospital without medicine.

We should thank God and take courage upon every remembrance of the marvelous achievements of our Sunday school force and pray God's blessings upon them as they enter another year of kingdom expansion.

McKinley Norman

E. D. Dunlap

Source: *Proceedings*, Baptist General Convention of Texas, 1933, 129–31. Reprint courtesy of the Baptist General Convention of Texas.

9.12 BYPU

Thomas Cleveland Gardner served as the state director of the BYPU from 1916 until 1956. During his tenure, the BYPU grew at an incredible rate. Perhaps the most dramatic period of growth was the 1920s. During this period, the number of state BYPUs increased from 2193 to 4648. The very name of the group demonstrates its emphasis on the molding of Christian youth, but as the youth became adults many did not want to leave the organization. For this reason, the BYPU gave way to the age inclusive Baptist Training Union in 1934.

A Bright Future

One of America's greatest sculptors has portrayed "Time" as a great figure watching before an endless procession of human beings; some bowed with age or crippled with infirmity; some toiling ahead despite heavy burdens; children clutching the hands of plodding parents; and youth blithely treading along; all in a ceaseless parade.

Before that ever watchful eye of "Time" that passes generations after generation leaving behind only the ultimate fruits of their labors.

The B. Y. P. U.'s of the Pioneer 90s and the transition 1900s live only in the memory of the older members. The B. Y. P. U.'s of the Reconstruction 1920s and the Progressive 1930s hold fast to the guiding principles of the Pioneer days "Training for Service" and "We learn to do by doing." The spirit of the B. Y. P. U., "Unselfishness" and the plan "To utilize all members" have built and are building the Modern B. Y. P. U. of today.

In such a life panorama have been those, who, these forty years, have sought to keep alive and growing the ideals and purposes for which the B. Y. P. U.'s of Texas were founded forty years ago. During certain periods in this span of years, "Time" must have witnessed them, beset as they were by changing thought, and developments in the world about them. He must have seen them falter or fall, leaving the ranks then and straggling. But, now, he must be seeing again a throng of eager, exultant youth awakened anew to the opportunities of service and accomplishment in Kingdom building tasks.

Texas, the home of 4,648 B. Y. P. U.'s with a membership of 122,774, is just now approaching the time when the B. Y. P. U. is to have its most rapid growth and development. The Primary Union, the Adult Union, the General Organization and the Departmental organizations have all proven their value. These organizations re-enforcing, magnifying and enlarging the Junior, Intermediates and Senior B. Y. P. U.'s have also enlarged and magnified the Training Service to the extent that a place is now made in its organization for every member of the family.

It seems from the most accurate records that the first B. Y. P. U. was organized in 1888. This organization included only young people from the ages of 15 to 25. In the early days no one thought of an organization to train groups of other ages. It was thought that one union would suffice for any Church.

"Time" has seen the organization change and develop into a mighty Training Service department including the Primary, Junior, Intermediate, Senior and Adult departments with a program suited for each age.

May the 125,000 B. Y. P. U. members of Texas, the State B. Y. P. U. Convention, the State B. Y. P. U. Executive Board, and the State B. Y. P. U. department continue to discover, develop and disseminate better methods and materials, thereby, realizing the most for Texas Baptists. This will call for untiring effort from those officially identified with the state organizations, from its numerous co-workers and friends and from those whom it serves.

Source: *Proceedings*, Baptist General Convention of Texas, 1930, 103–4. Reprint courtesy of the Baptist General Convention of Texas.

9.13 WMU

During this era of ministerial progress, the WMU continued to make advances in the realm of helping the poor, ministering to children, and the support of missionaries. Under the leadership of Mrs. F. S. Davis, the WMU was divided into seventeen districts to simplify the work, stewardship and tithing were stressed and to be carried out each week, and the Lottie Moon Christmas Offering was largely gathered each year by their tireless workers.

Report of the WMU Corresponding Secretary, Mrs. J. E. Leigh, 1930

"Speak unto the children of Israel that they go forward" was not more plainly spoken to Moses by the Lord than the command is given today to His people. Today is a day of action. Work comes unto its original meaning now as never before. "My father worketh hitherto and I work," the meaning it had in pioneer days when the religious founders rose early and worked late to lay the foundation on which we are building.

Then vision is needed to guide the work of our hands. We need to lift up our eyes and get a clear perspective of the soundness and saneness of our cooperative effort in our W. M. U. and then forge forward with a certainty of success, born from above. We are to guard against becoming so inured with the picture that we fail to see the hours of labor that lie between vision and reality. I must admit that looking upon the work of Texas Baptists of tomorrow, through our young people, with their limitless possibilities and the amazing branches of constructive tasks, is calculated to set one to day-dreaming. Texas Baptists are charged with husbanding one of the greatest organizations in the world. Texas seems to have been reserved and preserved for an "experimental station in religious democracy." Our pioneer preachers attacked Texas with the spirit of love to tame a new frontier, we partake of this spirit today in an era of religious development which demands all our latent strength and endurance. The challenge nearest us now, that of our Lottie Moon Christmas Offering, sounds with insistent note over the plains of West Texas and reverberates through the hills of East Texas, is caught up, echoed and reechoed through South and North Texas. "Tis a call to brain, brawn, and heart, to loyalty and ingenuity, to the determination and endurance of every Baptist woman in Texas." In bringing the report of the year's work in Texas, one scarcely knows where to begin. The most hopeful feature has been the faithfulness of the women all over Texas. The fearful financial depression, instead of discouraging has drawn them closer to each other and to God. Meetings have been more largely attended and more spiritual than ever before. The manner in which women have responded to special calls denotes the presence of a sacrificial spirit.

The goal set for our Lottie Moon Christmas Offering in Beaumont last November was twice as much as was ever attempted before and we missed the goal of $45,000 by only a few hundred dollars. I have been privileged to do more work than ever before in the history of my eight years of service. For the first time I attended all district meetings and these were large and well planned. My work in teaching has been largely along the lines of Institutes, in districts and associations. More opportunities have been offered me to speak before the churches than in former years, and this has proven helpful in causing a better understanding of the missionary organizations. Stewardship has been stressed as vital to the success of the W. M. U. and I am happy to say that many men have become tithers on account of the women's zeal to follow the Bible plan. The cooperative program has been faithfully urged on every occasion. This plan has not had a fair trial as yet. There have been so many necessary campaigns for our institutions that divert, that missions have suffered but the small per cent of churches that have held to the budget plan have saved the situation.

Texas has two daughters in the W. M. U. Training School in Louisville who are holding our standard high. Miss Elizabeth Durham of Dallas and Miss Ruby Lea Johnson, graduate of Baylor College for Women, who is using the scholarship given by Mrs. S. E. Woody.

Source: *Proceedings*, Woman's Missionary Union of Texas, 1930, 7–8. Reprint courtesy of the Woman's Missionary Union of Texas.

9.14 Baptist Student Union

When children went to college and had their first taste of independence, they all too often forgot their church life. The Baptist Student Union was created to help these collegians remain in church and grow spiritually. Since the majority of Baptist students were attending state Universities rather than private Baptist Universities or colleges, the BSU began to operate in virtually all Texas Colleges. In addition, Bible Chairs were created at various institutions both public and private. Though supported by local churches, the men who held these Bible Chairs did not fall directly under the administration of those who financially supported them. Since they were not an official part of the faculty of the institution, and they were not under the administration of the BGCT, for this reason Bible Chairs received sporadic and limited financial assistance. As a consequence, financial support of several of these Bible Chairs was discontinued.

A. Bible Chairs

THE COMMITTEE'S APPROACH

Realizing the importance of our task in helping to determine a well defined policy in our denominational service to the Baptist students in our State schools, your Committee sought the opinions of a representative group of Pastors, College Presidents, Teachers and denominational leaders regarding the policy that should be recommended. We have also made investigation of every situation where there is a State school of senior rating to ascertain the attitude and desires of the Baptist constituency adjacent to them.

The response received and the opinions expressed revealed agreement as follows:

1. That our denomination in the matter of future leadership is dependent in a large degree on the Baptist Students of Texas.

2. That the study of the Bible is essential in the teaching and training of the students who will become leaders in our churches and in our denominational work.

3. That inasmuch as three-fourths or more of our Baptist Students are now in State and independent schools and these will constitute a large percent of the enlightened leadership in the churches and in the denomination in the future, the Executive Board is obligated to adopt a permanent policy in this far-reaching denominational opportunity.

4. The churches adjacent to our State schools cannot fulfill this obligation, and should not be expected to do so, without the assistance of the other churches as provided through our State Cooperative Program and directed by our Executive Board.

THE COMMITTEE'S INVESTIGATION

Your Committee, as instructed, has made a study of the John C. Townes Bible Chair at the University of Texas. A brief historical and statistical statement was placed in our hands. This chair was launched at the opening of the University in September, 1919. The enrollment for the college year 1940–1941 was 397. The lowest enrollment for any one year during the last six years was 276 students.

Your Committee held an open meeting in the Educational Building of the University Baptist Church, Austin, with the local Bible Chair Committee on January 27, 1942. The facts brought before this meeting and the personal testimonies given revealed the following facts:

1. The Chairs of Bible at the University of Texas exerted a most helpful and far reaching religious and moralizing influence upon the student body and the Faculty of the University.

2. The Teaching of the Bible through accredited courses of instruction places Christianity on a high plane with intellectual people. The study of the Bible on the part of Christian students enables these students to integrate their Christian life with other phases of life.

3. The Bible Chair teacher's function is not adequate to meet all the religious needs of the Baptist students in such an institution. The program of religious work should include a vital relationship to the church and all lines of religious activity as promoted by our Executive Board.

Your Committee made a study of the Baptist Chair at Denton, established by the Executive Board in December, 1934. This Chair of Bible serves the students of the Texas State College for Women and the North Texas State Teachers College. The enrollment in this Chair was 146 the first year and this year is 430. The average enrollment has been 409. A far-reaching service is being rendered by this Baptist Chair of Bible. A strong conviction was expressed on the part of the Deans of the two colleges that the Bible Chair be continued and enlarged. As an evidence of the importance and standard of the teaching done in the Bible Chair, the North Texas Teachers College will accept a major of work in Bible (30 semester hours toward graduation).

Your Committee made a study of the Bible Chair at Huntsville, established in 1936, and serving the students of Sam Houston State Teachers College. The first enrollment was 82; the present enrollment is 67, and the average enrollment has been 83. Requests for the continuing of this work have come to us from the President of the college and a Committee of the Tryon-Evergreen Association.

THE COMMITTEE'S RECOMMENDATIONS

I. Your Committee expresses a deep conviction and recommends that the denominational program for the Baptist Students in our State schools should be continued and enlarged from year to year. We recognize a three-fold obligation:

1. To win these students to Christ and our churches.
2. To teach the Bible to these students during their college days.
3. To train these students to be future supporters and leaders in our worldwide denominational program.

II. We recommend that the policy of the Executive Board regarding the denominational work for the Baptist students of the State schools should include the following:

1. That the policy, though definite and well defined, does not necessarily call for the uniformity of the program at all institutions.
2. That the aim of the Program shall be Christian and denominational in terms of Christian character, Christian education and denominational service.
3. That the Plan of the Program shall include:
   1) The Baptist Student Union organization fully set out at all Baptist Student Centers maintaining a proper connection with the Baptist church or churches adjacent to the campus, and with the University or College.
   2) The recognition, strengthening and cooperation with the Baptist churches as a religious and denominational center of power and influence.
   3) The establishment and maintaining of Baptist Chairs of Bible at the State Schools wherever such a setup is deemed essential and can be properly carried on, and these chairs shall be in proper connection and cooperation with the church or churches adjacent to the campus.
4. That the direction of the Program shall be by the State Executive Board in the following manner:
   1) The election and guidance of the Instructors in Bible Chairs and Student Religious workers supported in part or in full

through the appropriation of funds entrusted to the State Executive Board.

2) A General Committee shall be provided, consisting of six members to be elected in classes annually by the Executive Board so that the terms for one class only shall expire with each annual meeting. The term for each member elected shall be for three years.

    (1) This General Committee shall make a careful and sympathetic survey of all the denominational work carried on for the Baptist Students of State Schools and shall determine the type of service to be rendered at each school center. The need for establishing or discontinuing Chairs of Bible shall be entrusted to this Committee.

    (2) This Committee shall make an annual report to the Board and nominate Bible Chair Instructors and religious workers to the Executive Committee of the State Board for election.

3) The Bible Chairs maintained or established shall be properly related to the college or university in the educational standards required so that college credit can be given when courses in Bible study have been completed.

    (1) The content of the courses and the interpretation of the Scripture shall be under the direction of the General Committee, elected by the Executive Board, and carefully safeguarded.

4) A local Committee of three members shall be elected by the church or association adjacent to the institution, one member of which shall be chosen from the General Committee. This Committee shall maintain helpful oversight of the Bible Chair and render assistance to all religious programs promoted and carried on by the Baptist Student Union and church or churches adjacent to the institution. This Committee shall make its recommendations to the General Committee.

III. We recommend the Appropriation and Distribution of funds be as follows:

1. That an annual appropriation shall be made by the Appropriation Committee out of the amount adopted by the Convention for State Missions in the annual Budget.
2. That the distribution of this fund shall be made by the General Committee in cooperation with the Executive Secretary of the State Board.

IV. We recommend that the General Committee be provided at this meeting of the Executive Board so that action may be taken in regard to present Bible Chairs in time for proper announcement to be made in the catalogues of the Institutions.

Source: *Minutes*, Executive Board of the Baptist General Convention of Texas, 3 March 1942. Reprint courtesy of the Baptist General Convention of Texas.

B. The Salaries of Bible Chairs

Your Committee on Bible Chairs created at the March session of the Board, appointed as directed, met in San Antonio, Texas, in the Plaza Hotel, at 2 p. m., on May 18, 1942. Five of the members were present. After due consideration and realizing that some action should be taken now as the former action of the Board relative to the Bible chairs covered the period up to June 1, the Committee recommends the continuation of the three Bible chairs and the three instructors as follows: Dr. W. C. Rains, instructor of John C. Townes Chair of Bible, Austin, Texas; Dr. W. T. Rouse, instructor of Bible chair at North Texas State Teachers College and Texas State College for Women, Denton, Texas; Dr. J. T. Luper, serving at the Sam Houston State Teachers College, Huntsville, Texas. The Committee recommended that the salaries up to the annual meeting of the Board be the same, namely, $2100 at Austin, $1500 at Denton, and $600 as of the salary at Huntsville.

The Committee was unanimous in its opinion that further study of the salaries of these teachers in the Bible Chairs should be made and that a further recommendation shall be made to the Annual Meeting of the Board regarding the financial matters pertaining to these Bible Chairs.

Respectfully submitted,

Joseph P. Boone, Chairman

J. M. Price, Secretary of Committee

S. G. Posey

G. Kearnie Keegan

Source: *Minutes*, Executive Board of the Baptist General Convention of Texas, 2 June 1942. Reprint courtesy of the Baptist General Convention of Texas.

C. Baptist Student Union Report, 1934

Before making the report of the progress and accomplishments of the Baptist Student Union for the year, it will be well to give the four foundation principles of the organization as stated recently by our Southern Baptist Convention secretary, Mr. Frank Leavell:

First.—To take the students themselves into the activities and make the work their own movement. Therefore students have presided over every general meeting. They have also materially assisted in producing the literature and establishing the goal and ideals.

Second.—To offer the students nothing but the best. In this matter we have won the following of the best element of the Baptist students of the South. Whether it be speakers for their meetings, or leaders, or paper upon which the messages are printed, or a choice between one or two colors of ink, we have given them the best. If necessary give them less, but give them the best.

Third.—To uncompromisingly hold up the eternal verities of God's Word. There has been no substitute for the essence of religion, and that upon the highest planes of spiritual emphasis.

Fourth.—To encourage the prayer life of the individual students and to inspire them to hold a morning prayer service on every campus, thus raising the spiritual life on the campus. . . .

Here in Texas we have twenty-two Baptist Student Union organizations, ten in denominational schools, ten in State schools and two in private schools. We have ten student workers, two part-time student workers who serve in many instances as church secretaries or teach in colleges. Sixteen of our schools promoted special student revivals last year; seven of these were in State schools. The report indicates there were at any given time about 3,400 students enlisted in our Sunday

schools throughout the Baptist Student Union, 2,000 in the Baptist Training Service and 500 in the Young Woman's Auxiliary. An average of 390
students attended the daily prayer meetings throughout the last college
year. Seventy-five students were converted in these prayer services. Five
hundred sixty-five subscribed for the monthly magazine, The Baptist
Student: although our quota was only 550 for the State. In June we had
a record attendance at Ridgecrest of eighty-five students from Texas.
Our summer missionary visitation campaign included forty-six counties and about 200 programs.

We are justly proud of the interest and the excellent record of our
State activities in this realm of religious work. We recommend that the
Convention suggest to the Executive Board that they carefully consider
the advisability of employing a State student secretary, if it is at all possible that the Executive Board make this appointment at its own convention.

C. Roy Angell,

Mary Rust,

Robert Fling

Source: *Proceedings*, Baptist General Convention of Texas, 1934, 136–
37. Reprint courtesy of the Baptist General Convention of Texas.

9.15 Brotherhood

Not to be outdone by the WMU, the Brotherhood organization was started
in 1938. Though not as clear in a purpose as the WMU, the Brotherhood
sought to help the church and denomination in whatever way possible. Generally, this aid came in the form of building, finances, and emergency work.
In 1939, L. H. Tapscott became the first full-time Brotherhood Director in
Texas.

Local Church Brotherhoods

As is the case of every movement among Baptists, it is not worth
while until it becomes helpful in the local church. We have tried to organize our work in such a way that every department of church activity
will feel the influence of this new emphasis among the men. We have
scores of interesting testimonies regarding the value to the local church.

One in particular I would like to relate. Mr. B. F. Adams, former president of the Brotherhood in the church at Corrigan in East Texas (which section of the state is sometimes considered conservative), states that the Men's Bible Class, which had been averaging from five to fifteen in attendance increased from twenty to fifty after the Brotherhood was organized. Other testimonies state that the evangelistic spirit, the finances, the Training Union, and the missionary emphasis of the church have increased. We shall not be content with anything less than effective enlistment in every Baptist church in our great state. We have now approximately seven hundred organizations in the state, with a membership of about thirty thousand. It is true that some of these have majored in fellowship and food. Our challenge is to bring the correct emphasis on the main thing—service.

One of the most effective plans of activity we have found is to organize the Brotherhood into a working unit so that every family of the church is on the responsibility list of some member of the Brotherhood. The First Baptist Church of Amarillo has found this particularly helpful. In that church, there are 1,027 families represented in the church membership. The enlistment vice president of the Brotherhood has formed a giant committee, asking first, six to help him, and then six to help each of those six, making thirty-six; and then five to help each of the 36, making 180 men. This contemplated the use of 223 men. No man has a responsibility of more than six families, and in most cases, only five, in other words, the enlistment chairman works with his commitment; each of those six works with his commitment, etc. The 180 men have five families each. These men endeavor to secure regular Sunday school, Training Union, and preaching attendance on the part of these families. Also they encourage spirituality in each of the families, and ascertain if there is any way in which the church can serve. Thus 223 men are definitely interested in the church and are talking about it in the homes. The minimum requirement of these men is a visit in the home quarterly. It does not take much imagination to visualize what a force this can be. Other churches in Texas are using this plan, but of course, are varying it in keeping with the size of the church. The remarkable record made by these churches is to some degree at least attributable to this layman activity.

One Brotherhood meeting I attended had 80% of its membership present. In that church there were ten men enrolled in the church, and eight were present. In still another, there were over six hundred present. So this movement is catching fire in both the large and small churches.

One of the most outstanding activities of our local Brotherhoods has been the sponsoring of mission Sunday schools and evangelistic services. Among those who have been particularly active have been the First Church, Abilene; Diamond Hill Church, Fort Worth; First Church, Sweetwater; and others.

We say with Dr. Dodd, "God wants his men to be utilized. The men themselves want to be utilized. There is a great need for their utilization, and there is a great field in which they may be utilized. When the man-power of our churches comes forward in wholehearted consecration, then the wheels of the Kingdom of God will move forward with accelerated speed, and 'the earth shall be full of the knowledge of the Lord, as the waters cover the sea.'"

Source: *Proceedings*, Baptist General Convention of Texas, 1939, 142–43. Reprint courtesy of the Baptist General Convention of Texas.

9.16 Church Music

Music has always played a prominent role in Texas Baptist worship services and improvement in this area of ministry was always sought. Under the leadership of R. H. Coleman of the First Baptist Church of Dallas, publishing hymnals and songbooks became common place in twentieth-century Texas. Church music became denominationally unified in 1940 with the advent of the *Broadman Hymnal*. With the ever-increasing importance of music in Baptist churches, the BGCT formed a department of Church Music in 1945. J. D. Riddle was named to lead this new department.

A. Resolution on Church Music, 1934

Offered before the Texas Baptist State Convention session, November 5–9, 1934, San Antonio, Texas, by I. E. Reynolds.

Whereas, Music has such a large and vital place in the regular church worship and service and related activities, and,

Whereas, There is such a dire need for improving the music programs in the average church, in respect to grade of music used and its rendition, and,

Whereas, Nothing is being done by the denomination in an educational way to assist the local churches with their music programs,

Therefore, be it resolved, That this Convention asks its Executive Board at its next session to give prayerful consideration to the establishment of some agency for the purpose of aiding the churches of this Convention in improving their music programs.

Source: *Proceedings*, Baptist General Convention of Texas, 1934, 26. Reprint courtesy of the Baptist General Convention of Texas.

B. Report of the Committee on Music

J. A. Ellis read the report of the Committee on Music as follows:

Upon instruction of the Baptist General Convention at El Paso, the Board at its December meeting appointed the undersigned committee to study the question of Church Music with a view to improving the quality, spirituality and effectiveness of its rendition in our worship and related activities.

As we understand it, the Convention desired that our people be brought to the selection and use of such music as would fit the genius of our faith and express more nearly the spirit of a true Baptist Church, avoiding on the one hand the music which conforms to the highly formalistic music of strictly ritualistic churches, and on the other hand the cheap, tawdry, glittering swing of nondescript cults and sects.

This action of the Convention was in line with the action of the Southern Baptist Convention which for two years has given serious consideration to this subject, appointing a large representative committee to make a survey of the actual conditions in the churches and offer any suggestions looking to possible improvement.

That Committee has made extended suggestions which were adopted at the meeting of the Southern Baptist Convention in Richmond, as recorded on page 20 of our Convention Annual. It would well repay any member of this Board to re-read these suggestions and recommendations. We do not here attempt to reproduce or go beyond these recommendations, but we do wish to urge that this whole matter be given its due consideration by us and that we keep in view the inauguration of a proper church music educational program.

Source: *Minutes*, Executive Board of the Baptist General Convention of Texas, 6 December 1938. Reprint courtesy of the Baptist General Convention of Texas.

9.17 Baptist Colleges

By 1930 there were nine Baptist colleges in Texas. These colleges were divided into three levels: academy, junior college, and senior college. The nine schools reported a collective enrollment of 6,113 in 1939. During the Depression these schools suffered financially, but made a dramatic recovery in the late 1930s. This period of recovery saw schools change their academic status and upon occasion, the name of the institute. For instance, Marshall College moved from junior college status to a senior college standing and Simmons College was renamed Hardin-Simmons University.

Report on Baptist Schools, 1939

In bringing to you this report on our Baptist Schools, we are seeking to present a factual resume that will be of practical value. To that end we are making it as brief as possible. By way of explanation, let it be said that several weeks ago a questionnaire, prepared with the assistance and suggestion of the President of the Convention, Dr. J. Howard Williams, was placed in the hands of each of the Presidents of our nine schools. All of these were filled out and returned with the exception of Baylor University. Facts concerning that institution were gathered from the report of President Neff to the Convention.

At the present time there are 6,113 students in our Baptist institutions. If we add to this enrollment approximately 500 in Buckner's; 125 nurses in the Memorial Hospital; and 60 in the hospital in Abilene, we have a total of 6,789. Of those in the regular schools, there are (6,113), 3,225 are men and 2,888 are women. In the one Academy there are 250; in the University 625 Graduate Students; in the Colleges 2,013 Freshmen, 1,288 Sophomores, 874 Juniors, 636 Seniors, and 401 Special Students.

In the total student body are 90 who plan to enter some form of Missionary Service and 380 Ministerial Students.

The total number of professors and teachers (not including Baylor Medical School) is 305. Of this number 60 have the Ph. D. Degree, and

122 the Master's Degree.

During the past year, in scholarships, students aid, etc., the sum of $136,470.28 was granted by the institutions to worthy and outstanding students. The total endowment of our schools is $3,921,886.65 with Baylor University leading with $1,638,196.51 and Hardin-Simmons second with $1,250,000.

Having no further information available concerning Baylor University and Baylor Medical School, the following interesting facts are compiled on the basis of the reports submitted by the remaining seven schools, representing 3,131 students:

The average salary of a Professor is $1,599.66. The total number of scholarship students is 701. Students paying part or all of their school expenses by some form of student or school employment number 1,687. Of the 3,131 students in these seven institutions only 1,071 are full pay patrons. The total amount paid to the schools during the year by the patrons was $770,934.45. To this amount the Denomination, as such, added a total of $50,656.21.

The total debt on all our Colleges and Universities (Baylor Medical School and San Marcos Academy excepted) is reported to be $146,545.61. During the twelve months just closed a reduction of $17,893.85 was made in this debt.

One other item to which attention well might be called is that the above mentioned institutions have on their books at the present time accounts receivable in the total of $216,813.40.

Several observations on the above report might be pertinent. The total number of students enrolled in all our Baptist Schools is only two-thirds the number of students in the University of Texas alone. Many of our own Baptist young people are in this latter group.

The salary schedule of the teachers in the schools is pitifully small and inadequate. Only thirty percent of those entering the Freshman Class each fall remain to graduate, and of all classes, too small a percentage are full pay students. The schools are paying their debts gradually, but it is an indictment against patrons of the schools that such a large amount in unpaid bills remains on the books of the institutions.

The Denomination, with an investment of a little more than $50,000 per year, is putting an average of $16.18 into each student. This, of course, does not include the amount of indebtedness already assumed by the State Board.

These actual facts and figures we believe will give a bird's eye view of our Baptist efforts in the field of Christian Education and we make no apology for the omission or injunction.

Source: *Proceedings*, Baptist General Convention of Texas, 1939, 30–31. Reprint courtesy of the Baptist General Convention of Texas.

9.18 World War II

On December 7, 1941, the Japanese bombed Pearl Harbor and the United States entered World War II. As in World War I, the Baptists wholeheartedly supported the war against the Axis powers. Young Baptist men left home, college, and jobs to enter the armed services. While they were gone, their pastors ministered to their families and prayed for their safe return. Due to the need for raw materials, very few churches were built in Texas during the war years. In addition, the 1945 Southern Baptist Convention was cancelled in order to conserve fuel.

A. Army Camp Work

In the light of the large amount of good that has been accomplished in the beginning of our army work, as is reflected by the many souls that have been won and the many additions to the local churches, brought about by the work of the camp pastors and local pastors, we recommend that we continue our soldier work with all vigor and that adjustment of policies be made from time to time in the light of new needs and new developments. We note the change in the status of the work of the Home Mission Board in maintaining liaison with the chaplains inside the camps, while the State Missions Boards of the various State Conventions will maintain work among the soldiers outside the camps. We commend heartily this arrangement and assume our responsibility for the work outside the Army camps, posts, and stations in Texas, working in close cooperation with the adjacent churches. We recommend that Army Camp Superintendent A. C. Miller, the Executive Secretary and the Executive Committee be empowered to elect camp pastors or directors and other employees and make other necessary expenditures from the budget for Army Camp work.

Source: *Minutes*, Executive Board of the Baptist General Convention of Texas, 2 December 1941. Reprint courtesy of the Baptist General Convention of Texas.

B. Soldier Work, 1943

Concerning the work among the soldiers, we are happy to report the organization of soldier centers in the many areas where camps are located and where large numbers of men congregate on the streets. Thousands are being reached through these centers, many souls have been saved, and much good has been done. We recommend the continuance of this work under the direction of Dr. A. C. Miller, and ask the churches contiguous to such centers to lend all possible assistance, and that the Executive Secretary and Treasurer be authorized to cooperate with Dr. Miller in the enlargement program of such work where it becomes necessary.

Source: *Minutes*, Executive Board of the Baptist General Convention of Texas, 7 December 1943. Reprint courtesy of the Baptist General Convention of Texas.

CHAPTER 10

Ready to Go Forward,
1945–1953

10.1 The Five-Year Plan

The Five-Year Plan was an outgrowth of the "Centennial Convention" of 1948. In an attempt to determine future endeavors for the BGCT, it was decided that the following areas of ministry should be significantly advanced: evangelism, missions, Christian education, benevolence, hospitals, and finances. The Five-Year Plan called for raising $50 million for these Texas Baptist causes from 1948 until 1953. Since evangelism has been the BGCT's primary concern from its existence, it was listed first, and thus, the evangelism report for 1949 follows.

Report of the Executive Board, 1949

In comparison with records for former years our report to the Convention this year is one of new peaks of achievement. In comparison with what needs to be done and what we might have done were we living at our best, there is room for repentance toward God and a pledging of better things for the future. The past year had been one of turmoil throughout the world. Some denominations have experienced marked recessions in various phases of their work. For years we have been majoring on and achieving, in comparison with others, unusual results in the field of evangelism. We are glad to note a new emphasis is being placed by others on this primal task.

This is the first year of our new century of Organized Convention life. We set for ourselves a monumental task in adopting the report of

Committee on Survey which was made to the Convention last year. That report, which envisioned a general advance along all lines, called for a five-year plan which has indeed become the program of the Convention. We give, herewith, a summary of the achievements along the lines proposed and offer what we believe are pertinent suggestions and recommendations with reference to the future.

The Committee on Survey made recommendations along six lines: Evangelism, Missions, Christian Education, Benevolences, Hospitals, and Finances.

1. Evangelism

In this primal task of our total work we have reasons for gratitude. During the past two years the churches have baptized an average of 50,000 persons per year. Dr. C. Wade Freeman, the superintendent of our Department of Evangelism, states that he estimates the number will reach 60,000 this year. A Department of Evangelism was created three years ago and charged with the full responsibility of promoting this all important work. Sixty-five associational campaigns were conducted this past year and the evangelistic staff has led in the preparation and promotion of these crusades and conducted some of them personally. The members of the staff have conducted meetings in which there were 4,588 additions, 2,782 of this number coming from baptism. In cooperation with the south-wide effort Texas has been organized in the promotion of a simultaneous revival meeting in every Baptist church west of the Mississippi River during April, 1950. We recommend this whole effort to the churches. We believe there is a great value in concerted effort.

Source: *Proceedings*, Baptist General Convention of Texas, 1949, 56. Reprint courtesy of the Baptist General Convention of Texas.

10.2 Dollars and Sense

Texas Baptists were indeed fortunate to have J. Howard Williams accept a second term as Executive Secretary for the BGCT in 1948. A gifted fundraiser, Williams enlarged the budget of the BGCT from $3.3 million in his first year to $12 million in 1953. During this period, the Endowment and Baptist Foundation programs were significantly enhanced. The Endowment Program sought to acquire fiscal gifts for Baptist causes from wealthy philanthropists, wills, and trust funds. It proved to be quite successful. Directed by George Mason, the Baptist Foundation was established in 1930 to develop a permanent endowment for particular Texas Baptist institutes and ministries. Though difficult during the Depression, this endeavor was eventually accomplished through not only the gathering of funds, but also investing them in stocks and bonds to insure future monetary growth. These two programs were amalgamated in 1951, but problems began to appear and they were once again made separate programs in 1953.

A. Third Annual Meeting

Wisdom Exercised

The Baptist General Convention of Texas never exercised greater wisdom nor demonstrated better business judgment than in the creation of the Baptist Foundation of Texas, whose duty it is to administer the endowment of funds of its institutions. The Corporation, now three years old, was born in due time. The wisdom of its birth has been made manifest to all who are familiar with its activities. The directors of the Foundation and all institutional heads are gratified. The Foundation has labored to conserve investments made by the institutions during prosperous days and has been very cautious in its investments during depression days.

Institutions Blameless

No word of criticism is made against the institutions on investments made by them. They used as much wisdom as investment bankers and insurance companies, and more than most building and loan associations. They were doubtless as wise as the Foundation would have been, but all loan companies were too liberal when values were abnormally high and had to fall. But, the institutions were not equipped to handle investments through such strenuous times as we have been passing through for years. They did not have the help and equipment necessary. Every loan made during good times had to have personal and careful attention in days of adversity. Loans made when money was easy required little attention, but the same loans in tight times demanded painstaking and attentive handling. The Foundation hopes to be able to work these loans out with little loss to the institutions. Time is an important element. To be out of debt is glorious and to be in a position to wait is a saving factor. These endowment assets will be conserved.

Unheard of Declines

We have witnessed unheard of declines in real estate, both in the city and country. A house worth $10,000 in 1928 in many instances fell to $5,000, or less. Farms worth $150.00 per acre four years ago are selling today at $50.00 per acre, even as low as $25.00. This has brought about a condition where property is not worth the loan against it. Owners in some cases are throwing up their hands, saying, "Here is your property, come and take it." We are going and taking it but only after trying to work without it. Others are asking for time and it is being granted where possible. Still others are doing nothing and we are having to foreclose, but only as a last resort. We have had 24 foreclosures, the amount of money involved being $91,618,12.

Real Estate

The Foundation had considerable real estate from its beginning, most of which had been given to the institution previous to the creation of the Foundation. This has been added to by donations and foreclosures during the past three years until the total amount invested in real estate is $707,717.42.

This real estate is scattered widely, most in Texas but a few pieces in Oklahoma and two farms in New Mexico. This property has to be looked after. It must be kept rented and rents must be collected. Farms need to be visited. Your secretary and Mr. Moore have seen most of these farms together. The rest have been looked over by Mr. Moore. We know what we have and where it is. We are laboring hard to keep up with it. The crops on these farms this year are producing very well except in the dry section of West Texas where nothing is being harvested.

Farms Run Down

Most of these farms, particularly those under foreclosure, were in a run down condition. The houses and fences were in a bad state of repair and it was necessary to spend some money in order to get them in livable and rentable condition. It is and will be the policy of the Foundation to hold its real estate until farm lands and city property are again on the market. Little, if any, list is anticipated ultimately. However, the income during the years just ahead, after upkeep expenses are met, may be at a minimum.

Back Taxes

Taxes are burdensome. Land owners have been unable to pay them, and as a consequence, taxes have mounted high. In most of the foreclosures made it has developed that taxes were in arrears from years back. In order to clear the title and put the paper in order the Foundation was forced to consume income, in paying taxes, which otherwise would have been available to the institutions for running expenses.

Appreciation vs. Depreciation

During these years every effort will be made to conserve all farm lands and place them in a high state of cultivation. When and where it becomes necessary the land will be terraced to prevent erosion and loss in fertilization. If loss is to be avoided in the end these farms must be in A-1 condition when the market returns. There is to come a day when a "back to the farm" movement will be inaugurated. People starving to death in the cities will have to return to the farm where sustenance may be had from the earth. Idleness on the streets must be turned into productive labor on the land. When that day dawns real estate can be sold to advantage and profit. Until then we will labor to keep depreciation from setting in. We will seek rather to set up appreciations.

Much Travel Necessary

Considerable travel has been necessary during the past year. Mr. Moore has likely spent one-half of his time in his car looking after mortgage loans and real estate. He has traveled 40,000 miles. His expenses have been a little heavy, but the loss would have been inexcusable without it. With it any possible loss has been turned into a saving. Every dollar saved is a dollar made. It is not right to make it and then lose it. Conservation is the watchword.

Moratorium Law

The moratorium law has hindered operations in a few cases, but the directors of the Foundation are sympathetic with this law. It is rare that our debtors have tried to take advantage of, or hide behind, said law.

Bond Activities

We have had some activity in bonds held by the Foundation. We have sold a few. We have bought some. It has been a bad time to sell, but a good time to buy. The secret of success is in knowing when to sell and when to buy. The Investment Committee of the Foundation studies this problem constantly. We are fortunate in that we do not have to sell. When the market is down we can buy. When the market is up we can sell. The character of bonds held by the Foundation is with few exceptions of a high order. Few have defaulted in interest. The amount invested in bonds at the close of the fiscal year was $586,000.

The Investment Committee of the Foundation will not buy more than $5,000.00 of any one bond. Diversification is the criterion, so that in event of loss it will be negligible. The old adage, "Do not put all your eggs in one basket" is good.

Source: *Proceedings*, Baptist General Convention of Texas, 1933, 105–7. Reprint courtesy of the Baptist General Convention of Texas.

B. The Texas Baptist Foundation Leader: George J. Mason

We congratulate George J. Mason on the completion this October of twenty-five years of faithful and efficient service to Texas Baptists, having started as Field Secretary for the Seventy-Five Million Campaign in 1920 and then to State Treasurer in 1923, with the office of Executive Secretary of the Foundation being added in 1923, and then as full-time Executive Secretary of the Baptist Foundation since 1938. During all this time, he has served as Treasurer of our Book Stores. Dr. Mason has know the pulse beat of Texas Baptists. He has handled all funds entrusted to his care with extreme honesty and precision. His wise counsel in committee rooms, in Executive Board meetings, and in the courtroom has been invaluable. The fact that we now have thirteen million dollars in endowment for Texas Baptist institutions can largely be traced to efforts of Dr. Mason in this direction and to the confidence of our people in his integrity. Texas pioneered in establishing a Baptist Foundation and several other states are now following suit. We trust that an all-wise providence may see fit to leave Dr. Mason with us for many years to come.

Source: *Minutes*, Executive Board of the Baptist General Convention of Texas, 1945. Reprint courtesy of the Baptist General Convention of Texas.

C. The Achievements of J. W. Bruner, Endowment Secretary of the BGCT

Fifteen million dollars in thirteen years for the endowment of Texas Baptist institutions is quite an accomplishment. It would have been a splendid work even though many men had been responsible for securing it, but when we realize that it has been made possible in large measure by the efforts of one man, then it becomes astounding. Nevertheless, this is the record.

When Dr. J. W. Bruner became the Endowment Secretary of Texas Baptists in May 1940, the combined endowments of Baptist institutions were six and a half million dollars. In less than thirteen years, the total has reached more than twenty-two and one half million. In addition to this, the total property value of these institutions has increased by almost thirty million dollars. No person would say that Dr. Bruner alone has been responsible for all of this; but those of us who have kept up with his work do know that such accomplishments have been made possible in a large measure by his diligent efforts, Christian spirit and persistent encouragement to the whole Baptist constituency of Texas.

In the fall of 1938, The Baptist General Convention authorized the establishment of the Endowment Department and instructed the Executive Board to find a suitable man to direct it. In December 1939, the Executive Board called upon Dr. Bruner to lead the establishment of the new phase of Christian work. Never before had any denomination tried such an endowment plan. It was new and untried, but the Convention had called upon a man who was not afraid to undertake big things for the cause of the Savior. After many successful years in pastorates and with substantial experience in dealing with men of means, Dr. Bruner immediately became successful in his new undertaking; and each succeeding year has witnessed the increased effectiveness of his efforts.

In addition to the millions that have already come into the possession of the institutions, there are millions and millions to come in the future as a result of the wills and trust funds established by men and women who want God's Kingdom to get the benefit of their properties after they are gone. The Endowment Secretary has not asked the people for money, but he has given himself to counseling those who want to give to Christian causes; and with the knowledge he has of the various elements involved he has been of inestimable help to them, while at the same time he has led many to invest in the future of the Lord's work on earth.

This article is not intended to give a detailed account of the work done by the endowment secretary; nor does it seek to appraise the magnitude of his whole ministry. This has already been done in a book entitled, Life and Work of James W. Bruner. However, as he comes to the end of his tenure as a world leader in this field, it was the will of the endowment committee that the writer might pen some word of appreciation for him and the man who has been chosen to succeed him. The committee knows that God gave him to Texas Baptists at the right time to launch a most successful work; and the members of the committee feel that they express the feeling of most every Baptist within the state when they ascribe the highest honors to him for what he is and for what he has done as a great servant of the denomination.

In keeping with the policies of the Convention, Dr. Bruner was ready to retire from this work three years ago; but at that time a search had failed to reveal the right man to succeed him, and until very recently the committee did not feel that the right man had been located. Therefore, he has continued three years past the retirement age; and as he comes to the hour for relinquishing responsibilities, he does so with complete confidence in the leadership ability of his successor whom he will assist for a while in the office. He lays down this particular work with the satisfaction of knowing that now many other states have followed the Texas example and have established endowment departments for themselves. We believe that we may safely tell him now that he retires from denominational work with the confidence and love of a million Baptists of Texas and countless thousands in other states.

Source: *Minutes*, Executive Board of the Baptist General Convention of Texas, 2 December 1952. Reprint courtesy of the Baptist General Convention of Texas.

D. Separation of Programs for the Best Service

Dr. Williams explained that a year ago the Executive Board voted to reorganize the Endowment work and make it a part of the Baptist Foundation. He said that at the time the Foundation was not too sure that it was the right thing, but they said they would do it if requested. During this year their conviction has grown that it was not wise and they have been unable to find someone to work in their department. There seemed to come a solution and it was presented to all those involved in it. The Foundation passed a resolution which it asked to have presented and Mr. Wooten will make the statement in a moment. He then read the following statement given by Mr. Culbertson:

A year ago you requested that the duties theretofore and then being performed by the Endowment Department should be assumed by the Baptist Foundation of Texas coincident with the retirement of Dr. J. W. Bruner, Executive Secretary.

From its inception the Baptist Foundation has had no function to perform except to invest funds placed in its charge by Texas Baptists for specific purposes. We believe it has the confidence of Texas Baptists and has earned such confidence by attending diligently to the duties assigned it. Its directors, therefore, felt that it should not be given any promotional duties, but, at the request of this board, they did agree to undertake to organize a department of the Foundation to perform the duties theretofore resting upon the Endowment Program.

In making preliminary studies and laying preliminary plans, they have worked closely with Dr. J. Howard Williams, Executive Secretary, and have diligently undertaken to ascertain the best method of organization and to seek out the best available personnel.

In making these studies, in cooperation with Dr. Williams, Dr. J. W. Bruner, and others, it became apparent that the endowment work was of such magnitude, and the scope of its activities so important to all of our Baptist work, that the Endowment Department should be continued as a separate department, just as it has been in the past.

To give further study to the matter, the Endowment Committee was called in session and unanimously agreed that the endowment work could best be performed as a separate department and agreed that they would join the directors of the Baptist Foundation of Texas in recommending to the Executive Board that the Endowment Department be reestablished.

The directors of the Baptist Foundation have, therefore, authorized me, as Executive Vice President, to recommend to the Executive Board of the Baptist General Convention of Texas endowment work be removed from the Baptist Foundation of Texas and that the Endowment Department be reestablished and continued. I am informed that the Endowment Committee, upon approval of this recommendation, will be prepared to make a recommendation as to the department's continuance.

Source: *Minutes*, Executive Board of the Baptist General Convention of Texas, 9 December 1952. Reprint courtesy of the Baptist General Convention of Texas.

10.3 Ministry Departments

At the conclusion of World War II, almost every ministerial department in the BGCT experienced a postwar boost in growth. In particular, departmental growth was quite strong in the areas of Sunday School, Baptist Training, Baptist Student Union, and the Woman's Missionary Union.

A. Sunday School Report, 1948

The past year has been filled with opportunities and victories, in spite of obstacles which pastors and superintendents had to overcome. Enlargement has been one of the major problems. Some churches have already erected commodious buildings and others are now in building programs. Literally scores of churches are making plans to build. The principles followed should involve plans that will take care of the organization that churches should have to carry on their education program. The Sunday school organization very largely takes the shape of the building erected, but in spite of having inadequate buildings and other handicaps, our Sunday school work has forged forward in almost unbelievable manner.

The number of Training Awards earned by Texas Baptists is larger than that for any other year. There is every reason to believe that the increase in enrollment will make many rejoice when the final reports come in.

This department has enjoyed confidence, encouragement, and liberal support of our Mission Secretary, Dr. J. Howard Williams. The Baptist Sunday School Board at Nashville has been exceedingly helpful in a financial way, as well as furnishing talent when it was available. Our people rejoice over the contribution that the Sunday School Board has made to the progress of our work.

There is much gratitude in our hearts because of the fine cooperation that this department has enjoyed from the churches, and especially from our associational organizations. If it were not for the associational organizations, the report that is herein complied would not reach anything like the magnitude that it does. Each association should have no less than sixteen workers and if all of them had their organizations completed there would be an army of 1,840 people doing Sunday school work as associational units in Texas.

The Associational Missionaries have been generous in their efforts, as well as the District Missionaries and District Sunday School Superintendents.

Sources: *Proceedings*, Baptist General Convention of Texas, 1948, 131–32. Reprint courtesy of the Baptist General Convention of Texas.

B. Baptist Day Schools

In 1950, J. M. Price addressed the Executive Board about his concerns with the increased secularization of public schools. Following the lead of the Catholic church, Price stated that students were not receiving enough Christian education in Sunday School. One day a week would not suffice. He believed that a Baptist Day School program was the correct option. Price's idea of Baptist Day Schools was studied further but did not develop.

We have taken the liberty of broadening our assignments to include the entire field of weekday religious education. Studies have been made of developments in the Texas, Arizona, California, Kentucky, Tennessee, Virginia, and in the activities of the National Association of Evangelicals in promoting Christian Day Schools. The efforts of Mormons, Lutherans, Catholics, and others have also been kept in mind. We are presenting both the reason for and the types of these activities.

I. Occasion for Weekly Religious Education

1. The secularization of our public education

In the early years of our nation there was no need for religious education on weekdays by the churches since the elementary and secondary school systems provided it rather adequately. This was true in the charity schools of the Atlantic seaboard and the church-state schools of New England as well as the parish schools of the Middle Colonies.

For one thing the aim was definitely religious, namely to teach children to read, so that they could read the Bible, and to instruct them in the principles of religion. The purpose of the Massachusetts law of 1647, established schools, is typical: "It being one chiefe project of ye ould deluder Satan to keep men from a knowledge of ye scriptures."

Also the teachers were either the preachers or were licensed, recommended, and supervised by them. And their public school tasks included prayer at the opening and close of school, examining pupils on Monday on the pastor's sermon, catechizing them on Friday on Bible teachings, and punishing them for profanity and other sins. Often they helped with the church music, baptismal services, the Lord's Supper, and funerals.

And the texts were definitely religious. The New England Primer (1690) was religious throughout, the alphabet beginning learned through Scripture verses or truths, The Apostle's Creed, the Lord's Supper, Cotton Mather's Catechism, and other materials were included. Three million copies were sold. The Blue-back Speller (1783) had a circulation of probably sixty million and had biblical quotations and doctrinal statements on 36 of its 166 pages. McGuffey's six readers were both moral and religious and reached a total circulation of 135,000,000.

But as time has gone on, this picture has changed. The aim of public education has come to be developed of mental faculties, acquiring skills, and training for citizenship rather than biblical instruction, conversion, and church service. The teachers are no longer selected because of their Christian character. In fact, a Texas law even forbids a trustee to ask an applicant about his church affiliation. Bible reading and prayer are the exception, and in some places teachers are required to chaperone dances. The curriculum has become secularized so that the readers and spellers instead of showing 22 percent religious, 50 percent moral, and 28 percent secular, as in the early days, had recently 0 percent religious, 3 percent moral, and 97 percent secular. And a parent who publicized excerpts from an objectionable text to cre.te sentiment, was indicted for sending obscene matter through the mail.

Recently an atheistic mother backed by the Free-thinkers and others objected to weekday classes in religion in the public school building of Champaign, Illinois, by Jewish, Protestant, and Catholic teachers provided by the minister's organization on released time, and the system was declared illegal by the Supreme Court of the United States. Similar suits have been instituted in New York State against such teaching outside of school buildings. So we have just about completed the secularization of American education. And secularization is a stepping stone to materialism if not atheism, and it can turn to socialism if not communism.

2. The limitation of Sunday education

Religious teaching on Sunday has distinct advantages—the best day of the week, the very choicest personalities, graded materials and activities, and other values. Without in the least minimizing this magnificent work, the fact remains that it has certain natural limitations.

One is the limitation of time. While the worship period is very valuable, the actual time given to a study of the Sunday school or Training Union lesson is not over half an hour. And those studies come seven days apart, which is a definite pedagogical handicap.

Also there is a limitation in the curriculum, especially the Uniform Lessons. A study some time ago revealed that during forty-five years only a little over 35 percent of the Bible had been included in the lessons, with some entire books never touched. It is considerably better now.

Then there is a limitation in constituency. While Southern Baptists are leading the world in the number of people reached, it still remains true that three-fourths of the people are not being taught on Sunday. One-half of the public school population is not enlisted in church schools.

There is some limitation in trained leadership, especially as compared with the public schools. Many of our fine persons who teach voluntarily have never had the opportunity in high school or college courses in Bible, doctrine, psychology, and teaching methods.

And finally, there is a handicap in integrating the study of religion with the remainder of education. Sunday education is added to, rather than being put at the head of education. Catholics are right in saying that all studies should proceed from the religious viewpoint.

3. Religious and moral conditions

In spite of the splendid work we have done in teaching and training, we have had untold spiritual illiteracy. The average grade of 139 college freshmen taking a voluntary examination on eight simple questions on the Bible, was 40 percent. In fifty books written by chaplains and others there was general agreement that soldiers were sadly ignorant of Christianity and church membership.

While we are proud of our record of baptisms, we fail to take account of the lapses in faith. Of the 2,330,000 Southern Baptists baptized in a twenty-year period, we lost 756,000 or 32 percent by other means than death. And many on our church rolls attend irregularly, give spasmodically, and serve poorly. Dr. Hatcher wisely said: "It is as important to save what we have as to save the lost."

If one were to consider the prevalence of juvenile crime, the increase in divorce from 5 to 25 percent of marriages, and the widespread drinking and immorality, the moral picture is dark indeed. Certainly anything that can be done to make more efficient the work we are trying to do, should be welcomed. So we turn to some positive approaches.

II. Types of Weekday Religious Education

1. The Vacation Bible School

This is the easiest means of extending religious instruction into the week. It is the least expensive, involves no church-state relations, comes when public school pupils are free; and considering the outlay of time, money, and effort, it has accomplished marvelous results. Some time ago the Lutherans had 5,586 such schools with 233,381 enrolled. Last year there were schools in 2,443 of the 3,306 churches in Texas, 18,803 in the South with 1,363,213 enrolled, 40,000 conversions, and at a cost of 53 cents per pupil. Practically every church can maintain one and should do so. Its greatest weakness is its brief time. They should run two weeks or more.

2. Weekday Bible Classes

In spite of the Supreme Court's decision in the Champaign, Illinois, case, classes in Bible in elementary or high school grades, or both, are being maintained in various parts of the nation on released time both in and out of public school building. Sometimes they are taught daily in high school buildings as in Fort Worth where there are as many as 300 enrolled, and in Knoxville where nearly 900 are enrolled. These get a semester each in Old and New Testament. Sometimes they are once a week as in Chattanooga and vicinity, where 20,000 are being taught annually in all grades. In Virginia 48,972 were enrolled last year in 1545 classes. At one time 2,200 communities in the United State enrolled nearly 2 1/2 million pupils, one-fourth of whom were not in Sunday Schools.

These are supported by voluntary gifts of individuals and churches and are not expensive, especially when limited to high school grades. The Chattanooga classes cost a little over $2 per student, and the Virginia classes about $4 per capita. The Superintendent of City Schools in Chattanooga, the Chief of Police, principals, pastors, and others, praise the work most highly. Mormons have adopted this plan and have 88 Bible chairs with about 17,742 enrolled. Lutherans had 4,361 school enrolling 122,629. Texas Baptists should consider it carefully.

3. The Religious Day School

A third type of weekday religious instruction is that offered by religious day school corresponding to the Catholic parish school. More instruction in religion is a part of the daily schedule, and all other subjects are taught from the Christian point of view. Every argument for the Christian college applies to it, plus the fact that children and youth are more plastic and need such environment and instruction all the more. It is the most effective but the most costly. It is not a blight on democracy. Instead democracy must permit it. The National Union of Christian Schools reports fourteen with 3,700 pupils enrolled. Lutherans had 2,722 schools with 137,500 enrolled, and Catholics have over 10,700 schools with nearly 3,000,000 enrolled.

It may be on the preschool level in a church kindergarten and nursery school for three-, four-, and five-year-olds. Here the matter of the relation of church and state is not involved since no credit, released time, or use of buildings is required. Also it combines the value of a wholesome nursery for those whose parents are working or in school, along with definite instruction in religion and other subjects. A number of churches in the Southern Baptist Convention now have such (including four in Texas), and about sixty others are considering the plan. It is the natural starting point for a Christian day school and as far as many will be able to go.

Other religious day schools operate on the elementary school level including one or more of the first seven grades as well as the kindergarten. One in Louisville, Kentucky, and two of the six in Texas are doing this; and there are many in the North and West with splendid buildings. Baptists now maintain ten in the city of Los Angeles with about 900 enrolled. Church buildings may be used provided they come up to public school requirements as is true also of teachers and curricula. The cost is the biggest problem, the average being about $100 per year per pupil, with the parents paying about half. Segregation from public schools is another problem. Except in unusual cases it appears best for these to be operated by a group of churches in a section of the city rather than by individual churches.

The third type is the Christian high school. It may be either for the junior or senior grades or both. W. J. Bryan felt that these were more important than the Christian college. Naturally it is the most expensive and has been the last developed. There is one in Louisville, Kentucky, with 80 enrolled, operated by Baptists; one contemplated by Los Angeles Baptists; and none in Texas. In the light of evils in municipal high schools, such as dancing and immorality, it is very valuable. Here again the cost is the big problem with segregation also an issue. Where they are maintained, it seems that they should be operated on a city-or-association-wide basis rather than by an individual church, and be centrally located.

Catholics have come to them rather generally as a means of promotion, and much of their success is due to them. The messengers of light should be as aggressive as those of darkness. While we think that Baptists should go cautiously and take only the ground they can hold, we do feel that more should be done in weekday religious elementary grades, and weekday Bible Classes for high school students. Texas Baptists should lead the world in this program, and some communities may well consider Christian-day schools. In order to go further in the work, we recommend that Secretary Andrew Allen be asked to make further in-

vestigation and recommendations, aided by such a committee as he may
desire.

J. M. Price

E. L. Carnett

Source: *Minutes*, Executive Board of the Baptist General Convention of
Texas, 5 December 1950. Reprint courtesy of the Baptist General Convention of Texas.

C. Baptist Training Union Goals for 1947

Inspired by the achievements of the past, encouraged by the response
of the present and challenged always by the Holy Spirit, we desire to
suggest worthy and challenging goals for the year of 1947.

1. Additional church with Training Union 400
2. Increase enrollment in Training Union 40,000
3. Functioning associational organizations 114
4. Daily Bible Readers Enlisted by Training Union . 400,000
5. Study Course Awards 70,000
6. Associations with at least one study course 114
7. Churches with at least one study course 2,000
8. December 5, 1947 Associational Attendance Goal 25,000
9. Churches With Week Night Youth Meetings 3,301
10. Encourage towns and cities with five or more Baptist churches
    to have a zone, group or city Training Union with all churches
    cooperating each month.

It is interesting to observe that the above mentioned goals adopted
by the Executive Board of the Baptist Training Union Convention of
Texas are exactly one-fifth of the goals suggested for Southern Baptists.
To illustrate: Southern Baptists, through the Training Union organizations, will undertake to enlist 2,000,000 people to read the Bible. The
goal for Texas Baptists is one-fifth of that number, or 400,000.

To reach all of the goals mentioned above calls for prayer, cooperation and hard work.

The Years Ahead

The achievements of the Training Union during its life of fifty-eight years have inspired and challenged us all. The opportunities of the present are unlimited. If we are properly interpreting the signs of the times, a commanding day has dawned for the Baptist Training Union. Baptist pastors and denominational leaders seem to be of one mind that in this atomic age the Gospel of Jesus Christ should be proclaimed around this world. Baptist pastors and denominational leaders also have the conviction that unusual emphasis should be placed upon what Baptists believe, and training for heroic Christian service. The Training Union is designed to inform, indoctrinate and develop all of the members of our churches in such a manner that they will constantly make an effort to find and to do His will.

In the years ahead an effort should be made to parallel the Training Union organization with the Sunday School organization. Educational buildings should be erected to take care of both training and teaching needs. This calls for a new type of an educational building. Two or more Training Union schools should be conducted in each church annually and an all-out, all church, all-denominational program should be presented and adopted by the Training Union each year.

In presenting this report we wish to express our gratitude for the marvelous opportunity that has been ours to work with and for Texas Baptists. We appreciate the hearty cooperation of pastors and workers state-wide during the past year.

Respectfully submitted,

T. C. Gardner

Source: *Proceedings*, Baptist General Convention of Texas, 1946, 104. Reprint courtesy of the Baptist General Convention of Texas.

D. Baptist Training Union—The Advance Program

A study of the advance of Christianity here in the United States, in South America, in Japan, and in other countries, is both inspiring and challenging. We believe that if we continue our program of evangelism, as well as our program of training and indoctrination, Christianity will continue to advance. Some of the evidences of the advance of Christianity are as follows:

1. The increase of church membership from 50% to 59% of the population of the United States in the last ten years. This includes all

church members of all faiths. In Texas an average of one new Baptist church has been organized each week the last five years, and an average of 1,000 new members have been added to our Baptist churches each week for the last five years.

The Training Union enrollment in Texas increased 47,713 last year. This was an average of 917 each week.

2. A reverence for the name, person and teachings of Jesus our Savior. When the name of Christ is mentioned, people listen. As Baptists, we believe that there is only one way to be saved and that way is by the cross; that way is through repentance and faith. To be saved one must be born again.

The Training Union is a soul-winning agency. It is training its members to win the lost, and at the same time an effort is made to win all of those associate-members of the Training Union who are not Christians, to a living Christ.

3. The tremendous number of people who are searching the Scriptures. In Texas alone, Training Union members enlisted approximately 700,000 people to join the Bible Readers' Crusade this past year.

4. Scientists, educators, politicians, and statesmen alike, are saying there is a need for spiritual awakening around the world. This is a real evidence that Christianity is advancing. It will be a glorious day when all Christians become so interested in the winning of others to Christ that they will devote some of their time each day in an effort to win the lost.

5. The turning of the people in foreign lands to a living Christ. In Japan, Christianity is growing despite the end of American occupancy. Whenever the gospel is preached with conviction, lost men and women turn to Christ for their salvation.

With these evidences it seems to me that this advance program of Texas Baptists is the most timely program that they have ever launched. We are happy that the Training Union also has a Five-Year-Advance Program. This program has been set out in this report. It is a challenging program but is one that can be reached if all of us will work together the next five years. To be sure it is going to take team work. It is going to take consecrated and efficient leadership. Therefore, I call upon each Training Union officer in Texas to do the following:

1. Increase your vision and faith in God, in the church, and in your Training Union.
2. Give depth and enlightenment to everyday living.
3. Enlarge your concerns for others.

With the faith of our forefathers to inspire us, and the enthusiasm of our youth to challenge us, we believe that the Training Union will continue to enlarge its organizations, enroll new members, magnify the church of the living God, win the lost, and train its members to take their stand for God and for righteousness.

Training Union members have been on the march in Texas for sixty-two years. The organization has grown by leaps and bounds. We believe that the greatest day for the Training Union is yet to be. We believe that our Training Union leadership will continue to enlist new members, set up new organizations and promote our five-year advance program.

We suggest that every church in Texas, every association and every district adopt the six-point advance program for the Training Union, as given in this report. With this program adopted and the right leadership in every church, association and district to promote it, our goals will be reached, our organization enlarged, and humanity greatly blessed.

Respectfully submitted,
T. C. Gardner

Source: *Proceedings*, Baptist General Convention of Texas, 1953, 150–51. Reprint courtesy of the Baptist General Convention of Texas.

E. Training Union Convention: Enrolls 7,667

With typical western enthusiasm, Abilene entertained the Texas Training Union convention, March 31 through April 2. Attendance reached a new high for post-war conventions, and far-exceeded that when the body last met in the West Texas center in 1936.

Programmed around the theme, "Loyalty to Christ," speakers, both in general assemblies and the nine departmental conferences, stressed Christian faithfulness in a difficult-time.

Homes in the city aided the hotels and tourist courts in the entertaining the 8,000 registered in attendance, plus numbers of others who neglected to go by the registration booths.

Texas Baptists have had Training Union conventions since 1890, with meetings on alternate years from 1941 to 1949. By recent vote of the state executive board, both the Training Union and Sunday School Conventions will now meet annually. T. C. Gardner has been state director of Training Union work since 1916.

Interest in contests reached a high point not attained since Pearl Harbor. In addition to the pre-war contests of primary story-telling, junior memory verses, intermediate sword drill, declamations for young people and devotionals for adults, contests among singing groups have been added under the direction of J. D. Riddle, music department director for the state convention.

Rose Field House at Hardin-Simmons University, arranged to seat 5,000, was the location of general sessions. These were held each of the three mornings and Thursday and Friday evening. Afternoons were given to departmental conferences in First and University Baptist churches, and in First Christian, First Presbyterian, and St. Paul Methodist churches.

In cowboy attire, Pastor Jesse Northcutt of First church, Abilene, welcomed the visitors. Response was made by Pastor Byron Bryant of Harlandale church, San Antonio.

Convention President Guy Newman, now assistant to the president at Baylor University, said the answer to these perilous days is Jesus, the Way of Truth, the Light. "When the world is at its worst," he declared, "it is time for us to be at our best."

Keynoting the loyalty theme, Pastor J. Ralph Grant of Lubbock, First, asserted that Baptists are not going in for organic union with other denominations because the Training Union is church-related and Christ-centered. "All cannot be great," he told the great crowd, "but all can be loyal."

"Each year we are losing thousands of Southern Baptists to active membership," said Lattimore Ewing, Lubbock, "because they have not been enlisted, and trained and do not know the joy of Christian service."

Deepening the spiritual life will strengthen all other loyalties, Pastor Morris Ford, Longview, First, told an adult assembly that nearly filled the auditorium of Abilene's First church. He deplored the sin of shallowness and called for a five-fold service of clean living, answering God's call, preparation in training, evangelism, and support of the Cooperative Program.

President R. G. Lee of the Southern Baptist Convention was scheduled for two addresses. At the opening session he spoke of the suffering Savior, naming as the reason for Jesus' sorrow, homesickness for Heaven, misunderstandings, unrequited love, and undeserved suffering.

Source: T. C. Gardner, "Training Union Convention Enrolls 7,667," *Baptist Standard*, 14 April 1949, 15. Reprint courtesy of the *Baptist Standard*.

F. Woman's Missionary Union: Lifted Horizons

In little girl days when the joy of discovering—largely through pictures—the animals of the world was ours and we learned something of their characteristics, the giraffe stood high in the list of favorites. His height, his fleetness of foot, his long, tapering neck crowned by a small head enabled him to so manipulate his eyes that he could see almost as well behind his as before. These physical aspects were his chief defense against marauding enemies—he could "out-see" them. How this "seeing" far and near would intrigue my imagination.

Now Cicero tells us, "The eyes, being in the highest part, have the office of sentinels."

On the watch, some eyes see only enemies, troubles, pitfalls, miseries. Other eyes, better sentinels, see friends as well as foes, see blessings, beauties, mercies—in fact, see God.

We, as a W. M. U. have just passed though the Christmas for Christ season with its attendant Lottie Moon Offering, and while the figures are not all tabulated, the reports are encouraging. The most casual observer has seen in its programs, unparalleled missionary opportunities: needs—physical and spiritual—the direst with the memory of any of us. We have seen, too, if we have scaled the utmost height and caught a gleam of glory bright, wide open doors; opening doors; and tokens of tightly closed doors that Faith in God and faithful witnessing will yet open to him.

Let us make our watchword: "Look unto me and be ye saved all ye ends of the earth, for I am God There is none else," vital and living throughout the year. Our part in bringing about lasting peace is helping others know Christ.

War-weary and war-exhausted people in all ages, when worn out by fighting, have talked as we are now talking about peace and the abolition of war. Human nature is the most static thing in all the world; hate, prejudice and selfishness has ever ruled the unregenerate heart.

Peace will come when there are more peacemakers—sons of God. Only the power of Jesus Christ changing the hearts of individuals will make peacemakers. This change begins at home and in ever-widening circles is to reach the ends of the earth. Missions from beginning to end. "The only limit to our realization of Tomorrow will be our doubts of Today. Let us move forward with strong and active faith." (F. D. Roosevelt).

We will not forget that about 260,000 of our finest young men will never be coming home alive. Many have been maimed for life, and this for our freedom, for our independence. How humble and grateful we should be—the least war-scarred nation in the world. We should not—and most of us will not—forget the manifold miseries which afflict Europe and Asia, as a result of the war. Starvation and disease and fear stalk the nations, even though the guns are silent. What a golden opportunity for Christian America to be "good neighbor" to all the world as we enter the new year of a new century.

Source: "Lifted Horizons," *Baptist Standard*, 31 January 1946, 6. Reprint courtesy of the *Baptist Standard*.

10.4 Church Music

Following the lead of J. D. Riddle, Secretary of the BGCT Church Music Department, Texas Baptist music made significant advances in training, involvement, and leadership. Music training workshops were held all over the state. Soon, children's and youth choirs began to appear in churches of all sizes.

A. Music and Worship: J. D. Riddle

In considering this subject, let us first ask some questions; then discuss the subject. Have you ever seriously considered the relationship of music to worship? Would you like a church service without music? What does music do for the worshipers? Is music an aid to worship? Or is music worship within itself? How does music help the preaching of the Word? Why is congregational singing necessary? What kind of music should we use in worship? What do people do when they sing together? What are the final tests of music and worship?

The writer recognizes, with appreciation, "Let us Sing"—McKinney and Graves—from which quotations are taken. We believe the basic purpose of music in the church is for worship—yes, to aid in worship and as an act of worship. Every service in the church opens with music, Sunday school, Training Union, Missionary Meetings, Brotherhood meetings and preaching services all begin with music. Music gets people in a worshipful attitude. Sing a song; read a Bible passage; breathe a prayer. So we are concerned with Sunday school worship music, Training Union worship music, Brotherhood and W. M. U. worship music and preaching service music.

Music is the language of the soul. God is the author of music. God created our musical instrument—the human voice. It is a divine instrument. The voice is the only divine instrument. Other musical instruments are great and fine; and God created materials in them such as wood, ivory, strings, but with his own hand he created our voices. Christians ought to use them for His glory.

Music brings us into fellowship with each other and with God. It leads us up to the edge of the infinite and causes us to gaze for a time out into eternity. Man is by nature a three-fold being—body, mind and spirit. God created us so. Well-rounded Christian education should care for all three natures. The main efforts of Christian education both in the home, the church and the Christian school should be to look to the growth and development of body, mind and soul of individuals.

The writer believes that music is the only factor in our worship services that stimulates and appeals to all three-fold natures of man. No one would deny that music is physically stimulating. Who has not watched soldiers march to stimulated music? Or the football team spurred to greater action when the band plays? Many an audience has been led into action by rousing music. Even a tired man may become relaxed by directing or participating in a rousing song service.

Source: J. D. Riddle, "Music and Worship," *Baptist Standard*, 28 February 1946, 14. Reprint courtesy of the *Baptist Standard*.

B. Beware of Trends Toward Formalism in Music and Worship: J. D. Riddle

The writer's pastor, Dr. W. A. Criswell, of Dallas, delivered a message at the State-wide Conference on Evangelism on Seminary Hill last week that provoked the thought in this article.

I believe there are two extreme dangers that Baptist churches are facing in the matter of order of service. I believe that the danger in both cases comes from the type of music used and the order of service followed.

The first danger is the lighter type of semi-jazz music, as B. B. McKinney puts it, "heel music." Second: a trend toward cold formalism and ritualism. Baptists, being a free, non-liturgical denomination, should steer clear of both of these dangers.

There is a great danger in our churches toward ritualism. By ritualism, I mean a procedure of service which is the same Sunday after Sunday. A service of this kind becomes a recital largely between the pastor and the choir. There is a danger that the choir cannot assemble unless a certain song is played or sung. The worship cannot begin unless a certain call to worship is given by the choir. The opening prayer cannot be completed unless a certain response is sung by the choir. The offering cannot be taken unless a certain call to offering is sung by the choir. This is what I mean by a danger toward ritualism.

The scriptural form of music in the worship service is congregational singing. The admonition is to "let all the people sing." "Praise the Lord in the congregation of the Saints." The first purpose of every choir should be to lead the audience in singing. The second purpose should be to edify, uplift and inspire the congregation by special music.

Lest some should think that the writer is opposed to an order of service, let me hasten to say that if we do not have order, we will most assuredly have disorder in our worship procedure. There must be a beginning, a body and a conclusion to every worship service. The entire service should be planned in advance before the service starts. The planning, in the main, should be done by the pastor and the music director.

Let us hope that the trend in our churches shall ever be toward freedom of worship in which all the people are encouraged and trained in participation. Baptists have always been non-liturgical, democratic and free, and the worship of our services must continue to be thus if our services are to continue to be evangelistic and worshipful from the heart. Forms, dogmas, ritualism, cold formalism have no place in our worship services.

Source: J. D. Riddle, "Beware of Trends Toward Formalism and Ritualism in Music and Worship," *Baptist Standard*, 13 June 1946, 7. Reprint courtesy of the *Baptist Standard*.

10.5 Department of Evangelism

Since 1920 the BGCT had claimed that evangelism was its major purpose, but among the many boards, evangelism was not central and in many cases not to be found. This oversight was corrected in 1946 with the formation of the State Committee on Evangelism. With the creation of this department, Texas became the first state convention to have an evangelism department. Furthermore, the Southern Baptist Convention had no such department in place at this time. Under the leadership of C. E. Matthews, pastor of Travis Avenue Baptist Church, Fort Worth, individual revivals were held, youth revivals, and associational revivals became commonplace. The primary concern of rural evangelism was superseded by a more comprehensive plan, and the services of the old rural evangelists were no longer required. Following Matthews's resignation six months into 1946, Clifford Wade Freeman of Sulphur Springs was thrust into the role of leadership. Spurred by William Fleming, Freeman embarked on a statewide evangelistic crusade in 1951 to baptize 250,000 people. Inspired by the Billy Graham Crusade of 1950, Fleming desired to set the number at one million, but scaled the crusade back to a more reasonable goal. Though they fell short of their goal, 62,086 converts were added and this number was five thousand more than in any previous year.

A. The Development of an Evangelism Staff

Dr. Matthews spoke a few words of appreciation for the confidence in electing him Superintendent of Evangelism and said that unless he considered it the Lord's will he would not have resigned his church for it. He stated he would assume his responsibilities May 1 and would go to El Paso for the first week. He announced his intention to live in Arlington. He stated that he believed the staff of evangelists should be

limited to five and that it might take a while to select the right men.
Certainly a mistake must be avoided.

To lend definiteness to the program, Dr. Williams made the following recommendations:

1. That we commit ourselves to a program of evangelism, which majors on simultaneous campaigns.

2. That we seek to discover the right men for the staff; that it be limited to five; that recommendations for staff members be brought to the Executive Committee when such recommendations are ready; that only men who have special talents in promoting simultaneous campaigns will be recommended.

C. B. Jackson moved that we adopt these recommendations. This was seconded by J. P Boone and passed unanimously.

Source: *Minutes*, Executive Board of the Baptist General Convention of Texas, 19 April 1946. Reprint courtesy of the Baptist Standard.

B. Committee on Evangelism

The Committee on Evangelism, appointed by the State Executive Board, met in the Secretary's office at 10:00 A.M., January 14. Those present were C. E. Matthews, Chairman, C. Y. Dossey, D. D. Sumrall, James B. Leavell, Jr., the Secretary and Dr. A. B. White. After a season of prayer the conference, lasting all day, came to the following conclusions:

First, that the state should be thoroughly organized for a great evangelistic effort, having a state chairman and organizer and like officers for each district and each association.

Second, it was decided to have a state conference of the state and district leaders to convene at the Dallas headquarters at 10:00 A.M., February 15.

Third, the district missionaries were requested to confer with the President of the District Convention and Chairman of the District Board in the selection of a District Chairman of Evangelism. It was thought that likely either the District President or the District Chairman might serve unless someone else in the district has special gifts and interests in the field of evangelism.

Fourth, it was suggested that these same three men, the District Missionary, the District President, the Chairman of the District Board select the associational chairman and organizer and that all such selections be subject to confirmation of the District Board in the case of district leaders and of the associational board in case of the associational leaders.

Fifth, it was decided that we should have a State Evangelistic Conference at Seminary Hill on or about June 1st, the time to be referred to Brother Matthews and the State Secretary after consultation with the Seminary authorities.

Sixth, after a full discussion of the broad outlines of our future evangelistic work in Texas and long, thoughtful and prayerful consideration of the future of our staff of evangelists, the following action was passed unanimously:

In keeping with the action of the Executive Board in its December 1945 meeting, in which it stated, "We commend our evangelists for their work during the past year and recommend that a committee of five be appointed to restudy the entire work of evangelism and that this committee working with the Executive Committee, be empowered to act," and in compliance with the action of the Executive Committee in its meeting of January 3, 1946, we, the Committee on Evangelism, go on record as follows:—

In view of the fact that the present staff of evangelists have been serving with a view to emphasis on rural evangelism, we ask that each one on the staff be notified that his employment on the staff be continued up to but not after May 1, 1946. We recommend that the members of the staff be given the assistance of our secretary and associate secretary in adjusting themselves if they so desire. The reason for this change is that the new program of evangelism contemplated will require a different personnel on the part of evangelists in the future.

Source: *Minutes*, Executive Board of the Baptist General Convention of Texas, 3 January 1946. Reprint courtesy of the Baptist General Convention of Texas.

10.6 Radio Department

Always looking for a way to present the gospel to as many people as possible, in 1946 the BGCT began to use radio stations to get out the good news. With the AM stations too expensive, local Baptist churches and associations bought several small FM stations and began to broadcast preaching and gospel music throughout the state. By 1949, however, the radio emphasis had declined due to the introduction of television into many homes.

A. Baptist FM Network Recommended

The matter of establishing a Baptist network of Frequency Modulation radio stations, which was presented to the general convention at Mineral Wells by Chairman R. Alton Reed of the radio committee, will come up for consideration by the state executive board at the December 3, meeting.

Frequency modulation, usually shortened to FM, is a new type of radio which eliminates static, and makes possible a greater number of stations. It is limited in coverage, the smaller stations reaching only 35 miles and the more powerful up to 75 miles.

The report of Dr. Reed, pastor of Park Cities church, Dallas, envisioned FM stations in key places in the state, owned and operated locally by incorporated Baptist groups, Baptist institutions, and Baptist laymen who want to cooperate with a Baptist network. The local stations would be free to set up their own schedule for local broadcasts and for network times.

The minimum cost of an FM station is estimated at around $11,000, with an annual operation cost of double that amount. Larger stations may cost up to $40,000 or more. It is expected that commercial advertising will carry much or all of the operating costs.

The plan provides for a convention-related FM network organization which will provide programs for 100 hours weekly, 15 hours daily for six days, and 10 hours, with no commercial broadcasts, on Sundays.

Several Baptist groups and institutions have already made applications for a station license; and others have signified interest, Dr. Reed pointed out. By a special arrangement, the radio committee is able to provide the engineering necessary in making an application for an FM station for $750, which is much less than some Baptist schools have already paid for such service. This is all the cash which must be put up until materials are ordered, which may be one or two years hence, the committee stated.

The Texas plan, furnished to the Southern Baptist radio committee, of which Dr. Reed is a member, was adopted in substance by the Georgia convention on November 15. Chairman Reed, who was in the radio industry before entering the ministry, has given much time to exploration of the possibilities of this new venture.

The radio committee of the convention, as enlarged at Mineral Wells, consists of R. Alton Reed, Julian Atwood, Odell Jamison, W. A. Criswell, and C. E. Colton, all of Dallas, and acting as an executive subcommittee. Other members are C. Wade Freeman, Sulphur Springs; T. Hollis Epton, Gainesville; Earl Hankamer, Houston, and Jas. N. Morgan, Fort Worth.

Communities interested in having a part in the network are urged to contact the chairman or some other member of the committee immediately.

Source: "Baptist FM Network Recommended," *Baptist Standard*, 28 November 1946, 1, 5. Reprint courtesy of the *Baptist Standard*.

B. KYBS—Your Radio Station

Dr. Feezor, chairman of the Radio Committee, stated that it was anything but easy for the Committee to perform its task. The radio picture now is not too clear. Television is entering in. The Committee undertook to appraise every factor: the cost of installation, the cost of operation, the size of the audience to begin with, and every element that entered into the radio picture. The Committee had two meetings, each lasting at least three hours. Dr. Feezor stated that he had never worked with a committee that had upon their hearts the sense of responsibilities that this Committee had and manifested a frankness and Christian attitude in opinions. "The Committee did not fully agree upon the motion I present as a recommendation. Two dissented from the motion, but in a gracious attitude. There was no feeling that we should discontinue the radio program as we had set it up. The two felt it would be the point of wisdom if we would wait another year, but we have waited more than a year and the picture is not any clearer now. I present this recommendation from the Committee: We authorize the Radio Department to establish, build, and operate a station in Dallas for the Baptist General Convention of Texas.

Source: *Minutes*, Executive Board of the Baptist General Convention of Texas, 12 July 1949. Reprint courtesy of the *Baptist Standard*.

10.7 Church Loan Department

The purpose of the Church Building and Loan Association was to give affordable loans to financially challenged local churches in order to enlarge, refurbish, or build new buildings. Created in 1951, this organization was a rousing success as it closed 28 loans in Texas by the end of 1952.

A. The Need

We, your committee appointed at the June Board Meeting for the purpose of making a study of the proposed Church Building and Loan Association, wish to submit the following report:

From the survey recently made by Dr. Williams and his associates, we have discovered that there is a need for some three hundred new churches to be built in the twenty-five larger cities of Texas. Many additional church buildings are needed in the smaller cities, villages and rural places throughout our state. These small congregations do not possess sufficient collateral to enable them to obtain satisfactory commercial loans. After careful consideration we have come to the conclusion that our denomination can and should extend help to such churches in their building needs. We therefore wish to offer the following recommendations:

(1) We recommend that the Executive Board authorize the establishment of a Church Building and Loan Agency for the purpose of making available funds to be loaned to churches throughout our state.

(2) We recommend that the Executive Board make available to said Building and Loan Agency the sum of $250,000, which is now held in the form of bonds, to be temporarily used as initial capital.

(3) We recommend that the committee be continued to work out the details of operation for such an agency and bring back a full report to the next meeting of the Board.

Source: *Minutes*, Executive Board of the Baptist General Convention of Texas, 4 September 1951. Reprint courtesy of the *Baptist Standard*.

B. A Resolution for Aid

Chairman, E. S. James, called the meeting to order, and after a prayer, called on Dr. Williams to present the matters to be discussed. Dr. Williams stated that one of the matters was to be discussed previously and stated that the committee appointed to study the matter was ready to report. He presented A. B. White, who brought the following report of the committee:

Whereas, the Executive Board has heretofore appointed a special committee for the purpose of considering the advisability of setting up an organization for assisting in financing Baptist churches of the Convention in the construction and improvement of church buildings, and which committee made its report to the Executive Board recommending the creation of a corporation for such purpose with twelve directors, which report was approved by the Executive Board on September 4, 1951, and

Whereas, the Convention recognizes the importance of assisting Baptist churches in the constitution of buildings or in the improvement of existing buildings for the purpose of public worship and religious education, through the making of loans to such churches from a special fund created for the purpose; and

Whereas, it is desired to have such funds handled and loans made through a separate corporation organized under the direction of this Convention, which corporation shall be authorized to accept gifts and bequests for such purpose and to maintain said fund on a permanent basis, and operate the same without profit as a religious and charitable organization. Therefore,

"Be it resolved by the Baptist General Convention of Texas that it ratifies and confirms the action of the Executive Board in approving the report of the special committee recommending the setting up of a separate corporation with twelve directors, as in said report specified, and that a charitable and religious corporation be organized under the laws of Texas to be named 'CHURCH BUILDING AND LOAN ASSOCIATION OF THE BAPTIST GENERAL CONVENTION OF TEXAS' for the purpose of administering funds entrusted to it, and from such funds to make loans to Baptist churches cooperating with and having the official sanction of the Baptist General Convention of Texas, to aid such churches in constructing buildings and improving existing buildings for public worship and religious education, upon such terms as the directors of said corporation may determine;

Be it further resolved that until further ordered by the Executive Board of this Convention, the number of directors of said corporation shall be twelve, such directors for the first year being as follows:

Dr. James H. Landes, Wichita Falls	Mr. A. B. Culbertson, Dallas
Dr. Guy Newman, Brownwood	Mr. Jim Wittenberg, Amarillo
Mr. Luman W. Holman, Jacksonville	Mr. Homer Covey, Fort Worth
Dr. Carlyle Marney, Austin	Mr. J. T. Luther, Fort Worth
Mr. John S. Tanner, Dallas	Mr. T. C. Bateson, Dallas
Mr. Herbert Burleson, Dallas	

and that any three or more of the persons above named shall be and they are hereby authorized to execute and file with the Secretary of State articles of incorporation in the form exhibited at this meeting and filed with the Secretary of the Convention, they being given authority to make such changes in the articles of incorporation and to do such other things as in their judgment may be deemed advisable to effectuate the purposes of this resolution."

Source: *Minutes*, Executive Board of the Baptist General Convention of Texas, 23 October 1951. Reprint courtesy of the Baptist General Convention of Texas.

C. Success of the Church Loan Program

Gentlemen:

The Church Loan Association is pleased to submit the following report. From the beginning of our operation January 21 last to date in Texas we have closed 28 loans, totaling $611,785.00. We have made commitments to 30 churches totaling $613,500.00. We have served 58 churches and the total amount of money involved is $1,225,285.00, or an average of $21,124.50 per church.

The Baptist Church Loan Corporation, operating in the west, has closed loans, totaling $99,500.00. We have made commitments to 8 churches in the amount of $224,000.00. Total money involved is $323,500.00, or an average of $29,450.00 per church.

Our expenses for salaries, travel, office equipment and general overhead total $11,527.07. Our income from interest, donations and money advanced by the Executive Board totals $14,608.62, leaving an operating balance of $3,081.55.

The western offering as of today is $673,225.04. This leaves $553,225.04 for our work in the west.

Respectfully submitted,

A. B. White, Executive Vice-President

Source: *Minutes*, Executive Board of the Baptist General Convention of Texas, 9 December 1952. Reprint courtesy of the Baptist General Convention of Texas.

10.8 Western Missions

Texas Baptist aid in the funding of loans for church buildings was not limited to their own borders. Due to the birth of Glorieta Conference Center in New Mexico and the fact that many pastors in the Baptist pioneer states of Washington, California, and New Mexico were originally from West Texas, the BGCT decided to help these western churches acquire or improve church buildings. The Southern Baptist Convention chose not to participate in this endeavor. Texas Baptists, however, led by William Fleming, chose to act on their own and provided substantial financial aid to these developing regions.

A. Much-needed Aid

On July 17, 1952, the Church Loan Department of the Baptist General Convention of Texas was asked by the executive board to assume the responsibility for the establishment and operation of the Baptist Church Loan Corporation, a new institution created and owned by Texas Baptists for the purpose of making loans to Baptist Churches located in the West and Northwestern states now cooperating with the Southern Baptist Convention. The creation of this new corporation has presented a tremendous challenge to us all. During August and September Texas Baptists engaged in a campaign to raise a million dollars which is to be used as capital assets by the corporation. Much time has been devoted to travel and study in an effort to work out practical plans for the administration of these funds. We have already received many requests for loans. The total amount requested up to date is approximately $695,000.00.

The first loan in this new program was made to the First Southern Baptist Church of Seattle, Washington, in the amount of $9,500.00 and was closed on October, 2nd. Among the first to receive our letter of commitment was the First Southern Baptist Church of Hollywood, California. This is a very new rapidly growing congregation. These people certainly have a mind to work and by the help of the Lord they will present the gospel honestly and faithfully to the people of a very needy city.

Perhaps the Parkview Church of Phoenix, Arizona, has presented us the most pathetic call we have received to this date. They have for weeks been meeting in an old tent. With sandy streets and dust covering the ground one is able to visualize the extreme difficulties under which this group is trying to meet. It will be a pleasure indeed to help them in their needed building.

Like every other phase of our state mission program this department seeks to help. We appreciate the generous cooperation we have received from the people throughout the state and we hope to be able to greatly enlarge our scope of usefulness during the forthcoming years.

Source: *Proceedings*, Baptist General Convention of Texas, 1952, 134–35. Reprint courtesy of the Baptist General Convention of Texas.

B. Application for Aid

Resolutions meeting legal requirements together with application blanks shall be furnished to the churches by the Loan Department, the application blanks shall be sufficiently extensive to provide essential information regarding the church, its location, present status, and future opportunities. Space shall be provided on the application blank for the appraisal of real estate values, the same to be provided by an independent individual firm engaged in this field of business.

A church making application for a loan must be located in a community which presents opportunities for building and maintaining a church, based upon a religious census made during the ninety day period preceding the application for loan. Such locations are to be agreed upon by representatives of the state convention and by the Loan Association. It is necessary for churches to be well located in their communities and ample space sufficient to provide for contemplated expansion. The church making application for loan must be in full fellowship and cooperation with an association which is affiliated with a state Baptist Convention and with the Southern Baptist Convention. Such church must be contributing to or agree to contribute to missions through the Cooperative Program regularly and systematically. It must subscribe to Southern Baptist principles of doctrine and polity. The church desiring a loan shall authorize the application to be made in a regular business meeting of the church. Resolutions must be adopted which meet legal requirements, the same to be furnished by the Loan Department. The church shall continue in cooperation with its association, with the state convention and with the Southern Baptist Convention throughout the life of the loan, otherwise the indebtedness shall become due and payable immediately. Non-cooperation shall be determined by the association and state convention with which the church is affiliated or by the Church Loan Department of the Baptist General Convention of Texas.

We recognize the freedom and absolute autonomy of each Baptist Church and would in no sense encroach upon the liberties of any church and yet we must acknowledge the importance of proper pastoral leadership. With this in mind preference will be given to applications for loans where pastors are well balanced in their doctrine, thoroughly cooperative and in complete accord with their state convention and with the Southern Baptist Convention.

Source: *Minutes*, Executive Board of the Baptist General Convention of Texas, 17 July 1952. Reprint courtesy of the Baptist General Convention of Texas.

10.9 Christian Life Commission

From their first days in Texas, Baptists have been concerned with the moral issues such as drinking, gambling, and women riding men's bicycles.

Despite their concerns, there was no specific venue in which they might pursue these issues. For this reason, the Christian Life Commission was formed in 1951. Under the leadership of J. Howard Williams, T. B. Maston, and A. C. Miller six distinct areas were to be examined: 1) scriptural basis on moral issues, 2) the family, 3) race relations, 4) public morals, 5) economic life, and 6) world order. Foy Valentine succeeded Miller in 1953 and under his leadership the Texas Baptist Christian Life Commission continued to develop and address these concepts.

A. State Convention Committee Reports: Progress in Its Work

At the meeting of our State convention at El Paso last November, our executive secretary made this statement: "I missed the convention at Houston last year because of illness. As I listened to the proceedings by radio, I saw our work more objectively than I ever had before. I rejoiced in the fine work that was reported, but I was disappointed in much that we did not do. The followers of Christ in our day are pressed on every side with problems and movements which pull at the anchors of their faith and call for Christian interpretation. It is my conviction that this convention should initiate some plan by which we can help our people understand the grave issues of our day in terms of Christian faith and practice."

A Movement Begun

This statement caught the imagination of the entire convention and enlisted its unanimous support of a motion for the president to appoint a committee to bring a report on the secretary's proposal.

The recommendation was made that a committee of seven be appointed to bring a report to the next annual session of this convention recommending methods and plans that might be used to meet the needs of our people in every phase of their lives and to apply the spirit of Christ and his teachings to every area of individual and community.

Committee Holds Meeting

The convention accepted this report with interest. President Bassett appointed the following committee: T. B. Maston, chairman, J. A. Ellis, W. R. White, Herbert Howard, A. B. Rutledge, Jesse Northcutt and the writer. Under the very able leadership of Dr. Maston, this group has had two meetings and will hold a third one this month.

In the first session, we organized the committee, agreed upon plans of procedure, and assigned specific fields of study to each member. Our second meeting was held at the seminary on the afternoon and night of May 18, and on the morning of May 19. At this time we discussed critically each member's report of his particular field of study. Our third meeting will be held on Tuesday, June 27, at which time we will endeavor to shape up these various studies into the report and recommendations to be presented to our state convention in its meeting at Fort Worth in November.

Source: A. C. Miller, "Committee Reports Progress in Its Work," *Baptist Standard*, 15 June 1950, 3. Reprint courtesy of the *Baptist Standard*.

B. The Contemporary Acuteness of Racial Tension

There are abundant evidences of seriousness and racial conflict and the acuteness of racial tension around the world. The underprivileged masses of the world are moving uneasily and possibly somewhat uncertainly. The stirring among the Negroes and other colored peoples is a part of a world-changing people's revolution. Pearl Buck concludes that "the deep patience of colored peoples is at an end. Everywhere among them is the same resolve for freedom and equality that white Americans and British have." This is true of the masses regardless of color. They are on the march and the march seems to be inevitable.

The situation is increasingly acute in the United States, as well as in the world at large. There are many factors that have tended to heighten racial tension in the contemporary period. World War II, in which race and racial theories played an important part, and the subsequent crisis "have tended to accentuate interest in the meaning of democracy and equality." There has arisen a greater demand for the consistent application of basic democratic principles to Negro and other minority groups. Recent court decisions, particularly the Supreme Court decisions abolishing segregation in the public schools, have speeded the movement toward the achievement of first-class citizenship for the Negro; but these decisions have also, in some areas, increased considerably the tension between the races. . . .

Deepening racial tensions have not only created serious problems for our world and for our nation but also for the Christian movement.

Harry V. Richardson considers the race problem "American Christianity's test case." Gallagher correctly concludes that the present crisis, of which the race problem is an important factor, will not threaten the essential genius of Christianity but that it does threaten the present organized forms of Christianity. If the Christian church will not dare to be the church in the fullest possible sense, if it will not take seriously the Christian ethic, applying its principles to race and other areas of life; then it will lose its own soul. Without the Christian ethic the Christian church becomes an empty shell, a corpse that has lost its power to give life because the life principle no longer resides in it.

The Christian forces of the United States have a "rendezvous with destiny." The future of the Christian cause in America and in the world may be determined, to a considerable degree, by what American Christian groups and individuals do in the immediate future about the racial tensions of our communities and our country. If we do not attempt honestly to apply the Christian spirit and Christian principles to race relations, how can we expect others to respect our Christian claims or to hear and accept the message we proclaim?

Source: T. B. Maston, *Christianity and World Issues* (New York: Macmillan Company, 1957), 81–83.

10.10 Assembly in the West

For decades Southern Baptists gathered at Ridgecrest Baptist Assembly in North Carolina for meetings, revivals, and training conferences. Due to the large number of Southern Baptists west of the Mississippi River, the poor conditions of roads and quality of cars, coupled with the underlining desire to anchor these western Baptists to the Southern Baptist Convention, a western assembly was deemed necessary. Texas Baptists pushed hard for the old cowboy meeting camp at Paisano, Texas, but the Convention opted for Glorieta, New Mexico. Despite the very disappointing Paisano loss, Texas Baptists have gathered at Glorieta in large numbers since its opening in 1952.

The Paisano Bid

Paisano is close to the Rio Grande, and though natives speak of "wet Mexicans" there are no mosquitos in that mile-high altitude, for Paisano is the highest point from New Orleans to San Francisco on the

Southern Pacific Railway. Close to the Big Bend Park, only an hour away, and also near the Carlsbad Cavern, some three hours to the north, the whole country is filled with scenic attractions.

There is old Fort Davis with its thick adobe walls tumbled down, and nestled in the mountains, an "Indian Village," and a modern hotel on the road to McDonald Observatory. This observatory on Mount Locke, some 6,700 feet high, is breathtaking in the vision it affords. Spread out below are the cattle and horse ranches, dude ranches, and race horse ranches, and in the distance Mount Livermore with its near 9,000 feet of altitude.

Paisano—here for once the Baptists were on the ground floor and have the choice of all resort locations. A railroad and a national highway pass through this 1,000 acres of Baptist land. Amazing, yes, a well of water that furnishes 60 gallons a minute from a well 150 feet deep dug on top of the mountain. Will the wonders of the west never cease? Overcoats in August in Texas! The climate is not as cold as New Mexico or Colorado, and yet the air is brisk, piercing, and invigorating as only mountain air can be.

Paisano—a place where preacher wearied, not by contrary waves as Paul was tired, by contrary folks; a place where preachers may rest. The Master said, "Come ye apart and rest a little." Rest equals refreshment, refreshing the body and soul. Here is a place where deacons, worn out by much labor and wearied by the world, may take their wives and children and rest in a rare air and look to the mountains whence comes their help and health and come back refreshed for another year of struggle with the stubborn old world. Mountains on which to build summer homes and trees in the valley under which to nestle a cottage. A mountain peak to climb and watch the golden glory of the sunset, and, if the conscience be right, then watch the stars twinkle in clarity as the pale moon turns into a silversmith as it covers the sagebrush with eerie light.

Dreams—"it's great to believe a dream but a greater thing to live life through and in the end make dreams come true." The Kokernots, the Mitchells, the Millicans, the Truetts, and a host of others whose names I do not know, dreamed a long dream. Theirs was the vision of empire founders who would not be satisfied with a small encampment of 40 or 50 acres, sufficient for the crowds they now have; but they built it larger, their castles and dreams. An assembly that would last for three months and fill our spiritual and physical needs must be built there. The spirit of the west must be caught. Does not that word Paisano, traveler, have it? That western spirit more to be admired than Texas flowers; sturdier than the persisting cacti; sharper than its spines; more graceful than the beautiful antelope; more gracious than the west's own hospitality; more enduring than the granite of the mountains that surrounds them, is the spirit that our children need, and which will refresh.

Paisano—the South needs it; perhaps, the other states will not be willing to go that far. Then Texas must do it. All of our state needs it. From East Texas and their pines and South Texas let them come, on highway 90 from New Orleans to Los Angeles, via Houston and San Antonio, and on highway 80 from Dallas. If preferred come by railroad or by air, as an airport is but six miles away. A program there ought to run for three months, for Paisano is a place to rest and to recuperate, to inspire with a religious atmosphere that has something for every group in our churches.

Imagine Paisano with its master-planned streets laid out, houses built according to the architect's outlook of plans, and all of the buildings conforming to the master plan—buildings of rock, or adobe or stucco, or logs, that will blend with the mountains—in the valleys, a lake like a jewel against the mountains. Let the assembly be run as a business; a good hotel with tourist cabins would pay the upkeep for nine months.

Source: R. A. Clifton, "Paisano, A Service Center, Bids for Southern Assembly," *Baptist Standard*, 11 July 1946, 5. Reprint courtesy of the *Baptist Standard*.

10.11 Orphans

The Buckner Orphanage had cared for Texas orphans since the 1870s. The ministry and memory of the beloved "Father" Buckner was expanded in 1948 and renamed "Buckner Baptist Benevolences." This new organization not only embraced the traditional orphanage, but also a retirement home, a Welfare Mission, and a Boys' Ranch. During this same period, four new orphanages were born: San Antonio (1944), Round Rock (1950), Beeville (1952), and a Mexican Orphanage in San Antonio (1946).

A. Mexican Baptist Orphanage Plans Cottage Dedication

Our first two cottages will be formally opened and dedicated in a special ceremony on Friday, September 6, at 6:00 p.m. Large crowds have attended the other public functions of this the newest of Texas Baptist institutions, and it is expected that this one will far surpass all others in attendance.

Dr. Hal F. Buckner will present the cottage donated by Buckner Orphans Home and Mrs. Copass will present the one given by the W. M. U. of Texas. Full details of the program will appear soon.

The public in general is invited. Churches and their organizations are urged to sendrepresentatives. A special Mexican Baptist Orphans Home Day will be announced soon. Watch the Baptist Standard and El Paso El Bautista Mexicano for this announcement.

Source: E. J. Gregory, "Mexican Baptist Orphanage Plans Cottage Dedication," *Baptist Standard*, 5 September 1946, 2. Reprint courtesy of the *Baptist Standard*.

B. Benevolent Institutions

We now have two Orphans' Homes in the State: Buckner's at Dallas, and the Mexican Baptist Home in San Antonio. It is proposed that three additional social institutions shall be established under the Buckner Home Baptist Benevolences.

> (1) A Home for the Aged. Dr. Buckner has already met with interested groups of Baptist leaders in Houston. The Houston Pastor's Conference has unanimously approved tentative plans for the establishment of such a needed institution. The Committee is encouraged to believe that within a very short time Buckner Home Baptist Benevolences would join the Houston brethren in a campaign for the completion of this worthy project.

> (2) A Welfare Mission for Unwed Mothers. This home is to be located at San Antonio. The Buckner Board has approved this project and proposes to join the San Antonio people in providing funds for this institution which is already established and augmented its gracious ministry at an early date.

A beautiful site for the new location of this home has already been selected.

(3) A Baptist Boys' Ranch. Two thousand acres of land, beautifully situated in the hill country of south, central Texas, with adequate fresh water frontage has already been contracted for, and an initial payment for the property has already been made by Buckner Home Baptist Benevolences. The ranch men in this area have shown great enthusiasm about this project of providing a character-building institution for under-privileged boys.

These three contemplated benevolences added to the work of the Buckner Home in Dallas cover the broad range of the Buckner Home Baptist Benevolences now envisioned by Dr. Hal Buckner. It is their persuasion and ours, as thousands of others who will likewise be interested as they receive knowledge concerning them.

Source: *Minutes*, Executive Board of the Baptist General Convention of Texas, 7 September 1948. Reprint courtesy of the Baptist General Convention of Texas.

10.12 The Sick

Texas Baptists have always felt that they should look after the physical as well as spiritual needs of people. Since acquiring the Houston Baptist Sanatorium in 1907, the BGCT expanded this benevolent ministry with five more hospitals by close of 1952. In addition, several of these hospitals were equipped with nursing schools. Several communities wanted the BGCT to take over their hospitals, but the overriding cost was too high and their offers were turned down.

Report on Hospitals

The healing of humanity's hurt has ever been a cause dear to the heart of God. In recording the early ministry of Christ, Matthew says:

"And Jesus went about all Galilee, teaching in their synagogues, and preaching the gospel of the kingdom, and healing all manner of sickness and manner of disease among the people"—(Matt. 4:23).

In fact, the healing of men's minds and bodies was such a vital part of His ministry that the Great Physician gave His twelve apostles special power and authority to minister to humanity's physical and mental needs. Luke tells us that following the healing of the daughter of Jairus, Jesus "called the twelve disciples together, and gave them power and authority over all demons, and to cure diseases and He sent them to preach the kingdom of God and to heal the sick"—(Lk. 9:1–2).

From that day until this hour the ministry of healing has gone hand in hand with the ministries of teaching and preaching. The healing of the body was never substituted by the Master for the salvation of the soul, but it was evident He often used physical healing as a means of ministering to the spiritual needs of the lost.

So it is in our Baptist institutions of healing. Our hospitals, like our Baptist colleges and seminaries, are more than by-products of evangelism, they are also denominational agencies for evangelism. Thousands of students are converted each year in our denominational schools, and are reclaimed for Christ and His service as a result of the spiritual ministry of our educational institutions. Similar results are manifested in the reports from our Baptist hospitals. Our seven Texas hospitals report for this year 602 conversions and 3,752 reclamations. Thus our hospitals have not only rendered medical treatment to some 88,522 persons they have also won some 4,354 to faith in Christ or to a renewed loyalty to His service. This is the New Testament program—healing plus evangelism.

Texas Baptists have every reason to be grateful to God for the great teaching and healing ministry of their seven hospitals. These institutions are: Baylor Hospital of Dallas, Memorial Hospital of Houston, Hendrick Hospital of Abilene, Hillcrest Memorial Hospital of Waco, Valley Baptist Hospital of Harlingen, Southeastern Texas Hospital of San Antonio, formerly owned and operated by the Southern Baptist Convention but which has become the property of The Baptist General Convention of Texas during this year.

These seven Baptist hospitals which participate in the funds of the Convention, now have a total capacity of 1,789 beds and 319 bassinets. They admitted this past year a total of 88,522 patients—a gain of 23,094 over the preceding year, with 12,782 of this gain being due to the addition of the San Antonio Hospital during the year. There were born in these institutions 15,853 babies during the year—which represents an increase of 4,212 over last year. These seven hospitals gave $510,759.04 in hospital care and treatment to some 17,832 charity patients, plus $86,554.84 in discounts. The income of our hospitals for the year totals $11,557,969.64. The San Antonio hospital accounting for $1,749,566.98, thus leaving for the other six hospitals a gain of $907,175.22 over the last year's receipts.

The property value of our hospitals has increased $4,104,174.72 of which $4,000,000 is due to the acceptance of the new hospital at San Antonio. The total value of our seven Texas Baptist hospitals now stand at $23,153,460.44 and with a total endowment of $1,629,837.91 on five of these institutions. When we add to all this the inestimable value of 602 precious souls won to Christ and an additional 3,752 Christian lives that have been reclaimed to the Master's service, computations of ministries of these institutions are far beyond comprehension. Neither must we overlook the vast importance of training Christian nurses in our schools of nursing. Five of our seven hospitals now have schools of nursing with a total enrollment of 420. These splendid Christian young women, trained in our Baptist schools of nursing, will go out to minister—not only to diseased and broken bodies—but to souls that are diseased with sin and to hearts broken by tragedy that only the healing touch of the Great Physician can cleanse and make whole. They shall become not only His hands ministering to their physical well-being, but His voice to bring the message of salvation to their souls. If the life and well-being of our Baptist churches, colleges and seminaries is dependant upon trained Baptist leadership, so is the spiritual life and well-being of our Baptist hospitals. We must have a trained and consecrated Baptist personnel to man our Baptist hospitals if they are to continue as Baptist institutions to minister to both the physical and spiritual needs of suffering humanity. Your Committee believes this is what Texas Baptists want and what our Baptist hospital leadership is trying to accomplish and maintain.

The spiritual aspects of the ministries of our Texas Baptist hospitals are so important that we should like to urge that each institution employ a chaplain with as many assistants as may be necessary to meet the needs of the patients and employed personnel, and to assist in every way possible in the enlistment and training of consecrated Baptist young women in our Baptist schools of nursing.

Source: *Proceedings*, Baptist General Convention of Texas, 1952, 118–19. Reprint courtesy of the Baptist General Convention of Texas.

10.13 The Baptist Building

Despite the great growth of all BGCT ministries in the twentieth century, Texas Baptists had no permanent building to serve as their headquarters. Since the period of the BSC and the BGA, Texas Baptists had rented space while periodically moving from building to building and often city to city. Following a generous donation designated for the purpose of establishing a permanent Baptist building, the BGCT decided to erect a permanent headquarters in 1948. Completed in 1952, the Baptist building was located at Evray and San Jacinto across from the First Baptist Church of Dallas.

Financing the Baptist Building

Dr. Feezor called on Dr. Williams to present the agenda. He asked Dr. Bassett to report on the progress of building plans, as chairman of the Building Committee. Dr. Bassett stated that they had representatives from the Executive Board, the Foundation and Relief and Annuity Board. It was tentatively agreed that there should be a building put up with the state Board paying one-half, the Foundation one-fourth, and the Relief and Annuity Board one-fourth. Each one should work out the space needed, then add some for expansion and everyone pay for the amount of space they occupied. The Baptist Standard and Book Store may want to come in. He stated that we might put up space on the ground floor for rentals. The committee did not do anything definite but finally decided to set up a joint committee and ask Mr. Springer to serve from this Board, Dr. Mason from the Foundation and Mr. Groner from the Relief and Annuity Board and work out something definite. Dr. Bassett brought out the fact that we have a five year lease and cannot be put out for five years. He said that the committee would make a full survey and have something definite to report later on.

Dr. Cockrell said Dr. Criswell had been appointed to see about getting space in the building for the Standard. Dr. Bassett said he could meet with the committee of three. Dr. Feezor said this committee was created by the Executive Committee. Dr. Bassett stated that the Relief and Annuity Board was making enough profit in the sale of the building to pay their part in the new one.

Source: *Minutes*, Executive Board of the Baptist General Convention of Texas, 8 March 1949. Reprint courtesy of the Baptist General Convention of Texas.

CHAPTER 11

New Directions,
1953–1960

11.1 Forrest Feezor

Following the resignation of J. H. Williams as Executive Secretary in 1953, Forrest Feezor, pastor of the First Baptist Church of Waco for the previous seven years, was elected Executive Secretary on the third ballot. During his seven-year tenure, the most important survey in the history of the BGCT, the Booz, Allen & Hamilton Report, was taken, the Wadley Memorial Hospital became a BGCT institute, and another five-year plan was implemented.

Executive Secretary for Texas Baptists

After going to Waco I was elected and served as a trustee of Baylor University, a trustee of the Baptist Hospital, and a member and chairman of the one-hundred and ninety-three member Executive Committee of the Convention. One year I preached the convention's annual sermon. Once I served as president. The pastorate at Waco involved me deeply in the work of the denomination.

The Baptist General Convention of Texas was to replace its Executive Secretary, Dr. Howard Williams, who had resigned to become president of Southwestern Baptist Theological Seminary.

It was a practice of the Executive Board of the Convention to select a leader without using a nominating committee. They would meet and pray about it. Then each member would vote for his choice. At that meeting we had more than one hundred and fifty of the one hundred and ninety-three members present. After a first ballot all nominees except the three getting the most votes would be dropped from consideration.

That day I was one of the three getting the largest vote on the first ballot. On the second ballot only Dr. E. S. James and I were in the running. On the third ballot I was elected. I stood up and asked permission to withdraw my name. Dr. W. R. White responded, "You ought not to do this."

We were sitting together. I prayed. I decided to accept the responsibility of becoming Executive Secretary. The decision by the members of the Executive Board had been made on a high spiritual level. I had never sought the office. Jessica's first response was, "You can't do that. You can't even keep your own checkbook straight." Then Jessica and I prayed about it, and we agreed that it was the right thing to do.

I believed that the Holy Spirit was instrumental in this and that I could count upon the Holy Spirit for whatever help I would need in making wise decisions. I knew that I must be always on the alert about how to deal with sensitive issues.

One of my first tasks was to lead in the reorganization of the Executive Board's work. Some agencies of the Southern Baptist Convention had employed a professional research group, Booz, Allen, and Hamilton of Chicago, to assist in planning ahead. We were favorably impressed with their studies and reports. So, at a cost of $90,000 we contracted with them to study our colleges, missions activities, child care programs, organization of the Board, welfare plans, and Christian Education Commission—everything we were undertaking. They would make practical suggestions about how we might improve the work.

There were many questions at first about getting an outside firm to do this study and about spending so much money. But, Dr. Wallace Bassett explained to the members of the Board how they would work and what good results we might expect. After his explanation there was no opposition on the part of Board members.

When the study was completed, a report was made with practical suggestions. We studied each item and debated it thoroughly. With the exception of the title for our program, we adopted the report in full.

In the 1940s and 1950s there was a great deal of discussion about the term "social gospel." Some Baptists came to be afraid that we would substitute "social" for "spiritual." The report of Booz, Allen and Hamilton suggested that we refer to our hospital and children's homes as "Social Welfare Division." I suggested that we create a "Division of Human Welfare." That was satisfactory. The work of our convention was duly reorganized along lines which have been in effect, for the most part, to this day.

When he was secretary, Dr. Williams had started a Christian Life Commission. It proved to be so helpful and so effective in its ministry that it has been continued through the unfolding years, and the Southern Baptist Convention modeled a nationwide program after it.

We took over the operation of the Junior College which formed the nucleus of the Baptist College which is now Dallas Baptist University. At first there was some difficulty about its location. Some people felt that it should be located in the Buckner Orphanage. There was opposition, and it was located at its present site. It was hoped that Fort Worth might be served by the new location.

We accepted Corpus Christi University and operated it for some time. The property had been a military establishment and some of the facilities were not appropriate for use by a university. The upkeep was very expensive. Later it proved to be impractical to continue it as a part of our program of higher education. We accepted as gifts the Round Rock Children's Home and the Beeville Children's Home.

We took over the operation of a geriatric facility in San Angelo. This was a new kind of facility and created a new ministry for Texas Baptists. It was given to the Convention along with a cash donation of $50,000 and a plot of land. A woman who studied nursing at Baylor University had prayed while she was a student and made a covenant with God that if He would help her finish her course in nursing she would do something to honor Him. God answered her prayer. Later, in San Angelo she nursed a wealthy man. He was so favorably impressed with her devotion to God, and so appreciative of her care of him that through her he provided the hospital, the money and the land on the condition that we would support it and develop it. Today the hospital is one of the outstanding institutions of its nature in America. The manner in which it came to us was: he gave the facility to the nurse, then she gave it to Texas Baptists.

We organized the education institutions into a Council on Christian Education. It was structured so that a request from a college or university would be studied by the Council. Their findings would be passed on to a coordinating committee for further study and refinement. Then the matter was presented to the Executive Board.

The same general procedure prevailed with the Human Welfare agencies, also.

One interesting development while I was there was the approach by Baptist churches outside the jurisdiction of the Texas Baptist Convention, requesting that they be permitted to become participating members of our Convention.

Some Mexican Baptists came and requested membership. Bringing in groups from the outside of our well defined geographic boundaries, or not in keeping with our traditional procedures and policies could become a real problem for our State Convention and for other groups within the Southern Baptist Convention. Some of our best leaders objected. In some areas there was a good deal of prejudice towards the Mexicans. Should we reject their appeals outright, or could we find a way to receive them?

I suggested that they take the initiative and make a formal application for membership in our Convention on the same basis as any other Baptist churches. It worked out fine over a period of time. All the way through I felt that the Holy Spirit was leading all of us who were involved in the matter.

Two churches in Wisconsin and Minnesota wanted to become a part of our convention. I led them to take the initiative and instructed them as to how to make a request. We accepted them.

When I went to Texas, Frank Norris had been denied fellowship in our State Convention. At several annual sessions of the Convention he worked through some henchmen to try to disrupt our work. At Amarillo, Louie Newton was the guest speaker. Norris did not like Newton. He sent a man to the platform to speak against Newton. Somebody started singing, "All Hail The Power of Jesus Name." The whole congregation joined in the singing and drowned him out. Finally, two men went to the platform, picked up the man, and carried him out.

Norris was continually trying to embarrass George W. Truett. Truett ignored his attacks. I learned that this was the best treatment any of us could give him.

I had been sixty-one years of age when I accepted the position as Executive Director in 1953. Retirement at the age of sixty-eight was the policy of the Board. For seven and a half years I was able to hold this position through an era of relative harmony.

During the time I never had a major recommendation turned down. In one instance when there was a great deal of difference of opinion as to whether we should accept responsibility for operating a hospital, I asked that our offer to accept the institution be withdrawn, and it was. I had the good will of the members of the Board. We were able to communicate by understanding each other. I had a staff of workers that any executive would have been proud of. They were cooperative, spiritually oriented and sacrificial.

If I may say it with proper modesty, we had a good overall working relationship all the way through my tenure. Not always was a decision unanimous. We had lengthy debate on some issues. But we always go together and worked together. To the glory and honor of the Holy Spirit I am able to say that I never received a critical letter or a serious complaint from any member of our Board.

There was always and in all matters an undergirding awareness that Christ was my Lord and the Holy Spirit was my inspiration, teacher and guide.

Source: Forrest Feezor, *Spirit-Led Man of God: My Autobiography Walking With God Through Life on Earth Beginning in the Year 1892* (Boiling Springs, NC: Gardner-Webb College Press, 1986), 47–51. Reprint courtesy of Gardner-Webb University.

11.2 Commendations and Causes

The Plans and Policies Committee was optimistic concerning the future of the BGCT in 1954, but they were also cautious about expenditures. The BGCT had inherited institutions and had been given other establishments which it was expected to support financially. While commending the general prudence of the BGCT, the Plans and Policies Committee recommended that no new institutions be founded, especially if the Convention was expected to pay for them. BGCT programs and membership continued to grow at a quick pace, but the leadership was careful not to overextend the budget. The giving of undesignated gifts and tithes was highly encouraged.

Methods of Work

1. With reference to the Institutional program of Baptists in Texas, your committee could do no better than to bring up to date and restate the excellent expression of the 1952 Plans and Policies Committee with reference to general institutional work and particularly as it relates to founding of new institutions:

In times of prosperity it is easy for new institutions to be born. Well meaning brethren, utterly sincere, thinking the services of a particular type of institution are needed may start such institutions. Sometimes this is done with a view to calling upon their Baptist brethren elsewhere to support the new institution. We all recognize the right of any individual Baptist or church, or group of churches, to start such an institution, but we question the wisdom of such a movement if they are to make general appeals to the churches and people without first conferring with the responsible Board or committee of the Board from which they expect help. It is always much easier to start an institution than it is to sustain it. We have now our Education Commission with its Executive Coordinator, our standing Committees on Hospitals and Benevolent Institutions. We believe, therefore, that no movement looking toward the establishment of any institution should be launched without the recommendation of the proper committee and the approval of the Convention or its Executive Board if said institution expects any support from the Baptist General Convention of Texas.

2. We observe that there is a continued tendency for churches to include various institutions in their budgets for specified amounts, which institutions are already receiving generous appropriations from the cooperative program offerings. Your committee believes that this trend will, if not checked, soon jeopardize the work of our overall cooperative plan of mission work. We would commend the Education Commission on

the allocation formula worked out by the College Administrators for the division of total funds available this year in our budget for Christian Education. We would at the same time encourage our standing committee on Hospitals to continue working with the heads of these institutions seeking to find acceptable equitable basis for allocation of the total cooperative funds available for the hospitals.

We recommend an equitable division be made of the Easter offering and other undesignated offerings for Children's homes sent through the Dallas office upon a basis agreed upon and adjusted from time to time by the administrators in consultation with the responsible committee for this phase of our work.

This statement is not to be construed as implying that churches may not give directly to the homes if they so desire.

3. As in other years, we invite the attention of all institutions to the agreement with the Board that no institution is to initiate a campaign for funds without the permission of the Convention or its Executive Board, and that all campaigns so recommended by the committee on institutions and approved by the Board be published in the *Baptist Standard* for the guidance of all our churches and Baptist people.

4. We recommend that it be the continued policy of this Board that no new grants of money be made except they be cleared through the Finance Committee. We further recommend that the Finance Committee be authorized to make such grants as it may deem necessary for emergencies so long as the requests are not for major sums and are to be paid within the current convention year within the budget allocated amounts for emergency and miscellaneous funds.

Your committee would call to the attention of the members of this Board the growing practice of making continuing commitments of large sums to be paid on buildings and institutions over a period of years. Already your Finance Committee faces an exceedingly difficult task of working out an equitable budget due to current operation demands and these long term commitments. The time is near at hand when State Missions and mission causes beyond Texas cannot go forward but will rather be forced to greatly reduce their ministry and missionary forces in order to honorably uphold the continuing commitments made by this Board. Your committee recommends that before action is taken by this Board on any future grant or commitment involving funds beyond the current year that our Treasurer be required to read before the Board each commitment now outstanding, including the amount per year and the number of years for which the Board is obligated.

Source: *Minutes*, Executive Board of the Baptist General Convention of Texas, 8 December 1953. Reprint courtesy of the Baptist General Convention of Texas.

11.3 The New Advance Committee: Changes in State Missions

Since the advent of the Five-Year Program, the Executive Board had planned their ministries and budget in five-year segments. At the conclusion of each segment, the Executive Board would present the results of its work to the Convention. In 1953, it was time once again for the next five-year plan. New and ambitious goals were set for evangelism, stewardship, and all other areas of ministerial work.

Recommendations: State Missions

1. In view of the continued expanding assets and increased responsibility falling on the Directors of the Baptist Foundation of Texas, we would recommend that the number of directors be increased to eighteen members, three of whom shall be active Baptist pastors.

We would further recommend that in the future selection of these members care should be exercised to provide that not more than two members be elected from the existing Boards of Trustees of any institution or agency whose endowment funds are handled by the Foundation. This provision shall not affect the status of the present members of the Board.

2. We recommend that the Trustees of Hardin-Simmons be requested to give serious consideration to the matter of entrusting their endowment funds with the Baptist Foundation of Texas.

3. Looking forward to the ideal of a 50-50 division of local church funds, our committee would recommend that the churches strive for a 2% increase of budget receipts to the Cooperative Program for each of the next four years and a 3% increase in 1958.

4. We would further recommend that as the percentage given through the churches to the Cooperative Program increases, that a proportionate percentage increase be sent undesignated to South-wide causes, looking forward to a 50-50 division of funds as soon as possible.

5. We would recommend that the department heads of our state mission work hold regular meetings with the State Secretary as may be designated by the Secretary and that quarterly reports of the work of each department be submitted to his office.

6. That the Executive Secretary through the Public Relations department prepare and distribute to the pastors and other workers a Texas Baptist Handbook giving information regarding all phases of our work and incorporating the information gained from the questionnaire distributed to the New Advance Committee. Such handbook would carry the five-year goals as adopted by our 1953 Convention and any other vital information regarding our future programs. It is desirable that such handbook be distributed as soon after January 1, 1954, as feasible and possible.

7. We would further recommend that the benevolent institutions, including children's homes, home for unwed mothers, and the haven for the aged, make a unified appeal to our churches for such support as may be needed on the Sunday preceding Easter each year. The Executive Secretary is asked to designate some member of his staff to aid in the coordination and the promotion of this offering. Information about all the homes should be given and our Baptist constituency should be urged to give to all of them. That for 1954 the Texas W. M. U. be asked to plan and promote the pre-Easter offering for the homes.

That the undesignated funds sent to the Dallas office for the homes be divided on a percentage basis agreed upon by the Benevolence Committee and the heads of the institutions.

It is understood that this procedure will in no way hinder the approach to certain individuals who may have a deep interest in one of the institutions and who may be impressed to give liberally to its work.

The superintendents of the various institutions are urged to continue their plans to form an organization among themselves, for the pur-

pose of regular meetings to share ideas and coordinate their work looking toward increased efficiency in every sphere of operation.

We recommend that the Benevolence Committee, in Cooperation
with the heads of the institutions give serious study to the possibility of
including the children's homes and related institutions in the Cooperative Program for either full support or for additional supplementary support, thereby decreasing the multiplying number of special appeals
necessary to support these institutions.

8. We recommend that the churchmen increase their interest in and
their support of the Mother's Day offering for the charity work of the
hospitals.

The Benevolence Committee is asked to cooperate with the administrators in plans to secure a larger response to their appeal and that, for
the present, Mr. Andrew Allen of the Baptist Sunday School Department, continue to assist in the promotion of this offering.

9. In view of the great investment Baptists have in benevolent institutions and in view of the extensive operations involved, we recommend
that the Benevolent Committee become a standing committee on the
Executive Board.

10. We recommend that the Education Commission, in cooperation
with the department of Direct Missions, give careful study to the possibility of providing a permanent type of college education for Spanish people.

11. We recommend that a committee consisting of the Executive
Secretary, the chairman and vice chairman of the Executive Board, the
Editor and the chairman of the Board of the Baptist Standard, and the
chairman of the New Advance Committee be asked to study the relationships of the Baptist Standard to the Convention and the Executive
Board and bring the results of their findings, along with any recommendations they may desire to make, to a subsequent meeting of the Executive Board.

12. We recommend that our churches be encouraged to set up a
Memorial Education Fund for scholarships for worthy students and that
our members be encouraged to contribute to such funds as a memorial
to a loved one.

13. We recommend that the Finance Committee in cooperation with the Executive Secretary and the Treasurer be requested to make a study of the distribution of our state mission dollars as regards state mission work, education and healing to discover whether we are maintaining a proper balance in the percentage allocations to the principal units of our work. Their findings, along with any necessary adjustments, will be reported at a subsequent meeting of the Executive Board.

14. In the realm of Christian education, we recommend the following: Progressive development of a unified cooperative program of Christian Education under the direction of the Texas Baptist Christian Education Commission and the Texas Baptist Association of College Administrators. A gain of a minimum of 2,500 full-time students in the Texas Baptist Educational institutions.

15. Planned expansion and enrichment of curricula through interaction and coordination.

16. Improved faculty welfare through better salary scales, tenure policies, retirement benefits, group insurance, faculty housing, etc.

17. A unified program of public relations through the office of our Executive Coordinator promoting Christian Education on a state-wide level—advantage to be taken of South-wide emphasis on Christian Education scheduled for the spring of 1954 and the continuing emphases thereafter.

18. The accreditation of all Texas Baptist Colleges by the Southern Association of Colleges and Universities.

Five-year budgetary goals for the twelve educational institutions to be realized out of Program receipts as follows:

> Current operation
> Endowment
> Capital needs

19. Serious study should be given to the status of our present rural works and the possible need for expansion. In view of the limited time and for lack of adequate information, no definite recommendation could be formulated at this time. We would recommend that either the ser-

vices of this committee be extended or that a new committee be appointed to give further study to this problem and to any other problem which may arise in the execution of the recommendations made in this report.

We offer this report to the Executive Board, mindful of the fact that it contains serious limitations due to the gigantic scope of the work of our Convention. Texas Baptists comprise a mighty host and our many phases of work constitute a major enterprise. We can be grateful for the "growing pains" that indicate the rapid development and progress of our denominational life. We rejoice in the fact of the favor of God resting on our labors. In all humility, we should dedicate ourselves afresh to the glorious service of our Savior and Lord and face toward the challenging future with vision of faith.

Let us beware lest we become complacent and self-satisfied with our present achievements. We hold only a "green border" of the inheritance which is our Lord's bequest to His followers. Let us say with Joshua of old as he gazed toward the rolling hills and fertile valleys of Canaan's fair and happy land, "There remaineth yet very much land to be possessed." Joshua 13:1.

> "Before us lie the hills, sunlit with promise
> Fairer fulfillment than the past could know,
> New growths of soul, new leadings of the Spirit
> And all the glad surprises God will show."

Humbly submitted by the New Advance Committee of the Executive Board of the Texas Baptist General Convention, September 8, 1953.

Source: *Minutes*, Executive Board of the Baptist General Convention of Texas, 8 September 1953. Reprint courtesy of the Baptist General Convention of Texas.

11.4 Missions beyond Texas

During most of the nineteenth century, Texas Baptists largely depended on other states for funds, missionaries, and educational materials. By the mid-twentieth century, Texas was assisting several churches, Baptist colleges, and associations in the west. In particular, Grand Canyon College,

Phoenix, Arizona, received a substantial amount of aid in its infancy from the BGCT as did the Colorado Baptist Convention after its creation in 1954. Lacking their own state conventions, Baptist churches in Minnesota and Wisconsin applied for BGCT membership in 1956 and were accepted. By the end of the 1950s, Texas Baptist influence could be felt well beyond the southwest.

Wisconsin and Minnesota

A. B. White, J. Woodrow Fuller, and R. A. Springer had just returned from a week's tour of the churches and mission points in the Wisconsin-Minnesota area and they were asked to make a brief report to the Board.

R. A. Springer reported on a trip to Hastings where he was present for a fellowship meeting in the basement home of a Southern Baptist family. There were 29 present, and likely it will result in a mission of the Southtown Church of Minneapolis. Woodrow Fuller spoke on the work in Minneapolis and St. Paul. While there, he and Mr. Springer participated in the dedication of the Southern Baptist Church of Minneapolis. He said that two years ago Ross Dillon of the Union Association had recommended the placement of four churches in the twin-city area. Already, we are cooperating in getting property in three locations and are looking for the fourth in a quadrant position. Dr. Springer and Dr. White and Dr. Fuller participated in the organization of a new church in Racine, Wisconsin, with 17 charter members. They reported that a new building would be started in Milwaukee in April. Also a new building will be started in Kenosha, Wisconsin. The pastors, along with the Superintendent of Missions, Frank Burress, were commended highly for their work in that area, in spite of the many difficulties present. Prayers were urged for their work.

Source: *Minutes*, Executive Board of the Baptist General Convention of Texas, 3 March 1959. Reprint courtesy of the Baptist General Convention of Texas.

11.5 Christian Education

Texas Baptists took a keen interest in education with the birth of Baylor University at Independence in 1845. By the 1950s, Texas Baptists had seven senior colleges, one academy, and one junior college with accumulated assets of $64 million. All schools were to be accredited by the Southern Association of Colleges and Schools by 1960 or their financial support from the Cooperative Program was to cease. In addition, two new schools joined their Texas Baptist brethren, Houston Baptist University in 1962 and Dallas Baptist College in 1954. As noted by the Booz, Allen, Hamilton Report, only 20 percent of Baptist students attended Baptist colleges while 80 percent were attending state schools.

A. Booz, Allen, and Hamilton Report: Student Coverage

(1) The Convention, through Its Sponsored Institutions, Should Continuously Seek To Enroll at Least 20% of All Baptist and Baptist Preference Students Who Attend College in Texas

Exhibit III showed that the percentage of Baptist students in Baptist schools has declined from 25% to 18% in the past ten years. If this proportion is not to decline further, the Convention must take active steps now to insure that its educational institutions will be able to enroll adequate numbers of students in the future.

In view of the recent enrollment experience of Texas Baptist institutions as illustrated by the figures of Exhibit III, mentioned above, an aggregate enrollment goal of 20% of all Baptist students in Texas colleges would appear to be a challenging goal for the future. A goal of at least this magnitude is essential if the Convention's educational system is to assert enough educational influence to make its continued support by the denomination worthwhile. If Convention institutions are to contribute effectively to the leadership needs of the denomination, they should consistently reach at least one out of every five of the college students in Texas who come from Baptist families.

(2) Texas Baptist Institutions Should Actively Recruit the Most Able Baptist Students for Enrollment in Baptist Educational Institutions

For best leadership results, the Convention should be concerned with the quality of students enrolled in its institutions as well as with their members. If one Baptist student out of every five is enrolled in a Baptist institution, there should be effort expended to see that the best student of the five is the one enrolled.

The best Baptist students cannot be enrolled in Baptist institutions unless the institutions themselves engage in an active program of recruitment. Pastors and church members in the surrounding area should be made aware of the nearby Baptist colleges' programs and should be urged to help establish contacts between their outstanding young people and the Baptist colleges. Although overall advertising and promotion of all institutions by the Convention is helpful, it cannot take the place of active recruitment on the part of the institution. Each institution bears ultimate responsibility for the number and quality of the students it enrolls.

Although it can be said that the Convention should be interested in seeing that the "best" Baptist students are enrolled in its institutions, the criteria for determining what type of student is "best" may vary for different kinds of institutions.

(2.1) Admission Standards for Undergraduate Studies Should Stress High Leadership Potential

As was mentioned in Chapter I, the primary concern of the Convention's liberal arts colleges should be with the leadership potential of their students. High scholastic aptitude is one important factor in leadership potential, but is not the only one. In setting admission standards, Baptist liberal arts colleges should try to identify the major factors contributing to leadership potential in students and should develop definite sets of criteria around these factors. Particular effort should then be made to recruit students who will meet the criteria best, and the criteria should be used to select appropriate kinds of students from among all those who apply.

(2.2) Admission Standards for Graduate and Professional Work Should Stress Academic Competence as the Single Most Important Criterion for Admission

Graduate and professional programs are different from liberal arts programs in that the leadership potential of students at the higher levels of training is most closely related to their academic achievement. Since leadership in an academic or professional field is tied so directly to the experience achieved in the field, students selected for these types of programs should have demonstrated high degrees of academic competence in undergraduate work. Therefore, the criteria used for recruiting and selecting students at the graduate and professional level should be weighted most heavily in the direction of scholastic aptitude and previous academic achievement.

(3) Each Institution Should Seek to Establish Suitable Proportions of Baptist and Non-Baptist Students in Each Year's Enrollment

The proportion of Baptist students in each institution's enrollment is also a matter of importance to the Convention. Since the Convention sponsors educational institutions for the primary purpose of developing future leadership for the denomination, it must be concerned with the extent to which this purpose is being carried out. The proportion of Baptist students enrolled is one indication of the extent to which the Convention's obligation to the denomination is being fulfilled.

Despite the apparent direct relation between denominational welfare and numbers of Baptist students taught, it is not necessarily true than an institution whose enrollment is 100% Baptist is doing the best job for the denomination. Other factors also influence the proportions of Baptist and non-Baptists students that are desirable for Convention-sponsored institutions. The necessity for avoiding denominational ingrownness is educational stimulation to be derived from school contacts with other social and religious groups. A proportion of Baptist students somewhat less than 100% for all Convention institutions is desirable. In addition, the enrollment of non-Baptist students on Baptist campuses affords an opportunity for on-campus witnessing.

Source: *Booz, Allen, Hamilton Report*, Vol. 3, 141–45. Reprint courtesy of the Baptist General Convention of Texas.

B. The Christian College

The Christian college or university has a unique function which cannot be performed by secular educational institutions or even by other distinctly Christian institutions, including the churches.

The distinctive mark of the Christian college is that it finds its integrating principle and philosophy in the Christian faith. It is a school for higher education facing the responsibility to achieve academic excellence like any other college, but bearing the added responsibility of maintaining Christian commitment in policy and action.

The Convention's Christian education program is based upon commitment. It is committed to God as He is known through revelation, but it is also committed to learn more of God as He expresses Himself in creation. It is committed to the quest for the truth of God as He revealed Himself in Jesus Christ as Savior and Lord and as He makes Himself known through the World He has created. These commitments are viewed as consistent and complementary. The Christian college should combine a respect for reason and science with a reverence for total Biblical revelation.

The Christian college should maintain the respect of other institutions of higher learning as well as the respect of students and the sponsoring denomination.

This presents a real challenge, especially in the atomic and space age. The president of a Texas Baptist college recently described this difficulty to his Board of Trustees in these words, "Our college, if it is to be an institution of integrity, must offer learning that is contemporary and comprehensive. Never in history has attention been so concentrated on science. The top billing of our American scene goes to rockets, space craft, computers, and super-highways. . . . In the realm of academics we face a very difficult problem, for an institution of higher learning which bears the name of Christ must give the best in contemporary knowledge."

Source: Edward N. Jones, ed., *The Future Development of the Christian Education Program of the Baptist General Convention of Texas* (Dallas: Baptist General Convention of Texas, 1964), 7–8. Reprint courtesy of the Baptist General Convention of Texas.

C. Christian Education Commission

Facing the indisputable fact that in ten years there will be twice as many Baptist youth of college age in Texas as there are today, the Executive Board of the Texas Baptist General Convention in its March meeting instructed the Christian Education Commission to continue studying the possibilities of expansion into the metropolitan areas not adequately served by existing institutions and the conditions upon which the establishment of new institutions might be approved. The Education Commission has given serious thought to this question for more than two years. Long hours of study, research and committee work have gone into the analysis of the problem. At a major planning conference, held in Dallas on May 10 and 11, we sought the counsel and advice of educators of national reputation. We have shared our thinking in numerous conferences with Convention officials, the educational leadership, pastors and laymen of local associations and churches and civic organizations. Our thinking has crystallized into the resolution we now lay before you.

I. Whereas the Education Commission of the Baptist General Convention of Texas desiring to reaffirm the primary importance of the existing educational program of Texas Baptists, built upon more than 100 years of experience in operating residential liberal arts colleges which we believe have and will continue to offer the highest quality collegiate program in the nation, be it reaffirmed that the principles set forth in the first Five Year Plan enunciated by the Education Commission covering the years 1955 through 1959 shall continue to be the guiding policies of our Educational program; namely, that all educational funds contributed through the Cooperative Program shall be used to improve and expand our present educational institutions to the end that each shall fully be accredited by the Southern Association of Colleges and Universities before January 1, 1960.

And, be it further affirmed that it shall be the continued policy of the Baptist General Convention to support and undergird these existing institutions in so far as they continue to fulfill the objectives for which they were created; namely, to educate Baptist youth in a Christian environment and to provide secular and lay leadership for our Convention at home and abroad.

Be it further affirmed that continued support of individual units in the existing program shall be contingent upon reasonably uniform costs of instruction to the Convention when compared with the group as a whole.

II. Whereas approximately one-half of all Texas Baptist youth now reside in the metropolitan areas, and

Whereas the present trends indicate that an even larger percentage of the state's future college age population will reside in these centers, the Education Commission suggests that such areas be designated as strategic for future expansion of our educational program.

III. Whereas it is advisable that any expansion of our educational program should be effected with the least interference with our existing program, it would seem wise to stagger the dates when each new unit could begin to share in Cooperative Program funds.

IV. Whereas the most simplified form of a higher educational institution is the junior college, and

Whereas this form of instruction is most economical to the sponsoring agency and the recipient, and

Whereas other desirable benefits accrue to new institutions operating at the junior college level, the Education Commission recommends that any expansion of our educational program be on the junior college level.

V. Whereas, an aggressive, strong, educational institution is an asset to any growing community, and

Whereas accrediting standards require an attractive, adequate physical plant and economic funds commensurate with the value of the property,

Therefore, the Education Commission reaffirms the statement of minimum criteria enunciated in 1954 for the establishment of metropolitan educational facilities; namely, that prior to the issuing of a charter of incorporation the institution shall posses an unencumbered title to a desirably located campus consisting of a suggested minimum of $1,500,000 for endowment, and, further, that assurance be given to such institutions that they would be accepted into the educational program sponsored by the Convention.

Now, be it therefore resolved:

"That the Education Commission present the above as a statement of policy to the Executive Board of the Baptist General Convention of Texas and recommend its adoption."

Dr. Landes said that all the committee had signed this report, and he moved that it be accepted in the Statement of Principles and that the Executive Board adopt the Statement. This was seconded by W. M. Shamburger, and the motion carried.

Source: *Minutes*, Executive Board of the Baptist General Convention of Texas, 5 June 1956. Reprint courtesy of the Baptist General Convention of Texas.

11.6 Baptist Benevolences

Aided by the findings of the Booz, Allen, and Hamilton Report of 1957, Texas Baptists broadened their benevolent ministries. Due to the continued influence of the Buckner Orphanage, childcare was always a chief concern and by 1959 the BGCT operated six orphanages. In addition, hospitals and homes for the elderly were becoming more common. This ministry was highlighted by the opening of the Baptist Memorial Geriatrics Hospital in San Angelo in 1957. The number of Baptist hospitals also continued to grow. After a strenuous debate over church-state relations, the BGCT accepted the state of the art Wadley Memorial Hospital in Texarkana in 1959.

A. The Booz, Allen, and Hamilton Report: Care for the Elderly

The task of helping people in an effective manner has always been difficult because it involves such a variety of psychological problems relating to dependency and wounded self-esteem on the one hand and a lack of humility and selfless motivation on the other. While the impact of economic dependency has been diminished by substituting the principle of insurance for the principle of charity, the tasks of helping people have grown even more complex. As human needs become more closely identified with the concept of disability than with the concept of poverty, the importance of medical care, rehabilitation, and preventative medicine have greatly increased. And even in the field of medical care there has been an increasing amount of attention to problems of mental illness. The problems of social maladjustment have also produced a need for various forms of social casework, but this type of effort may be more closely related to the preventive medical programs and health guidance centers of future medical institutions.

The special problems of youth have produced a wide variety of community service institutions, but it is not yet clear whether many of these institutions will in the future be more closely associated with the field of education than with the field of human welfare service. While the disruption of family life has created a need for the care of children from broken homes, as well as orphans, it is likely that all children who are not afflicted with serious handicaps will either be adopted or placed in foster homes. The need for placement services will increase, but institutional child care will either be temporary or limited to the care of the handicapped.

The special problems of elderly people have not as yet been met in a very adequate manner. Improvements in the field of medical care have increased the span of life and the ratio of older people in the general population. But hospitals have not yet developed adequate facilities or services to meet their medical needs. Many of the old age homes that were established primarily to take care of the poor are gradually being transformed into nursing homes and special hospitals. The rapidly increasing need for a new type of residence for elderly people has received even less attention than the need for better medical facilities.

The development of large, complex community service institutions presents a new problem and a new challenge. As these institutions have grown larger and more complex, they have tended to develop an impersonal character that is inconsistent with their basic purpose. In some cases, this impersonality produces a degree of inhumanity that represents a new form of human need.

Source: Booz, Allen, and Hamilton Report, Vol. 4., 24–25. Reprint courtesy of the Baptist General Convention of Texas.

B. Report of Special Committee on Orphanages

Carl McGinnis read the report of the special committee on orphanages:

The special committee appointed some months ago to make a survey of our four Children's Homes and their needs has met six times. The first meeting was during the Convention in Houston and was preliminary. Four of the subsequent meetings were held in visits to each of the homes and the last meeting with the Executive Secretary in Dallas.

We wish to commend to you the personnel of the administrative staffs of all the homes. Each of these men has a high sense of mission in relation to the work over which he has supervision, and each of them has the work of his home in the best of condition.

The four homes are caring for a total of approximately eleven hundred children. The total income of all four homes in 1955 was $1,495,949.96, of which amount $363,877.75 was received from churches which have the homes in their monthly budgets. The remainder was received from special bequests and wills of individuals, special offerings from churches and associations, and in some cases, from endowment and income-producing property. This last classification is largely from the Buckner Home. This is to be expected, since three of the homes are of such recent origin as not to have had time to accumulate either much endowment or income-producing property.

We found that our benevolent program, as related to dependent children, presents a far different picture than at the time our several state conventions (and notably Texas) started homes to care for orphans. There are now comparatively few full orphans. The overwhelming majority of children in our homes are either half orphans with one parent living, or are children from broken homes with both parents living. This fact does not relieve us of our benevolent responsibility, but it does raise the question as to what our maximum expenditure should be in the direction of providing additional equipment and personnel to deal with this increasing social problem.

We call the attention of the Board to the large and unselfish service rendered by the men and women who give of their time and influence to serve on the boards of trustees of these four homes. We suggest that it would greatly correlate the general spirit and interest of the work of all the homes if the four administrators and the executive committee of their boards of trustees could have a semi-annual meeting together for the exchange of ideas and the discussion of their common problems.

In view of some discussion to put these four homes in the Cooperative Program, we studied this matter in our survey. We do not believe this is the solution to the financing of these homes at the present time. It would require a minimum of one million dollars per year for operation cost, and their capital needs for buildings and equipment would be above this figure. Three of the institutions are comparatively in their infancy. If they grow to a reasonable maximum size, they will need several additional buildings and equipment over a period of a few years.

It is our opinion that the financial requirements of all four of the institutions will not pose any major problem, nor will support of the homes by the churches prove any detriment to the receipts for the causes represented in the Cooperative Program if they can be kept before the churches. We do believe they should share in the overall promotion of our work, and that such promotion should make it clear that these institutions receive no support from Cooperative Program funds. We would, therefore, recommend that a man adapted by training and (or) experience, be added to the personnel of our State Public Relations Department and that he be under the supervision of the director of the department, and that his explicit duties be the promotion of the work of all four of our Children's Homes. The expense of adding this individual to the Public Relations Department to be born out of the state Cooperative Program funds.

We also recommend that the personnel of the benevolence committee of our Convention be selected for their interest in and insight of the needs of our child-caring institutions; that the size of the committee be a minimum of nine members; and that in order for this committee to do more effective work, they be appointed for a five-year tenure.

We recommend that, as soon as is practical and possible, the charters of all these institutions be amended or changed to provide for the widest possible representation on their boards of trustees or directors, so as to include laymen and pastors and women, a wise combination which we believe will tend to a more widespread interest in and knowledge of the work of these important institutions.

We recommend finally that the formula for distribution of undesignated Children's Home funds be sent to the Dallas office, be studied by the benevolence committee of the Convention in cooperation with the four Children's Homes administrations and in counsel with the Executive Secretary for the purpose of an equitable distribution of these funds, based upon the needs of the four homes.

Source: *Minutes*, Executive Board of the Baptist General Convention of

Texas, 5 June 1956. Reprint courtesy of the Baptist General Convention of Texas.

C. Wadley Memorial Hospital

In the August 26 issue of the *Baptist Standard* the editor of the *Standard* wrote a lengthy editorial in opposition to the Baptist General Convention of Texas accepting Texarkana's magnificent Wadley hospital as a gift and an addition to the convention's already marvelous hospital ministry.

Feeling that the editor, in all good faith, does not wish to take the full responsibility for impeding the progress of that worthwhile and Christ-like-ministry, we have asked for equal space and equal position in the *Standard* to answer his editorial. He has very graciously accorded us the space and the position.

The editor of the *Standard* takes the position in his editorial that acceptance of the hospital would be a violation of the age-old Baptist principle of separation of church and state, basing his argument on the fact that Hill-Burton funds were used in the construction of the hospital.

Let us point out in the beginning that Wadley hospital was not constructed by the Baptists but by the people of Texarkana who realized the need of this city and its area for more hospital beds for the treatment of the sick and injured. It is true that Mr. and Mrs. J. L. Wadley, widely known Baptist philanthropists, contributed their time and their money in generous portion for the realization of this dream. Their contributions, however, were generously supplemented by the contributions of the Texarkanians of many denominations.

The fund-raising for the hospital was directed by the old Texarkana Hospital board; and as a matter of fact, some of the funds were derived from the sale of the old hospital and from the assets held by that institution. The Hill-Burton funds merely matched the contributions of the Texarkana people and the old hospital. The Baptist denomination was in no way involved in the action.

Because the people of Texarkana have observed with great satisfaction and admiration the hospital ministry of the Baptist General Convention of Texas, they chose the Baptists as the best qualified people to

administer the hospital and offer this magnificent plant and its personnel to the Convention as a bountiful gift with no strings attached.

A five-man committee, composed of some of the most outstanding
Baptist leaders in Texas were appointed by the convention's Hospital
committee to look over the Wadley hospital and to make a recommendation concerning the proposed gift. This committee, composed of Robert
Naylor, president of Southwestern Seminary; Frank Rayburn, legal counsel of the convention; E. H. Westmoreland, pastor of South Main Church
at Houston and a past president of the convention; H. K. Crawley, a
physician in Kilgore, and Vernon Elmore of San Antonio, investigated
the matter and unanimously recommended to the Executive board that
the hospital be accepted.

John Rasco, pastor of First church of Odessa and chairman of the
Hospital commission, has this to say about the gift:

"When the matter of the Texarkana hospital first arose, it was presented to the Hospital commission. It was my privilege to be a member
of the commission then, and from the first discussions of the Wadley
hospital I felt that it would be a wonderful opportunity for Texas Baptists and that it would be properly in keeping with the historic principles
to accept it from the PEOPLE OF TEXARKANA.

We are all cognizant of dangers involved in federal funds for many
interests of our committee. As I understand it, this is a different proposition. The people of Texarkana as a community group have built and
begun operation of a hospital. Now they offer it to Texas Baptists. It is
my conviction that we will be doing no wrong in accepting it for a Christian ministry of healing.

If we should go deep into the background of many other matters, we
might find ourselves more involved with the federal government than
many people seem to think we will become if we accept the Wadley
hospital.

One wrong would not justify another wrong. My position, therefore, is not based on this preceding statement but rather upon the simple
fact of the community offering to us a wonderful opportunity for a Christian ministry of healing."

Here is how Doctor Naylor feels about the gift:

"When we consider the question of accepting the Wadley hospital in Texarkana as a service and pressing opportunity for Texas Baptists, there is one point at which we are all agreed: We believe in the basic Baptist principle of separation of church and state. This is not lip service we pay, but it must be accepted as genuine if there is any basis for discussion.

These are the basic questions in determining whether or not this principle would be violated: What does the denomination benefit financially in areas of capital gains? Second, does the convention in receiving the hospital subject itself to government interference and control? Third, would the convention be bound to an irrevocable relationship if the fears of some proved well founded?

The answers to these are clear-cut in my mind. Texas Baptists would accept a financial obligation. The operation of hospitals costs money. It has been said again and again that the hospital would be put into our hands without strings. There would be no more government supervision than if we built the hospital ourselves. In the next place, it is clearly stated in every discussion that if we find ourselves compromised at any point we can immediately relinquish the hospital. In the light of these considerations, I feel that Texas Baptists should accept the hospital. May I add that I think we would be remiss in our obligation if we failed to do so as long as we give support to a hospital ministry in the earth."

Dr. Crawley says:

"After careful consideration of the editorial by Dr. James, I feel that he has failed in finding the point at hand. There would be no collusion between the Baptist General Convention of Texas and the federal government . . . and not a much-different situation . . . than calling the local fire department to control a fire in a non-taxpaying structure in case the church caught on fire."

Forrest C. Feezor, executive secretary of the Baptist General Convention of Texas, said:

"In my judgment you will be doing one of the finest things for the Baptist denomination you could do, and at the same time you will be adding to our facilities for caring for the sick. You have set aside $720,000 for hospital work in the proposed 1960 budget. It is entirely possible that the division of $720,000 would be enough and that no additional money will be needed from Cooperative Program funds."

James E. Coggin, pastor of First church of Texarkana:

"It is my conviction that there would be no violation of our Baptist principle of the separation of church and state in having our convention accept the Wadley hospital in Texarkana. This was a program initiated by the citizens of this area. The Baptists have made no requests of the federal government. These citizens have brought a great institution to us and asked us to become administrators of it. It is theirs to do with as they please. There are no government restrictions in regard to it. Neither would there be if we chose to accept it.

It will be tragic indeed to deprive the Baptists of this four-state area of this great ministry of healing. There is nothing that could so enhance the ministry of Baptists as this institution. What a tragedy it will be to lose such an opportunity on the basis of such a highly questionable subject.

Let us keep in mind that some of the greatest leaders of our convention feel that we are completely justified in acceptance of the hospital."

The Red River-Texarkana association has adopted a resolution favoring the acceptance of the hospital.

So we see this entire matter rests upon the decisions of the convention as to whose opinion it will follow: the opinion of the editor of the *Baptist Standard* in an extreme and, in our opinion, and unwarranted interpretation of our valued principle . . . or the opinion of an overwhelming majority of our denomination leaders in a reasonable interpretation of the principle.

The editor of the *Standard* intimates that the convention would be setting a dangerous precedent if it accepts the hospital. Agreeing with Doctor Rasco that two wrongs do not make a right, we nevertheless respectfully point out to the editor that when an extreme view is taken of this matter, the precedents are overwhelming.

If we followed the *Standard* editor's reasoning, it would be necessary, in order to preserve the separation of church and state, for the Baptists to render all of their churches and other property, municipal, county, and state taxes. It would be necessary to remind all givers of gifts to the church that they cannot in all good conscience accept deductions for income tax purpose. It would be necessary for our colleges to turn down all students who were there by virtue of government loans.

Shall we as Baptists busy ourselves with faulty unwarranted excuses for not doing the work of our Lord, or shall we throw ourselves enthusiastically into that work, filled with the fire of these words: "For as much as ye have done it unto one of the least of these, my brethren ye have done it unto me."

Source: J. Q. Mahaffey, "Texarkana's Wadley Hospital," *Baptist Standard*, 16 September 1959, 4–6. Reprint courtesy of the *Baptist Standard*.

D. A Hospital Decision

This I believe, the walls of the separation of church and state must be kept strong. Deteriorating influences must be resisted. To breach or destroy this wall will be to our hurt.

Therefore, I am positively in agreement with efforts to sustain our cherished Baptist position. Let me specify. A little while ago a physician called by long distance to ask, "If we apply, get government money, and build a hospital will Texas Baptists operate it." My answer was "No." Texas Baptists could not become a part of a plan to get government money to acquire an institution. The doctor went on to say that there was a Catholic hospital in his town and as a Baptist he could not conform to the requirements imposed. He said, "I'll have to move to some other city and start a practice there."

Texas Baptists are in the hospital business. This I believe, they are in the hospital business as a fulfillment of our Lord's pattern of life. "And Jesus went about healing all manner of sickness and all manner of disease among the people" (Matt. 4:23). We are motivated by the desire to help others.

We have not always operated hospitals. The late George W. Truett was the key factor in our entering the healing ministry. He made a plea for it, and Baylor hospital, Dallas, is the outcome. Doctor Truett believed in the spiritual ministry of the hospital. At one board meeting the convention obligated itself for a million dollars for Baylor's expansion.

Now, the convention has six additional hospitals. This desirable ministry has led the convention to make large capital investments in hospitals. On acquiring Memorial hospital in San Antonio, the convention agreed to add 100 beds. The cost of a hospital bed at that time was $10,000. The cost now is $18,000.

A decision faces the executive board at this point.

A modern hospital has been built in Texarkana. It is one of the most modern in the Southwest or nation. It was built by a community board of trustees with the aid of (1) private contributions, (2) a community campaign and (3) money given by the government. One Baptist couple, Mr. and Mrs. J. K. Wadley, gave in excess of $700,000 toward its construction. This couple are the donors of the Wadley Blood center in Dallas.

Through the influence, largely, of Mr. Wadley and his pastor, James Coggin, the hospital has been offered to the Baptist General Convention of Texas, fully equipped and without a dime of indebtedness. No other hospital has ever been so acquired without capital outlay.

Because these private trustees of the Texarkana Hospital, Inc. applied and received government money, there are those of our fellowship who feel that we would be violating the principle of the separation of church and state to accept their gift. There was appointed a committee, consisting of Robert Naylor, chairman, the late J. Howard Williams (replaced by E. H. Westmoreland) and Judge R. M. Ryburn, chairman of the deacons of First Church, Dallas, James K. Crawford, Kilgore, and Vernon Elmore of San Antonio.

After lengthy, careful study, this committee believes that in our accepting a hospital we would not be in violation of the principle of church and state. For one thing—no one ever encouraged or had any knowledge that the trustees were applying for government funds. It was done legally by a civic group of trustees. Had we been advised by them that they would build a hospital provided Texas Baptists would operate it, our answer would have been no.

The hospital has been offered to the convention. There have been no negotiations with any government agency. The committee, after long study, recommend its acceptance. Because of the church-state issue, the committee was asked to further study the matter. The committee has and is continuing its study. The report will be given October 1 to the executive board. If the board approves, the recommendation will go to the convention. Only the convention has the authority to accept new institutions.

Source: *Baptist Standard*, 16 September 1959, 6. Reprint courtesy of the *Baptist Standard*.

11.7 Booz, Allen, and Hamilton Report

> Due to the continued growth of all aspects of the BGCT, the accounting firm of Booz, Allen, and Hamilton was employed to examine the policies and procedures of the convention in 1957. They were then to propose a plan to streamline the work and make the convention more efficient on all fronts. When completed in 1959, the one-thousand-page report made several recommendations, some of which were enacted while others were ignored. This report demonstrated that the BGCT was one of the top 230 corporations in America and that it might have a financial base stronger than the Southern Baptist Convention.

A. Survey Report

A 51% membership and 130% giving increase reported by Texas Baptist churches during the past ten years are common among the nation's top religious growth statistics. Blessed by this unusual growth and faced with unparalleled opportunities, leaders from churches and areas of missionary work were asked by the Executive Board of our Convention in 1956 to make specific expansion plans for the next several years.

During 1957, it became more and more apparent that with the growth of Texas Baptist institutions and numerous requests for the admission of new ones, a thorough study should be made to determine how far the programs sponsored by the Baptist General Convention of Texas could be extended. The Hospital Commission started giving serious consideration to such a project. The Education Commission was thinking of a similar study. After conferences and discussions, it was decided that the most satisfactory approach to our planning task would be to make a study of the entire Texas Baptist program.

The Plans and Policies Committee was asked to give consideration not only to this proposal but also the employment of management consultants to assist in the study. On December 3, 1957, the committee brought its findings to the Executive Board and recommended the employment of the firm of Booz, Allen & Hamilton. The Board gave its approval.

At the time this action was taken, a committee charged with the responsibility of preparing and presenting a six-year program for the Baptist General Convention of Texas was already at work. It was enlarged to 25 members and asked to give direction to the contemplated survey of our Convention's work.

The membership of the committee constituted a cross-section of Texas Baptist life, with almost every geographical area and every phase of the work represented. It was made up of the following: T. A. Patterson, chairman; W. A. Criswell, Grady Metcalf, J. H. Landes, Charles Wellborn, W. M. Browing, Mrs. Clem Hardy, Lattimore Ewing, W. Fred Swank, A. J. Ballard, Mrs. Marie Mathis, H. E. Butt, Jr., Orba Lee Malone, L. L. Morriss, Gus Jackson, R. B. Smith, Groner Pitts, S. N. Reed, Elwin Skiles, W. L. Martin, W. M. Shamburger, C. E. Hereford, Vernon Elmore, Carroll B. Ray, and Rex Baker, Jr. Ex-officio members were Carl Bates (later replaced by M. B. Carroll) and E. Hermond Westmoreland.

Source: *Proceedings*, Baptist General Convention of Texas, 1959, 1. Reprint courtesy of the Baptist General Convention of Texas.

B. Texas Survey Committee: Preliminary Report

At the Louisville Convention, Southern Baptists adopted the report of their survey committee. Now that this has been completed and is ready for implementation, the next matter on the agenda for Texas Baptists is their own survey committee report which will be submitted, at least in part, to the state convention.

For 14 months a committee of 25, under the leadership of Dr. T. A. Patterson, has worked tirelessly on the survey of all Baptist work in this state. They have been ably assisted by the consultation firm of Booz, Allen, and Hamilton, and the findings of the consultants is under study by the sub-committees now. The report is long enough to fill five large volumes, and it is comprehensive enough to cover every phase of the Baptist endeavor. The editor has been asked to examine the report and make his observations known to the committee. Much of it is so technical and statistical that a great deal of time is required for a careful examination of it; but we hold that those who are going to make recommendations to Texas Baptists about their work in the future are obligated to give it their best thought and complete energy because that part of the report that shall be accepted by the convention may determine the course of Texas Baptists until the Lord shall come again.

After the committee has completed the studies and is ready for its recommendations, the substance of their conclusions will probably be published in the *Standard*. Until that time comes, all Texas Baptists are urged to make this a matter of much prayer. The report is tremendously important. The *Standard* expresses high appreciation for the extensive survey they have made and for many of their suggestions about our work in the future.

In many instances the Booz, Allen, and Hamilton report offers pertinent suggestions for the coordination and improvement of our organized endeavors. On the whole, it should be of a great value to the Patterson committee and the convention as they seek to filter the report and make their own decisions about what they desire to accept or reject. We have great confidence in the wisdom of the 25 persons on the Texas Baptist committee, and we believe enough in their integrity to express confidence now that they will make no recommendation unless they honestly believe it to be best for the future of the Baptist people of this state. The *Standard* looks forward to evaluating the findings of the committee.

Source: E. S. James, "Texas Survey Committee Report," *Baptist Standard*, 31 May 1959, 26. Reprint courtesy of the *Baptist Standard*.

C. A New General Administration Needed

> (1) <u>The Executive Board Should Be Responsible for Developing the Administrative Means of Achieving Convention Objectives</u>

The Executive Board's responsibilities for formulating objectives and program plans are the most important of its responsibilities. However, it should also be responsible for developing the administrative means of achieving Convention objectives.

To meet its responsibilities in the area of overall administration the Executive Board should:

- Select the executive secretary—the Convention's chief administrative officer—and define his functions and responsibilities.

- Establish the committees necessary to advise it on administrative affairs.

- Establish general personnel policies concerning the staff of the board and authorize the executive secretary to carry them out.

- Make certain that adequate program and budget planning procedures are followed and plans developed for each area.

- Establish financial policies looking toward adequate financial support of Convention programs and ample safeguard of financial resources.

- Recommend the allocation of undesignated financial resources of the Convention to broad program areas and to overall administrative purposes.

- Review annual reports of institutions for content and comparability before they are presented to the Convention. Evaluate progress of institutions in achieving denominational, community, and professional objectives and report on this progress to the Convention.

To meet its important responsibilities in these vital areas, the Executive Board should have the assistance of its committees, the executive secretary, and the service staff.

(2) The Program Coordinating Committee Should Be
    Responsible for Advising and Assisting the Executive
    Board in Coordinating the Work of the Convention
    in All Major Program Areas

The program coordinating committee of the Executive Board should be concerned with many key aspects of the administration of the Convention's work, including program and budget planning, program policies, administrative policies related to the conduct of programs, and the evaluation of program results and financial results.

Among the many responsibilities of the program coordinating committee should be those of:

- Formulating general policies for the conduct program.

- Formulating general personnel policies.

- Formulating criteria for the allocation of undesignated financial resources of the Convention, including the allocation of cooperative program funds.

- Formulating annual budgetary allocations of undesignated financial resources on a program basis.

- Reviewing plans and evaluating progress toward the achievement of goals in all program areas.

With these responsibilities, the committee is vitally concerned with the recommendations in this volume related to personnel administration, budgeting, and reporting.

(3) The Administration and Audit Committee Should Advise
and Assist the Executive Board on Administrative Matters

The Executive Board's administration and audit committee should be the group primarily responsible for advising the board on administrative matters.

The specific responsibilities of the administration and audit committee should be to:

- Formulate administrative policies, except personnel policies.

- Review and approve the accounting practices of the Executive Board.

- Foster the development and installation of sound accounting practices and adequate measures of internal financial control by all agencies of the Convention.

- Formulate auditing criteria and foster the effective use of competent public auditing firms.

- Review the annual audits to determine the soundness of financial operations.

- Appraise the treasurer's activities and work with him in strengthening the work of his department.

The administration and audit committee should act for the Executive Board in overseeing the administrative aspects of the activities of the Convention and its agencies, with particular emphasis on assuring that proper financial controls and audit reports are developed in every agency that is sponsored by the Convention.

It has been recommended that commissions be appointed to formulate policies and review programs in the state missions, educational, and human welfare areas. Similarly the administration and audit committee should act for the Executive Board in reviewing administrative matters. This does not mean that the committee should assume responsibilities that should be assigned to individual executives. The executives should have clear responsibility and authority for administering their work.

However, the committee should review and approve administrative policies and should satisfy itself that the policies are being put into practice. Accounting policies, purchasing policies, and staff transportation policies are among those for which the committee should be responsible. The treasurer should assist the committee in formulating these policies and should act as staff adviser to the committee, under the direction of the executive secretary.

The administration and audit committee should also employ certified public accountants for the annual audit of the Executive Board's accounts. The auditors should present their report to the committee, including appropriate comments on the adequacy of the system of internal control and whether the accounts are being properly maintained. At present, the auditors address their report to the Executive Board, but because the Executive Board is too large to review it adequately, the report is presented in practice to the staff. The auditors should continue to work closely with the treasurer and should follow their usual practices with respect to advising the staff of their findings, but both the formal written report and the informal oral report should be made to the committee.

The committee should also approve the auditors employed by the institutions and the other agencies that are sponsored by the Convention. The auditors should be selected primarily on the basis of professional competence in auditing nonprofit enterprises. The auditors of each institution and other Convention agencies should continue to report directly to the board of trustees of the institution. The administration of each institution or agency should forward two copies of the audit report and audited statements to the treasurer. One copy should be used in preparing the comparative and consolidated financial statements of the Convention, and the other should be used for analysis and review by both the services staff and the administration and audit committee.

Source: Booz, Allen, and Hamilton Report, Vol. 5, 3–8. Reprint courtesy of the Baptist General Convention of Texas.

D. In Perspective: The Booz, Allen, Hamilton Report

The Baptist General convention's executive board has just concluded a comprehensive survey. A committee of 25 conducted the survey with the aid of professional consultants. The committee made its report Oct. 1 and 2. On every hand there was enthusiastic joy at the revelations of the work of the committee.

The scope of the work covered our institutional life, our State missions activities and our benevolence operations, including hospitals and homes. In some respects Texas Baptists have a larger operation than the Southern Baptist Convention.

For one thing, we minister to more students than our six Southern Baptist Convention seminaries. Our hospital ministry serves more patients than our two south-wide and our foreign mission hospitals. Our hospitals' annual budget is 20 million dollars. We have more orphans under our care than in all foreign lands where Southern Baptists operate.

Moreover, our Baptist foundation administers more than 43 million dollars in behalf of our Texas and south-wide institutions. This does not amount to the funds operated by the Relief and Annuity board. However, the Relief and Annuity board has in its assets our Texas retirement funds. Surely, this I believe: any and all Texas Baptists may well be proud of the program of mission activities directed by the convention and its executive board.

The survey report suggests the strengthening of our missionary and administrative operations. At present some 22 different organizations must report to the executive secretary. To this are added many outside responsibilities with our institutional family of colleges, homes, and hospitals. This is humanly impossible for one man.

Moreover, one man has met the responsibilities as treasurer. It means the responsibility of nearly 12 million dollars per year to be handled according to the instructions of the board. Assistance will be provided for in this area.

This I believe: Texas Baptists are on the march. May our spirit be one of humility, simple trust in God's goodness, and steadfast loyalty to our Lord. The future is as bright as God's promise.

Source: Forrest Feezor, "This I Believe," *Baptist Standard*, 21 October 1959, 2. Reprint courtesy of the *Baptist Standard*.

CHAPTER 12

Onward and (Sometimes) Upward, 1960–1973

12.1 A New Day for Southern Baptists

For the first time in the history of the BGCT, the general growth of the organizations began to fall stagnant. Giving was on the decline, the Training Union was becoming more secular, there were not enough teachers for Vacation Bible School, and even the memberships of the local WMUs were falling. Television was now in the homes of most Americans. People were so enamored by television that they would watch whatever was on. In particular, Sunday afternoon professional football was hurting Sunday evening worship attendance. In addition, the Southern Baptist Convention was experiencing serious doctrinal debates that encompassed every aspect of the denomination.

A. You Can Help Reform TV

Now is the time for all the people who are agreed that too much television is rotten to swing into action. The road has been opened that can lead to reform of the industry.

Christians United for Responsible Entertainment (CURE) has been organized by some church leaders in Knoxville, Tenn. (Standard, June 24). They have a plan for petitions of protest to the stations, the networks, and finally to the advertisers who finance the junk. Lacking reform by the offending advertisers, petitioners will hit where it hurts in withholding their trade.

Television has been a major contributor to a decline in morals, an age of violence, and a thousand other sins. It loads its shows with scenes from the gutters of life. All this has made its impact or the industry must reverse its sales pitch to the advertisers. It is foolish to argue a commercial can increase sales and the next scene of violence lack in influence.

CURE is non-profit. Its staff is composed of volunteers. It needs the support of Christian groups across this nation.

The time has come to know that the industry is not going to cleanse itself. The Federal Communications Commission has been just as ineffective. But a hundred thousand or so people dedicated to protesting, and giving action to the protests, can win reforms.

Communicate with CURE, Box 9203, Knoxville, Tenn. 37920. Organize local groups and swing into action. Reward in our time goes to the vocal groups. Silence never won anything—or almost never.

Source: "You Can Help Reform TV," *Baptist Standard*, 31 July 1968, 6. Reprint courtesy of the *Baptist Standard*.

B. Crisis in the Churches

So much has been said about the crisis in national life, in institutional programs, and in other related areas that many have over-looked the most serious crisis of all, namely, the crisis of the churches. Perhaps it can be better understood by a few examples of what is happening in the state.

According to the study made by Charles Lee Williamson, in one metropolitan center population has increased approximately five percent per day during the last few years. Yet there has been among Baptists in that center a net loss of two churches.

Here is what has occurred the last few years in three strong churches.

Church A had 1,000 in Sunday school in 1960. This past year the average attendance was 900.

Church B averaged 1,900 in Sunday school in 1965. This past year the average attendance is 1,400.

Church C once had 1,300 in Sunday school. The figure has now dropped to 900.

This pattern is evident in many areas of the state. For the most part, the churches involved have been the life-blood of our denomination, for not only have they given strong support financially but they have helped in the establishing of new missions and churches. The convention owes it to these churches to do everything possible to encourage and to support them in their ministries.

In meeting this crisis, it is first of all necessary that we know it exists. Secondly, we need to talk more about evangelism, Christian teaching and training, and missionary outreach. Thirdly, we need to realize that the sums of money which we provide are inadequate to meet the needs of a rapidly expanding population.

Source: *Minutes*, Executive Board of the Baptist General Convention of Texas, 5 December 1969. Reprint courtesy of the Baptist General Convention of Texas.

12.2 Thomas Armour Patterson

Following thirty years as a pastor, Thomas Armour Patterson served as Secretary of the executive board from 1961 until 1973. Known as an administrative Executive Secretary, he spent a great deal of time advancing stewardship, church growth, and quarreling with E. S. James, the editor of the *Baptist Standard.* Forced to leave his position due to the BGCT's mandatory retirement age of 68, Patterson continued to influence missions and evangelism by accepting a position as the executive Vice-President of Dub Jackson's World Evangelism Foundation in Dallas.

A. Stewardship and Financial Development: Interview with Thomas Charlton

Patterson: Well, some of those administrators looked at us in anger and they said, "Where do you think we'd get the money to pay a development man?" We said to them, "If he's worth his salt he'd pay his own salary in no time at all." And so finally we sold every institution on a development program. I say, "we," the major responsibility goes to O. D. Martin. Mine was a supportive role. I was saying to him, "Go after it. This is what we want to do."

Now, I don't suppose the institutions, if you were to ask any of the leaders today, know that I was in back of promoting that. I gave more time to that than I did to evangelism.

Charlton: How did you work with O. D. Martin in working with this?

Patterson: I went with him in meetings of one kind or another. I sat down oftentimes with these administrators. I gave every encouragement through the Standard and every other that I possibly could and said, "This is the one thing we need to do."

Now, the colleges and universities are bringing in eighteen to twenty million dollars a year. On top of that, Bob Longshore has brought in this recommendation on the student foundation which has proved a great blessing. You're about it down at Baylor. And, to me, I feel that this was the major contribution I was able to make to the institutions.

Charlton: This is very interesting.

Patterson: But, nobody knows it.

Charlton: Then, you're saying that in the area of stewardship and financial development that this was a conscious effort you made that was, perhaps, unseen.

Patterson: That's right. I don't think it was known, and, after all, I don't guess it needs to be. Why go around and try to tell everybody? I spent more time traveling with Cecil Ray than I ever did with Wade Freeman of the Evangelism Division. Cecil Ray and I traveled hundreds and thousands of miles together in Texas. We'd meet with pastor groups and explain to them what the cooperative program was and why we ought to have it and let them ask questions we would answer in an effort to try to get across the cooperative program. I spent more time there than any other area.

Charlton: That's very interesting.

Patterson: But, you ask almost any person in Texas, he doesn't now that and he'd find it hard to believe.

Charlton: Do you believe it was because, perhaps, the Baptist Standard did not tell the people of Texas that this was one of your major emphases?

Patterson: Well, I guess two things: I didn't have a public relations man who would handle it; and in the second place, I was interested in getting the job done—not particularly interested in getting credit.

Charlton: Was this the kind of work that should have been kept quiet in any way?

Patterson: No, no. In fact, I think it would have been better if it had been known, as I think back to it now, because it might have given a better concept of what we were trying to do in the total program by Texas Baptists.

Charlton: Then, as you see your years as Executive Secretary, evangelism and stewardship stand out in your mind?

Patterson: Those were the major areas.

Charlton: I'm so glad you corrected me and included the latter.

Patterson: Yes. Those two go together. They're very close and you nearly have to have both of them because you can't operate institutions without money.

Source: *Oral Memoirs of Thomas Amour Patterson, A Series of Interviews Conducted August 1971– November 1976*, Thomas L. Charlton Interviewer. Texas Baptist Oral History Consortium, Printed Copy, 1978, in Roberts Library, Southwestern Baptist Theological Seminary, Fort Worth Texas, 226–28. Reprint courtesy of the Patterson family.

B. Working Relationships: Interview with Thomas Charlton

Charlton: Numerous persons have recorded and written and stated verbally, that the chief difference between Dr. Feezor as Executive Secretary, and you, as Executive Secretary, was that Dr. Feezor was much more interested in spiritual topics and that you were more the administrator, while, at the same time, you were interested in spiritual affairs as well. Is this a fair or correct assessment of the change that occurred in the office of Executive Secretary?

Patterson: Well, I don't know. Perhaps some people might not think of me as a strong administrator. It depends on your view of administration. I always felt that you ought to allow as much liberty as you possibly can to the people that work for you—work on the staff, because there's no purpose to bringing them on the staff if you're not going to allow them some freedom to develop their own particular abilities. If you go rubber-stamp everything, why bring them on the staff? I enlist them because they have something distinctive to contribute. And, I tried to allow as much freedom as possible to those who served on the staff.

Charlton: This is what I was asking, Dr. Patterson, did you have more of an eye for administrative detail than Dr. Feezor had?

Patterson: Well, I don't know, others would have to judge that.

Charlton: Well, I'm really asking, as you look back upon that period of transition.

Patterson: Well, I would simply say this, I do not see how on earth Dr.

Feezor got the job done. And I finally came to the conclusion that it was due to two things: he had an able associate in Woody Fuller who was then Associate Executive Secretary and turned over much of the work to him. Dr. Feezor himself was a strong man of prayer.

Charlton: As you became Executive Secretary, you, of course, were required to relate to the other persons in the Baptist Building such as Dr. E. S. James, as editor of the Standard and the secretaries of the commissions. I wonder if you might comment on the first period of time, perhaps the first year or so, as you settled into your new position and began to relate to the other commissions and agencies of the BGCT. For example, what about your relationship with Dr. James.

Patterson: I had, on the whole, a very good relationship with Dr. James. He, of course, is a strong individualist, as you know. I had great respect for him. And I think toward the close of his career as editor of the Baptist Standard, that perhaps we had a closer relationship than ever before. Now, there was a difference in our points of view but I always believed, though he was a journalist, he was a Christian first and I always believed that, to his best judgment, he would put his Christian concepts first, if he violated certain journalist principles.

Charlton: As Executive Secretary did you ever make any suggestions concerning editorial thrust or content of the Standard or any related subjects to Dr. James?

Patterson: We talked about some things and I at times gave him information. But Dr. James was not the person that you could make a suggestion to. For example, this is the difference in the way we operate, I'd write an article and hand it to my secretary and I'd tell her, "If I've got a misspelled word in there I want you to correct it if you find it. If I've got an error in punctuation, straighten it out. If there's a phrase that needs to be changed, you change it." If Dr. James had a secretary to do that he'd fire her. It's got to be just like he told her. So, you don't tell a man like Dr. James, or suggest to a man like Dr. James, what he should do and what he shouldn't do. Now, this is our difference in point of view, which I think he frankly recognized. He didn't think my column ought to be in the nature of an editorial.

Source: *Oral Memoirs of Thomas Armour Patterson, A Series of Inter-*

views Conducted August 1971–November 1976, Thomas L. Charlton, Interviewer. Texas Baptist Oral History Consortium, Printed Copy, 1978, in Roberts Library, Southwestern Baptist Theological Seminary, Fort Worth, Texas, 196–98. Reprint courtesy of the Patterson family.

12.3 Board and Budgets

The Executive Board of the BGCT was composed of 180 ministerial and lay members from all walks of Baptist life. The primary tasks of the Executive Board were to select an Executive Secretary, ratify policy, and approve fiscal budgets. Since the majority of the major decisions facing Texas Baptists were made by committees, certain members of the Board felt as if they were nothing more than a sounding board or rubber-stamp. A study was approved and it was decided that Board members would be given committee reports well before meetings and new members would be provided with orientation. The study, however, also indicated that churches where Executive Board members held membership had experienced a dramatic decrease in Cooperative Program giving. Furthermore, the BGCT failed to meet its budget for the first time in 1961. Though more money was being given to the BGCT, it often failed to meet budget goals in the 1960s.

Committee on Executive Board Involvement

The Committee was appointed by the Executive Board Chairman, Travis Barry, at the March meeting of the Executive Board. The following were named to the Committee:

> Charles Kelly, Beaumont
> Lamoin Champ, Burkburnett
> Lester Collins, Houston
> R. W. Eades, Hereford
> Gordon Bays, Austin (Chairman)

The Committee was instructed to study and bring recommendations on the following two areas of Executive Board involvement:

1. Find ways for the Executive Board members to be more involved in the decision-making process.

2. Find ways for Executive Board members to better represent the Executive Board and the Convention to the Associations and the

churches—this involves specifically the support of the Cooperative Program.

The Committee has had one meeting. All committee members were present. Travis Berry, Cecil Ray, and Bob McGinnis were invited to serve as resource persons. The Committee wishes to gratefully acknowledge the help of these three men.

The following information serves as a background for the committee's initial recommendations.

1. A study of Cooperative giving of the churches of Executive Board members, Commission members, and churches in general reveals that:

   38% of churches in Texas have made a percentage increase in their Cooperative Program giving for the years 1968–1971.

   26% of churches represented by Executive Board members made an increase in their percentage. (50% of the churches represented by Executive Board members show a decline.)

   18% of the churches represented by Convention officers, PCC, and the Commission members (77 churches involved) made a percentage increase (and 61% made a percentage decline).

   ("Percentage" is used in these references as referring to the percentage of the total church income. The causes for these variations are many, but one thing it clearly indicates is the <u>urgent need</u> of a <u>leadership</u> commitment.)

2. A study of the Cooperative giving of the churches, (1925–1971) reveals that 1967 was a turning point in Cooperative giving and that the percentage of church income channeled through the Cooperative Program is in decline to the point that a "turning around" is imperative.

The committee listed the major factors causing this trend as:

   (1) The squeeze of inflation on the church,
   (2) A generation of leaders who feel no part of the Cooperative Program,
   (3) Pastor-laymen conflicts in denominational life,

(4) People tend to equate feelings about the Convention with their feelings toward the Federal government,

(5) Reaction over institutions,

(6) Problems of communication,

(7) Crisis in the churches,

(8) Lack of information and understanding by the pastors.

But regardless of the factors causing the trend, leadership that will champion Cooperative Program giving is essential to reversing the trend.

The Committee recommends:

1. That the Executive Board of the Baptist General Convention of Texas reaffirm its commitment to the Cooperative Program as Baptists' most effective method of jointly supporting its total ministries and that the Board adopt for itself the task of promoting its total ministries and that the Board adopt for itself the task of promoting the Cooperative Program, and that the Board encourage the renewed loyalty, understanding, and active involvement of each Board member in behalf of Cooperative Program support.

2. That the members of this Board host meetings of pastors and laymen during the immediate months ahead (June–September). These group meetings will be scheduled, planned and promoted by the Executive Board members, and to which he or she invites a group of pastors and laymen. The purpose will be to discuss the total ministry needs of the Convention and to encourage renewed support of the Cooperative Program.

The Committee has asked Cecil Ray, Director of Stewardship Division, to assist the members with the presentation of the total Baptist ministries. Cecil Ray will attend or enlist either another staff member or the help of Missionaries, Grayson Tennison (for June-August) and James Teel (beginning in August).

The Committee emphasizes the responsibility of Board members to initiate these meetings and feels that the degree to which this is done is a measuring stick of the seriousness with which you act on these recommendations.

This is a partial report. The Committee anticipates a full report at the September Board meeting. At that time the Committee will speak specifically to the first of our two assignments and perhaps make further recommendations with regard to the second.

Source: *Minutes*, Executive Board of the Baptist General Convention of Texas, 30 May 1972. Reprint courtesy of the Baptist General Convention of Texas.

12.4 The Commissions

The Executive Committee accomplished its work through four commissions: State Missions, Christian Education, Human Welfare, and Christian Life. Each area of the BGCT's various ministries was classified as a division and placed in the Commission most appropriate to the nature of its work. Each commission, however, was not equal in standing. The State Missions and Christian Education Commissions were clearly the most prominent, while the Christian Life Commission and the Human Welfare Commission were considered secondary.

A. State Missions Commission

Created in 1958, the State Missions Commission worked closely with the local churches. It was composed of eleven divisions encompassing virtually all aspects of church life and evangelism.

1. Church Services Division

OBJECTIVES:

The objectives of the Church Services Division are to strengthen the work of Texas Baptist churches and missions through the Sunday School Training Union and Church Music programs. The division strengthens these programs through coordination, planning and evaluation.

PROGRAM SERVICES:

There are four program services which the division provides for the churches: (1) Develop materials, training opportunities and field services to assist the churches in establishing and strengthening church library work; (2) Provide materials and assistance to the churches in the program of church recreation; (3) Make available counsel and material to the churches in the church administration program; (4) Serve as a liaison between the Baptist General Convention of Texas and the 23 Baptist encampments.

MAJOR ACCOMPLISHMENTS, 1968

- Planned and conducted 3 camp leadership training conferences with 110 attending, representing 16 encampments.
- Planned and conducted 3 regional church library conventions with 505 workers in attendance. Helpful material, counsel and leadership in library work were furnished to 316 churches. 119 new church libraries were established during the year.
- Worked with the Church Library Department of the Sunday School Board in preparation for a Free Library Offer to be made available especially to Latin-American congregations. Assisted a selected Latin-American leader to attend Church Library Week at Glorieta for service as a library consultant. Assisted two Latin-American congregations in establishing a church library.

MAJOR GOALS, 1969

- Continue to develop strong relationships with the School of Religious Education at Southwestern Baptist Theological Seminary.
- Help establish 75 new church libraries.
- Assist 100 churches in the area of church administration.
- Provide program assistance to the 23 Baptist encampments with an attendance goal of 100,000 for the summer of 1969.
- Help relate the total resources of the Church Services Division to strengthen the Crusade of the Americas program.

Source: *Proceedings*, Baptist General Convention of Texas, 1968, 174. Reprint courtesy of the Baptist General Convention of Texas.

2. Sunday School Division

MAJOR ACCOMPLISHMENTS IN 1968

Three state Vacation Bible School clinics for associational leadership with 84 associations and 441 workers. Incomplete reports indicate a total of 2,270 Vacation Bible Schools held with enrollment of 518,173;

$49,103.11 gifts to the cooperative program and 8,264 professions of faith.

Conducted 18 Regional Sunday School Bible Conferences with more than 900 churches and 105 associations represented, with a total attendance of 5,000.

Three elementary workshops, training 842 Sunday School workers, representing 40 associations and 222 churches. Trained 1,230 Sunday School workers in 4 Adult Outreach Clinics, involving 30 associations and 200 churches.

Trained 90 Invincibles and student summer missionaries to conduct 188 Vacation Bible Schools with 14,434 enrolled and 934 won to Christ.

Conducted 32 Evangelism-Sunday School conferences in associations in cooperation with the Division of Evangelism.

Provided 6 one-night workshops in Minnesota-Wisconsin with all three associations represented, 28 churches represented and 353 in attendance. Provided additional one-night clinics in 4 associations, 53 churches represented, training 450 Sunday School workers.

Planned and assisted in conducting the Crusade of the Americas Rallies in 114 associations, 72 associations reporting 16,961 in attendance.

Conducted 7 Associational Enlargement Campaigns involving 62 churches and identifying 11,278 prospects. Participating churches made plans to begin 64 new departments, 112 new classes and enlisted 295 new workers.

MAJOR PROGRAM EMPHASES FOR 1969

Promote major use of the Sunday School in the Crusade of the Americas.

To promote the planning and conducting for associational witnessing campaigns.

Provide a major thrust for the enlargement of the Sunday Schools. Lead in organizing 100 new Sunday Schools.

Mobilize for the improvement of teaching in the Sunday School. Lead 3,000 Sunday School workers to attend Glorieta Sunday School Week.

Continue to give major attention to strengthen the love of the Bible and place of the Sunday School in the work of the churches.

Source: *Proceedings*, Baptist General Convention of Texas, 1968, 175. Reprint courtesy of the Baptist General Convention of Texas.

3. Church Music Division

OBJECTIVES: The objective of the Church Music Department is to assist churches in establishing, conducting, enlarging and improving a music program which

(1) teaches music to members

(2) trains persons to lead, sing and play music

(3) provides music in the church and community

(4) provides and interprets information regarding the work of the church and denominations.

MAJOR ACCOMPLISHMENTS

EVANGELISM CONFERENCE—Planned the music for the Evangelism Conference featuring the Texas Baptist Ministers of Music, Jo Anne Shelton, Robert Hale and Dean Wilder.

CHURCH MUSIC FESTIVALS—Assisted in promotion and conducting 135 Associational Music Festivals representing 81 associations and 500 churches with a total participation of 30,944.

STATE YOUTH CHOIR FESTIVALS—Conducted nine State Youth Choir Festivals, eight State Hymn Playing Festivals with 7,140 participants.

STATE CHILDREN'S CHOIR FESTIVALS—Conducted nine State Children's Choir Festivals and three State Children's Choir Retreats with a total participation of 6,500.

CHOIR ENROLLMENT—The department is happy to report another year of increased enrollment with 167,381 enrolled in the music program of Texas Baptist churches.

CAMPS AND WORKSHOPS—Conducted Highland Lakes Music Camp and Paisano Music Camp with a total participation of 746. Conducted five Regional Music Leadership Workshops with a total enrollment of 273.

RETREAT FOR MINISTERS OF MUSIC—Conducted one retreat for full-time ministers of music.

LATIN AMERICAN WORK—Assisted in planning and conducting the Music Conference at the Mexican Baptist Department Convention, which 200 persons attended, and assisted with music arrangements for the Mexican Baptist Convention in Fort Worth. Plans have been launched for a statewide Latin American Music Festival, April 6–7, 1973. Published the leaflet "El Himno Del Mes."

Source: *Proceedings*, Baptist General Convention of Texas, 1972, 186–87. Reprint courtesy of the Baptist General Convention of Texas.

4. Language Division

Cruzado Bautista Nueva Vida

Texas Baptists are stewards of the gospel for a mission field within her own borders of over two million Spanish speaking neighbors. There are 475 Spanish speaking Baptist congregations with a membership of 30,000.

In September and October, 1964, there will be an evangelistic crusade to reach every Latin American in Texas with the gospel of Jesus Christ. Five to six hundred revivals are anticipated. 1,000 laymen from Anglo churches and 500 laymen from Latin American churches will be needed. Radio, television, newspaper coverage will be used extensively as funds permit.

A 16mm color movie of the 1964 Crusade is available from the Language Missions Department.

Church Development

Church development programs are designed to encourage and accelerate the growth of Latin American missions to become self-supporting churches to win the Latin Americans to faith in Christ.

Salary support is provided for 225 missionary pastors and 15 kindergarten workers serving Latin American congregations.

Financial assistance is provided for building needs in strategic locations where there is a heavy concentration of Latin American population. Three congregations have been assisted with loans in the amount of $22,500.00. Churches at Eagle Pass, El Paso and Rio Hondo have received cash gifts for new buildings.

A magazine in Spanish, EL BAUTISTA MEXICANO, is published monthly and sent to approximately 3,000 Spanish speaking homes. The magazine reports news and information about all Southern Baptist work as well as news about local events in Spanish speaking churches.

Baptist Standard subscriptions are provided for 3,500 Spanish speaking homes.

Literature for W. M. U. and its youth organization is edited, published and distributed.

Leadership Training

Staff personnel in the Language Missions Department promote the programs of the Evangelism Division, Stewardship Division, Church Services Division and W. M. U. These programs are translated into Spanish, adapted to the needs of the Latin American congregations and presented to pastors and local leadership through area conferences and clinics.

Budget responsibility for the Mexican Bible Institute, San Antonio, and the Valley Baptist Academy in Harlingen is in the Language Missions Department. The Bible Institute trains Spanish speaking ministers who are not prepared for seminary study. This is the only such school for training Spanish speaking missionaries in the homeland. The Valley Baptist Academy provides Christian education on a high school level to Spanish speaking students who otherwise would be denied the privilege of a high school education.

A program of ministerial scholarships was begun in the fall of 1963, jointly supported by the Language Missions budget and a gift from Texas W. M. U. Mary Hill Davis Offering. Seven students were granted scholarships, ten applications are being processed.

Evangelism

LA HORA BAUTISTA is broadcast weekly over stations in El Paso, San Antonio and Harlingen. Leo Estrada is the evangelist. These stations have a potential audience of a million listeners.

A ministry is maintained for the Japanese through a program of visitation evangelism conducted on a regular basis by a Japanese pastor.

Converts are enlisted in the local English-speaking churches. There were ten saved this year.

A ministry to the deaf is maintained through salary support of a pastor to serve the state school for the deaf in Austin and the deaf congregation of the local church. An annual conference is conducted for the deaf and for the interpreters who minister to the deaf in the local churches. An annual camp is sponsored for the deaf youth.

Work among the Chinese is supported in El Paso, San Antonio and Houston.

Future Strength

Increased emphasis will be given to providing better building facilities. Good progress is being made but is painfully slow in many areas. Local support for needed buildings often is inadequate. Help can be given in two ways. A church or association can guarantee loans and assist with the monthly payments.

A language school to teach Spanish to Anglo volunteers for Latin American missions is a primary need. At present there is not such a language school in the United States. The Mexican Baptist Bible Institute is working with the Language Missions Department and the Home Mission Board in the development of a proposal for a language school as a part of the program of the Institute.

Source: *Proceedings*, Baptist General Convention of Texas, 1963, 212–13. Reprint courtesy of the Baptist General Convention of Texas.

5. The Area Program

In 1963 the Executive Board appointed a large Missions Study Committee under the leadership of W. E. Denham to examine the geographical divisions in the sub-structure of Texas Baptist organizational life. This committee reported to the Convention in 1963 that there was an imbalance in the "District" structure that had been developed about thirty years before. The Convention adopted their recommendation that associations group themselves into smaller units called Areas (one to four associations to an Area) with from fifty to one hundred churches in each Area (except in larger cities) and a resident membership of from 12,000 to 18,000 per area. A missionary would be secured for each Area. The

Convention noted that this plan would have to be developed over a period of several years, depending on the needs and initiative of the individual associations. It was agreed that the State Board would continue its financial policies with all associations and districts as long as these groups so desired or until the Area plan was adopted by a given Area or until there was a vacancy in personnel.

In 1964 it was reported to the Convention that the State Missions Commission had been working to implement the changeover from the District plan to the Area plan. In 1968 there were thirty-nine functioning Areas, each with a missionary, constituting over eighty-five percent of the Baptist churches in Texas.

Source: R. A. Baker, *The Blossoming Desert: A Concise History of Texas Baptists* (Waco: Word Books, 1970), 261.

B. The Christian Education Commission

The primary task of the Christian Education Commission was to centralize the work of the 8 Baptist colleges, one academy, 26 Bible Chairs at state universities, and 80 statewide Baptist Student Unions in order to avoid duplication of the educational work. With the greatest share of program money, the CEC was a powerful organization that was responsible for administering scholarships and grants to the Baptist schools of higher education. The CEC also authorized the infamous Carden Report of 1967. The purpose of the Carden Report was to provide a detailed analysis of the Baptist schools, describe their needs, present the cost for their improvements, and hopefully promote further giving to these institutions. The report turned out to be quite radical and was prematurely disseminated to a few trustees and educators before it had been examined by the Education Commission. The report was considered controversial and none of the suggestions were implemented.

1. Carden Report Proposes Cutback to Four Colleges

The Carden Report which is to have a year's study before any presentation to the Baptist General Convention of Texas concerning the future of the state's nine Baptist colleges recommends:

1. Howard Payne College at Brownwood and Wayland College at Plainview be sold to proposed tax districts and thereby separated from the convention.

2. East Texas Baptist College at Marshall shall be a "special pur-

pose junior college" primarily for those studying for religious vocations.

3. The University of Corpus Christi be given an "independent self-perpetuating" board and "allowed to determine its own future."

4. Mary Hardin-Baylor College for women be placed under the administrative control of Baylor University and at the end of two years its future reevaluated.

5. Hardin-Simmons University at Abilene drop its graduate program with some exceptions.

Coordinating Board

Additionally, the report proposed a Coordinating Board for the entire educational system which would "be largely a policy making organization" directed by a chancellor. Local trustees would be continued for the remaining institutions: Baylor University, Dallas Baptist College, Houston Baptist College, Hardin-Simmons University, and East Texas Baptist College in its new role.

Carden recommended that the convention reverse its policy and permit "government loans for buildings and government grants for equipment and programs." He suggested conditions which he said would keep the institutions free of government control.

Consistent in Policy

The convention has been consistent in its policy of prohibiting government grants. It reiterated in 1966 its policy against loans, turning down a committee recommendation which would have permitted them.

The recommendations were made in a voluminous report submitted through the Education Commission which had employed William R. Carden, Jr., for a year's analyses of the schools. The report now is in the hands of the committee of 12 (Standard, July 31) which is to report within a year. Homer Dean of Alice, an attorney, is committee chairman.

The committee report with recommendations presumably will go to the commission which would have recommendations for the convention at its session in 1969.

The report, which consists of 62 pages will be distributed to trustees of all the colleges. These pages include statistical tables concerning budgets, student enrollments, faculty salaries, and related items. Special sessions concerning each of the institutions will be added for transmission to the concerned institutions.

Carden introduced his report with a description of the problem ahead. Pointing to increased student enrollment, he said if Baptist institutions are to maintain 33 percent of Texas private school enrollments, they must grow from 22,352 students to 30,246 in three years, a greater increase than in the last decade. He added the situation would become more acute each year.

Carden centered on the budget problems, including inflation and larger appropriations for state schools.

"The cost squeeze from external factors has hit the Texas Baptist schools at the same time they had been faced with a declining percentage of gifts from the Baptist General Convention of Texas," he said. He explained that 26 percent of the convention income went to the schools in 1959 but that now the figure is only 21.6 percent. Dollar gifts increased, but percentages declined.

Critical of Expansion

Carden was critical of expansion in buildings at the schools without "sufficient consideration of the overall place of the facility in the educational program of the institutions and the flexibility of the building as regards the changing demands that will be made upon it in future years."

Carden said Baylor needed an endowment 10 times its $21 million and other schools had similar deficiencies. Student costs, he said, are as high as they can go except possibly at Baylor and Dallas. He also was critical of what he called a "premium price" charged students in all institutions without "first-class service."

The report then raised the question of a convention decision of "limited [financial] resources among nine" schools, an increased Baptist student ministry on other campuses, or both. He added that 700,000 students on Texas campuses by 1980 "constitutes the greatest mission field for Texas Baptist work."

Carden said the Texas Baptist colleges face a "quality gap" of $10 million in their annual operating budgets. He added that $15 million was needed for construction.

Optimistic Note

He sounded his optimistic note before turning to about 40 pages of statistics and recommendations:

"This is a grim picture, but there is much that it does not take into account. It omits, to begin with, the fact that there are some first-class students attending Texas Baptist colleges, and some first-rate faculty to instruct them. No institution, however small and poor, is not without a core of competent faculty and students. There are not now enough of either to convert the Baptist colleges into the institutions they must become, but there are some, and they constitute a foundation upon which to build."

Source: *Baptist Standard*, 7 August 1968, 3. Reprint courtesy of the *Baptist Standard*.

2. Defending the Carden Report

The Christian Education Commission of the Baptist General Convention of Texas was established in its present form when the Convention adopted the report of its Survey Committee in 1959. The Commission consists of fifteen Texas Baptists, both laymen and ministers, so ordered that at no time can there be less than six laymen or six ministers on the Commission. The relationship of the Christian Education Commission to the Convention and to the Texas Baptist schools is essentially one of serving as both a coupling and a buffer between the Convention and the schools. The necessity for such a dual relationship can be emphasized by noting three prime areas in which it is possible for misunderstanding to arise between the Convention and its schools.

Local School Autonomy and Division of Authority

A natural area of potential conflict exists in relating the local autonomy of the school and the authority of the Convention. On one hand the trustees and the school feel that the authority is properly placed with the local trustees; on the other hand the Convention feels that the schools are Convention institutions, and the Convention thus has some right to say what it expects of them. The Convention officially exercises its authority through the election of trustees, the approval of charters, and various other controls spelled out by the Survey Committee in its report.

There arises between these two ideas, then, a continuous possibility of conflict between what we might call the two supposed absolutes. The Education Commission has the responsibility of trying to relate the two to each other, resolve the misunderstandings, and promote an understanding that will keep right relationships between the schools and the Convention.

It is sometimes asked if the Commission's business is not representing the Convention but seeing that schools do what they ought to do. The Commission does not consider that this is its prime responsibility. The Commission has responsibility to the Convention since it was elected by it; at the same time the Commission cannot be faithfully responsible to the Convention without feeling an equal responsibility toward the schools. Thus, the Education Commission is a buffer and a coupling in relationship to matters of difference that arise from seeming conflict of the two absolute ideas as to the locus of authority.

Needs of the School and Limited Understanding of the Convention

The second area of potential conflict is that which involves the needs of the schools on one hand and the limited understanding of the Convention on the other. Dealing with great groups of people it is difficult to always get across many detailed items. The Convention wants a program of Christian Education, and the Commission is charged with the responsibility of such a development. The schools want that, too, but are deeply conscious of the economic barriers to such a development, and they are conscious of many other problems that lie in the pathway of the development of a Convention program, while at the same time realizing that looking to the needs of our schools hinders such development. The faculty salary increase plan which provides a definite system for all schools to increase salaries equitably rather than a hit or miss plan for each school to do as it desires, is illustrative of the type of action the Commission feels is absolutely essential if the Convention's ideal of a program of Christian Education is to be realized. It is one thing to say, "This we must have." It is another thing to say, "These are the implements by which this must come about." It then becomes the task of the Education Commission to provide these implements and lead in the utilization of them.

Texas Baptists must know the needs of their schools in regard to student body, physical facilities, and faculty requirements. The Crusade for Christian Education ought to be a clear indication that the Christian Education Commission is concerned vitally about the basic needs of our schools as they now exist. The Crusade is a measure to lead our state to contribute the $28,000,000 needed now for physical facilities of our schools, and also an effort to lead our people to such a deeper appreciation of our schools that we will also give them the finest of our young people and undergird them with our prayers. The Crusade is further designed to lead our schools to a stronger realization of belonging to the Convention. Texas Baptists must become conscious of the program of Education—Christian education—being carried out through the institutions that we call our schools.

Convention Purposes and Texas Baptist Schools

The third area of concern for the Christian Education Commission involves the purposes of the Convention in having these schools. Texas Baptists have definite spiritual and moral purposes to be realized through their schools. It is sometimes thought that these purposes are in conflict with the aim of academic excellence. These conflicts will always exist to some degree. There are some people who feel that every class ought to be an evangelistic service; others feel that the school as an educational institution should be concerned entirely with the achievement of academic excellence.

There are people who feel that they can send a regular, rebellious, maladjusted young person to one of our colleges and that the college is obligated to turn that person out as a perfect Christian gentleman, thoroughly oriented as to life, its purposes, and the ways of carrying them out. If for some reason the schools cannot do that, then, according to the interpretation of the parents, they are missing the mark completely. There is a certain degree of validity in this viewpoint. There ought to be something on our campuses and in our classrooms and in fellowship with the faculty that will make a vital contribution to the improvement of the spiritual and moral ideas and practice of every person. Most of those who are leading in the classrooms are in agreement with that concept! Yet, even the most dedicated Christian faculty member is apt to feel resentment when he is told in effect, "Forget about academic excellence. Just work on this lad of mine to see if you can make a gentleman out of him."

Texas Baptist schools are in the awkward position in one sense of the word of being both an educational institution and a church-related institution. The Education Commission feels very keenly the problem of making the Convention aware of the necessity for academic excellence. For example, no one wishes our schools to turn out public school teachers who are not, as far as institutional training is concerned, qualified to stand in the classrooms of our public schools. We hope that they will be top-notch Christian people, but they can't do the job if they have not received a good education, or are sadly lacking in academic achievement. We want Christian people as products of our schools, but if deepened spiritually is all they receive, we are failing in our ministry as educational institutions.

On the other hand, if our schools turn out educated people without Christianity, we are failing in our ministry as a denomination. While high quality instruction is essential, the overall development of Christian belief, the increasing of Christian dedication, and the total commitment to Christian life are both goals and represent characteristics which must always be an integral part of our campuses and our college life. This, then, is a part of the business of the Christian Education Commission—trying to bring together an understanding of the educational ideal of academic excellence and the Convention's spiritual and moral purposes in having these schools! I do not see that there is necessarily a conflict if we can realize that we are working in the same direction.

Texas Baptists must understand that in our colleges, universities, and academy we are working toward the development of Christian leaders for both our denomination and for our world, and that our schools are a vital means in the realization of both of these ideals.

Now, it is easily seen that the Education Commission works for the Convention, and works for the schools. It is the Commission's hope to bring the two into such a relationship that there will be a support of our schools unlike anything that any of us have ever dared to dream would come about. It is going to have to be, or what Baptists want in these schools can never become a reality.

Be assured of this: The Education Commission interprets its job as being a friend of the schools as well as a servant of the Convention.

Source: *Report of the Christian Education Commission and the Ministerial Aid Study Committee*, 14 November 1963, 72–74. Reprint courtesy of the Christian Education Commission.

3. Crusade for Christian Education

The years of 1961 and 1962 are a period of outstanding significance to the Texas Baptist colleges, universities, and academy of Texas and through them to the entire denomination. Education is now more important than ever due to the prevailing world condition.

Texas Baptist Crusade for Christian Education

Since the memorable decision at the 1960 Convention to approve the $28,000,000 campaign for buildings and equipment, the scope of the program has been enlarged. It has gradually become a Crusade for all phases of Christian Education. Thus, the overall purpose has increasingly become the improvement of the entire denominational program through the development of trained leadership.

That which started merely as a campaign for funds has taken on all of the characteristics of a Crusade: a Crusade that calls for the largest recruitment program of all time: the recruitment of students for Baptist schools, the enlistment of Baptist students in BSU programs, and the dedication of Baptist youth to vocational Christian service: A Crusade that calls for scholastic excellence, a general upgrading of our schools academically and above all a deepening of the spiritual resources and attitudes among staffs, faculties, students and Baptist constituencies. Pastors, church staff members, parents, Sunday School teachers, BSU directors, college faculty members, and young people themselves are to be a part of the Crusade. This is a convention-wide, all inclusive, all-out effort, for Christian Education and the future leadership of our denomination. This Crusade is predicated on the belief that our schools can and will fulfill their functions as an essential part of our Christian effort at home and around the world.

Our schools are all in dire need of improved and expanded facilities. The Crusade goal of $28,000,000 is not a figure pulled out of the air. It is based on careful study of the minimum itemized needs of each school. This amount will provide for a total of at least 36 now present buildings and completion of miscellaneous campus projects. To reach the enrollment objectives of our Convention, in light of the "population explosion" we must, by 1970, have facilities for 21,000 students. This will be 9,000 additional students over the 12,000 now enrolled in our Baptist schools.

The historical decision of our Executive Board to firmly assert our stand on church-state principles places additional responsibility on our Convention. We simply cannot take away a source of funds on the one hand without providing another avenue of support on the other. Ways and means must be found to build 15 new dormitories before 1965. This underlines the need not only to reach our goal, but to oversubscribe it emphatically.

All Crusade gifts will be credited to the church of the donor. Safeguards have been taken, through the ground rules governing the Crusade, to make sure there are no adverse affects on the income of the Cooperative Program. The Crusade must be an "over and above effort for Christ through Christian Education."

Source: *Proceedings*, Baptist General Convention of Texas, 1961, 96. Reprint courtesy of the Baptist General Convention of Texas.

4. An Educational Study: The Carden Report

William R. Carden, Jr., came to the Executive Board staff from Stetson University, Florida, where he had been serving as acting dean. He accepted an interim assignment for one year and was requested by the Education Commission to devote a major portion of his time to an efficiency survey of the nine Texas Baptist colleges and universities.

It was the opinion of the commission that he was well qualified for the assignment, not only because of his experience and training but also because of his deep commitment to Christian education. He brought with him some knowledge of the Texas Baptist campus for he was in one institution and was later a member of the faculty of another.

Distribution of Report

Carden's report was given to administrators and the Education Commission on July 22 at Salado. Several trustees from Baptist schools were present at the meeting.

The unfortunate and premature publication of a few details of the study had poised undue speculation and unwarranted conclusions. Neither now, nor ever, has it been the purpose of any committee or commission to withhold from the churches information which they ought to have.

When no decisions have been reached about a study, the dissemination of its contents can, and usually does, create serious problems. People become aroused over something that may never be recommended at all. A plethora of conflicting interpretations adds to the confusion, making it difficult for an objective appraisal to be made. When, eventually, recommendations are brought, they should be explained fully in order that those responsible for decisions will be in possession of all the facts.

Important Aspects

Let me point out several important aspects of the Carden report.

In my judgment, it is the finest study ever made of our Christian education program in Texas. The administrators meeting at Salado were unanimous in the opinion that it would be of great importance to all the schools. They were not agreed, of course, on all the conclusions and recommendations.

The communication media have insisted in considerable speculation about what will happen to some of our schools. Most of this is a priori reasoning based upon hearsay and rumors.

No decision has been made with respect to any recommendation which would affect the status of any Baptist school except Mary Hardin-Baylor. The Education Commission did recommend that the boards of Mary-Hardin Baylor and Baylor University enter into consultation with respect to a mutually beneficial alignment. However, should the boards fail to reach agreement, no change will be effected.

A committee of 12 men will make an intensive study of the Carden report. Perhaps a year will pass before the committee's findings and recommendations can go to the Education Commission. Every alternative will be considered, one of which undoubtedly will be that of strengthening and enlarging all our schools. In the meantime, it is to be hoped that the misinformation which has been circulated will not deter any student from enrolling in one of our Baptist colleges. He will have ample opportunity to pursue his education in any of them.

Source: T. A. Patterson, "The Carden Report," *Baptist Standard*, 7 August 1968, 7. Reprint courtesy of the *Baptist Standard*.

C. Human Welfare Commission

The Human Welfare Commission was responsible for the eight Baptist hospitals, four childcare homes, two geriatric homes, and a home for unwed mothers. James Basden was named Secretary of the Human Welfare Commission in 1961.

1. Child Care: Cooperation in the New Decade

New insight into the needs of these [orphan] children have led us from the "child centered" approach to a "family centered" one. We have come to understand that the child's affections are deeply rooted in his own family. Our work in recent years in claiming the resources of the child's family has produced gratifying results.

Since World War II we have to conceive of the program of a modern children's agency as involving a "treatment centered" approach. The distressing conditions of family life today have severely damaged many children and our Southern Baptist homes, along with the children's agencies across the country, are now accepting children who are deeply disturbed, many of whom will become delinquent and mentally ill. Some of these will require, of the agencies with the best trained staff, professional skills which must be secured beyond our doors. This will demand a much more expansive program of care and will likely mean, under the present budgets allowed for children's work in the Southern Baptist Convention, a greatly reduced number of children served, but our efforts will be intensified with fewer children.

These are trends, and as Christian child care is viewed as it is being conducted now and in the future by Southern Baptists, one cannot emphasize too strongly the need to hold fast to those aspects of our past and present programs which will continue to serve basic needs of children. In doing so we will labor together on the local, state, and world-wide level to prevent family breakdown, to major on preventive work, and gear our institutional, foster family care, adoptive and rehabilitative work to meet the complex and total needs of children who come through our doors.

It is only as the past and present Christian child care is appraised that trends in the future can be predicted. Several major factors have and will continue to influence this ministry of care in the future.

First, the increasing complexity of modern life has resulted in the entry of government in the field of welfare in the same manner in which public education and health required the resources of the state to share in the burdens beyond the strength of the Christian churches and private philanthropy. Democracy as we understand it and it is practiced has no other choice. The current public budget of twenty billion dollars is convincing evidence of that choice. The practice of Christian compassion and the insistence of the Christian church that democracy implement its Constitution and Bill of Rights played no small part in this choice. The claim of influencing this choice carried with it the responsibility of conducting participation in these services as citizens of both the state and Christian community.

Governmental support of the program of human welfare constitutes an additional area of our opportunity for service to people and at the same time our greatest peril. This is a lesson which is plainly recorded in the history of welfare services. The ever-present danger to peddle welfare services for political influence, to produce learners instead of lifters, and the temptation to decrease Christian benevolences in favor of more public support will ultimately defeat both private and public objectives.

Christian child care in the future, therefore, is seen as operating in special fields carefully defined along with a network of private, non-sectarian and governmental agencies for the common welfare of our children. The relationship will be complementary and compensatory; it will be inter-dependent and not dependent; voluntary and not compulsory; and it will be cooperative and not competitive.

This statement from the 1960 edition of the <u>Social Work Yearbook</u> on the objectives of Protestant welfare services seems to further clarify the relationship between public and Christian welfare services: "Social welfare is an integral part of the ministry of the church, not an optional part of its program, not an onerous duty which must reluctantly be undertaken, but a glad response to God in service of man . . . it cannot be evaluated in terms of its success in making Christians out of those whose need is served—while the church always desires to open people's lives to the love and power of Christ, it serves human need because it must as a response to faith."

This cooperative relationship will produce mutual respect and a willingness to see the areas of common and especial services of each. It will recognize new and unprovided areas—the "no man's land" that is fearful to tread. These are the areas entangled by the barbwires of community tensions and the bombshells of public opinion. As colleagues, public and private agencies must accept our share of the troubled areas of juvenile delinquency, illegitimacy and the ever-increasing mental and emotional incompetency which our civilization has produced. There will be many gaps unless the ranks are brought closer together.

This spirit of cooperation will provide a broader base for conducting research in the field of child care. There is need always for the courage to experiment—research which will examine old techniques, holding on to the tested and effective procedures and discarding those which no longer serve the needs of children. Together we can move with boldness toward the physical well being, emotional maturity, social competency and growth of the spiritual in the children served.

Source: *Proceedings*, Human Welfare Orientation Conferences, February 1960, 40–41. Reprint courtesy of the Baptist General Convention of Texas.

2. Mexican Baptist Children's Home

FACTUAL AND HISTORICAL INFORMATION:

The Mexican Baptist Children's Home came into being as a result of a long felt need. It has been the dream of several of our Mexican Baptist leaders as well as the Anglo Baptist missionaries. It became a must when death claimed some of our Baptist parents and their children became dependant upon us. The Home became a reality in June of 1944 when a charter was granted by the State Department of Public Welfare. Immediately thereafter an administrative staff was set up and the Home became a reality. The first children were officially received on September 1, 1944. In December of that year a little farm of 122 acres ten miles west of the courthouse in San Antonio was purchased and possession was given in March, 1945. Superintendent E. J. Gregory and family moved out and began plans for construction. The success of the movement has been largely due to the wholehearted response of churches and individuals throughout the entire state.

WHY AND HOW THE HOME BECOMES A PART OF THE NEW TESTAMENT PROGRAM OF EVANGELISM:

The Mexican Baptist Children's Home exists for the purpose of caring for the destitute Latin-American child, to the end that the child will come to know the true way of life and become a useful citizen in the Kingdom of God as well as of his country. The Mexican Baptist Children's Home has a distinct ministry which no other children's home has . . . it ministers to another race, culture and religious background, making it in the strictest sense a wonderful missionary opportunity. It is easy to show the love of God to a needy, love-starved, under nourished child after you give him nice clean, warm clothes, good food, adequate shelter and people who minister to his every need from a sense of divine vocation. This benevolent Home is positive proof that we want to help in a tangible way the ever increasing number of Latin Americans in our midst. Moreover, it serves as a strong tie between Mexico and the USA in better understanding between the two nations. Here is the good neighbor policy at work in a real way.

FUTURE PROJECTIONS:

Within the next five years we hope to raise $250,000 for capital improvements. That means an expenditure of an average of $50,000 per annum. The following are urgent requests and needs in order to maximize efficiency.

1. Superintendent's home.
2. Repair to eight older cottages.
3. Build four new cottages.
4. Paving for streets.
5. Gymnasium.

6. Youth activities building combined with laundry.

7. A well for the ranch.

PRESENT PROGRAM AND FACILITIES:

There are twelve cottages housing 144 children, an administrative-chapel building, a personnel building with four large apartments, dairy barn, three employees' dwellings, one large storage building, a large building used for repair and bus shed. The office employees include superintendent, Rev. J. Ivey Miller; assistant superintendent, Mr. Leland Hacker, secretary Miss Elizabeth Belton; bookkeeper, Mrs. Adelaide Germany; social worker, Mrs. Mildred Cooper. Other employees are purchaser, farmer, rancher, four utility men, musicians and dieticians. The operation expense is $142,000 yearly. It costs $3.05 per day to care for a child. (Ninety-six percent of the financial support comes from Anglo churches and four percent from Latin American churches) The Home is supported by the Cooperative Program and by designated giving by the churches.

Religious Program: A worship service is conducted twice weekly, Thursday and Sunday evenings. On Sunday mornings the children go to three Sunday Schools and churches, Prospect Hill (Anglo), Calvary Mexican, and Alta Vista Mission. The last two of which are Spanish speaking. RA's and GA's are conducted each Thursday on the campus and Training Union each Sunday evening on the campus. Personal counseling is a vital part of religious instruction.

Educational: The Home takes the children to the public schools in San Antonio, John B. Hood School (Elementary) and Sidney Lanier (Junior and Senior High). Students who desire and are qualified continue their studies in colleges with the support of the Home. Most of the students receive scholarships in our Baptist colleges.

Work Program: Every one works at Mexican Baptist Children's Home. Each child has his assigned house duties and the older ones earn a small amount each week with extra jobs on the campus as those working in dairy, grocery room, bus shed, etc. Each child is given a weekly allowance and taught to contribute to the church, the needy. Children are encouraged to save a little.

Recreation: In the summer swimming is the principal sport. A beautiful swimming pool affords moments of delight to the children. A concrete slab is used for skating, basketball and volleyball. Softball and hard ball are played also. Several of the boys join various Little League Baseball teams and play at the adjoining Lackland Air Force Base.

Social Work: Recently the Home employed a social worker who will work with not only the children and house parents but the parents and relatives of those in the Home.

FUTURE PROGRAM:

At the present we do not have an adoption and foster care program, but we believe that this field is one which should be entered. It will be more difficult in placing children in Latin-American homes, yet these are sufficient to justify such a program.

PRESENT NEEDS:

The following are suggested areas of cooperation between the Mexican Baptist Children's Home and the San Antonio Baptist Association.

1. Sponsorship program for hot lunches is in progress. Many go without lunch because they do not wish to take the usual sandwich and apple. For $6.00 a month a child can have a hot lunch. A child can be sponsored on his birthday.

2. Canned goods and produce are presently needed. Food is the largest expense of the Home. Any food whether canned or fresh will be used.

3. With the 794-acre ranch we could and should produce enough beef for home consumption. A calf could be put on the ranch and fattened out for a slaughtering.

4. The Home needs more endowment. People are needed who will place the Home in their wills. There is presently needed $100,000 to add to the $40,000 already on hand. The interest from the endowment can add greatly to the operation expense and secure the Home for possible unforeseen lean years.

Source: *Survey Report*, San Antonio Baptist Association, 1965, 135–37. Reprint courtesy of the San Antonio Baptist Association.

3. Department of Planning and Special Services

The co-sponsored Group Foster Home concept of child care continuous to furnish the vehicle for a variety of specialized care.

Under a pattern first begun with Green Acres Baptist Church of Tyler in 1968, the church or organization provides for the housing and daily living needs of the children, and Buckner assumes responsibilities for staffing and professional services. There are now five of these homes giving long-term resident care similar to that provided in Buckner's larger children's homes. Three new homes established this year provide a different type service.

In San Antonio and Lubbock, short-term, interim care facilities were begun with the supportive help of the San Antonio Baptist Association, and First Baptist Church, Lubbock. One home is specified for teenage girls, and one cares for boys and girls from ages three through 17. Descriptions of these homes are given in reports to follow, by Buckner units responsible for their administration.

In the north Texas town of Princeton, still another type of group foster home was begun, through the co-sponsorship of the Maranatha Corporation. This home is programmed as a transitional residence for boys. Its need became apparent when boys who had been living in the isolated environment of another specialized program, Trew Camp, were finding it difficult to make the transition back to a highly structured society and a large school system. Princeton, with its small schools, provides an ideal transitional setting to meet the needs of these boys, and also those who need a transitional living experience from their own home to the larger Buckner child care homes. Princeton can care for six boys.

Due to the decline in requests for maternity care, the number of adoptions for the year decreased to 85. Inquiries for adoption are accepted only during the month of January.

Included in the responsibilities of this Department is consultative work with Buckner's administrative staff for improvement and upgrade of services, and in planning and research for future programs and services. A major activity this past year was a first time conference, which brought together all staff involved in child care, for a workshop in Dallas.

From July 29 through August 2, more than 160 Buckner administrators, house staff, social workers, supervisory personnel, secretaries, cooks, maintenance people, and others in related work in child care from all over the state were in Dallas for this period of work and fellowship. Special guest lecturer and consultant for the conference was Dr. Alan Keith-Lucas, of the University of North Carolina, recognized as one of the most outstanding practitioners in child care today.

Evaluations from workers following the conference indicate that it was a success. Their suggestions will provide helpful direction for planning similar conferences in the future both for child care workers and employees engaged in other Buckner services.

Source: *Proceedings*, Baptist General Convention of Texas, 1973, 150–51. Reprint courtesy of the Baptist General Convention of Texas.

4. High Plains Baptist Hospital

God continues to bless the ministry of healing through High Plains Baptist Hospital. With a capacity of 240 beds and planned for easy expansion to 400 beds, the hospital is operating at near capacity. The Board of Trustees, under the leadership of Chairman R. Earle O'Keefe, in the fall of 1972, adopted a long-range comprehensive planning program. A planning council, headed by Trustee James Franklin, six major committees, and 13 task forces were appointed to develop the plan. Employees, physicians, 25 trustees, and a significant number of hospital friends, representing community interest, 160 in all, are working in the planning groups. Scheduled for completion in February, 1974, the long-range plan will detail patient care, education, and Christian effectiveness programs which seem desirable for the immediate, short-range and long-range future. Already much is resulting from the study. An example is the new "One Day Stay Unit" designed so patients may be admitted and discharged on the same day, so as to decrease the time—and money—spent in the hospital. Other new services installed during the year include a cardiac stress laboratory, a Department of Medical Social Work, and a service in clinical psychology. The Board has approved for early implementation a Department of Development.

Expansion for the immediate short-term future, planned during the summer of 1971, will include the addition of the seventh and eighth levels, completing the seventh level and leaving the eighth level unfinished. This will add 69 beds for a total of 305 beds. Federal Medicare regulations which became effective January 1, 1973, require all hospitals to obtain prior approval of regional, state and federal agencies before beds can be added. A request for approval is pending before the appropriate agencies. The addition will cost $1,800,000. Once completed, both the sixth and eighth levels will remain shelled-in for completion before 1978.

The trustees of High Plains Baptist Hospital have been active in the formation of several affiliations with other local institutions during the year. One such effort is the "Amarillo Emergency Receiving Center," an organization to provide one receiving center for all major emergencies, assuring the public of adequate facilities and physician back-ups in all the specialities for the proper care of patients. This is a cooperative effort between the boards of three hospitals, their medical staffs, and the County Medical Society. Another is the "Amarillo Area Academic Health Center Corporation." This is a consortium of five hospitals, the medical society, and the dental society for the integration and coordination of medical education in all the hospital facilities in Amarillo with special emphasis on education for medical students of Texas Tech University School of Medicine, and later, of interns and residents in the various specialities. Finally, the trustees have given leadership in the orderly formation and implementation of the "Panhandle Regional Health Council," a planning commission for health services, facilities and manpower for approximately 26 counties in the Panhandle of Texas. These affiliated efforts should lead ultimately to improved patient care and health education programs at reduced costs through the sharing and integration of programs between local hospitals, and the reduction to an optimal minimum of any unnecessary duplication of services.

Three positions on the Board of Trustees are vacant at the time this report is being made. They are occasioned by the retirement from active service of the "Dean of the Panhandle Pastors," W. R. Lawrence, formerly pastor of First Baptist Church of Clarendon, who has moved to the state of Washington for "retirement" to a mission field. A second position was vacated by Dr. Gerald Mann, formerly pastor of the First Baptist Church of Hereford, and now pastor of the University Baptist

Church in Austin: and the third, by the resignation of businessman Ed Myatt of Pampa. All three gave yeoman service to the Board. We are grateful.

A mountaintop experience occurred during the year when, through the fraternal partnership program between this hospital and the William Wallace Memorial Baptist Hospital in Pusan, Korea, Soo Lee, assistant administrator of that hospital, visited with us for two weeks, observing the management and organization of this hospital. Our fraternal partnership was strengthened by his visit, and we look forward to helpful experiences between our hospitals through future years. The pastoral care program was expanded this year with the addition of a third full-time chaplain intern position. The program is accredited by the Association of Clinical Pastoral Education and allows the hospital to provide much more extensive pastoral care to patients because of the services of these chaplain interns.

We look forward to seeing you in Amarillo at next year's Baptist General Convention of Texas. We want to show you what we have been trying to tell you through these reports during the last few years. Please pray God's love will be made real in the lives of our patients during the coming year.

Source: *Proceedings*, Baptist General Convention of Texas, 1973, 146–47. Reprint courtesy of the Baptist General Convention of Texas.

5. Hospital Study Committee: Troubles Ahead

Background information on the appointment of the Hospital Study Committee was given by Chairman Harris. Dr. Harris recognized James Basden, Secretary of the Human Welfare Commission, who expressed thanks to the committee for the work they had done and then introduced Dr. John Bagwell, Chairman of the Hospital Study Committee.

Dr. Bagwell expressed appreciation to the committee and then referred to several sections of the report before reading the four recommendations. (A copy of the entire report will be included in the 1971 Texas Baptist Annual.)

A. Recommendations as to the Relationship of Baptist Hospitals to Government

Recommendation #1—The committee recommends that the convention approve a policy allowing the boards of trustees of Texas Baptist hospitals to apply for and to accept capital grants for new and improved services where the hospital is using facilities in the care of recipients under federal or state programs.

Recommendation #2—The committee recommends that the convention approve a policy allowing the boards of trustees of Texas Baptist hospitals to utilize federal low interest, long-term loan arrangements where this will relieve the difference between payments for services for recipients of government programs and the cost for providing the facilities required for serving those patients.

B. Recommendation as to the Relationship of Hospitals to the Local Community

Recommendation #3—The committee recommends that the convention approve necessary constitutional changes allowing the Baptist members of each hospital's board of trustees to elect a number of non-Baptists to membership on the governing board with the provision that each board must have, at all times, at least three-fourths (3/4) of its members who are Baptist and elected by the convention.

C. Recommendation Regarding the Release of Hospitals from the Convention

Recommendation #4—The committee recommends that the Executive Board of the Baptist General Convention of Texas be authorized to approve arrangements for the transfer of any Texas Baptist hospital from Baptist ownership to a voluntary, non-profit corporation—at the request of the governing board for the hospital and subject to approval of the arrangements for the transfer by the Executive Board, provided the governing board has determined that the hospital needs to be separated and that delay of such action until the next annual session of the convention would severely jeopardize the hospital.

The committee recommends that, in the event a hospital is released, and prior to the release, the Human Welfare Commission and the Executive Board be authorized to negotiate contracts with these hospitals to conduct chaplaincy programs, education and such other activities of a hospital ministry as the convention from time to time may desire to sponsor.

Dr. Bagwell explained that James Semple, a member of the Hospital Study Committee, had asked to be allowed to bring a Minority Report and Dr. Bagwell relinquished the floor to Dr. Semple to bring this report.

Albert Brown asked if it were not out of order to have the discussion before a motion to adopt these recommendations. Chairman Harris explained that all of this was a presentation of the committee and it was his understanding that the committee had the privilege of the presentation of the issue before any discussion.

Dr. Semple read the Minority Report in full. This report had been handed out to all members present and had been mailed to the Board members prior to the meeting. Dr. Semple said he would like to move the adoption of this Minority Report at the proper time. The Chair ruled that Dr. Semple would be given time later but at this time Dr. Bagwell still had the floor.

Dr. Bagwell called on Travis Berry, Vice-Chairman of the Baptist Study Committee, to bring a further presentation of the report. At the close the comments, Dr. Berry moved that the Special Hospital Report be adopted. W. M. Shamburger seconded the motion.

Dr. Bagwell stated that since Dr. Semple's recommendations had never been presented and discussed in any meetings of the Hospital Study Committee, his report should be considered as an individual's opinion. He also stated that he, as Chairman, had not received any word from any committee member that they believed in a Minority Report.

Dr. Bagwell said he had asked Dr. E. D. Westbrook, a physician from Beaumont, to speak to the report. Also, W. A. Criswell, pastor of the First Baptist Church, Dallas, and, if time permitted, he had asked Dr. David Hitt, Baylor Medical Center, Dallas, to answer the allegation that this committee is incorrect in saying that the hospitals are losing money on government patients.

Because of the scheduling of other activities at 11:45 A.M., only Dr. Westbrook and Dr. Criswell were permitted to speak to the report.

Jay L. Skaggs led in prayer before the Board adjourned for Dedication Services of the Mobile Relief Unit. These services were held on the

Patterson Street side of the First Baptist Church where the new Mobile Unit was on display. W. M. Shamburger, Chairman of the State Missions Commission, presided at this program. At the conclusion of these services, lunch was served to the Board members by the First Baptist Church.

The Executive Board reconvened at 1:00 P.M. to hear further discussion of the Hospital Study Report and other matters of business on the Agenda.

James Semple spoke in opposition of the report and gave his reasons for writing the Minority Report, saying, among other things, that he had considered resigning from the committee but that would have been only a negative response and he wanted to do something positive, so he wrote the dissent.

Chairman Harris announced that if the recommendation of the Hospital Study Committee were approved by the Board, these recommendations would still go to the Convention. However, if the Board rejected any part of this report that part would be dead, unless the Convention itself wished to bring it up, or an individual messenger wished to bring it to the Convention.

The question was raised if the four recommendations were to be voted on separately or together. Chairman Harris said the motion to adopt the Report, made by Travis Berry, would require voting on the entire report unless a substitute motion was made asking that the recommendations be voted separately.

Charles Cockrell made a substitute motion that the four recommendations be voted on separately. There were several seconds and the motion carried. There was one opposing vote.

Dr. Bagwell again read Recommendation #1.

James Dunn, Secretary of the Christian Life Commission, spoke in opposition of this recommendation. He said the Christian Life Commission was polled and with one abstention, the Commission opposed recommendations one and two. (James Harris, a member of the Christian Life Commission, abstained from voting because of his position as Chairman of the Executive Board.)

Jack McCreary, a member of the Hospital Study Committee, but not a member of the Executive Board, spoke in favor of all four recommendations.

W. B. Etheridge spoke for the motion.

O. W. Summerlin spoke against the motion and made the following substitute motion: That should the governing board of any hospital affiliated with the Baptist General Convention of Texas desire separation from the Convention that (1) a request must be made known at least thirty days prior to the annual session of the Baptist General Convention of Texas, (2) that the Convention in its annual session must approve the request for severance, and (3) that the transfer of ownership be made to a voluntary non-profit corporation with the requests that the word "Baptist" be removed from the name of the hospital.

Chairman Harris ruled Mr. Summerlin out of order since Recommendation #1 was under discussion and that his substitute motion pertained to Recommendation #4 which was not being discussed.

Dr. Stonie Cotton spoke in favor of the first two recommendations but did not favor the last two.

Jimmy Allen spoke against Recommendation #1. Dr. Bagwell rebuked Dr. Allen's statements concerning Recommendation #1.

James Springfield moved the previous question and asked the floor without further debate to vote on Recommendation #1. This motion was seconded and it carried.

Recommendation #1 passed by a standing vote of 66–50. (Will be presented to the Convention in Houston in October.)

James Springfield moved the previous question and asked the floor without further debate to vote on Recommendation #2. This motion was seconded and it carried.

Recommendation #2 passed by a standing vote of 67–59. (Will be presented to the Convention in Houston in October.)

Oswin Chrisman spoke in favor of Recommendation #3.

J. B. Fowler, Jr. moved the previous question. The motion was seconded and it carried.

Recommendation #3 lost by a standing vote of 47–59.

No one spoke to Recommendation #4. Rufus Spraberry moved the previous question. This motion was seconded and it carried. A point of inquiry was asked by James Riley and he was permitted to proceed: Does this give blanket authority for emergency approach rather than a typical approach? The answer was "emergency approach." This was further explained by Dr. Bagwell.

Recommendation #4 lost by a standing vote of 57–59.

H. M. Jarrett made the following motion concerning Recommendation #3: That the one-fourth of non-Baptists on the membership of the governing body be elected by the convention, along with three-quarters of the members who are Baptists. There was a second to this motion. Charles Cockrell spoke in opposition to this motion. The motion lost.

Source: *Minutes*, Executive Board of the Baptist General Convention of Texas, 10 September 1971. Reprint courtesy of the Baptist General Convention of Texas.

D. Christian Life Commission

Led by Jimmy Allen until 1967, the Christian Life Commission was the smallest of the four commissions, but it still proved to be highly influential in Texas Baptist life. The primary responsibility of the CLC was to speak on moral issues, race relations, Christian citizenship, and to serve as a watchdog over the government concerning moral issues. The task of the CLC was to speak to Baptists, not for them. At no point were the statements made by the CLC to be understood as the official position of the BGCT.

Christian Life Commission Report, 1973

"For just as the body without the spirit is dead, so faith without works is dead" (James 2:26). Valid Christian faith should always express itself through the life of the believer. The Word of God demands that we apply the transforming message of our Lord to every avenue of life. The Christian Life Commission through various approaches attempts to speak to both individual Christians and local churches concerning ways to apply effectively the gospel to issues of everyday life.

One of the ways the Commission does this is through literature that is relevant and up-to-date. Thus, the Commission in cooperation with other Christian Life Commissions in the Southern Baptist Convention, just completed a rewrite of the old "Christian Answers to Family Problems" series and "Teen Talks" series. That rewrite, 21 pamphlets now under the title, "The Christian Life Styles Series," has been well received by Texas Baptists. More than 235,000 pamphlets were distributed in the first six months of availability.

The Commission also frequently prepares newsletters on critical areas of Christian concern. For example, to help pastors better understand now best to minister in regard to the abortion issue, the Commission mailed to every pastor in the state a major newsletter on abortion.

The Commission's statewide workshop, held in February of this year, had a record attendance. The workshop, entitled "Helping Churches Help Families," was designed to give pastors and others practical help in dealing with family problems. It featured such leading personalities as Dr. Joyce Brothers, Dr. R. Lofton Hudson, Dr. David Edens and Dr. Gerald Shedd. Dr. E. S. James was honored as the recipient of the Commission's Distinguished Service Award.

The 1974 Workshop is already scheduled at Southwestern Seminary for February 25–27.

Believing that we worship a God who is interested in all of life, the Christian Life Commission once again sought to have an influence in some of the political decisions of this state that affect so many of God's children. To this end, the Christian Life Commission seriously studied and finally actively endorsed a number of legislative items. To keep Texas Baptists informed on these issues, the Commission conducted legislative briefings in nine cities across the state. A legislative report was also mailed to all pastors in the state.

The Commission was vitally interested in the final outcome of a number of issues. In the last legislative session, the revisions of the Family Code, the passing of mandatory, transitional, bilingual education programs, the revision of the Penal Code, and the revision of Texas drug laws, all passed in acceptable forms. Stronger traffic safety regulations, which the Commission supported, failed to pass. The Commission stood against the strong effort to pass a gambling lottery in Texas. That legislation was defeated in committee in both Houses. The Christian Life Commission also indicated to the Constitutional Revision Commission its opposition to the deletion of the present constitutional prohibitions against certain forms of gambling.

The Commission again this year will prepare an analysis on how our legislators voted on many of these crucial issues during the last session.

In September, the Commission conducted a series of seminars on alcohol and drug abuse. The emphasis again was on practical help and information for pastors and parents. The seminars, held in five major Texas cities, featured Dr. R. Lofton Hudson and Ron Willis. Also present were representatives from the State Program on Drug Abuse, the Texas Commission on Alcoholism, and local experts on resources and referral.

Also, in cooperation with the State Mission Commission, the Commission sponsored a Mexican-American Citizenship meeting in San Antonio which was attended by Mexican-American pastors across the state.

A major part of the ministry of the Commission continues to be speaking on ethical issues in local churches, camps, and associational meetings, retreats and many other forums.

Resource and research services constitute another major function of the Commission in its effort to speak to difficult zones of practical Christianity. The staff responds with information, referrals, and direct assistance to daily telephone calls, letters and visits from those seeking help on ethical issues from a Christian perspective.

The present staff on the Christian Life Commission includes Dr. James M. Dunn, secretary; Phil D. Strickland, Director of Citizenship Education; and Ben E. Loring, Jr., Director of Research and Organization.

Source: *Proceedings*, Baptist General Convention of Texas, 1973, 139–40. Reprint courtesy of the Baptist General Convention of Texas.

12.5 Committee of 100

Instituted in 1966 and chaired by E. H. Westmoreland, the Committee of 100 was assigned the task of evaluating all aspects of the BGCT and then devising a way to implement the full resources of the Convention in order to better fulfill the Great Commission. The first report was delivered in 1967 and the recommendations of the Committee proved to be quite radical. As Texas Baptists had done with the Carden Report, the Committee of 100's suggestions were either ignored or outright rejected.

A. Formation

Fifty ministers and 50 laymen were chosen last week to form a committee to review and evaluate "all of the work of the Baptist General Convention of Texas, its boards, agencies, commissions, committees, and institutions."

E. Hermond Westmoreland, pastor of South Main Church, Houston, was named chairman of the committee at its initial meeting.

The committee was selected by the convention's president and two vice-presidents after being established by convention vote last year. The convention president is J. Carroll Chadwick, pastor of First Church, Center. The vice-presidents are Bruce McIver, pastor of Wilshire Church, Dallas, and Gordon Clinard, pastor of First Church, San Angelo.

While the committee was set up by the convention officers to have 50 laymen and 50 ministers this was not included in the convention's direction. It had been suggested prior to the convention, however.

Other officers of the committee are Jarman Bass of Dallas, vice-chairman, and Jack McCreary of Austin, secretary. T. A. Patterson, Executive Board executive secretary, was elected an ex-officio member of the committee.

There will be four main subcommittees, Chairman Westmoreland said. Three of these will be for the Executive Board's commissions; and the fourth will be for the Church Loan Board, the Baptist Foundation of Texas, and the *Baptist Standard*.

Officer of the subcommittees will be selected by officers of the convention and officers of the larger committee, it was indicated.

Much of the committee organization will be effected during a luncheon meeting in Dallas on Feb. 16, Westmoreland said. Subcommittees appointed at that time will begin their organizational meetings in the afternoon.

According to the schedule the committee hopes to follow, it would report at the convention in Lubbock this year; and its work would be finished.

The committee came into existence for the purpose of increasing "further participation on the part of both laymen and pastors in every area of our Baptist work . . ." It is expected to make a review and evaluation of all the work of the convention and "explore ways and means of enlisting the total resources of Texas Baptists in the implementation of the Great Commission through our churches and convention. . . ."

Westmoreland said the work of the committee will be constructive. It will not be a referee, he indicated, but will be used as an evaluation agency to see if adjustments are needed. "We hope to outline ways to enlist more persons in the work," he said.

"We hope to interest more laymen because this would be wholesome. We don't want a preacher-dominated convention," he concluded.

Chadwick said that Texas Baptists look up to Westmoreland as an elder statesman. "He has been called upon before to moderate, initiate, and give strength to the Baptist image." Westmoreland has served on three committees of survey type, and he is now president of the SBC Annuity Board. "He is loved and respected," Chadwick said.

Source: "'Committee of 100' is Formed to Evaluate BGCT Endeavors," Baptist *Standard*, 25 January 1967, 3. Reprint courtesy of the *Baptist Standard*.

B. Recommendations of the Committee of 100

The following recommendations were developed in the subcommittees, discussed and approved by the general committee and are presented to this convention for your approval, disapproval or modification:

Recommendations requiring constitutional changes:

1. The following recommendation was adopted. See items 61–65 in Convention proceedings.

1. Committee to nominate executive board members (Article VI, Section 9) which read, "Of the fifteen members, a minimum of five shall be ordained persons and a minium of 5 lay persons," be amended to read, "Of the 15 members, a minimum of 6 shall be ordained ministers or church staff members and a minimum of 6 lay persons."

2. Recommendation No. 2 was adopted. See item 73 in Convention proceedings; also further discussion items 182-184.

1. Committee on nominations for institution boards (Article VI, Section 10) which reads, "Of the 15 members, a minimum of 5 shall be ordained ministers and a minimum of five lay persons," be amended to read "In the election of the 15 members, a minimum of 6 shall be ordained ministers or church staff members and a minimum of 6 lay persons."

2. Convention officers (Article V) by the addition of Section 8 to read: "In the election of the president, first vice-president and second vice-president, at least one must be a layman."

Recommendations requiring changes in the 1959 Survey Report

1. Recommendation No. 1 passed; see items 77–83 in Convention proceedings.

1. The deletion of the statement on page 60 in the 1959 Book of Reports which reads: "They (Christian Life Commission) should look to the State Missions secretary for general administrative guidance between sessions of their governing groups." Also the deletion on page 87 of the 1959 Book of Reports which reads (1) The Christian Life Program and (2) Director of Christian Life Commission.

2. (1) Recommendation No. 2 (1) passed; see item 84 in convention proceedings.

1. Regarding the Committee on Nominations for Institution Boards, the following changes in the Survey Report are recommended:

(1) That paragraph 5, page 52, which reads: "The nominating subcommittee for each educational institution having a separate board of trustees should consist of five members: (1) a member of the Education Commission, (2) an alumnus of the institution, (3) an alumnus of another Baptist educational institution, (4) an alumnus of a non-Baptist institution or a member-at-large, and (5) a trustee of the institution. Not more than one member of a subcommittee should be a trustee of the institution involved and nor more than two should be alumni of the institution.". . . be changed to read "(3) a trustee of the institution, and (4) two members-at-large from the state Baptist constituency."

2. (2) Recommendation 2 (2) passed; see item 85.

(1) That paragraph 6, page 52 which reads: "The nominating subcommittees for each hospital or home board should include five members: (1) a member of the Human Welfare Commission, (2) a member-at-large from the state Baptist constituency, (3) a former or present trustee of a similar Baptist institution, (4) a prominent Baptist member of the community in which the institution is located, and (5) a trustee of the institution," be changed to read "(2) two members-at-large from the state Baptist constituency, (3) a Baptist member of the community in which the institution is located, and (4) a trustee of the institution."

3. Recommendation No. 3 passed; see items 86 and 87.

1. The administrative relationship of the State Missions Commission to the Church Loan Association and the Christian Life Commission recommended by the 1959 Survey Committee, be discontinued, leaving the above agencies responsible administratively to the Executive Secretary. This will eliminate the broken lines (Exhibit XV, page 72 of the 1959 Book of Reports).

4. Recommendation No. 4 failed; see items 88–92 in Convention proceedings.

1. The creation of three new divisions out of the present Church Services Division (1959 Book of Reports, pages 88–90); namely, Sunday School, Training Union and Church Music. The Training Union division will administer the special services now included in the Church Services Division, such as church recreation, church administration, church library and family life emphasis.

5. Recommendation No. 5 referred to Committee of 100 for further study. See items 94–97.

1. The nomination of directors of the Baptist Foundation. . . .

By action of the Baptist General Convention of Texas in 1960 annual session, the portion quoted (1) through (5) was deleted and the following was substituted:

The nominating subcommittee responsible for proposing persons for membership on the board of the directors of the Baptist Foundation will include five members: (1) the president of the Baptist General Convention of Texas, (2) the chairman of the Program Coordinating Committee of the Executive Board, (3) the president of the Baptist Foundation, and (4) two members of the Foundation's Board of Directors selected by the directors of the Foundation, but not including any member whose term of office is expiring. Persons nominated for membership on the Baptist Foundation's Board of Directors shall be active regular members of cooperating Baptist churches; shall have had successful experience in finance, farming, ranching, business, industry or commerce; and shall have the support of all five members of the nominating subcommittee. The Committee of 100 recommends that the foregoing be changed to read: "The board of directors of the Baptist Foundation of Texas shall be nominated and elected in the same manner and for the term as all education and human welfare institution boards of trustees: namely, Institution Boards and subsequently elected by the convention. The subcommittee to nominate directors to the Baptist Foundation board shall include five members consisting of (1) a member of the Human Welfare Commission, (2) a member of the Christian Education Commission, (3) the chairman of the Program Coordinating Committee, (4) a member of the Foundation's board of directors, and (5) one member-at-large from the state Baptist constituency.

Other Recommendations

1. and

2. Recommendations No. 1 and 2 adopted; see item 166 of Convention proceedings.

1. Increase the Christian Life Commission from 12 to 15 members elected for three-year terms. One-third of the membership shall rotate annually. A minimum of 6 laymen and a minimum of six pastors shall be required. Members should be permitted to serve two successive terms.

2. The expansion of the program of the Christian Life Commission to include adequate statistical services through research. This would require additional help because of the heavy load now carried by the present staff.

3. Recommendation No. 3 adopted; see item 167.

1. General recommendations to expand services of the Public Relations Department:

(1) Provide public relations services and guidance to churches and associations through methods workshops (state-wide, area-wide and association-wide); by offering direct advice and assistance to churches in need of professional public relations aid.

(2) Develop greater use of facilities offered by various media, to present the Baptist story in secular press, television, radio, limited circulation of publications directed to select audiences.

(3) Encourage all areas in advance program planning and enlisting of public relations advice and assistance.

(4) Seek opportunities to meet with other professional public relations people, other Baptist public relations agencies, and over-all religious public relations groups to keep informed in newest approaches, methods and opportunities.

4. Recommendation No 4. adopted; see item 168.

1. General recommendations regarding Christian Education program;

(1) The Executive Board lead in providing clarification and clear settlement of all questions concerning the solicitation by colleges for inclusion in church budgets.

(2) The Order of Business Committee of the convention and all related committees of the Baptist General Convention of Texas provide significant recognition of the Christian Education program on the annual calendar of the convention. Recommend the approval by the convention of a church scholarship plan to be prepared and presented by the Christian Education Commission.

(3) The Christian Education Commission be requested to place before the convention a clearly stated and mutually accepted statement of purpose for the colleges which could be used by presidents, trustees, and others in communicating to the churches the actual account of the work being done by the colleges. This same general but clearly understood philosophy would be used to enable our churches to relate more effectively to the Christian Education program.

5. Recommendation No. 5 adopted; see item 169–171.

1. Recommendations concerning certain areas to be studied by the Human Welfare Commission:

(1) Study the needs and possibility of establishing a chaplaincy program at the Texas Medical Center at Houston.

(2) Restudy Mayo Clinic chaplaincy program being conducted jointly with the Home Mission Board to determine the justification for continuing the program due to certain limitations.

(3) Study the need for and possibility of securing a clinically trained Spanish speaking assistant chaplain to assist with our work at John Sealy Hospital, Galveston.

(4) Conduct a study to determine whether all other agencies are being utilized to the fullest (such as hospitals and colleges), where these

agencies are available, in serving our childcare homes.

(5) Study the possibility of establishing a guideline for requesting support from the parents and/or responsible parties who, upon investigation, show ability to provide that support for children they are placing in our homes.

(6) Urge administrators and/or trustees to work out suitable "policy procedures" concerning admittance to homes, institutional care, etc., and that such procedures be publicized.

(7) Recommend to the trustees of each hospital that they request the medical staff of each hospital to select a committee of staff doctors to meet regularly with the trustees in an advisory capacity, solely for the purpose of giving advice where needed in the area of patient care and medical education.

(8) Seek out methods whereby the Baptist physicians, the medical missionary home on furlough, etc., be given staff priority in our Baptist hospitals (qualifications being equal).

6. Recommendation No. 6 adopted; see item 172.

1. The State Missions Commission to launch an immediate and a long range program for the Rio Grande River mission thrust. ("To determine the most immediate needs of this area and begin such a ministry using new methods and old to publicize effectively and carry out such a program; and, further, that the basic aim of this ministry be a long range program of coordinated missionary efforts in the fields of evangelism, church membership, teaching and training, with the objective of establishing permanent string centers of witness properly funded to accomplish the purpose.")

7. Recommendation No. 7—Substitute motion passed; see item 173 for substitute motion.

1. The State Missions Commission be encourage to inform Negro Baptist churches how our associations receive churches into fellowship, and encourage those desiring to do so to petition the local association for participation.

8. Recommendation No. 8 passed; see items 98–111 and items 121–123 of Convention proceedings.

TEXAS BAPTIST MEN

1. The creation of a new organization for men to be known as Texas Baptist Men, an auxiliary of the Baptist General Convention of Texas. This new organization would replace the Brotherhood department that now operates as a part of the State Missions Commission.

(1) The basic objectives of Texas Baptist Men shall be the teaching of missions, the involvement in missions and mission actions of Baptist men, young men and boys, with special emphasis placed on proper correlation of aid missions and mission actions and operations with the Baptist General Convention of Texas, its Executive Board, and the State Missions Commission of the Baptist General Convention of Texas.

(2) Members of Baptist men's units in Baptist churches affiliated with the Baptist General Convention of Texas shall comprise the membership of Texas Baptist Men.

(3) Baptist men of local Baptist churches, with their pastors, shall be the organization through which objectives of Texas Baptist Men are accomplished.

(4) The associational organization of Baptist Men shall be recognized as the liaison organization of Baptist church units and Texas Baptist Men.

(5) The executive board of Texas Baptist Men shall be composed as follows:

    a. The officers, elected at the annual meeting, and the executive secretary-treasurer;

    b. One man from each of the associations of the Baptist General Convention of Texas who shall be the duly elected Baptist Men's director;

    c. In the event that no associational director exists, the associational moderator shall appoint a man to represent that association on the Texas Baptist Men's executive board;

    d. Eighteen members-at-large, to be elected by the Texas Baptist Men's executive board, of whom 6 shall be pastors and church staff members;

    e. The Texas member of the Brotherhood Commission of the Southern Baptist Convention, and the immediate past president of Texas Baptist Men.

(6) The executive board shall have authority over the affairs of Texas Baptist Men during the interim between annual conventions, except that of modifying any action by Texas Baptist Men's convention.

(7) The executive board of Texas Baptist Men shall be responsible for formulating policies and for integrating the work of the staff and committees.

(8) That Texas Baptist Men continue to receive funds for the operating budget from the Cooperative Program by submitting an annual budget request to the State Missions Commission and the Program Coordinating Committee.

9. Recommendation No. 9 adopted; see item 174.

1. Expansion of the program of the Evangelism Division of the State Missions Commission in the following areas:

(1) Consideration be given to increasing the budget of the Evangelism Division as rapidly as possible.

(2) Give more attention to a ministry among the military personnel in Texas.

(3) Work with the Baptist Men in stimulating the laity to personal witnessing.

(4) Study ways and means of reaching people who have social problems.

(5) Increased effort in cooperative evangelism with National Baptists including consultations on evangelism methods, mutual exploration of avenues of increased communication concerning our common task of witnessing to our world, and correlating special evangelistic efforts with all the Baptist congregations in an area regardless of race.

10. Recommendation No. 10 did not require Convention action. See items 175 and 177.

1. Detailed budget information including a complete breakdown of administrative salaries is always available in the Dallas offices for any interested Texas Baptist or Texas Baptist church.

11. Recommendation No. 11 adopted; see item 176.

1. Bylaws shall be adopted by the Baptist Standard Publishing Company.

12. Recommendation No. 12 referred to Committee of 100 Sub-Committee for further consideration and later recommendation; see item 60 of Convention proceedings.

1. There should be created a relatively small (not over 6 members) Audit Committee of the Executive Board of the Baptist General Convention of Texas. These committeemen should be "outside" (non-staff management) members who have had substantial experience with quality work by independent public accountants. This Audit Committee should study and describe, in detail the qualifications that must be possessed by independent public accountants engaged to audit all Texas Baptist organizations. It should also describe generally the minimum scope of such audits.

The selections of auditors should remain the privilege and responsibility of the trustees of directors of each individual Texas Baptist organization subject to the advice and consent of the Audit Committee. Audit report must be made available promptly to the Baptist General Convention of Texas Audit Committee, which should meet privately, and at least annually, with the engagement partner of each audit firm performing work for Texas Baptist entities. These meetings will afford an opportunity to discuss audit matters independently, confidentially, and in such depth as may be warranted by the circumstances involved.

The Audit Committee shall be appointed by and responsible to the Executive Board and the Program Coordinating Committee.

The Audit Committee shall refer audit reports after review and evaluation back to each entity or institution for information, attention, and action as needed to correct error, to change off assets considered as losses or inadmissible in accordance with convention policy or the constitution and bylaws of the entity or institution examined and to have the power to require such attention and action to be taken.

The Audit Committee shall serve as conservator or receiver or appoint a conservator or receiver in cases of emergency, until such time as the Executive Board may appoint a conservator or receiver, to prevent undue loss of assets in the event of abandonment of office, negligence, criminal action, or any other situation of emergency in which it is necessary to take action to protect the properties of the convention from such undue loss.

Source: *Proceedings*, Baptist General Convention of Texas, 1967, 58–62. Reprint courtesy of the Baptist General Convention of Texas.

12.6 WMU

During the 1960s the WMU remained very active in virtually all aspects of convention life. The WMU aided in the formation of WMUs in Mexican churches, helped launch the River Ministry, championed the Mary Hill Davis offering, and raised funds for the 1964 Latin American Crusade.

New and Old Concerns

The Latin-American Crusade was a major prayer concern. At the Executive Board meeting March 11, 1962, "My hopes for the Latin-American Crusades," was the topic for Mrs. Epifanio Salazar, Mrs. Carlos Ramirez and Mrs. Carol Paredes.

Miss Henderson reported 7,992 Leadership Training Cards issued. There were 15,018 W. M. U. organizations reporting with a membership of 168,867. The GA Queen's Court had an attendance of 2,015. There were 74 Associational Sunbeam clinics for local leaders, and three YWA House Parties with more than 3,900 in attendance.

Mary Jane Nethery took three bus loads of girls to YWA Week in Ridgecrest. A letter came to her from Monroe, Louisiana which read; *"On behalf of the management and employees of the Piccadilly Cafeteria of Monroe, Louisiana, we'd like for you to know how nice and orderly your girls of the Baptist churches were that ate with us June 19* (1964). *Please let them know how much we appreciate young people like them."*

At the Annual Meeting held in Corpus Christi, Mrs. G. M. McNeilly of Austin was recognized for having attended thirty-one consecutive meetings. Mrs. Harold Branch, Stewardship Director of Corpus Christi Association, and a member of both the National and Baptist General Conventions, led a prayer session.

Since Districts had been abolished during the year, Mrs. Ernest H. Pierce presented to Eula Mae Henderson the W. M. U. pin formerly worn by District Five Presidents. Miss Henderson had been a District Five Scholarship girl at the Seminary.

Five-year service pens were awarded to Mary Jane Nethery, Joy Phillips and Noemi Cuevas.

The Mary Hill Davis Offering reached $408,610.03 and since the allocations were only $247,000, this gave $161,610.03 to the Latin-American Crusade. Additional gifts to the Offering raised the total to $190,000 plus and the women were grateful.

The first Annual Meeting for Wisconsin-Minnesota women was held with 83 women present from 17 of the 30 churches.

A significant change in the By-laws was voted in 1964. The tenure of Texas W. M. U. Leadership changed from six years to four years and Associational W. M. U. Presidents became members of the State W. M. U. Executive Board. Three of the women, Mrs. Tom Drewett, Recording Secretary, Mrs. Roy Cooper, State Community Missions Director, and Mrs. Howard Bennett, State Stewardship Director, had served four years. They were replaced by Mrs. Otto Dukes, Recording Secretary; Mrs. Howard Scott, State Stewardship Director; and Mrs. C. L. Peterson, Community Missions Director.

Mrs. C. J. Humphrey of Amarillo was elected President.

Source: Inez Boyle Hunt, *Century One A Pilgrimage of Faith: Woman's Missionary Union 1880–1980* (Dallas: Woman's Missionary Union, 1979), 72–73. Reprint courtesy of the Woman's Missionary Union of Texas.

12.7 The River Ministry

It was estimated that there were more than two million people living along the 800 miles of the Rio Grande in the 1960s. The River Ministry was the dream of T. A. Patterson and Elmin Howell who thought of ingenious ways to minister to people on both the Mexican and American side of the Rio Grande. Vacation Bible Schools, medical missionaries, and a Christmas airdrop of toys to isolated villages highlighted this endeavor. The financial concerns of the River Ministry were met by the WMU who funded the project out of the Mary Hill Davis Offering for Home Missions.

One of the Greatest Mission Fields in the World

The Rio Grande River Ministry was discussed by T. A. Patterson. He stated that this is one of the greatest mission fields in the world with very little being done about it through the years. Dr. Patterson introduced Charles McLaughlin, Secretary of the State Missions Commission, who gave background on the work and told of a recent trip taken with representatives of the W. M. U. along the Rio Grande. He said there are over a million people on each side of the border. Plans for the summer include 11 summer missionaries to work there this summer. Also several doctors and a number of young people from various churches to move from place to place this summer conducting clinics and Vacation Bible Schools.

T. A. Patterson introduced Mrs. C. J. Humphrey, President of the Woman's Missionary Union, who spoke concerning her own personal reaction to the River Ministry and its needs. She gave some vivid descriptions of her visit along the river and in closing announced that the girls attending the recent YWA House Parties had given $3,886.00 to pay expenses of young people to conduct Vacation Bible Schools along the Rio Grande this summer.

T. A. Patterson read the following recommendation on the Rio Grande River Proposal:

"Baptist pastors, missionaries, and lay leaders along the Mexican Border have increasingly given themselves to meet their immediate missions responsibilities. Their efforts have focused the attention of many others upon thousands suffering from spiritual starvation who live along the Texas-Mexican Border. On the premise that a massive missionary thrust in the interest of these lost neighbors should be generated, the following recommendation rests:"

"The State Missions Commission recommends that the Executive Board of the Baptist General Convention of Texas give approval and authorization to the State Missions Commission to join with the Texas Baptist Woman's Missionary Union, if so desired by the W. M. U., in the promotion of the Mary Hill Davis Offering for State Missions and that special consideration be directed to mission needs on the border of Texas from El Paso-Juarez to Brownsville-Matamoros."

Harry Trulove moved that the recommendation be approved. Seconded by Carroll Jackson.

H. J. Flanders raised the question, would this Mary Hill Davis Offering be used only on the Texas side of the river? Charles McLaughlin
answered that it would be anticipated that assistance would be given to
churches along the river sponsoring work on either side. And if the recommendation is passed, Dr. Patterson plans on corresponding with the
Foreign Mission Board to correlate whatever work is done with them,
the same thing would be true in working with the Home Mission Board.

Mrs. Humphrey was asked to briefly review what the W. M. U. did
last year and is doing this year in the Latin American area. Last year
$65,000 was allocated for Valley Baptist Academy, also the same amount
this year. Participating in "Share and Care," the building of Latin American church buildings. After this discussion, the motion carried.

Source: *Minutes*, Executive Board of the Baptist General Convention of
Texas, 7 March 1967. Reprint courtesy of the Baptist General Convention of Texas.

12.8 Controversy

> Dr. Ralph Elliott, an Old Testament professor at Midwestern Baptist Theo-
> logical Seminary, Kansas City, Missouri, published the *Message of Genesis* in
> 1961. In this text, Elliott questioned the historicity and traditional authorship
> of Genesis chapters one through eleven. This work was harshly critiqued by
> several prominent Texas Baptists, such as *Baptist Standard* editor E. S. James
> and K. Owen White who penned the infamous "Death in the Pot."

Death in the Pot

Since the parable includes the historical and non-historical, one can
say with Richardson: "We must learn to think of the stories of Genesis—the creation, the fall, Noah's ark, the Tower of Babel—in the same
way as we think of the parables of Jesus; they are profoundly symbolic
(although not allegorical) stories, which aren't to be taken as literally
true (like the words of the textbooks of geology), but which yet bear a
meaning that cannot be paraphrased or stated in any other way without
losing something of their quality of existential truth."

"Adam originally must have meant 'mankind,' not just one person."
"The particular problem of Chapter 5 is the longevity of the antediluvians.

It is difficult to believe that they actually lived as long as stated. In all probability, the Priestly writer simply exaggerated the ages in order to show the glory of an ancient civilization."

"'God took him' is not necessarily an indication that he disappeared suddenly and was nowhere to be found. It is the Old Testament expression of belief in the ideal of immortality."

"The tower of Babel parable shows the futility and emptiness of human effort divorced from the acknowledgment and service of God." "In other words, there are great many evidences which, while not giving conclusive proof, lend strong credence to the historicity of the patriarchs."

"Quite possibly some of the stories have been heightened and intensified by materials that are not literally historical, for the purpose of the Bible is not merely to give a factual account of events."

"This not to say that Abraham was a monotheist, but it is to say that he had a concept of God different from that of his pagan neighbors."

"If one cannot be certain of the facts of historicity, what is to be received from the stories?"

"It would appear, then, that in verse 19, Melchizedec was blessing Abraham by the Baal, whom Melchizedec considered to be the highest god of the city-state at Salem."

"Supposedly, during the prophetic period, the narrative was edited in such a way that it was made also to teach a fine lesson about God."

"There developed the tradition that this was what happened to Lot's wife—perhaps not exactly historical . . . "

"Suddenly, what had been a thought of meditation gripped the inner being of Abraham until he thought he heard it as a clear call from God, 'Go sacrifice Isaac.'"

Does this sound like Boyce, Broadus, Mullins, Robertson, Sampey, Gambrell, Carroll, Scarborough, and other great Southern Baptist leaders? The quotations listed above are from *The Message of Genesis,* written by Dr. Ralph Elliott, now teaching at Midwestern Seminary, Kansas City, Mo.

Being a graduate of Southern Seminary and having served as pastor of Southern Baptist churches for more than 30 years, I love and believe in my denomination and have a burning passion for it to remain true to the Bible as the Word of God. I have a deep concern that our seminaries shall sound a clear, ringing note in their interpretation of the Scriptures and that young preachers shall come from their halls without an "uncertain sound."

The book from which I have quoted is liberalism, pure and simple! It stems from the rationalistic theology of Wellhausen and his school which led Germany to become a materialistic godless nation. This is "the wisdom of the world" which seeks to find a "reasonable, acceptable" solution to every problem which involves the supernatural.

Several great denominations in the last generation have drifted from the faith of our fathers, have lost their conviction that the Bible is authoritative and dependable, and now have little evangelistic witness. The drift came from liberalism in their seminaries and their literature.

If the appeal is made for "academic freedom," let it be said that we gladly grant any man the right to believe what he wants to—but, we do not grant him the right to believe and express views in conflict with our historic position concerning the Bible as the Word of God while he is teaching in one of our schools, built and supported by Baptist funds.

The book in question is "poison." This sort of rationalistic criticism can lead only to further confusion, unbelief, deterioration, and ultimate disintegration as a great New Testament denomination. It has happened to other denominations; it can happen to us! Modernism is insidious, dangerous, and destructive.

What can be done?

- Invite men with great views to find a place of service with group or denominations of like theological inclinations.
- Ask the trustees of our institutions to consider seriously the dangers involved in such theological views and to exercise caution in their approval of faculty members.
- Urge our Sunday School Board to be alert to any trend in the direction of liberalism in our publications.

This is not an incidental matter. It involves the total responsibility of every one of us individually, of our churches and our denomination, in declaring plainly, positively, and unequivocally "the whole counsel of God."

In this brief statement I have made no attempt to review the book. The quotations speak for themselves. I have merely emphasized certain words and phrases in these quotations to shed light upon the particular doctrinal or historical truth in question. The influence of this sort of teaching would substitute intuition for inspiration, reason for revelation, and futility for faith. It is quite true of course that in our study and interpretation of God's Word we are not to forsake common sense, but we also need to remember the words of Isaiah 55:8, 9. "For my thoughts are not your thoughts, neither are your ways my ways, saith the Lord. For as the heavens are higher than your ways, and my thoughts than your thoughts."

"There is death in the pot!"

Source: K. Owen White, ". . . Death in the Pot," *Baptist Standard*, 10 January 1962, 6. Reprint courtesy of the *Baptist Standard*.

CHAPTER 13

Focus on Texas, 1974–1982

13.1 James Landes

Following the retirement of T. A. Patterson, James Landes was chosen as the next Executive Secretary of the BGCT in September of 1973. Landes believed that more emphasis should be placed on Texas missions rather than on foreign missions. In particular, Landes and the majority of his staff were not advocates of the Japanese Crusade. Under the leadership of Landes, the heads of the different commissions met weekly with the Executive Secretary in order to keep him appraised of their progress, their leadership skills were constantly evaluated, and an attempt to rescue Dallas Baptist College from debt was undertaken.

A. Thoughts on Patterson: Oral Interview

Pitts: How did you find things there as you went in to take the office?

Landes: The fact of the matter is that I was elected in September and by October 1, the men who work directly with me and are in category two—we have two categories there, insofar as leadership levels are concerned; we have five levels of people. There's only one person in level one and that's the Executive Director, but there are ten or eleven who are on level two. Those people began to come to visit me at the church, and I saw that it was absolutely necessary for me to set up conferences with them for planning for the year that was ahead. They wanted to know what I thought about everything, you know. So, I did go on down to the Baptist Building periodically from October 1, on. But you will recall that I stayed through stewardship time at the First Baptist Church of Richardson, which meant, I believe, through the first Sunday of November. On the first day of December I moved down to the building into an office on the first floor, not into Dr. Patterson's office, or the Executive Director's office, but into a vacant office on the first floor. By that time, I had already established a relationship with the men—all the men who were on level two, the administrators or the directors of the various commissions and coordinating boards and so forth.

I found things at the building in very interesting shape. Dr. Patterson was a strong man in many ways, and was a strong leader. He had one consuming ambition which is a very noble one; the same ambition as the apostle Paul had when he said, "I am willing to become all things to all men if, by any means, I might save some." Dr. Patterson's strong forte, and continuous forte and great dream was that he was going to save the world for Christ's sake, and he gave himself, during his tenure as Executive Secretary, which was the longest any man's ever had— thirteen years—to the matter of world evangelism. As you know, he's now with the World Evangelism Foundation, whose office is across the street from our building. In doing this, it was necessary for him to neglect some other things; no man can do all things, and in order to do this well, he had to let some of the other things go. I found that on the part of some of the men there was a earnest desire to get in close with the Executive Secretary. Dr. Patterson is a very warm man to meet personally, but as an administrator, he operated in a pretty lonely fashion, which is not my way of operating.

And so, I had to establish my personal relationships with each one of these men. It was not hard to do. They were hungry; they were anxious for a personal relationship with the executive director. He had met with them regularly, but, as I say—this is certainly not a reflection; it's a compliment—he was a man with one mind and one purpose, and going about one thing. That left the schools to run themselves; he left the other institutions to run themselves, and so forth. It was my job to move in immediately and work with Dr. Armes at the educational level. Dallas Baptist College was in desperate trouble, and the first year and a half I was there, I was consumed with the interests of Dallas Baptist College. We had some other institutional problems that I don't need to mention, but it's so generally known that Dallas Baptist College was about to fold that I don't mind mentioning that one. It was necessary, though it had been admirably handled, for me to move into the human welfare division, which are the hospitals and the child-care homes. They were all in good shape financially, but they were anxious to have the strong support of the executive director.

The first thing I had to do, Dr. Pitts, was to establish a personal relationship with these men; to sit with them long enough to set forth administrative directions; to let them know how I would operate; and to let them know that they were to stay out of each other's hair, that each would report directly to me, and that, in my absence, if one of them made a mistake, I would correct it.

Source: *Oral Memoirs of James Henry Landes, Jr.*, 2 vols. Texas Baptist Oral History Project, Baylor University, 1: 182–84. Reprint courtesy of the Baptist General Convention of Texas.

B. Trouble at Dallas Baptist College

At this time, Dr. Landes expressed appreciation to the members of the Executive Board for being present for this called meeting. He also expressed appreciation for the Christian Education Commission, Administrative Committee, administration from Dallas Baptist College, Chairman of the Executive Board, members of the Board of Baylor University, including Dr. Abner McCall and Dr. Herb Reynolds, for the many hours all had devoted to this cause.

Dr. Landes reviewed his first four months as Executive Secretary saying he had crisscrossed the state by automobile, plane, both commercial and private, trying to strengthen our total mission thrust through our mission division and the missionary work of all our institutions of all types through the Cooperative Program as given to us by the BGCT last fall.

He continued, "When it became apparent several weeks ago that anticipated gifts to DBC were not forthcoming this spring, the Chairman of the Dallas Baptist College Board realized that the institution was again in financial trouble. Accordingly, at his request several consultative meetings were called with the elected officers of the Board, elected officers of the Convention, and the proper people from the institution itself. These were consulted across the brief span of weeks. It was obvious to all concerned that a series of difficult decisions were at hand. Finally it was felt by a majority of the DBC Board and those who had been consulted that possibly the DBC-Baylor merger was the most viable solution in view of the total work of the total Baptist family. From the outset I believed, not only I but all have taken the position, that we represent all institutions, each institution, and all programs. I will continue to do so as long as I serve our Lord, our churches, and our institutions, and you in this present office.

"We have called together procedurally proper groups, also various groups. We have consulted with the college presidents, individuals involved, the CEC, and the Administrative Committee. The CEC and the Administrative Committee had two meetings within the last week. Last night they were in session until 1:00 A.M. We recognize that a merger of any two institutions of the BGCT is a matter of great importance and must be approached with the utmost care. The impact of such a merger upon the institutions involved affects them and all other institutions and programs of the BGCT. Hasty decisions which could be irrevocable could be questioned for many years. The life of our institutions calls for the best judgment of a multitude of counselors over a sufficient period of time. Circumstances can alter from day to day.

"Changes in direction can be found perhaps. May I suggest that important as dollars are, and we know the power of dollars, the spirit of unity that prevails in our Convention is even more important. Trust and faith in one another is vital. Trust in the elected leadership, including the elected leadership of this convention, and boards, is vital to our functioning as a democratic group. This is not ever to preclude proper questions and truthful answers. I cannot speak for others though I feel I can, and I am sure I can for myself, but more prayers have been said and more heart searching agony has been experienced over this particular problem in recent weeks than are normally experienced over a period of years. The number of man hours that have been spent is unbelievable. Once again let me say that in my particular office, Mr. Chairman, I have striven to think in terms of the total mission thrust, the total BGCT-convention program. Inventory has been taken, analyses have been made and in a short time you will receive a recommendation from the Administrative Committee and the Christian Education Commission."

Source: *Minutes*, Executive Board of the Baptist General Convention of Texas, 16 July 1974. Reprint courtesy of the Baptist General Convention of Texas.

13.2 Ministry to Ministers

During this period of restructuring, the BGCT did not forget to take care of the needs of its four thousand pastors and hundreds of denominational employees. The most significant aid services were a ministers' counseling service, a ministerial placement service, and a ministers' retirement program.

A. Ministers' Counseling Service

Landes: And the younger ministers, Bill, are not in a very secure position anymore. This is true because there has been a demand that we accept the Chicago statement on theology—theological statement—as the statement, as over against the '63 statement, which was, of course, the '25 statement known back forever. And then there has been more and more emphasis on the big church, the megachurch, and their pastors have been used more and more in our evangelistic conferences and this sort of thing. And so stress for numbers and stress for commercial world success and the demand for obedience to a certain creed have heightened the thing that has always been there—tension. And as a consequence, we have men being fired right and left.

Pitts: I expect, from their point of view, they feel a lot more stress and burnout and so forth. At least we read a lot more about that. I know that you had in place counseling services for ministers in difficulty and that type of thing.

Landes: A lot of stress; a lot of need for someone to stand by. That's a very uncertain position one is in.

Pitts: Then, too, our procedure for moving people around is quite different, say, from the Methodists, where someone is guaranteed some work if he or she is a minister. And—

Landes: Yes, that's in there. We have something else, and I put it on tape. We have a very active placement organization in Southern Baptist life now, which we have never had before. If First Church, Richardson, gets without a pastor, they will receive three or four letters immediately, and they will be from someone in the ultrafundamentalist camp. Will simply say, if you want to know about this person, call Dr. W. A. Criswell, or call the Memphis pastor [Adrian Rogers]. And this is stress filled because some of these persons—not all of them—but some of these persons don't mind dropping heads. They just cut off your head if you don't agree with them, and that's hurt a lot, Bill, hurt a lot.

Source: *Oral Memoirs of James H. Landes, Jr.*, 2 vols. Texas Baptist Oral History Project, Baylor University, 2: 218–19. Reprint courtesy of the Baptist General Convention of Texas.

B. Ministerial Placement—Church/Staff Information Service

James L. Cooper, Chairman of the Staff Committee, appointed to study the needs for a Christian/Staff Information Service, brought the following report:

Purpose:

We suggest that the office of Church/Staff Information Service be implemented for the purpose of offering a liaison service between the Baptist General Convention of Texas churches and ministers, upon request, in the form of information and counseling. It is thoroughly understood that the principles of the sovereignty of God, the leadership of the Holy Spirit, the autonomy of the local church, and the freedom and responsibility of both ministers and churches be respected.

Function:

The functions of the office would be as follows:

1. To maintain factual and confidential biographical files on ministers who are willing to provide such information.

2. To offer assistance, when requested, to pastor-selection committees or other staff personnel committees, in helping them understand their responsibilities.

3. To secure information from churches which seek staff help from the service.

4. To provide names, when requested, for consideration by staff search committees, giving biographical information, service records, and non-interpretative factual material on such prospective staff members. Such information would not imply either endorsement or recommendation of the persons involved.

5. To assist in gathering information on prospective staff members when requested by the BGCT staff members, Directors of Missions, and other responsible persons who have been called upon by specific churches to assist them.

Staffing and Budgeting:

We suggest that W. E. Norman be named as Director of the Church/Staff Information Service along with his present duties as Statistician. It is suggested that $5,000 be allocated in the 1978 budget to facilitate beginning this ministry.

Related Information:

On October 18, 1971, the BGCT approved the establishing of a Church/Staff Information Service. Since that time twelve state conventions have tested and proven to be effective with a slightly different model. It is for this reason that the following recommendation for implementation of the Convention's previous action has been modified. It is our belief that these minor changes will greatly strengthen the program while fulfilling the Convention's intention and purpose in the original action.

Some Advantages of the Suggested Plan:

1. Church/Staff Information Service is the name already authorized by the Convention in 1971. This could be considered "pre-computer" start up, and so already adopted by the Convention. R. "Dusty" Crawford of Membership Services Incorporated has observed, "It would not be financially feasible to establish the Church/Staff Information Service as a computer operation with the limited number of names you will have at the beginning. As the service increases you may wish to give some consideration to transferring to a computer."

2. Low profile beginning makes it possible to begin immediately and on a small budget. The amount of $5,000 for 1978 is an estimate based on very minimal travel, supplies, materials, printing, postage . . . , etc.

3. The concepts, process, forms and letters have already been reported to the Administrative Staff and Administrative Committee (May, 1976). They have been "tested and proven worthy" in other conventions. Twelve states now have this kind of ministry, with the number being about equally divided between those who do this work full time and those who share other responsibilities.

4. The proposed plan could be easily related to the efforts of Directors of Missions. In fact, it could be a service to them when desired in their information help to churches.

5. It is flexible. Different churches with differing needs may use only those services requested. The initiative stays with the local church committee and the minister.

Source: *Minutes*, Executive Board of the Baptist General Convention of Texas, 13 September 1977. Reprint courtesy of the Baptist General Convention of Texas.

C. Ministerial Retirement—Annuity Study Committee

J. T. Luther, Chairman of the Annuity Study Committee, gave background on the committee stating that the committee had met several times and visited with a number of people before preparing the recommendations to be presented. He observed that the committee had agreed 100% this time that this committee of 15, one from each zone, should be appointed, organize from all over the state and get behind this program by encouraging all churches to enter their pastor and staff members as rapidly as possible.

RECOMMENDATIONS OF ANNUITY STUDY COMMITTEE

1. We recommend that a permanent Annuity Committee reflecting the 15 zones be established by the Executive Board to give continued attention to the following:

2. We recommend that a program of Annuity Education be implemented by the Executive Board Secretary and his staff. This will be coordinated through the Texas Annuity Board representative and our association missionaries.

3. We recommend that every Texas Baptist church be urged to accept its responsibility as employer.

    a. Enter every pastor and staff member in the Basis Plan "A" (or "B") as rapidly as possible.

    b. Move toward participation on 10% of base salary immediately.

    c. That up to $50,000 be budgeted by the Convention as their part to the fund due to the increased participation on the part of churches and staff members.

4. We recommend that a special Annuity Emergency Fund of $25,000 be established to meet emergency financial needs of present annuitants. This fund should be administered through the established Southern Baptist Convention Annuity Board channels.

5. We recommend that the Annuity Committee establish its own guidelines, utilizing the findings of the Study Committee and consulting the Executive Board and its staff.

> J. T. Luther, Chairman
> William H. Hinton
> Ned King
> John Rasco

Mr. Luther moved the adoption of this report. There were several seconds.

Questions, answers and observations pertaining to the report were made by the following:

Ed Thiele: This does not do anything for the person already retired as far as emergency needs. Do we have any plan for helping a person in need? What is my action in helping this person, do I go to Bill Roe, or do I go to that man and get him to apply personally? How do we get help to that man?

Luther: This is the purpose of setting up a committee from the 15 zones. A person could come, say, through the area missionary, then through the Annuity Board. Also, we (Annuity Study Committee) would like to meet with these 15 persons after they are appointed and share some of our observations with them.

Elder: Our Annuity Board representative is Bill Roe and he would work closely with Dr. Landes and with this committee that is being recommended.

Thiele: Could Bill Roe be given the opportunity to speak? He must have some data about men applying to his office, or knows of persons who should apply. This would help me to be satisfied with what we are doing as a temporary measure.

Bill Roe: Present procedure: Some person must call to our attention, either pastor, missionary, someone. We in turn through the Annuity Board forward a recommendation sheet to that person who made the contact. This is returned to the Annuity Board who handles these emergency needs. All information received is confidential.

Question: Has anything been done in asking the churches to contribute an extra amount, over and above what is paid for the pastor's retirement, to help these cases?

Luther: Once we get started with this committee of 15, Cates and I will be the first two people, if the committee will come to us, to start some kind of fund. Might be asking everyone to help us. We need a million dollars.

Elder: The Annuity Board does have flexibility to help us meet any Annuity needs that we are unable to meet.

Jack Harris: Does this 15-member committee eliminate the Study Committee?

Landes: This committee is offering its services beyond this point. They are saying, we have information we want to share it. I believe when we find out about these friends who need help, we will want to do two things: We don't want them to be embarrassed and we do want them to be helped. I believe we can do this, anyway, somehow.

Question: How much is the SBC budget for emergency action?

Roe: $200,000 with a possible $50,000 increase. In all probability we will spend all of this year's budget by the end of the year.

Elder: They're asking for a larger amount than, $200,000, are they not?

Roe: Have petitioned for more but have not had a response.

Observation: The persons who are suffering are the ones who are retired on a very small annuity. They're in an emergency day to day.

Ned King: I think we as Baptists should really get with it and sell our Annuity Board programs to all the people before they get sick, retire, etc. We have a great program as Baptists but we are also autonomous and unfortunately our autonomy is greater than our vision and wisdom. I think we are trying to say that if the pastors and laymen over the state will join with us, working through our missionaries, and start selling our churches to get involved in the retirement programs, rather than talking about those few deserving cases. And now we have to do something about them for we're under mandate from God to take care of our helpless. We need to get to the heart of the thing by taking care of the next generation by simply preparing in advance for living too long, dying too soon, or getting sick.

Observation: Either North Carolina or South Carolina gives $50,000 each month to each of its pastors in the Annuity Board's Plan A or B. Further discussions to this observation pointed out that even if this does this those in the most need would be penalized by having this amount deducted from their Social Security. Therefore, rather than increasing their income they would be paid just that much less by the government.

The question was called for and the motion to adopt the Annuity Study Committee report carried.

Source: *Minutes*, Executive Board of the Baptist General Convention of Texas, 10 September 1974. Reprint courtesy of the Baptist General Convention of Texas.

D. Proposed Annuity Committee Guidelines

The Executive Board of the Baptist General Convention of Texas voted in its quarterly meeting on September 10, 1974, to establish a permanent annuity committee.

These proposed guidelines are given to carry out the instructions of the Executive Board.

I. RELATION TO CHURCHES AND CHURCH STAFF

The Committee will function with the recognition that pastors and other church staff and employees are employed by the church and that each church is an autonomous body. This principle of relationship will guide the committee in efforts to:

1. Encourage the churches and staff members in a program of increased participation in the retirement and insurance programs administered by the Annuity Board.

2. Lead the Baptist General Convention of Texas in its role of responsible assistance to the churches because of the new voluntary ties of denominational life.

II. RELATIONSHIP TO THE ESTABLISHED CONVENTION PROGRAMS

The Committee will work with the established annuity programs of both the Southern Baptist Convention and the Baptist General Convention of Texas. The Annuity Board of the Southern Baptist Convention has the trustee responsibility for programs and the Baptist General Convention of Texas has a responsible role of contractual relationship with the Annuity Board relating to the basic retirement program involving the staff member, church and the Convention.

III. RESPONSE TO NEEDS OF INCREASED PARTICIPATION

The Committee recognizes the need for increased participation in the retirement programs by many churches and employees. This is reflected by the fact that 1,500 Texas pastors are not enrolled in an Annuity Board retirement plan and that about 65% of the churches would do well to consider increasing participation in the retirement plans.

The Annuity Committee shall request and encourage all churches in Texas to participate in the Southern Baptist Retirement Program at the minimum level and most churches to participate at the 10% level of salary deposit for all employees; request and encourage Texas churches to provide the insurance program administered by the Annuity Board for full-time employees, with the church paying at least 50% of the premium cost of the insurance.

IV. ALERTNESS TO NEEDS OF RETIRED CHURCH STAFF AND WIDOWS

The Committee will seek to serve both the Baptist General Convention of Texas and the Annuity Board by receiving and forwarding to the Annuity Board information concerning retired church staff and widows who are in need of financial assistance. As needed, recommendations will be presented to the Executive Board of the Baptist General Convention of Texas.

V. WORKING WITH THE ANNUITY DEPARTMENT OF THE BAPTIST GENERAL CONVENTION OF TEXAS

The Annuity Department functions within the structure of the State Missions Committee of the Baptist General Convention of Texas. Its budget and programs of work are approved by the State Missions Commission, the Administrative Committee and the Baptist General Convention of Texas. The Annuity Board of the Southern Baptist Convention funds approximately one-half of the Texas Annuity Department program.

The Annuity Committee shall receive reports on a regular basis by the Annuity Department of its work in the following areas:
1) Numbers of churches and persons enlisted in retirement programs.
2) Number of persons and churches adding to present retirement programs.
3) Special activities performed by the Annuity Department.
4) Number of persons assisted by the Annuity Board, Southern Baptist Convention, through the supplemental assistance program for retired church staff and widows.

VI. RECOMMENDATIONS RELATING TO SPECIAL GROUPS

The Annuity Committee shall meet annually to receive progress reports and evaluate needs, and at other times as deemed necessary to conduct Committee business. The Chairman of the Annuity Committee shall be empowered to call a special meeting of the Committee, in consultation with the Executive Secretary (Director) for the Baptist General Convention of Texas and the Secretary of the Annuity Department.

Source: *Minutes*, Executive Board of the Baptist General Convention of Texas, 11 March 1975. Reprint courtesy of the Baptist General Convention of Texas.

13.3 The River Ministry Revisited: Funding

Pitts: How is the River Ministry financed?

Howell: The base finance comes to the River Ministry from the Mary Hill Davis offering which is held each fall. Donations and special designations will also cover a good percentage of the needs. I wouldn't want to be held to a figure or percentage of what that would be. We could figure it out, but it varies from one year to the next. In some years we couldn't have accomplished anywhere near what we did if it had not been for special designations and donations that people have made. They have been out there and been involved and they want to, to put forth some money to meet special needs. The upstate churches have taken on big responsibilities. I can think of four missions right off where assisting churches made the difference. And now those, those missions are churches because of the good, solid relationship of an upstate church working with a local missionary. The upstate church saw that the local people were trained and that they had everything they needed for training, and now they're pretty well carrying their own load and the upstate church has gradually backed off and is now going in another direction. This is a beautiful thing to watch and be a part of.

Pitts: I see. You mentioned priorities awhile ago. How are these determined by the missionaries in the six associations and how are the needs met?

Howell: The missionaries will get together with their individual associational mission committees, and sometimes the members of their executive boards, and determine what their budget's going to be for the year. They'll review a list of unmet needs. These unmet needs have come to them from the pastors and from the area workers. From the list of unmet needs then will come a list of possible needs that may be met if the right circumstances take place with upstate sponsoring churches. For example, if the balance sheet shows over here that it looks like it's going to take ten thousand dollars to accomplish a project, then they would put that over on a priority list, saying that it appears at this point that in order to build an educational wing or to put on a full-time pastor, that a salary supplement or a certain amount of money will be needed for that particular priority.

That priority, then, among others, will be shared, or featured, when they meet with the churches at the retreats. At a retreat a missionary will just sit down across the table in a very informal setting and share his list, and he'll have copies available for the churches. Sometimes the missionary will have new churches coming to the retreats for the first time. Sometimes there will be the same churches sitting around the table that he's been working with for three or four years or more. They'll give the church leaders there a chance to say, Well, we'd like to take number two or three priority. Procedures move out from there in the planning to get those needs met. A lot of times, the priorities go unmet and so they to reevaluate and redesign. Their proposed programs may have to be postponed. I've talked with other missionaries on the foreign fields in a number of countries and I see that their problems are very similar to ours. They have hopes of getting moneys for the special priorities from Lottie Moon. And sometimes that money doesn't come in so they have to go back and redesign and reprioritize what they are going to be doing, and the same thing is true in our field.

Pitts: When the six associational missionaries coordinate their needs, do they work together at this point or do they work just directly with the churches.

Howell: They communicate with us, as we ask them to, to keep us informed as to what their priorities are—

Pitts: I see.

Howell: —that's when I'm in a church out in the field I can talk sensibly to a church who's asking me about a priority. A church might ask, We want to go into the Frio River Baptist Association. We understand they've got these three items that they need; are these valid? Well, I have to be able to say yes or no, so I have to stay in communication with the associational missions office. In that light, they keep in touch with us. As far as planning together, no, they don't, except when we have the annual retreats. We try to have a missionary fellowship planning retreat about every other year where Dr. McLaughlin, Dr. Landes, Dr. Greer, and others would meet with us and with our river missions team of missionaries. And at that point, each missionary gets to see about where other missionaries are and just to learn from some of their trials and errors, or from each other. We're able to grow, kind of, in a standard way.

Source: *Oral Memoirs of Elmin Kimboll Howell, Jr.* Texas Baptist Oral History Consortium, Institute for Oral History, Baylor University, 1980–1981, 126–29. Reprint courtesy of the Baptist General Convention of Texas.

13.4 Personal Involvement in Missions

Due to the success of the Japan New Life Crusade and the River Ministry, Texas Baptists began to desire additional opportunities for personal and volunteer involvement in missions. This desire was met with the birth of three integrated programs: Mission to Brazil, the Mission Service Corps, and Partnership Missions.

A. Mission to Brazil:1982 Annual Report

As Brazilian Baptists began to look forward to their centennial date, Oct. 15, 1982, they invited Texas Baptists to help them reach some challenging goals. The Mission to Brazil office was established to coordinate the effort, and to serve as a liaison between the Brazilian Baptist Convention, the Foreign Mission Board, and Texas Baptists.

It is estimated that by the centennial date 3,750 Texas Baptists will have participated in the effort and that 95,000 souls will have been won to Christ by volunteers. Ten major cities in Brazil were linked with 10 areas in Texas. Through this "sister city" relationship, numerous requests have been made for various types of partnership mission projects; simultaneous revivals, evangelistic efforts, church growth clinics, WIN schools, music, sports, construction, disaster relief, agriculture, and religious education.

The basic purpose of the Mission to Brazil program is to enable Texas Baptists to become personally involved as witnesses to Brazil. The partnership has been a real blessing for both Texas and Brazil. As Mission to Brazil came to a close, Texas Baptists have accepted the challenge of partnership missions in other countries, and will continue to minister through a new Partnership Missions office.

Source: *Proceedings*, Baptist General Convention of Texas, 1982, 150. Reprint courtesy of the Baptist General Convention of Texas.

B. Mission Service Corps: 1982 Annual Report

Mission Service Corps has the assignment of enlisting volunteers to assist churches and associations in mission outreach and to generate service opportunity requests for mission volunteers from churches and associations.

Mission Service Corps response in Texas continues to be the pacesetter for Southern Baptists. At the present rate of enlistment, there is a distinct possibility of achieving the Texas goal of 1,000 MSC volunteers by the close of 1982. Mission Service Corps personnel presently serve in 20 states and 13 foreign countries. Six orientation meetings for Texans were conducted by MSC personnel in the past year. Sixteen regional consultants serve in Texas and are available to churches, associations, and related organizations for Mission Service Corps presentations and to recruit and counsel volunteers.

W.M.U. leadership Conference (Houseparty) provided conference time for MSC as did the Church Library Conventions, Retiree retreats, Campers on Missions, Senior Adult Meetings, River Ministry and Baptist Student Union Convention. Texas Baptist Men have worked closely with MSC in the enlistment of volunteers.

A prayer chain was formed with retired missionaries throughout the state. Prayer requests from MSC personnel are shared with Texas Baptists as is praise for answered prayer through "Prayer and Praise Newsletter."

Three pilot projects were conducted during the past year with good success and will be continued throughout next year. While serving on MSC assignment, several volunteers have found leadership for career missions.

A recent survey indicates 45% of MSC personnel are male and 55% female with 24% of the group under 30 years of age and 31% above 60 years of age. Professions of faith average 9 per volunteer.

Source: *Proceedings*, Baptist General Convention of Texas, 1982, 151. Reprint courtesy of the Baptist General Convention of Texas.

C. Bold Mission Thrust

Chairman Heflin (Administrative Committee) presented the following Resolution concerning the Bold Mission Thrust:

WHEREAS, the Southern Baptist Convention meeting in Kansas City adopted the following resolution:

"We recommend that the Southern Baptist Convention, working in cooperation with the state conventions, seek to enlist by 1982, 5,000 persons, groups of churches, or churches who would agree to provide and fund 5,000 mission volunteers who would go for one or two years, either in the United States or overseas, in an effort to reach the objectives of the Bold Mission Thrust."

WHEREAS, this expresses the determination of the Convention to take seriously our purpose to preach the gospel to all the people in the world by the year 2000; and

WHEREAS, the Executive Board of the Baptist General Convention of Texas is enthusiastically involved in planning models for the use of volunteers on the mission fields in the homeland and around the world;

BE IT THEREFORE RESOLVED:

THAT the Executive Board of the Baptist General Convention of Texas today affirm its wholehearted commitment to the ideals and objectives envisioned in the new Mission Service Corps program as evidenced by the Board's instructing the Executive Director to proceed in studying structures and the relationships for the BGCT's proper involvement.

W. Ray Parmer moved that this Resolution be approved. There were several seconds and the motion carried.

The following mimeographed material on the <u>Principles of Bold Mission Thrust</u> has been mailed to all Executive Board members.

1. That the name of the project be Mission Service Corps of the Southern Baptist Convention and that it become a vital part of the larger Bold Missions Thrust.

2. That the objective be to enlist by 1982 five thousand persons, groups of churches, or churches who will agree to provide and fund 5,000 mission volunteers to serve for one or two years, either in the United States or overseas, in an effort to reach the objectives of the Bold Missions Thrust. It is hoped that the churches will also encourage an increase in Cooperative Program giving by some percentage each year and the churches will seek as a goal to double their Cooperative Program gifts during the same period of time.

3. That the two mission boards and the state conventions jointly work out administrative procedures having to do with the enlistment and utilization of volunteers.

4. That all funds flow through normal channels and that those not designated for specific activities or persons be divided by formulae to be agreed upon by the SBC and state conventions, recognizing the importance of identification of church or individual support with the Mission Service Corps personnel.

5. That the two mission boards, state conventions and associations, administer all personnel assigned to them.

6. That the state conventions, in cooperation with the appropriate SBC agencies, take the leadership in planning with churches and associations the development of Mission Service Corps opportunities.

7. That the two mission boards, W.M.U., Brotherhood and Sunday School Board work with the state conventions in the promotion of the Mission Service Corps and the enlistment of volunteers.

8. That the Executive Committee relate to the Mission Service Corps in keeping with Missions Challenge Recommendation #10 and Bold Missions Thrust Task Force Recommendation #4 approved by the Convention.

9. That the Executive Committee work with the two mission boards, the state conventions, W.M.U., Brotherhood and Sunday School Board for the evaluation of the Mission Service Corps beyond 1982.

10. That the chairman with the responsible groups appoint a Steering Committee to coordinate MSC activities (This committee will also report to the MSC committee on literature and other matters in February).

11. That the Mission Service Corps Committee be continued until the February meeting of the Executive Committee.

Source: *Minutes*, Executive Board of the Baptist General Convention of Texas, 13 September 1977. Reprint courtesy of the Baptist General Convention of Texas.

D. Partnership Missions: Annual Report, 1982

The Baptist General Convention of Texas, responding to the request of the Foreign Mission Board, initiated the Partnership Missions office effective January 1, 1983. The Coordinator began preparation work on September 1, 1982. Partnership Missions is an extension of the Mission to Brazil idea and is designed to focus specialized missions efforts to foreign fields in cooperation with the total strategy of the Foreign Mission Board of the Southern Baptist Convention.

Beginning in 1983, Texas Baptists are responding through this office to an invitation of the National Baptist Convention of Mexico to work in their country. This is a part of the Baptists' Bold Mission Thrust and is designed to run through the year 1985 and possibly beyond. Also, through this office, Texas Baptists will be responding to an invitation from Australian Baptists in the year 1984.

Source: *Proceedings*, Baptist General Convention of Texas, 1982, 150. Reprint courtesy of the Baptist General Convention of Texas.

E. A Proposal for the Partnership Missions through the BGCT

I. Theological and Structural Foundations

The Baptist General Convention of Texas recognizes the Great Commission as its authority seeking to evangelize and congregationalize persons all around the world. The mandate of Jesus to "go therefore and make disciples of all nations" must be taken seriously by all believers. Southern Baptists in Texas are committed to the objectives of Jesus that are clearly implied in the words, "make disciples of all nations." These words are understood to mean evangelism, Christian nurture, teaching, training and ministry to persons and cultures.

To accomplish these objectives, Southern Baptists in Texas are committed to establishing and strengthening local churches in Texas which have the primary responsibility for ministering in their own geographical setting and additional responsibility for cooperating with other Southern Baptist churches to minister in the state, the nation and the world.

Texas Baptists are committed to the purposes and procedures of the Southern Baptist Convention in ministering outside the United States of America. The Foreign Mission Board is recognized to be the channel through which Southern Baptist Convention churches bear witness in foreign nations. Texas Baptists subscribe to the philosophy that career missionaries living and ministering in foreign cultures on a long term basis is the primary methodology for doing foreign mission work. Furthermore, Baptists in Texas subscribe to the philosophy that supportive ministries by lay volunteers in foreign countries supplement the work of career missionaries and should be used as a method to increase the tempo of reaching the nations for Christ.

II. Historical Background

On December 9, 1980, the Foreign Mission Board voted to engage in a program of partnership in missions. Based on this vote, and because of its commitment to partnership evangelism, World Evangelism Foundation, an independent organization of Southern Baptist mission leaders led by W. H. Jackson, voted unilaterally to close its doors and turn over to the Foreign Mission Board its partnership efforts for 1982 and beyond.

The Baptist General Convention of Texas had already begun a partnership relationship with Brazil at the invitation of the Brazilian Baptist Convention, channeled to Texas Baptists through the Foreign Mission Board. Texas Baptists were asked to help meet the goal of doubling the work in Brazil from 1977 until 1982. That invitation, forwarded through the Foreign Mission Board, led to the development of the Mission to Brazil office, a tri-parte liaison office between the Brazilian Baptist Convention, the Foreign Mission Board and the Baptist General Convention of Texas, with responsibility for coordination of the projects.

The Mission to Brazil office developed its program along five lines: structure, personnel, funding, materials and methods. The 1982 program proposals of the Mission to Brazil office outlined the present structure. Experience has been gained as 2,000 volunteers have gone to Brazil on close to 100 projects since 1978, with very encouraging results.

As a result of its commitment to partnership missions, and knowing of the deep interest on the part of the Baptists of Texas, the Foreign Mission Board presented to the Baptist General Convention of Texas requests from Mexico, Senegal and Australia for partnership efforts of 1983 and beyond.

The following proposal is a possible response to that challenge. The Baptist General Convention of Texas desires to support the Foreign Mission Board in its efforts to meet the needs of the world and take advantage of the interests, energies and the God-given resources of Texas Baptists.

III. Proposal

The Partnership Missions Study Committee recommends that the Executive Board of the Baptist General Convention of Texas establish a Partnership Missions Office to respond to invitations from the Foreign Mission Board to coordinate volunteer partnership mission projects in foreign countries; that the Partnership Missions Office begin its work in January 1983 and continue so long as the need exists or until the Executive Board determines that the program should be terminated; that the Partnership Missions Office be supervised by the Assistant to the Executive Director and assisted by the State Missions Commission Director; and that the funding be obtained through the Mary Hill Davis State Missions Offering.

IV. Personnel

The Partnership Missions Office will be staffed by two employees: a coordinator and a secretary. Field consultants will be employed as needed. Additional staff may be required when large Partnership Missions (such as Mission to Brazil) are adopted. Such staff would be temporary or part-time and consist of personnel jointly approved by the appropriate Foreign Mission Board staff and Administrative Committee of the Executive Board of the Baptist General Convention of Texas.

V. Finances

It is suggested that the Executive Board of the Woman's Missionary Union consider funding the Partnership Missions Office through the Mary Hill Davis Offering for State Missions.

Volunteer participants will arrange financing for their own expenses relating to plane passages, hotel, meals, ground transfers, insurance, airport taxes and some incidental expenses.

The Partnership Missions Office will provide enlistment materials, preparation materials, witnessing materials, as well as provide the other services outlined in the program proposals.

It is the conviction of this committee that requests from foreign fields for financial involvement should be channeled to the Foreign Mission Board. Any further attempts to promote fund-raising such as a Lottie Moon Plus Offering for foreign missions should be carefully considered and approached cautiously before any commitment is made to such a program.

VI. Relationship

1. Foreign Mission Board

The Partnership Missions Office will work through the Foreign Mission Board with missionaries and National Baptist leaders in countries involved.

2. River Ministry

The River Ministry would continue to be treated as a separate program, but would be called upon to share its expertise with the Partnership Missions Office on all projects in Mexico.

3. Mexican Baptist Convention of Texas

The Partnership Missions Office would work closely with the officers of the Mexican Baptist Convention of Texas to utilize their unique gifts related to projects in Mexico and other Spanish-speaking countries.

4. The Partnership Missions Office would work closely with all departments and divisions of the Baptist General Convention of Texas as requests come from the Foreign Mission Board for various types of partnership activities (for example: Evangelism, Division of Student Work, Woman's Missionary Union, Texas Baptist Men, Church Music, Sunday School, Church Training, Stewardship, Church Extension, Church Building, Language Missions, etc.).

5. Brazil

The Partnership Missions Office would service requests from Brazil where the need exists, and to the extent where the possibilities in Texas permit.

VII. Program Proposals

Objective: To promote and coordinate the response of Texas Baptists through the Foreign Mission Board of the Southern Baptist Convention to invitations received from Baptist entities of other countries to cooperate in partnership mission efforts.

Assumption: That requests have been received from the Foreign Mission Board and that relationships have been defined by the Administration of the Baptist General Convention of Texas.

Goal 1:   Inform Texas Baptists of partnership requests.
Strategy 1: Utilize available publications that inform Texas Baptists.
Strategy 2: Publish a special information piece.

Goal 2:   Enlist volunteers from Texas Baptist churches to fill every request from other countries.
Strategy 1: Present each request to an association or area in Texas that would seek to meet it.
Strategy 2: Provide materials for use in enlistment of volunteers.
Strategy 3: Utilize missionaries of the Foreign Mission Board, both furloughed and emeritus, as well as pastors and laymen who have been to other countries, and others, for speaking in the associations or churches.
Strategy 4: Maintain a volunteer personnel file.
Strategy 5: Assist the Foreign Mission Board with enlistment of vol-

unteers for projects other than those approved by the Baptist General Convention of Texas.

Goal 3: Make available to the Baptist churches of Texas furloughing missionary Field Consultants to represent the Partnership Missions Office for the purpose of promoting the partnership efforts, and to assist associational and area missionaries with the enlistment and orientation of volunteers. The Field Consultant would also serve as Project Consultants.

Strategy 1: Enlist Field Consultants from furloughing missionaries.

Strategy 2: Provide adequate training for each consultant.

Goal 4: Make available to Texas Baptist churches on a project by project basis Project Consultants who would assist them in efforts they have undertaken.

Strategy 1: Enlist a corps of people who could serve as Project Consultants for the Partnership Missions Office.

1. Enlist consultants from among furloughing or emeritus missionaries in Texas.

2. Enlist consultants from among lay persons and/or ministers who have traveled or worked in partnership efforts in other countries.

Strategy 2: Provide adequate training for each Project Consultant.

Goal 5: Enable every volunteer who goes to another country to witness and minister effectively through a uniform program of comprehensive preparation.

Strategy 1: Provide materials for preparation of each volunteer.

Strategy 2: Conduct an adequate number of preparation meetings for volunteers for each project.

Goal 6: Provide every Texas participant with materials for effective witnessing.

Goal 7: Promote and encourage intercessory prayer through a program of prayer support.

Strategy 1: Provide special materials for the promotion of the prayer support program.

Strategy 2: Promote the prayer support program through the use of the special materials, the <u>Baptist</u> <u>Standard</u>, <u>lead-er-ship</u>, and <u>El</u> <u>Bautista</u> <u>Mexicano</u> magazines.

Goal 8: Aid field personnel in other countries, both nationals and missionaries, in their preparation to receive the Texas mission volunteers.

Strategy 1: Assist the Baptist entities of other countries in the enlistment and orientation of a   project supervisor for every effort that involves volunteers from Texas.

Strategy 2: Conduct bilateral planning sessions with missionaries and national leaders.

Goal 9: Where possible, secure the participation of Baptist leaders of other countries in promotion of the partnership efforts in Texas.

Strategy 1: In cooperation with the Foreign Mission Board, missionaries and National Baptist leaders select representatives, jointly approved, who may assist in promotion of the effort.

Goal 10: Evaluate and preserve for history the results of each effort.

Strategy 1: Evaluate the efficiency of each project.

Strategy 2: Secure an evaluation and a testimony from each project participant. Send selected testimonies to the Public Relations departments of the Baptist General Convention of Texas and the Foreign Mission Board.

Strategy 3: Produce a statistical and historical report of each project.

Ed Stewart moved that these Proposals for Partnership Missions be adopted. The motion was seconded by Floyd Bradley. A brief discussion followed with Mrs. Maurice Johnston reporting that the Woman's Missionary Union's Executive Board would be in session next week and would be considering the financial structure of this Proposal, of which she spoke enthusiastically.

The motion carried.

Schmeltekopf presented two additional recommendations from the Partnership Missions Study Committee, as approved by the Administrative Committee:

1. That the requests from the Foreign Mission Board to the Baptist General Convention of Texas to become involved with the National Baptist Convention, Mexico, in a three-year partnership, 1983-1985, be approved and during the time of this partnership the committee will restudy to see if a second three-year partnership should be undertaken.

2. That a short-term partnership with Australia be approved for the summer of 1983 involving about 55 teams.

O. O. Erwin moved that these recommendations be approved. There were several seconds and the motion carried.

Source: *Minutes*, Executive Board of the Baptist General Convention of Texas, 9 March 1982. Reprint courtesy of the Baptist General Convention of Texas.

13.5 Good News Texas

Launched in 1977, Good News Texas was the largest Texas Baptist evangelistic endeavor to date. The goal of Good News Texas was to tell everyone in the state about the saving power of Jesus Christ before the end of the year. A public relations firm was employed and an intensive media blitz blanketed Texas with testimonies from famous people describing how Jesus had changed their lives. The number of baptisms, however, did not significantly increase.

A. Media Campaign Unveiled at Evangelism Meeting

A million dollar mass media campaign to support the Good News Texas evangelistic effort was unveiled at the annual Texas Baptist Evangelism Conference last week.

More than 8,000 church leaders from throughout the state were shown television and radio spot announcements that the Bloom Advertising Agency of Dallas predicts will be seen 40 times by the average Texan this spring.

The television and radio spots, focus of the "Living Proof" media campaign, will feature 10 widely known persons telling how their lives were changed through a redemptive experience with Jesus Christ.

JAMES H. LANDES, executive director of the Baptist General Convention of Texas, speaking after the premiere showing of the spots, said the media campaign will support local church revivals and other evangelistic efforts. He challenged churches to gear into the media campaign by contacting every Texan who has spiritual and physical needs.

Leighton Ford, brother-in-law of evangelist Billy Graham and a member of his evangelistic team, told the audience.

"The biggest question that you will be asked during Good News Texas is 'can someone tell me how to find God?' The important thing now is not how many people come forward for decisions. It's how many Christians are discipled and trained to share their faith."

DARRELL ROBINSON, pastor of First Church, Pasadena, said his church will have two Witness Involvement Now schools simultaneously to train members for participation in Good News Texas.

"When we go into homes, there is always a noticeable difference in attitudes right after a Billy Graham television crusade. Just think what can be done through the 'Living Proof' spots. It will be the greatest tragedy if one home is missed."

The opening session was crowned with the live "Living Proof" testimony of war hero Col. (ret.) Heath Bottomly of California.

His son, now a student at Dallas seminary, led his father to Christ during a telephone conversation between Vietnam and Indiana.

Other speakers included Southern Baptist Convention President James L. Sullivan; Vance Havner of North Carolina; evangelist Luis Palau; A. Louis Patterson, a black pastor from Houston; and J. Sidlow Baxter of California who led a Bible study at each session.

Source: "Media Campaign Unveiled at Evangelism Meet," *Baptist Standard*, 26 January 1977, 5. Reprint courtesy of the *Baptist Standard*.

B. Enthusiasm, Decisions Mark Good News Revivals

Renewed enthusiasm and large numbers of professions of faith have marked the first wave of Good News Texas revivals, according to L. L. Morriss, chairman of the Good News Texas steering committee.

Churches all across the state have either completed revivals, are now engaged in them or will begin soon, coordinating them with the "Living Proof" media campaign now blanketing the state with the message of Christ.

The media campaign, a $1.5 million effort designed to present the gospel to 4.7 unsaved Texans through radio and television testimonies and newspaper ads, began Feb. 21 in North Texas, March 7 in South Texas and March 28 in West Texas.

The testimonies and ads have been planned to make people receptive to the gospel; the revivals, suggested to begin the last week of the media thrust in the three areas, are planned to capitalize on that opportunity.

Morriss said more than 1,000 persons have responded to the Living Proof testimonies by writing to Box 1000, Dallas.

While there has been write-in response, the primary goal of the Living Proof campaign has always been to create an atmosphere in which church members can minister most effectively, person-to-person, Morriss said.

Dramatic results of that goal are flowing in from around the state.

While attending a family reunion near Corpus Christi, an Indiana man saw the Living Proof spot announcements. He called Bill Brown, pastor of First Church, Flour Bluff, and asked him to visit. Brown shared Christ at the reunion, and seven adults accepted Christ as Savior.

Charles Higgs, pastor at Forrest Park church, Corpus Christi, reports four adults won to Christ after seeing the testimonies.

A man living near the church was the first in Corpus Christi to write to Box 1000. "I would like to know more about the Living Proof and would like to know if there is a group of people here in Corpus Christi whom I could talk to or who could come by my house so that I can understand more about it," he wrote. "I want to be saved. I'm looking for help and need help and I hope you can help me . . . "

The letter was relayed promptly from the Good News Office in Dallas to the Forrest Park church, which sent the help requested. The man accepted Christ as Savior and said he would be in church the following Sunday and with his wife and two children.

A Living Proof lapel pin provided a witnessing opportunity that resulted in a young woman coming to Christ.

An airline stewardess saw the pin worn by Pastor Benny King of Oak Lawn church, Texarkana, and told him she had seen the testimonies on TV. "Can you tell me what it's all about," she asked.

King shared his faith in Christ and asked the young woman if she would like the peace of the people in the commercials. She said she would and received Christ on the plane.

Living Proof has also been felt in some unusual ways through other media.

A San Antonio TV executive reports that he called the information operator in Dallas and said he wanted to know whom to talk to about the Living Proof spots.

"I'm in charge of that," said the operator, "because I'm living proof that Jesus has changed my life." Then she added, "I know what you are asking," and she gave him the telephone number. But she got her message across.

THEN THERE were the two truckers overheard by Evangelist Charles Massagee on their CB radios.

"What's all this I'm hearing about Living Proof," asked one trucker.

"I don't know, but it must have something to do with Jimmy Carter and being born again," responded the other.

The impact of the media campaign is also being felt by other denominations.

At Princeton near Dallas, the Baptists were joined in the Living Proof Crusade by Catholics, Methodists, Assembly of God and the Christian church.

Princeton is a community of about 1,100 and there were more than 700 in one of the services under a tent on the high school parking lot, reports Gil Stricklin, evangelist for the meeting.

Source: Orville Scott, "Enthusiasm, Decisions Mark Good News Revivals," *Baptist Standard*, 3 March 1977, 4. Reprint courtesy of the *Baptist Standard*.

C. Accomplishment of Goals and Objectives

The media evangelism purpose was stated in terms of seven, single-word goals and interpretive objectives. The goals were: awareness, response, conversion, discipleship, membership, Baptist image, and Christian groups (Elder and Morriss, 1976:1). Each of these will be discussed with evidence presented as to the degree of accomplishment. A major problem is encountered and was acknowledged by the Bloom Agency (1977:7) in the failure to quantify objectives.

Awareness

The objective behind <u>awareness</u> was to make every Texan aware of the gospel of Jesus Christ. Louis, Bowles, and Groves, Inc. (1977:1) found that 60 percent of the sample recalled seeing or hearing some religious advertisement recently. Sixty-three percent of these were able to recall at least the name of the themes of the Living Proof campaign. Zachry, Naill and Associated, Inc. (1977:12) also concluded that awareness of faith in Jesus Christ had been increased. In the Marshall, Texas, study (see Chapter IV), conducted by the authors, 73 percent of the respondents recalled seeing the Living Proof logo. Seventy percent of them gave a correct meaning for the logo. Fifty-three percent could identify one or more of the ten Living Proof "personalities." Of these, 77 percent correctly identified the message of the personality or personalities that they recalled seeing. These percentages are a long way from "every Texan." However, it must be kept in mind that all of these studies majored on the television and radio presentations. The exposure of the other media and the work of the local churches are not measured. It can be concluded that awareness of the gospel of Jesus Christ was heightened and intensified to a large degree even if "every Texan" did not hear the message.

Response

Response was interpreted as calling for and providing an opportunity to respond to the gospel. While only one mechanism was provided through the media campaign, Box 1000, another strategy was through the invitations of the local churches. Box 1000, Dallas, Texas, proved to be a disappointment in light of the expectations. Only 921 letters and clippings were received whereas 200,000 were anticipated (see Chapter IV). But, results were reported by the churches (see Chapter V). Eighteen percent of the pastors in the sample survey of Texas Baptist churches conducted by the authors (see Chapter V), reported that they had additions directly related to the Living Proof media campaign. Twelve percent claimed that they had reached people after their revivals as a result of Living Proof. Two Directors of Associational Missions wrote that response from Blacks and Mexican/Americans will be slow until Southern Baptists decide to welcome them into their churches. No measure is available to indicate what response may have been made by the invitations of other denominations. As was noted earlier, lack of quantified objectives as well as adequate measures makes it difficult to totally assess the response.

Conversion

At the heart of all evangelism is <u>conversion</u>, therefore, a central objective was to lead to salvation those searching for new life in Christ. The study by Belden Associates (1976:8) had concluded that persons who rated 0 to 1 on a six point scale in church going, and who rated 0 to 2 on a six point scale of religiousness would be too difficult to attract and thus should not be the target group. Louis, Bowles and Grove, Inc. (1976:1,1, 2.2) listed as poor prospects those who were non-Christian or unaffiliated. Louis, Bowles, and Grove, Inc. (1976c:1), in a latter study, also concluded that the non-Christians were probably too difficult to reach. Louis, Bowles and Grove, Inc. (1976a:2.1) even argued, "The limited resources available for mass media evangelism must necessarily be directed initially at those persons who seem more likely to be attracted by the media"—not at the lost.

And yet, it is this group for which the television commercials were targeted. In fact, the testimonial format was chosen, to a large degree, because the unaffiliated in the study rated it higher than other formats for the television commercials. In the light of the above research one has difficulty understanding the decision to target the non-Christians and non-affiliated. Only in recognizing the strong commitment to this objective can one understand the decision. Marty (1961:138-140) provides a rationale for the decision that may have escaped the researchers. "The most salutary function of mass communications for telling the healing and reconciling story, from the Christian point of view might properly be termed 'pre-evangelical.'" He adds:

> It merely prepares the soil. It intrigues and raises curiosity. Not ashamed of the gospel of Christ, it participates sufficiently in the agonies of human existence on the plan of salvation to speak realistically to the world, and avoids cheap grace in the church. It avoids

pat verbalization of the gospel and avoids extensive systematic presentation of the good news, leaving that for the proclaimers of the
Word within the Christian community . . .

What better description of Good News Texas with its Living Proof testi-
monials and the local church simultaneous revivals.

Documentation of conversion as a result of Living Proof is not easy.
In discussing response, indication was given of those whom pastors reported as having been reached as a direct result of Living Proof. In
addition, data in Chapter V, from the sampled Texas Baptist churches,
reveals that churches which financially supported Living Proof and held
a revival during or near the GNT designated period baptized more people
than churches that did not. Also, data from the analysis of all Texas
Baptist churches revealed that churches that supported Living Proof baptized more people in 1977 than in 1976. While these figures are less
than conclusive, they are indicators of conversion.

Discipleship

The fourth goal, discipleship, was interpreted as to encourage every
Christian in his daily discipleship and witnessing. No direct measures
of this were available, however, several indicators may be utilized. In
Chapter V, pastors in the authors' sample survey reported on the churches'
involvement in outreach and witnessing activities. Twenty-eight percent
of those who had spring revivals conducted a WIN SCHOOL (Witness
Involvement Now), a training program for personal sharing of one's faith
with non-Christians. Forty-eight percent of these rated their school as
having some measure of success. Thirty percent conducted the Action
Plan for enrolling new prospects in Bible study. Sixty-nine percent of
these felt the activity had some success. Thirty-two people conducted a
People Search, a seeking of prospects. Seventy-three percent found it at
least somewhat effective. Sixty-seven percent of those pastors who had
spring revivals saw the spiritual interest and involvement of their people
as encouraging or at a high level.

Membership

Discipleship and membership are goals that are highly related. The
interpretation of the goal set forth the objective to strengthen the local

Baptist church through direct, personal involvement. In discussing discipleship, several indicators were set forth that could also serve to indicate a degree of success in reaching this goal. Especially is this true in the measure of spiritual interest and involvement. An additional indicator may be found in Chapter V in the high percentage of pastors who indicated their revival had been a "church revival and had an impact mostly on the members." Sixty-four percent made this claim.

Baptist Image

The goal, Baptist image, was translated into an objective by the statement, to communicate with others as a caring/sharing sector in Texas life. In discussing the public relations aspect of Living Proof, earlier in this chapter, reference was made to the good image created by the commercials. Baptists postured themselves, in the Living Proof commercials, not as a religious group seeking proselytes but as a people who could identify with the personal needs of mankind and could share a message of hope. Needs such as hopelessness, purposefulness, and lack of peace of mind, discovered through research, became a focal point around which the testimonies were built. Elder and Morriss (1976:1) state "The purpose of the media is not to launch a good will campaign for the Convention, nor to advertise the local churches." The low key sponsorship by-line, "the Baptists of Texas," used on the television commercials was a fulfillment of that claim. The decision not to include the Box 1000 response mechanism in the television commercials grew out of the commitment to share the gospel free of personal gain motives. This decision, however, probably explains the low amount of response and thus hindered, to some degree, the accomplishment of that goal.

Christian Groups

The last goal, Christian groups, was stated as the objective, to enhance and strengthen the work of other Christian churches or groups. Earlier in this chapter, in discussing public relation benefits of Living Proof, a number of different Christian groups were indicated that had made contact with the BGCT either to praise the effort or to find out if they could use the materials. However, most of these groups were not Texas based. Some were. Many Baptist pastors reported praise from both pastors and laymen from other denominations within their local communities. In the post-Living Proof study by Louis, Bowles and Grove, Inc. (1977:3.72) they documented an increase in favorableness toward religious advertising for Christians of non-Baptist preference when pre-test and post-test data were compared. There is a virtual absence of criticism and a strong climate of praise from other denominational groups that would indicate that this objective too has been accomplished to some degree.

Conclusion

What was Good News Texas? It was, in its broadest interpretation, the continuing ministry of 4,400 Texas Baptist churches, the influence of over one million resident members of those Baptist churches, the direct work of 114 Baptist Associations and the total ministry of the Baptist General Convention of Texas involved in an all-inclusive evangelism approach because of the challenge for a state with nearly five million Texans who need Christ, utilizing a combined strategy of a statewide media campaign with local church involvement (Elder and Morriss, (1976:2.1)). In reality it was somewhat less than that and yet it might well be summed up with the comment that it was Texas Baptists doing what they have always been doing, but doing it on a larger scale and using new methods. Secular methods seemed to have proven effective once again in the churches' struggle to combat secularism and in calling some back to sacred values.

What did it accomplish? This study has tried to analyze data that would shed light on that question. The conclusion was drawn that every goal was achieved to some degree. Some, perhaps, more than others. No quantifiable measure is available to say to what degree any good was achieved. One Director of Missions wrote, "If one soul has been saved as a result of this, then every effort has been worth it all." He may have summed up the feelings of most, if not all, Baptists who cared enough to become involved in Good News Texas.

Source: James and Janet Palmer, *Good News Texas: A Study of Intensive Evangelism through Media and Churches* (Marshall, TX: East Texas Baptist College, 1978), 135–40. Reprint courtesy of James Palmer.

13.6 Church-State Issues

During this period, Baptist Colleges and Universities in Texas refused to accept any financial aid, scholarships, or grants from the federal government. The federal government, however, believed that it still had the right to enforce hiring policies at Baptist schools. True to form, the Baptists refused to give in to this overt breach of the policy of the separation of church and state. At one point, the situation became so acute that Southwestern Seminary was forced to defend itself at the Supreme Court for refusing to hand over its hiring records so that the government could see if the school was in compliance with federal hiring practices. Southwestern won the case.

A. Federal Interference: Dr. Donald Anthony

I believe, however, that there are some problems that are becoming more serious by the year—specifically with respect to the church-state issue. Our convention has long been sensitive to the issue of accepting federal funds by our institutions. Guidelines have been written and revised and currently a committee is working to update these guidelines. Certainly this matter merits our continuing concern.

But, the coin of church-state separation has another side to it. I refer specifically to the matter of recognition by the state, of the right of the church and its institutions, to exercise their historic role in our society, without undue government interference. Recent years have seen a very significant change in the relationship of the federal government to higher education, particularly in the private sector. The accelerated growth of a federal bureaucracy, with increasing regulatory power, but not responsible to the electorate, has resulted in the rapid extension of federal controls into areas which have traditionally been the prerogatives of the institutions. To a great degree these controls are essentially unrelated to the issue of federal funding.

In all sincerity, I believe that the greatest threat to religious freedom in America is the growth of a massive federal bureaucracy whose regulations take on the force of law and have resulted in an increasing interference in the affairs of our constitutions. I view this trend with a great deal of concern.

Our convention has in the past voiced its concern that the church by its actions not intrude upon the proper role of the state. I believe that we now need to speak with a loud and clear voice against the tendency of the state to intrude unduly upon the proper role of the church and its institutions.

Our Texas Baptist colleges are led by men of dedication and commitment to historic Baptist principles. They need our help and support as never before. Let us help them.

Source: *Minutes*, Executive Board of the Baptist General Convention of Texas, 14 September 1976. Reprint courtesy of the Baptist General Convention of Texas.

13.7 Tensions in Texas

Though the majority of the BGCT programs were growing and proving to be effective, all was not well in Texas Baptist life. There were certain tensions in the air that threatened to destroy the delicate fabric of the BGCT. The most significant of these tensions included missionary priorities (Japan or Texas), the decreasing role of associations, the funding of Baptist colleges, in particular the perpetually financially strapped Dallas Baptist College, and a resurgence of fundamentalism.

A. Missionary Priorities: Landes Interview

Stricklin: You mentioned a minute ago, in talking about the difficulties replacing Wade Freeman, the factionalism that was developing in the seventies, and that would come as a surprise to some people who think that that's a more recent phenomenon than that. Can you kind of trace some of that.

Landes: No. Yes, I can do that. That arose around Dr. Pat.

Pitts: This was a state issue.

Landes: Yes, this was a state. It arose around Dr. Pat. Many people did not agree with Dr. Pat on his Japan crusade. There were many pastors across the state who said, You are doing what the Foreign Mission Board ought to be doing; you're stepping out of your rights, and were rather censorious of it. But you could not turn Dr. Pat away at all. He was a very strong-willed man and had a heart as big as the world. There was no way to turn him around. He asked me, as president of Hardin-Simmons, to send the Cowboy Band to Japan. I said, "No way." But I'm so much more reserved and so much quieter than Pat was, and I just wouldn't do it at all. Though I never—I was the only college president, so far as I know, who was supporting Dr. Pat at that time. He took money away from all other programs. A lot of things go back to money, David. He took money away from a lot of the programs in order to have this Japan crusade and still wound up owing a half million dollars. It was a very expensive gesture. In the long term, he established, or helped to establish, partnership missions. When I went into the office, I immediately got in touch with the Foreign Mission Board and said, "Because Dr. Pat has stressed evangelism direct from Texas to the world, I have no choice but to have partnership missions, but it's going to be through you. And you are going to tell me how to do it, and you are going to get the credit or the blame." So that was—that created a tension earlier. And the tension was there very much. As a matter of fact, I don't think I want to put any more on the—when you turn that thing off, I'll share a little more about that.

Stricklin: And these may be things the two of you have covered in other interviews.

Pitts: No, we've not, but, you know, we've talked as family before.

Stricklin: Yeah. Well, that's very helpful. It wasn't—what I thought you were saying was—

Landes: It's not this present controversy.

Stricklin: —precursors of the—

Landes: No, no, it was really Texas, and it was purely strategy. It was over strategy.

Stricklin: I see, okay. Well, thanks, that clears that up.

Source: *Oral Memoirs of James H. Landes, Jr.*, 2 vols. Texas Baptist Oral History Project, Baylor University, 2:76–77. Reprint courtesy of the Baptist General Convention of Texas.

B. Role of Associations: The Area Program

Baptists realize that the association is the basis unit of denominational cooperation. The Area Program of missions support was started in 1963 by Texas Baptists as a means toward strengthening associational work.

An area is composed of one, two, three, or four associations. Each area is served by a Director of Missions.

This voluntary arrangement of associations into areas has been effective in helping the churches fulfill their New Testament destinies. It is, therefore, recommended that all associations seriously consider becoming part of an area program.

RATIONALE ON AREA/ASSOCIATIONAL SUPPORT PROGRAM:

This support program is designed to provide the most elemental and basic needs (salary, housing, travel, office) for a director of missions to be made available to each area/association. The percentage calculation for this funding support uses the percentage of 1.5 of undesignated receipts in the churches as gifts to the association. For an association to have a worthy program of promotion and service, the receipts from the church should be more approximate to 3 to 4 percent on the average for all the churches in a given association.

BASIC PRINCIPLES

1. The Baptist position regarding independence and interdependence of all Baptist bodies should be recognized and treated accordingly.

2. There is a stewardship responsibility regarding time, money, and personnel; therefore, each area is encouraged to look toward financial independence as a worthy goal.

3. The primary purpose of an association's existence is to serve the churches; therefore, it is proposed that the needs of the churches be the focal point in the development of each association's program.

4. It should be noted that cooperation in the promotion of various programs has not diminished as program support funding has decreased.

ORGANIZATIONAL PLAN

To ask associations to group themselves into area units (one to four associations to an area) under the following general categories with the total number of churches (except metropolitan areas) at least 50 with an Area Director of Missions or Associational Director of Missions serving each such area:

1. Town and Country—one, two, three, or four associations.
   a. Multiple Associations
   b. Single Association

2. Urban—a core city with a population of at least 25,000 and/or a total population of 50,000.

3. Metropolitan—a core city with a population of at least 75,000.

RECOMMENDATIONS

1. That the state Executive Board continue to encourage area groupings as the primary source of cooperation with the understanding that the individual associations assume responsibility of initiating this relationship.

2. That the state Executive Board adopt the financial support schedules as outlined herein with the understanding that variable needs exist. Executive Board staff and the area committees should respond accordingly, recognizing that there are always more demands than there are resources.

3. That the State Executive Board reconfirm its enthusiastic endorsement of associational work and encourage the churches to support their association through percentage giving to the association throughout the year. The suggested percentage is determined by each association according to its need and resources.

4. That the Baptist Association be recognized and promoted as the denominational entity of Baptist life more closely associated with the churches than any other. The traditional boundaries of associational relationships in Texas have not changed with the vast technological changes over the past 30 years.

5. That the State Missions Commission encourage associational realignments which might go beyond the traditional county line boundaries.

6. That the special mission opportunities should be given special consideration.

7. That these policies should be reviewed periodically, at least every five years.

FINANCIAL SUPPORT SCHEDULES

1. Metropolitan areas would be on a declining scale based upon 1982 program support from state board funding with anticipated 100% phase out of this funding by December 31, 1988. The convention recognizes the unique missionary dimensions and challenges which are integral to three metropolitan associations in particular; i.e., Rio Grande Valley, El Paso and Corpus Christi. It is, therefore, recommended that the phase out schedule for metropolitan associations not apply in these three cases.

2. Urban areas would be on a declining scale based upon 1982 program support from state board funding with anticipated 100% phase out of this funding by December 31, 1988.

3. Town and Country

   Multiple associations/areas

Two, three, or four associations which have a combined number of churches of at least 50. The program support would be on one of the following bases with a maximum funding from the state board of $11,000 per year;

1. Where there is sufficient funding provided by 1.5% of undesignated receipts from the churches plus the current state funding to meet the costs of the Director of Missions and his office, the state support will continue at the 1982 level.

2. Where there is sufficient funding for associational support from the churches of 1.5% of their undesignated giving without the state funding to meet the costs of the Director of Missions and office, the state support will decline at a rate not to exceed 15% per year beginning in 1984.

3. Where there is insufficient associational support from the churches of 1.5% of their undesignated gifts plus state funding to meet the costs of the Director of Missions and office, the state support may increase at a rate not to exceed 15% per year beginning in 1984.

4. Where the associational gifts are less than 1.5% of the undesignated gifts to the churches, the state program support will decline at a rate not to exceed 15% per year beginning in 1984.

5. Administration: These policies will be administered through a consultative process with the areas with the final decisions to rest with the State Missions Commission.

Single Associations

a. An association with an exceptionally large geographical area, such as 8,000 square miles, may apply and receive the same funding consideration as a multiple association-area but with maximum funding for a year at $5,000.

b. An association which is unable to align with a multiple association-area but cannot carry on a full-time program individually may apply for program support. Such support would be provided up to $3,000 per year from the state board.

c. An association which, since 1963, has formed from two or more associations for a more efficient operation may apply and receive program support which would be decreased or accelerated in terms of the net funding available from the churches as noted under multiple associations above (a, b, c, d).

d. If none of the above applies to an association, there is a possibility that the association could consider a part-time or combination leaders such as moderator/missionary, student director/missionary, or some other arrangement. Funding could be requested and negotiated in terms of the amount of time the particular person in mind would devote to the Director of Missions responsibility.

New Work

1. No assistance would be given to areas with fewer than 50 churches unless there is unusual potential (such as a new military installation).

2. A financial agreement would be established in three phases:

a. Phase 1—years 1 and 2, the Convention would supply up to 2/3 of the cost of the Director of Missions and office, but not to exceed $24,000 as the Convention's share.

b. Phase 2—years 3 and 4, the Convention's share would decline 20% a year.

c. Phase 3—year 5 and following, agreement would be reached on basic relationship in accordance with existing policy as outlined above.

Exceptions

Should there be extenuating circumstances for any areas as outlined above, a rationale and appeal could be made through the State Missions Commission for an exception to the funding policy.

SUGGESTED POSITION DESCRIPTION

Position Assignment

Position Title:	Director of Missions
Organization Unit:	Area
Salary Scale:	Recommended by the Area Committee and set by Associational Board(s)
Recruited by:	Associational Committee
Elected by:	Associational Board(s) of the Area

Working Relationships

Reports to:	Associational Board(s) of the Area with copy to Area Committee

Basic Functions

To provide continuous program guidance in the association(s) to help churches achieve their individual and cooperative objectives.

Responsibilities

1. Recommend objectives and goals to the association(s) based on the needs of the churches.

2. Counsel regularly with associational leaders to plan, coordinate, conduct, and evaluate programs needed to help the churches.

3. Work cooperatively with state leadership to interpret, adapt, formulate, and initiate program resources to carry on selected activities to help the churches.

4. Where the Director of Missions is responsible for more than one as-

sociation, he shall concentrate on the several associations separately and shall hold area-wide meetings only where the association deems it wise.

5. Work with moderators and appropriate associational leadership to screen and evaluate requests for various financial assistance through state programs.

6. Assist associational leaders in the performance of their responsibilities.

7. Provide necessary assistance in the development of annual associational program budgets in his area.

8. Provide necessary assistance in the development of any annual budget for his office.

9. Counsel churches and pastors when necessary during times of stress and with pastorless churches as needed.

10. Serve as a representative in the area to interpret and promote programs of (1) State Mission, (2) Christian Education, (3) Human Welfare, (4) Christian Life Commission, and (5) other agencies of the Baptist General Convention of Texas.

11. Serve as the denominational coordinator and promoter for state, home, foreign missions, and other related Southern Baptist emphases.

12. Serve as denominational public relations officer with the general public and churches in matters concerning the understanding and welfare of the total program of work and cooperation.

13. Make quarterly and annual program and budget progress reports toward goals of the associational mission programs to each board to whom he is responsible.

14. Accept other special assignments and duties as they may be outlined by the associational board(s) to whom he is responsible.

Source: *Minutes*, Executive Board of the Baptist General Convention of Texas, 7 December 1982. Reprint courtesy of the Baptist General Convention of Texas.

B. Financially Rescuing Dallas Baptist College

Proposal Re: Dallas Baptist College—Morriss gave background information on DBC Study Committee, which was named at December 8, 1981 Executive Board meeting. He read the names of the committee members and said this committee had met many times since it was appointed. He introduced Alvin Burns, Chairman of the DBC Study Committee, who presented the formal proposal.

Proposal

In consideration of the $1,000,000 pledge which Mary Crowley had made this year to Dallas Baptist College (DBC), and in anticipation and contingent upon a pledge of a $3,000,000 offer of endowment from anonymous donors, we propose that the Baptist General Convention of Texas (BGCT), as soon as reasonably possible after approval by the Executive Board, provide a total funding of $3,000,000 to Dallas Baptist College as follows:

1. A BGCT contribution of $500,000 to the Dallas Baptist College Unrestricted Current Fund to apply in reduction of its accumulated deficit.
2. BGCT loan of $2,500,000 to Dallas Baptist College on the following terms:
    a. Principal amount due in ten years.
    b. All property released as collateral by paying of Dallas Baptist College's most recent bond issue (Heitner bond) is to be pledged as collateral. (This is the entire campus real estate except for 3.37 acres on which three dormitories are located.)
    c. No interest during the first five years.
    d. Interest at 8% per annum during the remaining five years. However, if Dallas Baptist College raises a net additional $5,000,000 in endowment funds during the first five years (in addition to the $3,000,000 from anonymous donors) then interest during the remaining five years is waived.
3. Immediately upon receipt of the funding proceeds, Dallas Baptist College must apply $2,500,000 to pay off the Heitner bonds and $250,000 to reduce the principal balance of its note to Republic Bank of Oak Cliff. The remaining $250,000 may, at the option of

the Dallas Baptist College, be held for general use until January 31, 1983, at which time it must be applied in full to further reduce the principal balance of its note to Republic Bank of Oak Cliff.

We also propose that this study committee, or a similar study committee, review the financial progress of Dallas Baptist College for each of the next two years and make annual reports to the Executive Board at its regular meeting in March of each year, together with any additional proposals it may deem appropriate.

Source: *Minutes*, Executive Board of the Baptist General Convention of Texas, 8 June 1982. Reprint courtesy of the Baptist General Convention of Texas.

D. Fundamentalist Resurgence: Landes Interview

Stricklin: Yes, indeed. And the other thing is, it's hard to sit here and think back fifteen years to the kind of hallway gossip and things, but I wonder if you and your friends and associates were—if there was any discussion then that this might be a harbinger of things to come with the possible ultraconservative men?

Landes: One of the conservative, yet very bright, men in Texas Baptist life, who is now gone, was J. D. Grey. J. D. Grey and I had many differences, but we had many things we saw alike, and were very close friends. J. D. came to me about fifteen years ago and said, "Jimmy, I'm for evangelism conferences. I'm for Pastors' Conferences at the SBC, but I do not like the direction it's taking. It's becoming a political monster." That was J. D. Grey. He's in heaven now. If he were here, he would come in and say, "Yeah, Jim, I said that to you." So the answer to your question is yes, we saw what was happening, though the other side of it is, those of us who were in positions of leadership were so busy that we did not know as much was going on as it was. In the beginning, the movement that has come to be known as fundamentalist-conservative movement was a very quiet movement, and we were deliberately kept uninformed.

Stricklin: I remember when Adrian Rogers won the presidency in 79; there was a lot of wringing of hands then, but we'll get to that after a bit, but—

Landes: Yes. Well, let's see, somewhere in here our friend from Lubbock was elected president of the—

Pitts: Yes, Jaroy Weber in this year. Actually, he was reelected this year.

Landes: Yes, yes. Well, the first time we realized—first time I realized— the first time Landrum Leavell realized, for example, and some of us who were in the heart of everything at that time realized—came along about here when Jaroy was elected. We did not now what had gone on beforehand, and most of us expected Landrum Leavell to be elected.

Pitts: That was something of a surprise to a lot of people, wasn't it?

Landes: Oh, it was a tremendous surprise. It was a shock to all of us who were close to Landrum and who had encouraged Landrum. It made Landrum ill. Landrum came to me after that election and said, "I'm leaving the convention." And I said, "Oh, (chuckles) what do you mean?" Because it scared me when he said that. He said, "Oh, no, I just mean, I'm leaving this convention. I'm going to Hawaii. I'm getting away from this thing." Well, he had gotten word of what had happened the night before, the many secret meetings and all that sort of thing. And so it's right at this time that we became aware that something was happening, but we didn't know, yet, how much had happened. We'll get to this later on, I'm sure, but let me pause just a moment to say, I did not realize how thoroughly that thing was organized until about 1978—this was three years later—at which time I received a letter from Paige Patterson. Now, Paige was always very respectful to me. His father had been ahead of me, you know. I had succeeded him. And he was very respectful to me, but he wrote me when I wrote an editorial on the Cooperative Program. I supported all of our institutions and this sort of thing. And he said, "Dr. Landes, I want you to know that the Cooperative Program is in trouble," or something of that essence, and said, "If you push it too hard, there will be thousands that will rise from the country places around the state." I looked at that letter. I was stunned. At the end of it he said, "Now, I know this letter sounds very negative. I want you to know I am support- ing you," and all this kind of thing, "as my executive director, but I just thing [sic] I ought to share with you that there are lots of them that are out there that are unhappy." I shared it with W. A. Criswell. I was that innocent. I don't know if W. A. knew what was going on or not. He was the head of the thing, but, anyway, that was three or four years later. They operated very quietly, one-on-one basis. They used the good old democratic process, and they took over.

Source: *Oral Memoirs of James Henry Landes, Jr.*, 2 Vols., Texas Baptist Oral History Project, Baylor University, 2:96–98. Reprint courtesy of the Baptist General Convention of Texas.

E. The Dangers of Fundamentalism

Fundamentalism is more dangerous than Liberalism because everything is done in the name of the Lord. In the name of the Lord, the Fundamentalist condemns all who disagree with him. . . . He uses the Bible as a club with which to beat people over the head, rather than as a means of personal strength and a revealer of God. To the Fundamentalist, the test of fellowship is correct doctrine. If you do not agree with his doctrinal position, he writes you off and will not have fellowship with you. There is no room in his world for those who have a different persuasion. He feels threatened by diverse convictions and writes them off as sinister and heretical. As long as you support his position, he is with you. Cross him, and he has no use whatsoever for you. . . . The Fundamentalist tactic is simple: hatred, bitterness, and condemnation of all whom they despise. . . . In the name of the Lord they will launch vehement attacks on individuals and churches. In the name of the Lord they attempt to assassinate the character of those whom they oppose. They direct their attack most often on other Christian leaders with whom they find disagreement.

Source: James Draper, *The Church Christ Approves* (Nashville: Broadman Press, 1974), 38, 39, 43. Reprint courtesy of Broadman and Holman Press.

CHAPTER 14

Continuity Amidst Change, 1982–1998

14.1 William Pinson, Jr.

In 1982, Bill Pinson, Jr., replaced James Landes as Executive Secretary of the BGCT. In the history of the BGCT, Bill Pinson may have been the most qualified man to hold the office. After receiving his M. Div. and Ph.D. from Southwestern Seminary, he had been a professor of Christian Ethics at Southwestern Seminary, Associate Secretary of the BGCT Christian Life Commission, President of Golden Gate Seminary in San Francisco, and along with Clyde Fant, he authored *Twenty-Centuries of Great Preaching*. Along with his academic and administrative training, Pinson was also known as a deeply spiritual man. He would need all of these traits to lead the BGCT through one of its most controversial periods.

A. The Unanimous Selection of Bill Pinson

Bill Pinson is perhaps the finest urban strategist we have in our Convention. He took his sabbatical to work with the Home Mission Board in the area of urban strategy. His mission zeal is second to none. He is remarkable, fair, obviously brilliant and unquestionably committed to Scripture.

Our nominee and his lovely wife were invited back for a meeting with the full committee on April 28, 1982. The formal vote was in their presence. The motion was made, the chair noted thirteen seconds to the motion, and the vote was unanimous.

Presley summarized Pinson's accomplishments, as outlined in the Resume distributed to the Board members.

Our recommendation is that the Board elect Dr. William Pinson, Jr., Executive Director effective July 1, 1982, through December 31, 1982. This will give him opportunity to serve with Executive Director James H. Landes for a period of six months, as which time Dr. Pinson can review the policies, programs and procedures of the Convention, visit and become reacquainted with our institutions, commissions and boards and their leadership. It will afford him time to meet with pastors and lay leaders in different areas of the state, and a period to attend a management seminar as a refresher for new management and executive skills.

Then effective January 1, 1983, our proposal calls for Dr. Pinson to be the Executive Director following Dr. Landes' formal and official retirement. Dr. Landes will be the Chief Executive for all of 1982. He and Dr. Pinson are in harmony on the manner in which they would serve together. For example, Dr. Landes has advised Dr. Pinson that no decisions regarding professional personnel will be made without joint consultation.

They will make an excellent team during the interim period, and the result will be that the Baptist General Convention of Texas will benefit because there will be no loss of momentum in this change of leadership.

Presley asked Judge Oswin Chrisman to present a formal resolution:

Executive Board Resolution
Employment of Executive Director-Elect

Whereas the Executive Director Search Committee of the Executive Board of the Baptist General Convention of Texas has been duly constituted and

Whereas the said Search Committee has prayerfully and carefully sought the appropriate person for the Executive Leadership of the Baptist General Convention of Texas,

Be It Therefore Resolved That:

1) Dr. William M. Pinson be elected Executive Director-Elect of the Baptist General Convention of Texas effective July 1, 1982.

2) Dr. William M. Pinson will become Executive Director of the Baptist General Convention of Texas January 1, 1983.

3) The Executive Director-Elect's compensation will be $41,788.00 and a housing allowance which, when combined with

the said salary, will equal the compensation (including housing allowance) and deferred compensation of the present Executive Director of the Baptists General Convention of Texas, plus the following benefits.

a) Convention related life and health insurance premiums.

b) A 15% of total compensation contributed by the Baptist General Convention of Texas to retirement program of the Southern Baptist Convention. Dr. Pinson must match the 5% beyond the basic 10% in order to reach 20%. The maximum contribution from the Convention is 15%.

c) A car and actual expense.

Judge Chrisman moved that this resolution be adopted. Ed Rogers seconded the motion.

Winfred Moore, James Draper and Ed. B. Bowles, members of the Executive Committee, spoke to the motion.

Chairman McIver opened the meeting for discussion. The following Board members spoke the motion: Charles Kemble, Mrs. Earl Johnston and Charles Dodson. Rudy Sanchez and Elvis Egge also spoke.

D. L. Lowrie led in prayer. Board members were asked to register their vote by standing. It was a unanimous vote. Others were asked to stand and the congregation sang, "To God Be the Glory."

Welton Gaddy made the following motion: That the Executive Board go on record commending the integrity of the selection process, both from its inception in naming the members of the committee through its search, to its report today. Further, that we thank the members of this committee not only for bringing us Bill Pinson to a position of leadership, but for modeling for Texas Baptists, and for all who watch Texas Baptists, how the unity of seeking and doing God's will can grow out of and transcend the diversity of differences. Mark Briggs seconded the motion and it carried.

Kenneth Hall made the following motion: That our Chairman write a letter expressing our Board's appreciation and prayerful concern for Golden Gate Seminary in these hours as they now began searching for a new President for that institution. There were several seconds and the motion carried.

Chairman McIver introduced James H. Landes. (Standing ovation) Dr. Landes thanked the Board in appointing the Search Committee and thanked the Committee for its work. He expressed a warm welcome to Bill, Bobbie, Meredith and Allison Pinson—we welcome them with prayerful spirit, we welcome them with a scripturally "merry heart" and we welcome them with open arms. I believe we can tell Bill Pinson where we are—we are in the will of God. I believe we can tell him where we want to go—we want to win the world to Jesus Christ. We want to begin at home and carry the gospel to the ends of the earth. We will do our best to help him know where we are in all the workings of our Convention. Texas Baptists have a great heritage of Christian leadership. Look around the Southern Baptist Convention and you will see how strong our Texas Baptist leadership is and has been. I am confident this morning that it will continue unto the man you have chosen as your Executive Director-Elect today.

Dr. Pinson, one of the joys of serving as Executive Director of the BGCT is that you will have the most delightful time working with men who are honest, who will express themselves openly and who will pray for you earnestly because they know the responsibility you will be carrying. As we welcome him, let us assure him of our prayers. Let us share with him such wisdom as we have, after we have prayed, let us give him continuing support and great good will. Thus, we will honor our past and we will assure the present. The blessings of the Holy Spirit will be upon us today and tomorrow with God's grace resting upon us. Let us do all that we can to make this time the best time in the long and wonderful history of the Baptist General Convention of Texas. God love you and bless you.

Dr. and Mrs. Bill Pinson were welcomed to the meeting by Mr. Presley. Dr. Pinson in accepting his election as Executive Director-Elect said, "This is without a doubt the most humbling and terrifying moment of my life. There has been many tasks God has called me to that I have somehow felt prepared for, and even perhaps adequate to tackle. But, this one I must confess to you is one far, far beyond my ability, experience or background and if I did not feel God was in it, I would stay in California regardless of the threat of earthquake!

"But, there has been a growing feeling on my part, as well as you have heard expressed from the committee, that this is indeed what God wants and, therefore, humbly and with great desire for your prayer and support that I accept the election of this Board to the position of Executive Director-Elect."

Dr. Pinson expressed his appreciation to the Search Committee, his family, Golden Gate Seminary and Texas Baptists. He said, "I see this as a continuing unfolding of God's purposes in missions for my life. I come therefore on mission, not on ceremony and ritual and second-rate agendas, but rather to a mission. I see Texas as the cornerstone of our mission to the world."

In closing, Dr. Pinson asked for the prayers and support of all. "God has called us to unity," he said. He read Ephesians 6:18–19: "Praying always with all prayer and supplication in the Spirit, and watching thereunto with all perseverance and supplication for all saints; And for me, that utterance may be given unto me, that I may open my mouth boldly, to make known the mystery of the gospel.

"That is what I ask you to pray for as we come together to commit ourselves to the task which God has called us together," said Dr. Pinson.

Mrs. Pinson spoke briefly and the meeting closed with prayer by Chairman McIver.

Source: *Minutes*, Executive Board of the Baptist General Convention of Texas, 18 May 1982. Reprint courtesy of the Baptist General Convention of Texas.

B. Texas Baptist Schools Are Centers of Missions Activity

Those in the past and in the present who have been part of the Baptist General Convention of Texas have believed in the close relationship of missions and education. Both are viewed as necessary for the fulfillment of the Great Commission of the Lord Jesus Christ.

Institutions, such as mission boards and schools, were developed to provide structures for carrying out the Lord's command. Upon first arriving in Texas in the 1830s, Texas Baptists established churches and associations of churches—the primary organizations in Baptist life. Shortly afterward, they established two other organizations, one for missions and one for education. These early Texas Baptists saw the need for both and realized the relationship of each to the other.

That need and relationship continue to exist. Baptist educational institutions remain a vital part of the missions enterprise. As the schools function in the way their founders intended, they contribute to the mission efforts of Baptists in multiple ways. Thus, support for such schools is support for missions.

Texas Baptist schools help to "call out the called" for international and domestic missions service. A large number of missionaries serving around the world and throughout our nation have received their call to missions service while in a Texas Baptist school.

In addition, the schools help to develop the leaders for Baptist churches who will be missions-minded and provide the prayer and financial support necessary for missionary activity. Some of these will serve as pastors and church staff members. Others will be lay leaders in churches. Together, these persons make a potent force for missions through churches. They encourage prayer and missions education. They provide financial support through the Cooperative Program and special missions offerings. They often lead out in missions projects locally and in various parts of the state, nation and world.

The Texas Baptist schools also are centers for missionary activity. By enrolling and evangelizing lost students, they help add to the army of the redeemed. By providing training and opportunities for students, faculty and staff to be involved in missions outreach, they share the gospel with a multitude of people each year. By making available resources for Christian growth and discipleship, they develop effective witnesses for today and tomorrow.

Texas Baptist school presidents help maintain this missions focus while providing quality education. Their goal is for the schools to be distinctly Christian, unapologetically Baptist and academically excellent. Through that combination, students are molded into an effective force for missions. Working with the presidents toward that end are faculty, staff, student leaders and graduates. Providing basic direction are the trustees charged with the responsibility of seeing that missions and education remain dynamically wed.

Please pray for the missions and education efforts of Texas Baptist schools. Pray for all involved in maintaining their strength and focus. And pray that this year a host of persons in Texas and around the world will come to faith in Jesus Christ as Lord and Savior because Texas Baptist schools have focused on missions and education.

Source: "Texas Baptist Schools are Centers of Missions Activity," *Baptist Standard*, 25 February 1998, 5. Reprint courtesy of the *Baptist Standard*.

14.2 A New Leadership Team

Realizing that his task was great, Pinson developed a strong team to aid him in his administrative duties. This team included Doris Ann Tinker, executive associate; Ed Schmeltekopf, associate executive director; Jay Skaggs, treasurer; and Thomas J. Brannon, director of public relations. Several members would remain in their positions until Pinson's retirement in 1986. Pinson's administration would always be marked by a strong support staff.

A. Office of Associate Executive Director, Ed Schmeltekopf, 1996

Implementing Texas 2000 continues to have a major impact upon the work of the Associate Executive Director. Heightening awareness in the churches across our state and coordinating the work of the staff in these matters are responsibilities which claim priority.

Art Hodge, a volunteer who assists the Associate President and Chair of the Executive Board claim much time in the work of this office. The Effectiveness/Efficiency Committee has met four times this year and has scheduled five meetings for 1997. Also, the Theological Education Transition Committee is working to finalize the work earlier assigned. The Associate Executive Director coordinates the work of these committees as a staff liaison.

The Associate Executive Director is responsible for implementing the Salary Administration Plan of the Executive Board. During this past year, the Associate Executive Director has worked with a professional administration consultant in the restudy of the Salary Administration Plan of the BGCT. The report of this study is submitted to the Administrative Committee for their decision in regard to determining an appropriate Salary Structure.

The Office of Associate Executive Director maintains the continuing responsibility of working with organization, structure and coordination of the Executive Board Staff. Supervision of Cooperative Program Promotion, Human Resources, Partnership Missions and Mission Service Corps are part of this responsibility. Detailed reports of these areas of work are included in this Book of Reports.

The Associate Executive Director is responsible for planning meetings which are the responsibility of the Executive Director and serves as an advisor to the Executive Director. During the past year the Associate Executive Director has led in planning four Executive Board meetings, four regular Administrative Committee meetings, two general Staff Planning Weeks and two additional Staff Planning Days.

The Associate Executive Director works closely with Convention elected leadership. He assists the officers as they appoint Convention committees of the Convention and of the Executive Board.

Source: *Proceedings*, Book of Reports of the Baptist General Convention of Texas, 1996, 75. Reprint courtesy of the Baptist General Convention of Texas.

B. Treasurer's Report, 1989

Roger Hall reported that at the end of 10 months, Cooperative Program receipts were 91.8% of budget and expenditures were about 89.8%. November's receipts were in excess of our budget which put the budget receipts at 92.8%. This is 3.1% ahead of last year's giving to the Cooperative Program. The summarization of the Cooperative Program's giving this year, four words apply: stability, faithfulness, recommitment and gratitude. All four designated offerings showed increases in the month of November. Arthur Anderson & Co. representatives are in the process of auditing our records and reports of that audit will be brought to you in the future as we try to be accountable for the way funds are utilized.

Source: *Minutes*, Executive Board of the Baptist General Convention of Texas, 5 December 1989. Reprint courtesy of the Baptist General Convention of Texas.

14.3 Mission Texas, 1985–1990

Since the 1930s, the BGCT has implemented its programs in five-year increments. The goal of Mission Texas was threefold: evangelism, enlistment and training in Christian Living, and missionary giving. The primary goal of Mission Texas was to train 89,000 witnesses from 3,000 churches in the hopes of winning one million Texans to Christ. This intention was to be met by implementing four practical facets that corresponded to the three primary goals. These facets included Reaching People, Developing Believers, Strengthening Missions, and Spiritual Awakening. Extremely ambitious goals were set for each facet with each falling short of its goal. Tremendous advances, however, were still accomplished in each area.

They Too Can Believe

Sacrifice and Courage always have characterized Texans. From the sacrifice of the Alamo martyrs to the courage of the homesteaders who tamed the plains, Texans have struggled against the odds to carve out their destiny.

These same qualities have characterized Texas Baptists from the days of Z. N. Morrell and Noah T. Byars to the present. As surely as the pioneer preachers and lay leaders were a people of destiny waging spiritual warfare for the souls of Texas, the battle still rages today, demanding no less courage and no less sacrifice.

Today's Texas is a multi-cultural, religiously pluralistic, greatly diverse state. It is also a largely unchurched state. At least one half of its population claims no church affiliation whatsoever. Reaching out with the gospel to the Texan of today means speaking in more than 100 different languages and dialects. It means crossing cultural, racial and economic barriers. And it means offering a compassionate response to the struggling farmer, the unemployed worker, the chronically poor and other hurting people.

Confronted with this challenge many Texas Baptists are launching out in unprecedented ways . . . so they too can believe. They are the rallying goals of MISSION TEXAS—prayer for spiritual awakening, stewardship growth, strengthening missions, developing believers and reaching people through 2,000 new churches and missions by 1990.

Many Texas Baptists are taking part in this effort through a unique missions giving opportunity—the Mary Hill Davis Centennial Offering for State Missions. To reach the goal of $30 million in seed money to help start 2,000 churches, Texas Baptists have been encouraged as individuals and churches to TRIPLE-TRIPLE—triple their 1984 offerings in 1985 and then triple their 1985 offerings in 1986. Nearly 1,000 churches and countless individuals took the first step of faith last year by tripling their 1984 giving to the state missions offering.

This year the goal is unprecedented—$22.8 million. This once-in-a-lifetime goal includes more than $18.8 million for new mission/church assistance. Many other ongoing state missions programs will be funded through the basis goal of $3,989,179. Many of these support and undergird the work of the new churches and missions. They include scholarships for ethnic students, Hispanic Baptist Theological Seminary, Valley Baptist Academy, Rio Grande River Ministry, Partnership Missions, Mission Service Corps and many other ministries.

From the Rio Grande to the Panhandle, from the Sabine River to the Davis Mountains, Texas Baptists are taking the gospel to a state that needs the Good News of Jesus Christ. This special section offers a look at some of the work that is being made possible through your gifts to the Mary Hill Davis Centennial Offering for State Missions.

Source: "So They Too Can Believe," *Baptist Standard*, 10 September 1986, 9. Reprint courtesy of the *Baptist Standard*.

14.4 Baptist Building

Since the Convention moved its headquarters to Dallas in 1896, the BGCT had rented space for its denominational leadership to carry out its work. In 1952, the BGCT purchased its own building, which it soon outgrew, and an even larger structure became necessary. A new spacious building located on the corner of Washington and Race in Dallas, which was completed totally free of debt, was dedicated on December 6, 1988. The state-of-the-art building houses the offices of the WMU, Texas Baptist Men, Baptist Church Loan Corporation, State Missions Commission, Christian Life Commission, Christian Education Coordinating Board, Human Welfare Coordinating Board, the director of Church/Minister relations, the Baptist Leadership Center, and a myriad other BGCT offices.

No Cooperative Program Money Was Spent!

The Baptist General Convention of Texas has a new building to house employees of the Executive Board, the Baptist Church Loan Corporation, Texas Baptist Men and Woman's Missionary Union. The building will be dedicated Dec. 6.

The $10.9 million building is debt-free. You read it right, and no Cooperative Program money was used to build the building.

Then how was such a feat in Baptist life accomplished? Give God all the glory and praise, and be thankful for some Texas Baptists who had foresight and wisdom, along with the Annuity Board, to sell the 511 Akard Baptist building in downtown Dallas when real estate was at its peak price. Some names should be mentioned such as William M. Pinson, director of the Executive Board, and Roger Hall, treasurer of the board, who have had much to do with the successful project. Ed Rogers, pastor of First Church, Dumas, and chairman of the building committee, along with all of its members is congratulated. Also some laymen should be mentioned including Dewey Presley of Dallas, Fred Roach of Dallas and J. T. Luther of Fort Worth, who helped put together the package of selling the old property and selecting the new site. Others? Sure. Many.

Texas Baptists have reason to be thankful for the building which is only a tool to be used to help Baptists do their work.

Remember, the building on Washington Street in Dallas is the Baptist Building. It is not Baptist headquarters. Headquarters for Baptists is the local church.

Congratulations to all Texas Baptists on their new Baptist Building.—PHW

Source: Presnall H. Wood, "New Baptist Building," *Baptist Standard*, 30 November 1988, 6. Reprint courtesy of the *Baptist Standard*.

14.5 Volunteers on Mission

Under the leadership of Bill Pinson, Texas Baptists continued to volunteer in a number of missionary endeavors. In particular, the Rio Grande River Ministry, Partnership Missions, and the Mission Service Corps grew in popularity and continued to flourish. The River Ministry continued to attend to the needs of those on both sides of the Rio Grande by means of Vacation Bible Schools, medical aid, and student evangelism. Partnership Missions developed new missions avenues in the District of Columbia, Estonia, and Australia. The Mission Service Corps restructured its consultant program, advanced the River Ministry, and continued to aid the Minnesota-Wisconsin Baptist Convention.

A. River Ministry: Reaching the Unreached

A prostitute and a drug addict, Norma kept her two young daughters in an outhouse until social workers in Ojinaga, Chihuahua, Mexico, intervened and placed the girls in a new children's home opened in Ojinaga by Bethel Baptist Church.

The home's director, Olivia Medina Terranga, had come to know the Lord through the ministry of Bethel and its pastor, Edmundo Valenzuela. Olivia and her brother, Julian, studied at the Theological Training Institute at Bethel.

Whenever Norma came to the children's home to visit her daughters, Olivia prayed and shared Christ with her. Eventually Norma wanted to know the Jesus Olivia knew, and Olivia led her to the Lord.

Soon Norma took pastor Edmundo Valenzuela to witness to her drug-addicted friends. At first their response was jeers and scoffing, but Norma cried and prayed for them and kept witnessing to them.

Soon they began coming to her secretly, asking questions and seeking help. Today, 17 of her friends are active members of Bethel Church. Children of some of Norma's friends lived at the children's home before their parents' lives were changed through the power of Jesus Christ.

Norma is studying at the Theological Training Institute at Bethel and continues to minister among drug addicts and prison inmates.

The children's home in Ojinaga is one of six which Texas Baptists through their Rio Grande River Ministry and Mary Hill Davis Offering for State Missions help support along the 900 mile stretch of the Rio Grande River between Brownsville and Matamoros. Piedras Negras, across the Rio Grande from Eagle Pass, has two child-care homes, and others are in Juarez, Nuevo Laredo and Matamoros.

Since Texas Baptists launched the River Ministry in 1967, tens of thousands of people along the Great River have been introduced to Jesus through the ministry of thousands of volunteers from upstate churches.

Ironically it was a disaster that focused the attention on millions of spiritually lost people living along the River. Hurricane Beulah struck the Gulf Coast and wreaked major damage to population centers far up the Rio Grande. In aiding storm victims, Texas Baptists caught the vision to begin the River Ministry, as well as a program of disaster relief for which the denomination's Texas Baptist Men are known around the world.

Since the River Ministry began, more than 670 new churches have been started along both sides of the River. Among the thousands of missions volunteers helping to conduct Vacation Bible Schools, construct church buildings, dig water wells and perform other ministries were more than 900 college and seminary students who served as summer missionaries along the border. Many of these are now involved in vocational Christian service.

Each year, more than 400 church and college student groups are involved in some type of mission project along the border area.

The desperate need for medical and dental aid along the River led to mobile clinics that evolved into 67 permanent medical and dental clinics staffed by volunteers. A public health physician estimates that River Ministry's health-care programs have improved conditions along the Texas-Mexico border by about 300 percent in the last quarter century. Infant mortality has dropped from 65 percent to about 10 percent.

Elmin Howell, who served as director of the River Ministry department within the BGCT State Missions Commission for nearly 30 years, retired last year and was succeeded by Larry Eckeberger, who began his ministry as a River Ministry summer missionary.

"Through the River Ministry Texas Baptists have begun to write a great drama in the annals of Christian ministry, but their greatest challenge is ahead," Howell said. "We must share Jesus' gospel with 10 million people along the Rio Grande, more people than the total populations of many countries of the world."

An estimated 50 families a day move into Juarez, which already has a population of nearly 3 million. Colonias (neighborhoods) fan out across the region, providing fertile ground for planting hundreds of new churches.

Unfortunately, it provides an opportunity for the Communist Party as well. The Communists developed a stronghold in Colonia Manuel Valdez by promising better living conditions in an area which had no potable water, electricity, sewage disposal or mass transit.

"Just become a member, and we'll meet your needs," party leaders promised.

Into this scene came a family from Torreon, Mexico. When a daughter became ill, the mother sought medical aid at a free clinic staffed by River Ministry Health Care Service volunteers near Juarez in Cristo El Redentor Baptist Mission, Zaragosa. While waiting for the doctor to attend her daughter, the women accepted Christ as Lord and Savior.

Back home she shared her testimony with her husband, who also received Christ. They invited members of El Redentor to conduct a Bible study and invited neighbors to attend. Initially, because of the Communist influence, neighbors resisted. When Texas Baptist volunteers came to conduct Vacation Bible School, the Communists encouraged children in the colonia to throw rocks at the Texans' church vans.

But soon the neighbors were won over, and the Dios Es Amor (God is Love) Baptist Mission began in a home made of cardboard and packing materials. The family who began the work returned to Torreon, but their home, appropriately called "the cardboard church" continues to serve as the worship site for an average of about 40 people.

"Along the Rio Grande, from El Paso to Brownsville, from Juarez to Matamoros, missions volunteers are helping to bring the light of Christ into the lives of people who are spiritually and physically needy," said Eckeberger.

"Many have helped by giving to the Mary Hill Davis Offering for State Missions."

"But God is calling others to share their faith in this great mission field—the world's most populated transnational corridor—at our front door."

Source: *Texas Missions*, Fall 1997, 13–14. Reprint courtesy of the Baptist General Convention of Texas.

B. Partnership Missions

Partnership missions, student ministry and world hunger topped the agenda at the March 12 meeting of the Baptist General Convention of Texas' Executive Board.

Acting on a recommendation from the Texas Baptist Administrative Committee, the board renewed a three-year partnership missions agreement with the District of Columbia Baptist Convention and entered into a partnership with the Northwest Baptist Convention.

Lead partner in the relationship with the District of Columbia will be the Austin Association, reported Ed Schmeltekopf, the convention's associate director. He pointed to a similarity between the two capital cities and the success of "sister city" relationships in other partnership missions efforts.

The board also ratified a three-year partnership missions relationship between the BGCT and the Northwest Baptist Convention, which includes Oregon, Washington and the panhandle of Idaho.

In other business, the Executive Board approved a recommendation from the Christian Education Coordinating Board that Thomas M. Ruane, 50, be named director of the student ministry division. Ruane had been acting director of the division since Jack Greever's resignation last June, and he previously served as associate director.

Ruane directed Baptist student ministries at the University of Texas at Arlington, Howard Payne University and Tarleton State University.

The San Antonio native is a graduate of Howard Payne University in Brownwood and Southwestern Seminary in Fort Worth. He is working toward a doctor of ministry degree from New Orleans Seminary.

He and his wife, Mary Alice Wimberly Ruane, have two sons and a daughter.

The Executive Board also approved a recommendation from the Texas Baptist Christian Life Commission that moves the emphasis on world hunger relief giving from the second Sunday in October to the four consecutive Sundays leading up to Thanksgiving.

When asked if the emphasis would conflict with any other special offerings, CLC Director Phil Strickland noted the offering would fall between the Mary Hill Davis Offering for state missions in early September and the Lottie Moon Christmas Offering for foreign missions in December.

Joy Fenner, executive director-treasurer of Woman's Missionary Union of Texas, voiced her organization's support for the proposal "as long as we keep foreign missions strong, too."

Source: Ken Camp, "Northwesterners to be Texans' Next Partners,"

Baptist Standard, 20 March 1996, 5. Reprint courtesy of the *Baptist Standard*.

C. Partnership Missions: 1996 Report

While gearing up for the challenge of Texas 2000 "to present the gospel to every person in Texas by the year 2000," Texas Baptists did not diminish their efforts to reach our nation and our world for Christ. Through Partnership Missions they have touched people's lives, constructed building facilities for expanding work, healed broken bodies and trained others for optimal Christian service.

Throughout this Convention year, these achievements have been realized in Australia, Cuba, Estonia, the Dominican Republic, Taiwan (Union Association) and the District of Columbia Baptist Convention. In addition, we have worked with the Northwest Baptist Convention to establish a new partnership beginning Jan. 1, 1997. All these partnerships are channeled through the Southern Baptist Convention Foreign Mission Board, the national Baptist body involved, or the respective state convention. During the past year, 260 volunteers were involved in various aspects of ministry.

The Australian Crusade involved 95 Texas Baptists in 16 teams working in as many Australian Baptist churches in New South Wales. Although all reports are not in, professions of faith reported have totaled over 100. There were additional decisions seeking baptism and church membership. Reports continue to come from the Australian churches for decisions made after the Texans had left, but attributed to their ministry while there. The enthusiastic reaction of Australian Baptists has led them to set the dates of July 23 through August 5 for a 1997 crusade. Also, there were 12 BSM summer missionaries in teams of two that worked with six churches for 10 weeks.

In Estonia three construction groups worked on new construction of a church building, restoration of an existing church building and installations in the national camp ground. Fifteen BSM summer missionaries in teams of two spread out over the country to work with the individual churches. A dentist spent two weeks in dental work and teaching local dentists in current methodology, equipment and materials. Several volunteers were involved in teaching English as a second language. Two

consultants from the Executive Board staff served with the union to promote stewardship and cooperative giving.

A number of one-time projects in other countries in cooperation
with the Foreign Mission Board were undertaken such as restoration of
the new International Seminary's facilities in Prague, Czechoslovakia;
help in the move of the German Baptist Seminary from Hamburg to
Berlin; and a medical team of 32 serving in Romania.

Partnership Missions focuses the concern of Texas Baptists for the
world in areas approved by the Executive Board. Our volunteer outreach to a world in need enhances the aggressive pursuit of the goals of
Texas 2000.

Source: *Proceedings*, Baptist General Convention of Texas, 1996, 76.
Reprint courtesy of the Baptist General Convention of Texas.

D. Mission Service Corps: 1996 Report

The Mission Service Corps (MSC) office has the responsibility of
coordinating volunteer missions, long and short term, for volunteers to
serve at home, in Texas, the United States and overseas. This responsibility includes:

- Publicizing information on volunteer missions to groups and individuals.
- Assisting potential volunteers in determining the Lord's calling
  to positions of service.
- Encouraging and assisting churches and institutions to identify
  where volunteers can serve.

To carry out this task, there are 40 consultant units throughout the
state. These consultants—volunteers themselves—are fully trained and
highly motivated. One of the consultants primarily serves black churches.
Twelve associations/areas have their own individual churches. Twelve
associations/areas have their own individual consultants. Other consultants serve several associations. They recognize the importance of volunteer missions in helping churches, associations and institutions to reach
their goals as part of Texas 2000 and are continuing to enlist volunteers
in record numbers.

Mission Service Corps volunteer home missionaries are making a
difference in local churches. They are filling positions in such ministries

as outreach, pastor, church starter, senior adults, homebound, administrative, crisis, education, music, minister of missions and others.

International Service Corps volunteers serve overseas in a wide variety of positions.

These statistics (as of Jan. 1, 1996) show the growth of Mission Service Corps in Texas and the ministries performed by these volunteer missionaries. These people serve four months or longer, full time and provide/raise their financial support.

- 1,172 Serving in Texas and Texans outside the state (10% increase in 1995)
- 206 Serving overseas (FMB)
- 806 Serving in Texas
- 160 Serving in U.S. outside Texas
- 375 Local churches
- 80 Primary association staff positions
- 140 Association related positions
- 220 Assigned to or related to BGCT

The 806 MSCs serving in Texas provide almost $25 million annually in ministry and service.

Missions Service Corps volunteer missionaries who serve two years are included in the total missionary count of the Home and Foreign Mission Boards. One in four home missionaries is a Mission Service Corps volunteer. One in seven foreign missionaries is an International Service Corps worker or Journeyman.

Despite increases in the number of MSCs serving, there were 400 unfilled requests in Texas at the end of 1995.

The MSC office also supports Texas partnerships with Minnesota/Wisconsin and Washington D. C.

Persons interested or needing volunteer missionaries should contact their MSC consultant or the MSC office (214-828-5290).

Source: *Book of Reports*, Baptist General Convention of Texas, 1996, 76. Reprint courtesy of the Baptist General Convention of Texas.

E. Minnesota-Wisconsin Baptist Convention

As of July 1, 1997, 143 churches and missions in seven associations make up the MWBC. The estimated population of both states is approaching 10,000,000. The population is both changing and growing. This changing and growing population includes large numbers of adults who are unreached by any church. To reach these multitudes is the challenge facing the churches, pastors, and leadership of the Minnesota-Wisconsin Baptist Convention. This challenge gave birth to a Vision Statement.

VISION STATEMENT

Establish a mission base among the congregations of MWBC so that the convention and association are indigenous, self-supporting and contributing to world-wide missions through finances and personnel. Establish by the year 2010 more than 400 healthy, growing, reproducing congregations in Minnesota-Wisconsin, 75% of whom are led by upper-midwestern natives with 15 averaging more than 200, 12 averaging more than 400 and 3 averaging more than 1,000 in attendance, a total membership in excess of 40,000, total attendance or more than 25,000 and 4,000 baptisms per year.

TEXAS BAPTIST CHURCHES
EXPANDING
PARTNERSHIP

Churches of the Baptist General Convention of Texas have a long standing relationship with the Minnesota-Wisconsin Baptist Convention. In fact, MWBC began as an association of Texas Baptists in the 1960s. That relationship needs to be expanded during the next several years. There is a great need for churches of the BGCT who are willing to enter into a three-year partnership to help establish new churches in Minnesota-Wisconsin and see them develop into strong mission base congregations. There is also a need for churches of the BGCT to partner with existing churches of the MWBC to help them develop into stronger congregations.

THE PARTNERSHIP RELATIONSHIP
WOULD INVOLVE SOME OR ALL OF
THE FOLLOWING ASSISTANCE

- Sponsorship of new work
- Monthly financial assistance

- Assistance with leadership training
- Volunteer building teams
- Survey teams for new church starts
- Church development assistance
- Assistance for various mission and ministry needs

Source: Pamphlet, *Become a Partner in the Minnesota-Wisconsin Mission Challenge*, 1997. Reprint courtesy of the Baptist General Convention of Texas.

F. Mission Service Corps: Restructuring the Consultant System

The emphasis on the consultant system was continued and expanded. More consultants were recruited with training in April 1984. There were sixteen consultants units, a unit being either a couple or one individual. The system continued to expand. In 1987, there were twenty-four consultant positions, with every association assigned to a consultant. Spanish-speaking and African American consultants were added.

Training for consultants was also increased over time. Length of the original training was gradually increased as the position became more comprehensive and more of the total operation was computerized. It went from two days in 1984 to five days in 1993. As the emphasis on supporting other organizations took effect, it was necessary to include people from the Baptist Building who worked in these areas; i. e., Church Extension, River Ministry, Missions Development Council, etc.

In 1992 it was found that it was beneficial for an experienced consultant to spend a couple of days with a new consultant before the initial training. In this way, the new consultants had an idea of what their duties would encompass. This made the training more applicable and effective.

MSC orientations were also used for training. Experienced consultants were brought back as orientation staff members, giving them direct involvement in negotiation assignments there. New consultants were included in the orientation staff meetings. Both of these moves proved very effective.

As the number of consultants increased, direct supervision by the coordinator became more difficult. In 1987, working with Dr. Bob Mills, HMB/MSC Director, a supervisory structure was designed and implemented. Six experienced consultants were selected as supervising consultants. In a meeting, procedures were worked out to include supervisors in all events/communications except assignments. Supervisors would visit their consultants as least every six months and talk to them frequently.

Despite a concerted effort, this structure did not work. It was found that both supervision and training functions must follow the assignment chain. It was extremely difficult for the supervisor consultants to be very helpful if they were not part of each assignment action. This was not possible—or at least not feasible—so this supervisory consultant system was abandoned.

In October 1989 the consultant system was restructured to more greatly utilize the local knowledge and experience of consultants. These were the major changes. They placed responsibility at the level closest to the action. Consultants will:

- Negotiate local assignments between potential volunteers and supervisors. When completed, consultants advise the BGCT/MSC who notifies HMB to make the assignment. This was very significant because the HMB negotiated assignments in/for other states.
- Provide all necessary information to prospective volunteers.
- Respond to all invitations to speak. Seek invitations to special events such as senior adult functions, missions activities, etc.
- Serve as members of the Director of Missions staffing each of their assigned associations. They would attend as many meetings as possible. This meant being a part of association strategy planning, major committee meetings, reporting at Annual Meetings, etc.
- Monitor all prospective volunteers and assist them in every way possible. Follow up on orientation attendees.
- Take every possible action relative to their area of assignment. Refer situations to the BGCT/MSC when appropriate.

In turn the BGCT would provide necessary/appropriate information and publicity pieces to the consultant. This included:

- Copies of applications, SORs, orientation attendees, new assignment and concluding actions from the HMB and other pertinent information.

- Necessary computer products such as lists of interested people, serving MSCs, unfilled SORs
- Appropriate information pieces such as:
  - Why Should a Volunteer be MSC?
  - MSC Overview
  - Sample MSC Needs
  - Families as Volunteers
  - Determining the Will of God in Relation to Volunteer Service
  - Volunteers Serving as Missionaries
  - Volunteers in Local Churches
  - Why Supervisors Should Want their Volunteers to be MSC

These were later modified to include the consultant's name as part of the design. Consultants ran off copies as needed.

As part of the restructuring, consultants were asked annually to set specific numerical gains for their area. A monthly reporting system was implemented which tracked these goals.

This restructuring was implemented only after thorough discussion and modification at the January 1990 consultant meeting.

This process worked well. It required consultants to give priority to their duties and greatly increased their effectiveness. Some consultants resigned because they felt God was leading them to continue in other ministries. Rapid growth in the number of persons serving through MSC occurred after this change.

Source: Samuel P. Pearis IV, "Outline History of Mission Service Corps," unpublished paper dated January 22, 1997, 10–13. Reprint courtesy of Samuel P. Pearis.

14.6 Schools and Students

The job of the Christian Education Coordinating Board was to oversee the eight Baptist Colleges or Universities, one academy, and nearly one hundred campuses that maintained BSU programs. Lester L. Morriss who directed the work of the CECB for a number of years, retired from his post in 1985, and Jerry F. Dawson, former President of East Texas Baptist College, was chosen as his replacement. Dawson accepted the position during a period of great prosperity in the lives of the Texas Baptist schools. All the

Baptist schools were receiving adequate funding, polls showed that Baptists believed in the work of their schools, enrollment was up, and adequate presidents were in abundance. Even the Bible Chairs at the State Universities managed to survive in an increasingly secularized society. Under Dawson's leadership, Texas Baptist schools continued to prosper.

A. San Marcos Baptist Academy: 1996 Report

San Marcos Baptist Academy began its 89th school year on August 12th. The ministry of the academy continues to touch the lives of young people from around the world. Middle School and High School students from nine foreign countries and nine states comprise the fall class of 1996. The largest group continues to come from the major metropolitan centers of our state, but 86 different cities within Texas are represented by the students in attendance.

Enrollment for the 1996 spring semester was slightly lower (1%) than last year, and the summer and fall sessions are following a similar trend. The spirit of the faculty and staff is positive and optimistic, and the new school year promises to be an excellent one.

The importance of the spiritual dimension of life is continually emphasized at San Marcos. Regular worship and chapel services are held each Sunday and Wednesday. Additionally, five consecutive days of spiritual emphasis are scheduled each spring and fall semester. This past year's renewal weeks were particularly meaningful, and a number of young men and women publicly professed their faith in the Lord Jesus Christ. Many others made significant spiritual recommitments.

Adolescents have seldom, if ever, faced the kind of challenges inherent in today's real world environment. God has given the institution a unique opportunity and responsibility. The academy faculty and staff have a special sense of being called to touch young men's and women's hearts in a positive and spiritually healthy way at a teachable moment of their lives. A concern for our youth who will be the leaders of tomorrow called this school into existence in 1907. This same concern forms the basis of our witness and service today.

Dr. Jack E. Byrom, academy president since 1965, retired on May 31, 1996, after 31 years of faithful service. He continues to serve the institution as chancellor and president of the San Marcos Baptist Academy Foundation. Dr. Paul W. Armes, formerly pastor of the First Baptist Church of Corpus Christi, began his service as president of the school on June 1, 1996. Jimmie Scott, executive vice-president for 32 years, retired July 31, 1996. Dr. Don Davidson assumed the post vacated by Mr. Scott. Mr. Davidson has formerly served the academy as chaplain and academic dean.

Church youth and athletic camps continue to be a major feature of the summer's schedule. In 1996, 1,750 young men and women attended these camps, all of which were planned and conducted by the sponsoring churches. So many life-changing decisions are made during these special weeks. This fact has led the administrative staff to open additional dates for summer camps beginning in the summer of 1997.

The academy family wants to thank Texas Baptists for their generous and loving support. About 8% of our annual budget is supplied directly by the Baptist General Convention of Texas. We are grateful for the partnership which has existed between our state conventions and San Marcos Baptist Academy since 1911. Thank you for your prayers and your interest in and love for young people.

Source: *Book of Reports*, Baptist General Convention of Texas, 1996, 92. Reprint courtesy of the Baptist General Convention of Texas.

B. Christian Education Coordinating Board: 1984

Dr. D. L. Morriss gave a report on the recent survey made by the Public Relations Department of the Convention. The survey was made among the Texas Baptist educational institutions and results were that 99% of those surveyed said Christian education should remain high on the list of priorities of Texas Baptists. More than 90% of the 1,954 who were surveyed said they would encourage their children to attend a Texas Baptist school.

Reporting on Howard Payne University, Dr. Morriss told that the school now has a newly constructed Administrative Building which is debt-free. The university will have raised $250,000 by January 1985 thereby meeting the requirement for them to apply for the challenge grant in the amount of $250,000 from the Baptist General Convention of Texas.

Good news concerning Dallas Baptist College, which will become Dallas Baptist University, January 1, 1985, was reported. The school has operated in the black for the third consecutive year with an increase in endowment funds and for the last five years an increase in enrollment.

Source: *Minutes*, Executive Board of the Baptist General Convention of Texas, 4 December 1984. Reprint courtesy of the Baptist General Convention of Texas.

C. School Enrollment Increases 5.1 Percent

Nearly all of Texas Baptists' eight universities and San Marcos Academy have increased their 1990 spring enrollments over last spring's figures.

Total enrollment at the schools this spring is 23,420, a 5.1 percent growth over last spring's enrollment of 22,225.

Dallas Baptist University had the largest enrollment growth—2,254 students this spring compared with 1,978 last spring.

Wayland Baptist University, which recorded its largest enrollment in history last fall, a 17 percent gain, is in the winter semester and will not have spring enrollment figures until later, said the school's president, Lanny Hall. Enrollment last fall was 2,052, and winter enrollment is 1,834.

"We anticipate an enrollment increase this spring over last spring," Hall said.

Enrollments reported by the other schools were Baylor, 11,116 contrasted with 11,083 last spring; East Texas Baptist University, 807 compared 763 last spring; Hardin-Simmons, 1,757 compared with 1,787 last spring; Houston Baptist University 2,350 this spring compared with 2,210 last spring; Howard Payne University, 1,271 compared with 1,172 last spring; the University of Mary Hardin-Baylor, 1,732 compared with 1,553 last spring; and San Marcos Academy, 299 compared with 289 last spring.

"Texas Baptist schools are unusually blessed, because they are continuing to increase their enrollments far out of proportion to other private and public schools in our state," said Jerry Dawson, director of the Christian Education Coordinating Board.

"Although Wayland and Dallas Baptist University have relatively new administrations, each of them has shown rather spectacular strength," Dawson added.

Source: Orville Scott, "School Enrollments Increase 5.1 Percent," *Baptist Standard*, 28 February 1990, 11. Reprint courtesy of the *Baptist Standard*.

D. Bible Chair Ruling Gives Temporary Reprieve

Texas Baptist chairs of Bible at state universities seem to have received a reprieve, at least for a semester.

Thanks to clarification by Texas Attorney General Jim Mattox on the opinion he gave last fall concerning the constitutionality of the arrangement between the universities and the Bible chairs, schools that had decided to drop the programs have reinstated them.

Mattox's clarification came after he met with Baptist General Convention of Texas attorneys in Austin in December.

In a letter to Kenneth Ashworth, commissioner of the coordinating board of the Texas College and University System, Mattox emphasized that his earlier opinion "does not require the total severance of 'Bible Chair' programs from state colleges and universities," but only addressed the question of state schools appointing to a faculty position someone who is chosen or salaried by a religious organization.

"If a college or university wishes to integrate these courses into its official format, it must have total discretion over the selection and payment of teachers," Mattox wrote.

"Nevertheless, I remain convinced that we should explore the possibility that, within certain guidelines to preserve the separation of church and state, 'Bible Chair' programs may continue to offer religion courses to state college and university students."

Mattox said he looked forward to consulting with the state coordinating board on guidelines and hoped they could be implemented by the fall 1986 semester.

"In the interim, public institutions should be cautious about taking any drastic action regarding existing 'Bible Chair' programs," he wrote. "If courses have already been planned or advertised, issues arising under the Due Process Clauses of the Fifth and Fourteenth Amendments to the United States Constitution may be involved."

The Due Process clauses forbid the denial of life, liberty or property to anyone without due process of law.

Ashworth sent copies of Mattox's letter to all the state universities and colleges Dec. 27 to assist them in dealing with the Bible Chair situation. He said he hoped guidelines could be formulated in "early 1986."

One Baptist observer, who did not want to be quoted, said the reprieve is good news in the short term, but said the guidelines could turn out to be just as prohibitive as Mattox's original ruling.

But he noted that the ultimate outcome is hard to predict given the climate of an election year.

Bill Webb, an associate in the Texas Baptist Student Division, said some schools, which had reacted to Mattox's earlier opinion by canceling the Bible Chair programs, have reinstated them. Those schools were Stephen F. Austin, Angelo State, Sam Houston State, Southwest Texas State, The University of Texas at Austin, UT-El Paso, and UT-Arlington. Sul Ross was "up in the air" about it, Webb said.

After they received Mattox's second letter, Webb said, their regents began reversing those rulings.

"To my knowledge, there is not a single state university or college which has cancelled their spring 1986 Bible Chair courses, as a result of the attorney general's opinion," he said.

Two junior colleges have dropped the Bible Chair programs, Webb said, but discussions with those schools concerned other separation of church and state issues and were going on long before Mattox's first ruling. Other schools have dropped the program because of various disagreements and internal academic reasons—Texas A&M hasn't had the program for more than 15 years.

Each new administration at each school usually evaluated the Bible Chair program, Webb said. "That's their prerogative."

Enrollment in Baptist Bible Chair programs has declined in recent years, as has college enrollment in general. But Webb said the percentage of non-Baptist students in the program has remained at about 50 percent.

Source: John Rutledge, "Bible Chair Ruling Gives Temporary Reprieve," *Baptist Standard*, 22 January 1986, 4. Reprint courtesy of the Baptist Standard.

E. Division of Student Ministry

Individually and corporately, Texas Baptists make Student Ministry possible. Local churches, associations of churches and the Baptist General Convention of Texas cooperate in presenting each university student an opportunity to know Jesus Christ, to respond to His call and to minister in His world.

As Colossians 1:28 states, "We proclaim Him, admonishing and teaching everyone with all wisdom, so that we may present everyone perfect in Christ.". . . Student Ministry's purpose is to reach lost students, to help them develop as believers, to strengthen them in servanthood and in mission vision. To involve them in ministries to persons, Christian growth, discipleship, evangelism training, leadership development, mission education and action, stewardship, Bible study, denominational awareness and churchmanship are the priorities of Baptist Student Ministry.

Baptist Student Ministry (BSM)
Organizations

137 Baptist Student Ministry Units are located at:
- 8 Baptist institutions
- 34 senior tax-supported institutions
- 63 junior/community tax-supported institutions
- 16 medical, dental, nursing and special institutions
- 13 private/other denominational institutions

Salaries for Student Ministry personnel are provided through the Cooperative Program giving of Texas Baptist churches and include:
- 55 full-time BSM directors/associate directors
- 5 full-time BSM intern directors
- 33 part-time BSM directors
- 3 supplements
- 13 volunteers

Student Ministry Statistical Summary

Through the balanced program of Texas Baptist Student Ministry, reports indicate the following:
- 2,591 students baptized in Baptist churches

- 2,200 involved in Baptist Student Ministries
- 7,800 participated in Bible study groups
- 3,750 in witness training
- 4,200 in discipleship training
- 150 campuses reported having an evangelistic emphasis in 1996
- Texas students, through an over-and-above offering of $147,966 sent 108 Baptist Student Ministry summer missionaries:
- 37 to Texas projects in 11 different associations
- 32 to Home Mission Board locations in 17 states
- 39 to partnership locations in four foreign countries
- 8 students participated in the Adventure Program in Texas

In addition, $27,300 was given to overseas projects. Texas students again served with Cuban Baptists this summer and special teams were sent to Australia and Estonia. Preparation is being given to a special Estonia Challenge project to assist with resources and students in Tartu, where the Estonian Baptist Seminary is located.

Some 5,309 students have served in community mission projects off-campus, working in both Baptist Student Ministry and local church efforts. River Ministry, inner-city projects and other ministries during the spring and winter breaks have been very successful. The BEACH REACH evangelistic and help projects at Padre Island were especially fruitful, with more than 121 professions of faith, and attracted nation-wide attention through the media.

Baptist Student Centers and Facilities

Texas Baptists maintain 53 Baptist Student Centers or facilities, 24 titles are held by the Baptist General Convention of Texas, four are in the name of Baptist universities, and 25 are in the name of individual associations.

Student Ministry Committee

On Dec. 6, 1994, the Texas Baptist Executive Board appointed the Division of Student Ministry Committee. This is a new committee de-signed to give leadership and direction to our Texas Baptist Student Ministry.

Source: *Book of Reports*, Baptist General Convention of Texas, 1996, 84. Reprint courtesy of the Baptist General Convention of Texas.

14.7 Hospitals and Homes

In 1994, the Human Welfare Coordinating Board supervised the administration of seven hospitals, five geriatric homes, and four orphanages. In regard to hospitals, the BGCT did not own these hospitals, but sponsored them. This delicate relationship made issues such as abortion a touchy question for all parties. The Chaplaincy Program at these hospitals, however, remained distinctly Baptist. The orphanages received a small stipend from the BGCT, but the majority of their income they raised themselves. By this time, Buckner Baptist Benevolences encompassed an extensive number of entities other than orphanages, such as foster care centers, geriatric homes, and counseling centers.

A. Hendrick Medical Center, Abilene

While rooted in the mission to heal the sick in a spiritual setting, Hendrick Medical Center continues to expand to meet the needs of Midwest Texans from a 22-county region as a full-service regional health system.

On the main campus of Hendrick Medical Center, officials broke ground Aug. 12, 1997, for a freestanding outpatient cancer center to be affiliated with M. D. Anderson Cancer Center. Construction of the $5 million outpatient cancer treatment center has been totally funded by philanthropic efforts from both external resources and internal resources such as managers and employees who pledged their financial support for expanding the Hendrick mission through an outreach of this nature.

Hendrick also broke ground in 1997 for a 50,000-square-foot physician office complex. Other growth during the past year includes the completion of a massive 14-month expansion of Hendrick's cardiac services area, creating four cardiac catheterization labs.

Other new services and facilities include a 7-bed inpatient hospice unit; renovations of The BirthPlace at Hendrick; renovation of several patient floors; expanded skill nursing facilities and extended care services; plus the addition of several blocks of new guest and employee parking lots.

Hendrick is the only hospital in the Texas Midwest to offer air ambulance services, which in 1997, continued increasing the number of flights per week particularly to the region.

Along with advanced cardiac, cancer and birthing services, Hendrick offers such specialties as a free-standing rehabilitation hospital; pediatric intensive care unit; skilled nursing unit; extended care; and expanding rehabilitation services, including sports medicine.

FIRSTCARE, a health maintenance organization of which Hendrick shares ownership, continues to grow in the Texas Midwest. FIRSTCARE enrollment for the Abilene/San Angelo territory neared 16,000 in July 1997.

Hendrick Medical Center offers the full spectrum of care to Texas Midwest residents, from birth to retirement, including independent retirement living, assisted living and nursing care.

When part of Hendrick's retirement living network, people can access the Hendrick continuum of care quickly and easily. As the population of retired citizens grows, Hendrick continues to strive to meet the needs of seniors, and it does so with the Hendrick mission as the guide to provide for the healing ministry of Jesus Christ.

Source: *Care for Texas: Texas Baptist Hospitals*, Pamphlet, 1998. Reprint courtesy of the Baptist General Convention of Texas.

B. New Programs at Buckner

Dallas—say the word and you can almost hear your mind spin through images of glitz and glamour; of television shows, glass buildings, the Cowboys and corridors of money and power. But just off those hallways of high finance are closets of despair.

Consider these facts about Dallas and Dallas County:
- one in four children have no health insurance;
- one in three pregnant women have inadequate prenatal care;
- 5,500 babies were born to teenagers in 1993;
- one out of five children drop out of high school;
- 30,000 children in Dallas County are left without supervision during some part of every day;
- one out of every five children in Dallas County (91,000) live in poverty;

- more than one in 10 children are abused or neglected each year;
- 13,431 reports of alleged child abuse or neglect were made to Child Protective Services in 1994;
- 5,721 cases of abuse and neglect were confirmed in 1994

A report released in June by the Coalition for North Texas Children and Children's Medical Center for Dallas states that "long-term strategies that focus on preventing serious problems faced by our children ought to be a priority."

The report says the lack of investment in services which meet human needs "will place the future of our community in jeopardy."

Those gloomy observations and predictions are part of the reason Larry Mercer, administrator of Buckner Children and Family Services in Dallas, has launched a broad program of Community Based Services.

Mercer and his staff are expanding beyond the residential services traditionally associated with Buckner Baptist Children's Home.

That expansion has led the Buckner team to collaborate with a wide variety of schools, churches and other social service providers in the Greater Dallas area. Mercer said with the belief driving the growth of non-residential programs, which keep families together and strengthen them, Buckner can prevent the collapse of many at-risk homes.

Often, the prevention comes in the form of emergency relief or aid. Sometimes it is through family counseling.

But regardless of the form, Mercer said the goal remains the same as it has been for Buckner since 1879—helping families and children.

"Families are under enormous stress," Mercer said. "It's stress from struggling to make ends meet financially, and they're doing their very best to stay above the water. But it is affecting the infrastructure of the home. So many families have just been overwhelmed."

Mercer said stress in families often "works itself into the care of the children. Parents sometimes don't know how to work out the pressures." All too often, the result is abuse or neglect.

The whole idea behind a strong Community Based Service Program, according to Buckner experts like Mercer, is to strengthen families by giving them tools and resources to work through difficulties.

"There's no institution, there's no program, there's no agency that's going to be able to fill that vacuum better than the home," Mercer said. "I see families who need support and it takes different forms, whether it's families being taught and given insight in how to deal with the stresses and balance taking care of the kids, whether it's husbands and wives learning how to take advantage of community resources, or whether it's helping teachers in schools know how to address the complexities of the family structure. It's not like it used to be and the old approaches won't be effective anymore.

"We can't go back to the old option of taking a child out of a home and saying, 'We're just going to take the child out of that bad situation and put the child in an institutional setting.' That should not be and cannot be because it's not the best for the child and because from a cost standpoint, nobody can afford it. The best place for a child is in the home."

Mercer compares preventive programs to building protective measures along a dangerous mountain road. Rather than treat those injured after a wreck occurs, it is better to place speed bumps and guard rails along the road to prevent accidents.

"We're helping to avert the crisis," he said. "We're really trying to help families take care of kids and there is no substitute for the family."

At the same time, Mercer said Buckner remains committed to providing residential care as it has for 118 years.

"There will always be a need for long-term residential care," he said. "We want to be careful that we always maintain the ability to be there for children who need that kind of care."

Mercer said Dallas' response to the growth of Buckner's Community Based Services program has been "tremendous. They've really embraced us. Everybody knows that if we are able to strengthen and build families, it will ultimately result in helping children."

Source: *Buckner Today*, "Welcome to Big D," Fall 1996, 23. Reprint courtesy of Buckner Baptist Benevolences.

C. Round Rock Campus Children's Home

Residential Group Care

Recognizing that every child's needs are best met in a loving family environment, Texas Baptist Children's Home Strengthens the lives of children and families by providing distinguished professional services including residential group care.

Residential Group Care reaches the children of families in chronic conflict. Such families may face issues of alcohol or substance abuse, violence, ineffective parenting or other diminished communication skills. Through this program, care is provided in residential cottages to children and adolescents ages 6–18 who need long-term 24-hour supervised care. All children in residential group care receive individual, peer group, or family counseling.

At-Risk, Emergency Care

Services to at-risk and runaway youth (or Starry) give immediate care to the most helpless victims of our turbulent culture: the abused, the neglected, incested, angry, depressed, confused and lonely.
Every day Starry provides a safe haven for at-risk youth of Williamson and surrounding counties with food, shelter, loving concern and counseling. Starry's home-based therapy helps prevent child abuse and neglect, runaway and truancy problems, and parent-child conflict. Families learn how to work together to resolve difficult and sometimes volatile situations. This program is a cooperative effort between Texas Baptist Children's Home and the Texas Department of Protective and Regulatory Services. Partial funding is provided through TDPRS.

Single-Parent Family Care

Our acclaimed Single-Parent Family Care program keeps mothers and their children close together in times of extreme crisis.
Those receiving assistance come from diverse economic and social backgrounds. Each cottage houses up to four single-parent families with a caring staff family in residence to give counseling and support. Mothers care for their own children while at home, prepare family meals and participate in cottage activities. Single-parent support groups meet each week to share parenting issues, encourage personal growth and examine prospects for eventual independent living.

Foster Family Care

Foster Family Care provides temporary care within well-trained, loving families for infants and children whose safety and survival are at risk.

Central Texas families who genuinely care about the well-being of children provide in-home love and special care to many kids each year. Service plans for each child are carefully developed with frequent periodic review and specialized needs assessment. Foster Family Care is also available to children in residential group care with TBCH whose chances for reunification with their families seem unlikely. All clients with kids in Foster Family Care maintain full custody of their children.

Miracle Farm

A serene and picturesque 270-acre ranch just north of Brenham is the setting for Miracle Farm, our hands-on, task-intensive education and care center for pre-delinquent boys ages 10 to 17.

Placement of boys by parents or guardians is followed by a challenging outdoor Wilderness Adventure Camp that builds character through self-awareness, confidence and teamwork. Thereafter, each boy is placed in residential group care and carefully guided through a therapeutic work/study program. Enhanced family involvement and conflict resolution counseling are a vital part of the restorative ministries of Miracle Farm.

Values and Spiritual Growth

The universal need within each of us to know the redemptive power of faith and its attending values colors all aspects of Texas Baptist Children's Homes Services to children and families.

Who am I? Why am I here? Where am I going? Those questions test the fabric of the soul in greater measure for those who have been emotionally or physically abused and who need thoughtful, compassionate Christian care. In weekly chapel services, personal reflection journeys and one-on-one dialogue with trained staff, essential values—positive and negative, right and wrong, good and evil—are introduced and clarified. For many, the discovery of healing through God's unconditional love has meant a new way of seeing, a new beginning, a new life.

Source: Doing All We Can, "Texas Baptist Children's Home: Round Rock Campus, Miracle Farm," 1997. Reprint courtesy of the Baptist General Convention of Texas.

14.8 Facing Moral Concerns

The BGCT Christian Life Commission holds the responsibility of guiding Texas Baptist perspectives concerning moral issues. In 1980, Phil Strickland was placed in charge of the CLC. Strickland was highly qualified for this job as he had been a White House consultant, active in Texas child welfare programs, an advocate of fairness in employment, outspoken on the problem of world hunger, and a vigorous defendant of the Baptist principle of separation of church and state. In recent years, the CLC has taken firm stands against abortion (except in extreme circumstances), gambling, alcohol, and racism. Though on friendly terms with the Southern Baptist Christian Life Commission, the Texas CLC stands opposed to the larger body's move away from certain policies, in particular the issue of separation of church and state, race relations, and world hunger.

A. Texas CLC Rejects Views

The Texas Baptist Christian Life Commission issued a statement on Sept. 22 opposing "disturbing views" on race relations, world hunger, and peace expressed at the Sept. 13–14 meeting of the Southern Baptist Christian Life Commission.

"Some comments made . . . at the recent meeting of the Southern Baptist Christian Life Commission represent a radical departure from the historic positions of both the Southern Baptist Convention and the Texas Baptist Christian Life Commission," the Texas CLC stated.

According to the prepared statement, the Texas commission "unequivocally" rejects Caine's labeling of Martin Luther King Jr., as a "fraud" and his statement that "apartheid in South Africa . . . doesn't exist anymore and was beneficial when it did."

"The Texas and Southern Baptist Christian Life Commissions have consistently spoken against all forms of racial discrimination," the Texas CLC stated.

The statement also rejects "the cynical view of world hunger evidenced" in Caine's remark that, "starvation has been used since time immemorial to control people."

"Southern Baptists have prayed for and given to the starving of this world," the CLC stated. "Compassion wed to action is the model response to human need given to us by Jesus."

The statement also notes that the Texas CLC rejects Caine's idea that "peace means anything that promotes communism."

"Trivializing peace in this way ignores clear and important biblical teachings," the statement reads. "The Christian Life Commission has consistently urged Southern Baptists to pursue the vision of peace which permeates the Bible from the prophets to the Sermon on the Mount to the apostle Paul.

"To equate the use of the word peace with promoting communism belittles the identity of the Prince of Peace and the biblical mandate to be peacemakers."

"The Texas CLC statement commends newly elected CLC executive director Richard Land . . . for his stand in opposition to many of these disturbing views," pledges commitment to cooperating with the Southern Baptist CLC in efforts to promote applied Christianity, and urges Southern Baptist CLC members "to express their support of policies that reflect clear opposition to racism, support of peace with justice, commitment to minister to the poor and hungry and affirmation of the historic Baptist understanding of church-state separation."

Source: Ken Camp, "Texas CLC Rejects Views," *Baptist Standard*, 28 September 1988, 4. Reprint courtesy of the *Baptist Standard*.

B. CLC Interests and Positions

Citizenship

In our day biblical truth calls for political Christians. Some Christians are willing to die for freedom, but few are willing to live as constructive citizens working for democracy in a democratic society.

The real question is not whether Christians should be involved in working for good laws, freedom, peace, justice and clean government. The question is how they should be involved. Without active involvement by the people, the dream of democracy can never come true.

The Christian faith demands responsible citizenship. The Texas Baptist Christian Life Commission is deeply involved in the nature and nurture, theory and practice of Christian citizenship.

Citizenship requires participation, not mere observation. It requires effort and concern.

How can we—the Christians—fail to bring our very best to bear on the important matters relating to the lives and good of our fellow citizens?

Religious Liberty

Each citizen is a free individual before God with the freedom to select—without coercion—the path his faith will find, the method of his worship or even the right not to possess religious faith.

Neither the church nor the state has the right to coerce any citizen. If his choice is not a free choice, it is no choice at all.

Baptists traditionally have believed each person to be a free moral agent, not a puppet. We believe each one has soul consciousness—freedom—before God.

Church-state questions take the form of aid to nonpublic schools, state-enforced prayer in schools or public meetings, taxation of churches, church-related properties, the acceptance of public monies by religious institutions.

The heart of the matter is religious liberty; free people free to practice a free faith, no matter what faith it might be.

The Commission's task is to identify clearly any breakdown in the historic principles and to support vigorously the concept of religious liberty and separation of church and state.

Daily Work

Most of us who are Christians realize all too clearly that while we are not of this world, we most certainly live in it. Most of us spend a large part of our lives working—sweating, straining, struggling.

The Bible consistently speaks of daily work. It relates God's attitude toward it, its place in our lives and how we should approach it.

Many issues are involved in daily work. Some are simple, some incredibly complex. How does the Christian relate to issues of poverty, salaries, labor-management relationships, truth in advertising, honesty in merchandising, migrant workers, labor unions, discrimination in hiring because of race, age or sex?

There is a Christian view of the marketplace, too. The scriptures are uncompromising in their demand for ethical justice.

The aim of the Christian Life Commission is to stimulate Christian response to the practical issues of our daily work and to support the Christian as he tries to bring his "faith in action" to bear on his job.

Family Life

What is family?

A group of people who happen to live under the same roof? A group of people who happen to have had the same parents? A group of people tied together by "blood"?

Today, the question, "What is family?" has increased importance. Statistics tell us marriage and family are under a constant and increasing barrage of pressures. The family is disintegrating under the pressures of modern life.

Part of the assignment of the Christian Life Commission deals with the family. The assignment takes on many forms: marriage enrichment; printed materials; assistance to churches; associations and individuals; special training; study; special materials.

Preserving and protecting, affirming and esteeming, counseling and strengthening. The Christian Life Commission works to help the family in today's often confusing and conflicting world.

Race Relations

Christians should be concerned when others are deprived of their freedoms and legal rights, regarded as unacceptable, treated as subhuman and are aliens and outcasts in their homeland.

Christians should be particularly concerned because of what the Bible has to say about our relation with others.

The Bible describes our being of "one blood" because of the blood of Jesus Christ. It stresses our being one race, one family, one people, a peculiar people who God loves and cherishes.

Racism—with all of its ugly implications—has long been a matter of concern for the Christian Life Commission.

The Commission deals with matters of much concern: bilingual education, institutional racism, discrimination in employment, housing, education, migrant workers, illegal aliens, world hunger, politics, voting.

The Christian Life Commission helps us be aware of the Christian perspective on race and helps individuals and churches overcome their prejudices.

Moral Issues

A daisy in a bear trap?

It does look kind of silly. But the daisy represents some sweet, un-permitted fruit, made all the more delicious by its unlawfulness and forbiddenness.

The trap? It's simple. There's a hook hidden in every immoral act.

The New Testament expresses a very specific understanding of mo-rality. It places emphasis on the loved and valued individual. Loved and valued by God. The New Testament understanding of morality sees that any force which damages or destroys individuals takes on moral impli-cations. These moral issues have implications for the individual, for the family, for the nation, for church, for society.

The Christian Life Commission works to provide a foundation for decision making concerning social and personal issues, decisions which "put faith into action by producing the evidences of Christian living."

Source: Pamphlet, Christian Life Commission: Baptist General Con-vention of Texas. Reprint courtesy of the Baptist General Convention of Texas.

C. Four CLC Directors: Separation of Church and State

Under the leadership of four directors, the commission maintained the belief that separation of church and state is a cornerstone of free-dom. It was extremely sensitive to actions that eroded the principle. In 1951 the commission listed three dangers that threatened freedom of religion in the United States. The first was failure to teach the scriptural foundations for separation of church and state. The second was persis-tent attacks by the Roman Catholic hierarchy. The third was poor lead-ership by men in high places who chose expediency over principle. The commission warned that carelessness and apathy were just as dangerous to the principle of separation of church and state as were premeditated attacks on it.

In 1958 the Executive Board of the BGCT requested that the CLC prepare a study of the basis for the separation of church and state. The commission published Bases for Separation of Church and State the next year. This booklet presented the biblical, historical, and constitutional bases for separation of church and state. The section on biblical basis did not give proof-texts but stated principles, central to the Bible, concerning man, the church, and the state.

The booklet traced the relation of church and state in six historical periods. Three of these periods preceded the settlement of America. The other three covered the history of America from 1620 until the present.

The section on constitutional basis discussed the First Amendment along with several important U. S. Supreme Court decisions related to the separation of church and state. The treatment of each of these topics was brief and written for laymen. Each topic was published in the Baptist Standard on three successive weeks in 1959 to give them the most exposure possible.

Although the commission encouraged Baptists to be involved in politics, it acknowledged the limitations of political action. The 1960 commission report to the state convention pointed out that legislation cannot create religious dedication or moral purity. If churches depend on the state to finance them and to enforce their religious practices, they reveal their own spiritual bankruptcy to work through spiritual persuasion.

The 1961 convention report of the commission summarized well the commission's point of view on religious liberty, saying,

"A basic Baptist insight into the Word of God is soul liberty and the priesthood of the individual. The belief involves the absolute necessity for religious freedom. One should be able to support or not support, profess or not profess a religious faith free of coercion; otherwise his religious experience is meaningless. We stand for religious liberty not just for ourselves but for all the peoples of the world. We are grieved by the loss of freedom of our brethren in other lands who are constantly pressured by governments giving special privileges to ecclesiastical bodies or by governments controlled by atheistic communism. We believe that Christians should pray for and work toward attainment of complete religious freedom all over the world. We believe that complete religious liberty can be attained only where the relationships of church and state is [sic] separate."

The report went on to say that separation of church and state does not mean the separation of God from government or the encouragement of society to become materialistic and secular. It does not mean that Christians should not seek to influence the politics of that state. Christians ought to be good and responsible citizens. In fact, Baptists ought to examine candidates for public office at every level to determine their position on separation of church and state. This should be used as one legitimate factor in deciding for whom to vote.

Despite its support of Christian citizenship, the commission opposed the formation of a Christian party. It said that Christianity should not be limited by or tied to any political party or any government.

In 1974 the commission favorably quoted a statement by Glen Archer, head of Americans for the Separation of Church and State. Summarizing well the commission's point of view, it said,

> Why does the First Amendment come first? And of all the liberties guaranteed by the First Amendment, why does religious liberty come first? Because our country's founders believed that religious liberty was the most important of all and therefore should be put first.

Source: Phil Strickland, "An Interpretive History of the Christian Life Commission of the Baptist General Convention of Texas, 1950–1977" (Ph. D. dissertation, Baylor, 1981), 231–34.

D. Legislative Concerns

Chairman Price recognized David Becker, Chairman of the Christian Life Commission, to present this report. Becker recognized Phil Strickland, Director of the Christian Life Commission, to present an update on legislative concerns.

Strickland gave an update on the Religious Freedom Restoration Act, gambling, APPAC, abortion, and human services.

Becker requested the board commend Congressman John Bryant from Dallas who co-sponsored the Professional and Amateur Sports Protection Act legislation, for his efforts to control sports gambling in this country; and that we express to Congressman Bryant our appreciation for his good work in this matter.

Leroy Fenton made the motion to approve the recommendation and Charles McLaughlin seconded the motion. The motion carried in a voice vote with no opposition expressed. Randall Scott expressed a concern that Texas Baptists call their legislators, but call with intelligence and courtesy. Alan Wallace asked if there was a way to coordinate correspondence to the legislators. Strickland responded that the Christian Life Commission helps to coordinate such responses.

Asa Pease, Southside Baptist Church, Olney, asked that the Christian Life Commission to reconsider their stand on relaxing views on abortion. Becker responded that the Christian Life Commission's stand against abortion has not changed. Leroy Fenton spoke a word in support of the Christian Life Commission's stand.

Source: *Minutes*, Executive Board of the Baptist General Convention of Texas, 16 March 1993. Reprint courtesy of the Baptist General Convention of Texas.

E. Resolution on Pari-Mutuel Gambling

Whereas, the 68th session of the Texas State Legislature is in session, and

Whereas, bills proposing the legalization of a full range of gambling enterprises, including pari-mutuel racetrack gambling on horses and dogs, casino and lottery gambling have been introduced, and,

Whereas, the State Legislators are sworn to seek the general welfare of both the state of Texas and its citizens, and

Whereas, the harmful effects of the legalization of gambling are well known documented to the effect that when gambling is legalized,

> Illegal gambling increases,
> Organized crime prospers,
> Officials may be corrupted,
> Windfalls of tax revenue fail to materialize,
> New gamblers are created,
> Psychological addiction to gambling increases,
> Families suffer,
> The poor are victimized, and

Whereas, when the state becomes partners with investors in a profit-making endeavor which has always abused those who participate in it, the moral stature of the state is diminished, and

When the state punishes lawbreakers for gambling activities while the state itself sponsors gambling activities for its own profit, the moral stature of the state is diminished, and

When the state participates in the abuse of individuals, especially the poor, who are enticed to gamble, the moral stature of the state is diminished, and

When the state legislates an activity in which its share is called a "take," the moral stature of the state is diminished;

Therefore let it be resolved, that while we recognize that gambling as an individual activity is something which likely will always be a part of human behavior, we deplore the idea that the state of Texas should be a partner in it, or participate in tax revenues which come from its abuses of citizens, and

Be it further resolved, that the Executive Board of the Baptist General Convention of Texas urge the 68th Session of the Texas Legislature to reject the legalization of pari-mutuel racetrack gambling bills as well as the dog-racing, casino gambling and other gambling bills that are proposed, and

Be it finally resolved, that the enactment of any of these bills would be an error of judgement of incalculable consequence, while concern for good public policy will result in the Texas Legislature continuing its 44-year rejection of the legalization of pari-mutuel as well as other forms of gambling.

Source: *Minutes*, Executive Board of the Baptist General Convention of Texas, 15 March 1983. Reprint courtesy of the Baptist General Convention of Texas.

14.9 Strengthening Texas Churches

The State Missions Commission is the BGCT catalyst that works most directly with the local churches. The SMC directs areas such as church extension, church building planning, the River Ministry, neighborhood work, Discipleship Training, the Minnesota-Wisconsin Convention, as well as a myriad other local church endeavors. Charles McLaughlin ably headed up the SMC from 1964 until 1988. D. L. Lowrie then briefly headed up the SMC in 1988, but resigned later in the year to return to his native Tennessee. In late 1988, the evangelistic-minded James Semple of Paris, Texas, directed and advanced the work until his retirement in 1997.

A. Churches With Staying Power

"The weather was a frigid 20 degrees, it was dark and we were look-ing over our shoulders as we knocked on an apartment door in a high crime area of our city," said Lanny Elmore, minister of missions for First Church, Dallas.

The volunteers were doing visitation in the inner-city with the aim of starting apartment Bible studies there.

The door opened, and they were greeted by Jose Marti, a Cuban attorney, who, with his wife, Yvonne, had recently come to Dallas after 18 months as refugees at Guantanamo Naval Base in Cuba.

Marti, who'd been trained under the Communist regime, admitted he'd been to church only twice in his life, both times as a student study-ing architecture. But he and his wife agreed to allow First Baptist volun-teers to hold Bible studies in their apartment.

At the second Bible study, the Martis both accepted Christ as Lord and Savior and have joined El Buen Pastor Church, one of about 25 missions of First Church, Dallas.

Marti told Elmore, "If you'll teach me, I'll do what you're doing."

The former Cuban attorney has discussed with two attorneys who are members of First Church his plans to attain credentials for being a Texas attorney so he can help other Cubans, said Elmore.

"He has opened up the Cuban community to us, and he glows with his testimony of Jesus' salvation.

We knocked on his door fearfully, but in the dark of night the door opened, and the warmth of God's love transformed two lives to share Christ with numerous other lost persons."

Similar experiences can be repeated time and again by volunteers of First Church, Dallas, and First Church, San Antonio, two congrega-tions who are committed to remaining downtown.

"We provide a church home for the homeless, preach the gospel to different language groups and share biblical principles with executives," explains Lanny Elmore, who has led First Church, Dallas, in missions for 16 years. "I think we are under a spiritual mandate that if people won't come to us, then we have to go to them to minister in Christ's name."

R. B. Cooper, head of church and community ministries at First Church, San Antonio, for 26 years, agrees. "The church decided to be a good steward of our strategic location," he says. "It is hard to reach an entire city if you are located in the outskirts. Many churches have had to move because they ran out of space, but our earlier pastors and lay leaders had a vision and provided adequate land and buildings so we can stay in the center of town and still keep growing."

The Dallas program is built around Inner-City Chapel and the Dallas Life Foundation. "Our overriding purpose is evangelism," Elmore says, "but DLF focuses on providing human needs such as shelter and job training while ICC seeks to be the church home for the homeless."

DLF feeds 500 homeless people nightly and has agreements with two companies guaranteeing its training graduates a job.

ICC is one of the 28 missions of First Church, Dallas. Only one is located outside the city limits, and 11 worship in a language other than English.

Outreach to the business community includes lunch time Bible studies and providing athletic facilities.

In multi-cultural San Antonio, First Baptist's DOME Committee (Downtown Outreach Ministries Effort) is targeting the 80,000 people who work downtown keyed to a luncheon Bible study/outreach led by Callie Smith, retired CEO of the Baptist Memorial Hospital System.

Other outreach to the "velvet ghetto" is built around Wilson House, an historically protected, ornate 18th century mansion the church acquired in order to buy the surrounding land. "We open it for weddings, receptions and Bible studies for the community, host an annual arts and crafts show that attracted people from all over the city and Elderhostel uses it for classes. The idea is to build relationships with people who will not come into the church building and share Christ with them."

At the other end of the economic spectrum, the San Antonio church maintains strong ties with Victoria Courts, a housing project separated from the church by the business district. "While we are able to speak to the entire city because we are not identified with any one subdivision, we consider the Victoria Courts our 'neighborhood' and gratefully assume the role of neighbor to live out and share the gospel," Cooper explains.

Evangelism teams regularly visit juvenile detention centers and numerous church members serve as mentors for area students. In partnership with the San Antonio Baptist Association and Buckner Baptist Benevolences, the church has applied for an apartment in the complex to use as a permanent base, "to change the face of the whole community that is staggering under a load of violence, gangs, drugs, and teenage pregnancies," Cooper says.

Three blocks from the church a former servicemen's center, "is the only place downtown you can get a shower without spending the night." It feeds 40,000 homeless people each year. Each day begins with a devotion. Three mornings a week the ministry provides food, clothes and money for transportation. Tuesday and Thursday mornings newly professed Christians are discipled.

The Fourth Street Inn gives downtown workers a nice lunch option. It also provides hourly jobs for the homeless. A partnership with First Presbyterian provides free dental care.

Other services include English as a Second Language classes and assistance in getting GEDs and preparing for citizenship exams.

"We want to provide a church of, by and for street people," Cooper adds. "We had more than 250 professions of faith through community ministries last year."

"Nothing First Baptist Church in Dallas does legitimizes our ministry more than our efforts through our Dallas Life ministry to the homeless and often, hopeless, of our inner-city," said pastor O. S. Hawkins. "We presently conduct services every Sunday in 26 different localities in a dozen different languages, and we are asking God to give us a network of 100 satellite churches in every traditional neighborhood of Dallas over the next decade."

T. Don Guthrie, pastor of First Church, San Antonio, said, "It is thrilling how this church applies the culture-changing power of Jesus Christ to this city the same way missionaries do. 'Amazing Grace' can be sung in Swahili, and just as surely it can be sung in downtown America."

Source: Craig Bird, "Churches With Staying Power Reveal Christ in the Inner-city," *Texas Missions* (Fall 1996), 10–12. Reprint courtesy of *Texas Missions*.

B. Celebrating 40 Years of Working Together with Minnesota-Wisconsin Baptists

Wausau is at least a thousand miles from San Antonio, as the snowbird flies. But it's home now to Kevin Prather, a native of Alamo City, who has served the last two years as pastor of First Baptist Church in that central Wisconsin city.

"We know we've been called here. God has broken our hearts for this place," he said.

In fact, he's so at home there that he rooted for the Green Bay Packers in their 1996 NFC championship bout with the Dallas Cowboys. That's in spite of his wife, Priscilla, having been a former Cowboy's cheerleader five years ago.

Prather says God gave him a heart for the upper Midwest. And it's the same kind of divine love that has bound Texas Baptists to fellow believers in Minnesota and Wisconsin for four decades.

Texas Baptists began cooperating in "pioneer missions" in Minnesota-Wisconsin in 1956 when there were only seven Southern Baptist churches in the two states.

Since Frank Burress resigned as pastor of Central Church, Jacksonville, to become superintendent of missions for the work in Minnesota-Wisconsin in 1957, a succession of Texas Baptists have felt God leading them to minister there.

Some have served as pastors of churches, others have gone to help in revivals and others evangelistic outreach efforts. Volunteers, including Texas Baptist Men Retiree Church Builders, helped construct buildings.

"Celebrating the 40th anniversary of our joint missions effort in Minnesota-Wisconsin is especially exciting for many Texas Baptists who have supported the work through prayer, giving and going to do missions there," said Texas Mission Service Corps volunteer Carl Elder, part time consultant for Minnesota-Wisconsin liaison.

Currently, the Minnesota-Wisconsin Baptist Convention includes 130 churches and missions, according to Executive Director Bill Tinsley. But the two-state convention has a goal of 200 churches by 2000 and 400 by 2010.

Through the years, Texas Baptists have supported missions in Minnesota-Wisconsin through their gifts to the Mary Hill Davis Offering for State Missions. A growing number of Texas churches are also linked in direct partnerships with sister congregations in Minnesota-Wisconsin.

Over the past seven years, churches in Sabine Neches Area in East Texas have sent at least 70 volunteers and $60,000 to partner in the Duluth, Minn., region.

"The partnership has made our area more aware of pioneer missions. It has broadened our churches' view of being part of a national ministry and given them a sense of responsibility beyond our borders," said B. C. McCoy, director of missions for Sabine Neches Area.

For at least the past three decades, Texas Baptists have funded a pastor's-wives retreat each February at the Green Lake Conference Center in Wisconsin. The retreat provides a great source of encouragement and renewal for the couples, Tinsley said.

"Many pastors and their families serve congregations far from any other Southern Baptist church," he noted. "Western Association covers the entire southwestern fourth of Minnesota, but it includes only four churches affiliated with the Minnesota-Wisconsin Convention."

"The retreat offers pastors and wives a good opportunity for sharing information, networking and relaxing," said Bobby Sinclair, pastor of Mt. Hermon Baptist Church, a mostly African-American congregation in Milwaukee, Wis.

"The timing is just right, coming about a month after the holidays, when many of these couples are ready for a 'get away' time," said Sinclair, vice president of the Minnesota-Wisconsin Convention. Sinclair has lived in the area 40 years, having moved as a child to the upper Midwest from Tennessee.

"There is a unique culture here in the upper Midwest that is best understood if you grew up in it," said Glen Land, pastor of the Valley Baptist Church, Appleton, Wis., and president of the two-state convention.

While a German-Scandinavian heritage dominates the area, the cities—particularly Minneapolis-St. Paul and Milwaukee—are increasingly multi-cultural. Minnesota-Wisconsin has the largest Hmong congregation in the nation. Through the Mary Hill Davis Offering, Texas Baptists helped produce the first translation of John's Gospel into the Hmong language. It is being used in the Hmong's native Laos, as well as in the United States.

Church techniques transplanted from the South and Southwest don't take root well in the region, according to Minnesota-Wisconsin Baptists.

"Theology doesn't change whether you're from Minnesota, Wisconsin, Texas or Brazil. But the cultural context of doing ministry does change," said Land, a former church extension field missionary with the Home Mission Board.

Minnesota-Wisconsin Baptists are committed to developing an indigenous model for "doing church," he said.

"I can't think of any place in the convention where I'd rather be serving," Land said. "There is such energy here, such a rapid pace of change, and such an openness to explore new models and new approaches.

"It's a great place to be," he said, pausing to think about the sub-zero temperatures of a week earlier, "if you can just handle the weather."

Source: Ken Camp, "Giving, Praying, Going: Celebrating 40 Years of Working Together with Minnesota-Wisconsin Baptists," *Texas Missions* (Spring 1996), 4–5.

C. State Missions Commission Report, 1991

We have all been shocked by the sudden death on April 2 of our beloved friend and co-laborer Dr. Carlos McLeod. His legacy in Evangelism lives on. The programs he proposed and developed for this year are going well. We are trusting that God will continue His blessings as we seek to reach people for Christ.

Evangelism Division highlights for the past quarter include: the use by 180 churches of the Giving An Invitation tape; involvement of 248 churches in revival preparation with materials; one Hispanic Crusade, 84 professions of faith; 44 Youth Power Source Rallies, 15,000 attendance, 490 accepting Christ as Savior and 584 making decisions of re-dedication.

The Discipleship Training Department conducted state events for 1,991 participants in this years Bible Drill and Speakers Tournaments.

February through April 1991 there were 42 Cooperative Agreements for new works approved by the Missions Funding Committee. The total Cooperative Agreements approved from October 1990 through April 1991 is 84.

Approved 12 Small Church Loans totaling $157,000 and 5 Care and Share Grants totaling $37,000.

Conducted 176 Field Consultations and 81 office consultations for building needs of churches.

Conducted 254 new Work Revivals, 97 Resource Discovery Meetings, 79 Feasibility Studies, 23 New Work Surveys, 1,156 personal conferences, 1 Laser Thrust, and 5 Mission Committee training sessions.

Participated in the Texas Baptist State Convention, Jacksonville, Texas, consulted with pastors and brought greetings to the Convention.

Developed and conducted a Seminar on Rebuilding the Black Family with eleven couples present.

Processed 3 No Interest Loan applications for a total of $85,000.

Conducted 4 Regional Church Building and Finance Conferences with 258 in attendance from 83 churches.

Prepared Space Studies for 30 churches and Master Site plans for 19 churches.

Conducted a Cooperative Program Pilot project for Black leadership with 11 of the 12 churches present which were invited. Attendance 43.

A Key Church Report on MISSION TEXAS 1984–1990 was made showing 43 total Key Churches; 584 missions/churches sponsored. In 1990, 383 churches reported with 16,295 average Sunday School attendance; $868,588 monthly tithes and offerings and 6,206 baptisms.

Trained and assigned 34 River Ministry student summer missionaries for service in 1991.

Church Administration conducted and participated in 3 Preaching Enrichment Workshops with 78 in attendance.

The Church Ministries Department has completed the first training seminar for Volunteer Chaplains, consisting of 22 trainees. This group was composed of persons who are and will be serving as Volunteer Chaplains for local police departments, county jails, hospitals, nursing homes and in industry. The seminar was taught by Director of Volunteer Chaplaincy Development, Clayton Watkins and Director of Volunteer Chaplaincy Training, Howard Linton.

Completed 3 River Ministry Training Retreats where a significant number of first-time church groups and Hispanic churches were represented to train for River Ministry involvement in 1991.

The Seminary Extension program under the program assistance of Pastor In-Service Training, has introduced new diploma programs. Classes are offered that can be applied to an accredited Bachelor's Degree as well as accepted by Southwestern Baptist Theological Seminary and be applied to either a Diploma in Theology or toward the Master of Divinity. This new program can be accomplished through a Seminary Extension Center in the local association. BGCT now has 57 certified Seminary Extension Centers in Texas.

The Church Music Department provided leadership for 167 Ministers of Music, members of the Singing Men of Texas, to participate in Praising II in Nashville, Tennessee.

The Church Stewardship Department conducted 238 conferences, Seminars and Stewardship Rallies with 1,566 in attendance, representing 360 churches.

Conducted 2 Associational Sunday School Revivals—25 churches and 2,285 participants in sessions and 4 Regional Maintenance-to-Growth conferences—included people from 41 associations: 314 churches, 402 persons in attendance.

One hundred-ten Associational Sunday School Convention Planning Meetings with 802 persons attending from more than 500 churches were held in preparation for the 1991 Sunday School Convention to be conducted in the Associations.

Aired 260 radio broadcasts in Spanish over 20 radio stations and distributed 432 Spanish Bibles.

Source: *Minutes*, Executive Board of the Baptist General Convention of Texas, 2 April 1991. Reprint courtesy of the Baptist General Convention of Texas.

14.10 New Churches in Texas

Under the leadership of Bill Pinson, the churches remained at the heart of the BGCT. Pinson was not only concerned about strengthening the existing churches, but also in the formation of new churches as Texas' population continued to swell. The first endeavor to meet this goal was MISSION TEXAS. The goal of MISSION TEXAS was to create 2,000 new churches between 1985 and 1990. This goal was reached. Texas 2000 was the second major endeavor. Its goal was to create 1,400 new churches between 1995 and 2000. This goal was also met. The Key Church Program also proved to be an important factor in beginning new churches. The program called for larger churches to sponsor smaller mission churches and help them become financially stable. Of course, the WMU went far beyond the call of duty and raised a tremendous 1985 Mary Hill Davis Offering in order to help meet these needs.

A. Church Extension Department Report, 1995

Texas Baptists believe in church starting! Great Commission churches are being born all across the state. New church sponsorship is becoming a way of life for many churches. What a great testimony to their missions commitment!

From September 1994, through August 1995, Texas Baptists entered into New Church Development Covenants with the Church Extension Department to begin 148 new congregations. These were, by ethnicity, 44 Anglo, one Arabic, one Asian American, one Asian Indian, 34 Black, one Chinese, one Ethiopian, 54 Hispanic, seven Korean, one Iranian, one Native American and two Vietnamese.

During this first year of implementation of the Vision 2000 Church Starting Strategy, there was a significant increase in Hispanic new churches. In the year 1995-1996, the strategy will focus more effort on Hispanics. There is one Hispanic Baptist church for 5,884 Hispanic missions in Texas. This compares to one church for 2,799 non-Hispanic persons.

The current population of Texas is over 18 million persons. Our church to population ratio, therefore, is approximately one to 3,260 persons. In 1900, this ratio was one church for 1,110 persons. To attain the same ratio in 1995, it would take 16,280 churches. To attain the same ratio as Texas Baptists had in 1950, it would take 7,727 churches. There are currently 5,544 congregations in the Baptist General Convention of Texas.

Considering the statistics above, Texas Baptists face a great challenge. The starting of new churches must be undergirded with fervent prayer, willingness to leave the comfort of existing churches to participate in new church starts and sacrificial giving.

The Church Extension Department celebrates the great accomplishments of sponsor churches and associations as they focus on unreached people in church starting. Many churches are moving beyond their walls to do missions where God has planted them.

Texas 2000 challenges Texas Baptists to share Jesus Christ with every person in Texas. We must evangelize and congregationalize people as never before. By the grace of God we will do it!

Source: *Annual*, Baptist General Convention of Texas, 1995, 118. Reprint courtesy of the Baptist General Convention of Texas.

B. Key Church Ministry: J. V. Thomas

Seeing the Key Church Strategy develop through the SBC has been a real joy. The opportunity to work with Key Church pastors, ministers of missions, association leaders, and the state convention staffs has been a great privilege for me.

Key Church as a strategy has already proven itself an effective evangelism, ministry, and church starting strategy. My prayer is that associations will begin to see it as a viable strategy.

My first place of denominational ministry was to serve as the director of missions for the New Bethel Association of Texas. I still feel, even thirty-six years later, that the association is the most important place of denominational service.

The major problem that I faced, while serving as director of missions, was the constant turn-over of lay leaders elected to serve as mission leaders in churches. Most did not serve more than one year at a time. By the time these persons had a few months of experience, and their training was little more than an orientation or introduction to missions, they were replaced and the process had to be started all over again. I have often thought of this problem while developing Key Church Strategy.

Another problem was the lack of stability in the church's local mission budget. When the church was enlisted to sponsor a mission project, the church would have to wait until the next year's budget planning to include money for the new project. This always made a long delay in responding to open doors.

When the sponsoring church completed the project, usually the money budgeted for the local mission project was removed from the budget the next year because, in the view of many church leaders, it was not needed.

The Key Church Strategy solves both of these problems for pastors and the director of missions. Key Church leaders are asked to make a long-term commitment to the Key Church's priorities. They become the church's missionaries. This gives time to train them and time for them to gain valuable experience. Over a period of years the pastor, minister of missions, and association leadership can work with lay leaders from the Key Churches to enlist, train, plan and involve them in missions. The association director of missions is able to develop trained experienced mission leaders who, not only impact their church, but become available to help all of the churches.

Key Churches are encouraged to put three to five percent of their undesignated budget receipts into Key Church to reach the local mission field. These funds are to be administered by the Key Church component program committees, or the Missions Development Council. When association leaders are confronted with mission opportunity open doors, there are Key Churches with trained leadership and resources ready to respond.

The association that is serious about being on mission in their local setting should give serious consideration to this strategy. Associations like Greater New Orleans, Dallas, Tarrant and Union have used Key Church as an effective evangelism, ministry, and church starting strategy.

This office would be happy to work with your association to develop the Key Church Strategy. This will be done in cooperation with the state convention's mission leadership. Please contact you state director of missions if you would like to schedule someone to talk with your association about a mission strategy.

Source: *Focus*, September/October 1996, 1. Reprint courtesy of *Focus*.

C. Key Church Report

Mr. Thomas reported that 99 sites for new churches now have loans with the Baptist Church Loan Corporation. Using the Key Church Strategy plan, a key church will sponsor a large number of missions with a minimum of six. The goal is to have 100 key churches. At the end of September, there were 26 key churches. The year 1984–85 ended with 282 cooperative agreements, which are official requests which come through the Mission Funding Committee for sponsorship of a new church, as well as the key churches.

In October and November the Mission Funding Committee approved four sites for loans and four key churches. There were 77 cooperative agreements in two months. There is the need to average 58 cooperative agreements per month, to start 700 new churches. Over the five year period there needs to be an average of 33 cooperative agreements each month.

Source: *Minutes*, Executive Board of the Baptist General Convention of Texas, 10 December 1985. Reprint courtesy of the Baptist General Convention of Texas.

D. Cooperative Program Gifts Boost New Church Fund

Texas Baptists have added to the financial resources needed to start more churches and missions.

The goal for new churches this year is 300. "We are doing well at this point," said E. B. Brooks, director of church extension for the Baptist General Convention of Texas, "but we must not slack up or we will lose the ground we have gained."

Texas Baptists have adopted an ambitious program called *Texas 2000.* Goals include the beginning of 1,400 new churches by the year 2000 and to share Christ with every Texan by then.

New churches can call for a minimum of financial help in getting started. Bills must be paid, supplies purchased, and sometimes property obtained. In the start-up period, all of this must be done with no reservoir of funds for the extra expenditures. New churches and missions must look to missionary-minded Texas Baptists for short-term financial assistance.

This year the BGCT Executive Board has made available extra funds for starting new churches.

First, the convention voted to use half of any excess over the 1996 budget for this special purpose. Cooperative Program gifts exceeded the budget by $70,769. Half of that amount was added to the fund for new churches.

The Executive Board also allocated $100,000 of unrestricted funds to help support new churches and another $100,000 to strengthen existing churches. The board further allocated additional funds in the amount of $75,000 to support the *Texas 2000* campaign.

"The stated goal of Texas Baptists is to share Jesus with every person in Texas by the year 2000," says William M. Pinson Jr., BGCT executive director. "We must be sure there is a congregation of believers for new converts just after they come to know Jesus."

The new church fund and all monies for the *Texas 2000* campaign are helping to establish new congregations.

Source: *New Church News*, Spring 1997, 1.

14.11 Criminal Justice Ministry

In their attempts to meet the evangelistic goals of Texas 2000, Texas Baptists did not forget those who were in prison. The WMU, Brotherhood, and the BGCT's new department of Criminal Justice Ministries attempted to minister to the needs of Texas' extremely large prison population. The most successful rehabilitative ministries have proven to be MasterLife and Discipleship Training Seminars. In addition, the Texas Baptist Men built the "Huntsville Hospitality House" near the prison in Huntsville for families of prisoners to lodge while they visit their incarcerated relatives.

Ministry Program at Jester II Makes History

Last Saturday was an innovative and historic day in the field of criminal rehabilitation for the U. S. Criminal Justice system.

Wardens, prison chaplains and inmates took special notice as about 40 outsiders entered the Jester II unit and spent three hours in Christian fellowship.

What was so innovative and unique about this event was that mothers, wives, sisters, brothers and friends received a chance to go beyond the gates and razor-sharp barbed wire fences and worship with their locked-up family members and representatives of the Kairos Prison Ministry.

The relatives went beyond the regular visitation area and through the gates, past cells occupied by inmates, through the cafeteria and into the gymnasium. At that location, three guards stood by as 42 inmates, their families and members of Kairos Prison Ministry gathered in song and praise.

The program was part of the Texas Department of Criminal Justice's InnerChange program, which has as its goal the rehabilitation of inmates through spiritual cleansing together with family and community spiritual involvement.

Saturday's fellowship was the first time that family members were allowed to go into prison and take part in religious services with their incarcerated relatives.

In the past, prison officials have allowed different faith-based groups to go in the prison and have religious activities with the inmates. One of those groups has been the Kairos Prison Ministry.

The fellowship was something InnerChange program director Ray Roberts believes is the best way to keep inmates from coming back to prison after they are released on parole. He said they try to get the family and community involved in the inmates' lives.

Roberts, who has more than 20 years of experience in criminal corrections, said the InnerChange program has worked in several South American countries and that in those programs, inmate recidivism is low.

Saturday's event happened thanks in part to Jester II Assistant Warden Bruce August, Roberts, and Kairos outside coordinator Stephanie Moran.

"I believe in God and working through God to help these inmates," August said. "I'd like to see a program like ours at every prison in the state and around the country."

Moran has worked with inmates and their families and coordinated the fellowship. Setting up the event, Moran orchestrated several meetings and a retreat involving the family members of inmates. She also worked with the inmates and chaplains outside the prison.

"It was a huge blessing for us having been able to bring the inmates and their families together in fellowship and prayer," Moran said. "This reunion gave the family members and inmates an opportunity to share where they were in their religious walk."

Moran said the response of prison officials, inmates and family members has been positive. Kairos is an established religious group in 21 prisons in the state. The group is in about 26 states around the country. Bill Auvenshine, a member of the Texas Kairos Board of Trustees, took part in the history-making event. He said the group came to Texas about 11 years ago after establishing programs around the country.

The program has garnished state and national recognition. Anyone interested in taking part in the event can call Stephanie Moran at 281-344-9151.

Source: *Informs*, December 1997, 4.

14.12 Responsible Stewardship

During the 1990s, Bobby Ecklund headed up the Church Stewardship Division of the SMC. Ecklund's primary responsibility was to encourage Texas Baptists to give generously to the Cooperative Program. Though fiscal gifts continued to rise in the 1990s, the percentage of their income continued to decline. The work of the CSD was concentrated in three areas: the Baptist Church Loan Corporation, the Baptist Foundation of Texas, and later the Texas Baptist Missions Foundation. Providing low interest loans to churches for either new buildings or expansion remained the job of the Baptist Church Loan Corporation. The Baptist Foundation invests monies from virtually every BGCT department and gives them the interest accrued over the period of investment.

A. Baptist Foundation Investments

The following charts and comments relate to the Statement of Earnings for the fiscal years ended June 30, 1996, 1995, and 1994.

Year Ended June 30, 1996, compared to Year Ended June 30, 1995

For year ended	1996	1995	% Change
Interest Income	$9,143,739	$7,223,805	26.6%
Interest Expense	$4,456,100	$3,720,060	19.8%
Operating Expense	$798,042	$685,989	16.3%
Net Earnings	$3,947,747	$2,856,322	38.2%

For the year ended June 30, 1996, the increase in interest income resulted from a combination of the increase in total loans outstanding and increase in prime rate resulting in rate increases on loans at rate change option dates. Interest expense increased primarily due to an increase in borrowed funds. During fiscal year ended June 30, 1996, a charge was taken to operating expense, as required by SFAS 121, to write down property held for salve to current estimated fair value sales cost. Other items resulting in an increase in operating expense were increases in expenses related to needed maintenance and repair of property held for sale, increase in legal and professional expenses related to obtaining legal and professional opinions, and an increase in expenses related to meetings and travel. Net earnings increased primarily as a result of the increased interest income.

Year Ended June 30, 1995, compared to Year Ended June 30, 1994

For year ended	1995	1994	% Change
Interest Income	$7,223,895	$6,059,451	19.2%
Interest Expense	$3,720,060	$3,370,501	10.0%
Operating Expense	$685,989	$607,808	12.9%
Net Earnings	$2,856,322	$2,060,940	38.6%

For the year ended June 30,1995, the increase in interest income reflects an increase in loans outstanding and an increase in prime rate resulting in rate increases on loans at rate change option dates. Interest expense increased during this same period due primarily to an increase in borrowed funds. The increase in operating expenses was a net result of fluctuations in several expenses during the year. During the fiscal 1995 the Corporation assumed the expenses related to maintaining the property held for sale sites resulting in increased expenses. Legal and Professional expenses increased due to costs related to securing legal opinions and board meeting expenses increased due to two additional called meetings during the year. During this same period salaries and employee benefits decreased due to a reduction in staff. Net earnings increased due primarily to reduced interest expense and loan loss provision.

Year Ended June 30, 1994, compared to
Year ended June 30, 1993

For year ended	1994	1993	% Change
Interest Income	$6,059,451	$6,229,634	(2.7%)
Interest Expense	$3,370,501	$3,726,663	(9.6%)
Operating Expense	$607,808	$498,121	(22.0%)
Net Earnings	$2,060,940	$1,896,941	8.7%

For the year ended June 30, 1994, interest income decreased from fiscal year 1993 due to rate reductions on loans at rate change option dates. Interest expense decreased primarily because the Corporation was able to reduce interest expense by calling the 13th issue bonds and re-structure bank loans at a lower rate. Total operating expenses increased primarily due to an increase in personnel expense and bond issuing expense. An increase in salaries and benefits resulted from the addition of staff members in June 1993. Bond issuing expense increased primarily because all accrued costs related to the 13th issue bonds were expensed during this fiscal year. Net earnings reflect a one-time charge to establish a liability for post-retirement benefits other than pensions as required by SFAS No. 106. The net earnings increase is due primarily to reduced interest expense and loan loss provisions.

Source: *Annual Report*, Baptist Loan Corporation, 1996, 16–17. Reprint courtesy of the Baptist General Convention of Texas.

B. Baptist Foundation of Texas

Since 1930, Baptist Foundation of Texas has served Baptist causes across Texas and around the world by encouraging, facilitating, receiving and managing gifts for the multitude of ministries Baptists support. Through the investment and management of funds which have been set aside for these purposes, the Foundation continues to be an integral part of these ministries.

The role of the Foundation and its endowment management is vital. The institutions and agencies which have been given the responsibility of carrying out these ministries must have the financial resources to meet needs and opportunities as they are presented. Through their gifts designated for endowment, donors from all walks of life have responded. They have given out of their accumulated resources—over and above their gifts to the local church—in order to ensure that the ministries being funded today will continue to be funded in the future.

Some highlights from 1996:

- Funds under management exceeded $1.3 billion—an increase of $137 million over the previous year, and the largest increase in the Foundation's history.
- Consolidated net income of $48 million.
- $49.1 million was distributed to Baptist causes, and $8.4 million was paid to life insurance and annuity beneficiaries.
- Establishment of Concord Trust Company, a wholly-owned subsidiary which will greatly enhance the Foundation's ability to serve its client institutions and their donors.
- Recipient of the "Outstanding Philanthropic Organization" Award, 1996.

We've grown in exciting and measurable ways vital to the Christian education, human welfare, missions and other ministries in which we play a part. We look forward to continuing that mission in the years to come.

Source: *Annual*, Baptist General Convention of Texas, 1997, 92. Reprint courtesy of the Baptist General Convention of Texas.

14.13 WMU

Under the direction of Joy Lynn Phillips Fenner, the WMU of Texas is currently at its peak in creative missions and influence. In charge of the Mary Hill Davis Offering for State Missions, the WMU has significantly enlarged the fiscal gifts virtually each year. A dramatic example may be seen in the comparison of the 1994 and 1995 Mary Hill Davis Offerings. In 1994, the offering raised $3.2 million and in 1995, the Mary Hill Davis Offering reached an unprecedented $7.6 million. The offering, therefore, increased 235% in one year. The WMU is also a practical, hands-on evangelistic force in Texas. In recent years, the WMU has developed prison ministries, nursing ministries, and has attempted to strengthen Hispanic families.

A. WMU Steers Evangelism

Characterized by Baylor University President Herbert Reynolds as the "rudder" of the convention, "steering us, keeping us on the course of missions and evangelism," nearly 1,700 Baptist women gathered for the first session of the Texas Leadership Conference (House Party) Aug. 11–13.

More than 1,200 pre-registered for the second session of the 33rd annual meeting at Baylor University, Aug. 13–15.

In a convocation address, William M. Pinson, Jr., executive director, Baptist General Convention of Texas, called the commitment to missions and evangelism "not a peripheral part but the focal part of my life."

Pinson listed a number of basic commitments that eliminate much decision-making and determine the course of life. He named among others the commitment to Mission Texas, and he said the Mary Hill Davis Centennial Offering for State Missions is "not just another offering" but is "a priority call to sacrifice."

This year Texas Baptists are seeking to raise $22.8 million through the Mary Hill Davis Centennial Offering for State Missions to help start 2,000 new churches and missions as part of the Mission Texas emphasis.

Charles McLaughlin, director, State Missions Commission, cited examples of how the offering for state missions is being put to use to reach the lost half of the Texas population to whom "the light of God has not reached yet."

Focusing on home missions, Don Seigler, told convocation participants about his experiences as director of missions in Mountain and Western Associations, New Mexico. He related how pastors, in face of witchcraft, superstition and persecution, are seeking to minister to Pueblo and Navajo Indians, Hispanics, Anglos and others in the rugged rural areas of western New Mexico.

"If it were not for the support of home missions, many of our mission churches would not exist, and much of our work would go undone," said Seigler.

L'nola Hall, director of the Stewart Baptist Center in inner-city, Atlanta, Ga., focuses on I Timothy 4:13–16 as she told of lessons she had learned working in the poor, predominantly black neighborhood.

"Until you realize who you are in Jesus Christ and what he has done for you, missions will always be something somebody else does," she said.

Foreign missionary Helen Ruchti told how she felt the call to missions as a GA at Highland Church, Dallas, but did not respond until much later. She served with her husband, W. C. Ruchti, Jr. for twenty-five years in Rome, Italy.

In a Bible study on the 1986-87 W.M.U. emphasis, "Gifted to Serve, Called to Act," national W.M.U. President Marjorie Jones McCullough said that while prophecy is the most important gift of the Holy Spirit, teaching is the most basic gift.

"I'm so sorry that in our denomination somewhere along the way we've lost our priorities and let Church Training largely go down the drain. How many of our own children don't know doctrine?" said Mrs. McCullough, a former foreign missionary now living in Alexandria, La., "We need to zero in on the art of the gift of teaching."

Listing about a dozen gifts of the Spirit, Mrs. McCullough said God gives these gifts in order to edify, to evangelize and equip Christians to do the work as the body of Christ.

Source: Ken Camp, "W.M.U. Steers Missions, Evangelism Course," *Baptist Standard*, 20 August 1996, 5. Reprint courtesy of the *Baptist Standard*.

B. Week of Prayer for Home Missions

Chairman Earnest Duncan presented Joy Fenner to speak on the emphasis of the 1986 Week of Prayer for Home Missions. Mrs. Fenner spoke of a young woman who fearfully stood before a group to present the program and materials of the Week of Prayer for Home Missions. After the presentation she shared her testimony in which she indicated that she wanted a heart for missions but lacked the knowledge to develop it. After involvement with missionaries, she prayed that God would give her the heart for missions He wanted her to have. She began to pray for them with the same burden that she had for her own family.

It is important that the W.M.U. Director, the Pastor of the church, the chairman of Good News America have the same desire—to have the heart that God wants for that person for missions. Joy Fenner expressed that desire to have the same burden for missions and missionaries as she has for her own family.

Source: *Minutes*, Executive Board of the Baptist General Convention of Texas, 4 March 1986. Reprint courtesy of the Baptist General Convention of Texas.

14.14 Brotherhood

Robert E. Dixon has led the Texas Baptist Men since 1970. Under Dixon's innovative leadership the TBM has been involved with projects such as disaster relief, retirees on mission, day camping, and Church Renewal Journey. Furthermore, Texas Baptists are not confined to the borders of the Lone Star State. They have provided food for the Kurds in Northern Iraq, coats for the children of North Korea, and sent a water-purifying system to Kenya. The TBM, however, is most well known for its building endeavors. Over the last twenty years, the TBM has built more than four hundred churches in Texas.

A. Builders Begin Work on Village

Tyler—More than 300 Texas Baptist Men Builders began construction last week on the first eight buildings near Tyler at Breckenridge Village, Texas Baptists' first campus for mentally handicapped adults.

Calling the event a "builders reunion," the volunteers from Texas Baptist churches throughout the state are constructing six residences—each with private rooms for eight adults with mild to moderate mental retardation and facilities for house parents—plus administration and vocational buildings.

"We expect to finish by the end of October," said Wilton Davis, coordinator of Texas Baptist Men Builders, most of whom already have helped construct a record 41 buildings this year.

Since their founding by the late Olen Miles of Austin about 20 years ago, the retiree builders have constructed more than 400 buildings for churches that usually couldn't otherwise afford to build.

Volunteers at Breckenridge Village include 87-year-old Pop White of First Church Lubbock, who has helped build 56 churches plus facilities for Texas Baptist encampments, and 84-year-old carpenter Abner

Bryant of Westwood Church in Tyler, who has helped construct about 130 buildings.

Breckenridge Village is sponsored by Baptist Child and Family Services of San Antonio. The village is being constructed on 70 acres of land donated by Jean Breckenridge of Tyler, who has a mentally challenged son.

The planned community near the Tyler municipal airport already has a waiting list of about 200 prospective residents from all over Texas and eight other states, reported Dwight Evans, executive director of the new campus.

The Baptist General Convention of Texas Executive Board approved a $6.9 million bond package to finance the project.

Ultimately, plans call for expanding facilities to care for more than 100 mentally challenged adults.

"They'll have the satisfaction of doing things with other people and earning a paycheck," Evans said.

"Society tends to 'disable' people more than they are. God has given each of them something special. If we put them in the right setting, it's amazing what they can accomplish."

Texas Baptist involvement in creating a care facility for adults with mental disabilities grew out of concerns expressed by parents at the annual Special Friends Retreat for mentally challenged adults and their parents.

The retreat is supported by the Mary Hill Davis Offering for state missions.

The retreat's camp pastor, James Aldridge of Northwestern Church in Midland, appealed to the BGCT Human Welfare Coordinating Board in 1992 on the parents' behalf. Aldridge, who has a daughter with mental disabilities, asked the board to consider creating a residential facility that could care for mentally challenged adults.

The board created a study committee that presented its findings to the BGCT Executive Board in 1993.

Based on that report, the BGCT and Baptist Child and Family Services of San Antonio commissioned a feasibility study to explore the possibilities of developing such a facility.

Source: Orville Scott, "Builders Begin Work on Village," *Baptist Stan-dard*, 8 October 1997, 1, 3. Reprint courtesy of the *Baptist Standard*.

B. Update on Texas Baptist Men's Activity in Criminal Justice Ministry

Texas Baptist Men has been involved in prison ministries for over 15 years. The building of the Hospitality house in Huntsville, Texas, 10 years ago increased our involvement. In May of 1990 under God's lead-ership we felt led to sponsor the first Criminal Justice Awareness Meet-ing at Belton, Texas, on the campus of Mary Hardin-Baylor. The purpose was to find out what was going on in Criminal Justice Ministry in Texas from those already involved in this type of ministry. God's direction and leading was clear to all who attended this meeting. Since that time, the following has occurred:

1. Later in 1990 we had the second state-wide Criminal Justice Awareness Meeting. In 1991, we had three meetings; in 1992 we had two meetings; in 1993 we had three meetings; and in 1994 we had five meetings. In 1995 we hosted four meetings. So far in 1996 we have sponsored 2 awareness meetings. The purpose for all twenty of these statewide and associational meetings is to help churches understand the potential ministry opportunities that they have in the area of Criminal Justice Ministry with volunteers. Our purpose is to motivate and edu-cate the church to become personally involved in the mission field of 3 million + people. We believe God has invited us to do this.

2. In April of 1994 Texas Baptist Men was asked to pilot the Expe-riencing God Weekends in prison. This was done in the Wynn Unit in Huntsville, Texas. Other weekends followed at the Coffield Unit in Au-gust and the Gurney Unit in December. The Experiencing God Week-ends in prison have brought many new volunteers into Criminal Justice Ministry. About 75% of all the men involved are first time volunteers. In 1995 we conducted twelve weekends. Five of them were on one week-end in South Texas. These weekends have involved hundreds of volun-teers from our Baptist churches. Hundreds of inmates have responded by making commitments to go through the twelve-week study of Expe-riencing God. God is truly at work in these weekends. What an opportu-nity for the church to join God in His activity. It would be just like God to send revival to prisoners before it happens in the church. God is at

work, let's join Him as He invites us to. Thus far in 1996 we have completed five weekends and have nine more scheduled.

3. February 10–11, 1995, in Austin, Texas, INFORMS (Emmett Solomon) and Texas Baptist Men hosted the largest Criminal Justice Ministry Conference ever held in Texas. Over 400 attended and 11 different denominations were present. There were 30 different ministry groups represented.

4. INFORMS and Texas Baptist Men were co-hosts once again to a statewide, non-denominational Criminal Justice Ministry Conference in cooperation with other Criminal Justice Ministry groups. This meeting was held February 2–3, 1996, in Dallas, Texas. An ice storm greatly affected the attendance but all in all it was a major CJM event.

5. The updated 1995 Criminal Justice Ministry Manual is now available from Texas Baptist Men. This is a "how-to" manual describing 17 different types of Criminal Justice Ministries that churches and associations can become involved in. Each chapter was written by the person in the state that is responsible for that particular area of ministry. The first chapter explains the Experiencing God Weekend in prisons. This manual was published by the Brotherhood Commission, SBC.

6. We would encourage everyone to read "Pathways to Hope," a new brochure just published by the Church Ministries Department of the Baptist General Convention of Texas.

7. Four national training events are planned for 1996 to introduce the Criminal Justice Ministry opportunities to Kentucky, Tennessee, Arkansas and Alabama. The Baptist Men in each state are hosting these training events. Baptist Men in most states will become more involved in Criminal Justice Ministry as it relates directly to the purpose statements assigned to Baptist Men by the SBC. These are being cosponsored by the Brotherhood Commission of the SBC.

8. June 13–15, 1996, Texas Baptist Men will be sponsoring two Experiencing God Weekends in Amarillo at the Clements Unit (men) and the Neal Unit (women). Henry Blackaby will be doing some of the resource training. We anticipate about 50 volunteers, mostly from within a 75 mile radius to Amarillo to be team members.

9. We have a sixty-minute video on Criminal Justice Ministry that describes the various ministry areas. Included on the video are testimo-

nies from ex-offenders who have been recipients of these particular ministries. This video is excellent for showing what can happen as a result of the church and associational involvement in these ministries.

10. It is also our desire to continue to network all of the various ministries throughout the state in connection with what is happening in Criminal Justice Ministries. Texas Baptist Men would like to become more non-denominational in our relationship with all those involved in this ministry. We all can walk across the same bridge to do this ministry. We want to cooperate with all denominations.

We believe that God has truly invited Texas Baptist Men to accept His invitation to join Him in His activity. Since the building of the Hospitality House in 1986 we have accepted all of God's invitations to be involved with Him in the area of Criminal Justice Ministry. We will continue to accept any invitation we are asked to do whatever the assignment may be. Involving men in any form of redemptive ministry is our assignment from the Father. We want to live and model out Matthew 25: 31–46.

Source: Update on Texas Baptist Men's Activities in Criminal Justice Ministry, Texas Baptist Men, 17 July 1996. Reprint courtesy of the Baptist General Convention of Texas.

14.15 Challenge and Response

During the 1980s and 1990s a number of new issues appeared that challenged the leadership of the BGCT. The first issue concerned whether the convention owned their many satellite entities or were they just affiliated with them. For the most part, the question concerned who would be responsible for the debt if the program developed financial problems that demanded immediate payment. The major issue was the touchy subject of pre-convention meetings. Prior to the traditional Tuesday opening of the regular session of the BGCT, ultraconservative members were meeting on Monday and developing a political platform, drumming up support, and attempting to gain votes for the nominees to the various power positions. Known as the "Pastor's Conference," this pre-convention meeting led to a political, rather than a spiritual BGCT. Though the BGCT asked that these meetings end, the ultraconservatives have continued to meet prior to the convention. Meetings of this nature occurred on the national level as well.

A. Ownership or Affiliation?

The 34-member Constitution Review Committee held its organizational meeting in Dallas last week, and while many concerns were aired at least one consensus appeared to have already surfaced—given a choice between (1) relinquishing control of Texas Baptist institutions to avoid the problem of ascending liability and (2) maintaining control and assuming liability, the committee will choose the later.

At least that was the thrust of many of the comments as Chairman James Semple, pastor of First Church, Paris, asked each committee member to share his feelings about their assignment in an initial three-hour meeting at the Executive Inn in Dallas.

The committee is the result of a motion at the annual meeting of the Baptist General Convention of Texas in San Antonio last November when a proposed slate of changes in the constitution and bylaws was approved by messengers but failed to get the required two-thirds majority.

Eleven changes were proposed, five dealing with terminology and grammar and the other six growing out of the report of a debt study committee concerned about a half a billion dollars in debt existing or proposed by the institutions. The changes would have substituted the words, "affiliated with" for "owned and controlled" in some portions of the constitution in an effort to insulate the convention from the problem of ascending liability—the convention being held accountable for institutional defaults or lawsuits.

However, several messengers spoke out against the changes, expressing the fear that "affiliated with" would make it easier for an institution to sever its relationship with the convention. (Procedures for institution/convention separation were approved by the convention in 1975 and require a lengthy process involving consideration by the appropriate coordinating board, the Executive Board and the convention). The changes were approved by a vote of 808 to 577, short of the two-thirds majority required for constitutional changes.

The messengers subsequently approved a motion for a committee to re-consider the changes and report to the 1986 convention in El Paso.

The committee was authorized by the Executive Board in December and appointed by then chairman Ed Rogers, pastor First Church, Dumas.

Semple, named chairman of the committee by Rogers, reviewed the assignment given the panel at last week's initial meeting, noting it is a "constitutional review committee, not a constitution revision committee." The action of the Executive Board authorizing the committee specified it is to review only essential changes and is not to attempt to "rewrite the constitution."

The committee approved three more meetings of the full committee on Feb. 4, March 11 and May 6 when it hopes to complete its report to the Executive Board. A workgroup was approved to work between those sessions and includes, Semple, James H. Landes, and L. L. Morriss, Dallas; W. M Shamburger, Tyler; Travis Berry, Plano; James T. Draper, Jr., Euless; Amelia Bishop, Plainview; Jack Riddlehoover, Abilene; and Maston Courtney, Amarillo. Shamburger was elected vice-chairman.

Semple said the committee would continue to invite written communications from any interested Texas Baptists. His address is P. O. Box 489, Paris, TX 75460.

The chairman told the committee he had received three letters and one telephone call, all from persons concerned about the recent Wake Forest University case in which trustees of the North Carolina school voted to become a self-perpetuating board, naming their own successors without input from the state convention.

D. L. Lowrie, pastor of First Church, Lubbock, and president of the convention, 1982-83, set the tone for much of the comments, noting he had asked for a review of constitutional language during his tenure, feels it is "in good shape," and the committee should concern itself with the changes that were at issue at San Antonio.

Messengers to that convention, he said, saw the debt study committee recommendations as a problem, that while trying to find a way to build protection for the convention, it jeopardized control.

"If I have to make a choice on liability and control." Lowrie said, "I'll assume liability and keep control."

Many committee members affirmed Lowrie's statement in subsequent remarks. Dallas Baptist University President W. Marvin Watson said he felt that control of convention institutions is what Baptists of Texas want, "anytime that is questioned, it is doomed to failure."

David Slover, pastor of University Church, Houston, and chairman

of the Administrative Committee which last year studied and recommended approval of the debt study committee recommendations, noted—
as did others—that at no time in the discussion of the proposals was
separation of any institutions or a diminishing control considered. In
fact, he said, the debt approval process suggested was meant to strengthen
the convention's control.

Berry, pastor of First Church, Plano, noted, however, that some of
the changes were perceived as diminishing convention control and "per-
ception is reality" and must be dealt with.

Other concerns expressed included the differences in health care
and educational institutions and federal government control of the health
care industry; the need to define "control"; the rising cost of liability
coverage; what kind of liability (indebtedness, lawsuits, etc.) should be
considered; the need to do a better job of communicating with churches;
the review process where institutional indebtedness is examined; the
relationship between the institutions and the convention, as outlined in
the institutional charters; the need to permit health care institutions to
keep up with their competition; and the complications that can arise
with the regional accrediting agencies of educational institutions over
the matter of "control."

Roy Cole of Dallas, longtime legal counsel for the convention, noted
that if control is maintained by the convention it will have liability, but
added that in his opinion at this time the problem of ascending liability
is not a problem in Texas.

He added, however, that while he sees little difference in the terms
"affiliated with" and "owned and controlled by," in Texas a charitable
organization such as Texas Baptist child care institution, a hospital or a
college cannot legally be "owned" by the convention; it can only be
owned by the corporation under which it is chartered.

Source: Toby Druin, "Panel Begins Constitutional Review Process,"
Baptist Standard, 15 January 1986, 5, 15. Reprint courtesy of the *Baptist Standard*.

B. Pre-Convention Meetings

Kansas City—"Shrewd brokers of power" were accused of manipu-
lating "the democratic process of this convention in order to promote

themselves" last week during the annual meeting of the Southern Baptist Convention.

The stinging rebuke came from Russell H. Dilday, Jr., president of Southwestern Baptist Theological Seminary who delivered the annual convention sermon. When he finished, messengers gave him a 40-second standing ovation.

He called on convention messengers to stay on the heights of God's "higher ground."

"Be faithful to your historic heritage," Dilday encouraged. "Don't dabble in controversies, don't exhaust your energies arm-wrestling for denominational control. This denomination is too valuable to let it become a volleyball bounced back and forth across the political net by shrewd game players."

Messengers interrupted his sermon six times with applause.

Earlier in his sermon he had urged the 14.1 million-member denomination to leave the "misty flats" of "suspicion, rumor, criticism, innuendos, guilty by association and the entire demonic family of forced uniformity."

Dilday said he shudders "when I see a coterie of orthodox watching to catch a brother in a statement that sounds heretical, careless categorizing churches as liberal or fundamentalist, unmindful of the effect that criticism may have on God's work." He said such actions are reminiscent of the omnipresent "Big Brother" of George Orwell's best-selling book "1984."

"I wonder what Jesus would think if he were here today, the one who rebuked James and John for their egoistic self-interest?" Dilday asked, referring to the incident in Matthew 20 when the disciples' mother asked special kingdom positions for her sons.

"What would he think of this convention as he watched our blatant scramble for denominational seats today. Don't we sound like the Sons of Thunder (the nicknames of James and John)? We've been left out. It's our turn to be elected. Put us on the boards and committees, give us the positions."

"I say this brokenheartedly but I say it plainly: When shrewd brokers of power manipulate the democratic processes of this convention in order to promote themselves, they've slipped from God's high ground to the barren plains of selfish ambition and conceit."

Dilday noted that Baptists have always upheld individual autonomy, or the "priesthood of the believer." But he said that today "there are some among us who, fearful of standing alone, and determined to get ahead in denominational life, surrender that sacred privilege of individualism."

These persons, he said, play to the gallery and flow with the tide.

"How much better," he said, "to be a Godly individualist who with open mind listens to all sides of an issue, prayerfully measures those issues by the Word of God, and then humbly takes a position and stands courageously by it no matter what others think."

Dilday also warned against those who would breach the historic Baptist principle of separation of church and state.

"Call on Big Brother in Washington to help you witness and worship, and Big Brother's going to trivialize your Lord, reducing his sacred birth to nothing more than a folk festival and giving Bethlehem's manger no more significance than Santa's sleigh or Rudolph's red nose," he warned.

Some day in the future, he added, other political forces hostile to religious liberty will have "the political clout you have today, and they may breach that crack you casually made in the wall of separation, and circumvent the guarantees you brazenly bent a little bit, and they may steal away the liberty you carelessly abused."

Source: "Annual Sermon Warns of 'Shrewd Brokers of Power,'" *Baptist Message*, 21 June 1984, 4. Reprint courtesy of the *Baptist Message*.

14.16 Helping the Helpers

The BGCT has always been concerned for the needs of its ministers. The Ministers' Counseling Service and the Minster/Church Relations Office have proven to be two of the most helpful programs that meet this need. The Ministers' Counseling Service provides psychological, financial, and spiritual aid for ministers who have been terminated. The MCS also administers a psychological test for all ministerial students in Texas Baptist Colleges so that students may either get help in a potential area of need, or be pointed in the direction of another career. The Minister/Church Relations Office was created in 1994 to help churches and their ministers resolve problems before the ministry of the church is damaged.

A. Ministers' Counseling Service Marks 25 Years

Dallas—In a quarter-century of counseling ministers, some things haven't changed.

Marriages suffer when spouses don't communicate. Wives feel neglected when their husbands spend all their time and energy on church-related duties. And ministers feel pulled apart by conflicting demands.

Those are conclusions shared by the two men who have coordinated the Ministers' Counseling Service, a ministry of the Baptist General Convention of Texas that was launched 25 years ago this summer.

The Ministers' Counseling Service provides crisis intervention ministries, such as individual, marriage or family counseling; preventative ministries, such as marriage enrichment retreats and conferences, stress and time; and consultation services for ministers who are involved in counseling.

Supported by the Texas Baptists' Cooperative Program universal budget, these services are made available to all ministers and their families in churches affiliated with the BGCT.

James Cooper, former pastor of First Church of Oak Cliff in Dallas, became coordinator of the service in 1972. When Cooper retired in 1988, Glenn Booth, then associate pastor for counseling and family enrichment at Green Acres Church in Tyler, was named as his successor.

"Probably 75 percent of my counseling sessions are spent trying to help ministers have more fulfilling and intimate relationships with their own families," Booth said.

Cooper agreed that at least half of his time was spent dealing with problems related to families.

"Usually, the basic problem was a lack of communication," he said. "That's what most counselors would find anywhere."

Closely related to marital problems are the job-related pressures of ministry that come from "being pulled in so many different directions and having to wear so many hats," Cooper added.

Booth underscored that same point. "It's not the work of ministry that gets a man down," he said. "It's the pressure he feels put on him, either by the congregation or by himself, to do the work."

Too often, ministers place extremely unrealistic expectations upon themselves out of a sense of "oughtness" and "shouldness," he noted.

"Sometimes, I feel their expectations even exceed what God Himself would demand of a man in the ministry."

Booth's approach is to "help the minister buy back the margins of life, those slots of time where he can plug in personal enrichment experiences, marriage enrichment experiences and family enrichment experiences."

Time invested in personal and family growth does not take away from ministry. It strengthens ministry, he insisted.

"If a minister provides both quantity and quality time for his family, it enhances the effectiveness of his ministry," he said.

While issues related to family have remained fairly constant throughout the Ministers' Counseling Services' 25 years, forced termination of church staff has seemed to increase significantly. Booth notes that about 300 Texas Baptist church staff members are fired annually.

"I try to help them through the pain, hurt, anger and bitterness that sometimes results," Booth said.

The service also offers limited financial assistance during the transitional period and career assessment to help the out-of-work minister discover his strengths, ministry profile, spiritual gifts, natural abilities and goals for self-fulfillment. All of the work is done to help facilitate the minister's re-entry into ministry.

"I would say that 99 and 44/100ths percent of those who go through the process of career assessment revalidate their calling," Booth said.

Source: Ken Camp, "Ministers' Counseling Service Marks 25 Years," *Baptist Standard*, 6 August 1997, 2. Reprint courtesy of the *Baptist Standard*.

B. Ministers' Counseling Service Report

During the past quarter the Coordinator counseled with 36 clients in 61 sessions. Many others were referred to counselors around the state. The Coordinator participated in the following conferences/workshops: Ministers Wives Conference, Baylor University; Volunteers Celebration Conference for the Home Mission Board, Arlington, Texas; and Youth Ministers Conclave, Dallas. The Coordinator also conducted the Ministerial Student Testing Program on 7 Baptist university campuses, and was denominational speaker for the annual meetings of Cooke and Sabine associations.

Source: *Minutes*, Executive Board of the Baptist General Convention of Texas, 5 December 1995. Reprint courtesy of the Baptist General Convention of Texas.

C. Minister/Church Relations Committee

There is a growing crisis of staggering proportions in Southern Baptists and Texas Baptist churches which is undermining the denomination's effectiveness in fulfilling the Great Commission. The crisis is the destructive conflict within many of our congregations which threatens to shatter fragile fellowships and impair or end the careers of faithful, God-called ministers of the gospel. This conflict negatively affects the witness of the church and leaves broken and hurting church members, ministers and ministers' families in its wake. Though many of our churches are doing well and this problem is not universal (in every ministry and church), it is general enough to demand consideration on the part of our Convention.

I. Defining the Problem

The Minister/Church Relationship Committee has sought to address this problem by surveying approximately 1,200 Baptist ministers and ministers' wives. Additionally, we have spent numerous hours listening to and interviewing ministers, ministers' wives, laypersons, directors of missions, seminary professors, members of the BGCT Executive Board staff, and therapists who deal with hurting ministers and their families.

We have discovered a growing erosion of trust and a lack of communication between ministers and their congregations. We have found churches in turmoil and communities where the good name "Baptist" has been the object of ridicule and contempt. We have discovered an epidemic of forced terminations of ministers and widespread discouragement and disillusionment among ministers in all size churches, even those who are in no apparent danger of termination.

We have found that the average church member does not begin to understand the pain and grief which a terminated minister and family experiences, nor the tremendous difficulty a terminated minister faces in being called to another church. For many good and dedicated ministers termination means the end of their ministry as other churches are hesitant to consider a "fired" minister, regardless of the reason for termination.

The problem also expresses itself in the pain and alienation of lay people who have had unfortunate experiences with ministers and have lost confidence in the Christian ministry. We have discovered a great deal of unresolved grief and anger in our churches which must be resolved so that congregations and future ministers may work together productively.

We have observed the repercussions of minister/church conflicts inflicting damage on the relationship between devout and faithful laypersons. Inevitably, these occurrences create situations in which church members who have loved and served with each other for years find themselves on opposite sides of a bitter disagreement. Friendships are devastated, church fellowships are fractured and the cause of Christ suffers immeasurable loss.

It is the prayer of this committee that ministers and churches will learn to deal constructively with conflict and manage it in a Christ-like manner. Our hope is that ministers will learn to deal better with problems which may occur within fellowships by developing more effective human relationship skills. It is our desire that congregations will learn to solve problems with their ministers in a fair and compassionate spirit, and when termination is the only recourse, the needs of the minister and his/her family are given due consideration. We believe that through improved relationships between ministers and the churches, the work of Christ will be advanced as energies are focused on a world which is lost. Finally, it is our prayer that the name of Jesus Christ will be glorified as non-believers say of our churches, "Behold, how they love one another."

What follows is an attempt (1) to outline the factors which contribute to destructive relationships between ministers and churches in our convention, (2) to offer suggestions to improve those vital relationships and (3) to strengthen the witness of our churches.

II. Prominent Factors that Contribute to Destructive
Relationships Between Ministers and Churches

A. Factors Related to Ministers that Contribute to the Destructive Processes

1. Leadership Style

One of the factors in leadership style that is contributing to stress in many cases is the authoritarian, often autocratic and dictatorial style that has become somewhat common. This a departure from the Biblical concept of "shepherd" leader. The authoritarian style places the pastor in the mode of "Chief Executive Officer." Though some churches are comfortable in that model, it seems that distress often comes when a church not accustomed to that type of operation is placed in that mode. Many persons perceive the authoritarian model is being demonstrated by some of the "super church" leaders. This is often adopted as a role model for young pastors. The difficulty frequently arises when pastors in churches not accustomed to this type of operation attempt to implement it, often resulting in polarization with the congregation.

2. Lack of Skills in Communication, Interpersonal Relationships and Conflict Management

In our committee's surveys, group listening sessions and personal interviews, this factor came to the forefront. It was often expressed that formal training in these areas is inadequate and sometimes non-existent. It should be noted that a significant percentage of the ministers in SBC churches have not attended Baptist institutions of higher learning.

3. Failure to Study and Understand the Traditions and Mission of the Particular Church They are Serving

This factor includes the minister attempting to bring about change too rapidly or to begin at the place the church should be rather than starting at the place where it is. It also includes the stress inadvertently caused by the minister's lack of recognition of past experiences of the church.

4. Emotional and Mental Problems

Emotional inadequacies related to ministry are often aggravated or brought forcefully to the surface by the pace and stress of today's church development. Factors that contribute to the highlighting of these inadequacies include:

1) <u>Models of success</u> held up by Convention and Conference leadership. Recognition for professional success is often related only to numerical growth.

2) <u>The role models</u> adopted by ministers to compare the success or failure of their ministry.

3) <u>Unrealized or undefined expectations</u> of the congregation. These can either be real or perceived on the part of the minister.

4) <u>Psychological problems</u> may include any of a full range of psychiatric disorders that have not been recognized or addressed. Under many circumstances some of these may not be destructive, but prove to be so when associated with the highly visible role of leader.

5. Moral Problems

This factor is contributing greatly to destructiveness by its growing prevalence. No attempt has been made to ascertain how much of this may be related to stress in marriage caused by the demands of ministry, lust brought on by today's permissive society or secret desires to be relieved of ministry.

6. Low Morale Problems

Numerous ministers have stated to committee members their own discouragement and disillusionment are feelings with which they constantly struggle.

7. Physical and Emotional Fatigue

Burnout appears to be a major problem for many ministers.

8. Pent up Anger

Like many other Christians, ministers seldom feel free to express anger in an open and constructive way. This may lead to frustration, depression and repression, which when it surfaces can create conflict and tension.

9. Multiplication of Ministerial Duties

The multiplication of ministerial duties in the modern fast paced church often leads to great frustration. This may lead to burnout.

B. Factors Related to Congregations That Contribute to the Destructive Processes

1.Threat of Change. This involves all the changes related to generational differences and entrenched leadership which influence church operation.

> 1) Generational. The gap between those who are senior citizens with pre-World War II values and the "baby boomer" is often more than just age. It is also a gap between concepts of how things should be achieved. This has led at times to polarization within the fellowship. Ministers may be perceived as being "for" one group or "against" another.

> Many seniors resist any kind of change. Some are extremely slow to accept it; so any change is too fast. To some younger groups any change is not fast enough. This difference sometimes leads to confrontation that may not directly involve the minister, but he/she can become the visible target for frustration and anger.

> Senior groups are often decision makers because of serving on key committees. They are the strongest financial base in the church. Sometimes this hinders progress as there is resistance to change in procedures, the accepting of new methods of nomination of new persons to serve on certain committees. The minister, when trying to change this to benefit the entire church, is frequently viewed negatively.

2. Private agendas or power exercised by certain individuals within the congregation. Often this approval must be secured for any program to succeed. Their goals may be undefined, or may not be the goals of the church. By the church empowering them, however, they wield significant influence and can be very destructive when in conflict with ministerial leadership.

3. Long existing divisions within the congregation. Former rifts have not been addressed and an uneasy peace exists among several factions, which are sometimes called "cliques." Each time a new minister comes things go well until it is perceived that he favors or listens to one side more than the other. This sometimes results in his being forced to leave and the process will then be repeated.

4. <u>Unresolved grief and anger within the congregation related to past ministerial conduct.</u> Often congregations choose not to acknowledge or address the grief and anger among members with regard to ministerial misconduct, believing that ignoring the problem would result in quicker healing. The consequences of not resolving these negative experiences and feelings can be lingering destructive forces within the congregation and in future relationships with ministers.

C. Factors Often Found with Both Ministers and Congregations that Contribute to Destructive Behavior

1. <u>A mismatch of the church to ministerial leadership style and abilities.</u> This mismatching can lead to great frustration on the part of one or both parties that can result in destructive relationships.

2. <u>Lack of clarity in expectations.</u> Either the minister or the church or perhaps both assume that the other understands their needs and expectations. It may be discovered too late that these expectations or their importance were not clearly stated or agreed upon.

D. Factors that Lead to Difficulties Within Staff Relationships

Difficulties in staff relationships may spill over into the congregation resulting in general distress, unpleasantness, polarizations, firings and church splits. Factors often relating to these are:

1. <u>Personality clashes</u> within the ministerial and support staff.

2. Pastors not possessing or using good <u>management skills</u>.

3. Lack of <u>recognition</u> on the part of staff that though they are called by the church, they are accountable to the pastor's leadership.

4. Staff attempting to develop their <u>preferred programs</u> instead of cooperating with the overall stated goals of the church ("Lone Rangerism").

5. Pastors who utilize the <u>CEO mode</u> often do not recognize that the other ministers are Christ's ministers, not their personal employees.

6. <u>Insensitivity</u> on the part of a new pastor who demands that exist-

ing staff be terminated or that they leave soon after he assumes leadership so that he might bring in his "own" staff.

7. Lack of <u>appropriate recognition</u> on the part of the congregation of the uniqueness of the ministry of each staff member. This is often related to compensation, benefits, vacation and conference times and special recognitions.

E. Factors That Can Lead to Destructive Effects Within the Minister's Family

1. The devastating effect of <u>forced termination</u> on the family. The ramifications of such terminations are often not realized by lay-persons. The home is lost if the minister lives in church property. The minister's children may experience ridicule, rejection, loss of friends and change of school. The loss of emotional support when relocated along with the loss of compensation adds to the stress. The length of time for those who find another place to serve is often over one year. Ministers are not covered by unemployment compensation.

2. The <u>unrealized and misunderstood expectations</u> placed on the minister's family by the congregation.

3. The family's inability to cope with <u>daily pressures</u> from within the congregation.

4. The family's <u>lack of support system</u> (peer group) within both the staff relationships and the congregation.

5. The family's challenge of often dealing with <u>inadequate income</u>.

Source: *Report*, Minster/Church Relations Committee, 14 September 1993, 1-4. Reprint courtesy of the Baptist General Convention of Texas.

D. Maples' Office to Face Minister/Church Crisis

With the election of their first coordinator of Minister/Church Relations, Texas Baptists are moving to help meet a crisis of pastors fired by churches, said Ed Schmeltekopf, associate executive director of the Baptist General Convention of Texas.

Under the direction of James R. "Dick" Maples, who was elected coordinator of the new office of Minister/Church Relations by the BGCT Executive Board in March, multiple ministries are being developed to meet the minister/church relations crisis.

Maples is former pastor of First Church, Bryan, and former BGCT president. He was chairman of the Minister/Church Relations Task Force established by the Executive Board after a study committee reported "an epidemic of forced terminations of ministers and widespread discouragement among ministers in all size churches."

The Committee reported that a Sunday School Board report revealed an average of about 2,000 Southern Baptist pastors a year are dismissed by their churches.

Maples will work closely with a 15-member advisory committee and with Glenn Booth, coordinator of the BGCT Ministers Counseling Service, and Richard Faling, director of the Church Services Division and Church Staff Information.

"God has blessed Texas Baptists by bringing to these key ministries such men of commitment and expertise to help our churches and church staffs to maximize their ministry for Christ," said BGCT Executive Director William M. Pinson, Jr.

"While they will not be in the position of placing pastors or even recommending persons to churches, they will provide referrals and assistance as requested."

The Task Force will continue to serve until the end of this year and will give way to an advisory committee which will include 11 members of the task force.

"I'm committed to working with every minister and congregation in our Texas Baptist Convention," Maples said, noting that Texas Baptists must approach the minister/church relations crisis with multiple ministries.

"This," he said, "involves seminary training in leadership, inter-personal relations and communications, as well as continuing education for pastors and other church staff.

Also, it would be our intent to offer education to congregations on the work of pulpit (search) committees and the development of realistic expectations on the part of church members concerning ministers and their families who serve in the churches."

"The whole matter of the terminated minister and his family must be addressed. We must help the terminated minister to return to the ministry or find secular employment," he said.

"I hope churches will determine to minister to the terminated minister and his family by providing a position, housing and a stipend until he can get on his feet and be called by another church."

Maples also cited a need for developing a network of ministers who can serve as intentional interim pastors in preparing congregations for the coming of a new minister to the church.

The first Conference for Intentional Interims, was held May 1–5.

Schmeltekopf said, "The new Office of Minister/Church Relations will help prepare people for this service and make them available to churches if they choose to use them."

Faling said that in his responsibility as director of Church Staff Information, he will continue to provide biographical information on prospective church staff members as churches request it.

But he will also offer assistance in strategic church planning, hoping to help churches in prevention of conflict and other problems.

The Church Services Division will sponsor a conference on leadership skills, one component of which is conflict management.

The Ministers' Counseling Service will continue to offer about 20 conferences, workshops and retreats each year, including marriage enrichment retreats for pastors and other church staff members and their spouses, Booth said.

Last year he counseled with 150 ministers and their wives and referred another 130 to members of a network of Christian counselors across the state. Through his office, the BGCT provided $47,000 of assistance in counseling subsidies.

"We're counseling for family problems, as well as church problems," Booth said.

Another goal of the new ministry, said Maples, is to develop a network of experienced pastors to serve as mentors for men entering the ministry.

"Experienced pastors, serving as resource persons and advisors to younger men, can help them avoid some of the pitfalls that inexperienced persons might fall into," he said.

"I am eternally grateful that when I graduated from seminary, I was privileged to serve for two years at First Church, Abilene, as assistant to Elwin Skiles (later president of Hardin-Simmons University) who helped me develop a philosophy of ministry and a leadership style."

Source: Orville Scott, "Maples' Office to Face Minister/Church Crisis," *Baptist Standard*, 17 May 1995, 10. Reprint courtesy of the *Baptist Standard*.

CHAPTER 15

Change Amidst Continuity, 1982–1998

15.1 Baylor and the Baptists

While the Southern Baptist Convention warred against itself on the national level, the Baptists of Texas girded themselves for the inevitable battle for BGCT entities. The first battle began on September 21, 1990, when Baylor University amended its charter so that trustees could elect their own successors. In effect, this cut Baylor off from the BGCT who had elected its trustees since 1886. Baylor president Herbert Reynolds and the board of trustees amended the charter in silence without informing any of the BGCT leadership. They hoped to amend the charter with as little resistance as possible and to keep the much beloved executive director, Bill Pinson, in the dark so that his reputation would not be soiled by the matter. Herbert Reynolds made it known that Baylor did not want to be taken over by the Fundamentalists as had the SBC. This event began a period of intense debate, argument, accusations, and castigations by several prominent ultraconservative Texas Baptists against Baylor University and its leadership. Joel Gregory, pastor of Travis Avenue Baptist Church, Fort Worth, claimed that no school that had severed its ties with its sponsoring denomination had remained true to its original course and thus, Baylor would lose its Baptist moorings. In this regard, Gregory would be proven wrong as Baylor University has remained true to its Baptist heritage.

A. Warning Signs at Baylor

A Melissa pastor said recently he is stepping aside from an effort to elect "conservative" trustees of Baylor University and to turn the Baylor alumni magazine toward a more "conservative" position but that the effort will be continued by a steering committee of United for a Better Baylor.

Donny Cortimilia, pastor of First Church, Melissa, said at the time the *Standard* contacted him, his wife was to have surgery and he will not be involved in the effort for the time being. He said the "steering committee" would be named soon but said he did not know when or where it would meet and he would not divulge the names of any other persons involved with him.

An advertisement in the July 1988 edition of the *Southern Baptist Advocate,* an independent paper edited by a North Carolina pastor, asked Baylor alumni and alumnae, "Are you mad at the liberal bent of the *Baylor Line?*" Then the ad urged alumni to write a P. O. Box in Dallas. The ad was signed "Alumni/ae for a Better Baylor."

Cortimilia told the *Standard* the ad was placed in reaction to a threat by Baylor President Herbert H. Reynolds to join the faculty in a lawsuit to preserve the school from Texas Baptists should it be threatened with "takeover by Fundamentalists."

The Melissa pastor said the story of Reynolds' threat in the May issue of the *Baylor Line,* a publication of the Baylor Alumni Association, was evidence of the magazine's liberalism. No "conservative" position is ever presented in the magazine, he said.

Cortimilia, who said he did not place the ad in the *Advocate* but answered the inquiries produced by it, in turn on Aug. 5 signed a six-page mailing to Baylor "Alumni/ae and Concerned Friends of Baylor" that went beyond the issue of "liberalism" in the magazine to Reynolds and the makeup of the trustee board.

The letter urged that its recipients get themselves elected as messengers to the state convention annual meeting in Austin, Oct. 25–26, and elect "conservative" trustees.

"The problem at Baylor is not just liberal professors and administrators, but a board of trustees that set the policy and support the present situation at Baylor," Cortimilia's letter said. "Baylor will never change until there is a board of trustees that will design and implement a new policy for a course correction at Baylor."

Winfred Moore, pastor of First Church, Amarillo, and chairman of the board of trustees of Baylor, told the *Standard* in regard to the board of trustees, "The Baylor board of trustees are all conservative; I have not seen a liberal among them." Saying no more "conservative bunch of people" could be found, Moore said, Baylor University already has "a conservative board of trustees and administration."

Concerning the need for "a course of correction" at Baylor, Moore said the course of Baylor is always being studied. Moore said: "Baylor University is doing a great job as a university. It is not a Bible college. It is a university. It is doing a super job. The school is in great shape."

Cortimilia also urged letter recipients to attend Baylor homecoming, to pay their alumni dues and attend the meeting of the alumni association on Nov. 4 to vote to change the editorial policy of the *Line*.

Cortimilia said he expected the steering committee of United for a Better Baylor to have 10 to 14 persons and would be announced soon, but he would reveal no names of any persons involved.

Funds for the *Advocate* ad and the mailing were provided by "concerned alumni" whom he also would not identify.

Asked for evidences of "escalating liberalism" in the *Line* at Baylor, Cortimilia cited the Reynolds lawsuit story and the fact that Baylor had substituted a weekly forum for chapel services.

He said he had not talked to the editor of the *Line* but had talked to some Baylor trustees, whom he declined to identify.

Jim Cole, executive director of the *Line* and director of the alumni association, said Cortimilia had not contacted him about the grievances.

"For that reason, we're disappointed," he said.

He described the controversy as "most unfortunate."

"I believe in his letter, he said something about dealing with the facts. I think there was an absence of facts as far as his letter was concerned," Cole said.

"The alumni association is doing in this century what it did in the last century. In fact a resolution was passed in 1879, where the alumni pledged to support and defend Baylor University, to make it a school of quality education, and that is certainly what we're doing today."

As far as Cortimilia's call for people to attend the alumni association meeting Nov. 4, Cole said, "He'll be welcome. Any alumnus is welcome."

Source: Toby Druin, "For 'Better Baylor': Warning Signs at Baylor, Group Urges Action on Baylor Trustees," *Baptist Standard*, 5 October 1988, 9. Reprint courtesy of the *Baptist Standard*.

B. More Trouble at Baylor

Baylor University, founded in 1845 while Texas was a republic, is owned and operated by the Baptist General Convention of Texas. Baylor is the oldest Texas Baptist institution. It is the largest Baptist university in the world with a controlled enrollment of 12,000 students. Almost 1,000 of its students are preparing for Christian ministries with more than 600 of them committed to home or foreign mission. Herbert H. Reynolds is president of Baylor.

Prior to the meeting of the Texas convention in Austin a group calling themselves "United for a Better Baylor" began to circulate some concerns in regard to Baylor and Reynolds, saying, "the problem at Baylor is not just liberal professors and administrators, but a board of trustees that set the policy and support the present situation at Baylor."

The present situation at Baylor? Winfred Moore, pastor of First Church, Amarillo, and chairman of the board of trustees at Baylor says the trustees as well as the administration are "conservative" and the school is "in great shape."

If a meeting of a laity group immediately prior to the Austin convention is any measure, many would agree with Moore concerning the conservative direction of Baylor.

With this as a background, Joel Gregory used part of his presidential address speaking to the issue.

Gregory came down hard on Baylor's critics saying they could not keep their credibility if they "criticize each supposed flaw or scrutinize every detail." The Fort Worth pastor spoke glowingly of Baylor, but also spoke to Baylor's supporters and leaders in urging them to hear and respond to some of the concerns offered by some "responsible Texas Baptists" who are not on the "edge but from the middle."

In a press conference prior to his address Gregory called for "enlarged and enhanced representation of credentialed, rational evangelistic scholarship" in "future accessions" to the department of religion.

Baylor University president Reynolds responded to the discussion concerning Baylor by releasing a positive statement which said, "Baylor will always strive to be a first-rate Christian institution of higher learning while engaging in self-renewal and improvements that come from its Baptist constituency and others who are committed to the welfare of the university."

There you have it. Baylor says they are conservative others say they are not. President Reynolds has vowed to keep Baylor from falling into the hands of those he called "Fundamentalists." Joel Gregory has given a word of caution and advice on the entire matter. Reynolds has issued a positive statement and is commended for doing so.

Should there be a committee to study the situation? No. There already is one called the trustees elected by the convention who have affirmed Reynolds and the direction of the university.

The situation at Baylor? Sure Baylor can and should do a better job in Christian higher education, but this does not take away from the job being done.

The *Baptist Standard* does not believe Texas Baptists want a perceived or real inquisition of Baylor or any of their institutions, but the *Standard* also believes Texas Baptists want their institutions to be Baptist and hold and teach the Bible as truth without any mixture of error.

Source: Presnall H. Wood, "What About the Situation at Baylor," *Baptist Standard*, 2 November 1988, 6. Reprint courtesy of the *Baptist Standard*.

C. Report of the Administrative Committee Concerning Baylor University

The Administrative Committee met in a special Called Meeting on October 2 from 9:30 a. m. until 4:45 p. m. Members present were: David Courtade; A. E. Fogle; Herbert Garrett, Jr.; George Gaston III; Rudy Gonzalez, Jr.; Hilton Hemphill; Maurice Johnston; Winfred Moore; Levi Price, Jr.; B. F. Risinger, Jr.; Mac Robinson; Gordon Thrall; and William White.

The committee heard a report by President Herbert Reynolds on the action of the Baylor Trustees on September 21 to establish a Board of Regents "with sole responsibility for governance of Baylor University."

The report was followed by a lengthy period in which committee members questioned President Reynolds about the action, expressed concerns, and raised objections. Winfred Moore, Chairman of the Baylor Board, spoke briefly stating the desire of Baylor University to remain close to the Baptist General Convention of Texas.

After Reynolds and Moore left, the members continued their discussion. Both pro and con statements were made concerning the Baylor action. Relational, legal, and financial issues were identified which must be addressed.

The following motions were passed by the Administrative Committee after considerable discussion:

1) That a formal study be made of the recent Baylor University charter action. The purpose of such a study is to clarify and determine what actually has occurred, assess the implications of what has taken place to include legal, relational, and financial and then determine what options are available to the BGCT for future action,

   that the Administrative Committee Chairman work with the Executive Board Chairman, Convention President and Executive Director to engage the necessary counsel and advisors to analyze carefully the facts and circumstances in this matter for careful documentation of the current situation before action is taken, and

   that authorization up to $30,000 from Contingency Funds be given for such use, a report on the use of these funds to be provided to the Administrative Committee as soon as possible. (Use of additional funds will need further Administrative Committee approval.)

The committee expressed hope that this study can lead to a continuing cooperative relationship with the institution while protecting and pursuing the mission and purpose of the Convention.

2) That the following people, in consultation with appropriate counsel, develop a proposal for a process to respond to the action by the Baylor University Board of Trustees on September 21, 1990, in which they took unilateral action to amend the charter of the

University: Phil Lineberger, BGCT President; Ed Rogers, 1st Vice-President; Billy Ray Parmer, 2nd Vice-President; Robert Parker, Executive Board Chairman; Levi Price, Jr., Executive Board Vice-Chairman; George Gaston, Administrative Committee Chairman; B. F. Risinger, Jr., Administrative Committee Vice-Chairman; Barbara Morrison, Christian Education Coordinating Board Chairman; Charles McIlveene, Human Welfare Coordinating Board Chairman,

that such a proposal include at least the following: (1) the persons to be part of the process, (2) the basic issues with which the process is to deal, (3) a suggested time framework for the process, and

that the proposal be presented at the Called Meeting of the Executive Board on October 17, 1990, for consideration by the Board.

3) That the 1990 Cooperative Program money due to be sent to Baylor University, with the exception of funds designated for Ministerial Tuition and Faculty Fellowship Funds, be escrowed with interest until such time as a Convention study of this funding matter can be completed. This action is not in any sense intended to be judgmental or punitive toward Baylor. The study is to receive priority attention and be completed as soon as possible.

4) That the 1991 Budget be presented to the Convention as prepared with the understanding that funds due to be distributed to Baylor University are subject to the completion of the Convention study of this funding matter.

The meeting concluded with the following statement by George Gaston, Chairman, and prayer;

"Baylor University is a highly esteemed, long-standing, valuable friend of Texas Baptists. The relationship of trust and cooperation which has existed between Baylor and the Baptist General Convention of Texas has been in place since 1886 and is worthy of preserving. Baylor has been the beneficiary of Texas Baptist prayer, the children of Baptist homes and churches, the cooperative gifts of Baptist stewardship, the wisdom and guidance of Baptist beliefs, the care of Baptist leadership, and the generosity of Baptist benefactors. Texas Baptists have received from Baylor a powerful influence for God's Kingdom in Texas and around the world. Christian leaders, trained and shaped by Baylor, fill the churches of Texas. Denominational leaders across the Southern Baptist Convention have been inspired to excellence through their Baylor heritage. The joy and pride spawned by Baylor in the hearts of Texas Baptists has served to strengthen greatly the ministry and stewardship of local churches across Texas."

"Every effort of prayer, discussion, and diligent concern must be exerted by Baylor and the Baptist General Convention of Texas to protect such a mutually productive relationship from being lost. Baylor and the Baptist General Convention of Texas need each other in an alliance of trust and mutual proclamation of the Gospel."

"The Executive Board of the BGCT has appointed a special committee to study the relational, legal and financial relationship of the BGCT and Baylor University. This committee is to report to the Executive Board and thereby the BGCT with all deliberate speed. Until such time as the report has been received and acted upon no action of the BGCT or any of its committees is intended to acquiesce in or consent to the action of Baylor University to pass judgment either way. Once the committee report has been received it will be acted upon by the Executive Board."

Source: *Minutes*, Administrative Committee of the Baptist General Convention of Texas, 2 October 1990. Reprint courtesy of the Baptist General Convention of Texas.

D. Joel Gregory's Statement

"I want to thank you Mr. Chairman. I am not a member of this board. I am pastor of Travis Avenue Baptist Church in Fort Worth, a Baylor alumnus with two degrees and a former officer of this convention. I would like to make a statement personally in light of personal remarks made concerning me and then read a statement with eight signatories to put into the record. First, let me say that I was surprised to find my comments as an undergraduate or graduate student of Baylor University germane to the issue before this body. As an undergraduate of Baylor University I would beg to differ with the distinguished President that I was among many who in classrooms and with professors debated the merits of theological positions at the University. I simply would like to make that as a matter of the record. Dr. Reynolds has raised a question of Religious Liberty, which it indeed is. In light of 2 plus million Texas Baptists' right to exercise their liberty, this is not a question of church and state, it is a question of convention and school and an adopted constitution by this body. For 145 years, Texas Baptists have given their trust, their money, their children to Baylor University. It has been argued by the distinguished Administrator that sole competency, priesthood of the believer and liberty are to the point. I would agree. That includes the sole competency of and the priesthood of more than 2 million Texas Baptists. I would call on this Board, before reading my statement, to recognize and to investigate this reality in American religious denominational higher learning. There is not a single incidence of a denominational university that has severed its ties of accountability with its sponsoring body that over decades has remained true to the vision of those sponsors. The evidence from Brown, Chicago, University of Richmond, not to mention the great colonial schools, is indisputable. I would call upon our special study committee, this body, and the requisite bodies to recognize that.

I asked that Chairman for the opportunity to read into the record here today, a statement with eight signatories. These are not comprehensive, but they are representative of perceived political parameters, lay pastors, graduates and non-graduates. I would like to read the signatories first and the brief statement.

I have signed it, Jack Graham, pastor of Prestonwood Baptist Church in Dallas; Don Willis, a layman and member of Park Cities Baptist Church in Dallas and a Baylor Trustee; Ralph Smith, pastor of Hyde Park Baptist Church in Austin and a Baylor Trustee; Neal Jeffrey, minister and graduate of Baylor; Jack Riddlehoover, pastor and graduate of Baylor; Bill Grubbs, layman and member of First Baptist Church in Dallas and a Baylor Trustee; and Fred Roach, a layman and a member of the church pastored by our convention president, Richardson Heights Baptist Church.

We simply place this statement before the leaders of Baylor University, its Trustees and the other requisite bodies. We prayerfully request the Trustees of Baylor University to reverse their action of September 21, 1990, and restore Baylor University to its traditional relationship of accountability to the Baptist General Convention of Texas. We call upon them to fulfill their fiduciary responsibility to the Baptist General Convention which elected them. Further, we call upon the Baptist General Convention of Texas, through its appropriate boards, committees and sessions, to pursue the recovery of its historical relationship with Baylor University.

This is a draft with those names having signed it. I thank you for the opportunity to speak as a personal privilege to the questions raised and to make this statement.

Source: *Minutes*, Executive Board of the Baptist General Convention of Texas, 19 October 1990. Reprint courtesy of the Baptist General Convention of Texas.

15.2 Earthquake at Southwestern Seminary

If Baylor University severing its ties with the state body caused tremors throughout the BGCT, the firing of Southwestern Baptist Seminary President Russell Dilday produced an earthquake of epic proportions. On March 4, 1994, Russell Dilday was fired in a very covert manner and with lightning speed. Southwestern trustees were immediately inundated with criticism for their action. They replied by listing several unproven reasons as to why Dilday was fired. This list included: the faculty not holding conservative views, the School of Church Music promoting a contemporary style of music, his failure to bring conservative speakers to chapel, his criticism of SBC leaders, and failure to teach the Inerrancy of the Bible. Dilday repudiated each of these accusations and the popular president soon found a home at Baylor University. The reputation of Southwestern Seminary, however, was severely damaged.

A. Dilday Fired as President at Southwestern

Trustees of Southwestern Seminary last week fired Russell H. Dilday, Jr. as sixth president of the institution, immediately changing the lock on his office door and telling him and his wife, Betty, to vacate the president's residence on campus by June 7.

The action closes out a fifteen year tenure by Dilday, who became president in August 1978, succeeding Robert E. Naylor, who retired at 69. Dilday will be 64 in September.

The five vice presidents of the seminary were asked to administer the school until an interim president can be chosen. A search committee was named to begin the process of seeking a new president.

No reason was given for Dilday's dismissal, which reportedly came on 26–7 ballot vote of the trustees at the last session of their spring meeting at the seminary March 9.

New trustee chairman Ralph W. Pulley, Jr., a member of First Church, Dallas, and who made the motion that Dilday be fired in a closed-door executive session, refused to answer repeated questions of "Why?" from seminary students and the media. He said only that the trustees felt the institution "needed new direction to move us into the 21st century."

Pulley was jeered by some 1,000 students as he read a letter from trustees about their action. The students and many faculty members had packed the foyer of Truett auditorium during the closed-door session, praying and singing songs and choruses to show their support for Dilday.

Later, in a press conference Pulley told reporters that the reaction had been expected and would subside with time. He declined comment on reasons for dismissal of the president, saying they were "not pertinent" and that charges Dilday had not been supportive of the fundamentalist-conservative movement in the Southern Baptist Convention or was too moderate were "past history" and he had no comment.

Two days after the firing the trustees issued a press release from the seminary public relations office saying that they and Dilday had "irreconcilable differences" but offering little more detail other than citing Dilday for continuing to speak out on political issues in contradiction of an agreement set down by them.

They gave Dilday "high marks for his personal skills and relationship," the release stated, but said they had reached a philosophical "stalemate" in working with him.

Dilday told reporters in a post-dismissal interview at the president's home that "the only word that ever cropped up that I heard (in the closed-door meeting) was insubordination, which I don't think is worthy."

Rumors had been rampant across the Southern Baptist Convention for several days before the meeting that the firing was imminent. Dilday said he had even had one call from European Baptist Seminary in Ruschlikon, Switzerland, about the rumor, another from his son, Robert, in Richmond, Va., and others from Nashville. The rumors were so persistent that Herb Hollinger, SBC Executive Committee vice president for Baptist Press, came to cover the meeting.

But such rumors have come with every board meeting in recent years, Dilday noted, and he dismissed them, especially after receiving high marks from the trustee executive committee in its annual appraisal of his performance on Tuesday evening, the night before his dismissal.

Source: Toby Druin, "Dilday Fired as President of Southwestern," *Baptist Standard*, 16 March 1994, 3. Reprint courtesy of the *Baptist Standard*.

B. Dilday Responds to Latest Charges of Trustees

Fort Worth, Texas(BP)—Russell H. Dilday, Jr., said every charge raised in a March 21 news release by trustees of Southwestern Baptist Theological Seminary is false. Dilday was president of the seminary until fired by the trustees March 9.

"All of these concerns would have been legitimate concerns to be raised at every (annual) personal review," Dilday told Baptist Press. "But this is the first time I have seen these. Last year's (evaluation by the trustees) was positive, and this year's."

"This is a group that took action precipitously and now they are trying to find reasons for (the firing)," Dilday said. "There is not one specific evidence (in their charges)."

Dilday did say the "golden parachute" offer was offered and was generous.

"But I refused it in integrity because it isn't right to be bought out."

Trustees said they offered Dilday, 63, a retirement package worth $400,000 if he would take early retirement "for the good of all concerned, but he refused."

Dilday took exception to every charge of mismanagement, disobedience, doctrinal differences, arrogance and gridlock.

"I was never disobedient," Dilday said. "Not one time did I refuse to carry out policy of the board. To individual trustees, I have not responded every time. The board governs only when it is in session. Those are the times when the board speaks. I would love to see a listing of when that (disobedience) has taken place."

Dilday said his style of management called arrogant and isolationist by trustees, is collegiality and shared governance.

"Anyone watching my work knows my approach has not been one of arrogance," Dilday said. "I secured Lily grants to help our board and the president to learn to work together. The 1989 covenant agreement was a great success, in spite of our differences."

Dilday said he had never discouraged dissent by trustees—"even if I had wanted to." Respecting dissent, he said, has been a hallmark of his life.

Also, Dilday said he had never been criticized by the board for being wrong doctrinally. And never, he said, has he refused to take direction from the board. "Give me one incident (where he did it)," Dilday said. Individuals might call and suggest something that I would not do but not the board, he said.

Dilday questioned the trustees' accusations that gridlock had enveloped the school.

"In spite of our differences, the school has moved to its greatest days. I don't see any evidence (of gridlock). They approved every recommendation I have ever brought, except for one faculty recommendation in the past, and then they deferred all of them at this meeting. But regularly and consistently, they have approved them."

Dilday said he hasn't criticized the Southern Baptist Convention or its officials since the 1989 covenant agreement, although "I spoke out strong about the takeover movement (in the SBC) before 1989."

Regarding the declining enrollment, Dilday said all six SBC seminaries have suffered about a 20 percent decline since 1985-86.

"I admit the staff has grown during that time, because of the complexity of our work. But I brought a major, drastic, reduction in staff to this meeting and they refused to accept it," Dilday said.

The Fort Worth, Texas, school is at its highest quality level and accreditation has just been completed, Dilday said. *Christianity Today* magazine named SWBTS the best school in the country, he added, and the Institute of Biblical Research just voted to build its library on campus because of the school's reputation.

"They (trustees) said I have damaged the school's reputation. I don't have any idea what they mean," Dilday said.

Source: Herb Hollinger, "Dilday Responds to Latest Charges of Trustees," *Alabama Baptist*, 24 March 1994, 1, 7. Reprint courtesy of the *Alabama Baptist*.

C. Firing Brings Letter of Censure from Accreditation Agency

A national accrediting agency rebuked trustees of Southwestern Seminary, March 17, for abruptly firing the school's president.

"We view with utmost seriousness the dismissal of Russell Dilday," said the Association of Theological Schools in a rare letter of censure. "Such precipitous action on the part of the board of trustees is a clear violation of accepted governance practices and places in jeopardy the vitality and basic integrity of the institution."

The agency called on trustees of the Fort Worth school to reconsider the firing but did not threaten to place the school on probation.

Southwestern's trustees chairman, Ralph Pulley, declined comment. Trustees did not cite a reason March 9 for firing Dilday, president of the 4,000-student school since 1978. They later said "irreconcilable differences" produced the impasse.

Trustees who opposed the action, however, said it was strictly political, reflecting a growing rift between Dilday and fundamental-conservative trustees bent on steering a new course for the nation's largest seminary.

ATS Executive Director James Waits, who wrote the letter of censure, said the trustees' March 9 action came without notice and without due process.

The ATS, which renewed Southwestern's status in 1990, is one of the two agencies that accredit the seminary. The other is the Southern Association of Colleges and Schools.

All six Southern Baptist seminaries are accredited by ATS and one of the regional non-theological agencies. Accreditation is the primary way schools demonstrate adherence to high academic standards.

Although ATS did not threaten Southwestern with probation March 17, a similar episode at Southeastern Seminary did result in probation.

The Southern Association of Colleges and Schools placed South-eastern on probation in December 1991 in part because of the administrative disruption that followed the sudden resignation of the seminary's president and top administrators in 1987.

Randall Lolley, president of Southeastern at the time, accused fundamental-conservative trustees of forcing the school to hire only biblical inerrantists to the faculty, a practice that drew the scrutiny of accreditors.

The Association of Theological Schools placed Southeastern on two-year probation in 1992. SACS lifted its probation last December.

Source: Greg Warner, "Firing Brings Letter of Censure from Accreditation Agency," *Baptist Standard*, 23 March 1994, 3. Reprint courtesy of the *Baptist Standard*.

D. Allen: Trustees Must Be Accountable, Apologize

Trustees of Southwestern Seminary must be held accountable for their actions in firing President Russell H. Dilday, Jr., and should apologize to Southern Baptists for "seven wrongs" permitted when they did it, says Wayne Allen.

Allen, pastor of First Church, Carrollton, and one of the seven trustees who voted against Dilday's dismissal March 9, has called for an emergency meeting of trustees to discuss the "wrongs" but has been thwarted by committee officers though at one time a majority were willing to re-convene, he said.

Southern Baptists have a right to demand an apology for these seven "wrongs," Allen said.

1- The plot to replace Dilday with an employment buyout or fire him was planned at least one week—probably weeks—before the trustee meeting with knowledge of only a part of the board.

2- Knowledge of the plan was deliberately kept from Allen and at least two other trustees. The chairman told Allen that it was kept from him because he would have gone to Dilday, "he would have told his friends, and we would have a mob scene." Allen said that instead of calling Dilday he would have demanded a meeting of the board to discuss the issue.

3- The impression was given to Allen, students, faculty and the president that no plot had been made. "This was deceit," said Allen.

4- Trustees were asked Monday, Tuesday and Wednesday before Dilday was fired about 11 A.M. Wednesday if there was a plan to fire him. They pretended they had no knowledge of it or denied it.

5- The trustee officers and another trustee who offered Dilday a "Golden Parachute" retirement package did not have the authority to make such an offer.

6- John Earl Seelig, who had requested early retirement rather than be fired in 1989, was back on campus as an employee the day of the firing, handling press releases. He was not approved by the trustees.

7- Changing the lock on the door of the president's office and denying him access to his computer, leaving the impression that some criminal act or an immoral act had been committed.

"Because of these 'wrongs' thousands of Southern Baptists feel bitter and betrayed and have every right to feel that way," Allen said in a press release. "As trustees elected by these Southern Baptists we owe them an apology. . . for the 'wrongs' committed. Failure to do so is to refuse to be accountable."

Seminary bylaws state that if a majority of the trustees request an emergency meeting, the chairman must call for it. Allen said that trustees Bob Anderson of Louisiana and Pat Campbell of South Carolina on April 13 had 20 of the 38 trustees who were willing to sign a letter requesting such a meeting.

However, two dropped out after receiving "very selected telephone calls," said Allen, and Chairman Ralph W. Pulley, Jr, of Dallas would not call a meeting.

Source: Toby Druin, "Allen: Trustees Must Be Accountable, Apologize," *Baptist Standard*, 27 April 1994, 5. Reprint courtesy of the *Baptist Standard*.

E. Executive Board Resolution

"Whereas Dr. Russell Dilday served as President of Southwestern Baptist Theological Seminary since 1977, after serving as pastor of Second Ponce de Leon Baptist Church in Atlanta, Georgia, Tallowood Baptist Church in Houston, Texas, First Baptist Church, Clifton, Texas, and Antelope Baptist Church, Antelope, Texas, and is a popular speaker and outstanding preacher at church, educational, and denominational meetings throughout the United States, and

"Whereas Dr. Dilday is a graduate of Southwestern Baptist Theological Seminary where he earned the Master of Divinity and Doctor of Philosophy degrees; including graduate studies at Baylor University and whereas Dr. Dilday was honored with Distinguished Alumnus Awards from both Baylor University and Southwestern Baptist Theological Seminary; and also received the Doctor of Divinity from Mercer University in Macon, Georgia, the Doctor of Humane Letters from William Jewell College in Liberty, Missouri, and the Doctor of Humanities from Dallas Baptist University; and

"Whereas Dr. Dilday was a leader among theological schools in the United States serving as president of the Association of Theological Schools from 1989–90, served on the Executive Committee of the Association of Theological Schools in 1992–93, and is a member of the American Academy of Religion, and

"Whereas Dr. Dilday led Southwestern Seminary, the largest Seminary in the world, to reach an enrollment of more than 5,000 in 1985, to expand the endowment fund from $4 million to $74 million, with total assets of $120 million, and achieved a balanced budget throughout his tenure, and

"Whereas Dr. Dilday has placed priority on developing Southwestern Seminary into a premier evangelical seminary through strategic planning, led in the building and renovation of numerous seminary structures, enlisted scholars in all theological disciplines including the practical aspects of education, and placed a premium on academic writing and research, we the Executive Board of the Baptist General Convention of Texas, therefore resolve:

"That Dr. Dilday be commended for his uncompromising integrity in upholding the character of the Gospel of our Lord Jesus Christ in the tradition of Carroll, Scarborough, Head, Williams, and Naylor while leading Southwestern Baptist Theological Seminary in its outstanding achievements in missions, ministry and evangelism, and

"That Dr. and Mrs. Dilday be commended for their sensitive Christian lifestyle in their personal leadership roles in the context of the Seminary family, the church, the community, and the Southern Baptist Convention; and their godly example for the minister's family in modeling the fruits of the Spirit; their constant witness to the unsaved in word and deed; and their unwavering commitment to their task of guidance of Southwestern Baptist Theological Seminary, and

"That Dr. Dilday be commended for his unbinding loyalty to the divinely inspired Holy Scripture as the written word of God, the 'perfect treasure of divine instruction' with 'God as its author, salvation for its end, and truth, without any mixture of error, for its matter' (Baptist Faith and Message), and

"That Dr. Dilday be commended for his noble and admirable leadership of Southwestern Seminary in its outstanding academic achievement, its acclaimed educational contribution to missions and evangelism, its astute training of men and women for ministry at home and around the world; his efforts in developing a superb faculty, his administrative skills and abilities, and his untiring commitment and support of the Kingdom of God through theological education.

"That Dr. Dilday be affirmed for his wisdom in sharing the Gospel as demonstrated in his preaching, administration, lifestyle, relationships, and denominational affairs; for his stance as a theological conservative in the finest heritage of Baptist doctrine and interpretation.

"That through this resolution, in light of the recent events surrounding his release as President from Southwestern Baptist Theological Seminary, Dr. Dilday be affirmed personally, academically, administratively, theologically, and denominationally for his Christian conviction, sacrifice, integrity and courage."

Clyde Glazener seconded the motion. The motion carried in a show of hands vote with some opposition expressed.

Source: *Minutes*, Executive Board of the Baptist General Convention of Texas, 7 June 1994. Reprint courtesy of the Baptist General Convention of Texas.

F. An Open Letter to the Alumni and Friends of Southwestern Seminary

As you know, the Executive Committee of the Board of Trustees was unanimous on March 29 when we announced the appointment of William B. Tolar as the Acting President of Southwestern Baptist Theological Seminary. He is deeply devoted to the Lord Jesus Christ and has a great love for the seminary where he has invested his life in the teaching ministry for almost 30 years. He is greatly loved by those who have worked with him on the seminary campus, by the students who have sat in the classroom and by thousands of Southern Baptists who have heard him preach in the pulpits of their churches over the years. We are most grateful that under the leadership of God's Spirit he has accepted this key position in such an important time in the life of the seminary.

We are pleased that the President's Search Committee has begun the work of finding "God's man" for the future. You will find a report along with a list of the members in this issue of the news. We ask each of you to pray with us for this important task.

For your understanding on how the SBC has directed the lines of responsibility for the seminary, we cite for you the Authority, Direction, Control, and Responsibilities of the trustees as outlined in the charter and the bylaws.

The Southwestern charter, Paragraph Ninth, provides: "Said corporation shall be under the patronage, general direction and control of the Southern Baptist Convention, which convention may establish articles of faith and permanent laws for the Seminary". . . which shall not be "altered, annulled, or abrogated by said Convention" except by the procedure provided in Paragraph Ninth. If there are matters not included in the articles of faith and permanent laws set out in Paragraph Ninth, "the corporation shall be subject to the rules and regulations of the Southern Baptist Convention, both general and specific, as these may be promulgated from time to time, and made a matter of record in the Minutes of said Convention." Paragraph Eleventh makes it clear that amendments to this charter are "made only with the advice and consent of the Southern Baptist Convention, which action must be duly recorded upon the minutes of the Convention."

The bylaws, Article I, Paragraph I, provides the ". . .members of the

Board of Trustees of the Seminary are those persons elected by the Southern Baptist Convention" in harmony with the requirements of the charter of the Seminary and the constitution of the Convention. *The President of the institution shall serve in an advisory capacity to the Board.*

Article II makes it clear as to the responsibility and authority of the trustees when it says; "The Southern Baptist Convention has committed to the Trustees the responsibility to operate the Seminary for the Convention and full authority in all matters of its operation. The basic ongoing policies of the Seminary are set out in the Seminary Policy Manual. The Board of Trustees is answerable only to the Convention for its acts in operating the Seminary."

Article V, Paragraph 1 (1) states: "The President shall be elected by the Board of Trustees. *His term of office and administration of affairs of the Seminary shall be under the direction and authority of the board.* The retirement policies, process, and benefits for the President shall be established by the Trustees." Article V, Paragraph 1 (2) indicates the President is . . . accountable only to the Board of Trustees.

Most educational institutions in the U. S. have self-perpetuating, nondenominational boards which results in a strong often unaccountable administration. This is not the way it works in the governance of Southern Baptist institutions. Our boards are selected democratically by state or national conventions and are responsible to the governing body, not to the administrator.

Southwestern Trustees come from thirty states. We, as trustees, have spent many hours in studying governance and trusteeship, most recently through a Lilly Foundation grant. An outgrowth of accountability has been improved communications and dialogue among the board members. The Trustees highly respect this trust and prayerfully perform the responsibility of governing Southwestern as instructed by the constitution and Bylaws of the Southern Baptist Convention and the Charter and Bylaws of Southwestern.

The board sets operating policies and the president is required to carry out those policies. Trustees by a vote of 27–7 felt there was no choice other than to require a change in executive leadership. While the action may have seemed sudden and without foundation, this is not the case. A strong attempt was continually made, particularly during the last five years, to work in concert with Dr. Dilday. It became increasingly impossible, the trust level between the Trustees and Dr. Dilday had widened rather than narrowed, and an impasse was reached.

The President's agenda was consistently in conflict with the direction desired by the Board of Trustees. He also had strong leanings toward an entity that calls itself the Cooperative Baptist Fellowship, an organization in competition with and adverse to the Southern Baptist Convention and the SBC Cooperative Program. This is a very serious matter, particularly considering the Southern Baptist Convention owns Southwestern and relies on gifts through the Cooperative Program of the SBC to undergird the ministries of the seminaries.

There were veiled threats that donors were attaching strings to gifts which would permit reevaluation if the president was dealt with by the Board. A large church in the metroplex voted to "cease contributions to the seminary in light of the action taken by the trustees . . . if the current president ceases to serve." Gifts with strings attached to the presidency are counter to the Cooperative Program and are an obvious attempt to sway trustees inappropriately. Records reveal this church has only given $3,729 since January 1, 1992.

We believe that God's work will always be supported by God's people. It is encouraging to note that actual cash gifts received by the seminary during the ten-week period beginning February 1, 1994, were $212,060.79. This compares to $183,709.11 received during the same ten-week period last year.

The leadership style was autocratic in his relationship to the Board. This is unacceptable. The chairman of an SBC agency was not permitted on campus without board action. There was open hostility to the Board, not only as a group, but in one on one confrontations by Dr. Dilday with board members.

Dr. Dilday gave every indication he intended to stay in office indefinitely. His stance made it impossible to have any kind of smooth transition. The problems were continuing to mount and a stalemate between the board and the president had been reached and could no longer be permitted to continue.

A situation had evolved where faculty and administrators were formulating policy, clearly contrary to acceptable collegial governance practices since trustees are assigned that role, and current trustee input was minimized.

All faculty members are elected by the board of trustees (not by one administrator) to serve the institution. Their allegiance should be to the institution and governing body, the board of trust.

An awareness report from *Christianity Today* released in recent years ranked SWBTS very high overall. However, Southwestern was ranked 15th in doctrinal soundness and 11th in spiritual atmosphere. These rankings are illuminating and disappointing.

While enrollment has declined, the number of administrative personnel has increased. An administration realignment combining the responsibilities and titles of three vice-president positions with the deans of the schools was not an acceptable plan to the Trustees.

The Southwestern Council, formerly the Advisory Council, was established many years ago to be encouragers and supporters of Southwestern. Yet, Dr. Dilday seemed to place more value and stock in this council than in the Board of Trustees. This has been confirmed by the adverse actions of the Southwestern Council leadership contrary to the well being of the Seminary since the Board action on March 9, 1994.

The action of the board of trustees has not placed in jeopardy the vitality and basic integrity of the seminary. The *purpose* and *mission* of Southwestern as determined by the Southern Baptist Convention is very much intact.

The seminary is alive and well. We anticipate what God is going to do with great expectancy with the assurance that He has great and wonderful things in store for us as we approach the Twenty-first Century. IT IS TIME FOR A REVIVAL AND RENEWAL OF THE GREAT SPIRIT OF SOUTHWESTERN.

The board is looking to the higher good and long-term ministry of the school. We are looking beyond personalities and believe our action has been met with satisfaction by a somewhat "silent majority." Our desire is to minister to the vast unreached world. We have confidence that God will bless the seminary and will foster harmony within the convention which will bring honor and glory to our Lord Jesus Christ.

THE BEST IS YET TO COME!

Cordially,

Ralph Pulley

Lee Weaver

T. Bob Davis

Source: *Southwestern News*, May-June 1994, 8, 9. Reprint courtesy of Southwestern Baptist Theological Seminary.

15.3 Theological Education in Texas

At the first Executive Board meeting following the firing of Russell Dilday, the Board made a motion for a study into new options for theological training in Texas. Within a year, the Executive Board created a Theological Education Committee and prepared to invest considerable money in university-based schools of theology. Even before the Dilday firing two Texas Baptist schools began to discern a need for new theological schools. Baylor University had already created Truett Seminary and Hardin-Simmons had formed the Logsdon School of Theology. Though these schools were already in existence, the troubles at the SBC-owned Southwestern Seminary had led the BGCT to embrace these new university-based schools sooner than many had expected.

A. Moderate Baptists Study Alternative Seminary

Greensboro, N. C.—Baptist moderates infuriated by the firing of the president of Southwestern Baptist Theological Seminary in Fort Worth are studying ways to establish an alternative seminary in Texas, a moderate leader said yesterday.

"We would ultimately need a seminary that would accommodate some 2,000 students," said Davie Currie of San Angelo, who is in Greensboro for a convention of the Cooperative Baptist Fellowship, a moderate organization formed three years ago to protest conservative control of the Southern Baptist Convention.

The Rev. George Mason, pastor of Wilshire Baptist Church in Dallas and a leader of the moderates' fellowship, said last night that Texas Baptists are discussing alternative seminary direction.

"There's very little doubt in our minds that Southwestern is terminally ill as far as moderate Baptists are concerned," Mason said. "We're not saying there are no good professors there now, but the future is clear.

It will be turned into a training ground for fundamentalists."

Although Texas Baptists are discussing many options, Mike Bishop, vice president of communications at Baylor University, said he believes that his school's George Washington Truett Theological Seminary, which will open in the fall, can meet the demand.

Originally Truett was expected to have only 50 students. But after seminary President Russell Dilday was fired, the number has been increased to more than 100.

"We were making small plans for a small seminary," Bishop said. "But God was moving in other ways."

A record crowd of more than 7,000 is expected for the fellowship convention, which opened last night. The meeting continues through tomorrow.

Fallout over Dilday's firing reflects the ongoing conservative-moderate, theological-political conflict that began 14 years ago and is splintering the 15.5 million-member Southern Baptist Convention, the nation's largest Protestant group.

The fellowship, supported by some 1,200 congregations, has received a surge of support since Dilday was fired March 9 by conservative trustees. He was fired after he refused to retire, according to Rev. Cecil Sherman, executive director of the fellowship.

Dilday isn't expected to attend the convention.

Although it declares itself as merely a "fellowship" of moderates, many see it becoming a separate denomination because it has its own funding agency, mission board and support for certain seminaries. Last year, churches sent $11.2 million through the fellowship.

Establishing a large moderate seminary in Texas is a long-range plan, Currie said. An immediate concern is providing more money to allow expansion of the Truett seminary, he said.

"It depends on how big Baylor wants to get," Currie said. "Either Baylor will decide to become much larger or Texas Baptists could establish their own seminary with branches in Fort Worth-Dallas and San Antonio."

Source: Jim Jones, "Moderates Propose Alternative Seminary," *Fort Worth Star Telegram* 6 May 1994. Reprint courtesy of the *Fort Worth Star Telegram*.

B. Recommendation to the Executive Board

Whereas many different schools in Texas are providing seminary education and training for pastors, church staff members, and other vocational Christian workers, such as Southwestern Baptist Theological Seminary, Truett Seminary, Dallas Theological Seminary, and Criswell College for which the Baptist General Convention of Texas does not provide governance, and

Whereas the Baptist universities in Texas for which the Baptist General Convention of Texas does not provide governance are involved in such training on a pre-seminary level, and

Whereas there is a need for a coordination of the best use of energy and financial resources, and

Whereas the nature of leadership of Baptist churches in Texas will be fashioned in large part by these various institutions,

Be it therefore recommended

That the Executive Board of the Baptist General Convention of Texas authorize the President of the Baptist General Convention of Texas and the Chairman of the Executive Board of the Baptist General Convention of Texas to appoint a committee of at least 15 to study the possible need for additional opportunities for theological education in Texas, and

That this committee evaluate the current theological education programs to determine their adequacies to meet the need of Baptist churches and other denominational entities in Texas, and

That this committee bring its recommendations to the Executive Board in its September 13, 1994 meeting and, if approved, to the Baptist General Convention of Texas, meeting in Amarillo, October-31-November-1, 1994.

Source: *Minutes*, Executive Board of Baptist General Convention of Texas, 7 June 1994. Reprint courtesy of the Baptist General Convention of Texas.

C. Theological Education Study Committee: Final Report

The Theological Education Study Committee began its work in June of 1994. BGCT president, Jerold McBride, and Executive Board Chair, Leroy Fenton, appointed the committee following the June Executive Board meeting, in which the concept of the committee was approved.

The committee has studied the present state and direction of theological education in America, reviewed the theological education available in Texas for training BGCT ministers, and sought to understand the desires of Texas Baptists concerning theological education. Along the way the committee has visited with leadership from all of our BGCT-related universities, conducted a theological education survey among Texas Baptists, and spent many hours in prayerful discussion.

The Theological Education Study Committee has sought to know the leadership of God concerning the role of the BGCT in providing theological education for men and women called to Christian ministry. On six occasions the entire committee has met. Numerous sub-committee meetings have been conducted to facilitate the work.

The committee has determined that the BGCT should strengthen its investment, in the delivery of theological education for ministers. After considering a wide-array of theological education options, the committee is now ready to recommend a preferred course of action for the Convention. In short, the committee recommends the establishment of an ongoing Theological Education Committee (TEC) for the BGCT. The TEC will work to encourage and facilitate an informal state-wide network of theological education endeavors, relating to and building upon ministry education already being offered through BGCT related educational institutions. The TEC will seek ways to undergird and stimulate theological education for persons with varying educational backgrounds, and for both vocational and lay ministers.

The following materials set forth our committee's conclusions and recommendation are submitted to the BGCT Executive Board, September 12, 1995.

George H. Gaston, III, Chair	Kenneth Cooper	Derrel Renfrow
Ron Lyles, Vice-Chair	Barbara Floyd	George Ritche
Paul Armes	Marvin Griffin	Dan Rivera
Bill Blackburn	Travis Hart	David Roberts
Lee Brewer	DavidKirkpatrick	Jim Shamburger
Kelly Brown	Terry Land	John Cash Smith
Waddy Bullion	Dan Murray	
Ex-Officio:	Jerold McBride, BGCT President	
	Leroy Fenton, Executive Board Chair	

Proposal For Formation of
Theological Education Committee

The Changing Status of Theological Education for Ministers:

For most of the twentieth century ministers related to the Southern Baptist Convention have received the majority of their formal theological education through the seminaries operated by the Southern Baptist Convention. By virtue of an unwritten arrangement, the state Baptist universities supplied the undergraduate curriculum for ministers while the SBC seminaries provided graduate level training. Recent decades have witnessed a clear shift away from that accepted arrangement. With the rise of Baptist training schools for ministers such as the Mid-America Baptist Seminary, Criswell Bible College, and the Luther Rice Seminary, a movement to train Southern Baptist ministers outside the SBC seminaries gained momentum. At the same time an increasing number of Southern Baptist ministry students began attending non-Baptist schools such as Fuller Seminary, California Graduate School of Theology, Dallas Theological Seminary and others. Alongside those departments, Bible/Christianity/Religion Departments of the state Baptist universities began to offer more training for ministers at the undergraduate level. Now, some of the SBC seminaries are considering offering undergraduate baccalaureate degrees for their students.

Another recent development is the emergence of graduate seminary training through Baptist universities related to the various Baptist state conventions. Beeson Divinity School at Samford University in Alabama, Gardner-Webb University and Wake Forest University in North Carolina, and Mercer University in Georgia are illustrative of this reality. Other Baptist universities are reportedly in the formative stages of developing graduate theological education. Obviously, such an emphasis by the universities is not new. They have historically demonstrated concern for and involvement in preparing persons for Christian ministry. Ministry training programs developed early in Baptist history largely through the efforts of the universities. Free-standing Baptist seminaries, as we know them today, are to some degree an off-spring of the universities.

A perceived need for broader involvement in training ministers at the university level is multi-faceted. The realization that many university ministry students are not seeking seminary preparation, is but one part of the issue. A desire to make available the vast interdisciplinary educational resources of the universities for ministry training is also a motivating factor. In addition, some of the universities involved in seminary training are seeking ways to prepare persons for the ministry in a more time-efficient manner, such as, crediting a portion of a student's undergraduate work toward the graduate degree.

Not to be denied is the reality that theological controversy in Baptist life has given some impetus to ministry training within some of the state Baptist universities. They have felt the need to insure the availability of training which they perceive prepares ministers within the context of traditional Baptist principles and doctrines.

Interestingly, the expansion of training by the universities parallels a trend throughout theological education. A movement to bring ministry training closer to the places where students live and minister is rapidly emerging. A number of factors seem to be fueling the trend. For one thing, today's seminarians are older, with the average age being 32/33. Older ministry students in need of seminary training quite often are established in homes with families and bi-vocational careers. Many find it impractical to uproot their lives, leave their places of ministry and move to a seminary campus. As theological education moves ever closer to the potential student, the possibility of training more ministers is increased. Another reason for more localized training programs is the increased emphasis on mentoring and hands-on training. Such emphases are better accomplished with smaller schools located in areas where students have ample opportunity to be involved in the practice of ministry.

Finally, the need for providing access to theological education for ministers without college degrees, and for lay persons needing and desiring theological education, can be met more readily through expanding localized training efforts. Such efforts have been underway in Texas for some time. The Hispanic Baptist Seminary with its various off-campus programs, the ELD (Ethnic Leadership Development) program, and seminary extension centers are examples of these efforts.

In Texas, the resurgence of graduate theological education at BGCT related universities, Hardin-Simmons and Baylor, marks a return to an educational emphasis of earlier years. Robert A. Baker wrote concerning the development of theological education among Texas Baptists:

> In 1893, in Baylor at Waco, the university trustees established a Department of Bible with (B. H.) Carroll in charge. In 1901 a Department of Theology was created under Carroll as Dean. A curriculum leading to the Bachelor of Theology degree was offered.... Early in 1905 Carroll came to the conviction that God wanted him to establish a theological seminary in Texas. . . . In 1907 the Baptist General Convention of Texas approved resolutions from the trustees of Baylor authorizing the chartering of the seminary, and its removal to a new location. On March 14, 1908, the charter was secured, creating Southwestern Baptist Theological Seminary. In the summer of 1910 the seminary moved to Fort Worth . . . . During the first year in Fort Worth, there were 190 ministerial students and a number of men and women studying for special Christian service, representing four foreign countries and eleven states and territories. The report to the Convention in 1914 showed 208 students matriculated, of whom 128 were ministers and 5 were laymen; and 75 young women were in the training school. (*The Blossoming Desert: A Concise History of Texas Baptists,* 180–81)

In 1925, during days of financial instability for the BGCT, the ownership and operation of Southwestern Baptist Theological Seminary was transferred to the Southern Baptist Convention. From that time forward, formal training for Texas Baptist ministers was accomplished primarily through the SBC seminaries. In time, Dallas Theological Seminary began to train an increasing number of Texas Baptist students preparing for the ministry, as did Criswell College.

Across a number of decades now, the BGCT related universities have been expanding their training for ministers. The Departments of Bible/Christianity/Religion have focused an increasing portion of their curriculum on ministry preparation. Helping students to clarify their call to ministry and understand the nature of ministry is a tradition of longstanding in our Texas schools. Agreements that provide for a portion of the seminary-bound student's credit hours to be earned at the university level are in place with a number of our schools and several seminaries.

Master of Divinity degrees are now being offered at Baylor University, through the George W. Truett Theological Seminary, and Hardin-Simmons, through the Logsdon School of Theology. Clearly, ministry training in Texas is once again in full-bloom among our BGCT related universities.

A Statement of Need:

Believing that God has been leading in the developing status of theological education in general, and within the BGCT, the Theological Education Study Committee has sensed the need for the Convention to strengthen this work. An ongoing Theological Education Committee could help the Convention in the following ways:

(1) Provide an organized forum in which BGCT theological education program leaders may dialogue and further strengthen the correlation of their efforts.

(2) Provide an ongoing forum for BGCT theological education program leaders to dialogue with members and ministers of the BGCT churches concerning ministry issues and needs in the local churches.

(3) Serve as a channel for financial assistance to ministry students pursuing theological education with BGCT related institutions.

(4) Seek to strengthen and recommend expansion of theological education within the BGCT and BGCT related institutions.

(5) Stay abreast of new developments in theological education and formulate future proposals to assist the Convention in undergirding this ministry.

(6) Keep the Convention informed on the combined progress of the BGCT theological education endeavors and assist in maintaining strong ties between the Convention and the theological education programs.

(7) Work with the BGCT and the various theological education programs in identifying and implementing opportunities for students to participate in the Convention's missions and endeavors.

The work of the TEC should greatly strengthen the Convention's efforts to reach the mission field of Texas. As more churches are planted, an ever increasing number of trained ministers and laypersons will be needed to serve the churches of Texas. Undoubtedly, those trained through the Texas Baptist theological education efforts will serve not only the churches of Texas but also will make a vital contribution to world-wide mission efforts. As the TEC assists BGCT educational institutions in strengthening their theological education efforts, ministry students throughout Texas will be given greater opportunities to participate in training where they live and serve.

Source: *Final Report*, Theological Education Study Committee of the Baptist General Convention of Texas, 12 September 1995. Reprint courtesy of the Baptist General Convention of Texas.

D. Maston Chair of Ethics, Logsdon School of Theology

A long-held goal of the T. B. Maston Foundation has been reached: the official establishment in a seminary or school of theology of a T. B. Maston Chair of Christian Ethics.

The Foundation and the Logsdon School of Theology at Hardin-Simmons University have been working together toward this goal since early 1996 and made a joint announcement of the establishment of the Chair in June 18, 1997, issue of the *Baptist Standard*.

The goal is to appoint a professor to fill the chair by the fall of 1998, assuming that funding of $500,000 is secured by that time. The T. B. Maston Foundation has provided initial funding of $100,000 and will raise an additional $100,000. The university will raise $300,000. Future fund-raising efforts by the Foundation and the University will increase the corpus to $750,000 by the year 2000 when the chair will be considered fully funded. Hopefully, the corpus will reach $1,000,000 in the first years of the new century.

Foundation board Chairman Weston Ware, board members, Browning Ware, Earl Rose, Patsy Ayres, Jimmy Allen, Hal Haralson and David Morgan, Hardin-Simmons University President Dr. Lanny Hall and members of his staff, Drs. H. K. Neely, Vernon Davis, Craig Turner and Rick Styles have all been involved in negotiations and strategy preparations for the chair.

University representatives have noted the far-reaching potential for this Chair: "Several areas of the University currently include courses in ethics as part of their curriculum. Nursing, Business, Physical Therapy, Philosophy, and Theology all have emphases in ethics. In addition, a minor in Leadership studies is available for selected students. Ethics is a key curriculum emphasis for the program as well. The professor who holds the Maston Chair in Christian Ethics would thus play a strategic role in enabling students throughout the University to develop the ability to think clearly concerning ethical issues, to make responsible decisions when facing moral choices, and to apply the Christian faith in life in the arenas of personal relationships and professional responsibilities.

"The primary impact of the Maston Chair of Christian Ethics will be on the students who take classes. Beyond this it is anticipated that wide-ranging influence will be experienced through conferences and workshops conducted both on campus and in other settings, such as churches, businesses, schools and agencies. The Chair might also develop a program of publication, which could stimulate research and writing in the field of ethics and provide materials which could be helpful to Christians dealing with ethical issues."

The Foundation believes the establishment of this Chair of Christian Ethics at Logsdon will be widely approved and supported. Those who are seeking ways to make investments in spiritual endeavors will find this Chair a most significant answer to their quest. We believe they will want a part in the funding of the T. B. Maston Chair of Christian Ethics endowment.

All of us who have been touched by Dr. Maston's life and teachings should be challenged to do our part in the establishment of this chair. Please begin by making plans for your significant participation in the immediate fund-raising effort. You should consider the possibility of including the T. B. Maston Chair of Christian Ethics in your will or other estate planning.

Source: *Abidingly Relevant: Newsletter of the T. B. Maston Foundation*, September 1997, 3.

15.4 Preserving Baptist Distinctives

Following the change of leadership in the Southern Baptist Convention in 1979, Texas Baptists began to show concern that certain traditional Baptist distinctives were in danger. The Fundamentalists and the Moderates held divergent views on the separation of church and state, sole competency, the priesthood of the believer, the role of women in the church, and pastoral leadership. At the 1994 BGCT, John F. Baugh was instructed to make available to Texas Baptists materials concerning traditional Baptist distinctives. Following the presentation of these materials, it became apparent that the two groups were even more diametrically opposed than anyone could have imagined. A prime example of the fundamentalist position concerning the separation of church and state may be seen in the teachings of W. A. Criswell. The moderate Baptist perspective is presented by the editors and contributors of the *Texas Baptists Committed* periodical.

A. Criswell Explains How to be a Good Pastor

Senior pastor among Southern Baptists W. A. Criswell offered his ideas on how to be a good pastor—and noted a couple of things he has changed his mind over—in a visit with about 30 pastors and guests at East Heights Church in Tupelo, Miss.

Beginning several of his statements with, "You may not agree with me but . . ." Criswell spoke for more than two hours.

"The man of God who is the pastor of the church is the ruler," he said, noting that three times in the New Testament Book of Hebrews the Bible says to obey those who have rule over you. "They can quarrel with God over that, not me," he said.

He said when he went to be pastor of First Church, Dallas, nearly 50 years ago, he told church leaders, "The pulpit is mine and I preach what God puts on my mind, and the staff is mine and I run that church." He added, "Remember, this is my idea of the pastoral role."

Criswell noted, "If you have a dynamic pastor guiding the destiny of that church, you'll have a godly church." If a church has "a wimp" who lets others dictate what he can preach, it will be "a slovenly and sorry and poor church," he said.

The size of a church depends on the size of the staff, Criswell said. "You can only put your arms around so many people," he said, comparing the church to a tree. In the middle is the pastor and his family. "You don't grow at the center, you grow at the periphery." He said at the height of the First Church growth the church had a paid staff of 344.

"The hardest thing in the world is finding consecrated, dedicated people (to put) on staff," he added.

A church needs choirs "plural," Criswell said. "Be sensitive to the comfort of the people and don't be afraid to change." When he was a country preacher, they would have month-long revival services in a tabernacle by the church. Now, he said, he doesn't attempt to have revivals. One can do the work through the Sunday School, visitation and bringing the lost to church, he said. Concerning broadcasting worship services, he said to do it if possible.

No matter how much money is given to the Lottie Moon Christmas Offering for foreign missions, Criswell commented, "We will never send out enough missionaries."

He said to enlist every family member at budget time. Everyone fills out a pledge card, he said. "Pin it on the diaper" of the baby. And allow the people to designate through the church to whatever worthy causes they like, he said, explaining it will keep them giving and, after a time, likely they'll stop designating and continue giving.

The church ought to encompass the entire life of the family, Criswell said. He reorganized First Church in Dallas, making workers responsible not just for youth Sunday School or discipleship training, "but responsible for them seven days a week."

He suggested starting an academy if a church can manage it so they can teach creation and have chapel services. He said it would be wonderful if a church could have drama schools and camps. "If I had been able to get the deacons to go along, we'd have had a football field and a baseball diamond and been the most inclusive of all organizations." He said the church started a Bible college and named it, against his will, Criswell College.

Besides dropping revival services, Criswell talked of the changes in the way he does things. For instance, he said at one time he would not perform weddings for divorced persons. Reading an article in a secular magazine initiated his change, he said. It dealt with other types of adultery. He said he knew a woman who came to church black and blue. "All kind of things destroy the family. . . . Thousands are better off when they break it up." He said it is a personal conviction that, after counseling, he will marry divorced persons.

He said his understanding concerning suicide has changed. "I have talked to pastors who think (suicides) are automatically damned in hell fire. I came to a heavenly understanding and explanation," he said, noting a person can be sick in the mind just as in the body. "Does God damn because we're sick?" he asked. Instead, he said he asks God's blessing of remembrance and compassionate memory.

OTHER ADVICE:

Finances: "You ought to live within that income."

Counseling: "Don't you talk to a woman about the intimacies of her life."

Baptism: "Dr. Truett (his predecessor at Dallas, George W. Truett) slam-dunked people. But Baptism is a burial service and I never saw anybody fling their dead into the ground." Instead, he said to do it gently and make a witness of the act. . . . "If one is to be baptized, talk to (witness to) the whole family."

Lord's Supper: "The pastor ought to present the elements with glorious acclaim."

Funerals: Make them personal. Have the family write out a summary of their lives.

The denomination: "The Cooperative Program was born in my lifetime. That does not mean you cannot support missionaries of your love and choice. We have 31 chapels. We tried to get those ethnic groups to our church but they wouldn't come. We're organizing the 32nd one (soon)."

Other preachers' material: He said he thought it was wrong to use another's experience but realized that his sermons would get thin if he did not do that. So he put references to preaching volumes in his Bible's margins "and my sermons got richer and richer and richer. If you have said anything that magnifies the Lord, I wish you would send it to me."

Baptist hymnal: "Two-thirds of those songs will never be sung. These tunes don't bless my heart."

The SBC: "We have won our attempt to turn the SBC back to the Bible, to its conservative nature. . . . The dichotomies lie in our state conventions. In Texas the conservatives tried to take over. But the convention is entirely in the hands of Baylor University. . . . You've got the same thing in this state (Mississippi). Practically all the states are in the hands of the liberals. God help us."

Affirming the pastoral preaching role, Criswell reiterated, "You're going to stand up there and call them out of the judgement that faces every soul. You'll call them out of Sodom and Gomorrah."

Source: Tim Nicholas, "Criswell Explains How to Be a Good Pastor," *Baptist Standard*, 12 January 1994, 11. Reprint courtesy of the *Baptist Standard*.

B. Dr. Criswell Spoke Too Quickly

I can still remember the day as if it were yesterday. On a white-hot September afternoon in 1955, I stepped off the KATY Railroad passenger car in Waco, Texas, to begin my freshman year at Baylor University. Completely enchanted with the school, with Texas and with the beckoning life before me, I moved from day to day as in a dream land.

One of my new friends, John Trueblood of Missouri, a sophomore transfer student, came bursting into my room at Mrs. Russell's rooming house right after church that first Sunday morning and said, "Let's go to First Baptist Church, Dallas, tonight, to hear Dr. Criswell!"

"How far away is Dallas?" I asked.

"Oh, about ninety miles," John replied, not even blinking.

"Ninety miles for Sunday night church?"

"Yeah, let's do it." And away we went, four or five of us in John's beige, dusty, vintage Plymouth.

Those twenty-nine years ago Dallas was just beginning to shake itself before bursting into the boom era of the fifties. Having grown up in Atlanta, the dozen tall buildings of the city did not impress me, but First Baptist Church did. The choir loft was full. The grand organ soared. Dr. W. A. Criswell, just back from a trip abroad, was in fine form. After a moving choral rendition of "When the Roll is Called Up Yonder," complete with a trio of Aida trumpets, the pastor preached a stirring sermon, the content of which I have forgotten but the flavor of which remains with me yet. Thereafter, as often as possible, I attended First Baptist Church—perhaps six or seven times in the last twenty-five years.

Though I have appreciated Dr. Criswell as a preacher and have always gained from worshiping in his church, I have not always agreed with him when he has spoken politically. As a seminarian and then as a pastor, I complained about the good pastor's political stands, but did nothing more than grumble. However, Dr. Criswell has really punched the wrong button this time.

During an interview on CBS television recently, the reporter asked Dr. Criswell what he thought of the idea of church/state separation. The Texas pastor shot right back, "I believe this notion of separation of church and state was the figment of some infidel's imagination."

Whoa, Dr. Criswell! Hold your rampaging Texas horses for just a cotton-pickin' moment, please, sir. Do you really mean that? Surely not.

For nearly two hundred years, Americans of every possible political and theological persuasion have held up the church-state separation principle as the greatest expression of and insurance for religious liberty. Dr. Criswell's own Texas colleague, Dr. J. M. Dawson, pastor, educator, and Baptist statesman, committed his life to the principle. He was no infidel. John Leland, Isaac Backus, Presidents Jefferson, Madison, Jackson, Buchanan, Grant, Garfield, Theodore Roosevelt, Kennedy and Carter all lauded the separation of church and state. Infidels? Senator Sam Ervin of North Carolina said ". . .there should be no official relationship of any character between government and any church or many churches, or all churches . . ." Infidel?

Perhaps Dr. Criswell was a bit hasty in his declaration. Coming on the heels of the Republican National Convention in Dallas, in which he participated, with the questionable mixing of religion into partisan politics, Dr. Criswell might have overreacted to the reporter's question. Let's hope so. I would hate to think that one of the nation's best known pastors would trash one of this nation's most treasured principles.

But Dr. Criswell is not alone in questioning, even ridiculing the separation of church and state. Other preachers and politicians, especially those who have jumped on Mr. Reagan's holy-rolling bandwagon, seem uncomfortably quick to toss aside the very tenet that has allowed this country's religious community to flourish as nowhere else on the earth.

Why this furious effort at rewriting? Why do respected religious leaders like Dr. Criswell jump to junk our liberties? One reason is that right now it is the "fad" among some historians and theologians to say "The Constitution does not teach separation. All it says is that government cannot establish a state church." And fads have a way of attracting adherents.

My answer to the faddists is, "How can we avoid establishing a religion if we abolish the separationist wall?"

More to the point, and more threatening is the drive by many of the revisionist, anti-separationists to enforce cultural, political and religious uniformity on our patch-work society. Apparently these surgeons of American history believe religion mandated, underwritten and enforced by the state can advance their monolithic conformity. Sure, the myriad of groups and ideologies are hard to deal with, but that's just who we are these days. Rather than attempt to squeeze us into one mold, let's try to find better ways for the creative energies of the various groups to freely bless and enrich the entire body politic.

Rather than denigrating the separation of church and state, let us celebrate it as a cherished reality of American life.

Please, Dr. Criswell, don't be so quick to toss away our liberties in the name of religion.

Source: Robert L. Maddox, "Dr. Criswell Spoke Too Quickly," *Church and State*, 37:23, October 1984. Reprint courtesy of *Church and State*.

C. What is Texas Baptists Committed?

The roots of the organization, Texas Baptists Committed (TBC), go back to 1845 and the birth of the Southern Baptist Convention. To understand TBC, you need to understand history.

The Southern Baptist Convention was formed in 1845 around a common purpose and a group of guiding principles. The various Baptist churches that came together in forming the SBC were very diverse. They united around the purpose of missions.

PURPOSE

The SBC Constitution of 1845 defines the purpose as follows:

"It is the purpose of the Convention to provide a general organization for Baptists in the United States and its territories for promotion of Christian missions at home and abroad and any other objects such as

Christian education, benevolent enterprises, and social services which it may deem proper and advisable for the furtherance of the Kingdom of God."

The charter, approved, December 27th, 1845, reads, "said corporation being created for the purpose of eliciting, combining, and directing the energies of the Baptist denomination of Christians, for the propagation of the gospel . . ."

The purpose of the founders of the convention was clear then and is clear now, "the propagation of the gospel . . . the promotion of Christian missions at home and abroad . . ."

The purpose revolved around the belief that every person on earth needed to believe or have the opportunity to believe in "Jesus Christ as Lord." While sharing Jesus was the responsibility of every believer and every local congregation, it was also important to spread the gospel through larger voluntary organizations.

GUIDING PRINCIPLES

The guiding principles of the SBC were based on limited authority, radical freedom and voluntary cooperation.

Limited Authority: The SBC Constitution states the limited authority of the SBC. "While independent and sovereign in its own sphere, the Convention does not claim and will never attempt to exercise any authority over any other Baptist body, whether church, auxiliary organizations, associations, or conventions."

Radical Freedom: Baptists were adamant about freedom. No convention had authority over a local church. There was no pope, no cardinals, no bishops, and hierarchical ecclesiology.

The commitment to freedom shaped the guiding principles. These principles are:

—the authority of Scripture. Baptists have no creeds. Scripture is the final authority for the individual and the local church.

—the priesthood of all believers. Each believer has the right and responsibility of being a priest. They are to interpret scripture for themselves and act as priests to each other.

—the autonomy of the local church. Each local congregation is free to choose its ministers, worship as it feels comfortable, and ordain whomever it believes is called of God to ministry. The church is a democracy where each member has equal rights, privileges and responsibilities. No other Baptist organization has authority over the local congregation.

—the separation of church and state/religious liberty. Here Baptists were the most radical. Their roots were in the Separatist movement in England and Holland. Baptists did not simply believe in religious toleration, but in religious liberty. No person, civil government, or religious system has the right to come between God and human beings. All religions, as well as the freedom to believe in no religion or not to worship, are equal before the law.

Undergirding these principles is the most distinctive Baptist belief, "the competency of the soul in religion." Soul competency excludes all human interference in religion such as episcopacy, infant baptism, religious proxy, and governmental authority in religion. Religion is a personal matter between the soul and God!

Voluntary Cooperation: Everything Southern Baptists did together was to be done on the basis of voluntary cooperation. Local churches make all the decisions. They choose to join associations, state conventions, or national conventions. They choose how much money to give to cooperative mission efforts. Coercion or authority from top down was not to exist.

Source: *Texas Baptists Committed*, June/July 1995, 1. Reprint courtesy of *Texas Baptists Committed*.

D. Distinctives Group Passes Reins

Founding members of the Baptist General Convention of Texas Baptist Distinctives Committee completed their three-year tenure last week and turned the reins over to a permanent continuing committee authorized by the BGCT Executive Board.

Texas Baptists created the committee in 1994.

Messengers to the BGCT annual meeting that year approved a motion calling for "materials for Texas Baptists on traditional Baptist distinctives and beliefs such as the authority of the scripture, the autonomy of the local church, Baptist polity and other beliefs, doctrines and tenets expressed in the unaltered Baptist Faith and Message Statement of 1963, and to maintain information on positions taken by other Baptist groups on these historic Baptist doctrines and beliefs."

Founding members of the committee, some of whom will continue on the permanent committee, include Amelia Bishop, Austin; Floyd Bradley, Plainview; Pat Carter, Kingwood; Bennie Carver, Wimberley; Betsy Goss, San Angelo; Brian Harbour, Richardson; Rolando Lopez, San Antonio; Glenn Majors, Dallas; Bill Pitts, Waco; Bruce Prescott, Houston; James Shields, Abilene; Paula Whitley, Gainesville; and Audrey Wimpee, Bryan.

Harbour, pastor of First Church in Richardson, was the first chairman of the committee. Members noted a number of reasons why the committee was needed. They included the huge influx of people into Texas Baptist churches with no Baptist background; the widespread lack of knowledge of Baptist polity, distinctives and history among younger Baptists; and a heritage worth preserving and enhancing.

The committee identified 13 concepts that are vital to the Baptist heritage:

- Priesthood of believers.
- Church-state separation.
- Believers' baptism.
- Authority of the Bible.
- Local-church autonomy.
- Salvation by Grace.
- Security of the believer.
- Cooperation.
- Soul competency.
- Believers' church.
- The Great Commission.
- Democratic church government.
- Symbolic understanding of ordinances.

BGCT Executive Director, William M. Pinson, Jr., praised the committee for its extensive work. "The initial committee under the very able leadership of Brian Harbour impacted Texas Baptists with excellent information and laid the plans to literally flood our Baptist family in Texas with inspiration and information about Baptists," he said.

"Always positive, never negative about other Christian groups, they nevertheless emphasized the beliefs and practices of Baptists which have made a difference not only in the lives of individuals but also in the world. We owe the initial committee much for their hard work and insightful plans and look forward to all that the permanent committee will accomplish to the advancement of our Lord's kingdom and to the glory of God."

The committee's accomplishments include publishing sermon helps on Baptist distinctives, topics to *Leadership* magazine, naming a speakers' bureau on Baptist distinctives, planning and staffing a booth at the annual state convention, providing a Baptist distinctive bibliography, supplying articles to the *Baptist Standard*, reprinting and distributing Baptist distinctive documents and encouraging youth writing and speaking contests on Baptist distinctive topics.

The goal of the committee's recommendations "must be nothing less than renewal of Baptist life in Texas and rededication to the principles and ideals that have shaped us," the committee said.

New members of the committee are Taylor Armstrong, Dallas; Robert Garcia, San Antonio; Glen Hilburn, Waco; Leon McBeth, Fort Worth; Ella Prichard, Corpus Christi; Wilma Reed, Cleburne; and Presnall Wood, Dallas.

Source: Dan Martin, "Enrollment in Texas Baptist Schools Tops 31,000," Baptist *Standard*, 22 October 1997, 3. Reprint courtesy of the *Baptist Standard*.

15.5 Texas Baptist Cooperative Program

The lifeblood of the Southern Baptist Convention and the Baptist General Convention of Texas is the Cooperative Program. From the birth of the Cooperative Program in 1925 until 1978, both designated and undesignated funds were counted as Cooperative Program contributions by the SBC. The BGCT and several other state conventions, however, continued to count undesignated gifts in their annual Cooperative Program receipts. In 1994, at the annual convention at Amarillo, the BGCT created the Texas Baptist Cooperative Program. This new program allowed churches to give to the SBC, Cooperative Baptist Fellowship, State Missions, the local church, either all or only some of these entities. The Amarillo resolution also slightly lowered the percentage of Cooperative Program money that was sent to Nashville. This was a small percentage, but a large amount of money remained in Texas for local ministries. A large minority of Texas Baptists were against this new division fearing this plan would further fragment an already fragmenting convention. Despite this fear, the Texas Baptist Cooperative Program has proven successful.

A. Cooperative Program Task Force, 1992

The meeting opened with prayer by Jim Herrington of Houston. Following the prayer, chairman Floyd Bradley reported on the actions of the last meeting which the Task Force had on August 14, 1990. He indicated that soon after the meeting of the Task Force, Baylor University announced its charter change and that action made heavy demands on Dr. Pinson and the staff in regard to convention life. The Task Force has not met for two years.

Chairman Bradley reviewed what had been done at the last meeting and what had been accomplished after the meeting. He indicated that the Task Force approved in principle the report regarding the Cooperative Program which appeared in the *Baptist Standard* on September 19, 1990. He also indicated that several questions and answers appeared in the same issue of the *Baptist Standard*. A copy of that report and the questions and answers are available for Task Force members in their packets.

Bradley further reported that at the meeting on August 14, 1990, the Task Force voted to approve a pilot project utilizing the plan that Stan Madden of Baylor University had developed regarding advocates or champions for the Cooperative Program in local churches.

Following the review of minutes, Dr. Pinson was asked to make comments. He cited the developments in Cooperative Program promotion and the commitment of churches to continue giving cooperatively. He spoke about the trends in Southern Baptist life and how that Texas was putting forth a major effort to increase giving through the Cooperative Program. He indicated that we now have a full time staff person in Bill Cathey, who is leading this work. Texas is doing more than any other state convention in Cooperative Program education and promotion. He indicated that Roger Hall could speak with specifics about how churches are utilizing opportunities given them by the actions of the Executive Board and Administrative Committee.

Roger Hall then reported on what is being done in 1992 with regard to Cooperative Program giving. He indicated that approximately 91% of the budget has been given through traditional Cooperative Program by the end of August, 1992. By adding "Texas Causes" receipts to this amount, the percentage is over 94% of the total budget. He spoke about the actions of the Administrative Committee and Executive Board to allow churches to exclude up to five line items in the budget and still count their contributions as Cooperative Program. He indicated that 138 Texas Baptist churches are utilizing the exclusion policy. The total amount being excluded and reallocated to other line items is approximately $75,000.

Roger Hall also indicated that approximately 90 churches are giving to "Texas Causes" only. These contributions are handled in the Texas budget as though they were Cooperative Program contributions, although they are listed as designated because they exclude SBC allocations. Less than 2% of our churches are excluding or redirecting their funds. Hall continued by stating that Texas convention related churches are continuing to show strong support for the traditional Cooperative Program and others are maintaining strong records of contributions through alternative methods of giving.

The Task Force was given opportunity to ask questions and make comments about the handling and reporting of funds.

Ed Schmeltekopf was asked to report on the pilot project utilizing the advocacy plan. Schmeltekopf reported that three associations in Texas were identified as associations where a pilot project would be tried— Fannin Association, Grayson Association, and Waco Association. He also indicated that Black congregations in the Union Baptist Association were also included in a pilot project. Fannin and Grayson Associations had approximately 20–25% of their churches involved in the pilot project while Waco Association had approximately 30–35% of its churches involved. The training sessions, led by Stan Madden, were good opportunities for Cooperative Program education and a number of "advocates" or champions were trained. Mention was made of the fact that it is too early to obtain information regarding the result of these efforts to increase Cooperative Program giving. Since we do not have records of the 1991–1992 Cooperative Program contributions of the churches who are utilizing the advocacy plan, no final evaluation is possible.

Stan Madden was asked to report on the training sessions and his observations regarding the advocacy plan. He indicated that Texas along with other state conventions, such as Tennessee, Mississippi, and Maryland, were contributing to a improved program of Cooperative Program growth and increases from the churches. Discussion followed regarding the developments of the advocacy plan and the entire Task Force participated in the discussion.

Bill Cathey was introduced by Ed Schmeltekopf as the new Director of Cooperative Program Promotion. He then led the group to examine an adjusted (or altered) usage of Stan Madden's plan. The basic concept developed by Stan Madden regarding the use of champions or advocates in local churches is being retained in the adjusted plan. Bill Cathey walked through the new plan called "Cooperative Program Representatives, Life Support System for Missions" (copy attached to minutes). Following the explanation of the adjusted program, opportunity was given for discussion. The discussion centered around utilizing church elected officers as representatives for the Cooperative Program. The group agreed that having both elected officers of the church and additional persons recruited by the pastor who would be mission advocates or champions, would provide significant lay leadership in the churches to make an impact on budget decisions regarding the percentage of giving through the Cooperative Program. There was strong affirmation given to Cathey's adjusted plan.

Mr. Cathey showed the new film, "The Magnitude of Cooperative Giving." Following the film, Mr. Cathey led the group to review all materials that are being utilized in Cooperative Program promotion and education. Time was then given for discussion and questions. One suggestion was that the video should be sent to youth directors to utilize with young people. This is in addition to BSU directors across the state. Another suggestion was made to consider reusing the four *Baptist Standard* pages of the report of the Task Force in 1990 and the questions and answers sheets. Consideration will be given by Mr. Cathey to utilizing again this good information.

The group agreed with the chairman's idea that the Task Force had completed its work. Expressions of gratitude for the work of the Task Force were given. The Task Force members were encouraged to continue to send ideas and suggestions to Mr. Cathey for utilization in his efforts to enhance Cooperative Program promotion.

The meeting was closed with prayer and the group shared lunch together.

Source: *Minutes*, Cooperative Program Task Force, 16 September 1992. Reprint courtesy of the Baptist General Convention of Texas.

B. Recommendations for the Texas Cooperative Program

1. That the Baptist General Convention of Texas continue to stress its constitutional objective which is "to awaken and stimulate among the churches the greatest possible activity in evangelism, missions, Christian education and benevolent work and enterprises; to cultivate a closer cooperation among the churches and promote harmony of feeling and concert of action in advancing all the interests of the Redeemer's Kingdom." (Article II, Baptist General Convention of Texas Constitution);

2. That the Baptist General Convention of Texas continue to assist all its affiliated churches in supporting Christian missions in Texas and throughout the world. "The Cooperative Program shall be the chief means through which this body shall support its missionary endeavors." (Article IV, Section 1, Baptist General Convention of Texas Constitution) The Cooperative Program will continue to be a church-directed program operated for the churches by the Baptist General Convention of Texas. In regard to financial matters, all churches giving to the Texas Cooperative Program budget shall be considered cooperating churches by the Baptist General Convention of Texas.

3. That the Baptist General Convention of Texas will recognize and distribute as Texas Cooperative Program contributions, funds from the churches given in any or all of the following ways:

(1) Gifts to the adopted budget of the Baptist General Convention of Texas (Texas missions and ministries) and the adopted budget of the Southern Baptist Convention according to the annually adopted percentage divisions between the two.

(2) Gifts to the adopted budget of the Baptist General Convention of Texas (Texas missions and ministries); and

Note: The Baptist General Convention of Texas will continue to recognize the decision of a church to delete up to five line items in the Baptist General Convention of Texas budget and the Southern Baptist Convention budget and still count the contributions as Cooperative Program.

(3) Gifts to the adopted budget of the Baptist General Convention of Texas and to other world-wide Baptist missions and ministries. These may include the Southern Baptist Convention, any agency of the Southern Baptist Convention, Woman's Missionary Union, the Cooperative Baptist Fellowship, the Baptist World Alliance and other missions and ministries within the Baptist family.

Note: It is understood that "other worldwide missions and ministries within the Baptist family" include (a) broad-based organizations which consider themselves Southern Baptist and which engage in or support missions, ministries or theological education, (b) items in the budget of the Baptist General Convention of Texas or the Southern Baptist Convention and not to include the local church, association or single issue programs, projects or ministries. Any additional entities may be added through the normal process of recommendation by the Administrative Committee and approved by the Executive Board.

4. That the Baptist General Convention of Texas continue to disburse gifts for special mission offerings and other contributions for Baptist causes by the churches.

5. That the Baptist General Convention of Texas budget continue to be adopted by the messengers from the churches attending the

annual meeting of the Baptist General Convention of Texas. The budget recommendation will include:

(1) The distribution of Cooperative Program contributions to the ministries supported by the Baptist General Convention of Texas and

(2) The percentage division of Cooperative Program contributions between the Baptist General Convention of Texas budget ministries and worldwide Baptist missions and ministries.

Note: This percentage division, as approved by the Baptist General Convention of Texas in its annual session will be the percentage division that applies to Recommendation 3 (1). While this percentage division is encouraged for use by churches electing recommendations 3 (3), it is not a required percentage.

6. That all contributions made by the churches through the Baptist General Convention of Texas will be recognized by appropriate reporting.

VI. UNDERSTANDING

In making the foregoing recommendations, it is the Committee's understanding that the Baptist General Convention of Texas staff will continue to provide:

1. Information about the adopted Baptist General Convention of Texas budget and information needed or requested by the churches about worldwide Baptist missions and ministries to assist them in determining their financial support;

2. Remittance forms annually to all the churches, so that Cooperative Program funds may be distributed as directed by the churches with churches being encouraged to limit changes to once a year;

3. Information to The Baptist Standard for reporting church missions gifts so as to reflect the church's purpose for their gifts;

4. Information about special missions offerings which will retain their identity;

5. Information about the policy of the Baptist General Convention of Texas regarding the church staff annuity/protection plan, since to receive matching funds for the ministerial protection plan support, the church must give at least a comparable amount to the Texas Baptist Cooperative Program budget.

Source: *Book of Reports*, Baptist General Convention of Texas, 1994, 148–49. Reprint courtesy of the Baptist General Convention of Texas.

15.6 Texas 2000

Under the able leadership of Bill Pinson, the BGCT began its greatest evangelistic campaign in its storied history in January 1996. Known as Texas 2000, the goal of the campaign was for everyone in the state to hear and have opportunity to respond to the gospel of Jesus Christ by the year 2000. Despite the distractions surrounding the new Baylor University regent system and the firing of Russell Dilday, Pinson kept the churches in the forefront and all of Texas was mobilized to meet the Texas 2000 endeavor.

A. Strategy Council Report

PREFACE

During the meeting of the Executive Board on September 15, 1992, Executive Director Bill Pinson requested that the Board authorize him, in conjunction with the President of the Convention and the Chairman of the Board, to appoint a Strategy Council whose responsibility would be to develop a strategic plan for Texas Baptists from 1995-2000. Dr. Pinson stated that in a rapidly changing state with a growing population and many needs, Texas Baptists must have a vision for what can be done from now until the end of this century to effectively carry out the Great Commission given to us by the Lord Jesus Christ.

1. APPROACH

Seventy-four persons were selected to serve on the Strategy Council. The 74 persons include a wide range of Texas Baptists. The process of selecting the Council began with an effort to enlist a man and a woman from each of the 15 geographical zones in Texas. From that point the leaders began selecting persons from all segments of Texas

Baptist life. D. L. Lowrie was appointed as chair of the Strategy Council.

A different concept was utilized by the Strategy Council in this work. The Council agreed not to become involved in setting numerical goals for the Convention or for affiliated churches, associations and institutions. Detailed annual planning will be done by the Executive Board staff, by associations and by institutions. The concept or approach of the Strategy Council has been to work on the development of a statement of purpose, priorities, values and vision. These ingredients will become the unifying force around which specific plans, goals and objectives will be developed by these different entities.

2. PROCESS

The Strategy Council met four times. A Steering Committee of nine persons from the Strategy Council was appointed to care for much of the detail for the Council. The Steering Committee met several times in addition to meetings of the Council and spent many hours in prayer, thought and planning to support the Strategy Council in its efforts. Following final adoption by the Council, the plan is hereby presented to the Executive Board for approval.

The Strategy Council's report focused on a time period that has great significance—the end of the century and the beginning of the third millennium of Christian history. The time frame of 1995 through 2000 calls for intensive efforts by Baptists in Texas to reach the state for Christ.

Everything that Texas Baptists do together cannot become convention-wide priorities for this five year time frame. The priorities which eventually rose to the top were developed through a process of utilizing the staff of the Executive Board and the persons of the Strategy Council. Every person had equal opportunity for input; a process was utilized to eliminate duplication and focus on what needs to be of highest priority during this five-year period.

The Strategy Council determined to develop a purpose statement, a limited number of priorities, a set of values and a vision that would guide Texas Baptists. The entire Strategy Council engaged in prayer repeatedly as God's direction was sought. The priorities which were finally agreed upon are the priorities the Council believes Texas Baptists must have as the year 2000 draws near.

The Great Commission is the biblical basis for this plan. Its major focus is "Make Disciples!" The Council was open to new directions and insights from the Holy Spirit. Considerable debate and dialogue took place in the process as a strategy was developed.

3. IMPLEMENTATION

After the Executive Board approves a plan for 1995–2000, each entity of the Baptist General Convention of Texas will be encouraged to develop its own statement of purpose and its vision in light of Convention approved purpose, priorities, values and vision. Specific goals and action plans will be developed by the different departments of work of the Executive Board. It is our desire that Baptist institutions, associations, and churches will evaluate their unique opportunities to be a part of Texas by 2000 and set specific goals and action plans to implement their involvement. The priorities that are being presented will be accomplished only by prayerful efforts of churches, associations of churches and Baptist institutions throughout Texas.

INTRODUCTION

The Baptist General Convention of Texas does not exist for itself, but rather it exists for the churches. The Lord of the churches made them aware of their interdependence and their need for cooperation in carrying out His Great Commission. The awareness prompted the churches to organize the Baptist General Convention of Texas and its institutions. Whenever a denomination forgets this fact about itself, it can do great harm to the churches.

It is wise for the Convention to restate its purpose periodically. It is helpful for the Convention to re-evaluate its priorities, to reaffirm its values, and renew its vision.

We have sought to do this. Our prayerful search compelled us to reaffirm our commitment to the Great Commission that the Lord Jesus Christ gave the churches, "Therefore go and make disciples of all nations, baptizing them in the name of the Father and the Son and of the Holy Spirit, and teaching them to obey everything I have commanded to you. And surely I am with you always, to the very end of the age" (NIV). Surely, this commission gives us the substance from which we will find our purpose, priorities and vision. It seemed good to the Holy Spirit and to us that set these forth in the brief paragraphs that follow. We invite all Texas Baptists to join us in a fresh commitment to this vision.

PURPOSE STATEMENT
BAPTIST GENERAL CONVENTION OF TEXAS

The Baptist General Convention of Texas exists to encourage and assist churches, associations of churches, institutions, and other Baptist entities in fulfilling the Great Commission of the Lord Jesus Christ.

- **"Baptist General Convention of Texas"** The Baptist General Convention of Texas is a chartered non-profit religious corporation. Its meetings are composed of members ("messengers") elected by cooperating Texas Baptist churches. They meet under their Constitution and Bylaws and the Texas Non-Profit Corporation Act to conduct the business of the Convention which includes providing organizations through which Texas Baptists can fulfill their purpose.

- **"encourage" and "assist"** The BGCT exists for the churches and will be aware of and sensitive to their needs and will respond with affirmation and resources. One means of assistance is to provide a way churches can cooperate to do more together than they can separately in carrying out the Great Commission.

- **"churches"** A Baptist church is an autonomous, local congregation of baptized believers which exists to fulfill the Great Commission.

- **"associations of churches"** The Convention carries out its purpose in Christian education, benevolence and missions through institutions and other entities. There are institutions such as educational institutions, healthcare systems, child care homes, retirement and nursing homes, a foundation and a state paper. In its Great Commission effort the Convention also relates to other entities such as missions, ethnic and various other organizations.

- **"the Great Commission"** The Lord Jesus Christ gave a mandate to all His followers to make disciples of persons throughout the world, baptizing, teaching, developing and equipping them for service and ministry in His name to the glory of God and by the power of the Holy Spirit.

Source: *Report*, Strategy Council, 8 March 1994. Reprint courtesy of the Baptist General Convention of Texas.

B. Evangelism Conference Spotlights Texas 2000

Texas Baptists' Texas 2000 strategy plan captured the spotlight at their 1996 Evangelism Conference last week in Fort Worth, as more than 10,000 people joined hearts and hands in the vision to reach 9 million unchurched Texans with the gospel by the end of the decade.

"The goal of Texas 2000 is humanly impossible," admitted William M. Pinson Jr., executive director of the Baptist General Convention of Texas.

Once known as the "buckle of the Bible Belt," Texas has become a mission field, Pinson said. With people coming from nearly every nation on the earth, Texas rapidly is becoming a secular state with the numbers of unchurched people growing faster than churches are reaching them, he added.

Pinson recalled, however, that the convention's Strategy Committee—74 men and women who drew up the plans and goals for Texas 2000—"wept as they realized God could do what we could not do."

Strategy Committee Chairman D. L. Lowrie, one of the opening speakers at the conference, asked, "How do we get the grace of God to these millions?"

"As Texas Baptists go across the state empowered by prayer, the Spirit of God will take the word of God, and there'll be sounds of resurrection all across this state," said Lowrie, pastor of First Church in Lubbock.

For more than 50 years, the Evangelism Conference, which features some of the world's best-known theologians, preachers and singers, has helped light the fires that helped the Texas Baptist convention grow from 873,000 members in 1945 to more than 2.6 million a half-century later.

World-renowned evangelist Billy Graham has preached at the conference several times across the years, but last week it was the time for his daughter Anne Graham Lotz.

Recalling the experiences of the prophet Isaiah, who saw a vision of Christ following the death of Jewish King Uzziah, Lotz said: "Sometimes we have to be shaken up before we look up and see who Jesus is. When was the last time you saw yourself and your service in the light of the majesty of Jesus Christ?"

Christians who have come to the cross of Christ for salvation also need to turn to Christ's sacrifice for sanctification, or spiritual cleansing, Lotz said.

"Before we can present the cross to Texas, perhaps you and I need to return and experience the cross ourselves in a deep, fresh new way," she explained.

Picking up the challenge, pastors Jack Graham of Prestonwood Church in Dallas and Dan Vestel of Tallowood Church in Houston urged Texas Baptists to take the necessary step of personal repentance so they can be effective witnesses for Christ.

Issuing a call for unity around the Texas 2000 vision, the two pastors encouraged total involvement in the goal of sharing the gospel with every Texan within the next five years.

"Now is the time to get right with God, get right with each other and go tell the good news of Jesus Christ," Graham said. "Now is the time for the people of this state to see the true heart of Texas Baptists—a heart for God, full of compassion."

The Texas 2000 vision demands the "individual participation of everyone on the team," Vestal said.

"We must be a team together—sharing Christ with every person in our state, depending on the power of the Holy Spirit to do what we cannot do and going forward with a oneness of purpose."

The Gospel of Jesus Christ has the power to renew, refresh and refill empty lives, said Ralph Bell, an associate with the Billy Graham Evangelistic Association.

"Today is always the appointed day to accept Jesus Christ," Bell said. "If you want to be refreshed, if you want to be regenerated deep within, if you want to be made whole in your innermost spirit, repentance must take place."

Spiritual awakening already has begun in Texas, according to speaker John Avant, pastor of Coggin Avenue Church in Brownwood.

Revival broke out in his church last January at a Sunday morning service that continued spontaneously for four hours with people confessing their sins, he said. Twenty-two people became Christian, and some committed their lives to the ministry.

The revival spread to nearby Howard Payne University and to Southwestern Seminary in Fort Worth, and it has continued to spread as students and others share its impact across the country, Avant said.

During an extended service at Southwestern Seminary, a white student came forward weeping and confessing, "I'm a racist."

Two African-American students threw their arms around him, weeping with him and exclaiming, "We love you, brother."

Later, one of the black students called to tell Avant, "He (the former racist) is my prayer partner now."

Another speaker, Rick Warren, who started Saddleback Valley Community Church in Mission Viejo, Calif., 16 years ago and has seen it grow to more than 11,000 members, urged Texas Baptists to start new churches to reach all kinds of people.

In its first 13 years, the Saddleback congregation met in 79 buildings, including a mental hospital, he said.

"Buildings don't build churches; people build churches," he insisted.

"So we put money into people and programs."

In September, the congregation moved into a building of its own, and attendance jumped from 9,000 to more than 11,000.

Stressing five principles of Jesus for being fishers of men—"know what you're fishing for, go where the fish are biting, learn to think like a fish, catch a fish on their terms and use more than one hook," Saddleback has started 25 new churches and has 80 ministries, Warren said.

Charles Redmond, pastor of First Church in Pasadena, said Texas Baptists must respond to the Holy Spirit without lengthy discussions and deliberation in order to achieve the goals of Texas 2000.

Noting that the worker is not the important thing, the gospel is the important thing, Redmond said, "When the gospel is shared, whatever the way, the gospel creates a need for itself.

"When the Spirit speaks to us, there's not time for deliberating, just obeying and delivering the message."

Leonard Sweet, dean of the School of Theology at Drew University in Madison, N. J., said the "new world" today is in many ways anti-Christian and requires a new reformation for sharing the gospel.

"The living water must be put into some different containers for the 'busters, the get-real generation,'" he said.

Stressing that people don't know what or whom they can trust, Sweet said: "There is One you can trust. . . . Whether you feel it or not, the Bible says, 'Trust and obey.'"

Spiritual Awakening leaders Richard Owen Roberts and Henry Blackaby said if Texas Baptists would repent and truly seek God, spiritual awakening would spread around the world this year.

"In order to truly seek the Lord, we must continually be broken and contrite," said Roberts, president of International Awakening Ministries in Wheaton, Ill.

"What we often seek are those things that satisfy ourselves," he said. "If your religion leaves you seeking yourself, it is not the religion of Jesus Christ. All other evil grows out of our failure to set our hearts to seek God. All the good and needed things we do are no substitute for seeking the Lord."

Blackaby, consultant for prayer and spiritual awakening with the Home Mission Board, said the call of God to repentance is addressed to His people throughout the Bible.

"When we put Him first and seek after Him, God will add everything else, and times of refreshing will come as we seek the Lord with all our heart," Blackaby said.

About 1,800 people attended a senior adult luncheon following the conference, and the Hispanic Evangelism Conference drew about 1,700 participants.

Source: Orville Scott, Ken Camp, Thomas J. Brannon, "Evangelism Conference Spotlights Texas 2000," *Baptist Standard*, 24 January 1996, 3–4. Reprint courtesy of the *Baptist Standard*.

15.7 A New State Convention

On November 20, 1997, the ultraconservative faction of Texas Baptists known as the "Southern Baptists of Texas" officially withdrew from the BGCT. It had become apparent that the "Southern Baptists of Texas" wanted to follow the fundamentalist principles of the Conservative Resurgence in the Southern Baptist Convention. The problem, however, was that the majority of Texas Baptists did not want to follow the lead of the national convention. Virtually all BGCT programs were thriving, people were coming to know the Lord, educational endeavors were at an all-time high, and churches were being built at an incredible pace. For all intents and purposes, it appeared that the fallout over Baylor University, the misquotation of Charles Wade at the 1997 Austin Convention, the election of Russell Dilday as BGCT president in 1997, and the findings of the Effectiveness/Efficiency committee became more than the "Southern Baptists of Texas" could bear.

A. Southern Baptists of Texas Vote to Form a New State Convention

Dallas (ABP)—Directors of Southern Baptists of Texas, the organization that has pushed for closer alignment of the Baptist General Convention of Texas with the Southern Baptist Convention, voted Nov. 20 instead to establish a new state convention.

Dee Slocum, pastor of Highland Baptist Church in Amarillo and vice president for the organization, said its 30-member board of directors voted unanimously to begin the process of setting up the new organization.

The directors and officers—executive director Ronnie Yarber of Mesquite, president Miles Seaborn of Fort Worth and Slocum— will serve as a "transitional team" to give it birth, Slocum said. He said no date has been set for an organizational meeting but that he anticipated it could come as early as spring.

Slocum said he had been appointed spokesman by Yarber, who declined to answer calls from *The Baptist Standard*. Seaborn is traveling in the Philippines.

William Pinson, executive director of the Baptist General Convention of Texas, said the reasons cited for establishing the new state convention "are not well founded and are not justification for such an act." **He said Texas Baptist leaders have worked to prevent a split and to maintain "togetherness for the sake of the gospel."**

Southern Baptists of Texas was first organized in 1991 as the Conservative Baptist Fellowship of Texas but changed its name two years ago.

Southern Baptists of Texas opposed passage of the Efficiency/Effectiveness report at the BGCT meeting in Austin last month because they contended it distanced the BGCT from the SBC, a claim denied by the committee which drafted it and by BGCT leaders.

Following approval of the E/E report, Yarber and Seaborn said the directors of Southern Baptists of Texas were almost unanimous in approving formation of a new state convention. The group conducted a written poll of some 400 persons attending a rally after the Monday night convention session in Austin.

Slocum said response to the poll was "overwhelmingly" in favor of beginning a new convention.

The purpose of the new body will be "to ensure and maintain a strong SBC presence in Texas," Slocum said.

"We saw that diminishing. We feel we have seen an erosion of the historic walk with the SBC on part of elected leadership of the BGCT as far back as the last Amarillo convention" in 1994, he said. "That concerns Southern Baptists across the state."

News of the decision to start the new convention was released by Baptist Press in a story written by Dave Parker, assistant editor of the *Oklahoma Baptist Messenger*. The new editor of the *Messenger* is John Yeats, who came to Oklahoma from the editorship of the *Indiana Baptist* and who has been a longtime spokesman for the group now controlling the SBC. Yeats is now SBC recording secretary.

Slocum was quoted by Parker as saying that an additional factor in the decision to establish a new convention "was outgoing BGCT President Charles Wade's comments regarding the historical accuracy of Scripture." In an interview with the *Austin American-Statesman*, Wade said, "Texas Baptists will support the Southern Baptist leaders if they focus on missions and evangelism instead of trying to force all Baptists to believe the Bible is factual and scientifically true."

Wade in fact had no interview with the Austin paper. The story carried by the paper was written from a manuscript provided to reporters by Wade. Wade's manuscript did not include the statement about the

Bible being factual and scientifically true. The Austin reporter who wrote the story said the statement about the Bible's accuracy was not a quote but a paraphrase of the position of the moderate Baptists on the Bible. But Wade said the paraphrase misrepresents his position.

In his speech Wade said: "Southern Baptist leaders will have our support if they will focus on missions and evangelism, but they will drive more and more Texas Baptists away if they focus on requiring uniformity as a condition of cooperation."

Wade said the use of the reporter's paraphrase by the SBT leaders was worse than a reporter's mistake. **"Those who claim they have an endless delight in the truth of Scripture are themselves guilty of deliberate misrepresentation of my remarks in the president's address to the Baptist General Convention of Texas."**

Source: *Texas Baptists Committed*, December 1997, 1–2. Reprint courtesy of *Texas Baptists Committed*.

B. A New Convention! Why?

Southern Baptists of Texas, a conservative group disenchanted with recent actions by the Baptist General Convention of Texas, has begun the process of creating a new state convention.

The move was initiated by a unanimous vote of the SBT board of directors in Dallas, November 20. Directors authorized the SBT officers and the administrative director to begin immediately the process of transitioning the organization into a new state convention.

Messengers to Baptist General Convention of Texas, Nov. 10–11 annual meeting in Austin approved an "Effectiveness/Efficiency Committee" plan that conservatives fought. **Portions of the E/E report must be adopted at next year's BGCT meeting in Houston before it will take effect.** [Editor's emphasis] Among the plan's recommendations was one that tied the BGCT membership more closely into giving to the BGCT. Conservative churches unhappy with the moderate lean of the BGCT had been exploring ways to bypass the state convention. Dee Slocum, pastor of Greenway Park Baptist Church, Amarillo, and vice-president of the SBT, said the action was due to what the SBT perceives as a "broadening and distancing of the BGCT from the SBC." He said the vote elevated the Cooperative Baptist Fellowship to "equal status with the SBC" and also elevated the BGCT to denominational status. The CBF is a group of moderate Baptists critical of the SBC leadership. "The CBF has always denied that it is a denomination, yet the E/E report elevated CBF to denominational status," Slocum said.

The E/E report consisted of 19 different motions, 15 of which were effective immediately. These included supporting Texas theological schools, creating Texas Sunday School literature, and expanding partnership missions to include the CBF.

The vote by Texas conservatives was the second such action this past year. In 1996, Southern Baptist Conservatives of Virginia formed in a split with the Baptist General Association of Virginia. "Texas declared itself as an independent Baptist convention," Slocum said. "It is their intent to affiliate in a limited way with the SBC and to expand their cooperation with agencies of the CBF. This is a radical departure of the BGCT from the SBC. This is denied by the BGCT, but the evidence is to the contrary," he said.

William M. Pinson, Jr., executive director of the BGCT, said its leaders "have stated again and again that they do not want any group to break fellowship with the BGCT. In my opinion, the reasons given are not well-founded and not justification for such an act," Pinson told the Baptist Press. "Certainly any Baptist group is free to do what it wills, but I pray that all Southern Baptists in Texas will find a way to continue to serve together."

BGCT officials quoted from former BGCT President Charles Wade in his presidential message as saying, "Southern Baptist leaders will have our support if they will focus on missions and evangelism, but they will drive more and more Texas Baptists away if they focus on requiring conformity as a condition of cooperation." In another statement attributed to Wade, Baptist Press reported, "It troubles many of us when women who feel God has called them to be ministers of God's gospel are told they must be mistaken, and they and their churches are not free to interpret and acknowledge God's call in their life, and no Southern Baptist leaders step forward to defend their freedom in Christ to respond to God's calling. The church where I am a member believes the world is too lost and the needs too great for us to be telling people, whom God has called and gifted, what they can't do rather than setting them free to do what God has gifted and called them to do."

Prior to the BGCT meeting, Slocum said the SBT Board of Directors had entertained a possible necessity of forming another state convention if the E/E Report was adopted. "We considered the state of affairs of the BGCT," he said. "We considered the condition of Southern Baptists in Texas. We have a desire to maintain a stronger relationship with the national Southern Baptist family. The Austin convention in and by itself is not the reason why our organization has made this decision," he added. "It has been a collective process across the last four or five conventions. The triggering device was that it became apparent to everyone that this is an attempt by the leadership of the BGCT to distance itself from the national SBC."

Slocum said, "We have been trying for years to reveal the fact that at the core is a theological issue, not a political one," he said. "The moderates, the liberals and the CBF have denied that there is a theological issue, until now. Since the E/E report first became public knowledge, SBT has received a great deal of interest from Baptists across Texas," Slocum said. After its passage, "We have been bombarded with telephone calls and faxes from across the state; the callers desire a new convention. They desire a stronger relationship with the SBC, not a weaker one. They want to move closer, not distance ourselves."

"Loyal Southern Baptists in Texas are going to remain just that; loyal Southern Baptists in Texas," Slocum said. "The BGCT has left us as Southern Baptists. It has done so under the auspices of autonomy.

"I don't dispute that BGCT has the latitude to set its own direction, but we have a choice, too. The rest of us have to make a choice, to either be Texas Baptists or Southern Baptists."

Source: *Plumbline*: Southern Baptists of Texas, December 1997, 1, 8. Reprint courtesy of the Southern Baptists of Texas.

C. Bill Pinson's Response

The Baptist General Convention of Texas has always been committed to all members of the Baptist family in Texas working together to promote God's Kingdom. BGCT leaders have stated again and again that they do not want any group to break fellowship with the BGCT.

Prior to the vote by the Southern Baptists of Texas board to form a new convention, as reported by Baptist Press, the BGCT president sent lengthy communication to their leaders stressing the importance of working together to help fulfill the Great Commission. Newly elected BGCT President Russell Dilday will continue to seek reconciliation in obedience to Scripture.

Neither I nor any officers of the BGCT have been supplied information directly from the SBT about any new state convention to be formed by them. Therefore, we do not know any details of what is proposed and cannot evaluate the matter. In my opinion, the reasons given in the press release for forming a new convention are not well founded and not justification for such an act. Certainly, any Baptist group is free to do what it wills, but I pray that all Southern Baptists in Texas will find a way to continue to serve together in the power and direction of the Holy Spirit to fulfill the Great Commission given us by the Lord Jesus Christ.

As a family of Baptists in Texas, we have endeavored to remain true to God's written Word, the Bible, and God's living Word, Jesus. While we may not agree on the interpretation of the Bible in every regard, we agree on essentials: We believe in God the Father, Son and Holy Spirit. We believe in Jesus as the virgin-born Son of God who lived a sinless life, died on the cross for our sins, rose from the grave, ascended to the right hand of the Father, and is coming again. We believe the Bible is truth and the sole authority for faith and practice. We believe in salvation by grace through faith; in believer's baptism; in the priesthood of the believer; in a regenerate church membership; in the governance of a church by members under the headship of the Lord Jesus Christ; in autonomous churches which cooperate with one another voluntarily for missions, evangelism, education and ministry; in religious freedom and soul competency.

While some believe a division would be best, I am not one of these. Neither is our BGCT president, chairman of the Executive Board or other leaders. If a new state convention is formed, it will not be because BGCT leaders have encouraged it. In fact, just the opposite will be the case. Written and spoken appeals have been and will be made for togetherness for the sake of the Gospel. Furthermore, the convention staff have made themselves and the resources of the convention available to all churches regardless of their political persuasion. Churches can send their Cooperative Program gifts through the BGCT with guidelines which provide flexibility. Churches related to the Southern Baptists of Texas have utilized this freedom extensively. Persons from the SBT serve on boards, committees and commissions of the BGCT. To depart would be to abandon Texas Baptist institutions, resources and ministries, Evangelism Conference, Super Summer, the River Ministry, starting and strengthening churches, and dozens of other ministries.

Those who speak of forming a new state convention have perhaps forgotten that it was the terrible disruption caused by having rival state conventions in Texas that led to the unification of these in 1886 and the forming of the BGCT. Later splits from the BGCT also caused division in churches and associations and disruptions of the Lord's work. Baptists have done this sort of thing before. But we hope the question for all of us is what is best for the advancement of our Lord's Kingdom.

As I have prayed about various possible options, I believe that continuing to cooperate for the sake of the Gospel would be most in keeping with the New Testament appeal to unity and to the prayer of the Lord Jesus for us as recorded in the 17th chapter of the Gospel of John. What a witness we would give to a lost world if we could join together in ministry and service—that the world may believe that the Father sent the Son to be Savior of the world!

I am committed to helping keep our Baptist family focused on the vision and priorities given us by the Lord. The BGCT will continue to be faithful to God's Word by cooperating to help fulfill the Great Commission of the Lord Jesus Christ.

Source: Statement from William M. Pinson, Jr., undated, issued by Thomas J. Brannon, Director of Communications for the BGCT, Dallas. Reprint courtesy of the Baptist General Convention of Texas.

15.8 Decisive Action

On February 24, 1998, the Executive Board, acting for the BGCT, expelled the University Baptist Church in Austin for receiving homosexuals into its membership and, in 1994, ordaining a homosexual man a deacon. For several different reasons, the BGCT failed to remove the church from its membership until five years after the ordination issue had been brought to light. In 1996, a motion was made to remove the church before the annual convention, but the church had sent no messengers, and thus the BGCT did not have the constitutional right to remove them. The BGCT, fearing that they might be viewed as pro-homosexual, finally felt compelled to remove the University Baptist Church after national media attention began to draw attention to the issue.

BGCT Marks Turf on Homosexuality

The Baptist General Convention of Texas has distanced itself from an Austin church that ordained a homosexual as a deacon.

The BGCT Executive Board voted Feb. 24 not to receive contributions from University Church in Austin. The board also asked the church to stop publishing materials indicating it is affiliated with the state convention.

The action additionally called on the convention to decline funds from "any other church which openly endorses moral views in conflict with biblical teaching."

The vote built a wall between the church and convention, but it did not remove the church from the convention, board Chairman Clyde Glazener noted.

According to Baptist practice, churches "affiliate" with the convention but are not members of the convention, explained Glazener, pastor of Gambrell Street Church in Fort Worth.

A church's official relationship with the convention is tested when a church sends "messengers"—what most groups call delegates—to the convention's annual meeting each fall, he said.

Only messengers to the convention's annual session can vote not to seat a church's messengers and thereby disassociate the convention from a church, Glazener said.

Under BGCT rules, a church need not contribute financially to the convention to send messengers to the annual meeting. So, the Austin church feasibly could present messengers for seating at the 1998 meeting in November.

But University Church has not tested that level of affiliation since it ordained a gay deacon and stepped into the denominational spotlight in 1995.

That fall, the church was removed from the Austin Association, and the state convention created a special committee to consider whether to amend its constitution to disallow affiliation with churches that ordain homosexuals.

In 1996, the BGCT declined to amend its constitution, noting the convention's credentials committee already had authority to refuse seating messengers from churches perceived to deviate from standard faith and practice. However, the convention approved a statement saying homosexual practice is "contrary to God's purposes and thus sinful" and "in conflict with the Bible."

The issue resurfaced last fall, when convention leaders became aware University Church's Internet site cites the congregation's affiliation with the BGCT but also reports the church has ordained a gay deacon and carries news about a homosexual group that meets at the church.

Early last month, the BGCT Administrative Committee voted to present the recommendation considered by the Executive Board last week.

Two factors shaped that decision, reported Administrative Committee Chairman Charles Davenport, pastor of First Church in Tulia.

"The convention clearly has spoken on the issue of homosexuality," Davenport said, citing the 1996 BGCT action and other convention resolutions.

In addition, the Austin church "clearly affirms a position—through the election of a homosexual as a deacon and through the public media—that is in conflict with the convention position," he said.

"If the church was simply ministering to the homosexual community, we could commend them for their effort," Davenport insisted. "But clearly, their position goes beyond ministry to homosexual persons and becomes an affirmation of their practice."

Although the church has an "autonomous right" to determine its ministries, "we need to remember that the convention also is an autonomous body and has the right and responsibility to determine those who will participate," he added.

The action is not "singling out homosexual persons for particular condemnation," Davenport said. He encouraged Texas Baptists to "lovingly minister to them and their families in the same way we minister to all persons."

Still, the convention cannot ethically receive the church's funds if it is not likely to seat the church's messengers, he stressed. He described the Executive Board action as an effort to "keep faith with the will of the convention as expressed . . .on homosexuality."

Larry Bethune, the church's pastor, pleaded with the board to defeat the proposal for three reasons.

"It sends one more damaging, damning message to homosexual persons and their families," he said. This action sounds "a message that can only be heard as hatred in the name of Christ."

"You may not agree with the way our church ministers with gays and lesbians and their families–in fact, we don't all agree at UBC—but we are creating one of the few safe places for your Baptist homosexual children to work out their salvation with fear and trembling."

The proposal should also be defeated because "it's not Baptist," since it overrules the autonomy of an individual congregation, Bethune added.

"One of the most important issues is that the BGCT continue to function as a servant—not an authoritarian—organization," he stressed. "Texas Baptists must continue to embrace historic Baptist principles that honor local-church decisions and individual religious freedom. . . ."

"To exclude a church in the name of harmony opens the door for other controversial church practices to be used as tests of fellowship, such as the ordination of women, the distribution of Christian Coalition voter guides or the denunciation of BGCT leadership from so many of our pulpits.

"Will we require all churches to agree on a matter of biblical inter-pretation?" Bethune asked. "If so, how long will the list be, or is this the only issue which will be used like a creed as a test of orthodoxy?"

Third, he urged a vote against the measure because "a biblical pro-cess has not been followed in this matter." The Administrative Commit-tee failed to follow conflict-resolution guidelines found the in the Gospel of Matthew, he said.

Debate on the recommendation lasted about 90 minutes, and Ex-ecutive Board members expressed strong feelings on both sides of the issue.

"Is there anything a church could do to cause us to ask that church to not be a part of the BGCT? Yes," insisted Debbie Chisolm, youth minister at First Church in Duncanville. She cited heretical teachings, such as the requirement of works for salvation, the idea that human documents are equal with scripture, the belief that Christians could lose their salvation and the practice of infant baptism.

But a church's right to ordain deacons and ministers is another matter, Chisolm contended. "I do not believe it is within our right to make that kind of decision for the local church," she said.

Bob Fagan, pastor of Memorial Church, Lubbock, contended moral issues comprise another matter which is properly censured.

"This is an open endorsement of a non-biblical lifestyle," he said of the church's action.

"Why this one issue?

She questioned the time of the action and convention leaders' asserting that the recommendation "has nothing to do with politics." Earlier in the meeting, BGCT Executive Director William M. Pinson, Jr., had noted statewide contribution of a false document (apparently linked in some cases to the break away Southern Baptists of Texas) claiming convention's leadership supports homosexuality.

"What's going to happen at our Executive Board meeting?" Vaughn asked. Will the convention distance itself from "churches whose membership would not have an African American, Hispanic American or Native American in their home for dinner?" Will the convention distance itself from the church "whose leaders would not tithe?"

"I don't like the racism or the thievery either," she stressed. "Why this one issue? Why now?"

BGCT President Russell Dilday insisted the Administrative Committee "did not act in haste, thoughtlessly, or carelessly, without undue consideration" in making its recommendation.

"Other issues—such as ordination of women for ministry—would not come up (for censure) unless the convention spoke clearly," said Dilday, distinguished professor of homiletics at Baylor University's Truett Seminary. "The attempt is to clarify an issue on which the convention has spoken clearly."

Source: Marv Knox, "BGCT Marks Turf on Homosexuality," *Baptist Standard*, 4 March 1998, 1, 6. Reprint courtesy of the *Baptist Standard*.

I N D E X